NEW ENGLISH HANDBOOK

Third Edition

Hans P. Guth

San Jose State University

Wadsworth Publishing Company
Belmont, California
A Division of Wadsworth, Inc.

English Editor: Angela M. Gantner
Editorial Assistant: Julie Johnson
Production Editor: Vicki Friedberg
Interior and Cover Design: James Chadwick
Print Buyer: Randy Hurst
Permissions Editor: Peggy Meehan
Copy Editor: Carolyn McGovern
Compositor: Thompson Type, San Diego

Credits

Barbara Meier Gatten for her research paper, "Women in Sports." Harper & Row, Publishers, Inc. for a dictionary entry (*brave*) from Funk & Wagnalls *Standard College Dictionary*. Copyright © 1977 by Harper & Row, Publishers, Inc. Reprinted by permission of the publisher. Houghton Mifflin Company for an entry (*impromptu*) from *American Heritage Dictionary, Second College Edition*. Copyright © 1982 by Houghton Mifflin Company. Reprinted by permission of the publisher. Merriam-Webster Inc. for entries (*call, feminism, media, populace, usage*) from *Webster's Ninth New Collegiate Dictionary*. © 1984 by Merriam-Webster Inc., publisher of the Merriam-Webster Dictionaries. Reprinted by permission of the publisher. Random House, Inc. for entries (*beauty, begin, belabor, belles-lettres, bene-, beneath, bent, better, brass, caliber*) from the *Random House College Dictionary, Revised Edition*. Copyright © 1984 by Random House, Inc. Reprinted by permission of the publisher. Simon & Schuster for entries (*alien, Gotham, mind, plan, produce*) from *Webster's New World Dictionary, Second College Edition*. Copyright © 1984 by Simon & Schuster, Inc. Reprinted by permission of the publisher. Sociological Abstracts Inc. for an entry (82M2679) from *Sociological Abstracts*. © 1982 Sociological Abstracts Inc. Reprinted by permission of the publisher.

Printed in the United States of America   34

2 3 4 5 6 7 8 9 10 — 94 93 92 91

Library of Congress Cataloging-in-Publication Data

Guth, Hans Paul
    New English handbook / Hans P. Guth.—3rd ed.
        p.   cm.
    ISBN 0-534-12774-6
    1. English language—Grammar—1950–   2. English language—
Rhetoric. I. Title.
808'.042—dc20   89-70563
                                                          CIP

Preface: To the Instructor

Teaching students to write can be the most frustrating or the most rewarding part of college education. At times, the teaching of writing seems a labor of Sisyphus, as we push the large rock called literacy up the hill, only to find the sentence fragments, *it's* misspelled, and shapeless unmotivated papers waiting for us again at the bottom of the hill come next term. At other times, a class that works well and student papers written with intelligence and conviction renew our faith that writing and thinking are at the core of a college education and that our students have a gift for language and an untapped potential of intelligence and imagination.

This book is designed to help teachers balance their concern with the basics of literacy and their commitment to the larger purposes that make the teaching of writing a rewarding professional enterprise. *New English Handbook* aims at a workable, teachable synthesis of the best in current composition theory, research, and classroom practice. It aims at being a step ahead of other texts in helping teachers meet the needs they encounter every day in today's classrooms.

Writing texts have become less like tablets from the mountain and more like books meant to be read, understood, and put to good use. Today's texts are much closer than yesterday's to how and why writers write, to what keeps them going in spite of writer's block and rewrite fatigue, and to how they develop the survival skills that help their writing meet the standards of editors, critics, and just plain readers. The books that promise to make our students better writers have come a long way toward helping both student and instructor overcome negative expectations. The best textbooks today share the assumption that many students may be poorly prepared but that they are willing to learn. They will work hard once they know that the teacher and the textbook are on their side.

Meeting Today's Classroom Needs

The following features of the *New English Handbook* are designed to help teachers meet the needs of today's composition students:

POSITIVE MOTIVATION This book does more than other handbooks to give students a reason to write. From the initial treatment of the writing process through the treatment of expository strategies and kinds of argument to the research paper, the book stresses the *purposes* that set writing in motion and give meaning to the rules and conventions we teach. An exceptional range of writing assignments and writing activities is designed to help students discover the rewards and satisfactions of using language effectively for their own needs.

EMPHASIS ON APPLICATION At every stage of the writing process, *New English Handbook* shows graphically how prewriting, writing, and revision strategies produce better student papers. Student models covering a range of current topics illustrate different major kinds of writing and assure that good student writing does not remain a myth for our students.

WRITING AND THINKING The hardest yet most basic part of our task is to teach the thinking that goes into writing. This book puts special emphasis on the thinking that goes into organizing a paper or guides major revision decisions. In the treatment of both expository patterns and argumentative writing, the focus is not on formal logic but on the reasoning that helps us process information or structure an argument.

PLAIN-ENGLISH EXPLANATIONS *New English Handbook* makes a special effort to make essential grammatical and rhetorical terms accessible to students who need help with basics. With large numbers of nontraditional or inadequately prepared students, we need to make sure that we do not allow terminology to become an end in itself. In this book, essential grammatical and rhetorical concepts are presented one at a time with explanations accessible to the learner. Students encounter first things first, with the focus on basic survival skills for the student writer and with major exceptions and finer points following later.

ACTIVE PARTICIPATION A special feature of this book is the mix of varied and productive exercises and activities to help students bridge the gap between rules and practice. *Writing workshop* activities help students implement and test rhetorical concepts and compare notes with fellow student writers. *Discourse exercises* show principles of grammar or punctuation at work in the authentic rhetorical context of short lively passages. *Peer editor exercises* provide practice in sentence-by-sentence editing. An exceptional mix of productive *sentence work* (sentence combining, sentence imitation, sentence revision) establishes the missing link between grammar and composition.

Highlights of the Third Edition

The new third edition has been thoroughly rewritten and reorganized in the light of classroom experience and changing emphases in classroom practice. Some highlights of the revision:

Chapter 1. The book starts with a greatly expanded overview of "The Writing Process," with emphasis on how techniques like journal writing, brainstorming, interviewing, discovery frames, and genuine revision pay off in better student writing. This new Chapter 1 moves from purpose (finding a reason to write) and finding material (working up a subject) through organizing and drafting to more-than-cosmetic revision and final editing. The chapter includes graphic demonstration of how writers push toward a thesis and put to use major expository strategies (classification, process, comparison and contrast) that structure much academic writing.

Chapter 3. This new chapter on "Argument and Persuasion" focuses on the thinking that gives shape and direction to writing. While it helps students avoid the faulty syllogism and other logical fallacies, the chapter concentrates on demonstrating the reasoning that structures different kinds of argumentative papers. The chapter moves from the inductive argument, arguing from principle, and weighing the pro and con to tracing cause and effect, eliminating alternatives, and writing the "Yes, but" paper. The chapter concludes with pointed guidelines for persuasive papers that involve and motivate an audience while respecting its intelligence.

Chapter 4. This chapter, "Grammar for Writers," starts with sentence basics (parts of speech and the basic sentence patterns that put them to use), goes on to the essentials of literacy (fragments, comma splices, standard verb forms), and then covers the requirements of serious written English from agreement to parallel structure. Like the later chapters on sentence style, word choice, punctuation, and spelling, this chapter follows a streamlined pattern for effective teaching and reference. Each section (such as **14** for fragments or **16** for agreement) starts with an *overview* (spotting and illustrating the problem) and moves on to pointed guidelines covering major *applications*, followed as necessary by attention to *finer points*.

Chapter 6. The chapter on "The Right Word" includes timely new material on sexist language, clichés, jargon, and other abuses of language (**30, 32**).

Chapter 7. This chapter stresses the "When and Why" that give meaning to punctuation rules. The chapter is organized according to the major *functions* that punctuation serves in a sentence—the *needs* for punctuation that arise in a sentence. The focus is on the choices writers make when punctuating, for instance, clauses linked by different kinds of conjunctions—comma or semicolon? comma or no comma? (A chart summarizing rules according to punctuation marks—comma rules, semicolon rules—appears at the beginning of the chapter.)

Chapter 9. The updated and expanded chapter on "The Research Paper" pays equal attention to writing a paper worth documenting and to the purposes served by documentation. A clear and comprehensive guide to documentation aims at demystifying the principles and details of the MLA style (*MLA Handbook*, Third Edition). A quick-check *MLA directory* presents more than 50 sample entries (both "Works Cited" format and sample parenthetical reference). Entries are easy to find under three major headings: books, articles, and nonprint sources. The sample research paper is accompanied by a "paper trail" on the making of the paper, with planning report, search record, trial outline, and a note on revision strategy. An introduction to the alternate APA style concludes the chapter.

Note: Chapter 1 includes a state-of-the-art section on *word processing* and computer writing (**6**) designed to help students utilize the full potential of the word processor, with special attention to prewriting techniques, genuine revision, proofreading problems, and new technology for instructor feedback and peer interaction.

A Coordinated Support Package

The support package for *New English Handbook* furnishes exceptionally well-coordinated backup and follow-through for the main text:

■ *The Wadsworth English Essentials Kit.* This compact guide to minimum proficiencies for the composition student is free to students with their copies of *New English Handbook*. It defines a successful student paper, goes on to minimum guidelines for revision, and provides pointed, graphic help with basic literacy, sentence basics, and essentials of spelling and punctuation. The focus is on the problems that instructors mark most frequently in student papers and that are most frequently tested in placement tests and proficiency tests in English composition. Sample test questions are included.

■ *New English Workbook,* Third Edition. More than a routine, "more-of-same" workbook, this companion text provides backup explanations and follow-up exercises for students with limited preparation or special needs. Writing activities are presented in a workshop format. Grammar and mechanics worksheets are formatted for quick scoring by the instructor or peer-marking by members of a class.

■ *Student Voices: The Writer's Range.* This anthology and mini-rhetoric of student writing helps the instructor bridge the gap between the writing of the professional and the beginner. Intended as models and inspiration for student writers, the papers in this collection dramatize issues, reconsider familiar assumptions, and offer new perspectives on people and ideas. Major sections move from experience to exposition and on to argument and persuasion, with additional sections devoted to writing across the curriculum. Varied writing topics and essays for peer review round out the volume.

■ *The Wadsworth English Proficiency Test.* This is a 100-item multiple-choice test that stresses simplicity of format and that can be administered during one conventional class period. In addition to the overall score, this test will yield subscores in the areas of basic literacy, standard English, sentence structure, punctuation, spelling, and paragraphs. The test is accompanied by instructions and topics for a *writing sample* (diagnostic essay) requiring an additional conventional class period.

Resources for Teaching

The *New English Manual*, Third Edition, provides professional background and resources for orientation of new faculty, as well as ample teaching helps and a complete answer key for *New English Handbook*. The initial overview, "Teaching Composition Today," covers topics including the writing process, writing and thinking, making the teaching of grammar productive in today's classroom, sentence work (sentence combining, sentence imitation) as the missing link between grammar and composition, and guidelines for teaching usage and mechanics. Guest essays include "Responding to Student Writing," "Toward the Interactive Classroom," "A Guide to Holistic Scoring," and "A Professional Bookshelf for the Writing Teacher." Teaching helps and answer key include suggested class activities and sample student responses.

A Word of Thanks

This book owes a large debt to composition teachers around the country. I have learned much from working with them in workshops on their campuses, from listening to them at national and regional conferences, and from collaborating with them on enterprises like the Young Rhetoricians' Conference. Like many other teachers, I have found an antidote to disillusionment and burnout in the spirit of solidarity and common purpose inspired by the writing movement that has revitalized our profession and has begun to secure overdue recognition for writing teachers in the English department and in the institution at large. My greatest debt is to the students who have allowed me to use their writing. They have taught me as much about writing as I have taught them, and their candor, good humor, youthful enthusiasm, and love of language have cheered me over the years.

Hans Guth

Acknowledgments

The author and the editors of this book wish to acknowledge gratefully the contributions of the following reviewers:

Paula Beck
Nassau Community College

Sister Mary Ann Benoit
College of Great Falls

Mary Boseman
Pensacola Junior College

Philip Boshoff
Skidmore College

Alma Bryant
University of South Florida, Tampa

Douglas Butturff
University of Central Arkansas

Jeannie Campanelli
American River College

Barbara Carpenter
Marist College

Duncan Carter
Portland State University

Ed Chute
University of North Dakota

Robert Cosgrove
Saddleback College

Peter Dusenbery
Bradley University

Eileen Evans
Western Michigan University

Patricia Ferrara
Oglethorpe University

George Findlen
Northwest Missouri State University

Lois Fisher
*Southwestern Oklahoma State
    University*

Kim Flachmann
California State University, Bakersfield

Dorothy Friedman
University of the District of Columbia

Peter Gingiss
University of Houston

William Gracie
Miami University of Ohio

John Grass
Western Wisconsin Technological College

Jeffrey Gross
University of Mississippi

Martha Hadsel
Pennsylvania State University

George Haich
Georgia State University

Jim Hanlon
Shippensburg State University

George Hayhoe
Virginia Polytechnic and State University

Richard Hespin
Henry Ford Community College

Gene Hollahan
Georgia State University

Barbara Johnston

Philip Keith
Saint Cloud University

Joseph Kolpake
Henry Ford Community College

Dolores laGuardia
University of San Francisco

Becky Mann
Wilkes Community College

Celest Martin
University of Rhode Island

Jeanette Morgan
University of Houston

Lorraine Murphy
University of Dayton

Sandra I. Nagy
Arizona State University

Peter Neumeyer
San Diego State University

Frank O'Hare
Ohio State University

Leota Palmer
William Rainey Harper College

Elizabeth Penfield
University of New Orleans

Vince Piro
San Jose State University

William Pixton
Oklahoma State University

Mary Beth Pringle
Wright State University

John Reuter
Florida Southern College

Kenneth Risdon
University of Minnesota, Duluth

Mark Rollins
Ohio University

Arthrell Sanders
North Carolina Central University

Katherine Scully
Tulsa Junior College

Jeanne Simpson
Eastern Illinois University

Edgar Slotkin
University of Cincinnati

Beth Stiffler
Western Illinois University

Judith Stockton
Oregon State University

Edgar E. Thompson
Northwest Mississippi Junior College

Joseph Trimmer
Ball State University

Dorothy Vella
University of Hawaii, Manoa

Richard Verrell
Boston University

Charles Wagner
Sinclair Community College

Jack White
Mississippi State University

Linda Woodson
University of Texas, San Antonio

About the Author

Hans P. Guth is Professor of English at San Jose State University, where he has been honored as Outstanding Professor and Professor of the Year. He wrote his doctoral dissertation at the University of Michigan on Kenneth Burke and other moderns. He has worked with composition faculties in workshops and institutes in most of the 50 states, and has been a visiting professor at Stanford University, the University of Illinois, and the University of Hawaii.

His articles on Spenser, Kafka, and other literary subjects have appeared in *PMLA, Anglia,* and *Symposium*; his articles on rhetoric and composition include "The Politics of Rhetoric" (1972), "Composition Then and Now" (*Rhetoric Quarterly*, 1980), and "How I Write: Five Ways of Looking at the Blackbird" in Tom Waldrep's *Writers on Writing* (1985). Guth's writing texts and professional books include *Words and Ideas, English Today and Tomorrow, English for a New Generation, The Writer's Agenda,* and *Essay: Reading with the Writer's Eye*.

Guth is co-director and program chair of the Young Rhetoricians' Conference sponsored by San Jose State University, which each year brings together composition teachers from around the country for a lively festival of the art of rhetoric.

Brief Contents

Contents

9 *The Research Paper* 548

10 *Practical Prose Forms* 682

NEW ENGLISH HANDBOOK

INTRODUCTION

To the Student

A key benefit of a college education is the ability to express yourself effectively in writing. True literacy means using the written language well for your own purposes. As a college student, you are expected to write effective **expository** prose—the kind of writing you use to inform, to explain, to argue, or to persuade. You use it when you explain how solar energy works, or when you sound the alarm about an endangered species. You use it to show the need for fairer taxes, more student aid, mandatory seat belts, or regulation of machine guns. You use it in letters of application and on written tests, as well as in memos and reports.

Good writing is the result of a creative process. To write effectively, you need to bring a subject into focus and do it justice. You need to explore a subject—to work up a rich supply of relevant material. A key phase in the process of writing is thinking the matter through—sorting out your ideas and beginning to see important connections. You can then lay out your material for the reader, following up each point with explanations and examples. As you revise your first rough draft, you strengthen your overall plan and fill in missing links. An important survival skill for every writer is final editing to make sure the finished product meets the standards of educated written English—so it will be print ready and assured of a respectful hearing.

The instructions in this book are meant to help you make the process of writing and revising a paper a productive and satisfying task. In working on a paper, ask yourself five basic questions:

■ **"What am I trying to do?"** What will writing the paper do for *you*—what is the "personal connection"? Who is your audience—and what will the paper do for your *reader*? The purposes writing serves range from

3

the practical to the political and inspirational. We write to give instructions and directions or to give advice. We write to tell our side of a story, to set the record straight, or to clear up confusion. We write to expose shortcomings, rally opposition to a misguided scheme, or enlist support for a cause.

■ **"What do I know?"** Effective writers know how to mobilize their resources. They know where to turn for *material*. Suppose you are writing a paper on how our society treats the disabled. Ask yourself: "What disabled people have I known? What do I remember about them? What were their problems, and how do they cope with them? What have I read that confirms or goes beyond my own observations? Could I talk to someone who could give me an expert opinion or the inside story?"

■ **"What do I think?"** A successful paper has a *point*. As you explore your subject, you have to ask yourself how things add up. How do the different parts of the picture fit together? Start pushing toward an overall conclusion that your materials suggest. Try to sum up in one sentence your answer for the reader who asks: "What are you trying to show? What are you trying to prove?" We call the statement summing up the key idea of a paper the **thesis**. The rest of the paper will have to offer support or evidence backing up the claim made in the thesis. The thesis of your paper might look like this:

THESIS: Disabled people are beginning to play a more visible and independent role in American life.

THESIS: Much as cyclists hate the idea, the ghastly injuries and traumas of motorcycle accidents make the wearing of helmets mandatory.

THESIS: Young women are barraged with confusing advice on how to dress for success.

■ **"What is my plan?"** A successful paper has a plan that the reader can follow. The writer has *organized* a confusing mass of material and laid it out in such a way that it makes sense. Early in the process of exploring a subject, start drawing up a scratch outline or rough working outline. Adjust it as necessary as you think more about your subject. Your readers will need a mental road map that tells them: "We are going to trace this process through four major stages." Or "We are going to look at the three most important qualities that make a job satisfying or worthwhile." Or "This paper on job opportunities for women will start with a look back at the situation *then* and then will go on to the contrasting situation *now*."

Often a successful paper provides an early preview or overview to steer the reader in the right direction. Often the thesis hints at the way the paper is put together.

■ **"Am I reaching my reader?"** An effective paper is well written; it carries its message well. To write effectively, you have to be able to imagine yourself in the reader's shoes. If you make a claim on your readers' time and attention, your part of the bargain is to provide a piece of writing that they can understand and that they can follow. Take time to find the right word. Take time to rewrite an awkward sentence. Provide signals that show where you are headed. Make sure word choice and sentence structure meet the standards of educated written English. Do not let misspelled words or confusing punctuation come between you and your reader.

Becoming a better writer will benefit you both in and out of school. Student, citizen, and private individual alike profit from being able to express themselves purposefully and forcefully in plain English. Few occupations are left that do not generate a constant stream of forms, memos, reports, newsletters, and studies. For many people, work means paperwork. Computers, far from making writing obsolete, are turning people all around us into writers, typists, and editors. In the century ahead, as in the century that is coming to an end, customer, jobholder, and voter alike will profit from the ability to make competent and confident use of the written word.

DIAGNOSTIC ESSAY

Read the following topics carefully. Choose one that you can relate to your own observation, experience, and reading. Write an essay in which you draw on what you have seen, heard, and read. State your central idea or overall point of view early in your paper. Work out a plan of organization that your reader can follow. Use detailed examples to support your points. Write for the concerned general reader.

Take a few minutes at the beginning to think, to gather material, and to prepare a working outline. If you wish, jot down some preliminary notes. Take a few moments at the end to correct spelling errors and punctuation problems. (You will not have time to copy over your complete paper.) Your essay should run to about 450 or 500 words.

1. Is prejudice on the decline? (Or is it merely taking more contemporary and perhaps more subtle forms?)

2. Does physical fitness build character? (Is exercise or athletic competition good merely for the body or also for the mind or the soul?)

3. Are public manners breaking down? (Minor annoyances produce assaults; people fight over parking spaces; public facilities are vandalized or covered with graffiti. Are we turning into a nation of bullies and louts?)

4. Do the media create an unfavorable image of American business? (What picture of people in business would visitors from outer space form if they knew them only from watching television?)

5. Have Americans lost the sense of home? (Is it true that American families move so often or split up so easily that many young Americans have lost a sense of belonging? What, for you, is the meaning of "home"?)

6. Do you believe in ceremonies? (Some people believe in graduation exercises, traditional weddings, church holidays. Others consider them artificial and old-fashioned. Where do you stand?)

7. Do current movies glorify war? (Is there a common denominator or recurrent message in recent movies about war?)

8. Does current popular entertainment tend to demean or belittle women?

1

The Writing Process

OVERVIEW Every writer starts with blank sheets of paper (or a blank screen) and vague, half-formed ideas. The assignment is to get from the blank sheets to a piece of writing that gives the reader something worth thinking about or good to know. Experienced writers develop their personal ways of working up a subject, gathering material, and pulling it into shape. They develop working habits that make writing a productive, rewarding enterprise.

Try out and adapt for your own purposes the procedures that experienced writers follow to move from the preliminary (or **prewriting**) stage to the finished product. Think of your writing as a creative process that moves through five intermeshing stages:

TRIGGERING Why are you writing this paper? What are you trying to do? Who is the audience? What will this piece of writing do for the writer and for the reader?

GATHERING Where are you going to turn for material? What do you already know, and how can you learn more? What opportunities will you have for drawing on personal experience, taking a firsthand look, talking to insiders, or consulting authoritative sources?

SHAPING How are you going to lay out your material? How does it add up—what is the point? How are you going to proceed—what is your strategy?

REVISING As you read your first draft, where does it say what you are trying to say, and where does it fall short? Can the reader follow your train of thought, or do you need to reshuffle parts of your paper? Do you need to do more to show connections between ideas?

EDITING   Where should the wording be more pointed or more vivid? Which sentences need work because they are wordy, roundabout, or confused? Did you check spelling and punctuation to make sure your writing is ready-to-print?

As you write your own papers, be sure not to neglect the first step. As you embark on a writing project, ask: What sets it in motion? Will it generate enough interest and commitment to keep the process moving forward and to make your work worthwhile? Make sure the papers you write are worth writing and rewriting, worth revising and editing.

1a   A Reason to Write

Make sure you have a reason to write.

Good writing has a purpose. When we read a successful paper, we sense that the writer set out to accomplish something. (Although it may have started as an assignment, it was not written *just* as an assignment.) People write best when they tackle a topic that they care about, that they can get involved in personally. For instance, you are likely to write with conviction when you

- share your expertise about cars, Mexican cooking, or computers;
- prove a point about student loans or about the homeless that has been overlooked;
- explain something that has confused or bothered you in the past;
- challenge a stereotype about a group to which you belong (Italians, Southerners, Mormons, fraternity brothers, jocks);
- tell the inside story of something that has been kept from the public;
- enlist support for a cause.

Even when you write on an assigned subject, try to find the personal connection—the tie-in with your own experience or convictions. It should not surprise us, for instance, that an author who writes eloquently about physical fitness had parents who smoked and drank and had severe health problems as a result. Health and fitness became an urgent personal issue

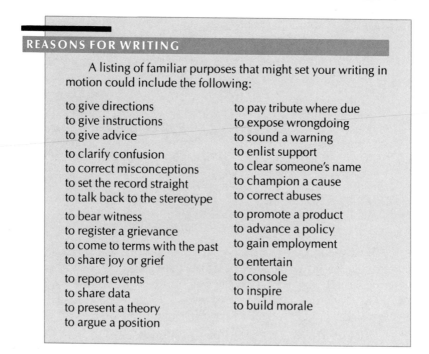

REASONS FOR WRITING

A listing of familiar purposes that might set your writing in motion could include the following:

to give directions	to pay tribute where due
to give instructions	to expose wrongdoing
to give advice	to sound a warning
to clarify confusion	to enlist support
to correct misconceptions	to clear someone's name
to set the record straight	to champion a cause
to talk back to the stereotype	to correct abuses
to bear witness	to promote a product
to register a grievance	to advance a policy
to come to terms with the past	to gain employment
to share joy or grief	
to report events	to entertain
to share data	to console
to present a theory	to inspire
to argue a position	to build morale

in the writer's life, a part of her personal agenda. You are likely to write best when you can similarly write as the eyewitness, the insider, or the advocate.

Here are motives that may activate different kinds of papers:

■ The strength of much autobiographical writing is that the events being told have a personal meaning for the author. People often write eloquently when they write to *register a grievance* or when they write about a recurrent problem they have had to confront. In writing an auto-biographical paper, you may be telling your story *to bear witness:* You may have been present at the arrest of a friend, getting into trouble for what the officers considered interference. By giving a faithful account of the events, you may be trying to show what you learned about police procedures.

■ Much informative writing is set in motion by a need *to clear up confusion* or *to correct misunderstanding*. On a subject you know well—

sports, diets, country music, child custody—you may listen to other people and say: "No, that is not the way it is at all!" You will feel the urge to set the record straight. The following passage is from a paper that aims at correcting a misunderstanding:

> Human beings have used food additives since ancient times to keep meat from spoiling or fat from turning rancid. They used salting, sugar curing, and smoking to keep their food edible. Today, health food advocates object to the addition of chemical preservatives to such common delights as T.V. dinners, cooking pouch entrées, frozen prepared potatoes, and ready-to-bake doughs. We are told that such chemicals are not as "natural" as the methods used in earlier times. What we have to realize is that salt, sugar, and smoke are not wonder substances that magically preserve food. The sodium and chloride in salt chemically bind water so that it cannot interact with the air to initiate spoilage.

■We often decide to embark on a systematic argument when an important issue has generated more heat than light. For instance, a discussion of changing immigration laws easily gets bogged down in ethnic prejudices, old allegiances, and ulterior motives. We may decide to *clarify the options* by tracing the consequences of different possible courses of action. By examining statistics and precedents, by studying causes and effects, we may set up the projections that would help a voter make an intelligent choice.

■In some kinds of writing, the writer's motives are more obvious than in other kinds of writing. The writer's aim may be to persuade us *to correct abuses* (fleecing of the elderly, overcrowding in prisons); *to condemn evildoers* (as in an exposé of bribes in high places); or *to support a good cause* (a peace initiative, opportunities for the disabled).

Study the following *student editorial* as an example of purposeful writing. It shows how writing gathers momentum when we justify something we do or when we defend something we value. As you read the editorial, ask yourself: What was the author's purpose? How does she set her editorial in motion? Where does she state her main point? What are major stages in her argument? How effectively does she reach a student audience?

The Press Pass and Compassion

> Journalists are hard of heart, nose, and head, according to many people. They worship bylines and headlines, clambering over people's feelings and lives to make it to the top.

"It's the press," the secretary whispers, hand covering the phone. "Should I say you're not in?" The pesticide industry executive ponders for a moment, then winks and says, "I'm gone for the day." After the secretary hangs up the receiver, the boss says, "Doesn't matter anyway. Those damn scribblers will put whatever they want."

Across town, a man lies on the ground, groaning in agony, his life's blood forming in pools on the gravel. His wife, uninjured by the now-dead sniper, stands nearby, screaming at reporters to stand back.

In the state capital, a defeated politician sits in his office, wandering the path to the polls over and over again in his mind, while a reporter conducts an interview. The reporter asks questions that seem to imply the politician's very hopes and dreams belong in another era.

In each situation the reporter seemed an enemy or an intruder to the people involved. It's not surprising. Journalists prod, probe, and pry for a living. They are salaried tellers of tales, but unfortunately, much news is unhappy, and those stories often hurt the subjects.

However, journalists also feel bad when they must ask the hard questions of the injured, the bereaved, and the defeated. Reporters see more than most human beings' share of certain things: mangled cars and airplanes, drowned children, young ambition slain by the assassin's bullet, to name but a few.

At such scenes, journalists often wear their hearts on their sleeves. Tear-stained notes mark the print reporter's feelings, while a radio announcer on the scene may sound his concern via a husky voice during the newscast.

Compassion and empathy do not forestall the journalist's duty to record current events for all to know. Reporters must provide readers the history of today so they'll be aware of what's going on in the world, but also so they can share the feelings of others. Knowing what another mother feels like, whether she's two states or two continents away, helps to foster an understanding of other people, whether it's joy over a child's recovery from illness or shared sorrow in the child's death.

When a tot drowns in a backyard pool, it's rough to ask the parents how long they left the boy or girl alone, why there was no enclosure around the swimming area, and whether the child knew how to swim. But it has to be done. It is news, and it may well prevent another drowning by alerting other parents to the dangers involved when toddlers and water mix.

Less tragic but still difficult circumstances also present challenges for reporters, who serve as the public's representative in places the public cannot or does not go. When something's amiss, whether in city hall, student government, or the church business office, journalists serve as surrogate eyes and ears for other citizens. It's a professional and civic duty to study the situation and report on it, no matter how reticent officials are to discuss the matter, and reticent is a true understatement.

To go where few ever go, to report the facts and to keep one's sanity—that's the duty of all reporters, and it's one few would willingly relinquish, despite the lousy pay, fierce competition, and ulcer-producing environment.

There's no better feeling than to find out and expose fraud, to tell a story of smile-invoking good times, or to write of a life well lived. It makes up by far for the sleepless election nights and ambulance chasing.   Maria J. Gunter, *Spartan Daily*

WRITING WORKSHOP 1   In the following *planning reports*, student writers explain what they are trying to do in a paper in progress. What is each trying to do? What do you think triggered the student's writing? What do you think explains the student's interest in the topic? What kind of paper does the planning report make you expect? What kind of reader would make a good audience for the paper? Would you?

1.   **Farmers in White Coats**

New varieties of crops are being engineered in sterile laboratories by biochemists and chemical engineers instead of being developed by years of planting and selective breeding in the fields. A new kind of "farmer" in a white coat and surgical gloves is replacing the one in overalls and boots. I will point out the tremendous advantages of the new plant varieties with such features as increased resistance to disease and a sharply reduced need for the use of herbicides and pesticides that damage the environment.

2.   **The Endangered Middle Class**

Is the traditional middle class on the way down? Are high-paying jobs in steel or auto manufacturing being replaced by low-status, low-pay work like hamburger flipping? Will the next generation of young Americans have jobs sweeping up in factories owned and run by the Japanese? I am going to present and explain statistics showing that the gloomy picture of tomorrow's job prospects familiar to newspaper readers may be wrong.

3.   **Fitness as a Way of Life**

Fitness has been a way of life for me for years. The benefits have always been obvious to me—improved health and an improved sense of well-being. This in turn leads to a certain self-assurance in other, unrelated endeavors. I have played competitive tennis and have been and still am an avid jogger and hiker. I jog every morning before 6 a.m. My family has a poor health and physical fitness record. My mother, a non-athlete, chain smoker, and heavy coffee drinker most of her life, died at age 54. My older brother, also a non-athlete, has been a heavy drinker and "drug dabbler" and has had a heart attack. In my essay, I will explain this background as the motivation for my lifetime commitment to physical fitness.

4. **A Special Day**

I want to describe the ridiculous Valentine's Day phenomenon. It is unfortunate that we need to set aside a special day to tell others that we care about them. I want to tell the people who every year dart frantically from card shops to candy stores that this annual behavior is absurd. We should find better ways to show others that we care about them. I want to give my supporting arguments first and then finish with my key point. I believe this will be a better approach than to start with my main point, which might at the beginning sound preachy or sugary and lose some of the audience immediately. If I save the main point for the last, readers may at least be ready to consider it.

5. **Empathy, Not Sympathy**

I am currently involved with volunteer work with the Special Olympics. I want to explain an organization that strives to perfect itself in helping mentally retarded people to perform and achieve to the best of their ability. My main point will be that people tend to be afraid of or feel sorry for the mentally limited. My paper will be directed at people who have a problem communicating with or understanding retarded individuals. Working with the organization, I have learned that the important thing is to have empathy for certain situations rather than sympathy. Feeling sorry is unnecessary and does not help. I hope some of my readers will become more interested or even involed as I did. (I have a sister who is "mentally limited" but did not let that limit her; she is married and works hard at her job at a card company.)

1b Kinds of Writing

Recognize major kinds of writing.

Traditionally, the first question student writers have been encouraged to ask themselves has been: "What kind of writing am I going to do?" You may write to tell a story, to give readers a vivid accounting of events (narration). You may write to take them to a scene or to make them see objects or people (description). You may write to explain or instruct—to make your readers understand a process or an idea (exposition). You may write to convince—to change the reader's mind (argument). You may go beyond logical argument to sway readers by appealing to their emotions and values (persuasion).

Remember that these traditional kinds of writing (or **modes of discourse**) are the means to further ends. They focus attention on the how rather than on the underlying why. Ultimately, you will have to ask: "*Why* am I telling this story? *Why* am I describing this scene?"

NARRATION **Narration** tells the story of events. It focuses on what people do and say, telling us when, where, who, what, and why. You are likely to use narration in *autobiographical* writing, in papers taking stock of personal experience. You may be telling the story of a backpacking trip, of a neighborhood party that turned ugly, of a tragic accident, or of false arrest. The following is a sample of autobiographical narrative:

> Almost every detail of that night stands out very clearly in my memory. I even remember the name of the movie we saw because its title impressed me as being so patly ironical. It was a movie about the German occupation of France, starring Maureen O'Hara and Charles Laughton and called *This Land Is Mine*. I remember the name of the diner we walked into when the movie ended: it was the "American Diner." When we walked in the counterman asked what we wanted and I remember answering with the casual sharpness which had become my habit: "We want a hamburger and a cup of coffee, what do you think we want?" I do not know why, after a year of such rebuffs, I so completely failed to anticipate his answer, which was, of course, "We don't serve Negroes here." This reply failed to discompose me, at least for the moment. I made some sardonic comment about the name of the diner and we walked out into the streets.   James Baldwin, *Notes of a Native Son*

Like other autobiographical narrative, this passage sets the scene. It seizes on revealing details. It tells us not only what people do and say but also what they think and feel.

DESCRIPTION **Description** is the record of close firsthand observation. Your aim may be to describe an object or a piece of machinery in such a way that we can visualize it, understand it, and put it to use. Or your aim may be to describe a scene—a wilderness area, a rush-hour traffic jam—in order to make us share in the sights, sounds, and feelings the scene inspires. The following is an example of description based on firsthand observation:

Clouds are streaming off the ocean, and the metal legs of the tripod are cold against my hands as I set up the spotting scope. I'm out for birds, and the lagoon is thick with them. Grebes and canvasbacks, buffleheads and mergansers work the shallow water for fish, and coots honk and dodge like little black taxicabs in the reeds along the shore.

Across the lagoon, a great blue heron flaps and glides along the shoreline, scouting a likely feeding station. Its thin, improbable legs trail out behind—tools of the trade, in tow from one fishing spot to the next. It lands now, gracefully, delicately for a bird the height of a six-year-old child. Herons are all stilts and feathers and this old giant—which looks as if it could wrap its wings around a Honda—is likely no heavier than a wailing human newborn. Fiddling with the scope until the bird fills my vision, I find it transfixed, surveying the shallows for frogs or cruising fish.   William E. Poole, "For the Birds," *San Francisco Chronicle*

This passage uses specific, exact names for the birds (and for features of the landscape). It shows that the author has an eye for striking, characteristic detail (the thin, "improbable" trailing legs of the bird that is all "stilts and feathers"). It uses words that call up for us authentic sights, sounds, and motions ("honk and dodge," "flaps and glides"). It employs vivid, imaginative comparisons ("like little black taxicabs").

EXPOSITION **Exposition** "sets forth," or lays out, information and ideas. Its aim is to inform, to explain, to instruct. You may be writing to show what the frog's eye tells the frog's brain (and what we can learn from frogs about human vision). You may be writing to show what makes Japanese production techniques superior to American ones. You may be writing to sort out career interests of today's college students. Much exposition aims at making us see how things work, how they compare, or how they fit into a pattern. The following is an example of exposition:

The importation of plants is the primary agent in the modern spread of species, for animals have almost invariably gone along with the plants, quarantine being a comparatively recent and not completely effective innovation. The United States Office of Plant Introduction alone has introduced almost 200,000 species and varieties of plants from all over the world. Nearly half of the 180 or so major insect enemies of plants in the United States are accidental imports from abroad, and most of them have come as hitchhikers on plants. In new territory, out of reach of the restraining hand of the natural enemies that kept down its numbers in its native land, an invading plant or animal is able to become enormously abundant. Thus it is no accident that our most troublesome insects are introduced species.   Rachel Carson, *Silent Spring*

17

This passage traces an important process (the spread, in modern times, of insect species beyond their natural habitat). It uses authoritative factual information; it translates technical information into striking everyday language (many undesirable insects came to this country as "hitchhikers" on plants).

> FOR PATTERNS OF EXPOSITION—CLASSIFICATION, PROCESS, COMPARISON AND CONTRAST—SEE 7.

ARGUMENT **Argument** is the use of systematic, step-by-step reasoning to prove a point. We try to structure an argument in such a way that a reader examining the evidence and following our reasoning will reach the same conclusions that we did. A writer may be systematically examining cause and effect to prove a connection between government policies and recessions. Or a writer may weigh the pros and cons of a proposed immigration law to help readers reach a balanced conclusion.

The following passage from a student paper on gun control is an example of systematic argument:

> In a recent year, 65 percent of the murders, 63 percent of the robberies, and 24 percent of the aggravated assaults involved guns. A government commission found that parts of the country with the highest level of gun ownership have the highest incidence of gun-related violence. When stronger gun control laws are enacted, robberies and homicides tend to decrease. When Massachusetts enacted a stricter gun control law, homicides decreased an unbelievable 55 percent during the two following years. Our rate of violent crimes is 100 percent higher than that of Great Britain, which has stricter gun control laws, and it is 200 percent higher than that of Japan, which outlaws private ownership of handguns. All the available evidence shows that the easy availability of handguns in this country is one of the main causes of violent crime.

This passage shows several features of systematic argument: The writer has collected relevant evidence; she presents an array of facts and figures; she draws conclusions.

> FOR PATTERNS OF ARGUMENTATIVE WRITING—THE INDUCTIVE ARGUMENT, ARGUING FROM PRINCIPLE, CAUSE AND EFFECT, PRO AND CON—SEE 11.

PERSUASION **Persuasion** is the kind of writing that most directly aims at results. Persuasive writers want to change our minds, but they also want us to take action. They want a vote, a sale, a change in our habits. Persuasive writing goes beyond logical argument to appeal to our emotions and to shared values. It often stirs our compassion or indignation; it may appeal strongly to our sense of fairness or to self-interest. The following is a sample of effective persuasive writing:

> EXTINCTION—IT'S FOREVER. One quarter of all species of animals and plants on earth may disappear in the next thirty years because of our destruction of their habitat. The rate of extinction is increasing enormously as forests are destroyed and other wild areas are lost. Organisms that evolved over hundreds of millions of years will be gone forever. The complex interdependence of all creatures, from the largest animals to the smallest plants, is being shattered. We face a crisis with profound implications for the survival of all life. Unfortunately, little is being done to save our planet's natural heritage. The ark is sinking. We need the help of every concerned citizen to conserve the diversity of life on earth. Help save the endangered species.

This passage makes a strong plea for the reader's help. It uses strong emotional language to create alarm, fear, or a sense of loss: *destruction, extinction, forever, shattered*. It uses words with rich positive overtones to appeal to the reader's values: *interdependence, survival, heritage, diversity*.

Note: In practice, the traditional modes overlap. Writers often use them in combination. To help us understand the "new poor" (exposition), a writer may tell the story of a woman who lost her job, her health, and her place to live (narration). Effective argument often dramatizes the issue by vivid accounts of people and events, by using the story of a representative individual as a case history.

WRITING WORKSHOP 2 How would you *classify* each of the following writing samples? Does it illustrate narration, description, exposition, argument, persuasion? Defend your choice. (What were the author's more specific or more personal motives in each passage?)

1. *From a book about the great railroads of Europe and Asia:*

> Venice, like a drawing room in a gas station, is approached through a vast apron of infertile industrial flatlands, crisscrossed with black sewer troughs and stinking of oil, the gigantic sinks and stoves of refineries and factories, all intimidating the delicate dwarfed city beyond. The graffiti along the way are professionally executed as the names of the firms. . . . The lagoon with its luminous patches of oil slick, as if hopelessly retouched by Canaletto, has a yard-wide tidewrack of rubble, plastic bottles, broken toilet seats, raw sewage, and that bone white

factory froth the wind beats into drifts of foam. The edges of the city have succumbed to industry's erosion, and what shows are the cracked back windows and derelict posterns of water-logged villas, a few brittle Venetian steeples, and farther in, but low and almost visibly sinking, walls of spaghetti-colored stucco and red roofs over which flocks of soaring swallows are teaching pigeons to fly.   Paul Theroux, *The Great Railway Bazaar*

2. *From a book on the skills and crafts needed for rural living:*

There's a lot more to building than just hammering nails, but it's a good place to start. These are some useful things to know: To drive a nail, hold the nail in your left hand (if you're right-handed), and tap directly on the head of it a few times with the hammer to set it. Hold the nail at a slight angle—it is less likely to bend and it makes a stronger joint. Then, take away your left hand and hammer it the rest of the way in. It's most important to hammer directly on the nail head, so that the nail doesn't bend. This sounds simple and it is, but it requires developing coordination and a sense of the hammer, its weight and its force. It is best to hold the hammer near the end of the handle. This gives you more leverage and, therefore, more force.   Jeanne Tetrault and Sherry Thomas, *Country Women*

3. *From an article about the future of Social Security:*

The demographic shift most important to long-term deficits is the dramatic decline in fertility rates for members of the Baby Boom generation. Much more than any increase or decrease in longevity, fertility rates affect the eventual age distribution of a population. In recent years the American fertility rate has ticked up slightly, but it is still close to the record low, reached in 1976, of 65.8 live births per 1,000 women of childbearing age. The low fertility rate guarantees that the median age of the American population will rise dramatically in the years ahead— barring, of course, an enormous increase in immigration. As the population ages, the demands on the budget will become extreme.   Philip Longman, "Justice Between Generations," *Atlantic*

4. *From an editorial on drug traffic:*

Illegal drugs are not some mysterious and uncontrollable plague seeping north from the tropics. They are commodities that are imported because there is an American market for them. The surest way to stop the illegal drug trade is to make that market dry up. This is where the prevailing drug-control strategy is hypocritical. It exempts from all blame the one class of people ultimately responsible for this brutal business: American drug users. Every time an American does a line of coke, he or she is directly subsidizing murder across the hemisphere. It doesn't matter if the user is a legislative aide to a compassionate congressman or an inner-city pimp. As Colombian drug lord Roberto Suarez Gomez boasts, his fortune came entirely from "the depravity of the Yanquis." "The Dope Dilemma," *The New Republic*

1c   The Audience Profile

Keep your audience in mind as you write.

Who is your intended reader? Sometimes we write mainly for ourselves, recording our thoughts and feelings. But most writing is meant to be read. How you size up the needs and expectations of your target audience will help shape what you do and how you proceed.

THE EDUCATED READER Much of your writing will aim at an imaginary educated reader. Both your instructors and your peers at their best will try to serve as stand-ins for the reasonable, well-informed general reader. Ideally, educated readers are thinking readers; they look for a thoughtful, well-worked-out piece of writing rather than glib talk. They care about issues of public interest and are open to new ideas. They frown on name-calling (*redneck*, *bleeding-heart liberal*), sexist language (*just like a woman*), slanted evidence, and cheap shots of all kinds.

THE LAY AUDIENCE In informative writing, we play the role of the expert who explains specialized information to a lay audience. We assume a receptive audience that likes to be kept up to date on new developments—for instance, in science or medicine. We shed light on matters that interest or worry our readers but that they lack time to research on their own: security systems for cars, new treatments for mental illness. Our responsibility is to show patience with the needs of the outsider: We provide necessary background, explain technical terms to the uninitiated, and present new ideas one step at a time.

THE IN-GROUP AUDIENCE When we write for an in-group, we write for a limited audience that shares a common interest or believes in a common cause. Groups that share a common purpose include unions, Rotarians, art associations, *Star Trek* aficionados, Elvis Presley fan clubs, and the like. Writers will find such a group a willing audience if they know the history and the lore of the group, if they can show their commitment to its shared

21

values. A writer writing for an in-group audience of movie buffs, for instance, is likely to speak with affection of legendary early stars, of the great foreign directors, and of the great critics, such as Pauline Kael. At the same time, in-group readers are likely to be sticklers for accuracy; they will expect the writer to get the facts right concerning such movie classics as *Gone with the Wind* or *Citizen Kane.*

SPECIAL AUDIENCES   Much writing targets a special audience identified by age, sex, occupation, religion, or ethnic background (or by a combination of these). Much advertising, for instance, singles out a particular range of customers and works on their special needs or vulnerability. When you aim your own writing at a particular age group or occupational group, you will have to take into account differences like the following:

- Many young people have only recently staged their rebellion against parental control; they are less likely than older people to applaud calls for discipline, supervision, "cracking down," law and order.
- Social workers and teachers will tend to favor spending to alleviate social problems (for instance, money to shelter the homeless or to provide child care). However, property owners or operators of small business tend to be suspicious of initiatives that would raise their taxes.

Your relationship with the audience will help set the **tone** of your writing. If your audience expects you to take it and the subject seriously, you will write a fairly formal kind of English. If your audience expects to be entertained, you will move toward a more informal, a more relaxed or chummy style. For most of your writing in a composition class, the right level is between two extremes—neither hyperformal nor disrespectful and slangy. The best modern prose is *moderately formal*—formal without being stiff or pompous. The following passage is an example of effective modern prose that is never too far removed from plain talk. (Note words and phrases like *picture phone, whisked, cheap, come and gone.*)

Looking Back at the Future

The future was to have been a wondrous time, with a picture phone in every home and an atomic-powered car or a personal airplane in every garage. Conveyor-belt sidewalks were to have whisked us through space-age cities while atomic power plants generated clean energy so cheap there would be no need to meter it. But the future, as envisioned a generation ago, has come and gone. Picture phones, atomic cars, and moving sidewalks have all died on the drawing board. Nuclear energy is here, but it has not exactly lived up to its expectations.   John Flinn, *San Francisco Examiner*

WRITING WORKSHOP 3   Work alone or with a group to prepare an *audience profile*. Study closely one recent issue of a publication that aims at a distinct audience. Prepare a portrait of the imaginary ideal reader for a publication like the following: *Sports Illustrated, Popular Science, The Wall Street Journal, The New Yorker, Ms., McCall's, New York, The New Republic, Rolling Stone.* What common background or shared interests do the editors assume? Do they cater to shared likes and dislikes? Do they appeal to shared values? (Is there any "outgrouping"—that is, are any groups treated as outsiders?) Use detailed evidence or illustrations.

The following is a sample passage from one student's report:

> Increasingly, the advertisements in *McCall's* are designed to catch the eye of a woman who has a career as well as a home. A perfect example is the back cover, featuring a woman telling about her first day at a new job. The woman looks like a housewife who has decided, for whatever reason, to go to work after twelve years. We don't know if she's married, divorced, separated, widowed, or what, so a woman in any of these circumstances could easily identify with her. New York Life Insurance has an ad on page 95 with the woman behind the desk with pictures of kids and husband. (Is he dead? Or is it a boyfriend?) The headline says "for people with big responsibilities." Obviously New York Life thinks enough career women read *McCall's* for it to be worth its money to advertise in the magazine. On page 211 is an ad promoting nuclear power plants with a woman being the spokesperson, billed as a Nuclear Cost Accountant.

WRITING TOPICS 1

On which of the following topics do you have something to say? Choose a topic that you can relate to your own experience, observation, reading, and viewing. Write a paper that has a point, that has a plan, and that will reach your intended reader.

1. Have you ever felt the need to correct misinformation or to clear up a *misunderstanding*? What was the problem? Why did you care? What did you say, or what should you have said?

2. Have you ever been able to provide a helpful warning or useful *advice*? Is there a subject on which you think you could give helpful pointers to other people? Sketch out the advice.

3. Have you ever felt the need to alert others to the significance of something that is often overlooked or *ignored*? Why is it important?

4. Have you ever felt like a *whistleblower*—knowing that something highly touted does not work or is badly flawed? Or wanting to expose incompetence or deception? What could or should have been your report to those in charge?

5. Have you ever wanted to pay tribute to *unsung heroes*? What men or women do you think deserve more recognition than they receive? Why is their contribution overlooked? What can you say to right the balance?

6. Have you been involved in promoting a *good cause*? Why should your readers care? What could you say to break through the crust of apathy?

7. Have you ever reacted negatively to being *stereotyped*? Have you ever felt put down not as an individual but as a member of an ethnic, racial, religious, or other similar group? What is the stereotype? What would you say to counteract the stereotype?

8. Do you hold an *unpopular view* on a current issue? Why are you out of step with prevailing opinion? How do you defend the stand you take?

2   Finding Material

OVERVIEW   Where should you turn for material? How does a writer gather the material for a paper, a magazine article, or a chapter in a book? Experienced writers know how to explore a topic, how to work up a subject. When you work up a subject, you mobilize resources you already have, and you turn for help to outside sources. You draw on the right mix of personal experience, firsthand investigation, relevant reading and viewing, and consultation with insiders or people in the know.

Jog your memory for incidents, details, and figures that tie in with your topic. Search for possible connections with what you have recently read in newspapers or magazines and with what you have heard and seen on news broadcasts or documentaries. Follow up promising leads—read and listen as much as time allows. Usually you will be able to draw on one or more of the following sources of material:

OBSERVATION Good writers are alert observers. Like scouts or spies, they notice revealing details and register quotable quotations. For instance, when they walk through a new shopping mall, they note for future reference the plastic ferns, the piped-in muzak, or the cute names of the boutiques.

EXPERIENCE Good writers know how to draw on the memory bank of past experience. They use prewriting techniques like brainstorming and clustering to bring to mind memories that are to the point. For example, when they write about the disabled, they mobilize memories of contacts with disabled people in their family, among their friends, or in the larger community.

INFORMED OPINION Good writers listen to people in a position to know. They look for the testimony of the insider or the eyewitness. They read what experts and pundits have to say. They listen to people with the inside story—whether in informal conversation or in a structured interview.

RESEARCH Research is a more systematized version of the learning and finding out that are always part of working up a subject. Good writers know their way around a library. They know how to sift records, documents, and a range of print and nonprint sources. They know how to weigh the conflicting testimony of interested parties.

Remember: Exploit the full range of resources from the *personal* to the *public*. Our writing about personal experience gains in depth and interest if we can at the right moment branch out to similar experiences of others and to informed opinion on related trends. Our writing about public issues becomes less theoretical and more authentic if at the right moment we turn back for support to something we have personally witnessed or experienced.

2a Prewriting Techniques

Use the techniques that will help you work up a rich fund of material for your paper.

Writers develop their own ways of working up a subject. They jot down rough ideas, prepare a scratch outline, or start a preliminary file on their word processors. They collect clippings or photocopies, and they take systematic notes on their reading. Study and practice different techniques for generating material for your papers.

JOURNAL WRITING   Many professional writers use **journals**, diaries, or logs to record ideas and impressions from day to day. The entries in your journal or writer's log might deal with family occasions, chance encounters, jobs, childhood memories, friendships, or personal problems. You might devote entries to current reading, public events, or TV shows and movies. Use such entries as raw materials for more formal, more structured kinds of writing. A journal entry like the following could form the basis for a paper about the work ethic or about the needy:

> When I was sixteen years old, I worked for the Pope, in a manner of speaking. My first job was that of a part-time receptionist at the St. John rectory. The rectory, a Spanish-style building, white-washed and topped with a red tile roof, was the nerve center of the parish. As one of three part-time receptionists, I needed tact and courtesy, decent communication skills, and a basically friendly outlook toward the rest of humanity. My duties included answering the telephone and writing messages; stuffing, sealing, and organizing mountains of envelopes; running errands; closing the church at night; and often helping with the dishes. It wasn't a bad job for a sixteen-year-old. I also had free access to the refrigerator and baked goods. I performed my job with a happy-go-lucky attitude, but I was often troubled and surprised by the number of people who were in need of food and shelter. Before I worked at the rectory, I thought I had been living in a prosperous middle-class parish.

WRITING PRACTICE 4   Start a *journal*. Write in it regularly to record observations, thoughts, memories, or notes on current viewing and reading. Include the kind of detail that would provide promising raw material for future papers:

- graphic details on a *setting* where events take place
- capsule portraits of *people*
- dramatic highlights of *events*
- striking *quotations:* what people actually said
- your candid *reactions* or feelings (*how* you reacted, and also *why*)

BRAINSTORMING   **Brainstorming** is the process of jotting down, in rough unsorted form, the ideas and associations that a topic brings to mind. Jog your memory for relevant observations, incidents, data, slogans, headlines, remarks. Worry later about how a statement will sound or how well an example will fit. Right now, let things come to the surface. Work up a fund of material for later use. Remember a few simple guidelines:

(1) **Keep moving.** Put down anything that might possibly be useful. Leave the sorting out and any second thoughts for later.

(2) **Let one thing lead to another.** Often one remembered incident will jog your memory and bring to mind other related events or details from the memory banks of the brain.

(3) **Push toward specifics.** Include scenes we can visualize, snatches of dialogue we can hear.

Develop your own format for your preliminary brainstorming on a topic. The following examples show some common varieties. For each example, ask yourself: What kind of paper might result from these first exploratory jottings?

  ■ CHAIN OF ASSOCIATION—letting one thing lead to another, jotting down key terms and phrases:

(Fitness)

Running races—fitness routines—balanced diet—counting calories—cholesterol—high blood pressure—drinking/smoking—overdoing it—fit for life, not just spurts of exercise—anorexia/bulimia—appetite suppressants—caffeine—aerobic workout tapes—jogging—lifting weights—rowing machines—health clubs

  ■ IDEA INVENTORY—listing possibly relevant points:

(American business)

failing in the world market
unable to compete
unable to produce quality goods—VCRs, televisions, digital watches
moving production overseas
employer vs. employee
employee apathy
Atari: moving production overseas, eliminating American jobs
Dow: people exposed to chemical contamination
the bigger we are the harder we fall
violating personal freedoms: mandatory drug testing, required polygraph tests
Ivan Boesky and insider trading—anything to make a buck

■ THINKING OUT LOUD—ranging over the subject, recording preliminary thoughts as they come to mind:

(The macho male)

Macho: Big, muscular, unfeeling, rough—harsh, moves to kill. (Sylvester Stallone: I hate what he promotes.) Negative impression. Hard craggy faces with mean eyes that bore holes in you.

Men who have to prove themselves through acts of violence. The man who is disconnected from his feelings, insensitive to women's needs—cannot express himself in a feeling manner.

The word seems to have negative connotations for me because I work part-time in a bar. I am forever seeing these perfectly tanned types who come on to a woman. As a child, macho meant a strong male type who would take care of me—paternal, warmth in eyes. John Wayne: gruff, yet you feel secure knowing someone like this was around.

Crude, huge—the body, not the heart—tendency to violence always seems close to the surface. Looks are very important. Craggy face. Bloodshed excites them. Arnold Schwarzenegger muscles, gross.

Tend to dominate in relationships—desire for control. "Me Tarzan—you Jane."

In the following paper, the author of the brainstorming sample has sorted out the material and formulated the conclusions it suggests. Compare the paper with the brainstorming notes.

Misconceptions of Macho

"Macho"—the word makes me see yet another prototype of the muscular tanned male walk through the doors of the establishment where I work. He glides past me, lean and smooth. Dressed to kill, not a hair out of place, he lets his eyes dart this way and that, trying to zero in on his female prey of the evening. Suddenly, some woman catches his eye. He saunters over, makes some unintelligible remark, and the courting dance has begun.

The stereotype of the macho is the tough man who proves his maleness through acts of violence or through dominant behavior. Sylvester Stallone as Rambo creates the stereotypical image, complete with mayhem, blood, guts, and brute strength. The price the macho pays is that he is incapable of expressing himself in a caring, feeling manner. He is insensitive to a woman's needs. He may be the strongest, toughest, most handsome, and best-at-everything kind of person in the world, but he lacks emotional qualities that would link him with the rest of humanity.

Macho is as much a state of mind as a matter of physical appearance. A macho male can be a five-foot-tall, ninety-eight pound weakling and still have that condescending attitude toward a woman, looking down on her as if she were nothing more than a vehicle put here by God for his own pleasure. As a woman who works in the bar and restaurant business, I have seen this scenario played out many times: A lone woman comes into a bar, perhaps to meet a friend, and finds that she is fair game. The macho male will invade her space immediately; he will not be put off even with a blunt "Get lost!" He thinks all women are little Barbie dolls equipped to satisfy his every whim. This man operates from a "Me Tarzan, you Jane" mentality. His desire to dominate and control is too great to allow any real intimacy to develop.

Yet I remember that when I was a child the image of the strong male held different associations for me. The macho ideal of my childhood was more of a gentle giant. Though tall, strong, and gruff in his John Wayne manner, he was not afraid to show emotion in his "manly" way. Yes, he was tough. But he was never openly condescending towards women, because roles were still definitely defined. He took charge of his wife and family, but he was paternal and at the same time respectful. He had that Jimmy Stewart twinkle of warmth that I remember seeing in the old movies. He represented security, he inspired trust, and he seemed open and genuine. These qualities are missing in today's macho male.

WRITING WORKSHOP 5   As a *brainstorming* exercise, jot down any ideas, memories, observations, or associations that come to mind on one of the following topics. Keep writing—leave the sorting out of material for a later stage. Share the result with a group of your peers. What kind of paper might come out of this exercise? Choose one:

fitness	Disneyland	evangelists
diets	vandals	game shows
guns	the police	dress for success
charity	drunk drivers	long hair
celebrities	ex-friends	the aged

CLUSTERING   **Clustering** is a kind of free-association writing taught by Gabriele Rico in her book *Writing the Natural Way*. When clustering, a writer starts with a central stimulus word that becomes the core of the cluster. Different lines of association then branch out from the center. A network of images and thoughts takes shape that the writer then turns into a finished piece of writing. The ideas called up by the clustering technique often arrange themselves into a satisfying pattern. Here is a sample cluster and the writing sample based on it:

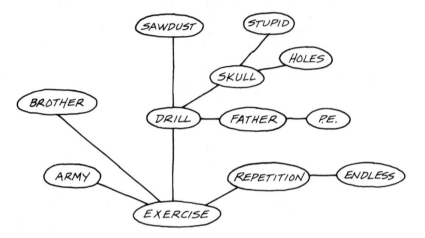

Drill

Drill to me is a nightmare. I never minded arithmetic or grammar drills in school; I could do them, and they gave me a sense of security. But I can't think of those drills without a crowd of images bursting forth. I see my father bending close to my face saying with horrible enunciation: "Can't-you-drill-that-into-your-thick-skull?" At the same time I see an overlaid image of a real drill, drilling into plywood and showering sawdust everywhere. And I see, too, my brother in green, marching endlessly, with the drill sergeant barking orders at him. For good reason, the word *drill* rhymes with *kill*.

WRITING WORKSHOP 6   From the list that follows, choose a word or phrase that is rich in meaning for you. Make sure it calls up memories or starts a train of thought. First, get your ideas down on paper by *clustering*, letting your ideas branch out from the word as a central core. Then write a paragraph or longer passage in which you arrange your material in an order or pattern that makes sense to you. Choose one:

rivals	home	chance
divorce	veteran	alone
the team	free	addiction
bullies	being close	loyal
cheating	losing	success

INTERVIEWS Often you can learn much by listening to people close to your subject. Experienced writers listen attentively to witnesses, experts, and insiders. They often draw on informal interviews with people whose background or special commitments qualify them to speak with authority on a topic. Look at what is part of the interviewer's job:

(1) Get people to talk. Good interviewers know how to put people at their ease. They build trust, getting people to talk freely and confidentially. Often you will find that people turn eloquent when they can tell a sympathetic listener their grievances or when they can share their interest in a specialty or a cause.

(2) Structure your interview. Be ready to go with the flow of the conversation, but also prepare questions that will give the interview its general direction. Sometimes an interviewer will start with safe, nonthreatening factual questions and then push on to questions close to the other person's heart. Sometimes an interviewer will use more aggressive tactics to goad people into revealing what at first they were perhaps not ready to say. If you are writing on the problems of the elderly, you may approach the interview with a prepared set of questions like the following:

- What did you do before you retired?
- How or why did you retire?
- What do you like most about retirement?
- What do you like least about retirement?
- What do you think about mandatory retirement?
- How is retirement different from what you expected?
- If you could turn the clock back twenty years, what would you do differently?
- Do young people today live in a different world?

(3) Be an attentive listener. Use written notes (or your tape recorder) to capture key facts, revealing personal statements, and shades of opinion. Sometimes you may write up the results of an interview in a *question-and-answer* format. The following is part of an interview with a campus assistant at a high school:

Question: What are your duties—what does a campus assistant do?
Answer: Well, the job entails enforcing the rules that they have here at the school, and it requires some vigilance looking around if anyone is causing trouble or committing crimes. It involves opening and locking doors or windows, also helping teachers out and giving students whatever help or information they need from me.

Question: What is the best part of the job for you?

Answer: The best part is the people. I get to interact with a lot of people. We get to talk with them. I walk around a lot and meet new people. My last job was in the kitchen, in the back at McDonald's, making hamburgers and cheeseburgers. I like this job better.

Question: When you were younger, what did you think work would be like?

Answer: I don't think my father enjoyed working very much. He used to come home tired. I mean, he didn't usually say, "I really had a great day at work today." So I thought work was going to be very unpleasant.

Question: Was your father right?

Answer: I guess he was right in a way. Most people wouldn't work without pay. I think it's a great incentive to pay people. But I need to do something I can enjoy. I want to be able to say, "I enjoy work."

You will often draw on interviews in a paper using both oral and printed sources. However, you may also devote a whole paper to the results of a fruitful interview. Study the following *interview paper* as a model:

Picking Up Garbage

Gabriel was born the youngest of thirteen children. He grew up in the old country and has been in the United States for three years. Every morning he goes to his job in the waste land-fill area. When I ask him about his work, he says: "I used to pick up papers in the area. Everybody starts out with that job. Some people are able to save some money that way. Then they go back to the old country, drink and relax for a few months, and then, when they run out of money, come back here. They will always be picking up papers. I don't want to go back. I drive a truck now, and I crush the garbage. I save money."

I ask him about the place where he lives. He is not living with family. "It is a small place with fifteen people living there. I feel bad because we all sleep together in two rooms. I am the first one to go to work in the morning. So when my alarm goes off at 5:30 AM, everybody is disturbed. I feel bad that everybody wakes up because of the noise from my alarm. But what can I do? I have to work."

Gabriel spends little time at the place where he "lives." He usually works more than five days and goes to school four evenings a week. What does he like least about his job? He says that he does a lot of thinking while he drives the truck. "You know that the American people throw out many things. Much of it is good stuff. I see toys that are brand new. I see radios that are not broken. I see many things that I would like to send to people in my own country. But I cannot pick up any of the things. There is a rule. The driver is not allowed to get out of the truck."

I assume that the company is trying to protect the drivers' health by not letting them handle items from the garbage cans. But Gabriel says that the rule is intended for the driver's safety: Once a driver who climbed out of the truck to pick up something was run over by another driver who did not see him.

"A few times," Gabriel says, "I have taken the chance of losing my job. I got out and picked up a tape recorder once. I brought it home, and it worked perfectly. The Americans throw away so many things like that. It's like throwing away money. Americans are very rich. The people in my country are very poor. Every day I see good things thrown away, and it breaks my heart to crush them. I am destroying what my people could use."

I am looking at the job of the garbage collector from a different perspective since I talked to Gabriel. I used to think that the filth and the smell would bother me most about the job. I found that what bothers Gabriel most is the idea of looking at "waste" all day.

WRITING WORKSHOP 7   Prepare a set of questions for an *interview* and try to get feedback or suggestions from a group. Conduct the interview and present the results first in a question-and-answer format. After discussion and feedback, write a paper interpreting the results of the interview. Make good use of brief, revealing quotations. Interview a person *outside* your own familiar world. For instance, interview

- a police officer working in a high-crime neighborhood
- a security guard for a posh apartment complex
- the owners of a mom-and-pop grocery store
- an illegal immigrant
- a member of a religious cult
- a guard in a correctional institution
- a nurse or technician in a psychiatric ward
- a clerk in an adult bookstore

READING NOTES   Learn to look at your reading with the writer's eye. Many professional writers keep a file of clippings that stores information, statistics, provocative comments, and revealing sidelights on topics in which they have a tentative interest. In reading a newspaper or news-magazine, an experienced writer will often decide, "Let me write this down" or "I should make a photocopy of this page."

Suppose you are working on a paper that will explore the cult of the star athlete. You should be able to glean material like the following from a few days' reading of current newspapers and magazines:

Inflated salaries

- A *Time* article listed players signed to million-dollar-a-year contracts during the last year. Even such figures pale compared with the earnings of athletic superstars like quarterback Steve Young, who garnered a $40 million lifetime contract from the now defunct USFL and then went on to sign another $5 million contract in the NFL.
- Sports columnist Glenn Dickey said that the signing of baseball great Jack Clark by the New York Yankees meant "a resumption of the giddy free-agent bidding that has sent player salaries through the roof."

The other side of the star system

- Arthur Ashe, first male black athlete to win the Wimbledon tennis tournament said in a widely quoted article in the *New York Times:* "For every star earning millions there are six or seven others making $20,000 or $30,000." Many others have their careers cut short by injuries. Most high school athletes never make it to the pros.

Parallel patterns in college athletics

- G. Ann Uhlir, dean at Texas Woman's University, says about women in college sports: "Opportunities for elite women athletes have improved, but total participation slots available for women have declined."

With notes such as these, you are well on the way toward a paper that will contrast the glamorous image of the star athlete created by the media with the sobering realities facing the rank and file. Study the way a student writer identifies and uses material from reading notes in the following paragraph. Look at the identification of each author and publication. Look at the use of *short* selected quotations (put in quotation marks), alternating with short summaries in the student writer's own words (indirect quotation or paraphrase).

People have long had false teeth, artificial limbs, and pacemakers—why not an artificial heart? For a while, the future looked right for another "breakthrough" or a "medical miracle." However, after the death of artificial-heart recipient William Shroeder, many observers had second thoughts about the outlook for the permanent artificial heart as "a long-term lifesaver." Doubts and reservations multiplied. As Robert Bazell said in *The New Republic*, "Exotic medical procedures make compelling news stories" but the "trouble is that they are indeed experimental, and often they do not work." The costs are horrendous: In an article in *Business Week*, Kathleen Deremy and Alan Hall estimated that the widespread use of artificial hearts could add up to $3 billion to the nation's health costs. And the procedure raises thorny questions of medical ethics: Who decides who gets the artificial heart and who is left out? What stand do we take on the "right-to-die" issue— does the patient have the right to suicide? (As Beth Vaughan-Cole and Helen Lee pointed out in *The American Journal of Nursing,* "the artificial-heart recipient has the key that turns off the machinery.")

WRITING WORKSHOP 8 Examine several issues of newspapers and newsmagazines to study the coverage of a topic currently in the news. Take *detailed notes:* Summarize information, jot down striking details, condense key statistics, quote provocative comments by experts or insiders. Choose a topic like the following:

1. *The Congested Future:* traffic problems and solutions
2. *Women's Sports:* toward equality?
3. *Health Alert:* a health hazard currently in the news
4. *Call the Police:* police work in today's communities
5. *Troubled Youth:* young people in trouble with the law
6. *To Build or Not to Build:* development pro and con
7. *Schools in the Red:* supporting your local schools
8. *Domestic Violence:* battered wives or abused children
9. *Red Tape:* regulation and deregulation
10. *Crisis Coverage:* a crisis currently in the news

Work out a general conclusion (or conclusions), and write a paper in which you use the material from your notes to support your general point (or points). Clearly identify each author and publication; put all directly quoted material in quotation marks. Hand in your reading notes with your paper.

DRAWING ON EXPERIENCE When you write about personal experience, you write about what you know best. You may be writing about personal experience to come to terms with some of the things that have happened to you or to take stock of who and what you are. But you may also be turning to personal experience in order to bring abstract ideas and theoretical issues to life for your reader.

Learn to mobilize your memory—learn to draw on a rich backlog of remembered events, thoughts, and feelings. Rack your brains; start the flow of material that might be useful. As you focus on a major strand or trace the common thread linking events that may have occurred years apart, let a *chain of association* lead you to half-forgotten incidents and details. Work up notes like the following about what you and the other people involved did and said and felt. Get close to actual situations, incidents, gestures, confrontations.

What material in these sample notes seems especially promising? What overall conclusion or direction do they suggest?

Declaration of Independence

"looking nice"
"don't carry the ice chest"
"get good grades in school"
dependence—having to go for rides in the car to get out of the house and my mother being angry and staring out the window, head on her hand and not saying a word the whole time—I always thought that was ridiculous.

My grandmother was an independent woman. In 1928, she sailed from Canada to Manila, by herself, so that my grandfather and she could get married on his next leave from the Navy.

My mother was always concerned with what the neighbors would say, about anything. When I was in high schol and went on a protest march, my mother wasn't concerned with the cause, if it was right or wrong, but "what will the neighbors say?"

Independence wasn't on the agenda for my mother's childhood. My grandmother, a woman of the 1920's, used her independence as a way and means. With the War, Depression, alone a lot and moving from base to base, she was outspoken, unconventional, and atypical of an officer's wife.

My mother in contrast seemed meek and shy, growing in the shadow of their only other child, a boy. He was the one destined to follow in my grandfather's footsteps (although he never did).

Growing up with uncertainty, my sister seemed to flourish. She set a goal and has stayed with that same goal for 15 years. My brother and I floundered under a dual message. My father was a lightpost. Always there, sturdy despite his appearance, methodical and self-satisfied with himself. When my mother got furious and started slamming the kitchen cabinets and doors, my father would calmly ride out the storm. Trying to do the best that we could was father's objective for his children.

Thanksgiving dinner was always the same at our house. The women cooked the meal, served the meal, and cleaned up after the meal, while the men sat down to watch the football game. Most of the women enjoyed this whole set-up. It was a chance to talk "girl talk": where the best bargains were, who was seeing whom (in terms of marriage), and what was happening on the soaps.

These notes, although still unsorted and written down as they came to mind, already focus on a common theme that echoes throughout: a daughter's dissatisfaction with the example of dependence set by her mother. Moving toward a first draft, the writer will work out the pattern that will trace the connecting thread and make sense of the materials.

PEER REVIEW 9 Study the way a student writer used *personal experience* in the following paper. Answer questions like the following:

- What was the writer's purpose or underlying motive? What did writing this paper do for the author?
- Did the writer bring the topic to life for you? Are there any striking or memorable details? Are there any telling phrases that you are going to remember?
- Does the paper have a plan or a strategy that becomes clear to the audience?
- What does reading this paper do for the reader? Are you a good audience for this author? Why or why not?

Free at Last

My memories of childhood are dim and hazy as if I lived in a fog or perhaps was only a casual observer in my life. My most vivid memory is not of an event but rather of a feeling which was with me at most of my waking moments. The feeling was that I lacked control of my life and actions. I suppose that all children feel this to some extent or another. The difference in me was that this feeling came not from my being told what to do, but rather from my inferring what my actions were to be and controlling myself to fit this image, all the while hating the restraints that I was placing on myself.

I suppose this bound feeling emanated from the attitudes of my parents. In my earliest memories, I can remember my parents creating an aura of superiority about our family. The actions of others, even relatives, were constantly viewed, reviewed, chastised, and condemned. When my aunt's children started getting in trouble with the law, when my cousin got divorced, when our close family friends became heavy drinkers, we secretly judged them and isolated ourselves from them, all the while professing our Christianity. I often participated in this, but gradually I came to resent being separated and elevated above those who did not live up to our standards. Still it was hard to isolate myself from this indoctrination, and more often than not, I would censor my own actions so as to live up to the ideals of my parents. In retrospect the events often seem small and petty but at the time they were enormous and life-shattering. I can remember once, as a junior in high school, I lied to my parents about the movie I was going to see. I wanted to see *Young Frankenstein*, a very popular "R" rated movie, but I told them I was going to see *Jeremiah Johnson* which was rated "G." I can still feel the guilt of slinking out of the door to taste the forbidden fruit. There was a feeling that someone else's will was being superimposed upon my own.

This feeling of guilt also affected me in other ways. I did things not because I wanted to, but because I felt it was expected of me. I went out for the football team even though I had no desire to play, and for three years I sat on the bench, finally earning a varsity letter because I was a senior, not because I was a good player. I joined the Air Force J.R.O.T.C. because my dad had been an Air Force pilot and I knew that was what he wanted. I did what my parents wanted, believed what my parents believed. I did not exist; the model child my parents had created was merely borrowing my shoes.

By the end of my senior year, things had reached an unbearable level. I had won an R.O.T.C. scholarship to the state university, another attempt to prove my sterling character. But it was clear that something was changing. I had attempted to pay rent while staying at home so as to gain some little freedom and ended up poorer but with no more freedom. One evening after we had finished dinner, my parents fell asleep in front of the television. I left the living room, with my parents snoring and M*A*S*H still playing, to go hang out with my friends. Time passed quickly, as it does when spent idly, and before I knew it, it was well after midnight. I was unsure what to do, but I decided to try and sneak back in the house. As I crept past the living room windows, I peered in trying to see if anyone was awake. Suddenly, I was blinded by a light. My mother had been sitting on the couch in the darkness waiting for me to return home. She pointed towards the door, gesturing for me to come inside. My mom and dad both questioned me for what seemed hours asking where I was, what I was doing, and who I was with.

I did not know it at the time, but the scholarship was to become my escape route. Through it I was able to glimpse the freedom I so badly needed. Once I had enrolled at the university, I no longer had to worry about the watchful eye of my parents. That is not to say that they did not try to control my behavior. There were countless conversations about whom I associated with, how often I studied, and how much beer I drank. But a phone call across five hundred miles has little power to discern the truth. Finally I could experiment with the freedom that had so long eluded me. I skipped classes. I drank till I fell down. I experimented with smoking pot.

This sounds as if I slipped into this new lifestyle quite easily, but the fact is that I was constantly torn between my desire for freedom and my guilt at experiencing it. I was beginning to feel sorry about my exploits and began discussing my intention to join the priesthood. This sounds rather melodramatic, but it was met with great applause. Fortunately the Jesuits suggested that I spend more time in school, gaining some life experience, before I join the order. My parents continued to call me, trying to keep tabs on my life, but these calls no longer had the same effect on me. I was beginning to feel no guilt about enjoying life.

2b The Structured Search

Ask the kinds of questions that will lead to a fruitful investigation.

Experienced writers ask themselves questions that help them cover an event or explore an issue. Many typical questions are applicable to different topics. We can often ask: What do I already know about this from *experience*? How is this issue covered in the *media*? Are there any popular stereotypes or *misunderstandings* that might have to be cleared up? What are some of the underlying *causes* of the current situation? What *authorities* could I turn to to confirm my tentative conclusions? We call such a set of questions for the systematic exploration of a topic a **discovery frame**—a framework or program for fruitful investigation.

ANALYZING AN EVENT Journalists are taught the traditional **journalistic formula** for covering news events:

- *Who* was involved?
- *What* happened?
- *When* and *where* did it happen?
- *Why* did things happen as they did?
- *How* did things happen or how were they done?

Often the lead sentence of a news report will answer all of these questions, telling us who, what, when, where, why, and how. (The reporter can then go on to answer each question in greater detail in subsequent paragraphs.)

Late last night, 400 chanting protesters were arrested by riot police at the Las Manes testing grounds after they tried to storm the main gate to protest the resumption of nuclear tests.

You might use a similar set of questions when writing a paper on a famous disaster, such as the sinking of the *Titanic*, the San Francisco earthquake, the Kennedy assassination, the *Challenger* tragedy. You would use a dicovery frame like the following to help you cover the event. Your finished paper would include a paragraph or more in response to each question.

> I. *What happened?* When and where? What are the bare facts? How would you summarize what took place to inform or remind your readers of the event?
>
> II. *What led up to it?* What background or perspective does the reader need? How would you put the event in context?
>
> III. *Who played a key role?* Who were the main actors in the drama? What were their assignments or responsibilities?
>
> IV. *How did people behave?* What did they do, or how did they perform? What did they do that was striking or unexpected?
>
> V. *Why did things happen the way they did?* Who or what is to blame? Are there different theories or explanations of what happened?
>
> VI. *What happened afterwards?* Was there an important sequel or aftermath? What were the consequences? Did people learn anything from the event?

WRITING WORKSHOP 10 The high points of much autobiographical writing are events that changed the writer's outlook or thinking—a first encounter, a turning point, a traumatic disappointment, a painful separation, a dramatic confrontation. Focus on an important incident or event in your own life. Work up material that will answer the five *storyteller's questions*:

> I. THE SETTING—Where are we? What will it take to make your readers visualize the setting, the scene?
>
> II. THE PEOPLE—Who are the key players in the drama? What do they look like; how do they talk and act?
>
> III. THE SITUATION—What led up to the event? What background or context do you need to fill in for your readers?
>
> IV. THE EVENT—What happened? How did things come to a head? How can you dramatize the high point of the story?
>
> V. THE POINT—What did you learn from the event? How did it change your thinking or your attitude? Why is it worth remembering?

Study the following story-with-a-point as a model for your own. How productive were the five storyteller's questions for this student writer?

The Devil Made Me Do It

THE SETTING: The house was one of those tract homes that are indistinguishable from their neighbors. It was always shadowy and smelled like a pantry. The room I had rented was down the hall, to the right. Coming home from football practice, I would timidly walk into the kitchen, make a bologna sandwich, and walk down the hall to eat it in my room, ready to put on a fake smile when I encountered the Westons, the couple who owned the house.

THE PEOPLE: My parents and I had agreed that I should live, at least to start with, with a Christian family (it was more their idea than mine), my parents being fairly religious people. The Westons both looked alike; he wore sweaters all the time, wore glasses, and spoke and moved softly; she always wore drab skirts, was always smiling, and had a hairdo that looked twenty years out of style. They were always holding hands and prayed over the tiniest things. They often said things like "Praise the Lord" and welcomed me as a "fine young Christian man" the first day.

THE SITUATION: When I moved in, I had no idea of what to bring besides clothes and necessities (the only thing the Westons had specified was no loud music, so my stereo and extensive collection of rock and roll records were out). I decided to bring my comic book collection and all my fantasy and horror novels. I was then at the peak of my collecting and had six or seven shoe boxes with titles like *Spiderman, Daredevil, Iron Man,* and *Moon Knight.* After I finished lugging the boxes with comics and paperbacks into my new room, I asked the Westons if they wanted to check out their backroom, which was now mine. They said "No, that's your room" and smiled.

THE EVENT: A week after I moved in, as I was walking down the hall munching my bologna sandwich on the way to my room, the Westons confronted me at the door to the room and said: "We'd like you to get rid of these . . . things." They pointed accusingly at the bookcase where my beloved books were stored. I looked at them in disbelief and said: "I'll do it in the morning." They said "No—right now." Without saying anything, I carefully carried each box across the street to my car, while the Westons stood by, looking distressed. When I approached the room after the last box was secure in my car, I saw the Westons kneeling, holding hands, and muttering prayers over the spot where my books had been. I remember slinking down the hall and into the bathroom, where I stayed until I heard them leave my room.

THE POINT: This event marked the beginning of my disillusionment with the kind of narrow religious attitude these people represented. I had been taught to think of them as the best kind of people: kind, decent. They sat glued to religious television, yet they couldn't stand to see a

Daredevil cover sticking out above the top of a shoebox. The Devil was in their house, and they were going to cleanse the spot where he had dwelled.

ANALYZING AN ISSUE   Suppose you want to alert your readers to a current issue. Perhaps you are aiming at an audience that is apathetic about the homeless, teenage pregnancies, junk food, high dropout rates, or violence in TV programing for children. A set of questions like the following could guide you to material that would make the issue real for your readers:

I. *What is the issue?* What striking event, example, or statistic would best dramatize the issue for your reader?

II. *How are the media dealing with the issue?* What are some striking recent examples of media coverage? Has the issue recently been the subject of newspaper articles, television shows or documentaries, interviews, talk show patter, movies, editorials in the campus daily, cartoons? What questions or points come up again and again?

III. *What popular misconceptions or prejudices cloud the issue?* Is the problem lack of information or traditional ways of thinking?

IV. *What are the experts saying?* Who *are* the experts? Do they agree, or are they divided?

V. *Where has the issue touched your own experience?* What do you know from firsthand observation? How has it touched the lives of people you know well?

VI. *What does the future hold?* What are the plans for action? Are there promising alternatives? Is the outlook good or discouraging?

WRITING WORKSHOP 11   Prepare to write a paper analyzing a *current trend.* Is it a passing development or does it represent some significant lasting change? Use or adapt a discovery frame like the following as a guide to material for a paper that would start with surface symptoms but go beyond them. If possible, arrange for feedback from a group to your choice of topic and your collection of preliminary material.

The Fitness Fad

1. *Surface Symptoms:* Where do you see telltale signs of the current fitness craze? What signs do you see in your neighborhood or on campus? How is it reflected in current advertising and, more generally, in the media? (For instance, how aware are you of runners on streets and highways, of ads for exercise bikes and rowing machines and running shoes, of health clubs and aerobics classes?)

2. *Firsthand Exposure:* Are you yourself a participant or merely an ob-
    server? Have you had a chance to take a close-up view at people seri-
    ously involved? (For instance, do you have close friends or family
    members who have taken up running, weight lifting, or aerobic danc-
    ing? What do they do? What do they say?)
3. *Background Facts:* In your studies or reading, what facts have you en-
    countered concerning the physical benefits of popular kinds of activity
    or exercise? What do the experts say about such benefits as weight
    control, stress reduction, or the prevention of heart disease? What are
    the comparative advantages of different kinds of activity? (For instance,
    is it true that one hour of running produces the same health benefits as
    three hours of walking?)
4. *Deeper Causes:* What are some of the underlying causes of the cult of
    physical fitness? What are revealing slogans, or what are key ideas in
    the mystique that surrounds it? (For instance, what is a "natural high"?
    Are we observing a reaction against a mechanized and plastic culture
    and a return to physical and biological basics? Is keeping in shape a
    natural ideal for the me generation?)
5. *Doubts or Second Thoughts:* What warnings by medical authorities have
    you read about the dangers of the fitness craze? What do doctors say
    about the need for stress tests and for medical supervision in general?

| WRITING TOPICS 2 |

Choose a topic for which you can work up ample material from a
range of sources: observation, experience, viewing, listening, reading. Include as much authentic firsthand detail as you can. Convince your reader
that you have made yourself somewhat of an authority on your topic.

1. How does our society treat the disabled? What is it like to be disabled
    in today's world? What difference have recent changes in attitudes,
    facilities, and opportunities made? Write for the concerned citizen and
    voter.

2. Does our society still have assumptions about "women's work"? What
    new challenges are women taking on? Where have they been especially
    successful? What barriers are especially serious? Decide whether to
    write mainly for a male or a female audience.

3. Have you experienced the meeting of two cultures? In your family or
    among your friends, have you seen the clash of two different tradi-
    tions—different ethnic backgrounds, different religious values, dif-
    ferent lifestyles? Explore the conflict or merging of different ways

of life. Write for fellow students from a conventional mainstream background.

4. At times something that was only hearsay becomes real. It becomes a vivid reality in our lives or in the lives of people close to us. Write about one such subject, and show how it became real for you through firsthand experience. For instance, you might write about violence, a lawsuit, being laid off, divorce, jail. Write as an insider initiating the outsider.

5. Find two articles that present similar or opposing views on a current issue. Write a paper in which you compare and contrast the two authors' positions. Go on to your own opinion on the issue and provide support from your own observation, experience, viewing, or reading. Some possible topics:

   - stiffer penalties for drunken driving
   - using lotteries to help finance education
   - the press and a candidate's privacy
   - rape prevention
   - shelters for the homeless
   - coeducational varsity sports
   - movie ratings

---

3   Organizing and Drafting

OVERVIEW How does a paper take shape? How do you move from scattered notes to a first draft? A well-organized paper pulls together material that was at first confusing or contradictory. It funnels evidence into conclusions you can support. This bringing of order out of chaos can be very frustrating in the early stages, but it can also be very rewarding as you begin to get your material under control.

How do you develop the strategy that will shape your paper as a whole? Keep in mind three questions that will help give shape and direction to your writing:

■ **What is your focus?** A writer has to learn how to focus attention on one limited topic or one major point. In practice, we do not write about birds in general, or about welfare as a large umbrella topic. We write because some part of our general subject is not well known, and we want to fill the gap. We write because an issue has come up, and we want to take a stand. We write because a question has come up, and we want to answer it.

■ **What is your point?** Your reader will want to know: "What are you trying to tell me?" Push toward a central **thesis**: The thesis of your paper sums up what the paper as a whole is trying to show. It summarizes the message of the paper or its central point. We lose the attention of an audience if we say a little something about many different points. We make an impact by concentrating on one major point and driving it home.

■ **What is your plan?** A well-planned paper moves through steps that you can outline and that your reader can follow. Even while gathering material, you will start sorting it out. You will be working out a strategy for putting it to use. Many writers try out different organizing strategies in their minds until they arrive at the one that seems right for the subject. They start with a rough **trial outline** and then scratch it to do another. They shuffle pages or note cards, arranging them in tentative patterns. Some writers work out a fairly detailed working outline to follow in their first draft. Some work from a master plan or grand design that exists in their heads.

Once you have worked out a tentative plan, you can start your first draft. Often a writer will already have bits and pieces or whole sections roughed out before the grand design for a paper or an article has really taken shape. If you work on a word processor, you can already have a file of preliminary material that you can transfer to the right spots in your draft. Some writers do a continuous first draft, following their tentative outline. Others draft key sections first, worrying about introduction, conclusion, and missing links later.

3a	From Notes to First Draft

Develop your sense of how a paper takes shape.

Many writers find that their minds are at work sorting and shaping the material for a piece of writing even while they are thinking about something else (while taking a shower or driving to work). Study the way a definite plan takes shape as a fellow student works on a paper. Study the way the following sample paper moves from the planning report through the note-taking stage to the first draft. How does the student writer accomplish the goals she sketches out in her planning report? How does she use her notes? How does she develop her overall strategy?

PREWRITING: PLANNING REPORT

> I have been stereotyped in the past because of my voice and the way I look. I have had instructors and fellow students form instant opinions of me that I have found hard to dispel. Having suffered from the dumb-blonde stereotype, I want to show the frustration of dealing with the stereotype and trying to change people's instant opinion of me. People need to be accepted and respected on their merits, and stereotyping causes people to be hurt and become less than they could be.

PREWRITING: NOTES

> The media stereotype: blonde dream girl in tight sweaters working as a maid for two leering men. Blonde airhead in *Three's Company*. More current shows: Diane in *Cheers* is smart and has a college education. At first she held her own, but in many later plots she was shown to be arrogant and often was made fun of as silly and presumptuous.

> Unsolicited advice: told to put my hair up in a bun, use no makeup, wear glasses. Student commenting on my "Barbie Doll" voice while working on a group project. Instructor's negative comments on oral report. Women as well as men: At least men have the excuse of being conditioned to react sexually to women who sound and act "feminine."

> Unfair focus on appearance: Brunettes are more likely to be taken seriously?

> Norman Mailer on Marilyn Monroe in *Marilyn*: "She was not the dark contract of the passionate brunette depths that speak of blood, vows taken for life, and the furies of vengeance . . . no, Marilyn suggested sex might be difficult or dangerous with others, but ice cream with her." (p. 15) "So we think of Marilyn who was every man's love affair . . . who was blonde and beautiful and had a sweet little rinky-dink of a voice . . . which carried such ripe overtones of erotic excitement and yet was the voice of a little child." (pp. 15–16)

> Note: Pitch of the voice is determined by size of the larynx and how tightly the muscles in it are stretched. Voiceprints like fingerprints: can be used for identification.

WRITING SAMPLE: FIRST DRAFT

Dream Girls

> The stereotype killed Marilyn Monroe, the blonde bombshell with the sexy voice. Marilyn wanted the role, so she played the game. She became, as Norman Mailer says in *Marilyn*, "every man's love affair,"

blonde and beautiful and "with the voice of a little child." As Mailer says, she "suggested sex might be difficult or dangerous with others, but ice cream with her." Marilyn used her looks; she lived in a role for the public that her inner self couldn't be, and she died of an overdose.

The stereotype is hard to fight. The idea of the dumb blonde is cut deep into the minds of men, bosses, those in power, other females. A blonde with good looks and a soft musical voice has a steeper climb to the top than her dark-haired sister.

TV perpetuates this idea by creating roles for blonde airheads. In one show, canceled at first because it offended women's groups but then brought back, the public could watch a blonde dream girl in tight sweaters and plastic gloves delight the two men who hired her as a maid. The role of Diane in *Cheers* was at first coveted by actresses because Diane was college-educated and had some depth to her character. In the end, Diane was a fool. She had an education that made her arrogant and presumptuous. There are serious roles for blonde women on TV, but the stereotype is hard to shake.

I am blonde. I have a soft musical voice. I have always had high grades. Working as a tutor, I have helped other students improve their work. I have worked as a bookkeeper and assistant personnel manager. Still, there are people who don't take me seriously because of the way I look and sound. I've been told to put my hair up in a bun, wear glasses, quit wearing makeup, and work to lower the pitch of my voice. I want to teach, but I don't want to play a role; I want to be myself.

Men are not the only ones doing the stereotyping. I had a female instructor criticize my voice as unprofessional during an oral report critique. I had a female student say in a group endeavor that I should go last because my "Barbie Doll" voice would leave an emotional impression on the audience.

All blonde hair does not come out of a bottle, and the pitch of the voice is determined by the size of the larynx and by how tightly the muscles in it are stretched. Voiceprints, like fingerprints, are highly individual and can be used as a means of identification.

The myth of the beautiful childlike blonde will probably always exist as long as men want to take care of women who give them pleasure and who need protection. The stereotype will wane when men begin to respect women who take care of themselves.

Contrast the promising raw material in her planning report and in her prewriting notes with the strategic use the author made of it in her draft. Here is a rough outline of the material in her notes:

(chunk 1) statement of the student's resentment and frustration with the dumb-blonde stereotype
(chunk 2) media exploitation of the stereotype

(chunk 3) personal experiences of the author with instructors and fellow students
(chunk 4) Norman Mailer on the Marilyn Monroe myth
(chunk 5) scientific or factual material

In the first draft, the material has been reshuffled to produce the *overall plan*:

1. The writer starts by using a widely quoted *authority* on the Monroe myth, thus helping validate her own concern with her topic—showing her topic to be of general concern. (chunk 4)

2. We look at the *media* next to show how widely Mailer's concern is reflected in popular entertainment. (chunk 2)

3. The writer reveals her *personal connection* with the topic (which if given away earlier might have made the paper sound too much like mere personal grievance). (chunk 1)

4. The writer traces the stereotype to the thinking of other *women* as well as men (she's not just berating males). (chunk 3)

5. The writer goes from personal, subjective impressions to objective *facts*. (chunk 5)

In the student writer's original notes, the materials appeared in the order in which they came to mind. In the draft, they appear in an order that makes sense and that serves the writer's purpose.

WRITING WORKSHOP 12   Our personal experience seems miscellaneous as it happens from day to day. But often when we look back years later, we notice a pattern. For instance, have you gone through several *stages or phases* in your attitude toward parents, school, relatives, church, police, sports, camping, or immigrants? Choose one of these or a similar topic. Write a planning report sketching out how a paper tracing several stages or phases would shape up.

Use the following planning report by a student writer as a possible model.

Empty Rituals—Vain Ceremonies?

stage 1   I have been on several sides of the argument over ritual and ceremony. As a child, like most children, I happily dressed up for special occasions and went through the familiar rituals of special holidays. Each Thanksgiving and each Christmas followed the same pre-scribed pattern.

stage 2

In high school, however, I soon adopted the view that most public ceremonies were meaningless charades carried on by mindless idiots. They showed people's in-ability to think for themselves, their tendency to operate on automatic pilot in accordance with some prescribed pattern set up by society. It seemed that no intelligent people really listened to commencement speeches or to the speakers at dedication ceremonies and the like. When my parents got very upset about the modernizing of traditional worship services at their church, my brother and I failed to see what the big fuss was about.

stage 3

Lately, I have started to take traditional ceremonies more seriously. Several of my friends want traditional weddings in order to make the event and the commitment seem *important*. I have been to funeral services that make the family feel someone *cares* and that give people a chance to express their fond memories and their sense of loss. I know many people just go through the motions, but others get some real personal satisfaction or mean-ing from the ceremonies in which they participate.

3b   *foc* | Sharpening Your Focus

Know strategies for bringing your subject into focus.

Our reader wants to know: "What are you trying to accomplish? What are you trying to say?" This kind of question helps us bring a paper into **focus**. It helps us pull things together. The more clearly focused a paper, the better the chance that our point will sink in or that our information will be put to use.

What can you do when your papers tend to be too sprawling and formless? Try the following strategies:

(1) Limit the area you are going to cover. No one can write a paper on a large sprawling subject like "Education in America." You will often have to narrow a broad general subject until you arrive at a topic that will allow you to take a closer look. With topics like the following, you are moving closer to issues that you could make real for your reader:

How Computers Teach
Math and the Woman Student
The English Language Is My Enemy
Busing: The Long Way to School
Prayer in the Public School

By narrowing the scope of your topic, you will be able to treat it in greater depth. You will be able to look at specifics. When you write on a topic of current concern, ask yourself: "How much narrowing should I do before I reach the level where people can see actual effects on their own lives? When would they begin to see what they themselves might be able to do about the problem?" Look at how the following general issue has been scaled down. The more specific topics make possible a paper that becomes specific enough to become real or convincing to your reader:

VERY GENERAL:	Improving the Quality of Life
LESS GENERAL:	Cleaning Up the Environment
	Solving Chronic Unemployment
	Transportation Fit for Human Beings
SPECIFIC:	Bottles vs. Cans: A Problem in Ecology
	Plastics That Decompose
	The Psychology of Litterbugs

(2) Concentrate on a key question that your paper will answer. The more specific the key question you choose, the more likely your paper is to have a clear focus. "How do crime comics shape their readers' attitudes?" is a very *general* question. Try to point your question at a more limited issue.

■ Is it true that the heroes look white, Anglo-Saxon, and Protestant, while villains look Latin, for instance, or Asian?
■ Is it true that in crime comics people are either all good or all bad?
■ Do crime comics reveal the political sympathies of their authors?

A pointed question is more likely to produce a focused paper than a question that is merely exploratory. Avoid questions like "What are some of the causes of adolescent crime?" The "What-are-some" kind of question may lead to a paper in which many different things are mentioned but few of them studied in detail. Try a "What-is-the-most" or "What-is-the-best" kind of question:

KEY QUESTION: What is the most serious obstacle to communication be-
                 tween teenagers and their parents?
KEY QUESTION: What are three key features shared by successful televi-
                 sion comedians?
KEY QUESTION: What is the best source of alternative energy?

Often you can bring a paper into focus by concentrating on a clear-cut "Should we? Or should we not?" question. The author of the following excerpted paper expressed a view that she expected to be unpopular with her audience of fellow students. She unified her paper by focusing on a clear-cut alternative:

An Unpopular View

During the typical first-day "introduce yourself" routine in my speech class, a young woman announced proudly that she had served a two-year enlistment in the armed forces and that "every kid should have to do it." Most of the classmates balked at her suggestion, but for some reason I found myself seriously considering her idea. . . .

Many students feel that enlistment would interfere with their plans for a college education. However, many high school students take a year off before entering college. Six more months would not make a great difference. The armed forces provide financial incentives that can make the difference between a junior college and a university, or a Bachelor's and a Master's degree. . . .

Other students feel that enlistment would sidetrack them from their careers by removing them from the "real world." However, high school and college classroom "wombs" may do less than military service to prepare them for the real world of specific skills and responsibilities. . . .

Still others are apprehensive of the use of women in combat. However, there are dozens of options available to women other than combat or clerical work. When I took the Armed Services Vocational Aptitude test, at least forty percent of those taking the test were women. Their interests ranged from nursing to flight control or working on a Coast Guard cutter. . . .

PEER EDITOR 13   Suppose the topics listed below had been suggested by your classmates as possible topics for short papers. Help *narrow* these to more specific topics that would allow the writer to zero in on a limited issue and do it justice. Here is an example of how such a formless general topic might be scaled down:

VERY GENERAL: How Technology Runs Our Lives

LESS GENERAL: The Spread of Automation
The Motorized Society
The Proliferation of Gadgets

SPECIFIC: The Automated Assembly Line
Your Checking Account and the Computer
How Appliances Put the Customer to Work

Suggest *one or more* manageable specific topics for each of the following:

Computers
The Plight of the City
The Future of Marriage
Educational Opportunities for Minorities
Jobs for the Class of 2001
Freedom of the Press
Protecting the Consumer
Sexism

PEER EDITOR 14   Suppose your classmates had been given a choice of the topics listed below. For each formulate one *pointed question* that might provide a take-off point for a focused paper:

student government
sexual harassment
welfare reform
abortion laws
urban renewal
the homeless
media stereotypes
comic strips

3c | Pushing Toward a Thesis

Use a strong thesis to help unify your paper.

A powerful tool for organizing related material is the **thesis**, or central idea. When you state a thesis, you take a stand; you commit yourself to a point of view. You answer the central question your paper raises, or you sum up your solution to the problem it has identified. Your thesis tells your readers: "This is what I have found. This is what I mean to show."

Practice summing up in a single sentence what you are trying to tell your readers. Thesis statements like the following are meant to satisfy the reader who asks: "What is the point?"

THESIS: The huge sales of Valentine's cards and gifts testify to a need for romance that most people do not openly admit.

THESIS: Lottery funds for schools allow people to feel virtuous about helping education, but almost none of the money is spent on classroom instruction.

THESIS: Colleges should shift the emphasis from spectator sports to active participation.

A thesis does not merely map out a topic; it sums up what you have to say:

TOPIC: Attitudes of young Americans toward work

THESIS: Young Americans today rarely find work in which they can take personal pride.

TOPIC: The treatment of youth in American advertising

THESIS: American advertising promotes a cult of youth that makes older people seem irrelevant and unwanted.

A good thesis is the result of a process of investigation, of thinking the matter through. It often pulls together materials that at first might have seemed to point in different directions. Suppose you are taking stock of what you have seen of the current fitness craze. You remember signing up for a workout program that became a horrendous drain on your pocketbook. You came to know well a woman obsessed with the "model look," who overexercised and undernourished her body. You have taken a close look at fitness magazines, with their endless stream of advertisements. You have read about appetite-suppressant pills, about anorexia and bulimia. On the next page is a rough chart of how these observations might feed into a general conclusion. Look especially at how the thesis emerges from the materials that feed into it.

In a well-focused paper, the thesis will often appear at the end of a brief introduction that raises the issue:

The Fitness Drain

The bill for my spa payment came in the mail again this month. When I signed up, First Lady Spa promised me that I could use their first-class weight-lifting machines and attend an endless number of aerobic classes for only $21.40 a month. I was handed a 20% discount card for

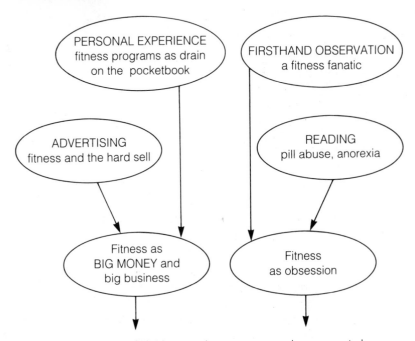

THESIS: In the name of looking good, women everywhere seem to be sacrificing their hard-earned money and jeopardizing their health.

Leotard World, and I was on my way to perfect fitness. I soon discovered that the more I went to the spa, the more items I was expected to buy. First of all, I needed special aerobic shoes, which cost about $45.00. *In the name of looking good, women everywhere seem to be sacrificing their hard-earned money—and jeopardizing their health.*

The body of the paper will then offer the evidence needed to support this charge. Often the conclusion will reinforce the initial thesis. The following conclusion is not just a lame restatement of the original idea. The writer has abandoned her original half-amused ironic tone to make us face up to the seriousness of the situation:

CONCLUSION: We discover the other side of the coin when we read about the abuse of appetite-suppressant pills and about teenagers who become victims of anorexia and bulimia in an attempt to become like the tanned perfect bodies that look at them from the covers of fitness magazines. Instead of working and working out in healthy outdoor surroundings, we look for the secret of perpetual good looks in capsules and machines. In the process, we drain our bank accounts and our energy. The pioneers of the American past would laugh at us.

The following guidelines will help you write a strong thesis and use it to advantage:

(1) Use your thesis to pull together your previous observations or available information. Suppose you have observed disabled students in your own classes and on your campus. You have observed changes designed to make buildings more accessible for such students. You have read about how schools are implementing laws about mainstreaming disabled students. Everything you have observed and read will influence your final conclusion:

THESIS: Everywhere in American education, disabled students are playing a more visible and more independent role.

(2) Whenever you can, sum up your thesis in a single sentence. A well-written thesis is a clear statement of a limited point. Whenever possible, state it in a single sentence:

TOPIC: Urban redevelopment
THESIS: Redeveloped neighborhoods lack the varied life of the grown neighborhoods they replace.

TOPIC: Violence in movies
THESIS: Too many of today's movies make killing seem quick and easy.

TOPIC: Raising the Iron Curtain
THESIS: People in Eastern Europe are fascinated by everything American.

(3) Revise a vague or open-ended thesis. A strong thesis points a definite direction. It provides a program for the paper as a whole; it provides us with a test of the relevance of what follows. Revise thesis statements that are too open-ended, that do not take a stand:

WEAK: Many today are searching for the perfect prescription for a happy family. There are **several necessary ingredients** if this prescription is to be filled.
REVISED: A happy family needs a firm basis in love and affection, constantly strengthened by shared joy and sorrow.

(4) Think of your thesis as a promise to the reader. Make it serve as a program for the paper as a whole. Suppose your thesis reads as follows:

THESIS: Nineteenth-century American fiction often lacks strong female characters.

To keep your promise to the reader, take a look at several striking examples. Major paragraphs in your paper might be devoted to examples like the following:

first example   In Mark Twain's *Huckleberry Finn*, the aunt is left behind, and the story revolves around the boy, his father, and Jim, the runaway slave. . . .

second example   In Melville's *Moby Dick*, we follow Ishmael and the all-male crew of the whaling ship in pursuit of the White Whale. . . .

third example   In Cooper's Leatherstocking novels, we move in a frontier world of hunters and scouts and braves. . . .

Avoid the *misleading* thesis, which mentions points at the beginning of a paper that are not taken up later. If your initial prescription for a happy family mentions affection, joy, and sorrow, your reader expects that all three of these will be taken up in your paper, to be illustrated and discussed.

(5) Make your thesis hint at the overall plan of the paper. Experiment with making your thesis a preview of your overall plan. An effective thesis often hints at the outline of the paper; it maps out the itinerary that the reader is to follow:

THESIS: Contrary to the stereotype of student apathy, political opinion on campus is a three-ring circus featuring the aggressive young conservative, the well-meaning liberal, and the activist radical left.

(Comment: The reader will expect key sections illustrating each of these three categories.)

WRITING WORKSHOP 15   Choose *three* of the following topics. Select topics that allow you to draw on relevant observation, experience, reading, or viewing. For each topic, formulate a *trial thesis* that you could support in a short paper. For each tentative thesis, write a paragraph to explain how you would support or defend the stand you take.

1. Parents in current situation comedy
2. Toys as a reflection of American values
3. Changing images of women in current American movies
4. The family in current television commercials
5. Newspaper coverage of crime
6. The typical or average student on your campus
7. Teachers' attitudes toward minority students
8. Adolescents in current television commercials
9. Changing images of native Americans in current movies or television programs
10. Idealism on campus—passé or alive
11. The decline of good manners
12. The arts—frills or essentials
13. Beauty pageants
14. Guns for self-defense
15. Pornography in the campus bookstore

PEER EDITOR 16   Study and evaluate each of the following statements as the possible thesis for a short paper. Answer the following questions about each:

■   What kind of support does the thesis need? What kind of follow-up does it make you expect? What would it take to make you respect or accept the writer's point of view?

■   If you were writing on the same subject, would you change the thesis to make it reflect your own point of view?

1. The self-service gas station points toward a future where service to the customer will be increasingly hard to find.
2. Fear of violence restricts the activities of many Americans.
3. Earlier immigrants were eager to assimilate; many new immigrants are proud of their separate identity.
4. The great whales have become a symbol of wildlife threatened with extinction by heedless humanity.
5. The typical amusement park has become an artificial wonderland of plastic smiles, faked nostalgic settings, and regimented crowds.
6. Most young Americans today are cynical about politicians and apathetic about elections.
7. Much of the current cult of health foods and healthful living is faddish and overdone.

PEER REVIEW 17   Study the following exceptionally well-focused student paper. Answer questions like the following:

- How does the *introduction* set the prevailing mood? How and where does it lead up to the central *thesis*?
- Where does the writer state his thesis? What does he do to *support,* follow up, or reinforce it?
- What strategy has the writer used to give this paper clear *focus* or unity?
- How does the *conclusion* echo the initial thesis? What does the conclusion add? What is its effect on the reader?
- How do you react to the paper? What kind of reader would make a good *audience* for it?

A Day in the Life

Quickly walking through the unending maze of unblemished ivory-white hallways, I see the familiar rectangular black sign on the wall, "This elevator for employee use only." I press the plastic button, suddenly the bell sounds, and the down arrow above the elevator door turns a bright red. Slowly the elevator door disappears into the wall. Making sure I do not overturn my shoulder-high polished-aluminum food-tray cart, I watch that the small black plastic wheels of the cart do not get caught in the crack between the elevator and the spotless tiled floor. Already in the capacious elevator is an orderly dressed in blue from cap to booties, standing next to a gurney with an unwrinkled snow-white sheet over a patient. As the door opens to the first floor, I pull my cart in to the hallway. As I turn to hold the door open, I notice a green tag dangling from the big toe of the patient, and I hear the orderly's voice: "Thanks, but I'm getting off in the basement."

The depression I always felt as a dietary technician (actually a dishwasher and gatherer of dirty dishes) at the Valley Hospital was a result of the dejecting atmosphere. Every day's sights and sounds reinforced my feeling of helplessness when confronted with pain and misery.

At six-thirty on a Sunday morning, the gentle hum of the giant black floor polishers seems to be the only sound audible in the hospital. As I enter the Intensive Care Unit, I see the nurse on duty engrossed in a book with a deserted beach on the cover—she is escaping for a short time from the suffering and dying around her. The patients have light-green name bands around their wrists. One has a cropped head of hair (impossible to tell the sex) and is chained to the bed by the drips, drains, and leads connected to a kidney machine and respirators.

I pass a cheerful young volunteer pushing a wheelchair-bound old woman past the bold red sign that reads, "Keep clear at all times—Emergency Access Area." I pick up some dirty food trays from the emergency room and move on.

"Code ninety-nine CCU east"—a calm voice breaks into the piped-in dentist's-office music that fills every hall and waiting room. As I move through the Coronary Care Unit, I see a defenseless gray-haired old man with tiny white stubs on his chin, lying in a fully automatic, do-everything, criblike bed. A doctor, a stethoscope around her neck, takes a pancake-shaped instrument with small plastic handles and black coiled wires to place on the old man's lean chest.

"For the protection of the patients, no matches, lighters, belts, ties, or drugs of any kind beyond this point." This sign appears at eye level on the locked door to a closed ward, my last place to pick up food trays for the day. I pick up the nearby white telephone and state my name, title, and business. A buzzer sounds, and I walk into the community "kitchen"—nothing more than a green sink, a light green refrigerator, a green formica table, and white plastic chairs. Four expressionless people sit around the table, as if they were not on this planet. They look as if they had been awake for days without sleep. They do not utter a word as I walk by.

After working in this environment for a time, I became used and perhaps immune to the depressing sights I saw around me. I gradually began to see the invigorating parts of life in the hospital, such as the maternity ward and the miracle of a dying patient's fighting and conquering a fatal disease. But these positive impressions will never quite balance the feelings of depression and helplessness that I felt in the beginning.

3d *plan* Organizing Your Paper

Work out a general organizing strategy for your paper.

A successful paper has an overall strategy that gives it shape. It has a master plan or grand design that you can outline for a reader or friendly critic: "First, I pinpoint the problem . . . then I clear up familiar misunderstandings . . . then I zero in on the root cause . . . then finally I point to a promising solution." Often your thesis will give your readers a strong hint of your organizing strategy: a contrast of then and now, a survey of different solutions to a problem.

Writers differ in how they do the mapping and charting that produces an organized paper. Some do all or most of their planning in their heads. Some work with rough scratch outlines, frequently revised. Some write their first draft from a detailed point-by-point outline they have prepared. In your own work, you are likely to find that a working outline, frequently updated and adjusted, is indispensable.

What will guide you in working out a ground plan for a paper? Although each paper is different, you will often be using or adapting basic organizing strategies that reflect the way our minds take in and process information.

CHRONOLOGY   When we use **chronological order**, we follow events or developments step by step as they happen in time. In much how-to writing—directions, instructions—we focus on telling the reader what to do next. For example, we may move from the choice of flour and other ingredients through the necessary steps in the process that produces good pasta. In a term paper on the French Revolution, we may trace major stages in the historical progression from the old monarchy through the revolutionary upheavals to the triumph of Napoleon.

The following excerpts from an autobiographical paper present, in chronological order, major stages in the writer's growing up:

Sports, Anyone?

Looking back, we sometimes find that our attitudes on something important have changed drastically over the years; we find ourselves in a different place. . . .

As a child, I had a marked disdain for sports. This was probably the result of my being very bad at them. While my grade school peers played Pop Warner football and Little League baseball, I went to art and music camp. This was no real problem until junior high school. There, adolescents were socially made or broken in gym class. People who were good at sports were cool. People who had the misfortune of having a pair of hands like masonry were seriously not cool. . . .

I cowered my way through seventh grade, my self-confidence plummeting as I was picked last for every sport. That summer I grew a few inches and wondered how I would survive. One way was to become a fan of sports. I took up basketball. I rooted hard, studied statistics daily, and learned about jump shots and layups. Eventually, my basketball prowess enabled teams to pick me second or first. The real status leap occurred in the ninth grade when I became a gym helper, assisting the gym teachers with the lowly seventh graders. . . .

Since, I have graduated from basketball, soccer, and stickball in high school to volleyball, bicycling, and jogging in college. Today I enjoy sports for the physical pleasure of doing something well with my body, of feeling healthy, of learning the limits of my physical capabilities. I have moved beyond the kind of jock mentality that knows sports only for winning, for dominating the other side.

EXEMPLIFICATION   Often our basic strategy is to lay down a barrage of convincing examples to support a point. We often find our way by grouping together parallel examples—instances that all point in the same direction. We can then funnel these into a thesis that sums up a pattern or a trend.

One student wrote about the gentrification of a quiet rural riverfront. He complained that for the new owners the small creatures living in this habitat were not wildlife to be cherished but the target of "pest control." In the body of the paper, the writer furnished the examples backing up the indictment. Different sections of the paper described the new residents' warfare against the beavers (who might damage trees), the muskrats (who might nest in the styrofoam used to float boat docks), the groundhogs (who might burrow in the high-priced riverfront), and the owls (whose hoots might disturb the new residents in their slumber).

Note: Often the laying out of related examples to build a case will combine with other organizing strategies to give shape and direction to a paper. For instance, a writer may present major examples in chronological order. Or a writer might go from the humorous to the serious, starting with amusing examples of a new trend but going on to examples that disturb us or make us think.

CLASSIFICATION To make sense of confusing information, we often need to set up major categories. We sort things out by putting what belongs together in the same bin. For instance, we classify sports as upper-class sports (polo, sailing), middle-class sports (football, baseball), and lower-class sports (wrestling). Here, we are using familiar established categories to help us chart the territory. **Classification** becomes a special challenge when we set up our *own* categories to do justice to the material at hand. We might classify sports in a very different way—according to how much gut-level physical contact they require or how much challenge and satisfaction they offer to the human spirit:

Sports and the Human Spirit

I. Grunt Sports: boxing, wrestling
II. Contact Sports: football, hockey
III. Skill Sports: basketball, tennis
IV. Inspirational Sports: track, mountaineering

SEE 7b FOR MORE ON CLASSIFICATION.

COMPARISON AND CONTRAST Often we organize information by focusing on how things are alike and how they differ. The following is a working outline for a paper developing a *then-and-now* contrast:

It's a Living

THESIS: Workers once were dissatisfied with jobs requiring hard physical labor; today workers often dislike their jobs because of
psychological pressures and frustrations.

   I.   YESTERDAY: Exhausting, dangerous physical work
   - field workers (stoop labor)
   - punch press operators
   - miners

   II.   TODAY: Psychological pressures
   - picky supervisors
   - unreasonable regulations
   - lack of praise or recognition
   - speed-up of operations

SEE 7d FOR MORE ON COMPARISON AND CONTRAST.

PROBLEM TO SOLUTION An effective strategy for capturing and steering
the reader's attention is to move from problem to solution, from an urgent
question to a needed answer. In the following overview, note the boldfaced
links, or **transitions**, that lead the reader from one step to the next.

Overworked and Underpaid

Day-care workers will remain underpaid unless not only parents
but government agencies and employers assume their part of the responsibility.

Day-care workers who care for preschoolers in a good program do
much the same work as kindergarten teachers but are likely to be paid
much less. . . .

Contrary to what one might expect, substandard salaries are not
limited to financially strapped centers in poor neighborhoods. In the
brightly painted, profit-making centers that dot suburban highways the
pay can be just as low. . . .

Why are the wages of day-care workers so low? **For one thing**, the
job has traditionally been considered woman's work. **In the past**, older
women seeking only to supplement their husband's incomes were not
deterred by the paltry wages. . . .

Today, the basic economics of running a center put the squeeze on
wages. **In the first place**, many centers must meet state-mandated
teacher-student ratios and still charge fees that parents can afford. . . .

In the second place, large day-care chains attract customers by
clean classrooms, cheery decor, and impressive toys and playground

equipment. Their ability to provide these attractions depends on their ability to keep wages very low. . . .

What is the answer? To raise salaries, day-care centers need higher fees from parents, or increased state aid, or contributions from corporations helping pay for day care for the children of their employees.

Certainly, some parents could afford to pay higher fees. . . .

However, in most families the cost of child care takes an enormous chunk out of the family income. . . .

As a result, parents have concentrated their efforts on getting state legislatures to provide increased support. . . .

Only recently have large corporations faced the need of helping their employees provide for satisfactory care. . . .

LEAST TO MOST One tried-and-true way of taking the reader along is to move from least to most, or from worst to best, or from unlikely to most probable. Our minds are prepared to follow a natural progression from one end to the other end of a scale. Suppose a baseball fan is trying to champion his favorite sport. He places different kinds of popular sports on a scale, from the most to the least violent:

The National Pastime

I. Boxing is an extreme example of a **violent sport**. Although sportswriters talk about a boxer's skill, spectators come to see a slugger; they want to see the knockout.

II. Football is a violent sport **masked as a contest of skill**. Although it is called a contact sport, it is really a collision sport.

III. Baseball is the **most civilized** of the major spectator sports. Although there are injuries in baseball, the spectator's attention is focused on the skill, the strategy, the beauty of the sport.

The following are rough notes showing a student paper in progress. To judge from these notes, what is going to be the *overall strategy* of the writer? How logical or how plausible is the overall pattern that is taking shape? What materials or details could you provide for some of the headings or topics that are sketched in only very briefly here? If you were writing on this topic, would you adapt a similar plan? How would you change it and why?

Starting the Clean-Up

Personal experience: A few weeks ago, I was running on the canal road by my house with the sun just coming over the hills when I looked ahead and for a moment thought I was hallucinating: A large white truck was about a quarter of a mile ahead and a being in an oversize white suit with a hood to match was standing by the truck holding on to an enormous hose that was spraying a white liquid into the air; another white-hooded apparition was flashing a large white light up and down in an apparent warning gesture. . . . Recently, when I climbed out of the pool after a workout with my swim team, an attendant was putting up a "Danger: High Chlorine" sign (someone had left a switch open all night and 85 pounds of chlorine was pumped into the pool).

Main reason for our apathy about the polluting of our living space: We accept it as if it were an act of God or a natural catastrophe. This is especially true when the exact causes are hard to pin down. Example: acid rain.

However, in many cases the actual agents can be identified and pinpointed. Examples: strip mining and toxic waste dumped in rivers or imperfectly buried in inadequate sites.

The basic solution is a long educational campaign to promote *awareness*—create the feeling that something *can* be done. Start with symbolic acts—carry your own refuse back out of a wilderness area. Participate in tree-planting campaigns.

Next step: Organize, agitate, lobby to help fight the intermediate battles. Support recycling laws. Smog checks on cars.

Long-range objectives: Prepare public for the big battles—offshore drilling, slowing down nuclear industry.

WRITING WORKSHOP 18　From the following topics, choose one that has a special meaning for you. Work up detailed material, relating the topic to your own observation, experience, and viewing or reading. Structure your material and prepare a detailed *working outline:*

- Include a thesis that sums up your general conclusion and sets a general direction for the paper.
- Set up major divisions or categories. (If you wish, include hints of details or examples to be used, putting them in parentheses.)
- After you revise your outline as necessary in response to your classmates' or your instructor's comments, use your revised outline as a guide in writing a first draft.

1. *O What a Feeling:* how car commercials sell cars
2. *You've Come a Long Way:* career opportunities for women
3. *Details at Eleven:* the predictable television news
4. *The Computer Invasion:* how computers are changing our lives
5. *The Throw-It-Away Society:* how products become obsolete

6. *I Know the Type:* victims of prejudice
7. *A Tale of More Than Two Cities:* different faces of the city
8. *The Fractured Family:* sources of friction in the modern family
9. *That's Not Funny:* objectionable humor or offensive jokes
10. *A Partygoer's Guide:* a guide to social occasions for young adults

---

3e   *plan*   Using Outlines

Work out an outline that fits your subject and serves your purpose.

At different stages in the writing of a paper, ask yourself if you can sketch out your master plan in an outline that you can take in at a glance and that will make sense to your reader. If you cannot, you need to streamline or clarify your plan, or else your readers will find your paper hard to stay with and hard to follow.

Outlines range from scribbled working outlines to the detailed formal outlines often required with major writing projects:

(1) Use an informal working outline to chart your course. A **working outline** is not like the architect's finished blueprint for a house, where every door, hallway, and sink are already in place. Think of your working outline as a **trial outline**—a first rough sketch that helps you see how things fit together and how they might have to be shifted around. Suppose you are writing a paper on the roots of the regulations that ensnarl us in our overregulated society. Your first trial outline may focus on the role of government and Big Brother agencies:

regulation by legislation:
    speed limit
    seat belts/air bag
regulation by government agencies:
    sexual imbalance in college sports
    special traffic lanes

As you explore the subject further, you may decide to add a third category that is sometimes overlooked:

regulation as the result of citizen initiatives:
    nonsmoking sections in restaurants

A working outline may start as a very rough tentative plan that slowly turns into a fairly detailed itinerary for the paper. Start thinking about your overall strategy *early*—and then adjust and rearrange your outline as you begin to see important connections or as you think about the needs of your reader.

Suppose you wanted to discuss an important common element in books that have enjoyed great popularity with adolescents. You might first jot down titles as they come to mind:

> *The Pigman*
> *Catcher in the Rye*
> *Catch-22*
> *The Prophet*
> *Lord of the Flies*

To arrange these titles in a plausible order, you might decide to start with a *classic* example: *Catcher in the Rye*, the book about a turned-off adolescent that at one time everyone had read. You could then discuss outstanding *later* examples, taking them up roughly in the order in which they became popular. Finally, you could discuss in detail a *personal* example—a book that meant a great deal to you as an adolescent. Your working outline might look like this:

> Classic example: *Catcher in the Rye*
> More recent examples:
>   *Lord of the Flies*
>   *Catch-22*
>   *The Pigman*
> My own favorite: *Slaughterhouse-Five*

(2) Use a formal outline as a final check on organization and as a guide to the reader. As your paper assumes more definite shape, your trial outline may develop into a final outline in which all divisions and subdivisions are clearly worked out. A **final outline** is often a well-worked-out chart, a detailed guide to the organization of a finished paper. The more substantial your paper, or the more ambitious your project, the more you may need a detailed outline that allows you to check the flow of your discussion or argument.

The first section of a formal outline for your paper on regulation and overregulation may look like this:

I. Regulation by legislation
   A. Speed limits
   B. Mandatory restraints
      1. Seat belts
      2. Air bags
II. . . . .

Formal outlines serve two different purposes. A writer may prepare a detailed final outline as an editorial aid, using it as a final check on coherence. But a detailed final outline may also serve as a guide to the reader; it is often part of the prescribed format for a report, research paper, or other major project. Your instructor may ask you to submit a final outline with a paper that presents a substantial argument or a substantial body of material. Two major forms are common:

■ **Use the topic outline to present, in logical order, the topics and subtopics that a paper covers.** Like other outlines, the **topic outline** often starts with a thesis sentence summarizing the central idea of the paper. Notice the use and placement of Roman numerals for the major categories, and of capital letters for the subdivisions in the following typed outline:

```
              To Join or Not to Join
THESIS:   For today's realistic, cost-conscious
          college student, joining a fraternity or
          sorority makes sense.
    I.    Academic benefits
          A. Inside information about teachers and
             classes
          B. Help with assignments
   II.    Social benefits
          A. Informal social life
          B. Organized activities
          C. Inside track in campus politics
  III.    Economic benefits
          A. Current living arrangements
          B. Future business contracts
```

Your Title

THESIS: Your thesis sentence appears here.
I. Roman numeral for first major section
   A. Capital for first subdivision
   B. Capital for second subdivision
      1. Arabic numeral for third-level subhead
         a. lowercase for fourth-level subhead
         b. lowercase for fourth-level subhead
      2. Arabic numeral for third-level subhead
   C. Capital for third subdivision
      1. Arabic numeral again
      2. Arabic numeral again
II. Roman numeral for second major section (and so on)

The following sample outline adds a third level—*sub-subdivisions* marked by Arabic numerals. Note that the outline as a whole charts a movement from then to now, or from traditional to modern:

Generations in Conflict

THESIS: The traditional conflict between parents and their teenage children is still with us.

I. The traditional generation gap
   A. Authoritarian fathers and rebellious sons
   B. Conformist mothers and independent daughters
II. Modern causes of conflict
   A. Freedom to be yourself
      1. Dress
      2. Hairstyle
   B. Unchaperoned outings
   C. Choice of part-time jobs
   D. Choice of friends and associates

■ **Use a sentence outline to sum up, in one complete sentence each, what you have to say on each topic and subtopic.** The sentence

outline forces us to think through our material more thoroughly than the topic outline, which merely indicates the ground to be covered.

The following is a sentence outline for a paper that systematically surveys the factors that have helped or hindered women in their struggle for equal pay. Notice the use of Arabic numerals for the entries that further subdivide the first subcategory in the second major section of the paper:

Why Women Earn Less Than Men

THESIS: While some traditional causes of women's low earning power are becoming less important, current patterns of professional advancement will have to change before true progress can take place.

I. Some traditional causes for the low earning power of women are becoming less important as a result of social change.
   A. Traditional prejudices about "men's work" and "women's work" are weakening.
   B. Large differences in educational opportunities for men and women have slowly disappeared.
   C. Traditional conceptions of women as short-term employees are changing as many women spend most of their adult lives in the labor force.
II. Current patterns of economic success and professional advancement continue to work against women, nevertheless.
   A. In most occupations, the years between age 25 and 35 are crucial to future success.
      1. Blue-collar workers discover the job openings and training opportunities that lead to highly paid skills.
      2. Corporations identify promising candidates for advancement in management.
      3. Professionals finish advanced degrees and compete for promising jobs.
   B. The years between age 25 and 35 are the most likely years for many women to be absent from the labor force or work part time because of family responsibilities.
III. For women to achieve more nearly equal earning power, society must revise its patterns of promotion and advancement to provide greater opportunities for mature women reentering the labor force.

Check your finished outlines against the following guidelines:

■ **Make your headings serve your purpose**. Writing about campus social life, you might divide students into Greeks, dorm dwellers, rent sharers, and loners. Writing about students' academic lives, you might divide them into grinds, crammers, prevaricators, and ad-libbers (who make up answers to exam questions as they go along).

■ **Avoid a confusing mixture of criteria.** What is the point of dividing students into graduates of local high schools, low-income students, and Catholics? Your readers can see the point of your categories if there is some common principle of selection, for example, geographic origin (local, rest of the state, out of state, foreign) or religious belief (Catholics, Protestants, Jews, Muslims, agnostics).

■ **Avoid single subdivisions.** Where there is a section A, you will need a section B; where there is a subdivision 1, you will need a subdivision 2. If in a paper on campus dress styles your section D ("Religious garb of the mysterious East") has only one subdivision ("Hare Krishna"), leave the section undivided.

■ **Reconsider a too-long sequence of parallel entries.** If you have eight or nine divisions under a single heading, see if you can set up subdivisions with two or three entries each.

■ **Use parallel wording to point up the relation between parallel ideas.** Your original wording might have been "I. Breaking the ice II. How to get acquainted III. A lasting relationship" and additional headings similarly mismatched. Try making each entry run along similar grammatical lines:

  I.   Breaking the ice
  II. Getting acquainted
  III. Cementing a relationship
  IV. Cooling off
  V.   Drifting away

Remember that outlines (like recipes) are a means to an end. They serve a double purpose: They help you clarify and channel your own thinking. They can also help readers find their way or help them check how well you have organized your thoughts.

WRITING WORKSHOP 19   The following interest inventory was adapted from a student paper. Arrange the items in a *topic outline*. Set up major headings and arrange them in an order that will make sense to the reader.

1. contact sports
2. coffee dates
3. religious retreats
4. taking a friend to the movies
5. work for worldwide disarmament
6. long hikes
7. beach barbecues
8. vacation trips
9. fellowship meetings
10. swimming
11. social work
12. student government

WRITING WORKSHOP 20 A student paper listed the following points as guidelines for parents. Prepare a *sentence outline* grouping these points under major headings.

1. Parents should avoid swearing or vulgarity.
2. Parents should not contradict each other in the presence of children.
3. Parents should provide encouragement when children do something constructive.
4. Punishment should be impartial when there are several children.
5. Parents should not shower their children with gifts.
6. One parent should not overrule the other in matters of discipline.
7. Parents should show affection, whether by a pat on the back or a good word.
8. Parents should respect children as individuals, letting them develop their own likes and dislikes.
9. Parents should not be overprotective.
10. Children should be allowed to learn from their own mistakes.
11. Parents should refrain from quarreling in the presence of their children.
12. Parents should teach good manners by example.
13. Parents should allow their children to choose their own friends.
14. Parents should not give vent to their frustrations or irritations by punishing their children.
15. Parents should not take notice of children only when they do something wrong.

WRITING WORKSHOP 21 Prepare both a *topic outline* and a *sentence outline* of a paper you have recently written. Observe conventional outline form.

WRITING TOPICS 3

Choose a topic that allows you to focus on a limited part of a larger subject. Push toward a thesis. Work out an overall plan. Sum up your central idea or thesis early in your paper and support it with specific details and examples.

1. People play different roles. Have you ever had to play a role that required you to change your behavior or assume a different personality? What did you learn from the experience? For instance, focus on playing the role of supervisor, camp counselor, scout, college athlete, poor relation, best friend, parent, or spouse.

2. Focus on a turning point in your life. Choose an event that had a lasting effect on you, a decision that made the difference, or an unexpected change for better or for worse. What did the event or the change mean for you? Make the people, situation, or events involved real for your reader.

3. Have you ever had to revise a stereotype about a group of people? (Or have you found a stereotype to be in part true?) Focus on a stereotype like the marine, the jock, the authoritarian father, or the housewife. Sum up a crucial change in your attitude and support it with ample details or examples.

4. About which of the following areas do you care enough to have definite opinions? Support as fully as you can one limited statement about one of the following. Provide a rich array of supporting examples. Write to provide guidance for a concerned audience: parents, fellow media watchers, people working in advertising, or the like.

    ■ toys as a reflection of American society
    ■ the role of women in current American movies
    ■ images of blacks or Hispanics in American advertising
    ■ the image of the native American in American Westerns
    ■ the treatment of conflict or violence in science fiction
    ■ guidance from teachers and counselors concerning jobs for women
    ■ teachers' attitudes toward children from bilingual backgrounds

5. College students are often accused of apathy on current social or political issues. Focus on a specific campus or community issue about

which you have been concerned. Present and support a concrete proposal for change or improvement. Write for the campus community or the larger local community.

4   Revising and Rethinking

OVERVIEW   A basic difference between the professional writer and the occasional writer is that the professional has learned to go beyond token revision. Writing teachers are frustrated when they give detailed instructions for revision but students attend only to the most obvious needs: dangling modifiers and missing commas, wrong words and sentences missing a verb. To profit from criticism (instead of just hating it), you have to learn how to respond to comments on the *larger elements* of a paper. You need to listen to comments about what you were trying to do, what sources you have drawn on, and how you have laid out your material. You need to act on comments on the purpose, substance, organization, and overall effectiveness of a paper.

Study the reader's comments on the following excerpt from a descriptive paper. The comments point to two kinds of revision needs:

- *missed opportunities*—places where the reader's interest is aroused but not satisfied;
- *barriers to communication*—features that distract or get in the way of what the writer is trying to share with the reader.

ORIGINAL:

improve colorless title? →   Trip to the Mountains

                Off in the distance, the beautiful

tone down   rustic mountains with elegantly fragranced
purple prose—   pine trees blended with the majestic blue
show us actual   sky that provided the setting for a trip
trees and   to the gold country in the sierra
mountains?   mountains. The winding road (provided the
                    path that) snaked (its way) through the

73

nice image, but very wordy sentence

slalom course of Mother Nature's mountainous creation. . . .

A two-story cabin provided a home for the trip. The small cabin reflected a warm homelike feeling with its outside boards

good – do more of this kind of concrete detail

painted blue and large pane-glass windows trimmed in white that allowed the sunlight to warm the place during the day. As I entered the cabin, I smelled a musty odor. However, soon the smell of the cedar boards took over after fresh air ran through the rooms.

The next day, as I went down to the stream that I had heard the night before, the morning air cleared my previously smog-filled lungs. I made my way along the muddy wet side while the stream rushed by at a great rippling pace. I continued until I came to a place where the shallow water was rippling over smooth rocks. A

redundant – avoid padding

bird chirped in the distance (representing its place in the local domain of the surrounding area). . . .

After lunch, I went back to the stream with my inner tube. As I entered the water, it cooled me off so fast that I

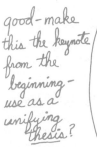

good – make this the keynote from the beginning – use as a unifying thesis?

felt numb and could not move without great effort. However, I pushed on and dodged in and out of the rocks in the stream. At the end of the workout in the icy, sparkling clean water, my whole body felt cleansed and refreshed.

When revised according to the reader's suggestions, the beginning of this paper might read like this. (Note the added thesis.)

REVISION:

High Country, White Water

The winding road snaked up into the mountains, retracing the slalom course that the waters of the mountain river had carved out over thousands of years. Off in the distance, successive ridges of pine-covered mountains blended with the hazy blue sky. I was heading up into the gold country of the sierra mountains. <u>I knew that ahead of me lay the kind of weekend that leaves the body exhausted but leaves the mind and the spirit refreshed</u>. Fresh mountain air would drive the city smog from my lungs. The rushing white water of streams swollen from melted snow would wash the grime of the city from the body. . . .

4a   *rev*   Revising for Larger Elements

Learn to do more than a cosmetic revision.

Much revision or correction of student writing deals with word choice, sentence structure, and punctuation. Remember instructions like the following when revising for the larger elements—purpose, substance, structure, and style:

(1) Strengthen your beginning. Is there a vivid introduction of the issue? Is there a pointed statement of a central thesis? Is there a helpful preview of what the paper is going to do? Study the following revision of an introduction in response to a reader's comments:

ORIGINAL:

South of the Border

Many times I have watched commercials and
television shows that supposedly show the lifestyle
of Mexicans south of the border. My friends have
often asked me if the way Mexicans are portrayed
there is true, and I have to say "no." Mexicans
aren't as old-fashioned as they are portrayed on
television and in movies; they are like any other
modern people.

COMMENT: Let us have a look at *one* striking commercial to give
us a vivid picture of what you have in mind. Then spell
out the central point for the rest of your paper more fully.
Make your thesis more of a preview of what your paper
is going to cover.

REVISION:

South of the Border

When people think of Mexico, they usually
remember a "Fly Mexicana" airline commercial and
picture a brown-skinned, black-haired person wearing
a white suit, sandals, and a sombrero. I often have
to tell my friends that the picture they get of Mexico
from commercials and television shows is not true.
Mexicans are not as old-fashioned as they are made to
look on our television screens or in movies. Most
people in Mexico are like any modern people. They
work, study, eat, have a social life, and dress as
Americans do; but then again, some of their customs
may differ somewhat from the American style.

(2) Restate key points clearly and forcefully. In a first draft, we are
often content to put our ideas on paper in an approximate way. As you
work on your revision, ask yourself: "What are some of the key points that
I want the reader to remember? Where in the paper are they stated in plain

English, in striking or memorable form?" Use your revision as an opportunity to rewrite awkward or roundabout sentences or to restate key ideas more directly:

WEAK:

> Unforeseen circumstances may make a relatively
> unimportant person seem all of a sudden very
> important.

STRONGER:

> A sudden turn of events may propel a nobody into the
> limelight; an obscure vice-president may overnight
> become President.

(3) Strengthen your overall plan. It is not too late to *rethink* your overall plan—to shuffle major sections for a more logical or more natural sequence. Suppose you have started a paper on ethnic humor by explaining and illustrating the new etiquette for the telling of ethnic jokes: People should not tell jokes to put down others; they should tell jokes only about their own ethnic group. People of British extraction will tell British jokes; people of German extraction will tell German jokes. (World's shortest book: *Four Centuries of German Humor.*) In your second section, you have contrasted the new etiquette with the offensive ethnic jokes—Polish jokes, Italian jokes, Arab jokes—of the past. In a third section, however, you have claimed that some jokes about other ethnic groups are meant to be affectionate rather than cutting or demeaning.

On second thought, you decide that the order of your paper is anticlimactic—it presents a provocative new idea first and then seems to backtrack and lose its punch. In your revision, you might reshuffle your major sections to *lead up* to the main point, going from the undesirable to the desirable:

REVISED:
Humor Is No Laughing Matter
  I. Truly offensive jokes about other ethnic groups
 II. Affectionate jokes about other ethnic groups
III. The new etiquette: jokes about one's own nationality

(4) Provide a stronger follow-through for key points. Build up supporting details and examples. In a first draft, you will often move on too fast—broaching one general idea and then going on to the next. The following passage, from a paper about the lack of role models for today's youth, moves too quickly from point to point:

TOO GENERAL:

> Young people today have no one to look up to. They are living in a time in our nation's history without true heroes. The only heroes young people see are in the movies. There is a big gap between the heroic figures in our history textbooks and the so-called "leaders" on our national scene. Because of the lack of true leadership, young people today easily follow false prophets, becoming involved in gangs or religious cults. . . .

By now there is already a backlog of questions in the reader's mind: What kind of heroes do young people see in the movies? What would be a good example of a textbook hero—and of a "so-called" current leader (and why are we inclined to be disappointed in the latter)? What do gangs offer or promise their followers? What is a good example of a religious cult that attracts young people? Remember that revision is your chance to answer the unanswered questions in the reader's mind.

Look for important points that lack striking detailed examples:

ORIGINAL:

> Television presents a constant stream of commercials promising to make us more attractive and to make our lives more glamorous. Advertisers seem to think that viewers are naive enough to expect a new toothpaste or a new shampoo to transform their love lives. . . .

REVISED:

> Television presents a constant stream of commercials promising to make us more attractive and to make our lives more glamorous. The man in a new compact picks up a woman on a street corner. She

likes his sun roof. A woman hunting for a lost earring under a table is joined by an admirer. He likes her fresh breath; she mentions her brand of toothpaste; they live happily ever after. Even the Tydee Bowl man lends an air of dignity to the toilet, as he wears his exquisitely tailored yachting togs. And, of course, whenever a commercial for clothes or makeup is presented, the gorgeous face of a famous model hints that Ultima II or Maybelline or Chardon jeans will transform the population at large into beauties.

(5) Clarify connections and strengthen transitions between points. Use each major paragraph to take a clear step forward in a description or in an argument. The following passage is from a paper that moves from point to point without signals clear or strong enough to let readers see where they are headed.

ORIGINAL (NO PARAGRAPH BREAK):

The first foreign exchange student who stayed with my family was Juan, who came from Argentina. My family and I soon started to notice the differences between the two cultures. Whenever someone new came to the house, Juan always stood up and gave the woman a hug or the man a big handshake. Juan explained to me that it was customary to stand up in the presence of an adult; young people who didn't were considered disrespectful. This was only one of many different barriers we were to encounter. Juan was used to staying out as late as he wanted. He explained that in his country there was no age limit to keep him out of bars or to keep him from buying alcoholic beverages. He soon became restless when he was kept from roaming the streets at all hours. . . .

REVISED (PARAGRAPH BREAK AND TRANSITION ADDED):

> The first foreign exchange student who stayed with my family was Juan, who came from Argentina. My family and I soon became aware of the differences between the two cultures. The first thing we noticed was that <u>his manners were more formal or more elaborate than those of most Americans</u>. He always stood up when someone new came to the house. He gave a woman a hug or a man a big handshake. . . .
>
> <u>On the other hand</u>, Juan was <u>used to considerably more freedom</u> than many American teenagers enjoy. He was used to roaming the streets at all hours of the evening. When he played basketball with the high school team, he would leave early in the morning and return late at night. He explained that in his country there was no age limit to keep him out of bars or to keep him from buying alcoholic beverages. . . .

Remember: Show connections; provide a bridge or transition from point to point. The following excerpts are from a paper with poorly marked turns:

Stereotypical Males

can you give more of a PREVIEW?

    The reruns of serials that in my youth filled television screens during the daytime mirrored perfectly the traditional ways of stereotyping the American male. **This stereotyping started in childhood.** From *The Little Rascals* to *Dennis the Menace*, it was always the boys (and never the girls) who got into mischief (and who had all the fun). . . .

prepare reader for CONTRAST

    These bad boys had to grow up to be men. From *I Love Lucy* to *The Dick Van Dyke Show*, the man was the stereotypical breadwinner who worked outside the home, while the housewife stayed home to cook and care for the children. . . .

weak link— show LOGICAL connection?

    Another favorite of the old serials was the professional man—the doctor, lawyer, or teacher giving everyone sage advice. . . .

> **Another old standby** was the kindly old grandfather or uncle who was grouchy on the surface at times but who really has a heart of gold. . . .

Look at the way the revised version provides the missing links:

The Cartoon Male

The reruns of serials that in my youth filled television screens during the daytime mirrored perfectly the traditional ways of stereotyping the American male. **This stereotyping started in childhood and followed the male into manhood and old age**. From *The Little Rascals* to *Dennis the Menace*, it was always the boys (and never the girls) who got into mischief (and who had all the fun). . . .

Paradoxically, these bad boys grew up to be the men **who were the traditional providers and heads of their households**. From *I Love Lucy* to *The Dick Van Dyke Show*, the man was the stereotypical breadwinner who worked outside the home, while the housewife stayed home to cook and care for the children. . . .

Closely related to the father responsible for the well-being of the family was the wise professional who represented a father image. He was the doctor, lawyer, or teacher giving everyone sage advice. . . .

At the end of his career, we would see the stereotypical male as the kindly old grandfather or uncle who under a sometimes grouchy surface carried a heart of gold. . . .

(6) Leave your reader with a strong final impression. A first draft often simply seems to run down, without a strong summing up or final pulling together of important points. Sometimes the writer at the end backs away from the issue, suddenly turning cautious or entertaining second thoughts ("Will there be stricter gun control laws, or will we all eventually own a gun?"). Replace a weak ending with a conclusion that has the courage of your convictions:

REVISED:

```
       Perhaps it is true that we only hear what we want
to hear, but I yet have to find an argument to counter
the statistics showing 200 gun-related deaths in this
country for every similar death in a country like
England.  Slogans that claim "Guns don't kill people"
are not my idea of a strong argument.  We need to
strengthen current laws concerning gun control
```

```
because the number of lives lost through the use of
handguns in this country is appalling.
```

WRITING WORKSHOP 22   Share a *first draft* of a paper with a group of your classmates. Ask them for candid oral or written comments. What help or guidance do their comments provide for a revision of your draft? Write a summary and evaluation of the feedback your received. Ask the group to answer questions like the following:

- In their opinion, what is your paper trying to do, and how successful is it?
- What are strong points of the paper?
- What are weak points?
- What specific suggestions for improvement do your readers have?
- How did they personally react to your paper, and why?
- What kind of audience do they think would react best? What kind is likely to react negatively, and why?

4b   A Paper from Notes to Revision

Trace a paper through the major stages of the writing process to final revision.

The following pages trace the history of a student paper from the initial notetaking, through a first draft and the instructor's comments, to a fairly substantial revision.

GETTING STARTED   The writer chose this subject from a list of possible topics because it was close to his own experience and interests. He himself had held various part-time jobs, and both his family and his friends often talked about what happened at work.

The author's general purpose was to write an informative paper about the *attitudes* of Americans at work—to take stock of his observations and show a general pattern that his readers could compare with what they had seen themselves. However, he had a more personal motive: He had been at times amused, annoyed, or angered by co-workers who did less than their share and depended on their colleagues to take up the slack. He had in mind an audience of his own generation. He was thinking of young people who wonder how they will fare in the world of work and who are interested in sharing experiences on the subject.

FROM NOTES TO OUTLINE Here are the student writer's working notes:

Constant refrain heard around the house when I was younger (mainly from my mother): "Finish the job. Do it right. Take pride in what you do."

Things people say: "I owe, I owe, so off to work I go." "I am doing it strictly for the money." "I love the work, but there is no money in it."

My restaurant job: some waiters/waitresses really put themselves into their jobs—always on their feet: extra glass of water, more bread, return change. Last dishwasher a real loser: piles of dishes always left for the next shift, "clean" dishes with chunks of food. Filthy silverware. Replacement: good worker.

Dad's job: engineer. Seldom brings home any work? Likes his work though. Always talks about people doing "useful work."

"Work ethic"? It really depends. Example, Fred: checked sales of magazines off magazine racks in supermarkets. Turned in reports—didn't even go to the stores! (Mention Amos: drifter, half of the time unemployed.)

Other side of the coin: dedicated physicists, scientists. Einstein. Computer whiz putting in fourteen hours a day.

Who else? Ellen has semiconductor job. Ask her about it—attitudes of workers?

As the student writer sorted out these notes, "That depends" began to stand out as the keynote. There seemed to be a range of attitudes, from the dedicated to the lackadaisical. In the following *trial outline*, his overall plan is beginning to take shape:

- truly dedicated (scientists, computer specialists)
- conscientious nine-to-five (Dad's engineering job, Ellen)
- strictly for the money (dishwasher, magazine checker)

THE FIRST DRAFT In his first draft, the writer expanded his scheme to include four categories instead of three. Read his first draft. Then study the comments the instructor wrote in the margin.

put this later when you give reasons for different attitudes? (start with a striking example?)

Is the Work Ethic Extinct?

The work ethic is an ideal that has never been embraced by the entire working population. Our attitude toward work is shaped in large part by what we observe our own parents' attitude toward work to be. If their attitude is "I owe, I owe, so off to work I go," we may also absorb the same attitude. If the parents' aim is to do as

83

little work as possible for the most amount of money, their children may also adopt this philosophy. My own parents taught me to take pride in my work, and no matter how hard I try, I cannot shake this attitude.

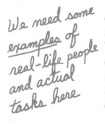

Good overview — but very dry (add a graphic touch or two)

To judge from my own experience, there are approximately four different attitudes that people have toward their work. One would be that of true lifelong devotion. Another would be sincere devotion for eight hours a day, five days a week. The third would be indifference, not really caring one way or the other. The last would be the attitude of people who deliberately do as little work as possible for the most amount of money.

We need some examples of real-life people and actual tasks here

Some people are totally absorbed in their work. A dedicated scientist may spend long hours thinking about an experiment, new data, or a challenged hypothesis. When taking physics and chemistry, I was told that in order to understand a scientific concept I should think about it continuously. Today's computer programmers and communications engineers also work long hours, driven by ambition and taking pride in what they do.

provide stronger link? tell us more about his work

The rank and file of the workforce includes a large number of people who do creditable work while on the job. My father is an engineer, and I know that his work requires hard work and concentration for eight hours a day, five days a week. An acquaintance of mine works in a semiconductor plant. She takes pride in her work and in being asked to help out in different production areas.

Good — do more of this kind of detail

I have had some firsthand observations of people who basically do not care. A dishwasher in the restaurant where I work part-time used to send out plates that still had chunks of food baked on to them, and he invariably left a pile of unfinished work for the next shift. The glasses he sent out were cloudy, and the silverware often hardly looked appetizing.

again good real-life example

Finally, there is the worker who milks the job for whatever it offers without feeling obligated to offer anything in return. I used to know someone who worked as a magazine checker. His job was to make the rounds of various supermarkets at the end of the week to count how many magazines had been sold and how many were left. It was his policy to make up approximate numbers, often not even visiting the store.

Is the work ethic a thing of the past? The answer depends on the examples we look at. In my family, it is not a thing of the past. But with some people I have known, the work ethic has gone into a total eclipse.

THE SECOND DRAFT The second draft of the work ethic paper follows the instructor's suggestions fairly closely. It builds on a first draft that had a workable overall plan and usable material. Check how the author's revision has accomplished the following:

- used the *introduction* to bring the subject into focus and to bring it to life;
- provided a clear *overview* with graphic touches;
- provided detailed follow-up with authentic *examples* from the author's reading, personal observation, and employment history;
- provided effective *transitions* that show the logical connection between one point and the next;
- added a new *conclusion*.

Is the Work Ethic Extinct?

The work ethic is an ideal that has never been embraced by the entire working population. Some people take a job only when they absolutely need it in order to help them pay their bills. ("I owe, I owe, so off to work I go.") Also, there have always been people who drift aimlessly from job to job. A friend of mine will take almost any job and work at it for a short while, then collect unemployment insurance until it dries up, then take another job. He continues this cycle with amazing regularity. When we ask whether the work ethic is still alive, we should disregard the drifter and take a look at workers who know they need a job and are not likely to move frequently from one job to another.

To judge from my experience, the attitudes of workers towards their jobs cover the whole range. Workers range from people who are obsessed with their work (the workaholics), through people who do the job from 9 to 5 (the rank and file), to people who do as little work as possible for the most amount of money (the shirkers).

Some people are totally absorbed in their work. A dedicated scientist may spend most of his or her waking hours thinking about an experiment, new data, or a challenged hypothesis. I remember a book about the Manhattan Project, responsible for the construction of the atom bomb during World War II. Many of the scientists involved worked long hours from early in the morning till late at night. I remember a story about one of them who was too preoccupied with the work to remember having eaten breakfast in the morning. Today, we read about computer programmers and communications engineers who work late into the night—young men and women dedicated to their work, driven by ambition, and taking pride in what they do.

Obviously, such total dedication and intense ambition are exceptional. The rank and file includes a large number of people who do creditable work while on the job. I know many people who devote eight hours a day, five days a week, to doing the best job they are capable of. My father is an engineer who will do his required work, do the necessary background research, and help a fellow worker who comes to him with a problem. His work requires a great deal of concentration eight hours a day, five days a week, but the rest of his time he has to himself. An acquaintance of mine works in a semiconductor plant. She takes pride in her work and in being asked to help out in different production areas when her experience and advice are needed.

These people illustrate the basic element in the work ethic, which is the satisfaction in a job well done. Not all of the people who share this satisfaction have jobs that are glamorous or highly paid. The dishwasher in the restaurant where I work part-time would not consider sending out dirty plates, greasy silverware, or cloudy glasses.

Unfortunately, many people do not care about the quality of their work. The previous dishwasher I worked with sent out plates that had chunks of food on them, and he invariably left a pile of unfinished work for the next shift. I have known waiters who considered it an imposition to be asked for a glass of water by a customer. People with this kind of attitude are often workers trapped in a job they do not like or want, and they continue strictly from economic necessity.

Finally, there is the worker who milks the job for whatever money or privileges it offers without feeling obligated to offer anything in return. I used to know a person who worked as a magazine checker. His job was to make the rounds of various supermarkets at the end of the week to count how many magazines had been sold and how many were left. His reports would tell the distributor how many copies of *Popular Mechanics, Good Housekeeping,* and *True Adventure* had been sold to eager readers. It was his policy to make up approximate numbers, often not even visiting a store while pretending he had been there. With people like him, the work ethic has gone into a total eclipse.

What accounts for such differences in attitude? Previous generations vividly remembered hardship and poverty. To them, hard work was the way to banish the spectre of poverty and deprivation. Often, our attitudes toward work are influenced by early training and the example of our parents. I will never forget the constant refrain I heard around the house when I was young: "Finish the job. Do it right. Any job worth doing is worth doing well." My parents taught me to take pride in my work, and I cannot shake this attitude, even when it might be convenient for me to care less and enjoy myself more.

FINAL REVISION In much professional writing, a third or perhaps fourth rewrite is not uncommon. Given a chance for final revision, the author of the work ethic paper might decide that some of the job descriptions in the paper are still too general and colorless. Here is a rewrite of the passage dealing with the author's father (in the fourth paragraph):

> My father is a **metallurgical engineer working for a company that produces marine turbines and similar gear. He works out and checks the specifications for the metals used—their strength, their ability to withstand corrosion, their capability of being welded, and so forth**. He will do his required work, do the necessary background research, and help a fellow worker who comes to him with a problem.

WRITING WORKSHOP 23 For a paper currently in process, prepare a *protocol*—a record of materials documenting how it took shape. Include a planning report, prewriting such as brainstorming or reading notes, trial outlines, successive drafts, and a record of instructor's comments or peer response. Annotate the different items—for each, provide a brief description and your comments.

4c   Peer Revision

Participate in peer revision of other students' writing.

Many professional writers revise and rework in response to feedback from editors, reviewers, agents, colleagues, and friends. They develop their sense of audience through reactions, warnings, and advice from readers who respond to early versions or trial drafts. When you participate in peer reviewing, you help provide other student writers with an audience other than the course instructor.

As a peer reviewer, you help others look at their writing from the reader's point of view. You will help them anticipate the likely reactions of their readers. What will make their readers pay attention, and what will make them lose interest? What will make them smile, and what will make them frown?

What will make your comments on others' writing helpful and constructive? Remember some general guidelines: Balance *positive and negative* criticism. A good editor identifies strengths (and helps the writer build on them) and weaknesses (and helps the writer overcome them). Pay attention to the *larger elements* as well as more limited points—examine overall purpose, content, and organization of the paper. Try to make *specific suggestions* for improvement.

Here is a brief *checklist* of features you might comment on:

1. Has the writer focused on a limited subject? What was the writer's purpose, and does the paper accomplish it? Who would make a good audience for this paper?

2. Does the paper get off to a good start? How effective are its title and introduction?

3. Is there a central idea or thesis? Does it provide a preview for the rest of the paper? Is there a clear plan, and does the writer help the reader see it?

4. Are the different parts of the paper well developed? Are key points supported with specific details? (Where is there strong supporting material? Where is the supporting material weak? How could it be strengthened?)

5. How well does the paper convey its message? Where is expression effective—clear and vivid? Where is it awkward or confusing?

6. Are there problems with sentence structure, grammatical usage, punctuation, spelling?

7. How effective is the conclusion?

WRITING WORKSHOP 24   Study the following first draft of a student paper. Give useful advice that would guide the student writer in preparing an improved final draft of this paper. Remember the two basic functions of a good editor: (a) to recognize and reinforce what a writer does well and (b) to give constructive suggestions for improving what is weak or needs revision in a piece of writing.

No Heroes

In todays society young people find few worthy objects or outlets for loyalty and devotion. They join groups ranging from neighborhood gangs to religeous cults because they need something to be loyalto or to believe in. To better understand this assessment we must look at the past and try to determine what worthy objects or outlets were available for young people to pledge their loyalty and devotion. To analyze these symbols for hero worship we will break them up into three categories: political, military, and sports figures. These seem to reflect well the more popular forms of hero worship in our society today.

In the past young adults had political figures to look up to and respect. Respect is the important word here. Today we still have the same offices to look up to but much of the offices themselves and their political occupants have been lost. Looking back we can easily have admired men like Teddy Roosevelt, Harry Truman, Woodrow Wilson, Franklin Roosevelt, Ike and even as recently as John Kennedy. Today we think of Lyndon Johnson and his relentless struggle with Vietnam, or Nixon and Watergate. It has become very easy to lose respect for the office of the presidency and our presidents.

The decline in loyalty toward our military is due largely to the fact that we have fought in unpopular wars for some thirty years. During these years weve fought the Korean and Vietnam Wars. We were no longer rallying around the flag as we had done for WWI and WWII. During these same years came the cause for our unpopular involvement the Cold War. Our reputation as the most powerful nation in the world is constantly being threatened, while our moral integrity is also being questioned. When we seek to aid another nation, is it for thier sake or ours? Why should we help another country while our own has unsolved problems? It is a shame when we lose respect for an institution such as the Military, an institution that has kept us a world leader for more than a century.

It also has become increasingly difficult to hero worship athletes in todays society. For this comparison well use baseball, America's national past time. We no longer have the Babe Ruths, Lou Gehrigs Willie Mays, Stan Musials or Mickey Mantles. Men who played the game with respect and a love for simply playing. Not with the major emphasis on baseball the business. Today we have players who have taken advantage of the bussiness aspect of baseball (the free agent draft). Players are being spoiled and pampered, thus they become much more temperamental. They perform below the standards their million dollar contracts seem to call for. This upsets the unsatisfied fans who feel cheated by sub par performances.

With all these problems in our society today, one can understand why young people search for new outlets to devote loyalties to. New institutions such as religeous cults (Moonies, Jonestown). Instead of Little League baseball, they get involved in neighborhood gangs. Young people are getting fed up with the so-called establishment and are finding it hard to find worthy alternatives.

WRITING TOPICS 4

Take a paper through a cycle of successive revisions in response to feedback from your instructor and to peer review. Aim at more than token revision of the larger elements: purpose, substance, organization, tone, and style. Choose one of the following topics:

1. Much biography focuses on how people rise to a challenge. Has a major challenge, issue, or obstacle played a role in your own life? How did it affect you? How did you cope with it?

2. Traditionally, home has meant to many people a central place in their lives that shaped their outlook and personalities and offered them a safe harbor to which to return. In the modern world, many people feel that this idea of "home" is extinct. People feel they are isolated or cast-off individuals; and home is simply a place where they find themselves at sundown. Which of these views is closest to your own? Describe your own concept of home, using detailed illustrations from your personal experience and observation.

3. The traditional American work ethic encouraged people to do their work with a sense of pride and satisfaction. In recent years, well-known authors have claimed that many Americans are dissatisfied with their work. Many Americans, we are told, hate their jobs. To judge from what you have seen of the world of work, how true are these charges? Draw on your own observation or experience.

4. Do you consider the police your friend or your enemy? In an emergency or in a difficult situation, would you expect the police to be on your side?

5. Does current popular entertainment glorify youth and create an unfavorable image of age? Are older people made to seem irrelevant or unwanted?

5   Final Editing

OVERVIEW When you edit your paper, you get it ready for print. Final editing is your chance to improve features of your writing that might come between you and the reader. An essential survival skill for you as a writer is to make a paper meet the standards of **edited written English**— the kind of English that will be acceptable to a large cross section of educated readers. Look for possible problems in three areas:

COMMUNICATION Look for words and sentences that get in the way of clear and direct communication. Some words are just plain wrong, and some are only half right. Your original wording may be **unidiomatic**—it may clash with the familiar natural way of saying something. Or the wording may be inflated—using too many unnecessary words or using disproportionately big words in a mistaken attempt to impress the reader.

CONFUSED:	Jean was not fully **convicted** [should be **convinced**] of the truth of the report.
UNIDIOMATIC:	Millions of immigrants have **stepped foot** [should be **set foot**] on this land of opportunity.
WORDY:	The launch was postponed **due to the fact that** [should be **because**] temperatures were unseasonably low.
INFLATED:	Mandatory verification of their attendance record was required of all personnel when exiting the work area. (All employees were required to punch time cards when they left.)

Look for sentences that slow down or confuse the reader. You can often improve an indirect or roundabout sentence by rewriting it on the "Who-does-what?" model:

AWKWARD:	Awareness of the need for gun control usually occurs when someone guns down an important public figure. (Who becomes aware?)
REVISED:	**The public** usually becomes aware of the need for gun control when someone guns down an important public figure.

USAGE The best modern prose is moderately formal, with an occasional lighter touch. Edited written English is more formal than casual speech, but it is not so hyperformal as to become stiff and pretentious. Formal and informal usage give different signals to the reader. "Leave now" and "Get out" say the same thing, but one is more respectful than the other. Look for passages where your wording might sound too informal for serious discussion:

TOO INFORMAL:	At times, even today's highly competitive students seem to suspect that **getting to the top of the heap** is not all that **it is cracked up to be**.
BETTER:	At times, even today's highly competitive students seem to suspect that those **climbing to the top** of the corporate ladder **pay a price**.

Much final editing aims at expressions where usage differs for informal talk and serious writing (*like* I said/*as* I said, between you and *I*/between you and *me*.)

MECHANICS Serious readers expect us to observe conventional ways of putting words on a page, including correct spelling and appropriate punctuation.

5a   An Editor's Checklist

Recognize high-priority items for final editing.

Many writers and editors have checklists or style sheets for a last-minute check of usage and mechanics. The following is such an **editor's checklist**, listing ten high-priority items that you should look for in final editing and proofreading of your papers.

To flag these and other editing problems for you in your papers, your instructor may use the numerical handbook key or the correction symbols employed throughout this handbook. Suppose you are carrying over to the written page the sentence fragments of stop-and-go conversation. (Fragments like this one.) The abbreviation *frag* or the guide number 14a will guide you to the section of this handbook that describes fragments and offers guidelines for revising them.

EDITOR'S CHECKLIST

KEY   SYMBOL

14a *frag* **(1) Correct sentence fragments.** Sentence fragments mirror the afterthoughts and asides of informal stop-and-go conversation. ("My friends would wear baggies. *Loose-fitting pants, usually a size too big*.") Many sentence fragments are isolated words or phrases that lack the subject and complete verb needed to turn them into sentences:

FRAGMENT: At the last moment. (Who did what at the last moment?)

COMPLETE: The mayor filed for reelection **at the last moment**.

Other sentence fragments do have a subject and a verb, but they start with a subordinator (subordinating conjunction) or a relative pronoun. They need to be hooked up to a main clause.

FRAGMENT: If the proposal succeeds.   (If it succeeds, then what?)
COMPLETE: Front Street will become a mall **if the proposal succeeds**.

FRAGMENT: Whose plane disappeared over the Pacific. (*Whose
plane?*)
COMPLETE: She admired Amelia Earhart, **whose plane disappeared
over the Pacific**.

14c *CS*   (2) Correct comma splices. A comma splice uses only a comma to
splice together two related statements. (Where the two statements join,
there is no coordinator like *and* or *but*, no subordinator like *if* or
whereas.) Use a semicolon instead of the comma:

COMMA SPLICE: We scratched the dog act, the poodle was ill.
SEMICOLON: We scratched the dog act; the poodle was ill.

Comma splices also result when only a comma appears between two statements joined by *therefore* or *however*. These and
similar conjunctive adverbs require a semicolon:

COMMA SPLICE: Peking seemed drab and bureaucratic, Shanghai
however seemed lively and sophisticated.
SEMICOLON: Peking seemed drab and bureaucratic; Shanghai,
however, seemed lively and sophisticated.

16d *agr*   (3) Correct faulty agreement. Agreement requires matching
forms for subject and verb: The *train stops* here (singular); the
trains stop here (plural). Blind agreement results when the verb
agrees with part of a wedge that came between it and the subject:

FAULTY: The credibility of these **witnesses are** open to question.
REVISED: The **credibility** of these witnesses **is** open to question.
(What is open to question? Their credibility **is**.)

19b *DM*   (4) Correct dangling or misplaced modifiers. A modifier is left
MM   dangling when it points to something that has been left out of the
sentence. (A modifier is misplaced when it seems to point to the
wrong thing.)

DANGLING: **Repossessed for nonpayment**, David claimed that the
terms of the contract had not been met. (*What* was
repossessed?)
REVISED: When **his car was repossessed** for nonpayment, David
claimed that the terms of the contract had not been met.

17e *ref* **(5) Correct vague or confusing pronoun reference.** Pronouns like *she* or *they* or *this* serve as shorthand references to people and things, but they need to point clearly to what they stand for. Avoid loose pronoun reference; especially, avoid shifts in the way you refer to a typical or representative person:

SHIFT: **The typical woman** today does not expect Prince Charming to take care of **their** every need. (We are looking at *one* typical woman.)

REVISED: The typical woman today does not expect Prince Charming to take care of **her** every need.

22d *ap, //* **(6) Correct faulty parallelism.** Sentences are parallel when several equal or similar sentence parts appear in a row, joined by a word like *and* or *or* or *but*. ("People were obsessed with *spies, conspiracies,* and *plots*.") But sometimes the second or third element in such a sequence snaps out of the pattern:

FAULTY: A rainy day makes people feel **tired**, **lazy**, and **in a gloomy mood**.

PARALLEL: A rainy day makes people feel **tired**, **lazy**, and **gloomy**.

43a *cap* **(7) Check for missing capital letters.** Capital letters, like apostrophes, do not show in speech and are therefore easily overlooked. Capitalize names of days, months, places, states, ships, schools. Especially, capitalize the names of nationalities and languages: *Mexican, Spanish, Italian, Canadian, Australian, Japanese, American*.

CAPITALS: The opera singer from Laurel, Mississippi, ended her 32-year career with a stunning farewell performance of Verdi's *Aida* at New York City's Metropolitan Opera.

42b *ap* **(8) Use the apostrophe for the possessive of nouns.** The possessive tells us *whose*: my *brother's* keeper, the *world's* safest airport; the *coach's* unexpired contract, the *cat's* meow. Remember the basic rule: apostrophe and *s* if you are talking about one; *s* and apostrophe if you are talking about several:

	SINGULAR	PLURAL
Whose?	a **friend's** BMW my **brother's** nose one **country's** history	the **tenants'** cars my **brothers'** noses other **countries'** problems
	a **week's** wage	two **months'** salary

Check for some often misspelled possessives: *today's* world, *yesterday's* newspaper, *tomorrow's* election. Check for unusual plurals: the *men's* locker room, *women's* rights, the *children's* hour.

42a *ap*   **(9) Distinguish between it's and its.** Use *it's* only when it's short for *it is: it's* too late, *it's* a plane, *it's* illegal. *Its* is a key exception to the rule that possessives require an apostrophe: the band and *its* instruments (whose?); the rifle and *its* parts.

39 *sp*   **(10) Check your spelling to catch the unforgivables.** Never misspell the following: *receive, believe, separate, definite, similar, athlete, perform, basically, probably, used to, a lot* (two words!), *writing, occurred.*

A final word: PROOFREAD. Never hand in a paper without giving it a slow, careful final reading. If at all possible, wait—half an hour, a day. (If you merely go over a paper quickly after you finish it, you will tend to see what you *meant* to write rather than what you actually did.) Read with grim determination to find typographical errors, garbled sentences, miscellaneous slipups, pages out of order.

5b   A Paper with Comments

Study—and act on—comments on your papers.

In practice, you will be doing much of your revising and final editing in response to your instructor's comments on your papers. Look for reinforcement of what you are doing right and for help with what needs work. Pay special attention to problems that come up several times in the same paper. From each set of comments, try to learn something that will help you not only in current revision but also in your future writing.

Here is a sample student paper with correction symbols and instructor's comments:

#98869   *wrong form?*

As a consequence of our (strive) for

better technology and efficiency, Americans

are becoming severely disatisfied with   *sp*

clarify what you mean?

their job environment and organization. This businesslike drive for profit and speed causes three serious problems *in or for?* in the American worker: lack of loyalty, lack of praise, and lack of knowing *or* youre needed.

Lack of loyalty is caused primarily by the very impersonal interaction that goes on between employee and boss. I started a job at a company where I <u>was referred to</u> as only "98869." I stayed for only a short while and quit. I felt no loss at leaving anybody behind, because they were just faces with numbers written on them. No one ever bothered you. It was more efficient that way! (22b) – *shift from I to you?*

good revealing detail – but give additional evidence?

Another major problem that causes dissatisfaction is the lack of praise for a job well done. After I quit my first job, I got a job as an assistant legal secretary. Each day I had to prepare wills, depositions, <u>and basically run the office.</u> Little by little I became more annoyed by my constant lack of any kind of praise. Then one day it hit me all at once. The lawyer called me from a phone in the city courtroom. He need me to prepare some things and bring them to him in court. He gave me half an hour. He proceeded to tell me all the things he needed. I had one hand on the typewriter, one on the copier, and one in my briefcase looking for my car keys! When I got downtown with one minute to spare, he

FP (22d)

(15a)

nice exaggeration (this whole paragraph is better developed) said: "I wish I could have looked this over before I got in there.   Was there a lot of traffic or something?"   Not once did he ever thank me for my help.   I felt that no matter what I did it wouldn't be appreciated.

sf

In my next job, as a bookkeeper/organizer, I realized what the lack of knowing that you are needed could do.   When I began this job I enjoyed each day.   I could use my organizing skills and keep the company and its employees all on

P schedule.   **SINGULAR** Each one had their own section, and I would organize it the best way possible.   I received a lot of praise from these employees and was told they couldn't do without me.

redundant? Sure! About ⑥ months later I was **46 b**
introduced to my new replacement.   He sat

nice image there with his lights blinking and little typed words flowing across the screen.   He

hy had a rainbow colored apple (with a bite

sf taken out of it) on its front.   "It's our

good use of direct quotations new computer," said the lady I knew only as "the computer lady."   "It can do everything.   Everyone will be able to write and read messages on it and it organizes things beautifully."   Well, it wasn't long before I felt very inadequate.   The computer could do what used to take me

MM **19b** an hour in 30 seconds. These feelings of

sp inadequacy really effected my sense of self-confidence.

98

p These three problems cause many
workers like me to keep looking hoping
that some day a job that offers a chance of
personal loyalty, accomplishment and
pride, and the feeling of being valued

awk will come along.

Your paper uses personal experience well to show what the thesis means. The organization is clear, and the transitions are smooth. The style is sometimes awkward (see the specific pointers above).

REVIEW REFERENCE OF PRONOUNS AND SHIFTS IN PRONOUN REFERENCE – 17e and 22b.

EDITING PRACTICE 25 Revise each of the following sentences to correct an editing problem that is common in student writing. If you need help, turn to the appropriate section of this book.

KEY SYMBOL

16d *agr*
agreement

43a *cap*
capitals

14a *frag*
fragment

40b *sp*
spelling

15b *vb*
verb

1. The typical diet article in newspapers and magazines *treat* food as if it were a foreign agent.
2. Alice Walker's *The Color Purple* won the Pulitzer Prize and was read by millions of *americans*.
3. The press chronicled his misadventures. *With great glee.*
4. Changes in our laws have not *detered* people from *commiting* crimes.
5. According to the inspector, someone else *could have wrote* the suicide note.

42b	*ap*	**6.** Stations use enticing "newsbriefs" to catch
	apostrophe	the *viewers* attention.
14c	*CS*	**7.** Blue jeans recognize no *classes, they* are
	comma splice	merely American.
18b	*ca*	**8.** Children may not know *who* to trust.
	case	
19b	*DM*	**9.** *Sitting on top of an animal filled with furious*
	dangling modifier	*energy,* the gate opens and the bronco
		dashes frantically for the other side of the
		stadium.
22d	*4P* or *//*	**10.** We went to the apartment to pick up the bills,
	faulty parallelism	financial statements, and *finally clean out*
		the refrigerator.
57U1	*gl*	**11.** A anchorwoman on a local TV station felt
	glossary	harassed because of her looks and age.
17e	*ref*	**12.** Although the study of techniques is helpful to
	pronoun reference	an artist, *they* do not need a degree to paint.
20b	*mx*	**13.** The *main objective* of the article *compared*
	mixed construction	the use of glittering generalities by the two
		candidates.
34e	*p*	**14.** Our retina, which has maybe 125 million
	punctuation	rods and cones performs the equivalent of
		10 billion calculations per second.
44c	*hy*	**15.** Vietnamese immigrants slowly transformed
	hyphen	our *low rent* district.

---

6   Word Processing

OVERVIEW   Many professional writers, including most journalists, today use word processors that allow them to draft and revise on a monitor screen, to store documents on disks for future reference, and to print out finished copy. Many students do most or all of their writing on a personal computer (PC) with word processing capability; others have access to workstations hooked up to large **mainframe** computers.

We turn a personal computer into a word processor by loading a word processing program and hooking up the computer with an electronic printer. What we compose takes shape on the computer screen. We can correct and revise it at will, getting it into final shape *before* we print it as finished copy—or as several copies of the same quality as the original.

Word processing is making it easier for writers to write and rewrite. The writer can simply type over wrong words, shift whole sentences or paragraphs without retyping, and add or delete without recopying a whole document. Increasingly, the software that programs the word processor includes editorial aids that help the writer start a paper, explore the subject, revise a first draft, spot spelling errors, and the like. Increasingly, writers will be able to call up on their screens input or feedback from peers, instructors, and computerized sources.

The following features make a word processor more than a glorified typewriter:

(1) You as a writer interact with the word processor. The word processor will repeatedly present you with a choice of commands—a menu of choices or options. For instance, you will have to select such functions as *insert, erase, store, retrieve,* or *print*. If you instruct your computer to do something drastic or irreversible (for example, to erase a whole paper), it may ask you for a second command to confirm the first (in case you pushed the wrong button by mistake).

(2) The computer will handle much of the work of arranging your text on a page.

■ It will automatically begin *a new line* when you reach the set margin. You will usually be able to fill in a very uneven right margin by going back over a block of text and hyphenating some words and shifting others. (You can also usually **justify** the lines—have the computer adjust and stretch the lines for an even right margin, as we are used to seeing in a printed text.)

■ Your word processor will automatically start *a new page* and number each page.

■ Your word processor will usually help you *center* titles or lines of poetry.

(3) A word processor allows you to get your writing into final shape before it appears on paper. The great advantage of word processing is that it allows you to erase, type over, or add and reshuffle material with ease—before your paper is printed. It thus eliminates the need for the retyping of revised drafts or of flawed copies of final documents.

(4) A word processor makes it easy to produce modified versions of the same document. If you are sending the same business letter to several people, you can use the word processor to insert the right name and address for each of the people. But you can also easily add the comments and greetings that will give each letter a personal touch.

| **6a** | Hardware and Software |

Familiarize yourself with your equipment and the software that runs it.

The hardware, or physical equipment, for your word processor includes familiar parts:

■ The *keyboard* resembles a typewriter keyboard but has additional function keys (or additional functions for the same keys). You use the keyboard not only to type your text but to give the commands that tell the computer to add, delete, and move; to italicize and **boldface** (print in bolder type); or to file and retrieve.

■ The *monitor* looks like a small television screen. It displays the text you are working on, text you have called up from your files, the index of the texts you have stored, or the **menu** of possible instructions from which the computer asks you to choose (for instance, to store or to print). Your word processing program may allow you to use a split screen to look at two parts of the same paper, or at two different documents, at the same time.

■ The *disk drives* accommodate the software (program disk) needed to program your word processor as well as the data disks that will store what you have written. Manufacturers are constantly expanding the **memory** of computers—their capacity for handling elaborate programs and bulky texts.

■ The *printer* produces the final printout, or **hard copy**. First-generation printers often produced unconventional lettering and hard-to-read pale print. Current equipment produces impressive professional-looking copy, with capacity for using different shapes and sizes of print (or **fonts**).

Software tells the hardware what to do. Word processing software varies in ease of use and range of features. Ideally, a program has simple key strokes for tasks ranging from deleting a paragraph to italicizing a phrase. It has simple commands that soon become second nature for the writer. Some programs take on chores like alphabetizing and formatting a list of sources for a research paper. If you are doing your writing in a computer lab, you may find yourself using software that came with the equipment. Whatever the strengths or limitations of the program you are using, any time you can spare to become thoroughly familiar with its features will be well spent.

WRITING WORKSHOP 26   Prepare to share your knowledge or your questions about word processing with your classmates. What software, if any, do you know? How do you add/insert? How do you delete/erase? How do you move/transpose? What is the meaning of recurrent commands like *return* or *escape*? How do you set up a file, index it, save it, and retrieve it? How do you handle margins, indenting, double-spacing? How do you underline, italicize, or boldface? What are special features or limitations of a word processing program that you know?

6b   Writing with a Word Processor

Make use of the full potential of your word processor.

Writers vary in how completely they become married to the word processor. Some will scribble a scratch outline or cluster a key term on a piece of paper before they turn on the machine. Some like to print out a trial draft to annotate by hand before they revise. Others will use the word processor at every stage of the writing process.

(1) Try brainstorming on the computer. The following might be your first jottings for a paper on the world mirrored in television commercials:

```
diet drinks: bouncy kids on beach, plastic smiles
(great teeth)
designer jeans: child prodigy celebrity models
"spend, spend; consume, consume"
happy wife-mother, cute all-American kids, a
shaggy dog
Bill "I'm-so-sensitive" Cosby
look and smell the best we can
```

On further thought, you might rearrange these notes and add to them as follows:

```
diet drinks, bouncy kids on beach, plastic smiles
(great teeth)
designer jeans: child prodigy celebrity models
look and smell the best we can
woman in slinky black dress selling vodka
thin is in
Diet Brew won't go to your waist
happy wife-mother, cute all-American kids
Bill "I'm-so-sensitive" Cosby
beaming white-haired Mom gets long-distance call
from young executive
```

(2) Store promising material for future use. Set up a file for anecdotes, statistics, and quotations that may prove useful for a planned writing project. A file of promising material for your paper on commercials might look like this:

---

commercial minidramas

In the small elegant apartment, the lights are dimming, music is playing softly, and a young woman sits by the telephone. "Tom?" she says in a provocative voice. "This is Julie . . . I have a bottle of Stanley's Bristol Cream Sherry and . . . you would? . . . great . . . 8:00."

Two teenagers are obviously attracted to each other, but things are still very uncomfortable. The boy comes to the rescue by bringing the girl an XYZ root beer. The commercial ends as the two walk away together singing "Nothing's so smooth and easy as XYZ root beer."

A couple is sitting romantically by a roaring fire. The man slowly opens a present, which turns out to be English Leather. He gazes into the woman's eyes as she turns to us and whispers, "All my men wear English Leather, or they wear nothing at all."

Professional writers early start filing possibly useful news clippings, quotations, or statistics, arranging them under tentative *headings* to make them accessible for future use. Use the word processor as an electronic note taker. Feed in data, statistics, lists, trial outlines, quotable quotes, summaries, tips on promising sources. Include with each item a key word or **retrieval code** that keys them to a writing assignment or to a subdivision of a project.

(3) Draw on stored material while writing your first draft. Transfer and adapt stored material for use in your paper. The following might be a quotation from a personal interview with a police officer:

```
Interview with Sergeant Jason

     "We see people at their worst all the time.
The general public just isn't exposed to the
violent situations or people out of control. Most
of the time, people don't know a police officer and
when they have contact with one, it is usually
negative:  they are getting a ticket, or their
house has been robbed.  They are frustrated, and
they take their frustrations out on the officer.
It is easy for police officers to become cynical.
They risk their lives and know that what they do is
not appreciated."
```

Here is how this passage might look after you have transferred it to your first draft, adding the necessary connecting links. Look at the inserted material:

```
     Sergeant Jason said, "We see people at their
worst all the time.  The general public just isn't
exposed to the violent situations and people out
of control."  Most people don't know any police
officers personally, "and when they have contact
with one, it is usually negative: they are getting
a ticket, or their house has been robbed.  They
are frustrated, and they take their frustrations
out on the officer."  As a result, "it is easy for
police officers to become cynical.  They risk
their lives and know that what they do is not
appreciated."
```

(4) Use the full potential of your word processor for both minor and major revision. Ease of revision is the great selling point of word processors. No more whiteout or messy erasures: You can delete or sometimes simply type over unwanted passages. You can add or insert examples and explanations, pushing back and reformatting the rest of the text. You can move or transpose whole passages or blocks of material as you rethink the organization of a paper.

Add, delete, and reshuffle material as you rewrite your first draft. Rereading a passage like the following in your first draft, you might decide that it badly needs real-life detail:

```
    Two of my brothers studied Karate and Aikido.
Often, I was called upon to act as the "live
dummy" for the prescribed movements my brothers
performed.  This early introduction to the
martial arts has remained etched in my memory.
```

Here is how the passage might read with some lifelike detail inserted:

```
    Two of my brothers studied Karate and Aikido.
Often, I was called upon to act as the "live
dummy" for the prescribed movements my brothers
performed.  For instance, one of my brothers would
ask me to throw a punch at him.  As soon as I
extended my arm, and before I could blink, I found
my limb precariously twisted behind my back with
my body twisting in wretched pain.  This early
introduction to the martial arts has remained
etched in my memory.
```

After you delete, add, or transpose, check your revised passages to be sure that your changes have not left sentences garbled or the flow of thought unclear. Look at the way the revision of the following paragraph *integrates* new material, filling in the right logical and grammatical links:

ORIGINAL:

> After the stark functional surfaces of the past, post-modern architecture signals a return to frivolity, to decoration for its own sake. At the top of tall buildings, we suddenly see sloping surfaces, curved gables, rosette windows, and curlicues. Some of them look like the playful shapes we might draw in an idle moment on a piece of paper.

REVISED:

> After the stark functional surfaces of the past, post-modern architecture signals a return to frivolity, to decoration <u>for the fun of it</u> and for its own sake. <u>In the heyday of modern (Bauhaus) architecture, architects built totally functional boxes of glass and steel that were all right angles. Today, we look up to</u> the top of tall <u>new</u> buildings <u>and</u> see sloping surfaces, curved gables, rosette windows, and curlicues. Some of them look like the playful shapes we might draw in an idle moment on a sheet of paper.

As you write and revise, do not lose sight of the *larger structure* of your paper. (Researchers report that students tend to write more fluently but also more disjointedly when they switch to the word processor.) Do not limit your view to the portion of a paper that appears on your screen. Scroll backward or forward as necessary to check how the passage you are working on fits into the larger whole. Experiment with moving blocks of material around to strengthen logical connections and to improve the flow of ideas.

(5) Edit with special care. In final editing of your work, you can correct many spelling errors and punctuation problems with the stroke of a key. You may also be able to instruct the computer to find and correct *all* occurrences of a misspelled word (like *mideval*) in your text. If a spelling check is part of your software, it will identify clear-cut misspellings like *identifed* and *should of* and query possible confusions (*to* or *too*? *there* or *their*?).

CAUTION: **Proofread.** Do not be fooled by the finished appearance of word-processed text. Your writing is likely to look ready-to-print both when you view it on the screen and when you print it out as a trial copy. But actually the speed and ease of typing on an electronic keyboard multiply transposed letters (*wrtier*), run-together words (*taggedon*), random misspellings, and miscellaneous glitches. Whenever you can, *double-proof* all text: Proofread it first when it is still on the screen, then again when you print out a trial copy.

Note: Your manual or user's guide will urge you to *store* your paper (or each major chunk of a bigger project), transferring it from the computer's memory to a storage disk to keep it from being accidentally erased.

WRITING PRACTICE 27   In recent years, a number of widely read books have raised the question of cultural literacy. How much do today's students know about their own history and the common traditions of their culture? The following is a typical anecdote told by writers who give a pessimistic answer to this kind of question. Enter the passage on your screen. Then go on typing, writing your reactions, comments, examples or counter-examples, arguments or counter-arguments.

> A history instructor found that an increasing number of her students could not understand what Hitler had done wrong. One student described Hitler as "a kid with a dream" who enjoyed "a pretty good run at the top of the charts."

REVISION PRACTICE 28   How are the sentences in the following paragraph related? Enter the paragraph on your screen. Then, at the beginning of as many sentences as you can, *insert* a missing link. Choose a transition like *also, for instance, similarly, finally, however, but, in fact, it is true that,* or *on the other hand.*

Our history textbooks have often pictured the Spaniards as a haughty and fanatical people. Every school child used to read about the cruelties of the Spanish Inquisition in hunting down the enemies of the true faith. Anglo historians have often blamed the Spanish conquistadores for wholesale massacres of the native populations of Mexico and Peru. Recently historians have asked us to revise this negative picture. Millions of Indians died in the fifty years after the Spanish conquest. Most of them died as victims of Old World diseases like smallpox, against which they had no immunity. Prominent leaders in the Spanish church argued that the Indians were not savages but had immortal souls and deserved our love as fellow human beings. More than other colonial nations, the Spaniards intermarried with the conquered peoples.

REVISION PRACTICE 29   Assume that you are editing a feature called "A Glimpse of the Past" for a student publication or a company newsletter. You have sent the following story of about 100 words to the printer, but there is space for only 80 words. Enter the complete passage on your screen. Then delete enough words to make the story fit the available space; make other adjustments as needed to make the story read smoothly.

In 1956, a member of Congress stood before the House of Representatives to report an outrage. He had come to say that a lobbyist had offered to pay him $2,500 for his vote on a bill deregulating the price of natural gas. Today this would be considered a paltry sum, not enough to bribe a building inspector. However, the congressman trembled with indignation and denounced the "pestilent stench of foul corruption." After the resulting outcry, the President vetoed the legislation. Another bill to deregulate the price of natural gas did not come before the House for twenty-two years.

REVISION PRACTICE 30   Study the following passage and enter it on your screen. Assume that you are the author and that you have decided to make two major changes. Move the second sentence to the end as a clincher sentence. Rearrange the order of the examples so that there will be a better flow from the least to the most serious.

Professionals often face a familiar dilemma: whether to reveal to others dark secrets that their clients have told them in the strictest confidence. Often the choice is to tell and feel like a rat or to keep silent and become an accomplice. Should a psychiatrist warn an ex-spouse that a patient is planning to "get even"? Should a priest tell the authorities that a parishioner has committed murder? Should a journalist go to jail for contempt of court rather than reveal to a judge the source for information about organized crime? Should a teacher tell parents about teenagers planning to elope?

6c	Computer-Aided Writing

Learn to make use of electronic writing aids and new technology.

Working in a writing course or in a writing lab, you may become familiar with developments like the following:

PREWRITING Publishers of word processing software promote a variety of computer programs designed to help writers write. Prewriting programs keep you thinking and writing through a set of prompts, asking you, for example, to spell out what you know about the background, expectations, values, expertise, and probable attitudes of your audience (**audience analysis**).

Often a program will map out a standard method for approaching different kinds of writing, such as autobiographical narrative, definition, or comparison and contrast. To help you develop an autobiographical paper, the program might ask:

```
Who is the most important character (other than
you) in your story?
```

The program might then follow up with a battery of questions: How does she look? What does her appearance tell us about her? What kinds of things does she say? How does she act? The computer can thus nudge you to flesh out the character—to make your readers see the character, to bring her to life.

ORGANIZATION The systematic questions asked by a program will often help you impose a preliminary structure on your materials—to create a kind of tentative order. A set of questions like the following might help you structure an argument:

111

What is the issue or controversy?

What stand are you taking on the issue?

What are your major reasons for taking this stand? What are the arguments on your side? What is the evidence for each?

What are the major opposing arguments? What is wrong with them? How would you show them to be wrong?

What doubts or questions might your audience have about the claim you are making? How would you answer their questions and reassure your audience?

A writing tutorial is likely to offer you ways of strengthening organization when you revise. A program may enable you to pull out and line up first (or perhaps first and last) sentences of paragraphs so you can check transitions and the flow of ideas. Or you may be able to **highlight** and then pull out key sentences (topic sentences)—not always necessarily the first sentence of a paragraph.

STYLE Much thought is going into the development of programs that would improve **style**—help you make your writing clearer and more direct.

■ You may be using software that provides a **jargon** alert—counting such telltale features as abstract nouns ending in *-tion* or *-sion* (*utilization, implementation, extrapolation, diminution*). The same program may flag for you frequent use of forms of *be*, such as *is, was,* and *were,* which help produce passive rather than active verbs ("The new immigrants *were deemed* undesirable" rather than "My family *disliked* the new immigrants").

■ A style check programed to detect **sexist language** may flag for you gender-specific terms like *landlady, chairman, stewardess,* and *bellboy.*

■ The strength of the computer is that it can quickly scan pages of material to alert you to *potential* trouble spots, including especially words easily confused, such as *accept* and *except* or *there* and *their.* Increasingly, on such items, you will be able to call up brief pointed instructions that help you make an informed choice. You may be able to call up *backup* instructions or additional examples to help explain the explanations.

NETWORKING Your personal computer or college workstation may already be part of a network that enables other students to see and to comment on or react to your writing at various stages. **Peer criticism** can thus help guide and shape your writing; **collaborative** writing projects of various kinds become possible.

Your instructor may already prefer to have you turn in papers or exams on a disk, so that comments and suggestions entered on the disk can take the place of handwritten comments. Or your writing may reach the instructor (and the instructor's comments reach you) through a network linking the word processors of teacher and students. Comments may be attached to a text as a whole or pinpointed (and coded) to a specific section of a paper.

DESKTOP PUBLISHING **Desktop publishing** makes possible the speedy local preparation of publications of professional quality. An editorial committee of your classmates may take in hand the assembling and production of a high-quality collection of the best student writing in your class, of a group research effort, of writing focused on a timely theme, or of the results of an essay contest.

WRITING WORKSHOP 31   Team up with a group to investigate state-of-the-art writing tutorial programs or editing software. Farm out to different members of the group such areas as starting a paper, audience analysis, brainstorming, developing a comparison, writing a narrative, analyzing the beginning of a story, or style analysis. Pool your findings in a group report.

---

7   Patterns of Exposition

OVERVIEW   The plan you work out for a paper depends on the task at hand. Suppose you are trying to show why in spite of traffic congestion and the risks of the road you prefer using your own car to using rapid transit. You could systematically line up the advantages of a car and the disadvantages of public transportation. You would take up in turn your main objections: being dependent on fixed schedules, having to wait for late buses or trains, facing fellow passengers whose problems you do not care to know. What guides you in laying out your material is the need to compare and contrast the two options in such a way that the reader can see the important differences.

113

Comparison and contrast is one of the basic patterns of **exposition**—of writing that explains, informs, reports, or instructs. You write exposition whenever you share information or clarify ideas. For instance, you write exposition when you show your fellow students how to convert to a vegetarian diet. A scientist writes exposition when explaining how the burning of fossil fuels produces a greenhouse effect. A psychologist writes exposition when analyzing our response to serious illness, tracing it through three major stages: denial, anger, acceptance.

Major patterns of expository writing mirror the way our minds process information. They reflect the sorting out and lining up that makes sense of miscellaneous data. Here are the key questions that guide us when we employ major organizing strategies for expository writing:

THESIS AND EXAMPLES "What does this mean in practice?"

CLASSIFICATION "What goes with what?"

PROCESS "How does it work?"

COMPARISON AND CONTRAST "How are two things similar? How do they differ?"

Exposition is a large umbrella heading for writing that sets forth information and ideas. Other patterns often included under the heading of exposition are cause and effect and definition.

SEE 11d FOR CAUSE AND EFFECT AND 11g FOR DEFINITION.

 ## Thesis and Examples

Support your thesis with well-chosen detailed examples.

The most basic pattern of exposition starts with a strong **thesis** and then presents a substantial array of authentic examples. A basic task of every writer is to provide examples that show what a theory or proposal means in practice. To make an idea meaningful, we provide **illustration**—one or more examples that show the principle in action.

For instance, your thesis may be that much of our food looks and tastes the way it does because it serves the needs, not of the customer, but of the distributor: Fresh, easily spoiling natural food is too much of a problem for modern marketing. You then illustrate by providing a series of examples, with each in turn serving as a case in point:

- additives extend the shelf-life of everything from bread to yogurt;
- barely ripened fruit protects dealers against spoilage;
- "gourmet" restaurant meals kept frozen and heated up by microwave eliminate the guesswork (and leftovers) of day-to-day cooking.

A well-written paper or article following this pattern has a cumulative effect. It builds a case. The first example that the writer gives us might be only an isolated instance. But with the third or fourth convincing example, we begin to feel that we are not dealing with isolated observations. We begin to believe that a pattern exists.

A paper following the *thesis-and-examples* pattern might proceed like this:

A National Disgrace

THESIS: How bad are our jails? **Critics of American prisons have found that concern for the physical and mental health of the inmates is often substandard.** . . .

first set of examples

Facilities are often primitive. One observer found thirty men confined in a cell with a single toilet. . . .

second set of examples

Health care is often totally inadequate. In a lawsuit filed in Alabama, an inmate reported what happened after prison doctors set her broken legs in a cast. After she repeatedly complained about excessive itching, doctors reluctantly removed the cast; they found roaches inside, eating her leg. . . .

third set of examples

Woe betide the prisoner having severe emotional problems or suffering from mental illness. In Colorado, a depressed prisoner who requested an appointment with the prison psychologist received a note asking: "What the hell do you want me to do?". . . .

Remember the following guidelines for an effective thesis-and-examples paper:

(1) Avoid a mere catalog effect. Suppose you are trying to show why many young people are disillusioned with political leaders. Do not merely list (and lump together) Presidents from Johnson and Nixon to Carter and Reagan. Discuss at least one of two of these examples *in detail*—to show what young people might have expected of them and where and how they fell short.

(2) Look for convincing representative examples. When we report on the lifestyles of a campus, our eye is tempted to rest on some of the most conspicuous (and eccentric) people we observe. Help your reader feel that the people you discuss as examples are indeed representative of different groups that make up the campus population.

(3) Arrange your examples in an effective order. One familiar strategy is to start with familiar examples (to put the reader in an assenting mood) and then go on to important less familiar ones. A writer discussing the menace from toxic chemicals might start by reminding us of familiar spectacular examples but might then go on to lesser known everyday examples to convince us that the problem is of urgent general concern.

(4) Avoid the hypothetical or made-up example. Use real-life examples whenever you can. If you do a composite portrait of the average student or the typical voter, try to buttress it with accounts of real-life people and real-life situations.

PEER REVIEW 32   Study the following *thesis-and-examples* paper. Answer the following questions:

- How does the writer lead up to the *thesis*? What is it?
- Take stock of the *examples* the writer uses to support the thesis. Are they skimpy or ample? Which seem fairly general? Which are most striking or convincing?
- Chart the *categories* the writer has set up to group the examples. What explains the order in which they appear?
- Is the *conclusion* expected or unexpected? Is it tagged on or well earned?

A Life of Crime

"Lawlessness" and the "breakdown of law and order" have long been clichés of conservative political oratory. Candidates to the right of the political spectrum have often run against "crime in the streets." Today many Americans find that reality has caught up with rhetoric. Crime is everywhere becoming a familiar facet of everyday life.

According to police statistics, professional crime is steadily increasing. Burglaries are now an everyday occurrence in what used to be "nice quiet neighborhoods." In spite of television cameras and other safety precautions, bank holdups have tripled in number during the last ten years in many parts of the country. Increasingly, major robberies are planned commando-style and executed with military precision and ruthlessness.

Just as disturbing is the steady growth in personal moral laxity on the part of ordinary people: petty pilfering, routine stealing, "ripping off" the employer or the customer. Dresses put on the clothesline to dry disappear. Watches and wallets disappear from high school locker rooms. Recently a principal was caught stealing petty change from vending machines.

In many areas of our lives, we see a steady increase of personal aggressiveness and vindictiveness. Students threaten and bully teachers. Customers settle an argument with the bartender by firebombing the establishment. People taken to court vow to "get" witnesses who testify against them.

We see the same trend toward more lawlessness on the political scene, where it is projected onto a larger screen. Newspaper readers and television viewers have become accustomed to assassinations, bombings, and reprisals as part of the daily news. For many years, terrorism has been a major unsolved political problem in places like Northern Ireland, Italy, and the Near East. People are not allowed on airplanes until they have been searched for deadly weapons. High government officials drive to work surrounded by bodyguards.

As the result of these and similar trends, many ordinary citizens are losing faith in traditional law enforcement. People are ready to join vigilante groups and to "take the law in their own hands." Can you blame them?

WRITING TOPICS 5

Write a *thesis-and-examples* paper. Formulate a strong thesis. Provide detailed and convincing examples or case histories. (Avoid hypothetical or made-up examples.) Your instructor may ask you to present a preliminary collection of material for group discussion. Choose one of the following:

1. Trend watchers are fond of charting trends that are *reversals* of what was once fashionable. Document such a reverse trend—a return to ceremonies, to formal dress, to patriotism, to religion, or to monogamous relationships. Provide a rich array of authentic examples.

2. Some of our most successful journalists and other media people practice the art of the *exposé*. They expose the shortcomings, weaknesses, or wrongdoings of people in positions of trust or authority—politicians, television evangelists, Supreme Court justices. Provide and discuss striking examples of this tendency in the media.

117

3. Admirers of George Orwell, the author of *1984*, scan the prose of government agencies (and of corporate America) for examples of *doublespeak*. Doublespeak is language used to deceive, cover up, or mislead (as when a missile is called the Peacemaker). Study reports on current doublespeak, or find examples of your own.

4. Is it true that *public manners* have deteriorated? Is it true that everywhere today we see examples of boorish, hostile, aggressive, contemptuous behavior? Formulate your own thesis, and support it with a rich array of striking instances.

5. During political campaigns, candidates like to invoke some of the *traditional American virtues*—neighborliness, tolerance, sympathy for the underdog, and the like. Are they prospering, or are they becoming extinct? Focus on one of these, and support your thesis with detailed convincing examples.

7b   Classification

Sort things out by establishing workable categories.

Much of the organizing we do for a short paper fits under the heading of **classification**. We sort things out to group together those that belong together. They share common qualities, or they work in similar ways, or they show the same basic principle in action.

Many subjects already have natural division or obvious parts. Sometimes, ready-made categories are well established: urban—suburban—rural; gifted—average—retarded; married—single—divorced. Often, however, we have to *set up* groupings that fit our subject. Suppose you are writing about the qualities that are most important in an effective teacher. In sorting out material from your own observation and experience, you may set up three major categories:

- evidence that shows knowledge of the *subject matter*;
- evidence that shows *ability to organize* and to present things in an intelligible fashion;
- evidence of a friendly and encouraging *manner* with students.

Remember the following guidelines for an effective classification paper:

(1) Start with established categories if appropriate, but modify or reject them as necessary. A subject may divide along established lines. For instance, people who have come to this country from abroad differ in legal status:

The Stranger in Our Midst

I. Temporary visitors (usually not allowed to work here and expected to return home)
II. Illegal aliens (who live and work here but have no valid papers)
III. Resident aliens (allowed to work here and often planning to become citizens)
IV. Naturalized U.S. citizens

This division is likely to prove useful in a debate on immigration policy. A different set of categories may become relevant in an argument over bilingual education:

I. Unassimilated (immigrants who live in foreign-speaking enclaves, where children hear little English)
II. Bicultural (bilingual immigrants who want their children to be equally at ease in both languages)
III. Assimilated (fully Americanized immigrants whose children may know only snatches of the parents' first language)

(2) Make sure your system of classification becomes clear to the reader. If possible, give a preview or an overview of your general scheme early in the paper. Make a brief introduction lead up to a thesis that spells out your general plan. The following might be a rough outline for a paper that treats its subject humorously but has a clear overall plan:

Making the Grade

THESIS: Among college students, especially the younger crowd, three types seem to stand out, each with a different attitude toward college.

I. *The Hardcores:* The Hardcores flock together in fraternity houses or in rundown homes that look like a scene from *Animal House.* They get loud, destructive, and obnoxious at parties. They do everything they can to show that they do not care about school or grades. Academic probation is a prerequisite for membership in this group. . . .
II. *The Preppies:* Preppies often live in dorms because their families won't let them live anywhere else. They outwardly emulate the

119

"hardcore" lifestyle, but within prudent limits. When asked, they will deny any interest in school or grades; however, they spend considerable time studying to keep their parents off their backs. . . .

III. *The Hackers:* The Hackers are the academic overachievers. They are so infatuated with the concept of the grade point average that they will do anything to squeeze an extra point or improved grade from an instructor for an exam or assignment. They consistently belong to organizations like predental or business clubs because membership in these groups will look good on a résumé. . . .

(3) Set up a consistent principle of classification. Are you applying the same basic question as you set up each category? For instance, in classifying the colorful variety of sports in contemporary life, you may ask, "What is the nature of the *competition*?" This way, you would focus on the underlying motives of the participants, setting up a scheme like the following. Notice that the thesis of the paper serves as a preview of the writer's major categories:

Meeting the Competition

THESIS: Sports offer us a means of testing ourselves by facing and overcoming opposition, whether human competitors, the forces of nature, animals, or our own human limits.

I. Competing with other human competitors
   A. football
   B. racquetball
   C. wrestling
II. Competing with the forces of nature
   A. rock climbing
   B. skiing
   C. sailing
III. Competing against animals
   A. rodeos
   B. bullfights
IV. Competing with ourselves
   A. marathon running
   B. body building
   C. golf, bowling

Note: Often several closely related factors will *combine* to help us set up our categories. In a marketing study of the "youth market," age level, occupational status, and marital status might combine to set up groups that have distinct buying patterns:

I. Late teens (still at home, with many of their needs provided for there but spending money on hobbies and entertainment)
II. College students (away from home and spending much money on snacks, sports equipment, traveling, long-distance calls)
III. Working singles (rent, eating out, sports, cars are major budget items)
IV. Young marrieds (conventional household expenses begin to play a major role)

(4) Arrange your major categories in a meaningful sequence. For instance, you might move from one extreme through intermediate stages to the opposite extreme. The following scheme for male stereotypes in popular entertainment starts with one extreme (the rugged macho type), then looks at in-between types (the authority figure, the well-intentioned father), and finally arrives at the opposite end of the scale:

I. The outdoor macho type
II. The male authority figure (doctor, professor, expert)
III. The harassed, well-meaning father
IV. The wimp

(5) Develop each category with detailed, convincing examples. Provide real-life details that will make your examples authentic and convincing. As in other writing, one key example treated in convincing detail and supported by several briefer examples may provide the most effective mix as you treat each category.

WRITING WORKSHOP 33   From among the following, choose one set of familiar or established categories that seem useful or instructive. (Revise or modify the categories if necessary.) For each category in your chosen set, fill in related material that would help flesh it out: observations that give it meaning, associations that cluster around it, images that it brings to mind.

- urban—suburban—rural
- child—adolescent—adult
- authoritarian—permissive—firm but kind
- unskilled—semiskilled—skilled
- married—single—divorced
- exclusive neighborhood—middle-class neighborhood—low-income neighborhood
- science fiction—fantasy—horror
- honor student—average student—dropout

PEER REVIEW 34 Study the following example of a *classification paper.* Look for answers to the following questions:

- How did the writer set the paper in motion? What is the thesis? Is there a *preview* or overview?
- What are the major categories? Does the *order* in which they appear make sense to you as the reader?
- Which *examples* are most striking or convincing? Which least?
- How adequate or effective are the *transitions* from point to point?

Meeting the Competition

Our word *athlete* is the Greek word for contestant. When we think of sports, we usually think of one contestant competing with another or others for a prize—an Olympic gold medal, a cherished trophy. On the surface, much of the world of sports presents human beings in contest with each other. When we go beyond the surface, however, we see that much of the time human contestants struggle against other kinds of opposition. Sports offer us a means of testing ourselves by facing and overcoming opposition, whether human competitors, natural forces, or animals. Often the adversary we are trying to overcome is our own human limits.

Obviously, many of the spectator sports that attract large crowds feature battles between teams of human competitors, with winners and losers, with victory celebrations and the consequences of defeat. In football, opponents literally face each other, with one player shoving the other down the field. Wrestling is one of the oldest of these symbolic confrontations between human contenders, as one contestant contends with another, trying to pin the opponent's shoulders to the ground.

On the other hand, some sports that seem to be a competition between human contestants really challenge athletes to test their own limits. For example, in marathon running the contest on the surface is between runners competing for first or second place. But many compete who have no chance to win and who are working toward a personal goal. Running the twenty-six miles is their challenge to themselves. An article in the *American Medical News* told the story of a twenty-three-year-old runner in the Triathlon World Championship in Hawaii:

> With only one hundred yards left between her and the finish, Moss fell to her knees. She then rose, ran a few more yards, and collapsed again. As TV cameras rolled, she lost control of her bodily functions. She got up again, ran, fell, and then started crawling. Passed by the second-place runner, she crawled across the finish line, stretched out her arm, and passed out.

This woman was in a race against herself, fighting the limitations of her own body. Other sports that seem competitive in the conventional sense also involve contestants who are basically testing their own limits. A golfer tries to get a lower score than in all previous games. A bowler tries to get a higher score than ever before.

In some sports, participants are pitting their own strength and skill against the forces of nature. In sailing, human beings struggle against the variables of wind and water. In the contest with nature, sports often cease to be play and become deadly serious instead: The mountain climber has to trust in a rope holding to break a fall; handholds and footholds in crevices or on ledges make the difference between life and death. Some three years ago, a brother of a friend of mine, in spite of warnings, went rock climbing alone and fell 150 feet to his death.

The grimly serious nature of the contest is strongest in sports that have their roots in prehistoric contests between human beings and animals. Modern rodeos entertain spectators by having riders try to control broncs and bulls, at danger to life and limb. In bullfighting, the matador kills the bull, and it appears that the animal is the inevitable loser. Yet according to Fodor's *Travel Guide to Spain* (1983),

> A bullfighter's chance of dying in the ring is one in ten. Chance of dying or being crippled is about one in four. They know, usually, what the horn ripping through the flesh feels like; no bullfighters finish their careers completely unscathed.

Wherever we look, the contest seems to be taking place on several levels. A race car driver is competing with other contestants for first place. At the same time, the driver is struggling to assert his or her mastery over a powerful, deadly machine. And the most basic contest is between pride, ambition, determination on the one hand and fear, fatigue, and human fallibility on the other.

WRITING TOPICS 6

Write a *classification paper* that sets up workable categories, supported by convincing examples. Your instructor may ask you to prepare a trial outline for group discussion. Choose a topic in one of the following categories:

1. No one wants to be a type; people resent labels that deny their individuality ("a typical jock"; "just like a woman"; "you know how Italians are"). Have you nevertheless been able to chart some major *personality types* that help you understand people you encounter? Write a paper

in which you divide a group of people into three or four major categories. For instance, you might classify people who give advice to others as supporters, friendly critics, hostile critics, and nitpickers. Make sure that your principle of classification becomes clear to your readers.

2. Set up a system of classification that could serve as a shopper's guide for a *concerned consumer*. (Your instructor may ask you to prepare a trial outline for class discussion.) Set up three or more major categories for one of the following:

   ■ kinds of restaurants
   ■ places to live (in your area or more generally)
   ■ major options in buying a car
   ■ kinds of parks
   ■ types of television shows for children
   ■ styles of tract homes
   ■ kinds of exercise
   ■ major choices in selecting a college

3. Set up a system of classification that would help a trend watcher understand *current trends*. (Your instructor may ask you to prepare a trial outline for class discussion.) Select an area like the following. Make sure your principle of classification becomes clear to your readers:

   ■ male stereotypes in commercial television
   ■ criminals in current crime shows
   ■ sports as symbols of social status
   ■ kinds of work open to women today
   ■ barriers to women's advancement in careers
   ■ how different types of men share in household duties
   ■ kinds of marriages
   ■ sports popular with young adults
   ■ levels of sophistication in local entertainment offerings
   ■ range of attitudes toward business among young Americans

---

7c   plan | Process

Trace essential steps in the right order to make your reader understand how something works.

To make a reader see how something works or how it came about, we often have to trace a **process**. We follow a process through its major stages so that the reader can understand it and see it as a whole. In tracing a process, we have to pay careful attention to how one thing leads to another. We have to decide what is essential and what is optional.

What we learn from the process paper has many applications. We apply it when we

- explain a *scientific* process:
  How energy of motion converts into electricity
  How sediments build up on the ocean floor
  How a translation machine scans a sentence

- give *directions*:
  How to plant a lawn
  How to make wine from your own grapes
  How to make pottery

- trace a *historical* chain of events:
  How nomads became villagers
  How the railroad transformed rural America

The following instructions will help you write better process papers:

(1) Explain the why as well as the how. Start by explaining the purpose or the benefits of the process:

The Natural Way to Eat Bread

Much of the bread we see on supermarket shelves is filled with preservatives so that it can stay on the shelves longer without spoiling. Much of it has an unnatural bleached appearance. It often has the consistency and the taste of a sponge. **To reduce the amount of dubious chemicals in our diet, we can learn to bake our own bread from natural ingredients. . . .**

(2) Pay patient attention to detail. Include the details that are needed to make things work. Provide necessary information about materials, tools, or procedures. Here is a student describing a stage in the making of homemade bread:

Yeast is composed of minute organisms that grow when exposed to moisture and heat. After the yeast has been dissolved in hot water and milk, mix it with the other ingredients of the dough. Turn the dough out on a lightly floured pastry cloth and knead it for about five minutes until it is smooth and elastic. The bread is now ready to rise, with the entire process taking about four or five hours. Place the dough in a lightly greased bowl, cover it with a damp cloth, and let it rise to about double its original bulk. Make sure the temperature is about 80 degrees: A higher temperature will produce a dry bread. If the room is too cold, put the dough in the oven with a pan of hot water under it. After the dough has risen to about double bulk, turn the dough out on a lightly floured cloth and knead it again for about five minutes. . . .

(3) Divide the process into major stages. Clear division into steps or parts lets your readers follow the process with a sense of direction; it makes them feel at each stage that they know where they are. When you give instructions or directions, dividing a process clearly into steps will build your readers' confidence, assuring them that they will be able to master one step at a time. The following might be the major stages for the paper on how to bake bread:

  I. Assembling the ingredients
  II. Mixing the dough
  III. Letting the dough rise
  IV. Baking the bread

(4) Make your reader see your overall plan. The opening of the following paper focuses on an essential principle and then previews the major stages of the process:

From Forest to Front Porch

Paper, or some form of thin material to write on, has been in use for at least five thousand years. Archaeologists have found evidence that the Egyptians were making papyrus sheets, made from the pith of the reedlike plant, three thousand years before Christ. In China, just as animal hairs had been matted to form felt, plant fibers—flax, hemp— were matted to form paper.

Today, papermaking is a highly mechanized process, going through several major steps: preparation of the stock or fiber; formation of the paper web by machine; removal of water by gravity, suction, or heat; and the rolling of the finished paper product. . . .

Where you can, make use of a pattern in time or space to help guide your reader. One writer, for example, wrote about a button factory that had three stories: *On the first floor,* liquid plastic was hardened into rubbery sheets, and blank buttons were punched out; *on the second floor,* holes were drilled, patterns carved, and the buttons polished; *on the third floor,* the buttons were sorted into cardboard boxes, ready to be shipped.

(5) Do justice to one major stage at a time. Give your readers a chance to concentrate on one essential step or one essential part of a procedure until it is clear in their minds. The following might be a selection from safety instructions for drivers. The writer's task would be to fix steps like the following firmly in the reader's mind:

first step

> To bring a skidding car back under control, you have to know how to use three different ways of controlling the movement of your car. **First**, turn the steering wheel as hard and fast as necessary. Use it to make your wheels point in the direction of the skid. Work your wheel rapidly if the skidding car keeps changing its direction. . . .

second step

> **Second**, make use of your gas pedal to help you control the car. Ease your foot off the pedal when the car first begins to skid, but keep your foot hovering over it. Press down on the pedal lightly when your front wheels seem to be pointing in the direction of the skid. . . .

(6) Clarify technical terms. In writing about navigation in space, have you taken for granted terms like *zero gravity, guidance system,* and *ecliptic plane*? Experienced writers routinely clarify terms that are new and difficult or familiar but only half understood:

> Green or partly green oranges are put into chambers where, for as much as four days, ethylene gas is circulated among them. The gas helps eliminate the chlorophyll in the **flavedo**, or **outer skin**, which is, in a sense, tiled with cells that contain both orange and green pigments.
>
> John McPhee

DISCOURSE EXERCISE 35   Study the following sample paragraph introducing the reader to essential technical terms for a manufacturing process. What does the writer do to make key terms intelligible to the newcomer or the outsider?

The Cheese Process

The first step in producing processed cheese is to sterilize the milk in a large metal vat, usually about the size of a Volkswagen bug. The milk is heated under pressure in order to destroy unwanted bacteria. It is then allowed to cool to about 70 to 78 degrees. The milk is now ready for the addition of the "starter" organism. The starter organism is a bacterial culture added to the sterilized milk to start the production of lactic acids—acids that form when milk sours. Like the starter used to produce sourdough bread, this culture is specifically nurtured to stimulate a spoiling of the milk that will not prove harmful to the health of the

127

consumer. Once the desired acid level is attained, the solution is said to be "ripe." This is the time to add rennet, an enzyme that causes the milk to coagulate, forming curds. Curds are large clumps of solidified milk from which the cheese will be eventually made; whey is the watery part of the solution that is left behind.

PEER REVIEW 36   Study the following example of a paper *tracing a process*. Look for answers to the following questions:

- How does the writer set the paper in motion? Is there an *overview* or preview of the whole process?
- What are the major *stages* in the process? Are they signaled by adequate transitions?
- What *explanations* are especially helpful or informative for the outsider?
- What *details* do most to bring the process to life?
- What does the *conclusion* add to the paper?

37 Flavors

Ice cream is not exactly a health food, for it is high in calories and rich in fat and sugar. For the most part, however, the general public is willing to overlook the health issue and the chemical additives. According to a recent estimate, every American eats about fifteen quarts of ice cream a year.

Ice cream is basically a mixture of milk solids and sugar. Mechanized manufacturing processes add numerous other natural and artificial ingredients, such as flavoring, coloring, stabilizers (which bind water and retard the growth of ice crystals) and emulsifiers (which coat the fat globules of cream during manufacturing in order to provide a more stable foam).

In an unassuming brown stucco building at six o'clock one morning, I witnessed vanilla ice cream being made at a local creamery. While most of us are asleep, a small group of people dressed in white shirts and trousers, yet bundled up in plaid jackets against the low temperature, makes ice cream from eleven at night till the next noon. The workers look like sailors dressed in service whites while working in what looks like an engine room, criss-crossed with stainless steel pipes and filled with circular vats and compressors. The floor is made of red tile, with a big brass drain cover as its centerpiece. The floor works like the bottom of a large kitchen sink, ready to swallow any liquids spilled from the vats.

The first step in the making of ice cream is to pipe in the basic ingredients from storage. In a separate room, two large holding tanks with doors like those of bank vaults hold one thousand gallons each of condensed skim milk and cream, which provide the milk solids for the ice cream. Next to them, sucrose and corn syrup are stored in upright holding cylinders of stainless steel.

The milk solids and sugars are piped out of their storage tanks into a "batching vat" and there pre-stirred according to the particular recipe. The raw product or "base mix" is then filtered out of the batching vat and heated at 362 degrees for twenty minutes. This heat treatment of the milk solids and sugars, called pasteurization, eliminates potentially dangerous bacteria, such as those that cause tuberculosis. However, as a result of pasteurization small fatty cream globules appear in the milk. These have to be broken down into smaller particles and spread evenly throughout the mixture. This breaking down of fat globules is called homogenization.

At this point, the pasteurized, homogenized liquid "ice cream" is still without special color or taste. The time has come to add flavoring, coloring, and special additives for the desired texture. For this purpose, the base mix is piped into one of several 200-gallon stainless steel mixing tanks that look like large washing machines with a catwalk that makes them accessible to workers. Here the necessary ingredients are mixed in by large blades beating the mix.

The final two steps of the process, freezing and packaging, go hand in hand. The still-liquid ice cream is transferred to freezers that are shaped like submarine torpedo tubes with an array of gauges and tubes. (Nuts and candies for the more exotic combinations are added at this stage.) The freezers whip the cream with a mixture of air, so that a semblance of body takes shape before the final and more intensive freezing. When the liquid is about 45 percent frozen, it is shot out through pipes leading directly to upright, folded-out cartons that move on an assembly line. The cartoned ice cream is then led out of the machinery room and into an ammonia freezer that is kept at minus fifty degrees. Several dozen cartons at a time are frozen for several minutes, until the ice cream is practically solid. Soon the hardened ice cream cartons are led down a conveyor belt and covered with plastic wrap, ready for transportation and distribution.

Like many products in our world of processed foods, ice cream is no longer always what it seems to be. Imitation ice cream has been in existence for over fifty years. Coconut oil is used as a substitute for butter fat in imitation ice cream. New kinds of ice cream are being marketed in health food stores and specialty shops. Made from bean curd or from rice, they promise "No sugar!" and "No cholesterol!" They also contain none of the dairy cream and eggs that made old-fashioned ice cream a sinfully delicious treat.

WRITING TOPICS 7

Among the following topics, choose one that allows you to draw on close observation or detailed investigation.

1.   Modern city dwellers have lost traditional skills that used to make people self-sufficient. Help your readers recover such a lost art or skill: baking their own bread, growing their own vegetables, making their own clothes, doing their own woodwork or cabinet work, making their own pottery, making their own wine, producing their own honey.

2.   Much has been written about synthetic products that over the years have taken the place of natural, home-grown, or homemade ones. Investigate and explain the process that produces one such replacement, substitute, or "improvement." Possible topics: processed cheese, soybean burgers, imitation ice cream, reconstituted orange juice, the rubber tomato, imitation crabmeat, decaffeinated coffee. Write for consumers who like to know what they are eating or using.

3.   Budget-conscious consumers look for do-it-yourself instructions that will help them do without highly paid skilled labor. Give detailed instructions for a task like the following: rebuilding an engine, renovating a house, doing cement work, installing wiring, arranging a do-it-yourself divorce.

4.   High-tech developments are transforming many traditional procedures and manufacturing processes. Investigate and explain some new or advanced process or technology. Possible topics: using robots on an assembly line, solar energy to heat a house, a computer to produce graphics, lasers in surgery. Write for the general reader; explain what is difficult to the newcomer or outsider.

5.   Investigate and explain a natural cycle, such as the life cycle of the butterfly, the frog, the salmon. Choose a cycle that moves through several major stages. Write for readers who have become removed from the world of nature.

6.   Are you a perfectionist? Do you believe that there is a right way to do a job that is often done too casually or imperfectly? Show your reader how to do an ordinary task right: how to brew a perfect cup of coffee, how to make the best pizza, how to pitch a tent right, how to make true old-style spaghetti.

7. A familiar type of science fiction describes the aftermath of a great catastrophe, with the survivors struggling to relearn the lost arts and skills of civilization. Prepare detailed instructions that would teach survivors how to make paper, sugar, steel, or some other staple product that is the result of a complex process.

7d *plan* | Comparison and Contrast

Use comparison and contrast to bring out similarities and differences.

In writing that explains or clarifies, the writer often has to look at several related things and show how they are similar or how they differ. Such **comparison or contrast** presents a special challenge: The writer has to lay out the relevant details in such a way that the reader can follow the cross-references and take in the overall picture that emerges.

Writing that compares and contrasts serves many purposes. Writers use it to

- make us see important *patterns*: How does a small college differ from a big university? How is the old-style family farm different from modern agribusiness?
- guide our *choices*: What are the advantages of a word processor over a typewriter? How does running compare with swimming as a boon to health?
- guide us in solving *problems*: What features set outstanding schools apart from poor ones? What do Japanese manufacturers know that Americans don't?

Remember the following guidelines in working on papers that compare and contrast:

(1) Discover your purpose. Why are you setting up the comparison or contrast the way you do? What is the reader supposed to learn from it? Perhaps you are trying to guide readers in a current crisis by tracing parallels with a similar situation in the past. Perhaps you want to warn customers of an innovation that has serious disadvantages compared with what it replaced.

131

(2) Systematically explore similarities and differences. Brainstorm; take notes. Writing about the contrast between traditional and modern marriages, for instance, you might line up distinct features in two columns:

TRADITIONAL	MODERN
church wedding	live together first
till death do us part	high divorce rate
virgin bride	family planning
subservient wife	both work
husband works	backyard weddings
take the good with the bad	equal relationships
husband handles finances	supportive, caring male
housewife cleans and cooks	share chores
wait on the husband	mixed marriages
sex on demand	marriage contract
talk about sex is taboo	mutual sex
marry your own kind	discuss problems
feminine wife	

(3) Consider tracing the comparison or contrast point by point. A **point-by-point** comparison reminds your reader at every major step that your purpose is to make *connections:* You look at the safety record, say, or the maintenance needs of a domestic car to see how that record compares with that of its Japanese counterpart. You then go through your set of major criteria or major features, asking for each: "*On this point*, what is the record of Car A? What is the record of Car B?"

Follow the Leader

THESIS: It is becoming harder to tell a best-selling imported car apart from its closest domestic competitor.

  I. Economy
    A. Initial cost (data for both cars)
    B. Cost of operation (data for both cars)
    C. Resale value (data for both cars)
  II. Comfort and convenience
    A. Space for passengers and luggage (data for both cars)
    B. Maneuverability (data for both cars)

III. Performance
    A. Acceleration and speed (data for both cars)
    B. Durability (data for both cars)
IV. Maintenance (data for both cars)

(4) Consider taking up two things separately—but covering the same points in the same order. Such a **parallel-order comparison** gives a coherent picture of each of the two things being compared. At the same time, it helps the reader see the connections between the two. The following is an outline for a parallel-order comparison of two famous heroes of classical antiquity: Odysseus (or Ulysses) and Achilles. In organizing the material, the writer starts with a basic similarity but then goes on to important differences:

The Fox and the Lion

THESIS: Odysseus and Achilles are both great warriors, but they differ in the other qualities that make an epic hero admirable.

I. Odysseus as epic hero
    A. Great warrior (unsurpassed in archery, etc.)
    B. Accomplished orator (successful in pleading his own cause)
    C. Shrewd counselor (carefully weighing facts and situations)
    D. Very human character (loves good food and wine)
II. Achilles as epic hero
    A. Great warrior (triumphs over Hector)
    B. Not a great speaker (tends to be haughty and insolent)
    C. Impulsive person (quick to yield to resentment)
    D. Half divine (indifferent to food)

(5) Group similarities and differences together if that seems the best strategy. In comparing the traditional Western with its modern offspring, you might first want to show the similarities: the setting, the familiar cast of two characters, the gunslingers intimidating the townspeople, the strong silent hero, the climactic shootout. Then you might go on to what makes a Clint Eastwood Western different.

(6) Mark the transition from point to point. As necessary, steer the reader toward similarities by using words and phrases such as *like, similarly, in parallel fashion, exact counterpart,* and *along similar lines.* Signal contrasts by words and phrases such as *whereas, however, by contrast, on the* *other hand, nearly opposite,* and *as a counterpoint.* Remember that comparison and contrast will test your ability to establish important connections and to make them clear to the reader.

WRITING WORKSHOP 37 Find a recent newspaper or magazine article focused on a *difference or contrast* of current interest. Summarize the contrast, pinpointing essential differences. Include key points, essential explanations, and selected examples. Choose a subject like the following:

- right brain and left brain
- Japanese and American work ethics
- word processor and typewriter
- agribusiness and family farm
- natural foods and imitation foods

PEER REVIEW 38 Study the following example of a *comparison-and-contrast* paper. Look for answers to the following questions:

- What is the *purpose* of this comparison? How does the writer lead up to the thesis?
- What is the *plan*? What are the major points, and in what order do they appear?
- How well are the major points developed or supported? What are the effective or striking *details*?
- How do you react as the reader?

Your Personality May Be Harmful to Your Health

In a famous study, cardiologist Meyer Friedman and Ray Rosenman linked cardiovascular disease to what they called the Type A personality. David Jenkins, an expert on the subject, describes the Type A person as marked by "competitiveness, striving for achievement, aggressiveness, haste, impatience, restlessness, and feelings of being under the pressure of time and under the challenge of responsibility." The Type B person is everything Type A is not: relatively passive, relaxed, noncompetitive, more patient, and quick to find time for recreation. A barrage of studies by psychologists and physicians has found connections between Type A behavior and ulcers, heart disease, headaches, asthma, and even cancer. My own experience with Type B people, however, tends to show that they suffer from just as many and similar health problems as their Type A counterparts.

One reason doctors find more wrong with Type A people may be that instead of going to a doctor a Type B person talks to a bartender. If a Type A person gets sick enough that her work is affected, she will take some money out of the bank and go to the doctor. A Type B person may want to see a doctor, but the chances are he has just spent his last hundred dollars on a triangular box kite or a pocket-size television set.

Type A people are known for pursuing money at the expense of their health, so it is not surprising that my mother, an upholsterer, has chronic back problems. My father, on the other hand, got his bad back and limp in a motorcycle accident. Type B personalities like my father tend to match in recreational injuries the damage Type A persons suffer from overexertion.

Many Type A problems are the result of substance abuse. The aspirin taken three at a time for tension headaches causes ulcers. The coffee that gets them through the day is hard on the digestive tract. They may drink to ease tension. But though these habits cause problems, they are at least kept in check by the need to perform. Type B people often have nothing to stop them from destroying their innards. The bar often is the focal point of what matters to them: conversation, friendship, laughter.

Type A ailments not shared by Type B people are balanced by unique Type B problems. Type A people at least tend to feed themselves and their families. Even during the hardest times there was always a gallon of milk, a loaf of bread, a block of cheese, and a sack of vegetables in my mother's refrigerator. While an upholsterer's wages usually keep her kitchen stocked like a bomb shelter, her ex-husband, my father, never has enough for groceries. His refrigerator is like half of a jigsaw puzzle. It holds hot sauce (no tortillas), pancake syrup (no flour or eggs), three bottles of imported mustard, the cardboard container from a six-pack, and a wedge of French cheese.

WRITING TOPICS 8

As you write on one of the following topics, make sure your comparison or contrast serves a purpose and meets the needs of the intended reader.

1. With pairs like the following, we are sometimes told not to confuse the two things being compared—they are very different. At other times, we are told the two overlap—they are more alike than they seem. What do *you* think? Choose a pair like the following for a detailed comparison and contrast:
   - city and suburb
   - school and business

- drinking and drugs
- army life and civilian life
- married life and life after divorce
- employees and management
- commercial and public television

2. Pairs like the following present options or *alternatives* in many people's lives. Prepare a detailed comparison and contrast that could help guide the reader's choice. Draw on your observation, experience, and reading. Choose a pair like the following:
   - a factory job and a service job
   - immigrant tradition and the American way
   - private school and public school
   - marriage and the single life
   - the business-oriented person versus the artist
   - small company and big corporations
   - small college and large university

3. The following pairs represent *opposite poles* in arguments over public issues or public policy. Choose one for investigation and prepare a detailed comparison and contrast that could guide a voter's or an official's choices:
   - private transportation and public transit
   - private affluence and public squalor
   - American and Japanese business practices or attitudes toward work
   - downtown: pedestrian malls or street traffic
   - wilderness areas or open parks

4. Many Americans believe in innovation and progress; many others look at them with a wary eye. Where do *you* stand? Prepare a detailed then-and-now contrast that reflects your preferences. Choose a pair like the following:
   - main street and shopping mall
   - Victorian houses and modern architecture
   - traditional and modern campus buildings
   - corner grocery and supermarket
   - the American car then and now
   - rerun versus current hit
   - war movies then and now

8 Coherence

OVERVIEW Effective writing moves ahead purposefully, taking us along. It has **coherence**; it "hangs together." The writer brings a topic into focus—and stays on the topic. The readers feel they know where the paper is headed. The turns in the road are well marked.

When a paper lacks coherence, readers lose their bearings. The writer's mind seems to wander; promising issues surface but disappear from view; the argument shifts ground or runs out of energy. The frustrated reader begins to ask: "Where are we headed? How does this fit in here? What is the plan?"

Here are some of the features that help us focus our readers' attention or keep our readers headed in the right direction:

TITLE AND INTRODUCTION A good title stakes out the territory and beckons to the reader. A good introduction capitalizes on the interest the title has created. It brings the subject to life for our readers and takes them to the central issue or idea to be treated in the paper. A weak beginning merely echoes the familiar or belabors the obvious:

WEAK: **A Nation of Immigrants**

> America has traditionally been a land of immigrants. The pilgrims came to these shores in search of religious freedom. The Statue of Liberty greeted the "huddled masses" that came from Ireland, Italy, or Russia to escape famine, poverty, or persecution. . . .

A strong beginning dramatizes the issue, uses a striking example, or ties the topic in with current concerns:

REVISED: **A Flood of Immigrants**

> Everywhere in American life, we see evidence of successive waves of immigration. When I took my first job, the owners of the restaurant where I worked were Hungarian immigrants. Of their twenty-two employees, four were from Central or South America, two from Taiwan, and one from India. Within a block of where I now live, Vietnamese and other Southeast Asian immigrants run a quick-lunch place, a shoe repair shop, and a cleaner's. Today with unemployment always around the corner, many Americans facing competition from immigrants ask: **Is it time to close the open door?**

CONCLUSION A weak ending merely repeats what the author has already said. A strong ending pulls together different strands of a paper and leaves the main point or the central plea imprinted on the reader's mind. Often the writer will save an exceptionally strong example for the last or circle back to a question or striking image from early in the paper.

KEY TERMS Once a topic has come into focus, key terms and their doubles (or **synonyms**) and close cousins can keep our attention centered on a key issue. In the following passage, note the network of terms that all relate to the idea of *good will*—of generosity, or "big-heartedness":

key term

follow-up

> Our **big-heartedness** is one of our proudest attributes. We like to think of the **New Deal** and the **Marshall Plan** as reflective of the American spirit. **Disaster relief** is among our most gratifying national pastimes. Nowhere else in the world has **philanthropy** become such big business. In our heart of hearts, we suspect that we are the most decent, **generous** people ever to grace the earth. Sure, we have shortcomings. Other nations, for instance, spend more on the arts and enjoy lower crime and infant mortality rates, but we ascribe such unpalatable facts either to our bigness or to our rugged individualism or to our **hospitality** to immigrants or to—anything, other than a shortage of **good intentions**.   Carll Tucker, "The Back Door," *Saturday Review*

TRANSITIONS Often writers keep us headed in the right direction by providing a bridge (or **transition**) from key point to key point. Transitions may help us move from one major stage to the next: "Even before the end of the war . . ."; "In the immediate postwar years . . ."; "During the period of postwar reconstruction . . ." Transitional phrases like *however, on the other hand,* or *nevertheless* may signal a major turn in an argument.

Provide the signals that help focus your readers' attention. Provide the signals that tell them what to expect. Help them follow from point to point.

8a   Titles

Use your title to attract the reader to your topic.

Effective titles stake out the subject. (Increasingly, writers include in their titles a key word that helps a computer retrieve publications relevant to a particular topic.) But good titles also hint at the writer's point of view;

they set the tone. To compete successfully for the reader's attention, an effective title often has a dramatic or humorous touch:

COLORLESS: A Look at Jogging
DRAMATIC: Run for Your Life

Ask yourself about your own tentative title: Is it likely to be noticed and remembered? A good title often has a satisfying pattern; it may use a striking image or play on words:

Aerodynamics: Cheating the Wind
The Art of Teaching Science
Looking for a Job Is a Job
Questioning Quotas
Good News for Bad Backs

Make sure that your title sounds like your personal choice, not like a ready-made, colorless general category. Avoid weak general titles that give no hint of your personal point of view:

WEAK: Urban Decay
BETTER: Neighborhood or Turf?
             No One Is Safe
             The Uncertainties of Gentrification

WEAK: Business Success
BETTER: Red Ink, Black Ink
             The Customer Is Rarely Right
             Stretching Your Credit

WRITING WORKSHOP 39   With a group of your fellow students, discuss your reactions to the following *book titles*. How effective is each title? What kind of book does it seem to promise? What seems to be the writer's agenda? What do you think would be a good audience or an ideal reader for each book?

Strategies for Women at Work
Easy Basics for Good Cooking
Our Bodies, Ourselves
Computer Programing for the Compleat Idiot
Number: The Language of Science
Make Your Money Grow
A Place Called School
Nuclear War, Nuclear Peace
Lost Worlds of Africa
The Marital Arts

8b | Introductions

Use your introduction to attract the reader but also to do important groundwork for your paper.

An effective introduction creates interest; it hooks the reader into the essay or story. It sketches out the territory to be covered, often by narrowing down a more general subject. It sets the tone for the rest of the essay. Above all, it heads straight for the central idea to be developed in the rest of the paper.

You will seldom write a paper requiring more than one short introductory paragraph. Study the following examples of effective introductions. Look at how each writer dramatizes the issue and leads directly to the **thesis** or central idea of the paper.

(1) Start with a striking example. To bring your subject to life, select one vivid example to catch the attention or arouse the indignation of the reader:

Test-Tube Food

Extrusion is the method of chopping or powdering foodstuffs and then reforming them to make them look whole. A striking example of extruded products is a foot-long rod of hard-cooked egg used by many caterers, restaurants, and institutions that want to bypass the cost of shelling real eggs. One of these rods enables a busy chef to cut seventy-five perfect center slices. Amazingly, the yolks of these high-tech eggs do not slip out of their white rims. Unfortunately, the slices have a rubbery texture and a vaguely sulfurous aftertaste. **Everywhere today, we encounter processed foods that have been adapted to give them eternal shelf life, to make them more profitable, and to destroy their original texture and taste.**

(2) Start with an event currently in the news. Relate your general subject to widely publicized recent events; show that it is the subject of current public concern:

Programed for Failure

A few weeks ago, Malcolm Hyde, a graduate of Oakmont High School, sued the Oakmont Unified School District for having failed to teach him to read and write. Malcolm had been one of the estimated 20 to 30 percent of the students in our public schools who "mark time or drop out." For the parents of such children, it is not enough to be content when a student "passes" and "stays out of trouble." **Parents of educationally deprived youngsters must start taking a direct interest in what happens in the classroom from day to day.**

(3) Relate your subject to firsthand personal experience. Show that your subject is not just of academic interest to you; show that it has a personal meaning:

A Thicket of Regulations

Shortly after my eighteenth birthday, my father died of hypertension. At that time, medication that would have controlled his illness was available in Canada but banned in the United States by the Federal Drug Administration. Less than one year after his death it was made available through a belated clearance by the agency. **Every year, promising experimental drugs are delayed because of a maze of bureaucratic regulations and the horrendous cost of extensive testing and trial use.**

(4) Start with striking symptoms of a current trend. Use telltale signs of current developments to lead the reader into an analysis of key features or underlying causes:

Patriotism Back in Style

Across the land, people are turning out in record numbers for holidays such as Flag Day and the Fourth of July. High school students are again entering patriotic essay contests sponsored by service organizations. ROTC programs, once scorned, are making a comeback on college campuses. **Old-time patriotism is coming back into style.**

(5) Use a striking quotation as the keynote for the rest of your paper. Set your paper in motion by quoting an eyewitness, authority, or insider:

Be Happy in Your Work

"64,000 hours are at stake!" That is what Richard Bolles, author of *What Color Is Your Parachute?*, tells readers trying to choose a profession. His figure represents the number of hours that an average person will work during a lifetime. **In spite of such warnings, many people drift into kinds of work that they dislike.**

(6) Use a striking contrast to lead up to your key point. For instance, use a *then-and-now* contrast to point up a change:

We Are What We Wear

The late sixties was the height of the love affair between the media and youth. Movies, magazines, pop music, and advertising extolled the teenage girl—a long-haired, blank-faced disco-dancing adolescent wearing a mini-skirt and thin as a stick. Today, most women no longer want to look like teenagers. The new ideal is the woman with both a career and a family. She's in her thirties or forties; she has character—you can see it in her face. **The media are struggling toward a new image of the mature woman, wearing a classic suit.**

(7) Use striking statistics to dramatize the issue:

Growing Up a Little Faster

According to one recent survey, seven out of ten children of divorced parents had not seen their real father in more than a year. **The traditional practice of awarding custody of children to the mother left a whole generation of children of divorce without the natural father as a model and a guide.**

(8) Use your introduction to set the tone. For instance, alert your readers that you will treat your subject with a humorous touch:

Captain of My Own Ship

Worker dissatisfaction has been with us for a long time. There must have been days when stone-age hunters felt weary as they set out on the trail of another mammoth, when Napoleon's soldiers balked at the scheduling of yet another battle, or when Columbus's sailors cringed at the thought of more days out at sea. In the past, however, most of the employed had no choice of how or where they worked. Education was limited, and most people were more or less confined to the same geographical location for a lifetime. **Today people have more freedom to choose the kind of work they want to do; they have more freedom to move on when they are dissatisfied.**

Avoid weak or ineffective introductions:

- *Repeating the assignment* (often word for word).
- *A dictionary definition* (unless you turn to a dictionary definition to bring out something important that is often overlooked): "*Webster's Dictionary* [which one?] defines *discrimination* as 'prejudiced or prejudicial outlook, action, or treatment.'"
- *A dutiful summary:* "Computers have changed our lives in many important ways. They have brought about a revolution in communications, bookkeeping, and entertainment. . . ."
- *Puffing up the subject:* "Bird-watching is a wonderful hobby. I have spent countless hours of untold pleasure watching the ways and antics of birds. . . ."
- *Complaints or apologies:* "Many contradictory opinions abound on the subject of the perfect interview. I find it hard to give a candidate for a job meaningful advice in a paper of 500 words. . . ."

WRITING WORKSHOP 40   Find three recent magazine articles whose *titles* and *introductions* you consider exceptionally effective. Explain how they attract the reader's attention and what strategy they use to lead the reader into the subject.

PEER EDITOR 41   Study the following *titles* and *introductions*. Which are effective, and how? Which are weak, and why? Answer questions like the following:

- What function does the title serve? How does it attract the reader's attention?
- How does the introduction lead up to the key issue or central thesis? What method or strategy does it illustrate?
- What kind of paper does the introduction make you expect, and why? (What is the tone of the introduction?)
- What kind of reader do you think would make a good audience for the writer?

1.   **Dangerous Books**

Any list of the books most frequently banned in American schools is sure to strike a chord in the reader's mind. One title I recently saw listed took me back to my junior year in high school. An English teacher who trusted me took me to the storage room to give me a brand-new copy of Kurt Vonnegut's *Slaughterhouse-Five*. There on the shelves were two hundred more brand-new copies that had never been given to students. The principal had decided these books were "unsuitable" for young minds. It seems that often the books that are censored are the ones students would be most likely to read on their own, as "unre-quired" reading.

2. ## Job Dissatisfaction

In this day and age, Americans feel that the benefits they receive from their occupation are not quite in accord with the efforts they ex-pend. Why do Americans feel this way? The answer probably lies in the American culture. Job dissatisfaction is in part due to the way Americans live at the present time.

3. ## Ordeal by Fire

Sooner or later, we may expect to see a candidate for the office of the President of the United States pitted against a bear. The engagement could take place in Madison Square Garden or any other arena conve-nient for the television cameras. Over the years, the presidential cam-paign has become an increasingly trying ordeal for the candidates and for the public. . . .

4. ## Television Shows

Many of my friends watch the music shows that are popular on television. There are also exercise shows, the news, situation comedies, specials, children's shows. The list could go on and on. What I am trying to show is that there are different types of shows on television, and I will try to describe a few of them in the following pages.

5. ## Freeze!

The average police officer fires a gun at a criminal perhaps once in a lifetime of service. In the typical crime show on television, there is hardly an episode without a climactic shootout, with police officers' guns blazing away. The net results of these programs is not to promote respect for the law but to make the viewer accept guns and gunplay as an ever-present fact of city life.

| Conclusions

Use your conclusion to tie together different parts of your paper and reinforce its central message.

Avoid conclusions that are merely lame restatements of points already clear. Make sure your conclusion *adds* something to the effectiveness of your paper. For instance,

- use your conclusion for a more *confident* affirmation of points made more tentatively before;
- pull together and highlight the *essential* points when an argument has moved through various steps or through a number of complications;
- *circle back* to the beginning by fulfilling an expectation created earlier in the paper. For instance, the writer may sum up the answer to a question raised in the title or introduction. Or the writer may return to a symbolic incident or key example used at the start of the paper.

Here are some examples of effective conclusions:

(1) Use a final anecdote to reinforce the central idea. Close with an incident or situation that gives dramatic form to your main point:

(*From an article on the growing pains of Third-World countries*)

    . . . My Nigerian friend looked out over the congested traffic as we sat in the stalled car. "Money," he said suddenly. "When we don't have it, it bothers you. When you get it, it worries you." He had summed up the story of his country, caught between ancient poverty and sudden wealth.

(2) Make striking details serve as symbols of an idea or a trend. For example, hobbies or styles of dress may symbolize more general attitudes:

(*From a paper on prevailing conservative trends on campus*)

    . . . In the shopping area across from the main entrance to the campus, head shops have been replaced by stores that sell roller skates

145

and running shoes. Conservative styles of dress are coming back: tweed sports jackets and skirts. Some of the students dress up to go to the library.

(3) Use a strong final quotation to reinforce your main point. Quote an authority or insider who has stated your point in a striking or memorable way:

(*From a paper on commercialism and the artist*)

. . . Some of the world's leading artists and performers have managed to solve this age-old dilemma: how to reach a large audience without pandering to popular taste. Toward the end of her career, the great gospel singer Mahalia Jackson was asked about several albums she had done for a "commercial" label. She said: "All my life, I have sung for my supper as well as for the Lord."

(4) Conclude with a suggestion for remedial action. Give your readers realistic pointers on what they can *do*:

(*From an article on prison reform*)

. . . If the leading citizens in a community would make it a point to visit their state prison, talk with the warden, then return to their communities with a better understanding of actual down-to-earth prison problems, they would have taken one of the most important and most effective steps toward a solution of our crime problem.   Erle Stanley Gardner, "Parole and the Prisons—An Opportunity Wasted," *Atlantic*

Avoid ineffective conclusions like the following:

- The well-meaning *platitude:* "Making our neighborhoods safe will require the vigilance of every concerned citizen."
- The *silver lining:* "Humanity in the past has survived earthquakes, famines, and the plague. And after all, we have already lived with the threat of nuclear war almost half a century."
- The *panacea:* "The restoration of old-fashioned discipline in our schools will make juvenile delinquency a thing of the past."
- The *sidestepped question:* "Death is sometimes more merciful than a life of suffering. But who decides, and on what grounds? These are moral questions, and, as with all moral questions, the answers will have to come with time."

- The *lame afterthought:* "Of course, if we burn more coal rather than rely on nuclear power, we will further pollute our atmosphere. This is a problem for the engineers of the future to resolve."

Note: Do not feel obligated to write your beginning first and your conclusion last. Writers often rough out the main part of a paper first. They leave for a later stage the task of leading the reader into the subject and of taking leave of the reader.

PEER EDITOR 42 Study the following *conclusions.* Which seem like a strong summing up or wrapping up, and why? Which are weak, and why?

1. *From a paper on trade barriers American businesses encounter in Japan:*

. . . Americans as well as Japanese know the pleasures of pointing the finger at someone else. It is frustrating for us Americans to have to think about matters that are our own responsibility, such as balancing our federal accounts or adapting to changing foreign markets. It is much easier to point the finger at our trading partners and shout "foul."

2. *From a paper warning against excessive emphasis on careers in a college education:*

. . . Students today have an almost hypnotic fascination with the subject of careers. They eat, drink, sleep, and, above all, sweat jobs. As a dean of students said at a Midwestern school, "I sometimes think that if I stopped one of these students on the street and asked, 'Who are you?' the answer would be 'I'm prelaw.'"

3. *From a paper on appeals used by American advertisers:*

. . . Advertisers know how to exploit our love of gadgets and our desire for a more glamorous life. They exploit the customer's yearning to be attractive, upwardly mobile, and forever young. Moral lectures will not stop advertisers from using methods that work. If we object to being exploited, we as consumers must learn to take a good look at what we really want. We must decide whether we want trendiness and surface glamor or value for the dollar.

4. *From a paper on test-tube babies:*

. . . Do doctors have a right to produce life in a laboratory? Nobody knows who is right or wrong on this issue, but what is important is that humanity still has the desire to learn more and to explore this field of unknowns, trying to find answers in our never-ending quest for knowledge.

5. *From a paper on the way television mirrors the American family:*

> . . . The image of the American family has changed from one extreme to the other. Viewers used to watch the happy lives of ideal families. Now they watch the trauma-filled lives of families that are unstable. One cannot help wonder what direction the image of the American family will take from here.

WRITING TOPICS 9

Choose a topic that you can relate to your own observation, experience, viewing, or reading. Pay special attention to beginning and ending. Provide an attractive but also informative *title*. Write an effective *introduction*, for example, one leading into the topic from a personal experience or from an event of current interest. Write a strong *conclusion* that does not merely repeat but instead reinforces your key point.

1. A writer discussing American schools divided students into two kinds: "answerers" and "questioners." The first kind always tries to give the right answer to the teachers' questions. The second kind asks questions that show curiosity and willingness to learn. To judge from your own experience, which of the two kinds of students receives more encouragement or reward in American schools?

2. Thomas Carlyle, a nineteenth-century British writer, wrote about the role of outstanding personalities in history. He once said, "Hero worship exists, has existed, and will forever exist, among mankind." What kinds of heroes do young Americans look for today?

3. One theory about people who get into trouble with authorities or with society is that there are born "troublemakers." According to this view, some people have a special aptitude for getting into trouble. How much truth do you think there is in this view?

4. Some people claim that differences in dress, hair length, and other matters of outward appearance are merely superficial. However, other people claim that such outward signs often show something impor-

tant about the attitudes or values of a person. What is *your* opinion? Support or defend your point of view.

5. For a time, it was fashionable for writers about the future to stress how different the future was likely to be from anything we had known in the past. What qualities or aptitudes do you think will be most essential for people to help them succeed or survive in the years ahead?

6. In the seventies, about 50 percent of college freshmen felt "there is too much concern in the courts for the rights of criminals." Ten years later, the proportion had grown to 65 percent. What explains this shift in attitude? Where do *you* stand? Back up your point of view.

8d   *coh*   Synonyms and Recurrent Terms

Use key terms and their synonyms to focus the reader's attention.

Often, the coherence of a paper shows in a network of closely related terms. **Synonyms**—words that mean almost the same—keep our attention focused on the same issue: *crime, lawlessness, transgression, felony.* Other related terms may reassure us that the writer is sticking to the subject: *violence, enforcement, gunplay.* Suppose you are reading an article on the psychological effects that *overcrowding* has on people in modern cities. In a well-focused article, other terms and phrases will echo the central term: "overpopulation," "penned up," "massive congestion," "great numbers," "rush-hour crush," "cramped quarters," and the like. Such synonyms or closely related terms show that the writer is never straying far from the central point.

Study the repetition of key terms like *work, toil,* or *labor* in the following excerpts selected to help you see the development of a long passage. In addition to such close synonyms, look at the other expressions that in some way paraphrase or echo the idea of work: "striving," "daily grind."

> What elements of the national character are attributable to this long-time agrarian environment? First and foremost is the **habit of work**. For the colonial farmer, **ceaseless striving** constituted the price of survival. . . .

The **tradition of toil** so begun found new sustenance as settlers opened up the boundless stretches of the interior. "In the free States," wrote Harriet Martineau in 1837, "**labour** is more really and heartily honoured. . . ."

One source of Northern antagonism to the system of human bondage was the fear that it was jeopardizing this basic tenet of the American creed. "Wherever **labor** is mainly performed by slaves," Daniel Webster told the United States Senate, "it is regarded as. . . ."

Probably no legacy from our farmer forebears has entered more deeply into the national psychology. If an American has no **purposeful work** on hand. . . .

This **worship of work** has made it difficult for Americans to learn how to play. As Poor Richard saw it, "Leisure is. . . ."

The first mitigations of the **daily grind** took the form of hunting, fishing, barnraisings, and logrollings—activities that had no social stigma because they contributed to the basic needs of living. . . .

The importance attached to **useful work** had the further effect of helping to make "this new man" indifferent to aesthetic considerations. . . .   Arthur M. Schlesinger, *Paths to the Present*

DISCOURSE EXERCISE 43   Study the following passage. Trace the *network of related terms* or expressions that refer in some way to the sending or reception of signals.

Satellite Television

The transmission of television and other signals by satellite has become a technological commonplace. Communications satellites now ring the globe. They have made possible improved navigation and flight control, worldwide high-speed data transmission, business teleconferencing, and increased telephone service. (The annoying little delay in most international and many domestic phone calls is the time it takes a microwave, traveling at the speed of light, to zip back and forth between Earth and a satellite.) They have also brought about the rapid expansion of cable television, the wild proliferation of new programming, and in the past four or five years a brand-new industry aimed at enabling people to receive satellite signals in their homes. Perhaps a million Americans own satellite antennas of varying shapes and sizes. They use them to receive as many as a hundred different television channels bearing everything from X-rated movies to unedited network news stories to Russian weather reports to talk shows whose hosts are nuns.

Ten years ago no regular American television programming was transmitted by satellite. Today almost every viewer, whether or not he owns a satellite antenna, watches shows that have spent at least part of their lives bouncing through outer space.   David Owen, *Atlantic*

8e   *trans*   Transitions

Provide a bridge from one point to the next and from one subtopic to another.

Effective writing provides smooth **transitions**—signals that help the reader move on from one part of a paper to the next. In writing, but especially also in revising a paper, provide the links that help the reader follow:

(1) Spell out the logical connection between one paragraph and the next. Study the way experienced writers make the beginning of a new paragraph point back to what came before and point forward to what is to follow:

THESIS:	The diversity of higher education in the United States is unprecedented. . . .
first problem is taken up; one alternative is considered	**Consider the question of size.** The small campus offers . . .
second alternative is considered	**Others feel hemmed in by these very qualities.** They welcome the comparative anonymity and impersonality of the big university. . . .
second problem is taken up; first alternative is considered	**Another familiar question is whether** the student should go to a college next door, in the next city, or a thousand miles away. By living at home . . .
second alternative is considered	**Balanced against this,** there are considerable advantages for a youngster in seeing and living in an unfamiliar region of the country. . . .
alternatives are weighed	**But this question too must be decided** on the basis of individual preference. . . .

(2) Use transitional phrases to help the reader move smoothly from one point to the next. The connection between parts of a paper is

COMMON TRANSITIONAL PHRASES	
ILLUSTRATION:	for example, for instance, to illustrate
ADDITION:	similarly, furthermore, moreover, too, besides
EXPLANATION:	that is, in other words
REINFORCEMENT:	indeed, in fact, above all
LOGICAL RESULT:	so, therefore, thus, accordingly, consequently, as a result, hence
CONTRAST OR OBJECTION:	but, yet, however, nevertheless, on the other hand, conversely, on the contrary
CONCESSION:	granted, admittedly, to be sure, no doubt, it is true that
SUMMARY:	in short, in brief, to sum up
CONCLUSION:	finally, in conclusion, to conclude
CHRONOLOGY:	first, next, later, soon, meanwhile, in the end

seldom as obvious as the writer thinks. **Transitional phrases** are directional signals that help the reader move along without stumbling. Words like *similarly, moreover,* and *furthermore* signal that an additional example or a further reason is about to reinforce the same point. *Indeed* and *in fact* signal that an exceptionally telling example or clinching argument will follow. *Admittedly* and *granted* tell the reader that we are about to recognize a legitimate objection; we are ready to grant or concede a point. Links like *nevertheless* or *however* show that we are ready to take on or refute the objection.

(3) Avoid a lame *also* or *another.* Weak transitions, often using *also* or *another,* merely add without showing why. If you can, show the logical connection with what went before:

WEAK LINK: **Another** misleading image created by television is that of the typical married male. . . .

BETTER: **After marriage**, the carefree young male of televisionland turns into the stereotypical middle-aged television male worried about insurance. . . .

Finer Points Transitional words or phrases are effective when they are used strategically, at a point where they are needed. Overused, they can become too obtrusive—they stand out like the pipes that run across the ceiling and down the walls in a converted basement apartment. Effective writers know how to use other ways of showing what goes with what. For instance, when two sentences are **parallel** in structure—exceptionally similar in form—we sense that they may be related examples or applications of the same basic point:

> The family is the seedbed of economic skills, money habits, attitudes toward work. . . . **The family is a stronger** agency **of** educational success **than the school. The family is a stronger** teacher **of** the religious imagination **than the** church.   Michael Novak

DISCOURSE EXERCISE 44   Study the two following passages from a discussion of sexual stereotypes. Find all the *transitional phrases*. Explain how they are used—how they steer the attention of the reader.

Less Than a Person

When people respond to one of the many stereotypes of women, they are reacting to an idea rather than to the real person. Therefore, their impressions are often wrong, and their behavior is often inappropriate. For example, if people think a woman is a soft and delicate creature incapable of reason, they may defend, protect, and think for her. They may substitute their reality for hers and deny her own experience its validity.

But worse than having her individuality denied by others, is the way she herself may identify with the stereotypes, treating herself as less than a person. . . .

Women have traditionally had their roles and their worth defined for them by their usefulness in the family. The woman who pours great energy and talent into the task of rearing children and making a home for her family fulfills a role which is vital to society's survival. However, she is unlikely to be paid or given any positive public recognition. Instead, she is known as "just a housewife," a label which belittles all her dedication and effort as well as the vital role she performs.

153

Although traditional roles for women are undervalued, they may nevertheless be very attractive. For one reason, these roles are systematically taught. For another, they deal with women's potential ability to create and shape human life and are thus a symbol of creative power. As a result, the woman who becomes a wife and mother is often responded to on the symbolic level alone.   James Hall, Nancy J. Jones, and Janet R. Sutherland, *Women: Portraits*

WRITING TOPICS 10

In writing on one of the following topics, pay special attention to the overall *coherence* of your paper. Focus your discussion on a unifying key term. Give special thought to the pattern you set up. Provide the signals that will steer your readers' attention.

1. Write a paper in which a central term, with its synonyms and related terms, helps focus the readers' attention. Write to answer (or to agree with) critics of current American life or society. Choose one:
    - the myth of American goodwill
    - the demise of cultural literacy
    - the computerization of America
    - the tradition of being a good neighbor
    - the lost war on poverty
    - the macho mystique
    - the feminization of poverty
    - the cult of youth

2. Write a paper in which you lead your reader from the familiar to the unexpected, or from the least important to the most important. Write for readers looking for advice. Choose one:
    - what we learn in school
    - the secret of a happy marriage
    - how to lose friends
    - how to keep a job
    - how to enjoy the outdoors
    - how to improve relations between police and community
    - how to fight depression

3. Write a paper in which you go from problem to solution. Write for readers skeptical of the "quick fix." Choose a problem like the following:

   - peer pressure and drugs
   - graffiti
   - dropouts
   - teenage pregnancy
   - managing on a tight budget
   - poor self-image
   - recruiting scandals
   - cheating on tests

2

Writing Better Paragraphs

Instructions Read each of the three paragraphs carefully. Answer the questions that follow each paragraph. Put the letter for the right answer after the number of the question.

> **A.**   We are becoming more aware of our kinship with other animals that share the earth with us. Animals were not created to be used and abused by human beings; they have a right to live with us on this planet. It is true that many of us are still unaware of the horrible conditions under which chickens or calves are pent up all their short lives in order to feed our insatiable appetite for meat. However, public opinion has changed drastically about such creatures of the wild as grizzlies, wolves, and coyotes. There has been a revulsion against the trapping of fur-bearing animals or the clubbing of baby seals for their pelts. Dog fanciers have changed their standards to make traditional barbaric practices like ear-cropping obsolete. In fact, the phrase *animal rights* is becoming more than a mere slogan; it is acquiring some legal clout.

1. Which of the following helps shape the overall pattern of this paragraph?
   a. initial claim followed by a detailed example;
   b. key idea supported by brief explanation and several examples;
   c. chronological tracing of a process.

2. The repetition of words like *animals, creatures of the wild,* and *animal rights* shows
   a. a lack of variety;
   b. a tendency to bring in irrelevant points;
   c. evidence of focus on a central topic.

3. Two of the transitional expressions in this paragraph introduce
   a. a concession followed by contrary evidence;
   b. theory followed by fact;
   c. a popular stereotype contradicted by expert testimony.

4. The phrase *in fact* at the beginning of the last sentence introduces
   a. factual evidence for the preceding sentence;
   b. a clincher sentence;
   c. an unnecessary restatement of an earlier point.

B. The objection to censorship has deep roots in American history and in the collective memory of Americans. It is true that the pilgrims who sought religious freedom here claimed that right for themselves without granting it to others. However, such leaders of the American revolution as Thomas Jefferson and Thomas Paine vigorously supported the right of others to their own opinions. Nineteenth-century writers like Emerson and Thoreau preached nonconformity and self-reliance. In this century, the book burnings that marked Hitler's rise to power left many Americans with an abhorrence for the suppression of dissent.

5. The major organizing principle in this paragraph is
   a. chronology;
   b. classification;
   c. cause and effect.

6. This paragraph uses familiar transitional expressions to signal each of the following *except*
   a. concession;
   b. summary;
   c. counterargument.

7. The topic sentence in this paragraph is the
   a. first sentence;
   b. third sentence;
   c. last sentence.

C. What has happened to America's mythical national heroes? For several generations, a legendary figure like Buffalo Bill could serve as a symbol of the gallant, reckless, sturdy independence of the Western frontier. At the same time, he was celebrated as a show business genius who made his Wild West show the most famous spectacle of its kind. Today, however, his name reminds us above all of the reckless destruction of the American buffalo. Whereas the Indians had regarded the animal with almost religious reverence, hunters like Buffalo Bill started the wholesale slaughter that decimated the herds and that destroyed the livelihood of the native Americans. Buffalo Bill is one of many mythical heroes who have been taken down from their pedestals as Americans have critically reevaluated their past.

8. What is unusual about the structure of this paragraph?
   a. no topic sentence;
   b. topic sentence at the end of the paragraph;
   c. key question left unanswered.

9. How is this paragraph developed?
   a. one single major example to prove the main point;
   b. a solid array of different examples;
   c. a chain of cause and effect.

10. Which of the following transitional expressions marks the major turning point in this paragraph?
    a. *at the same time*;
    b. *however*;
    c. *whereas*.

9   Writing the Paragraph

OVERVIEW In a well-written paragraph, we present and support one main idea. Paragraphs enable us to cover a subject one step at a time. Each well-written paragraph is a group of related sentences that focus on one part of a subject and do it justice. In a well-developed paragraph, we show that we are serious about what we are saying. A passing remark about the applications of solar energy is soon forgotten. But in a well-written paragraph, we can show how solar heating can meet most of the energy needs of a family. We can stay with one point long enough to show how things work, to show what is involved—to show what we mean.

A well-written paragraph satisfies readers who want to say: "Slow down. Move in for a closer look." It is true that in some kinds of writing a paragraph merely gives us a convenient break:

- In much *newspaper writing*, paragraphs are very short. There may be a paragraph break after every two or three sentences.
- In *dialogue*, a paragraph break signals a change from one speaker to another. If this book were written in the form of a dialogue, the next few lines might look like this:

"Why do some authors write very short paragraphs?"

"They write short paragraphs because they are skeptical about the attention span of their readers."

Nevertheless, in writing that explains, informs, or argues with the reader, the basic unit is the solidly developed paragraph that is a composition in miniature. Such a paragraph answers some basic questions in the reader's mind:

- It focuses on one limited point or issue. (What are we talking about?)
- It presents an overall idea or conclusion. (What is the point?)
- It backs up the main point with examples or other supporting material. (What makes you think so?)
- It provides signals that help the reader see how you have arranged your material. (How is your paragraph laid out?)

In your finished paper, your paragraphs are the major structural elements that determine the shape of the piece as a whole. In a well-developed paper, each major paragraph moves the presentation or the argument ahead one important step. It makes its point, explains it, illustrates it, supports it. Then the next paragraph goes on to the next point, often with a transition that spells out the logical connection.

The sequence of paragraphs in an article on television coverage of political conventions might in part proceed as follows:

Smile—You're on Camera

Television continues to change the look of political conventions. Speeches are fewer and shorter. Sweaty orators, bellowing and waving their arms for an hour or more, have yielded almost completely to TelePrompTer readers, younger and brisker, some of them very slick and many of them no fun. Both parties have shortened sign-waving, chanting demonstrations. . . .

While many of the changes may be for the best, there is something synthetic about this new kind of convention. There is a lack of spontaneity, a sense of stuffy self-consciousness. There is something unreal about seeing a well-known newscaster starting across the floor to interview a delegate and getting stopped for an autograph. . . .

Nevertheless, television coverage of conventions manages to get across to us a great deal about the way our political system works. We are still a nation of different parts. The conventions are the occasions that bring various coalitions together every four years to pull and haul at one another; to test old power centers and form new ones; to compromise and, yes, to raise a little hell together in a carnival atmosphere. . . .

9a   *dev*   Gathering Material

Use a paragraph to group together related material.

The raw material for a paragraph is a group of related data or observations. As we focus on one limited area of a subject, we bring together different details that seem to be part of the same general picture. Reading about sharks, for instance, we may notice several things that explain how sharks appear mysteriously whenever there seems to be a chance of food:

first observation	Sharks can smell blood from a quarter of a mile away, and they follow the faint scent to their prey.
second observation	Sharks sense motion in the water with special sense organs. Something thrashing about in the water is for sharks a signal of food.
third observation	Sharks are sensitive to bright light. They are attracted to bright and shiny objects, and to contrast between light and dark.

These observations all relate to the same basic topic: the food-tracking equipment of sharks. They add up to a general conclusion: Sharks are well equipped for identifying and tracking down food. In the finished paragraph, this conclusion will serve as the central idea that holds the paragraph together. We usually put such a central idea early in the paragraph as a **topic sentence**. The finished paragraph might look like this:

> **Sharks, known as voracious eaters, are well equipped for identifying and tracking down food**. As they prowl the water, they seem to sense the presence of unsuspecting prey from a considerable distance. There are several reasons why sharks are efficient at hunting down their prey. They can smell blood from a quarter of a mile away, and they follow the faint scent to a wounded creature. Sharks sense motion in the water with special sense organs; something thrashing about in the water is for them a signal of food. Finally, sharks are sensitive to bright light. Light reflected from something moving in the water alerts them, especially if it is the reflection from the shiny scaly surface of large fish.

Here is another set of related material drawn together for use in a paragraph:

first observation	People who have never been on a horse spend hundreds of dollars for elaborately decorated Texas-style boots.
second observation	They buy crafted leather belts with richly decorated silver buckles.

third observation	Passengers march onto airplanes wearing broad-brimmed cowboy hats.
fourth observation	Shirtmakers cultivate the urban-cowboy look.
fifth observation	Blue jeans, once worn mostly by ranch hands, are now the national uniform of the young.
conclusion	**Everywhere we look today, we see city people wearing cowboy fashions.**

When the material in a paragraph is related to the same basic idea, we say that it is **relevant**. It is to the point; it gives unity to a well-focused paragraph. The most basic requirement for successful paragraphs is your ability to pull together solid material from your observation, experience, and reading to turn what might have been a superficial opinion into a well-supported point worth thinking about.

PARAGRAPH WORK 1 What should be the topic sentence that is missing from each of the following paragraphs? In each of the following passages, related material has been brought together for a paragraph. However, the general conclusion suggested by the material has been left out. For each passage, write a sentence that could be used as the topic sentence of the complete paragraph.

1. _____ . The spines of cactuses are actually vestigial leaves. The bulb of an onion is a cluster of specialized leaves. Thorns of spiny plants and tendrils of climbing plants are often modified leaves, as are the needles of pine trees. The hard, woody sheathing of palm trees is a modified leaf, so large in one Amazonian plant that local tribes use it as a makeshift canoe.

2. _____ . Brown University's *Brown Daily Herald* prints run-downs of how much newspaper copy Brown rates, and *Issues*, a student monthly, leads off a big issue on Brown's future with speculation about what the school's "image-makers" will do now, after years of "exorbitant media coverage." A recent appeal to alums to come take classes included photos of staff with captions such as: "Giles Milhaven, Professor of Religious Studies, guest on 'CBS Sunday Morning.'" Every quarter the administration publishes a tabloid called *Brown in the News*, packed with the latest, including stories about student stars Amy Carter, Vanessa Vadim, and Cosima von Bulow.

3. _____ . In some arid countries, per capita consumption of water has risen tenfold thanks to improved sanitation. Underdeveloped countries need huge new water supplies for industrialization and irrigation. In the United States, many communities are facing water shortages. We have tapped most of the easily accessible sources of water in lakes,

rivers, springs, and wells, and the fresh water that remains will often be prohibitively expensive to collect and distribute.

4. _____ . People trying to protect whales have steered their small boats between the hunted whales and the sailors of catcher boats attempting to harpoon the animals. Other volunteers have harassed sealers on the harp seal breeding grounds on the ice of the Magdalen Islands. They have sprayed baby seals with organic dye that would make their pelts worthless for the hunters who club the defenseless cubs and then strip them of their fur. In one widely reported incident, an American released dolphins caught and penned up for slaughter by crews of Japanese fishing boats as threats to their catch.

5. _____ . Many companies now employ private security guards to protect business property. The sales of burglar alarms and other security equipment for private homes have increased steadily over the years. Locksmiths do a booming business fitting entrance doors with multiple locks, dead bolts, and the like. Increasing numbers of private citizens buy handguns intended as last-ditch protection of their families and their property.

9b   *foc*   The Topic Sentence

Use a topic sentence to sum up the major point of your paragraph.

The most basic question in your reader's mind is: "What is the point?" It is true that sometimes we want our readers to think about an issue and to reach their own conclusions. But in most well-written paragraphs, we include a clear statement that tells our readers: "This is what I am trying to show. This is what I am trying to prove." A **topic sentence** is a sentence that sums up the main point or key idea of a paragraph. Often the topic sentence is the very first sentence:

TOPIC SENTENCE: **Some of the job areas most popular with students are very small.** No more than 1,000 foresters will be hired this year, although perhaps twice as many students may get forestry degrees. Only 2,700 new architects will be needed to design all the buildings sprouting on the landscape, and almost twice that number graduated in a recent year. Everyone wants to design things, but, according to the Department of Labor, only about 300 industrial designers are added to the labor force during an

163

average year. Landscape architecture is appealing, too, because it combines creativity with outdoor work, but only 600 are expected to find jobs in the field this year.

Many paragraphs are constructed on this basic model: A topic sentence sums up the writer's claim, then the writer presents the evidence—the examples, details, statistics that back it up. Look at the way the author of the following paragraph backs up her claim about the role of slavery in ancient Greece:

TOPIC SENTENCE:

evidence

Greeks enslaved foreigners and other Greeks. Anyone captured in war was dragged back as a slave, even if he was a Greek of a neighboring polis. In Athens slaves, especially women, were often domestic servants, but of 150,000 adult male slaves, 20,000 were set to work in the silver mines, in ten-hour shifts, in tunnels three feet high, shackled and lashed; the forehead of a retrieved runaway was branded with a hot iron. Aristotle called slaves "animate tools," forever indispensable, he thought, unless you were a utopian who believed in some future invention of automatic machinery. In Athens it was understood that the most efficient administrator of many slaves was someone who had himself been born into slavery and then freed; such a man would know, out of his own oppressive experience with severity, how to bear down hard.   Cynthia Ozick, "The Moral Necessity of Metaphor," *Harper's*

Look at some common ways we vary the basic pattern of **statement and support**:

■ A topic sentence often carries its message most effectively if it is brief and to the point. However, it may call for some *explanation:* A second and perhaps a third sentence may restate the main idea, explaining a key term, spelling out how, when, or where. Then the paragraph may go on to *illustration:* The main point gets needed support from the examples or details that back it up:

TOPIC SENTENCE:
explanation

illustration

I always wished to be famous. As other people have an imagination for disaster, I have had an imagination for fame. I can remember as a boy of nine or ten returning home alone from the playground in the early evening after dinner, dodging, cutting, stiff-arming imaginary tacklers on my way to scoring imaginary touchdowns before enormous imaginary throngs who chanted my name. Practicing free throws alone in my backyard I would pretend that I was shooting them at a crucial moment in a big game at Madison Square Garden. Later, as a boy tennis player, before falling off to sleep, I imagined the Duchess of Kent presenting me with the winner's trophy on the center court at Wimbledon.   Aristides, "A Mere Journalist," *The American Scholar*

■ After providing illustration, the writer may decide to remind us of the point in a **clincher sentence**:

TOPIC SENTENCE:	**The new trend toward vocationalism is particularly counterproductive in an uncertain economy, when jobs are both scarce and changeable.** It makes slim indeed
explanation	the chances of picking the right specialization years in advance of actual entry into the labor market. The writer of an article in the *New York Times Magazine* extrava-
illustration	gantly extolling the virtues of New York's Aviation High School appeared unaware of its own ultimate contradiction: only 6 members of that year's 515-member gradu- ating class reported that they had found jobs in the
restatement	aviation industry. **The primary reason for youth unemployment is not lack of training but lack of jobs.** Fred M. Hechinger, "Murder in Academe," *Saturday Review*

■ Sometimes we delay the topic sentence *till the end* of the paragraph. We take our readers along, making them look at our evidence or examples, steering them toward a conclusion very similar to our own. To make such a paragraph work, we have to be especially careful that the details add up, so that the reader can follow our train of thought:

examples first	The shops of the border town are filled with many souvenirs, "pinatas," pottery, bullhorns, and "serapes," all made from cheap material and decorated in a gaudy manner that the tourist thinks represents true Mexican folk art. Tourists are everywhere, haggling with the shopkeepers, eager to get something for nothing, carrying huge packages and boxes filled with the treasures bought at the many shops. Car horns blare at the people who are too entranced with the sights to watch where they are going. Raucous tunes pour from the nightclubs, open in broad daylight. Few children are seen in the town, but some boys swim in the Rio Grande and dive to retrieve the coins that tourists throw as they cross the bridge

above. People come for a cheap thrill or cheap liquor. **A border town is the tourist's Mexico, a gaudy caricature of the real country.**

Remember what a good topic sentence does for the reader:

(1) A good topic sentence is like a promise to your readers. It gives them a sense of what to expect. In each of the following examples, the topic sentence steers the paragraph in a different direction:

TOPIC SENTENCE 1:   **Daytime TV commercials are increasingly bizarre.** They offer car insurance for even the most reckless and Visa cards for the most delinquent. Then there's the ad featuring a young fellow waiting for his friends to come and watch the Big Game on his new TV. How did he get the money? Well, Pharmakinetics will pay ambitious young men up to $1,000 to test the absorption rates of new drugs—on themselves. . . .

TOPIC SENTENCE 2:   **Like the sitcoms of the 50s, daytime TV commercials are far from gender-blind.** Men learn to be mechanics; women train to be nurses' aids. Men have a career in data entry; women attend the Washington School for Secretaries. Men worry about hair loss, women about weight gain. . . .

(2) A good topic sentence often hints at how the paragraph is going to be organized. It gives the reader a preview of points to be covered; it hints at the procedure the writer is going to follow. Look at the program implied in each of the following topic sentences:

TOPIC SENTENCE: Just as traffic lights may be red, amber, or green, so job interviews may be classified according to their probable results as hopeless, undecided, or promising. (We now expect a description of the **three kinds**.)

TOPIC SENTENCE: During my high school years, I saw a major change in the way schools treated bilingual students. (We now expect an account of the situation first **before** and then **after** the change.)

(3) In the paper as a whole, a good topic sentence moves the presentation or the argument ahead one essential step. Then the rest of the paragraph fills in, illustrates, and supports the point made. Then the next topic sentence again takes a step forward.

PARAGRAPH WORK 2   Study the following topic sentences. What is the author's point or intention? How might the author follow up the main point? What details, examples, statistics, or the like could you provide to help develop the rest of the paragraph?

1. It is becoming harder for the average high school graduate to get into and to stay in college.
2. The typical American car has many features that have nothing to do with providing cheap and efficient transportation.
3. Americans increasingly run into the ever-present computer during the business of an ordinary day.
4. A major industry can shape the quality of life of a whole town.
5. Violence in movies is getting more brutal.
6. Women in the judiciary are still the exception rather than the rule.
7. Many young people have negative attitudes toward the police.
8. Corporations ceaselessly develop marketing strategies designed to make what we already own obsolete.
9. At one time or another, most people's lives are touched or changed by divorce.
10. Terrorism, like auto accidents, has become a standard part of the news.

PARAGRAPH WORK 3   Choose one of the following statements. Complete it two different ways, each time filling in a *different comparison*. Use each of the two statements as a topic sentence. For each, write the complete paragraph filling in the examples or details that follow through. Choose one:

A college is like _____ .
A big city is like _____ .
A small town is like _____ .

| 9c | *dev* | Developing the Paragraph |

Build up your paragraph with a solid array of relevant detail.

In a well-developed paragraph, the topic sentence is backed up by details or examples. These show what is behind the general idea summed up in the topic sentence. Following through with specific examples or details is second nature for experienced writers; after making a point, they naturally go on to the "for example" or the "for instance."

167

Successful writers know how to pile on the examples that make the reader say, "Enough! I see what you mean." Notice how many different examples the writer has brought together in the following sample paragraph. Notice how directly they all relate to the author's central point:

> **Latin American culture has been and is a dynamic element in the development of our own.** It has, for example, furnished more than 2000 place names to the United States postal directory. Its languages have influenced American English, as such simple examples as "rodeo" and "vamoose" indicate. Its customs are part of our "Westerns" on television. Its housing, its music, its dances, its scenery, its ruins, and its romance have been imitated and admired in the United States. One third of the continental area of this republic was for a long period, as modern history goes, under the governance of Spanish viceroys or of Mexico. The largest single Christian church in the United States is identical with the dominant church in Latin America.   Howard Mumford Jones, "Goals for Americans," *Saturday Evening Post*

If you chart the supporting material in this paragraph, you see a solid array of details that all point in the same direction: Much in our culture has roots or parallels in Latin American culture and history. Here is a rough chart:

LATIN AMERICAN CULTURE AND OUR OWN

---

place names

Spanish words in English

"Western" customs

architectural styles, music, dances

former Spanish or Mexican territories

role of Catholic church

Here are some typical ways of backing up a topic sentence with convincing detail:

(1) Follow up your topic sentence with three or four parallel examples. The following is the kind of all-purpose paragraph that uses several different examples to illustrate the same general principle:

TOPIC SENTENCE:	**The deep sea has its stars, and perhaps here and there an eerie and transient equivalent of moonlight, for the mysterious phenomenon of luminescence is displayed by perhaps half of all the fishes that live in dimly lit or darkened waters, and by many of the lower forms**
first example	**as well.** Many fishes carry **luminous torches** that can be turned on or off at will, presumably helping them find or
second example	pursue their prey. Others have **rows of lights** over their bodies, in patterns that vary from species to species and may be a sort of recognition mark or badge by which the bearer can be known as friend or enemy. The deep-sea
third example	squid ejects a spurt of fluid that becomes a **luminous cloud,** the counterpart of the "ink" of his shallow-water relative. Rachel Carson, *The Sea Around Us*

(2) Use one exceptionally detailed example to drive home a point. Sometimes one striking example or summarized case history is remembered where more routine examples would be forgotten. Study the following sample paragraph:

TOPIC SENTENCE:	**As more and more clerical workers use computers, they increasingly find that their work is monitored from afar.** For example, computerization changed the working
key example	conditions in the accounting department of a large airline. The company hired a computer consultant to observe the work of clerks sifting through flight coupons and tabulating revenues. The consultant then devised a computerized system that enabled supervisors to keep exact count of how many tickets each clerk was processing each day. The system also identified periods during the day when productivity would dip while workers socialized or took breaks. The system enabled supervisors to set work quotas and to identify electronically those employees who fell short. Like the chickens on a computerized chicken farm, the workers were no longer allowed to waste the company's time.

(3) Choose one of several examples for especially detailed treatment. After giving more general examples, push toward specifics; move in for the closer look. In such a paragraph, you **downshift**—you move into a slower gear to allow the reader to take a closer look at one part of the scenery. An informative paragraph frequently moves through three levels: It starts with a fairly general statement or key idea (topic sentence).

It then takes one step toward specifics by following through with several brief examples (intermediate level). Finally, it zeroes in on one or more examples for more detailed treatment (specific level):

TOPIC SENTENCE: *(general point)*	**Most commercials succeed by working on the viewer's need to be loved and most commercials appeal to hidden fears. For example**, we have been schooled from
sample area *(intermediate)*	early childhood (sociologist David Riesman calls the American child a "consumer trainee") that our bodies produce numerous odors which "offend." Those who advertise deodorants, toothpastes, mouthwashes, colognes, and soaps have laid out billions of dollars to convince us that natural odors are unnatural. In an attempt
close-up example *(specific)*	to appeal to the environmentally conscious younger generation, the makers of Gillette Right Guard once announced: "A new anti-perspirant as natural as your clothes and makeup." David Burmester, "The Myths of Madison Avenue," *English Journal*

To help you visualize the downshifting that occurs in this kind of paragraph, imagine the paragraph laid out in a step pattern like the following:

1 GENERAL:	**We constantly expect more of computers.** Our tests for the artificial intelligence we build into electronic computers are constantly becoming more demanding. —————————————————▶
2 INTERMEDIATE:	When machines first performed simple calculations, people were amazed to see a collection of gears and levers add 2 and 2. —————————————▶
2 INTERMEDIATE:	Early computers amazed people by winning a game of tic-tac-toe. Today we are no longer surprised to see computers play chess, challenging world champions. —————————————————▶
3 SPECIFIC:	Current tests of computer intelligence ask a human subject to type questions and comments on a communication typewriter and then to judge which responses are being returned by another human being and which by a computer. For instance, a computer program called DOCTOR simulates the responses of a human therapist. According to a recent article on artificial intelligence, "some of the individuals interacting with DOCTOR thought they were getting typed responses from a real therapist."

(4) Draw on relevant statistics to help drive home a point. In many well-developed paragraphs, facts and figures assure the reader that the main point is not just one person's superficial impression. In the next paragraph, the main point is sandwiched in between statistics designed to make the author sound like an insider or an authority on the subject:

<table>
<tr><td>statistics</td><td>Four of the ten hardcover bestsellers last year were fitness books. Americans spent more than a billion dollars on exercise devices, and many people have turned their homes into private gymnasiums. Nevertheless, in</td></tr>
<tr><td>TOPIC SENTENCE:</td><td>spite of the fitness craze that has swept the nation, Americans are actually less physically fit than they were</td></tr>
<tr><td>statistics</td><td>five years ago. Between 80 and 90 percent of Americans still do not get enough exercise. (Exercise is defined as any activity that boosts heart and lung performance to 60 percent or more of its capacity for at least twenty minutes three times a week.) According to a study published by the Department of Health and Human Services, American children are fatter today than they were in the 1960s. Only 36 percent of our children today can pass minimum fitness standards set by the Amateur Athletic Union.</td></tr>
</table>

(5) Draw on well-chosen quotations for authoritative support. We often bolster a paragraph by the use of well-chosen quotations. We quote eyewitnesses, insiders, officials; we draw on authoritative printed sources. Look at the use of quotations in the following paragraph from a student editorial:

<table>
<tr><td>TOPIC SENTENCE:</td><td>For decades, Dali, the bizarre Spaniard with the erratic eyes and the antenna moustache, has been the uncontested leader of the art movement that expresses the unanalyzed subconscious. In their illogical and hallucinatory patterns, his paintings look like the record of extravagant dreams. These paintings bear such titles as</td></tr>
<tr><td>examples</td><td>"Rotting Mannequin in a Taxi" and "Debris of an Automobile Giving Birth to a Blind Horse Biting a Telephone." Images of ants, snails, melting watches, cauliflowers, lobsters, and women with chests of drawers in their abdomens appear throughout his work. When he first burst upon the art scene with an exhibition of surrealist paint-</td></tr>
<tr><td>quotations</td><td>ings in Paris, one critic said, "We have here a direct, unmistakable assault on sanity and decency." A French</td></tr>
</table>

poet called Dali "the great legislator of delirium." Dali has said of himself, "The only difference between me and a madman is that I am not mad."

PARAGRAPH WORK 4 How would you complete each of the following paragraphs? For each, *downshift* to one or more striking examples developed in detail. Modify or adapt the opening sentences if you wish.

1. *The fitness craze shows no signs of abating.* Sportswear stores carry twenty different kinds of running shoes, with the price of each pair representing three days' wages for the person working at MacDonald's or Burger King. . . .

2. *It is hard for young people to find heroes in the political arena.* Several recent Presidents have started in office with much popular support, only to be discredited or disgraced before they finished their duties. What Waterloo was to Napoleon, Watergate was to Richard Nixon, who resigned in disgrace when his White House "plumbers" were caught breaking and entering. . . .

3. *In our modern society, what cannot be counted does not count.* Numbers are the very models of modern facts. We expect to be served our customary diet of statistics—to be kept up to date with the latest swing in the unemployment rate, the consumer price index, or the President's standing in the polls. . . .

4. *Moviegoers and television viewers are fascinated by the possibility of extraterrestrial life.* Several years ago, the hit of the movie season was a spindly-fingered, child-size extraterrestrial who looked like an intelligent lizard. . . .

5. *Many outstanding athletes know that their careers may be brief or come to a premature end.* They know that their careers can be shortened with devastating swiftness by an injury. After a few seasons, broadcasters begin to refer to a player as a "veteran" while the club is acquiring high draft choices to groom for the older player's position. . . .

PARAGRAPH REVIEW 5 Study the way a central idea or main point is developed in the following paragraphs. Answer the following questions about each:

■ What is the main point? Is it stated in a topic sentence? Where in the paragraph?

■ Is any part of the paragraph a restatement or explanation of the main idea?

- What is the nature of the supporting material—multiple examples, one key example, downshifting to a more detailed example, statistics, or a variation of these? (What is the source of the supporting material?)
- Does the material follow a pattern, such as from familiar to new, or from less important to more important?
- How do you react to the paragraph as a reader? What kind of reader would make a good audience for the paragraph?

1.   The influx of women into the corporate world has generated its own small industry of advice and inspiration. Magazines like *Savvy* and *Working Woman* offer tips on everything from sex to software, plus the occasional instructive tale about a woman who rises effortlessly from managing a boutique to being the CEO of a multinational corporation. Scores of books published since the mid-1970s have told the aspiring managerial woman what to wear, how to flatter superiors, and, when necessary, fire subordinates. Even old-fashioned radicals like myself, for whom "CD" still means civil disobedience rather than an eight percent interest rate, can expect to receive a volume of second-class mail inviting them to join their corporate sisters at a "networking brunch" or to share the privileges available to the female frequent flier.   Barbara Ehrenreich, "Strategies of Corporate Women," *The New Republic*

2.   When I was in grade school, I had many friends. They often invited me over to their houses. My parents would let me go if I asked politely. They sent me off with the usual warnings about not riding my bike in the middle of the street or being back in time for supper. One year my mother and I were looking at my class picture, and I pointed out a good friend of mine whose house I had often visited. Looking at his picture, my mother realized he was of a different race. I was never given permission to visit his family again. When I complained, I was told my friend was not a desirable influence. I believe that we are born with no natural instinct for prejudice but that we learn prejudices later in life from others.

3.   Commercial fishing around the world can barely keep up with the growing demand for scarce protein. In a recent year, the total catch amounted to 74 million tons, which works out to 16 kilograms per person for the world, or almost a quarter of all animal protein consumed. More than a hundred species of finfish and shellfish are harvested commercially around the world, and 22 species provide 100,000 tons or more. However, per capita catches have been slowly dropping during the last decade. At least eleven major fisheries have been depleted to the point of collapse, ranging from the anchovy in Peru to the Alaska crab. In fact, only squid and the Antarctic krill are still underfished, since harvesters find it hard to make them palatable to new consumers.

4.   Outside the Arctic, which is my second home, I find little comprehension of the remarkable skill, work, and endurance it takes for Eskimos to live off the land and sea in one of the world's most inhospitable
climes. The whale has traditionally been, and still is, a large and important part of the Eskimo diet. Even today, natives usually hunt it as their
ancestors did—paddling up to the quarry in homemade driftwood-
framed sealskin boats, then dispatching the giant with a hand-thrust
harpoon or shoulder gun, the design of which was patented in the
1800's. As part of the hunt ritual, the Eskimos return the whale's skull to
the sea to appease the spirit of the magnificent beast. Since bowheads
are fairly wily, weigh a ton a foot, and sometimes grow to be 60 feet
long, the crews require considerable courage. Their primitive method
of hunting definitely limits the take, which, until 1978, was unrestricted
by law.   Lael Morgan, "Let the Eskimos Hunt," *Newsweek*

9d   *trans*   Transition

Use transitional expressions to help your reader follow from
step to step.

A good paragraph has built-in signals that help the reader follow. A
transition helps a reader "travel across" or move on from one point to the
next. It provides a bridge from one idea or detail to another. **Transitional
phrases** help your reader see how your paragraph is laid out; they help the
reader follow from point to point.

Use transitional phrases to steer the reader's attention in the right
direction. *For instance, for example,* and *to illustrate* steer us from general
point to specific example. *Similarly, furthermore, moreover,* and *in addition*
prepare us to continue the same line of thought. *But, however, on the other
hand, on the contrary,* and *by contrast* signal a turning point—objections
will follow; complications are about to set in. *It is true* or *admittedly* signals
a concession—the writer is (reluctantly) granting a point.

Here is a list of common transitional expressions:

ILLUSTRATION:	for example, for instance, to illustrate
ADDITION:	too, also, furthermore, similarly, moreover
EMPHASIS:	indeed, in fact, most important, above all
RESTATEMENT:	that is, in other words
SUMMARY:	in short, to sum up

LOGICAL RESULT:	therefore, so, consequently, as a result, thus, hence
COUNTERPOINT:	however, but, on the contrary, nevertheless
CONCESSION:	it is true, granted, admittedly, to be sure
ALTERNATIVES:	on the one hand . . . on the other hand

Trace the transitional expressions that guide the reader through the following paragraph:

TOPIC SENTENCE:	**Doctors have found that the way a drug is given can be important.** The commonly prescribed antibiotic tetra-
example	cycline is **one example**. It is completely absorbed when injected in a vein or muscle and fairly well absorbed in
caution	pill form on an empty stomach. **But** because the presence of food in the stomach interferes with absorption, pa-
additional point	tients are advised to take tetracycline before meals. **Fur-ther**, drugs are not absorbed equally after injection into
result	different muscles. **Therefore**, doctors now pay more at-tention to the site at which drugs are injected. **For exam-**
example	**ple**, in the case of a drug called lidocaine, which is used in the treatment of heart rhythm abnormalities, studies have shown that it was absorbed faster following its injec-tion into the deltoid muscle in the arm than into a muscle in the leg. Lawrence K. Altman, "Drugs—How Much Is Enough?" *New York Times*

PARAGRAPH WORK 6   In the blank spaces in each of the following para-graphs, fill in the missing transitions that will steer the reader in the right direction.

1.   Often, creativity and practicality go hand in hand. _____ , the cre-ative person might use the creative, pattern-forming right side of the brain to design a stained-glass window. _____ , the actual process of producing the window is painstakingly methodical, bringing into play the linear, systematic left side of the brain. The artist who creates a stained-glass window needs both imagination and highly developed technical skill. _____ , the pacemaker—a device that artificially stimu-lates the heart when the heartbeat is too slow—was at first someone's creative concept, requiring an imaginative leap beyond the tried and true. _____ , building a pacemaker is a practical process, requiring finely honed technical skill.

2.   The search for new sources of energy has often proved disappoint-ing. _____ , the extracting of oil from shale rock has proved less viable than its promoters had hoped. Companies looking for alternative

175

sources of oil started to mine shale, heat it to 900 degrees F, and draw off the raw shale oil, to be refined and made into petroleum. One ton of rock can yield 35 gallons of oil. One project was designed to produce as much oil as a medium-size oil field in Oklahoma. _____ , oil prices failed to rise as predicted, and development costs shot through the roof. _____ , oil companies put their shale projects on hold.

9e   *coh*   Coherence

Know how to improve coherence in a paragraph.

Paragraphs, like people, have to be coherent if we are to make sense of what they say. When a paragraph has **coherence**, it "hangs together"; the material in it is relevant—it helps the writer make the point. The reader can follow the major steps. In addition to clear transitions, use the following to strengthen coherence in your paragraphs:

(1) Use recurrent or related terms to help hold a paragraph together. In many paragraphs, a network of related terms makes for coherence and keeps the reader's attention focused on the point at issue. In a well-focused pararaph, the same central term, as well as various doubles or synonyms, may come up several times. Such **recurrent terms** form a semantic network—a network of words closely related in meaning.

In the following excerpt, notice the network of terms that relate to the idea of change:

> It is an ominous fact that in the long chain of evolution the latest link, man, has suddenly acquired alchemic powers to **alter** whatever he touches. No other species before has been able to **change** more than a tiny fraction of his habitat. Now there is but a tiny fraction that he has **left unchanged**. A bulldozer **undoes** in an hour the work of a million years. . . .   Paul Brooks, "Canyonlands," *Atlantic*

In the next paragraph, note the many words and phrases that echo the idea of purity: *naked—nude—pure—elemental—beyond corruption—natural—basic.*

> To the Greeks, who get the credit for inventing it, gymnastics was "the **naked** sport" (the word *gymnos*

TOPIC SENTENCE:

means **"nude"**), and the phrase manages to be both evocative and correct. There is something **pure about gymnastics**, something **so elemental** that the sport seems **beyond** either **corruption or adornment**. The athletes do not work against an opponent or against some arithmetical measure of time, distance, or weight. The gymnast works, instead, against the body's **natural** limits, with little protective clothing or equipment to help when courage or talent fails. The apparatuses of gymnastics are **basic** and symbolic, nothing more than artificial tree limbs, level tumbling lawns, and imitation saddles. When the sport advances, it is (for the most part) because a single athlete is able to make his or her body do something that no one has ever done before. Geoffrey Norman, "The Naked Sport," *Esquire*

(2) Use parallel structure to line up ideas of equal importance. Often, similar or parallel sentence structure signals to the reader that several ideas or details are closely related. In the following paragraph, the repetition of similar sentence openings signals that the writer is continuing the same trend of thought. The sentences starting "They are . . . They are . . . They tend . . ." each pinpoint something that is part of the same basic attitude on the part of reviewers. Later, two sentences that are again similar in structure describe the contrasting attitude of ordinary readers:

With a few splendid exceptions, professional reviewers do not really read books. **They are** in the book business. And that makes a big difference. **They are** so bored and so jaded with the sheer volume of books that pass through their hands that if they manage to respond freshly to one, it's nothing short of a miracle. **They tend** to regard all books as guilty until proven innocent. But readers are different. **They regard** each book with optimism. **They expect** their lives to be changed—and often write to tell me that they were.

In the following paragraph, similarity in sentence structure helps us take in the two parts of a comparison:

Baseball does not pay its officials nearly as well as basketball does. **In basketball, an NBA official with ten years' experience** may make perhaps $600 per game, with over eighty games on the schedule. The official would make over $45,000 a season. **In baseball, an umpire with ten years in the majors** until recently made closer to $200 a game, with a schedule of about 160 games. . . .

PARAGRAPH REVIEW 7 Study the devices that make for coherence in the following paragraphs. Which of these paragraphs relies mainly on *transitional expressions* to guide the reader? In which of these paragraphs is there a strong network of *related terms* that echo or reinforce the key idea? Which of these paragraphs relies strongly on *parallel sentence structure*?

1.   All the evidence indicates that the population upsurge in the under-developed countries is not helping them to advance economically. On the contrary, it may well be interfering with their economic growth. A surplus of labor on the farms holds back the mechanization of agriculture. A rapid rise in the number of people to be maintained uses up income that might otherwise be utilized for long-term investment in education, equipment, and other capital needs. To put it in concrete terms, it is difficult to give a child the basic education it needs to become an engineer when it is one of eight children of an illiterate farmer who must support the family with the produce of two acres of ground. Kingsley Davis, "Population," *Scientific American*

2.   Hate letters are a fact of life for anyone whose name appears in print or whose face is seen on television or whose voice is heard on radio. They are terribly disturbing—but after the first few, you begin to catch on to the fact that they have nothing whatever to do with you (or your book) but are sheer projections on the part of their writers. They are often unsigned. They often begin with sentences like: "My mother was a lady who never used four-letter words and ——s like you are what's rotting America and weakening our morale [*sic*] fiber. . . ." They are often misspelled and ungrammatical, and full of mixed metaphors and malapropisms. Erica Jong, "The Writer as Guru," *New York*

3.   Most often the male role in advertising is that of the strong, silent outdoorsman, athlete, or adventurer. The archetypal male figure in advertising is, of course, the Marlboro Man. This famous mythic figure was the product of an intensive campaign which transformed a poorly selling cigarette, originally aimed at women smokers, into the biggest selling filter-tip on the market. At the same time, it promoted an attitude about male roles still being sold in almost every cigarette ad currently in print. Commercials for beer also push the take-charge male image, showing men, generally in groups, participating in active, physically demanding sports or jobs and being rewarded with a cool bottle of beer. Rarely are women seen in these commercials other than as silent companions to these he-men. The Marlboro Man and his descendants exemplify the self-sufficient, highly individualistic male who provides the complement to the sexy, empty-headed female of toiletry commercials. David Burmester, "The Myths of Madison Avenue," *English Journal*

PARAGRAPH WORK 8   Regardless of the subject area, a basic tool of every writer is the expository paragraph that focuses on a limited point and supports it with detailed examples. Scan publications in an area of special interest to you for sample paragraphs. You might look at specialized magazines or textbooks, for instance. Share your choice of a statement-and-examples paragraph with a group of your classmates; have them discuss the sample paragraphs submitted and select those that best fit the type.

9f   *foc, dev*   Revising Paragraphs

Refocus and bolster weak paragraphs.

In much student writing, paragraphs are not developed fully enough to drive home a point. They are not detailed enough to give the reader a good grasp of what is involved. Revise weak paragraphs by highlighting the key idea, by strengthening the network of supporting details, and by streamlining the pattern that gives the paragraph direction and shape.

Remember the following guidelines for strengthening weak paragraphs:

(1) Revise paragraphs that lack a central focus.   Often a weak paragraph strays from one topic to the next. Remember that a good topic sentence gives unity to a paragraph. It can point out a logical connection that you previously missed or ignored:

RAMBLING: San Francisco is a city of beautiful parks and public buildings. Golden Gate Park, with its spacious lawns and graceful ponds, enjoys international fame. The city's bohemian section became the national headquarters for jazz-age poetry and philosophy. Every tourist must visit Fisherman's Wharf and Coit Tower. The city is famed for its cultural events and conventions.

UNIFIED: **Tourists and convention managers are irresistibly attracted to San Francisco.** Miles of varied waterfront, impressive public buildings, and spacious parks contribute to the city's unique appearance and cosmopolitan atmosphere. Fisherman's Wharf, with its seafood smells and colorful shops, attracts sightseeing crowds. Coit Tower affords a spectacular view of bay and city. Golden Gate Park, with its spacious lawns and graceful ponds, enjoys international fame.

(2) **Spell out a key idea that was only implied.** Look over your shoulder at the reader who wants to know: "What does this prove? What does this show? What is the point?" The following revision of a weak paragraph adds the topic sentence that spells out the point:

IMPLIED:

The Lone Ranger—what a man! He doesn't need anybody. Fearless and brave, he rides in on his white horse, sending the bad guys running for cover. After rescuing the heroine and saving the town, he rides off into the sunset, alone. How about Tarzan, Lord of the Jungle, or Dirty Harry Callahan with his .44 Magnum ablazing? My favorite heroes were the mountain men—rugged solitary men fighting Indians, wrestling bears, and discovering the only safe route through the mountains. I read every book I could lay my hands on about such giants as Jedediah Smith and Joseph Walker.

SPELLED OUT:

When I was growing up, I was totally taken in by movies and books that glorified the rugged outdoors type. The Lone Ranger—there was a man! Fearless and brave on his white horse, he sent the bad guys scrambling for cover. After rescuing the heroine and saving the town, he rode off into the sunset alone. Tarzan, Lord of the Jungle, another loner, single-handedly thwarted the evil designs of poachers or thieves of tribal treasure. My favorite reading was books about the mountain men—rugged solitary men fighting Indians, wrestling bears, and discovering the only safe route through the mountains, all in one day. I read every book I could find about such giants as Jedediah Smith and Joseph Walker. These men spent months, even years, in the mountains trapping beavers and living off the land, completely alone.

(3) **Build up the supporting material in weak paragraphs.** A basic weakness of many student-written paragraphs is the lack of concrete follow-through—a lack of specific scenes, incidents, and details. Readers need more than a general idea; they need things they can visualize and

imagine. Whenever you start a paragraph, remember that your ideas will not become real for your readers unless you get down to specifics.

Look at the following paragraph before and after revision:

GENERAL: **Images of blacks in the media have certainly changed.** They now sell deodorant and toothpaste and light beer, just like other people. Bill Cosby's show, which became a top-rated program on television, presents a comfortable middle-class family and its everyday problems. The family happens to be black, and we hardly notice.

SPECIFIC: **Blacks at one time were hardly visible in the media except as stereotypes (the field hand, the porter, the maid). That certainly has changed.** Blacks now sell deodorant and toothpaste and light beer. Bill Cosby's show, which became a top-rated program, shows a comfortable middle-class family and its everyday problems. Some black viewers have complained that Cosby's Dr. Huxtable doesn't represent the average black person. It is true that the average black family is not headed by a doctor father and a lawyer mother. On the other hand, neither is the average white family. But when Cosby identifies his son's room as "the room where clothes go to die," we don't think about whether this is a black family. We know it is a real family. And this seems to be the heart of the matter. When whites grow accustomed to the idea that blacks differ very little from them, it becomes more and more difficult to keep prejudice alive.

(4) Fit your supporting details into a pattern that the reader can follow. For instance, in writing designed to inform or explain, the first draft of a paragraph will often present interesting bit facts, facts that remain too miscellaneous. To help the reader grasp and remember the information, work details into a pattern that the reader can take in. Notice how the following paragraph answers questions about comets in the order in which these questions might arise in the reader's mind:

TOPIC SENTENCE: **Comets strew debris behind them in interplanetary space.** Some of it is seen from the earth as the zodiacal
where observed light, which is visible as a glow in the eastern sky before sunrise and in the western sky after sunset. (It is brightest

how produced

in the tropics.) Much of the zodiacal light near the plane of the earth's orbit is sunlight scattered by fine dust left behind by comets. Under ideal observing conditions, cometary dust also appears as the Gegenschein, or counterglow: a faint luminous patch in the night sky in a direction opposite that of the sun. Comets need to contribute about 10 tons of dust per second to the inner solar system

how ended

in order to maintain this level of illumination. Over a period of several thousand years, the particles are gradually broken down by collisions with other particles, or are blown away by solar radiation.   Fred L. Whipple, "The Nature of Comets," *Scientific American*

(5) Strengthen the transitional signals that will guide your reader. Set up clearer signposts for readers who might lose their way. Look at the way the signals in the following sample paragraph nudge the reader in the right direction:

then

Some of us are old enough to recall when the stereotype of a "liberated woman" was a disheveled radical, notoriously braless, and usually hoarse from denouncing

now

the twin evils of capitalism and patriarchy. **Today** the stereotype is more likely to be a tidy executive who carries an attaché case and is skilled in discussing market

emphatic reinforcement shares and leveraged buy-outs. **In fact**, thanks in no small part to the anger of the earlier, radical feminists, women have gained a real toehold in the corporate world: about 30 percent of managerial employees are women, as are 40 percent of the current MBA graduates. We have come a long way, as the expression goes, though clearly not in the same direction we set out. Barbara Ehrenreich, "Strategies of Corporate Women," *The New Republic*

Note: A series of short, two- or three-sentence paragraphs usually signals that you are skipping from one point to the next. (Sometimes a writer will use a one-sentence or two-sentence paragraph to make a key point stand out boldly from the rest.) A page or more without a paragraph break generally means that you are not laying your material out in the kind of step-by-step pattern that the reader can follow. Solid, well-developed paragraphs that average perhaps half a dozen sentences each show that you have brought your material under control and have followed up the key points you raise.

PARAGRAPH WORK 9   What is needed to strengthen each of the following paragraphs? For each of these, do a rewrite that would strongly present and support a central point.

1. Many parents think that once their children are at school anything they do is the responsibility of the school. Parents blame schools for not maintaining strict supervision on campus. However, although most schools have strong policies, these can also be broken. The staff cannot possibly watch all of the students all of the time. Parents should teach their children to have more respect for others.

2. Let us look at the average worker in an average American factory. Henry, an assembly worker, punches in at eight in the morning. On the line, he does the same repetitive job all day. At five o'clock, he punches out and heads home.

3. In many of my classes, teachers have asked me about my Irish heritage. Without my telling them that my father is Irish, they assume I am Irish from merely looking at my name. Many people admire the "fighting Irish" of the Notre Dame football team. On Irish holidays like St. Patrick's Day, many Americans share in the nostalgia for old customs and the old songs. Newspaper articles about the Irish often dwell fondly on their folklore and their love of song and story.

PARAGRAPH WORK 10   Practice *building up detail* in a multiple-example paragraph. Study the following paragraph as a model. Study its exceptionally ample use of relevant detail. (How many different examples can you identify?) Write a similar paragraph on a topic of your own choice.

A person's touch makes what the other senses take in more real to the memory. A wood carving appeals to the touch with deep grooves and parts that are rough as well as parts that are smooth. The fingers can interpret the richness of brocade and the rough warmth of wool. An ancient book becomes even older when one feels the fragile pages. A puppy tugging wildly at a leash feels like energy. Winter is felt in the hastily prepared snowball and the pine boughs that are brittle in the sharp air. A child must feel a hot stove before it becomes a thing to avoid touching. The energy of the sun becomes more apparent when one focuses a magnifying glass on one's fingers. A baby chick is something altogether new when one holds the cottonlike ball of feathers and feels its nervous heartbeat. An oil painting is only paint and canvas until one touches the swirls made by the artist's brush. A rose is only a flower until one holds it and pulls the petals from the intricate pattern. The surface of the rock is only light and shadow until one feels its ridges and ripples. Touching helps one to see and hear more clearly.

PARAGRAPH WORK 11   Choose a weak paragraph from a paper you have recently written. Revise it with three major goals in mind:

- providing a clearer statement and fuller explanation of the main point
- building up relevant examples and details
- helping the reader follow by strengthening the overall pattern or strengthening transitions

---

PARAGRAPH TOPICS 1

1. Write a paragraph that focuses on *one strand* in your growing up. Select an issue or important concern that will help your classmates know you better as a person. Show in vivid detail why it mattered to you. Study the following sample paragraph as a possible model:

> My personal Mexican-ness eventually produced serious problems for me. Upon entering grade school, I learned English rapidly and rather well, always ranking either first or second in my class; yet the hard core of me remained stubbornly Mexican. This chauvinism may have been a reaction to the constant racial prejudice we encountered on all sides. The neighborhood cops were always running us off the streets and calling us "dirty greasers," and most of our teachers frankly regarded us as totally inferior. I still remember the galling disdain of my sixth-grade teacher, whose constant mimicking of our heavily accented speech drove me to a desperate study of *Webster's Dictionary* in the hope of acquiring a vocabulary larger than hers. Sadly enough, I succeeded only too well, and for the next few years I spoke the most ridiculous high-flown rhetoric in the Denver public schools. One of my favorite words was "indubitably" and it must have driven everyone mad. I finally got rid of my accent by constantly reciting "Peter Piper picked a peck of pickled peppers" with little round pebbles in my mouth.   Enrique Hank Lopez, "Back to Bachimba," *Horizon*

2. Write a paragraph that follows up a key idea with *three or four well-chosen examples*. Choose one of the following topics for your paragraph:

   a. We hear much about species endangered by the results of human technology or civilization. Choose three or four examples of animals (other than domestic animals or pets) that have survived well *in spite of* the onslaught of human civilization. Start with a topic sentence that makes a general point about the examples you have chosen. Then follow through with your examples.

   b. It has been said that the flip side of progress is obsolescence. New inventions or technological breakthroughs gradually become old-fashioned and finally lose their usefulness. Choose three or four examples. Present them in a paragraph, using them to back up your topic sentence.

   c. Several recent American Presidents have come from outside the East Coast political establishment. They were not Easterners; they did not have Ivy League degrees; they did not have names suggesting inherited wealth or influence. Choose your own examples. Use them to back up your topic sentence in a well-developed paragraph.

3. Write a paragraph that explains a characteristic attitude or emotion of the young (frustration, rebellion, ambition) to older people—or that explains a characteristic attitude or emotion of the old to the young. Provide *an exceptionally detailed example* that will bring your key term to life for your reader.

4. Write a *details-first* paragraph that creates a setting or a mood likely to be unfamiliar to your readers. First, fill in striking, characteristic details. Then, at the end, fill in the meaning the place or the mood has for you. Study the following sample paragraph as a possible model:

   It is Friday night at any of ten thousand watering holes of the small towns and crossroads hamlets of the South. The room is a cacophony of the pingpong-ding-dingding of the pinball machine, the pop-fizz of another round of Pabst, the refrain of "Red Necks, White Socks and Blue Ribbon Beer" on the juke box, the insolent roar of a souped-up engine outside and, above it all, the sound of easy laughter. The good ole boys have gathered for their fraternal ritual—the aimless diversion that they have elevated into a life-style.   Bonnie Angelo, "Those Good Ole Boys," *Time*

5. Write a *multiple-example* paragraph documenting a current trend for the readers of a small-town newspaper. Focus on a topic that has become the center of media attention, the object of marketing efforts, a favorite topic of pundits and politicians, or the preoccupation of other trend makers. Sum up the trend in a topic sentence and pile on many striking examples.

6. Write a paragraph devoted to the exception to the rule. Remind readers who tend to share the opinions of the majority that there are important exceptions to something that is often claimed or something "everybody says." Present exceptions in striking detail, or concentrate on one especially striking exception.

10 Kinds of Paragraphs

OVERVIEW No two paragraphs are alike. The basic expository paragraph launches a main idea and then follows it up with examples or details. Other paragraphs follow a somewhat different pattern. Their organization mirrors their function: to trace a step in a process, to compare two related things, or to choose between alternatives.

The following two paragraphs trace the aftermath of a natural catastrophe. They illustrate the kinds of paragraphs we find in writing that traces natural or historical processes, with attention to patterns of cause and effect:

Aftermath

Mount St. Helens changed the way Northwesterners think about the land on which they live. It happened on the morning of May 18, 1980. The mountain launched an eruption that sent a square mile of pulverized rock 14 miles into the atmosphere and completely tore apart the perfect cone of the volcano. At least 62 people, including loggers and campers, lost their lives. Mudflows created by melting glaciers buried river valleys. And with the eruption came fast-moving flows of superheated steam, ash, and gases that killed everything in their path. Hundreds of square miles of timber and other vegetation were laid waste. Wildlife was wiped out, the landscape rendered barren and unrecognizable. Cities like Yakima, 80 miles away, were blanketed by ash.

But in the years since, plant life has regained a foothold on some of the ashen hillsides. A few animals have been sighted. This has happened faster than most biologists believed possible. Even some of the mud-choked rivers now show signs of returning salmon. Much of the blown-down timber has been harvested, except for a section set aside as a permanent memorial to the power of the blast.   Peter Potterfield, "God's Country U.S.A.," *Continental*

In writing that argues with the reader, a paragraph may move an important step forward in the argument. It may spell out two or three major reasons for a decision. Or it may line up the evidence pro and con on a key point. It may define an important term that could mislead the reader if it were left vague or ambiguous. Study the ways we lay out paragraphs that serve a special purpose.

| **10a** | *coh* | Narration, Description, Process |

Make your paragraphs follow a pattern appropriate to your subject.

In a narrative, in description, in explanations, or in instructions, a paragraph often traces a pattern that is built into the subject matter. In such a paragraph, we do justice to what is there, to what we are writing about. At the same time, we make sure we take our readers along. We trace a pattern that they can follow:

(1) Make a paragraph follow a pattern in time. In telling the story of something that happened, present major stages or key developments in **chronological** order—the way they followed one another in time. The following paragraph tells the story of a playground, from its opening to its gradual abandonment by the author and his friends. Notice that in a narrative the events often take shape without an introductory topic sentence. Notice the transitional phrases that help us follow the order of events in time:

beginnings   The orphanage across the street is torn down, a city housing project **begins to rise** in its place, and on the marvelous vacant lot next to the old orphanage they are building a playground. Much excitement and anticipa-
major event   tion as **Opening Day** draws near. Mayor LaGuardia himself comes to dedicate this great gesture of public

187

turning point

benevolence. He speaks of neighborliness and borrowing cups of sugar, and of the playground he says that children of all races, colors, and creeds will learn to live together in harmony. **A week later**, some of us are swatting flies on the playground's inadequate little ball field. A gang of Negro kids, pretty much our own age, enter from the other side and order us out of the park. We refuse, proudly and indignantly, with superb masculine fervor. There is a fight, they win, and we retreat, half whimpering, half with bravado—my first nauseating experience of cowardice, and my first appalled realization that there are people in the world who do not seem to be afraid of anything, who act as though they have nothing

intermediate stage

to lose. **Thereafter**, the playground becomes a battleground, sometimes quiet, sometimes the scene of athletic competition between Them and Us. But rocks are

end result

thrown as often as baseballs. **Gradually** we abandon the place and use the streets instead. The streets are safer, though we do not admit this to ourselves. We are not, after all, sissies—that most dreaded epithet of an American boyhood.   Norman Podhoretz, *Doings and Undoings*

Many accounts of events, trends, or developments follow an approximate order in time even when they do not follow an exact time sequence step by step. The following *Time*-style paragraph about opening day at Disneyland takes us from the beginnings (the glut of cars on the freeway) to the morning-after newspaper report:

TOPIC SENTENCE:

Disneyland was capitalism with a human face—or a smiling rodent's—and its opening day was set for July 17, 1955. **Even the mastermind recalled it as "Black Sunday"; everything went wrong.** The glut of visitors turned

getting in

the Santa Ana Freeway into a seven-mile parking lot. Refreshment stands ran out of food and drink for the

early snafus

nearly 30,000 invited guests and thousands more ticket counterfeiters who stormed the gates. Rides broke down immediately. A gas leak forced the shuttering of Fantasy-

high noon

land. The day's corrosive heat sent women's spiked heels sinking into the asphalt on Main Street. Nor was this debacle to be covered over with Tinkerbell dust: the whole sorry spectacle was broadcast on a live TV special

morning after

co-hosted by Ronald Reagan. WALT'S DREAM A NIGHTMARE, proclaimed the Los Angeles *Tidings*.   *Time*

(2) Make a paragraph follow a pattern in space. In describing a scene, lay out a pattern that the reader can easily visualize. The following model paragraph makes the eye travel gradually from what is close by (the house and its garden) to the far distance (the tropical forest):

TOPIC SENTENCE:	**The house stood in what was certainly the best position in Mamfe.** It was perched on top of a conical hill,
this side of gorge	one side of which formed part of the gorge through which the Cross River ran. From the edge of the garden, fringed with the hedge of the inevitable hibiscus bushes, I could **look down** four hundred feet into the gorge, to where a
river at bottom	tangle of low growth and taller trees perched precariously on thirty-foot cliffs. Round gleaming white sandbanks and strange, ribbed slabs of rock, the river wound its way like a brown sinuous muscle. **On the opposite**
opposite bank	**bank**, there were small patches of farmland along the edge of the river, and **after that** the forest reared up in a
distant forest	multitude of colors and textures, spreading endlessly back until it was turned into a dim, quivering, frothy green sea by distance and heat haze. Gerald M. Durrell, *A Zoo in My Luggage*

(3) Make a paragraph trace a process. To help us understand how something works (or how to make it work), a paragraph may trace a process step by step. The following paragraph traces the stages in a natural cycle. Notice the transitional expressions that take us a step forward in time:

TOPIC SENTENCE:	**Beavers often create forest ponds that for a time become the home of insects, reptiles, fish, otter, herons, and other animals.** Beavers can transform a pine forest
initial cause	into an entirely new habitat by damming a stream. The pond will flourish for a short time—perhaps a few decades. The pond's creatures adapt to seasonal changes.
seasonal pattern	**In the winter**, the pace slows beneath the frozen surface. Frogs and turtles bury themselves in the mud. **But soon after the ice thaws**, the natural rhythms accelerate. Dragonflies breed, fish spawn, and soon all the energies begin
reason for change	to prepare for another winter. **But when the food supply is exhausted**, the beavers will leave. Without their hard work and constant maintenance, the dam falls into disrepair and the water runs out. The area reverts to a
end of cycle	swamp, **then** a marsh, a meadow, and **finally** a forest once again in this never-ending natural cycle.

189

Much historical writing shows the chains of cause and effect that explain historical processes:

TOPIC SENTENCE:	**At the time of the migration to the North, the share-croppers in Mississippi were moving off the land, be-**
key cause	**cause they were being replaced in the fields by machines.** Heavy tractors and cotton-picking machines became common equipment on farms in the fifties; by 1960 what was once the work of fifty field hands could be done by only three or four. Typically, the sharecrop-
immediate result	pers were simply dismissed; white farmers in Canton who had dozens of people living on their property have
current reminders	no idea where they are today. Deserted sharecropper cabins are a common sight in the country outside Canton, falling down at the edges of open fields, some of them in rows, some half a mile from the nearest building or road. A few are still occupied, mostly by old people who sometimes still dress in homespun and use wood fires to warm themselves and cook. Nicholas Lemann, "The Origin of the Underclass," *Atlantic*

PARAGRAPH WORK 12   Write a paragraph that traces a central theme through several stages or sections of a movie or book. Make your paragraph follow a rough *chronological order*. Study the following student-written paragraph as a possible model:

In a scene from *The Odd Angry Shot*, an antiwar film directed by Tom Jefferey, Bung, a young naive army draftee, pulls off his shoes and socks to find that a fungus is eating away his feet. Bung is in Vietnam as part of his country's "peace-keeping" force. Throughout his tour of duty, Bung is faced with the horrors, pains, and hopelessness of war. On his first night in the jungle, his camp is attacked by guerrillas using rockets. One of the men that Bung is playing cards with has a hole blown through his back. He dies screaming. Later, on a mission to ambush guerrillas, Bung and his patrol are caught by surprise, and another of his friends dies screaming in agony. Bung is obviously shaken as he says over and over, "Why can't he stop screaming?" To the bitter end, the viewer follows Bung and his patrol through a duty consisting of horrible living conditions, terrifying encounters, and painful deaths.

10b   *coh*   Comparison and Contrast

Use a paragraph to develop a comparison or contrast.

We often use a paragraph to line up two things for comparison. Comparison can help a reader understand something difficult or new by showing how it is similar to something familiar. Contrast can alert the reader to important differences or distinctive features. Often comparison or contrast helps us evaluate things or make a choice.

(1) Line up similarities and differences. The following paragraph illustrates a common pattern for combined **comparison and contrast**, showing first similarities and then differences. Note the *however* that signals the turning point:

TOPIC SENTENCE:

People riding a moped should remember that it is not really a motorcycle but only a bicycle with a small motor attached. The moped may look like a lightweight
similarities
motorcycle, and it can weave through stalled traffic and crowded places like a motorcycle. Like a motorcycle, it is cheaper and easier to maintain than the bulky, gas-
differences
guzzling family car. **However**, the moped creates a real safety problem for people who ride it in ordinary traffic. It has much less weight and power than a real motorcycle. The driver depends on a very small, underpowered engine. The wind caused by a passing truck or bus can make the lightweight moped impossible to control.

(2) Set up a clear contrast. The following paragraph develops a **contrast** between two sides of police work. The writer makes us see the contrast as her paragraph takes shape, without using an introductory topic sentence. As in other paragraphs tracing a contrast, a transitional expression like *however, but,* or *on the other hand* takes us from one major part to the other:

first side
Like any other job, police work falls into set patterns: patrol this sector, cover this assignment, check this complaint, interview this man, this woman, this child, inves-
second side
tigate this company, work on this case. **But** always the

unexpected, the sudden violent event, it also part of the routine. If there is an undue hardness in the voice of a traffic cop stopping an offender for a minor violation, it might be because he remembers, in some deep part of his brain, hearing or reading of some cop, somewhere— stopping a light-jumper, a speeder, an improper turner— a cop who, summons book in hand, was shot dead for no reason. If there is a dictatorial tone in the command of a policeman who tells a group of curious onlookers at some unusual event to move on, it might be because he has seen a curious crowd grow into a menacing mob.   Dorothy Uhnak, *Policewoman*

(3) Trace a detailed analogy. An **analogy** is an exceptionally detailed comparison that traces a close parallel through several specifics. The two things being compared have to be alike in basic and instructive ways, not just similar in some superficial or isolated way. The following paragraph uses an analogy to make us think about an essential feature of growing up:

TOPIC SENTENCE: **We are not unlike a particularly hardy crustacean.** The lobster grows by developing and shedding a series of hard, protective shells. Each time it expands from within, the confining shell must be sloughed off. It is left exposed and vulnerable until, in time, a new covering grows to replace the old. With each passage from one stage of human growth to the next we, too, must shed a protective structure. We are left exposed and vulnerable—but also yeasty and embryonic again, capable of stretching in ways we hadn't known before. These sheddings may take several years or more. Coming out of each passage, though, we enter a longer and more stable period in which we can expect relative tranquility and a sense of equilibrium regained.   Gail Sheehy, *Passages*

PARAGRAPH WORK 13   Write a *then-and-now* paragraph that traces a contrast between old and new customs or patterns of behavior. Study the following paragraph as a possible model:

We have lost contact with many of our traditional rites of grieving. In rural America everybody had a role in the rites of death. Farm women dressed the body while the men built the casket. The body was buried on the family's land or in a nearby cemetery, by community members. Mourners wore black, or black armbands, for a long time—often a full year. The black would say, "I'm grieving; be gentle with me." Now, mourners are invisible. If a bank teller is short with me, there's no way to know that he is upset because his mother just died. For most of this society, grieving is set aside after a few days. Companies give three days bereavement leave for the death of an immediate family member, no time for the death of a friend. After three days, we are supposed to come back and perform as usual.

10c   *coh* | Argument

Write a paragraph that can serve as a step in an argument.

When we reason with a reader, we try to present our points in such a way that a reasonable or objective reader would have to agree. We present major steps in the argument in such a way that the reader can reach the same logical conclusion. Here are several kinds of paragraphs that follow familiar logical patterns designed to take the reader along:

(1) Write a paragraph that supports your point with convincing reasons. In the well-developed paragraph, you can first take a stand and then present solid **reasons** for your attitude or position. In the following student-written paragraph, the author presents reasons showing that her attitude toward convenience foods is more than a personal dislike:

TOPIC SENTENCE:

reasons

I object to convenience foods because they do not serve the cause of good nutrition. These expensive, elaborately packaged, highly processed products are usually a combination of many ingredients, some of which have nothing to do with nutrition. Often the extra ingredients are there to provide long-term preservation and to improve coloring, texture, or taste. Refined sugar is one example of an often unnecessary ingredient. We eat too much sugar without realizing that much of the sugar we consume is hidden sugar. Almost every processed foodstuff contains sugar in some form: honey, molasses, sucrose, corn syrup, dextrose, and the like. Too much sugar plays a role as a cause of heart disease, diabetes, and

193

high blood pressure. Salt is also abundantly used in processing beyond what is necessary for good health. The biggest argument against processed convenience foods is that during processing and packaging many of the original nutrients are lost and then artificially replaced by "enriching."

(2) Trace a pattern from cause to effect. We often explain something by first taking a look at its causes. Then we look at the results these causes have produced. The following paragraph follows a **cause-and-effect** pattern:

TOPIC SENTENCE:

cause

effect

Under primitive agricultural conditions the farmer had few insect problems. These arose with the intensification of agriculture—the devotion of immense acreages to a single crop. Such a system set the stage for explosive increases in specific insect populations. Single-crop farming does not take advantage of the principles by which nature works; it is agriculture as an engineer might conceive it to be. Nature has introduced great variety into the landscape, but man has displayed a passion for simplifying it. Thus we undo the built-in checks and balances by which nature holds the species within bounds. One important natural check is a limit on the amount of suitable habitat for each species. Obviously then, an insect that lives on wheat can build up its population to much higher levels on a farm devoted to wheat than on one in which wheat is intermingled with other crops to which the insect is not adapted.   Rachel Carson, *Silent Spring*

In the following paragraph, a crucial *therefore* takes us from cause to effect:

cause

effect

Japan is a nation that, lacking natural resources, must live by its wits, by social discipline, and by plain hard work. It is not surprising, **therefore**, to discover that during the last twenty years Japan has quietly been establishing a new, higher set of educational standards for the world. On a whole raft of international tests of achievement in science and math, Japanese students outperform all others. Japan's newspaper readership level is the world's highest. A considerably larger percentage of Japanese (90 percent) than Americans (75 percent) or Europeans (mostly below 50 percent) finish the twelfth grade, and a greater proportion of males complete university B.A. degrees in Japan than in other countries. Japanese children attend school about fifty more days each year than American students, which means that, by high-school graduation, they have been in school somewhere between three and four more years than their American counterparts.   Thomas P. Rohlen, "Japanese Education—If They Can Do It, Should We?" *The American Scholar*

(3) Use a paragraph to weigh the pro and con. A well-focused paragraph may line up the pros and cons that we need to weigh when faced with a decision. The following example lines up advantages and disadvantages in an exceptionally well-balanced way. Note the transitions that take us from the pro to the con in each set of examples:

TOPIC SENTENCE: **Like other modern inventions, computers have a capacity for use and abuse, a potential for good and bad.** Computers allow people to fly safely and quickly across continents, **but** they also make it possible to send missiles from one country to another. Computers can speed credit cards to us and help us use them with ease, **but** they can also be used to compile records that invade a citizen's privacy. Computers serve as electronic tutors; pocket-size electronic calculators can solve complicated problems with amazing speed. **However**, the students who start early to rely on calculators may see their own math abilities remain underdeveloped. The same computers that help administrators and accountants can ruin a student's class schedule or bill the wrong person for a thousand dollars' worth of merchandise.

(4) Use a paragraph to weigh alternatives. We sometimes start a paragraph by looking at one proposed solution or alternative and finding it wanting. We then go on to the more likely or more promising possibility. The following paragraph first looks at a desirable alternative but then goes on to the more likely prospect:

first alternative examined and rejected   History shows that wars between cities, states, and geographic regions cease once the originally independent units have amalgamated under the leadership of a single government with the power of making and enforcing laws that are binding upon individuals. **One might reason on this basis that** if all of the industrialized and

195

semi-industrialized regions of the world were to federate under a common government, the probability of another war would be greatly decreased. It seems likely that this conclusion would be valid if the resultant federation were as complete as was the federation formed by the original thirteen colonies in America. **On the other hand**, it is extremely unlikely that such a highly centralized federation could come into existence at the present time; nationalistic feelings of individuals and groups, and conflicts of economic interests, are too strong to permit rapid transition. **Also**, those nations which have high per capita reserves of resources and high per capita production would be most reluctant to delegate their sovereignties to higher authority and to abandon the economic barriers that now exist.   Harrison Brown, *The Challenge of Man's Future*

second alternative presented and supported

(5) **Use a paragraph to define an important term.** We often use a paragraph to explain an important technical term or pin down a word that has confusing or changing meanings. The following paragraph defines the term *conjunction* as used by astronomers and then illustrates its use:

explanation

In addition to Venus, there are four other planets visible to the naked eye—Mercury, Mars, Jupiter, and Saturn. During their movements across the sky, two planets may sometimes appear to pass very close to one another—though in reality, of course, they are millions of miles apart. **Such occurrences are called conjunctions**; on occasion they may be so close that the planets cannot be separated by the naked eye. This happened for Mars and Venus on October 4, 1953, when for a short while the two planets appeared to be fused together to give a single star. Such a spectacle is rare enough to be very striking, and the great astronomer Johannes Kepler devoted much time to proving that the Star of Bethlehem was a special conjunction of Jupiter and Saturn. Arthur C. Clarke, *Report on Planet Three*

key term

examples

In much argument, as in other kinds of purposeful writing, a key term helps us focus on an important idea. The term may help us focus on an important development or imply a program for action. A paragraph defining such a term will chart the territory the term covers; it will give concrete body to the abstract idea. Look at the way the following paragraph gives us a detailed, vivid look at what the author means by a "university without walls":

> It could be said that a women's **university-without-walls** exists already in America, in the shape of women reading and writing with a new purposefulness, and the growth of feminist bookstores, presses, bibliographic services, women's centers, medical clinics, libraries, art galleries, and workshops, all with a truly educational mission; and that the members of this university are working and studying out of intense concern for the quality of human life as distinct from the ego-bound achievement of individual success. With the help of the duplicating machine, documents, essays, poems, statistical tables are moving from hand to hand, passing through the mails; the dissemination of knowledge obtained from this study is not accountable in terms of the sales of a single edition or even dependent solely on commercial publication.   Adrienne Rich, "Toward a Woman-Centered University," *On Lies, Secrets, and Silence*

Finer Points   Obviously, paragraphs do not always follow a textbook pattern. You will often need to *combine or adapt* familiar patterns to accomplish your aims. For instance, you may trace causes and effects but at the same time present them in chronological order. The following paragraph combines a chronological pattern, contrast between then and now, and the tracing of important causes:

TOPIC SENTENCE:	**In many American colleges, intercollegiate athletics has become a big business.** How did these institutions
contrast with past	become as deeply involved as they are? **A hundred years ago**, athletic events at American colleges were true amateur events, with free admission. One of the first big
milestone event	stadiums was built **in 1903**, when the Harvard class of 1878, to celebrate its twenty-fifth anniversary, offered the university $100,000 to build a stadium for track and foot-
major factors	ball. As costs rose, spectators were **soon** charged for their seats. Institutions began to build bigger and bigger stadiums to outshine each other. Financial guarantees for visiting teams grew. The costs of scouting, recruiting, and
end result	traveling grew. **Today** a single large institution may employ forty coaches. The total athletic budget at a big football university may be between five and ten million dollars.

PARAGRAPH WORK 14   Write a definition paragraph that explains and illustrates a current buzzword, such as *lifestyle, quality time, the old boys' network, sexual harassment, primetime soap,* or *animal rights.* Study the following paragraph as a possible model:

> Examples of Doublespeak—the sometimes unwitting but more often deliberate misuse of words to cover up, rather than explain, reality—are easy to find almost everywhere. Government bureaus, for instance, have been instructed to eliminate the word *poverty* from official documents, replacing it with low-income, a term not nearly as alarming as poverty. For similar reasons, the unpleasantness of slums or ghettos has long given way to inner city. Instead of *prisons*, there are now only correctional facilities. U.S. State Department employees are not *fired* but *selected out*, a term that sounds like an award for excellence. Other government types tend to be terminated. In each instance, the aim is to make things appear better than they are or, in the case of correctional facilities, actually to seem what they decidedly are not. If all this were only a matter of semantics and style, there would be little cause for concern. Unfortunately, the truth is that the linguistic cosmetics are often used to create the impression that nasty problems have already been solved or were not really too nasty in the first place.   Fred M. Hechinger, "In the End Was the Euphemism," *Saturday Review/World*

PARAGRAPH WORK 15   In some kinds of writing, the function of each paragraph is exceptionally well defined. For instance, two related paragraphs may develop a contrast between then and now, or between the two stages of a process, or between two ways of accomplishing the same thing. Similarly, the first of two related paragraphs may present the surface advantages of a procedure or proposal, with the second paragraph pointing out the neglected other side—important disadvantages or unexpected side effects.

Write a *two-paragraph paper* with each paragraph serving a clearly defined function. Join with a group of your classmates to obtain reactions to your preliminary plans and feedback to your writing.

PARAGRAPH REVIEW 16   Study the following *sample paragraphs*. Ask about each:

■   What is the overall function of the paragraph?
■   What is the main point, and where and how is it stated?
■   What is the pattern of the paragraph—how is it organized?

- Does the paragraph serve a combination of purposes, or does it combine familiar patterns? Show how.
- What transitions help steer the reader?
- Who would make a good reader for the paragraph?

1.   Three fourths of the world's people receive very little attention from American reporters. They are the peasants, the three billion people who are still traditional subsistence cultivators of the land. There should be no doubt that these people are worth our attention: all the major contemporary revolutions—in Mexico, Russia, Cuba, Angola—have involved peasant societies. In almost every case, the revolution was preceded by cultural breakdown out in the villages, because the old peasant ways and views of life no longer worked. The 450 or so American foreign correspondents only rarely report on these billions, because the peasants live in the world's two million villages, while the governments, wealth, and power—as well as telephones, cable offices, files, and typewriters—are in the cities.   Richard Critchfield, *Columbia Journalism Review*

2.   The most disquieting aspect of the silicon chip is not that it distances us from nature; even before the Industrial Revolution, man was trying to do that. The more troubling fact is that electronic developments distance us from understanding. Any child of fifty years ago looking inside a household clock, with its escapement and weights or spring, could see in a few minutes how it worked. A child of today peering at a digital watch can learn nothing. Yesterday's children could appreciate that pushing a switch on a television set meant completing a circuit. Today's children, using remote control devices based on ultrasound or infrared radiation, can scarcely comprehend what they are doing. The real danger of the microelectronic era is posed by what was called, even in the days of macroelectronics, the black box mentality: passive acceptance of the idea that more and more areas of life will be taken over by little black boxes whose mysterious workings are beyond our comprehension.   Bernard Dixon, "Black Box Blues," *The Sciences*

3.   My mother once instructed me to say, "I am an American of Mexican descent." By the time I was nine or ten, I wanted to say, but dared not reply, "I am an American." Immigrants come to America and, against hostility or mere loneliness, they recreate a homeland in the parlor, tacking up postcards or calendars of some impossible blue—lake or sea or sky. Children of immigrant parents are supposed to perch on a hyphen between two countries. Relatives assume the achievement as much as anyone. Relatives are, in any case, surprised when the child begins losing old ways. One day at the family picnic the boy wanders away from their spiced food and faceless stories to watch other boys play baseball in the distance.   Richard Rodriguez, "Does America Exist?" *Harper's*

4.   When a beachcomber discovers a marooned marine mammal, center volunteers jump into their rescue truck to collect it. This can be a tricky business, because the arrival of humans is likely to excite the animal enough to stimulate his instinct to attack. The rescuers approach small seals and sea lions behind a "herding board" that protects the people and guides the animal into the rescue truck. They may briefly pop a blanket over the animal's head, says Schramm, "so they can't see where to bite." The uninitiated might be tempted to pet a young seal or sea lion with its invitingly thick coat and big cow eyes. But the animals are not as adorable as they look. Even the youngsters have very sharp teeth, and they're not afraid to use them. A larger elephant seal or sea lion is a bigger challenge and must be approached "with great caution," Schramm says. To collect the larger animals, rescuers use a "bull pull," a long pole with a rope on the end that is slipped over a large pinniped's neck to keep the biting end a safe distance from the people herding it into the truck.   Linda Currey Post, "Shelter from the Storm," *San Francisco Focus*

PARAGRAPH TOPICS 2

1. Write a paragraph that traces a clear pattern in space or time for the confused newcomer or outsider. Start with a topic sentence that sums up or previews what you describe. Choose a topic like the following:
   - the layout of a baseball field
   - building the foundation for a house
   - disassembling the engine of a car
   - the layout of your favorite park
   - typing a letter on a word processor or computerized typewriter

2. Write a paragraph that develops a comparison or contrast to help guide the choices of an undecided reader. Start with a topic sentence that sums up the comparison. Choose a topic like the following:
   - driving a car and riding a motorcycle
   - organic and ordinary food
   - downhill and cross-country skiing
   - jogging and walking
   - old-style and digital watches

3. Develop an analogy as a guide to the curious. Complete one of the following statements and use it as a topic sentence for a paragraph that

fills in the details or examples needed to follow up the analogy. (Or develop an analogy of your own choice.)

- Love is like _____ .
- Failure is like _____ .
- The army is like _____ .
- Marriage is like _____ .

4. Write a paragraph in which you take a stand and then give reasons for the position you have taken. Keep in mind the unconverted or hostile reader. Start your paragraph with a statement like the following: "I believe in ____ because ____ "; or "I object to ____ because ____ ." In the first blank in the sentence, fill in a topic like the following:

- large families
- stronger support for the U.S. military
- stricter speed limits
- rent control
- health foods
- financial aid to minority students
- more financial support for women's sports
- calculators in math classes

   Use the rest of your paragraph to present your most important reason or reasons.

5. Write a paragraph whose purpose is to explain cause and effect, to examine pros and cons, or to weigh alternatives. Write to convince a reluctant or unconverted reader. Choose a topic like the following:

- diets
- early retirement
- protecting nonsmokers
- cheating on exams
- a national speed limit
- mandatory helmets for cyclists
- graffiti

3

Argument and Persuasion

11	Structuring an Argument

OVERVIEW The purpose of a logical argument is to convince the reader. In a well-written argumentative paper, we argue an issue in such a way that the reader can follow along step by logical step. We try to convince our readers, not by appealing to their prejudices or exploiting their weaknesses, but by making them see the logic behind the position we take.

A successful argument depends on a basic mutual respect between writer and reader. As writers, we adopt toward our readers a stance that tells them: "If you look at these points and at this evidence along with me, you as a reasonable reader will reach the same conclusions I have reached." In turn, we expect the reader to feel: "Even if you have not made me change my mind, you have at least made me think."

What kind of thinking goes into a successful argument? Three basic reasoning patterns occur again and again when we think a subject through. They are at work again and again when we process information or try to make sense of a difficult situation. Alone or in combination, they give shape and direction to much argumentative writing.

INDUCTION In much of the writing we do, thinking the matter through means working out careful generalizations. It means looking for a common pattern in related examples. For instance, suppose you have studied reports of violence at soccer matches, riots after a football game, fistfights in bars, and shootouts over a parking space. Such reports of random violence gradually fall into a pattern. They point to a common element, a central clue: Many people in our society are constantly irritable as the result of the pressures of modern living. They suffer from a short fuse that may be touched off at any minute.

This bundling of related evidence is one of the basic reasoning patterns we use when we sort out information and make sense of data. This pattern takes us from the specific to the general, from isolated observations to a common clue. We call this generalizing kind of reasoning inductive reasoning, or **induction**.

Inductive reasoning helps us funnel related observations into a generalization that sums up a common pattern. It also helps us construct a **hypothesis** that explains puzzling data. A classic example from Monroe C. Beardsley's *Thinking Straight* looks as follows:

FACT 1:	The house across the street has shown no signs of life in some days.
FACT 2:	Some rolled-up, rain-soaked newspapers lie on the front steps.
FACT 3:	The grass needs cutting badly.
FACT 4:	Visitors who ring the doorbell get no answer.
HYPOTHESIS:	**The people across the street are away on a trip.**

All clues in the example point in the same direction: Papers are not picked up when the owner is away. The grass is not cut when the owner is away. No one answers the doorbell when the owner is away. (Other possible hypotheses: The people across the street have been the victims of foul play. Or the people across the street are in the basement, hiding from creditors.) In much of the writing we do, thinking the matter through means working out careful generalizations while taking apparent exceptions into account. It means constructing careful hypotheses to account for a state of affairs while not ruling out alternative explanations.

DEDUCTION   Often we go from the general to the specific. We spell out assumptions about appropriate behavior and then show how they should govern behavior in specific situations. We argue from principle, applying a general principle in order to decide individual cases.

For example, after asking when we should withhold life support from the terminally ill, a writer might formulate a rough contemporary consensus on what constitutes a meaningful life. She may then provide guidance for doctors and relatives by applying this concept to test cases of terminally ill patients. When we apply general principles to specific cases, we argue deductively. We employ deductive reasoning, or **deduction**.

In much of our reasoning, we work with what we already know. We bring previous knowledge to bear on current problems, apply general rules to specific instances, or invoke a prior law to judge a current crime. We move from shared assumptions, or shared **premises**, through logical steps to valid conclusions. An informal version of this deductive process guides us in everyday decisions:

GENERAL PREMISE:	All the design engineers I know look well groomed.
SPECIFIC FACT:	While in college, I have let my hair grow frizzy, and I tie it up with a bandana.
CONCLUSION:	Before I apply for a job as a design engineer, I should do something about my hair.

But similar reasoning determines the verdict on many matters of greater weight:

FIRST PREMISE:	Only native-born Americans are eligible to run for President.
SECOND PREMISE:	Dr. X is a naturalized citizen.
CONCLUSION:	Dr. X is not eligible to run for President.

PRO AND CON A third kind of reasoning is not always stressed in introductions to logic, but it is one of the basic ways we make up our minds. In many situations, we weigh the pro and con before making the right decision. The issue may be whether to live at home or away from home while in college; it may be whether to boycott a company that uses non-union labor. Typically in such situations, we have to balance conflicting advice or opposing views. The kind of reasoning that goes from *on the one hand* to *on the other hand* and on to a balanced conclusion is the process of **dialectic**.

A paper exploring the dialectic of contrasting views will often lead up to a turning point: A strategic *however, nevertheless,* or *on the other hand* signals that the writer will now look at the other side. Writing a paper on the role of ceremony in our lives, you may want to start with familiar objections: Audiences fidget at commencement speeches. Formulas recited by rote at weddings do not express sincere feelings; hard-earned money is spent to rent ill-fitting tuxedos. On the other hand, special occasions make us feel that we matter. They give us a chance to show that we care. They renew bonds of friendship and kinship. On balance, although ceremonies can be lifeless and boring, they can also make us feel good about ourselves and others.

The pro-and-con approach protects us against becoming too one-sided. It teaches us to look at the other side and to take opposing arguments into account.

Several other strategies for structuring an argument may also help you organize a paper as a whole:

CAUSE AND EFFECT Before suggesting remedies for acid rain, you may want to analyze key causes and project the consequences of different courses of action.

ELIMINATING ALTERNATIVES Which of the various suggested ways of relieving traffic gridlock is workable (and affordable)? You may want to look first at two or three clearly undesirable ones in order to make your readers opt for the choice you prefer.

YES, BUT The traditional assertive style of argument has been to take a strong stand and demolish the opposition. A less aggressive modern style of argument is to build respect and confidence first by meeting the reader halfway. We then change from a "No, you are wrong!" to a "Yes, but . . ." style of argument.

DEFINITION We can often clarify an important issue by defining a key term. We mark off its boundaries; we map out the territory it covers or the confusions it may cause.

11a *log* The Inductive Argument

Work out cautious generalizations and support them well.

When an issue has generated more heat than light, we may want our readers to suspend judgment while checking out the facts. We invite them to join us in the search; we ask them to generalize cautiously on the basis of what we know.

For instance, you may want to argue with fellow students who claim that young people today are more politically aware and responsible than their parents. You have been struck by the small turnouts for controversial speakers invited to your campus. You have studied the dismal statistics on recent elections for student government. You have seen reports on debates that fizzled. Your campus newspaper seems obsessed with the parking situation or the Ugliest-Man-on-Campus award. After reporting these and similar observations in vivid detail, you reach a general conclusion: A pervasive apathy toward political and social issues has overtaken your fellow students.

Normally, you would present this general conclusion first, as your unifying **thesis**, and then lay out the various striking examples you have collected. However, you may decide to involve the reader directly in the **inductive** process—in the *search* for a common pattern. If your readers follow you in your thinking step by step, the result may be more lasting conviction. When you start your paper with a strong initial claim, the skeptical reader's response may be: "Is that so?" When you make your whole paper lead up to a well-earned generalization, your readers may feel: "Yes, I have already reached the same conclusion."

As you experiment with papers that *lead up* to a general conclusion, remember the following advice:

(1) Work up a rich fund of supporting material. Buttress your conclusions with detailed examples, statistics, and expert testimony. Keep after your readers with facts, figures, and quotations:

> What is the main reason for the wretched conditions existing in our prisons today? When the two bloodiest prison riots in this country's history took place at Attica State Prison in New York and at Santa Fe prison in New Mexico, the population of these two prisons was at 50 percent over normal capacity. An official at the California Department of Correction said in April 1986, "Each day the population of the state's prisons shatters a record. The unprecedented numbers have caused a crisis that threatens to plunge an already violence-plagued system to new depths." The American Civil Liberties Union, in a study of prison conditions, found that "six inmates were sometimes housed in a 4 by 8 cell, with no beds, no lights, no running water, and a hole in the ground for a toilet." The effect of such conditions on the inmates was summed up by a chaplain at Riker's Island: "If you put a violent person in prison for a number of years, he will come out more violent than before." Overcrowding in our jails is the root cause of many of the problems that plague our prison system.

(2) Aim at a representative sample. A sample is **representative** when you have looked at a *range* of possible examples to make sure you do not generalize on the basis of unusual situations. What are the economic

fortunes of professional athletes? We should not base our answer on headlines about football stars signed to million-dollar contracts. We need to
investigate the salaries of the rank and file, of second-stringers; we need to
check into the fate of players whose careers are cut short by injuries or by
the changing policies of a team.

(3) Limit your generalizations. When reasoning inductively, we
tend to move ahead too fast, announcing the beginning of summer after
the arrival of one swallow. Avoid **hasty generalization**; limit your generalizations to what you can support by an array of convincing examples.
Make it a habit to scale down sweeping generalizations like the following:

SWEEPING: Americans are the most generous people on earth.
LIMITED: Although Americans are often accused of ulterior mo-
                 tives, other countries routinely turn to them for help in
                 times of famine, earthquake, or economic collapse.

(4) Be wary of inclusive terms and labels. Reconsider sentences
that begin with *every, all, anybody, always, nobody,* or *never.* ("Nobody really
wants war.") Use labels like *typical, normal,* or *average* with special care.
Where necessary, insert a cautious *maybe, frequently, in most cases,* or *at least
some of the time.*

(5) Lower the abstraction count. Abstractions "draw away" from
the messy detail of everyday reality toward general labels. Any paragraph
carrying several abstractions like *freedom, responsibility, integrity,* and *civic
duty* may already be in trouble. Tying one of these firmly to concrete reality
is already a major task.

WRITING WORKSHOP 1   Assume that you and your classmates are studying a report that an American educator has prepared on the Japanese educational system. Key sections of the report follow: a set of comparative
statistics on Japanese and American schools, and a summary of conditions
that provide the setting for Japanese education. Be prepared to discuss with
your classmates the central question raised by the report: What can American schools and American teachers learn from these findings? What justified
conclusions can we draw from them? What *un*justified conclusions should
we avoid?

Statistics

Students graduating from twelfth grade:	Japan	90%
	United States	77%
Average daily hours of homework during high school:	Japan	2.0
	United States	.5
Daily absentee rate:	Japan	very low
	United States	9%
Years required of high school mathematics:	Japan	3
	United States (typical)	1
Years required of foreign language (grades 7–12):	Japan	6
	United States	0–2
Engineering majors in undergraduate population:	Japan	20%
	United States	5%

The Setting

The country has few immigrants and minorities. The divorce and unemployment rates are low. Drug problems are minimal, and juvenile delinquency is not a serious problem. The national Ministry of Education sets standards and prescribes curriculum for the whole country. University entrance exams are extremely competitive; newsmagazines carry pages and pages of stories and statistics about the examinations.

WRITING WORKSHOP 2 Working with a group, test one debatable *generalization* about a current trend. Help plan and farm out different parts of the investigation: pooling personal experience of members of the group, arranging for firsthand observation, interviewing people in a position to know, or searching for published material. Help prepare a report that synthesizes the findings of the group. Test the generalization summed up in the following passage or a similar claim from an authoritative source.

Do women make better managers than men? According to a study by Marylee Bomboy of Cornell University, women are more effective in dealing with human relations and human interaction than men are. Female managers are likely to approach problem solving by considering the people and relationships involved, whereas men tend to approach the problem in terms of rules. Female supervisors are more likely to be rated "democratic" by employees; they are more aware than men of the need for creating a happy work environment.

PEER EDITOR 3 Study the generalizations in the following passages. On what level of generalization does the writer move? Which of the generalizations could you *support* with evidence of your own? Which would you *challenge*, and on what grounds? How would you scale down generalizations that are too sweeping?

1. Everywhere we see evidence of the new sobriety. Former martini drinkers drink white wine; former wine drinkers drink carrot juice; fraternities give parties without beer.
2. The turned-off, rebellious student questioning the educational establishment is an extinct species. Students today do not waste time arguing with a professor; they are eager to do what they are told.
3. We are all in favor of removing the traces of past discrimination. But the government has gone overboard in forcing the preferential hiring of minorities.
4. For the typical woman, divorce means financial insecurity and a lower standard of living.
5. Every week we read newspaper reports of college professors being challenged for teaching Marxist views. We are turning our colleges into centers of indoctrination in the Marxist view of economics and history.
6. Over and over we see movies that appeal to the vigilante mentality: First, we see a Charles Bronson type aroused by watching some ghastly unspeakable crime go unpunished; then we see him systematically hunt the criminals down.
7. The physical ideal for a woman in America today, I realized, was a man's body. The very curves and softness I had been trying to diet away were the natural qualities of a woman's body.
8. The TV manipulators of reality have discovered that Americans will trust anyone who is good-looking.
9. The mistakes of teachers are buried on the welfare rolls.
10. Never have as many people in our country lived openly in poverty and degradation.

11b   *log*   Arguing from Principle

Take your reader from accepted premises to justified conclusions.

Often a strong argument moves deductively from accepted assumptions to a triumphant *therefore*. When we reason deductively, we apply general principles to specific cases. We spell out basic assumptions or beliefs and show how they apply to a given situation. For instance, we may first spell out at what point pranks no longer express youthful exuberance but instead infringe on other people's rights. We then show how this principle applies to recent examples of Animal House-type behavior on campus.

Much argument on public issues applies legal or moral principles to specific questions of policy. Suppose you have become concerned by the current drive to revive the death penalty. In spite of strong arguments in its favor, capital punishment goes counter to some of your basic convictions. Writing a paper on the subject gives you a chance to sort out your thinking. You may decide to structure your argument as follows:

Thou Shalt Not

THESIS:

In spite of strong current arguments in favor of the death penalty, capital punishment violates several basic principles underlying the American system of justice.

first principle

Most basic to our legal system is our belief in even-handed justice. We believe that equal crimes should receive equal punishment. However, the death penalty has always been notorious for its "freakish unfairness." In the words of one study, "judicial safeguards for preventing the arbitrary administration of capital punishment are not working." Judges and juries apply widely differing standards. In one celebrated case, two partners in crime were convicted of the same capital crime on identical charges. One was executed; the other is in prison and will soon be eligible for parole.

second principle

We believe that all citizens are equal before the law. Justice should be "blind" to wealth, race, ethnic origin. However, poor defendants are many times more likely to receive the death penalty than wealthy ones, protected by highly paid teams of lawyers whose maneuvers stymie the prosecution and baffle the jury. Minority defendants convicted of capital crimes have a much higher statistical chance of being executed than white defendants.

third principle

Fairness demands that the judicial system make provision for correcting its own errors. If someone has been unjustly convicted, there should be a mechanism for reversing the verdict and setting the person free. However, in the case of the death penalty, such a correction of error is aborted. We are left with futile regrets, like the prosecutor who said, "Horrible as it is to contemplate, we may have executed the wrong man."

211

To give your paper an argumentative edge, keep your goal clearly in mind and pursue it in a determined manner. When trying to make a strong case, remember advice like the following:

(1) Pinpoint the issue. Focus the reader's attention on the point at issue. The issue should be an *open* issue—on which reasonable people have honest differences of opinion. The following passage effectively rekindles a current controversy:

The Right to Die

Does society have the legal right to force-feed aged or severely handicapped patients who are trying to end their pain-ridden lives? Should courts have the right to order life-prolonging surgery for infants doomed to a life of pain and severe retardation? Doctors have greatly extended their power to stave off death, but should there be limits on the use of this power? Should life be sustained by "heroic measures" and at any cost?

(2) Take a stand. What are you trying to prove? A strong argument needs a clear, well-supported thesis. The writer makes a definite claim or argues a definite **proposition**. (Remember that some arguments *lead up* to a strong final thesis.)

THESIS:	Maintaining the legal drinking age at 21 will save thousands of young lives every year.
THESIS:	Women have to ask for more than equal pay for equal work; they need to ask for comparable pay for work of comparable value.

(3) Examine your assumptions. If you start from shaky premises, your argument is likely to leave your reader behind. When you present an argument like the following, your readers may want to challenge your initial premise rather than your conclusion:

Students learn best in a relaxed, permissive atmosphere.
The present system of exams induces tensions and anxieties.
Therefore, exams work against true learning.

(But is it *true* that a relaxed atmosphere is best for learning? Do not at least some people perform better under pressure?)

Spell out **hidden premises**. Bringing unstated assumptions into the open forces you to take a good look at them. It gives your readers a chance to see what underlying assumptions they are asked to accept.

PREMISE:	Professor Metcalf is from a middle-class background.
CONCLUSION:	She cannot be expected to sympathize with the poor.
HIDDEN PREMISE:	(People cannot sympathize with someone from a different class?)

(4) Revise sweeping charges and exaggerated claims. Try to limit your claims to what you can support. For instance, modify or retract blanket charges. ("The average criminal is a brutal individual who deserves what he got.") Shelve cure-all remedies, or panaceas. ("To rid our streets of violent crime, we should lock up habitual criminals and throw the key away.")

(5) Take possible objections seriously. What counterarguments is the opposing side likely to offer? Can you refute them, showing their weaknesses, defusing potentially damaging charges? Suppose you are arguing that divorced fathers cut off from their children should more often be granted extended visiting rights or divided custody. Are you prepared for counterclaims that shuffling a child between homes has harmful effects? It would strengthen your case to anticipate this objection. If you can, cite authorities claiming that shared parenting arrangements demonstrate that both parents are devoted to their children.

Note: The generalizing, inductive kind of reasoning and the deductive kind that argues from principle are not mutually exclusive. They are both part of a larger overall picture and often go hand in hand. We generalize by finding the common element in related details or examples; that is, we proceed inductively. In turn, we apply our generalizations to specific instances; we make predictions on the basis of what we know. In other words, we reason deductively. The important thing for a successful argument is for us to show the reader how we moved from here to there, to help the reader follow.

FOR A DISCUSSION OF THE SYLLOGISM, SEE **11h**.

WRITING WORKSHOP 4   Suppose you were offered a chance to have the last word in a public discussion of one of the following issues, but time is limited. Team up with other members of a group; have each prepare a "closing statement" that would present his or her most important single argument on the issue. Have your group or your class as a whole discuss and evaluate the final arguments prepared by the group. Which seem forceful and why? Which seem weak and why? Have your group prepare arguments

- for or against school prayer
- for or against ROTC
- for or against marriage
- for or against fraternities and sororities
- for or against capital punishment
- for or against abolishing freshman English
- for or against keeping *Playboy* out of the campus bookstore
- for or against public financing of day-care centers
- for or against requiring students to have personal computers

PEER EDITOR 5   Which of the following passages makes you say, "I would like to argue this point"? Select one or more of these and prepare to argue for or against the point made in each passage. What would be your main argument or arguments? Where would you turn for support?

1. Many people realize that journalism is a business like any other. A television station structures its news programs to attract high ratings and well-paying sponsors. A newspaper packages its news so that it will attract buyers for the paper. The network or newspaper executive's job is the same as that of the corner grocer: to attract paying customers.

2. Negative views sit well with the public in the wake of two Presidents in a row—Carter and Reagan—who have campaigned "against Washington." Americans are by nature skeptical of authority and inclined to believe the worst about government. This makes an anti-Washington or anti-Big-Government campaign the easiest to sell to the voters.

3. On the subject of male nurses: If a man wants to be a nurse, let him find a job in a veterans' hospital. Men should confine their nursing to men only (or they should stay in man's work altogether). Women are by nature caretakers. We take care of family members when they are sick. In the end, we women take care of elderly patients. Men are too self-absorbed to provide care for others; a fair percentage of them are child molesters, wife beaters, serial murderers, and general all-around louses.

Weigh the arguments pro and con to reach a balanced conclusion.

In a systematic argument, we present our thinking or our reasoning on a subject in such a way that our readers can arrive at the same logical result as we did. One effective way to structure such writing is to line up the arguments on two sides of an issue. We first discuss the advantages of a proposal or a program, and then the disadvantages. We first present arguments in support of a new method or approach; then we look at possible objections. Ideally, as the strengths and weaknesses of the opposing arguments become apparent, a balanced conclusion will emerge that reasonable people can accept.

The successful **pro-and-con** paper is effective because it follows an exceptionally clear overall pattern. We expect that the arguments in the first half of the paper will all point in the same direction. Roughly halfway into the paper, a link like *however* or *nevertheless* or *on the other hand* will signal that it is time to turn to the arguments on the other side. Toward the end, we expect some phrase like "Weighing the arguments on both sides, we must conclude that. . . ." The writer is ready for summing up and balancing off the opposing arguments.

Here is how you might line up arguments for and against in a paper that moves from *on the one hand* to *on the other hand*:

Motorcycle Helmets

The Issue: Should protective helmets be required by law for all riders and passengers of motorcycles, motor scooters, mopeds, and any other two- or three-wheeled vehicles operated on public roads and highways?

Pros	Cons
1. Most motorcycle deaths and serious injuries are caused by injuries to the head. It is estimated that 20,000 lives could be saved nationally if all motorcycle drivers and passengers wore proper head protection.	1. Motorcycle riding in the open air is one of our last personal freedoms. If people choose to put themselves in harm's way there should be no law preventing it.

2. 86% of the cost of treating motorcycle injuries is ultimately borne by the State as motorcyclists typically don't have the insurance or resources to pay their own care—especially for head injuries where lengthy hospitalization and surgery are required.

3. Insurance rates could be reduced for both motorcyclists and auto drivers if costly medical care and legal assistance could be reduced.

4. California auto drivers are required by law to wear seatbelts—why not protective devices for motorcyclists?

5. Auto drivers need to be spared the personal, lifelong, responsibility for having seriously hurt or killed another in a collision when it could have been prevented by adequate protection.

2. Helmets make it difficult to hear sirens and other road noises and would actually make riding less safe except in a very serious accident.

3. Many motorcyclists are free spirits who find helmets needlessly restrictive. They enjoy the elements—the wind in their hair—too much to accept such a restrictive device as a helmet.

4. Helmets are not comfortable. They are hot, sweaty contraptions that are tight, ill-fitting, and plain uncomfortable.

5. Helmets are expensive. A good quality helmet costs $60 or more. Many motorcyclists are young people and students who can't afford such an expense.

6. Storing a helmet when not riding is a problem. Few motorcycles have a lockable storage area sufficient to hold a helmet.

Conclusion: All the reasons against requiring motorcycle helmets combined aren't worth the risk of a single life or the hurt and emotional pain of one auto driver who must live forever with the death or injury of another on his mind. The State has a vested interest in motorcycle safety since so many state dollars go for medical costs associated with accident injuries that are largely preventable. Driving a motorcycle, like an automobile, is a privilege, not a right. For that reason it is reasonable and appropriate to require helmets on all public roads.

Note that in writing a pro-and-con paper you may anticipate the outcome by stating your conclusion as your thesis early in the paper. This strategy takes away the suspense but shows that you know your destination. Or you may leave the issue open, involving your reader in the dialectic of conflicting claims, leading up to a balanced conclusion at the end.

To make a pro-and-con paper work, remember the following advice:

(1) Give roughly equal space to arguments on both sides. Even if you favor one side, show that you know and respect the arguments on the other side. Give credit for good intentions; recognize legitimate interests on either side of the issue.

(2) Avoid a strong judgmental tone. To make readers look at the issue rationally, lower the emotional thermostat. Try not to condemn or denounce; do not advertise the views you favor as those of all right-thinking Americans or truly responsible citizens.

(3) Avoid the brush-off effect. Revise passages where you might seem to be dismissing opposing views out of hand. ("This is another ridiculous proposal by our statehouse politicians." "Everyone knows that prison reform is a dead issue.")

WRITING PRACTICE 6   Choose a subject on which you hold strong opinions. Write a paragraph in which you describe as fully and as fairly as you can a point of view *different from or opposed to* yours. Sum up key arguments of the other side on a topic like registration of firearms, equal funding for women's sports, bilingual ballots, rent control, required courses outside your major, comparable pay, or resettlement of refugees in your community.

WRITING WORKSHOP 7   Working with a group or your class as a whole, explore the *pros and cons* of a current controversy. Have one team explore in depth and then present the arguments on the one side. Have a second team explore and present the arguments on the other side. Use the results as material for a group report or as background for your individual pro-and-con paper. Choose a topic like the following:

- Is compulsory drug testing compatible with American traditions of privacy?
- Are AIDS victims entitled to protection of their privacy? Should they be obligated to tell employers (or insurance companies) of the state of their

health? Are doctors and journalists justified in revealing the cause of death of prominent AIDS victims?

■ Are the institutions of American democracy incompatible with secret intelligence activities, or "covert operations"? Do Americans have faith in or are they distrustful of agencies like the CIA? Do they condone or condemn the secrecy and deceit of intelligence work?

WRITING TOPICS 11

In writing on one or more of the following topics, aim at a reader who is wary of hasty generalizations and sweeping claims. Show that you respect the intelligence of your audience—rely on convincing evidence and sound argument to influence your readers.

1. A well-known critic of American society said some years ago, "there get to be fewer jobs that are necessary or unquestionably useful; that require energy and draw on some of one's best capacities; and that can be done keeping one's honor and dignity." Test these generalizations against what you know and can find out.

2. Take a stand on an issue of current interest to students on your campus. What principles apply? On what principle are you going to take your stand? Argue your position and support it with appropriate evidence, ranging from personal experience and firsthand observation to authoritative sources. Choose an issue like the following:

   ■ Should students be forced to pay fees that support intercollegiate athletics—in particular, college football?

   ■ Should college bookstores be required to remove *Playboy* and *Penthouse* from their shelves?

   ■ Should colleges be required to offer equal support for men's and women's sports?

   ■ Does official recognition or support for fraternities and sororities constitute discrimination against students not affiliated with Greek organizations?

   ■ Should doctors, teachers, or counselors be obligated to pass on serious confidential information they have obtained from minors to their parents?

3. Write a pro-and-con paper about an issue on which there is something to be said on both sides. Do justice to arguments for and against. Aim at a balanced conclusion that will persuade a reasonable, well-informed reader. (You may want to state your conclusion as your thesis early in your paper, or you may want to lead up to it at the end.) Choose a topic like the following:

    ■ Should citizens have the right to use arms in defending themselves against attackers or intruders?

    ■ Should a major aim of instruction in the public schools be to promote one common national language?

    ■ Should expressways and freeways have special lanes reserved for buses and cars carrying several passengers?

    ■ Should government agencies be barred from damming the last remaining wild rivers?

    ■ Should government agencies be barred from helping finance abortions for the poor?

    ■ Should local governments be allowed to bar the homeless from their communities?

    ■ Should drug testing be compulsory for people holding sensitive jobs?

11d   *log*   Cause and Effect

Explain things by tracing causes and their effects.

We often feel we understand something after we see what caused it. As writers, it is often our task to trace a chain from cause to effect. In analyzing a problem, we often try to identify the causes that helped create it. Our readers will want to know: "What brought this on? What caused the present situation?" Once we sort out the major causes (or identify the main cause), our readers might be ready to listen to a possible solution.

The following might be preliminary notes for a **cause-and-effect** paper that goes beyond surface symptoms to underlying causes and then suggests possible remedies:

Hotheads and Short Fuses

Symptoms

A professor drives his car back to campus in the evening to pick up papers at his office. He is unable to avoid hitting a jaywalker who suddenly appears in front of his car. The incensed jaywalker drags the driver out of the car while the car careens wildly across the street and smashes into the shop window of a boutique.

After a narrow victory over a traditional rival in a championship football game, the celebrating fans rock and overturn cars driven by supporters of the visiting team; one car is set afire; dozens of people are hurt.

At a local school, vandals spray paint library books and walls and scatter records, causing $50,000 worth of damage.

Causes

According to zoologists, primates mark their territories by scent or visual display; humans similarly "leave their mark" on territory they are otherwise unable to control.

Gangs that vandalize schools or public property as a group effort reinforce their sense of mutual loyalty, producing a stronger degree of "social bonding."

Much "unprovoked" individual violence is caused by people striking back at a threatening or frustrating environment. An oppressive or frustrating environment produces pent-up anger. Anger causes people to lash out, often at the wrong target. People who feel thwarted or hemmed in strike back at others who they rightly or wrongly feel are invading their turf.

Cures

Traditional Response: Nebuchadnezzar tried to counteract vandalism by issuing edicts against the defacement of temples in Babylon. We try to discourage misbehavior by public outcry, threats of punishment—with dubious results.

Modern Behavior Modification: Psychologists ask us to think about the underlying psychological mechanisms that precipitate (or prevent) violent and destructive behavior. One landscape architect in Seattle wraps newly planted trees in gauze. The gauze bandage, suggesting something wounded or vulnerable, is designed to produce a caring rather than a destructive response.

The following might be a sentence outline of a magazine article on what has happened to the traditional family. The article would first trace major factors that have helped weaken the traditional structure of family life. It would then sort out some of the most important effects or results:

The Family Out of Favor

THESIS: Many forces in modern society weaken family ties and make people lose the traditional benefits of family life.

I.   Many forces in modern society weaken or work against the traditional family unit.
   A.   In our upwardly mobile society, success often means opportunities for travel and entertainment from which families are excluded.
   B.   The modern city, cut up by freeways and requiring long commuting hours, has lost the network of small local stores and local services that provided the framework for traditional family life.
   C.   To many modern individuals, self-fulfillment means liberation from traditional ties and obligations.
   D.   The mass media play up divorce statistics and play down the large number of lifelong marriages that continue to exist.
II.   The independent modern individual pays a price for the loss of traditional family ties.
   A.   Many people lack the sense of trust and belonging that children used to acquire in a closely knit family.
   B.   Many people today lack the network of kinship ties that used to be a source of economic and political support for many immigrant families.
   C.   People outside the large traditional family do not experience the process of conflict and reconciliation that teaches mutual tolerance and mutual adjustment.

Note: Be prepared to recognize *several* major causes. We would often like to find one root cause (and thereby simplify the matter). But in many situations, we have to recognize that several major factors may have contributed to a combined result.

WRITING WORKSHOP 8   On subjects like acid rain, erosion, lowered groundwater levels, or the deteriorating infrastructure, we encounter much writing that is long on finger pointing, scapegoating, or preaching but short on analysis of *cause and effect*. On one of these or on a similar topic, find a one-page or two-page excerpt from an article (or textbook) that seems a model for informative and helpful analysis of causes and effects. Present your find to members of a small group or to your class as a whole.

| **11e** | *log* | Eliminating Alternatives |

Arrive at the right or desirable solution by eliminating unsatisfactory alternatives.

An argument designed to lead the reader to the right conclusion often does so by eliminating undesirable alternatives. A writer might ask what can be done to reduce or eliminate sexual harassment on the job, including the many forms of belittling, condescension, and unwanted familiarity that many women object to. The writer might first take a detailed look at two familiar current remedies: 1) *rules* and regulations of all kinds—guidelines, ordinances, and the like; 2) *litigation*—lawsuits against employers, organizations, fellow workers. After showing the causes of her dissatisfaction with these two approaches, the writer might then go on to a more lasting solution: 3) *education*—ways to change the attitudes and expectations of a new generation.

We often have to *lead up* to our own solution by showing what is wrong with the conventional wisdom. By showing the limitations of the tried-but-only-half-true, we at the same time establish our credentials as writers. We show our familiarity with the issue, with familiar problems and suggested solutions.

The following might be the general scheme for a paper looking at alternative solutions to the overcrowding and obsolescence of the nation's system of prisons. The writer first takes a strongly negative look at two familiar solutions and then goes on to champion a third:

Too Late for Reform?

I. The traditional solution to the state of our overcrowded, dilapidated, understaffed prisons is to call for more maximum-security institutions where criminals can be warehoused and forgotten.

II. For lack of construction funds, what happens in practice is that prisoners jailed last year under "tough" sentencing laws are paroled or released early to provide even minimal space for this year's offenders.

III. The best hope for the future is the extension of programs that make possible some meaningful contribution or restitution by the offender, such as the fire camp program called by a Chief Justice one of the "best examples of productive incarceration."

PEER REVIEW 9   Study the following student paper and prepare an *outline*
for it. Ask yourself questions like the following:

- What is the problem to which the alternatives examined in this paper
  are the solutions?
- Which alternatives are found wanting, and why?
- Which alternatives does the writer endorse, and why?
- What transitional sentences or phrases help us see the overall pattern of
  the argument?
- Where has the author turned for material?
- Which parts of this paper are for you most striking and effective? Which
  least?

The Dilemma of Prison Reform

In earlier times, serious crimes were often dealt with by physical
punishments such as branding or mutilation. The ultimate punishment
was dispensed in very harsh forms, including burning, beheading, hanging, and crucifixion. Compared to these older forms of punishment, our
present system of imprisonment appears much more humane. However,
the cruel realities of detention in today's dehumanized prisons are almost as harsh and inhumane as the older forms of dealing with law-
breakers.

Few people on the outside can imagine what it is like to be locked
up for 24 hours day after day, and what a person in that situation goes
through both mentally and physically. The smells are by far the worst.
The fetid air with its odor of sweat, vomit, and urine seems to press in
on the visitor. Couple that with the ever-present undercurrent of violence
and the terrible noise of a large cellblock and the result is a slow torture
that is equal to anything that our ancestors inflicted.

What are the alternatives? Most of the literature written on penal
reform agrees on one basic point: The system fails to rehabilitate most
of the convicts, and an ex-convict is very likely to return to prison. The
most common complaint about rehabilitation programs in today's prisons is that the trades or skills taught are often unrealistic or outdated. In
one case, a prison in New York State provided prisoners with a course
in driving diesel trucks. The course was very popular and received support from local charity organizations. The irony of the situation was that,
once released, the ex-convicts found that the law barred them from
acquiring a Class 1 driver's license for more than five years in most cases.

Other countries have tried different approaches to rehabilitation. In
the province of Saskatchewan, in Canada, offenders have been allowed
to work off their fines. Another alternative to serving time is a system

that has been tried in Ottawa. This system is called diversion. In cases eligible for diversion, court proceedings may be halted if offender and victim agree on a settlement, as they do in the great majority of such cases. The offender pays his debt, in cash or work, to the individual victim or the community. The problem with such alternatives to incarceration is that public opinion in this country today pushes judges and parole boards in the opposite direction: The cry is for "getting tough" with criminals, for more prison sentences rather than fewer.

A system tried in Israel promises a solution to the problem of violence in prisons and fights among prisoners and to the sense of futility and lack of motivation that defeats many attempts at re-education and rehabilitation. The system divides the prison population into three groups, each with separate housing and differing privileges. The best-behaved prisoners are in the first group. Their privileges include longer visiting hours, the use of regular rooms to receive visitors, and unlimited movement within the prison. The second group has fewer privileges; the third group, the most violent, has the least.

The prisoners under this system are governed by the use of immediate rewards for good behavior according to a point system, and a prisoner can move from one group to another based on the accumulation of points. The system has caused violence to decrease as the result of the segregation of inmates and of the privileged prisoners' fear of losing their privileges.

Obviously prison reform is not a simple matter. What disturbs me is that in spite of the reports of numerous commissions and panels, few true reforms have been implemented in our overcrowded jails. Our record of failure makes me wonder whether our government is capable of dealing with more than the two or three popular issues that splash across the headlines during an election year.

11f   *log* | Yes, but

Establish areas of agreement before you disagree with the reader.

Often we have no chance to make our views prevail unless we counter strongly held opposing views first. One strategy for dealing with opposing views is the "Yes, but" style of argument—we acknowledge opposing arguments and meet the opposition part of the way. We concede what is true and reasonable in the opposing view—before we show what is really wrong with it.

Study the way the student writer implemented the "Yes, but" approach in the following paper. Ask yourself: Why did the writer use the "Yes, but" approach for this particular topic? How does she dramatize the issue? What are the three major applications of the "Yes, but" approach in her paper? (How do you react to this argument? Do you think it would sway a member of the NRA? Why or why not?)

The Law of the Gun

When a famous person is assassinated—President Kennedy, Martin Luther King, John Lennon—lawmakers for a time seem ready to make guns less accessible and more easily tracked. But soon we forget, and the powerful National Rifle Association is able to weaken or defeat laws aimed at more effective gun control.

One person who has been unable to forget is Sarah Brady, whose husband Jim suffered permanent brain damage when he was shot during an assassination attempt on President Reagan. As an outspoken member of Handgun Control, Inc., she has pointed out that John Hinckley, the would-be assassin, purchased his gun in a Dallas pawnshop with no difficulty. "Had there been a waiting period or background check," she says, "Hinckley would not have been able to get that gun."

It seems to be evident enough that, as the NRA claims, "guns don't kill people; people kill people." But because of the easy availability of guns, it is very easy for people to kill people with guns. In high school, a new boy enrolled one day, and within a week, everyone had heard that the reason he was so quiet was that a year earlier he had accidentally killed his brother with a gun. A week ago, we woke up to the news that a paroled murderer had held several people hostage in a downtown apartment and had shot and killed his girlfriend during the siege. Ten years ago, the same man had gunned down his wife in the parking lot of a hospital.

I am well aware that there are many people in the country who use guns and are not cold-blooded murderers. My brother learned to hunt from my grandfather. He respects not only his guns but the land on which he hunts and the animals that he stalks. He lives a simple life, subsisting on the vegetables he grows and the game he hunts. Laws intended to keep guns out of the hands of people like John Hinckley will not interfere with his lifestyle.

But, to hear the NRA tell it, anyone who wants to make the purchasing of a gun at least as serious a proposition as buying a car or applying for a credit card is intent on taking away my brother's means of survival. One gun enthusiast I knew had NRA magazines piled up next to his bed alongside his chemistry textbooks. He used to study the ads for mail-order guns the way house-bound gardeners study seed catalogs in January. Playing on the analogy of guns as a symbol of freedom, the NRA has perpetuated a scenario of a Communist takeover easily accomplished because the conquerors obtain the lists that tell them about everyone who has had to register a gun. Many gun enthusiasts truly believe that they are keeping America free for democracy and that to register their guns is to endanger our freedom.

Closer to home, many people feel that they have to have guns to protect their businesses or their families against armed intruders. It is true that every so often we read about an outraged citizen shooting down a burglar who brandished a gun. But police officers will tell you that most of the guns used by criminals were stolen by burglars in the homes of citizens who believe in the "right to bear arms."

WRITING WORKSHOP 10   On an issue that is currently generating much heated discussion, prepare two short presentations of your point of view—one in an assertive, aggressive style and one in the "Yes, but" mode. Try both out on members of a small group. Have them record their reactions. Possible topics might include abortion, sexual harassment, sex on TV, police treatment of rape victims, or pit bulls.

11g   *def*   Definition

Trace the basic meaning or the most important ramifications of an important term.

The success of an argument often hinges on our ability to clarify important terms. What do we mean by "rehabilitation" when we argue about prison reform? What does the term *elitist* mean when it is applied to education? Before we can make up our minds on an issue, we often need a clearer understanding of the key terms that seem to sum up conflicting positions or opposing goals. A **definition** paper can help the reader see the common element in different and confusing uses of the same word. Or it can make the reader see the different uses that make a word vague or confusing.

Your major purpose in defining a term can help you shape the organization of a definition paper:

(1) Show the common denominator that underlies different uses or meanings of the same word. For instance, you may want to pin down the basic common element that is present when we hear the label *permissive* applied in many different areas of our society. You could sum up the common element early in your paper. You could then devote major sections of your paper to the application of the word in several major areas of contemporary American life.

(2) Analyze key elements that together determine the meaning of a term. Sometimes a single criterion or requirement furnishes the central clue. More often, several key requirements combine to help us stake out the full meaning. The following excerpts are from a magazine article explaining key ingredients of the conservative temperament:

The True Conservatism

One autumn Saturday afternoon I was listening to the radio when the station switched to the Dartmouth-Harvard game. The game had not begun, and the announcer was rambling on about the nip in the air, the autumn colors, past games, this year's players, their names and hometowns. . . . Autumn, a new crop of players, New England: The world was **on a steady keel** after all. I could not remember having felt that **quiet sense of cycle**, of ongoing life and **the past** floating so serenely to the surface, in a long time.

That morning, anyway, I felt like a conservative. . . .

Two elementary attitudes underlie the conservative tradition. **The first** is a passionate sense of the need to conserve—the land, the culture, the institutions, codes of behavior—and to revere and protect those elements that constitute "civilization." The conservative looks to the enduring values of the past. . . .

The second attitude is a cautious view of raw democracy, or direct representational government. The conservative believes firmly in the rights of minorities and those institutions that protect minorities from the whims of the majority, such as the Supreme Court—an elite, appointed body—and the Constitution, particularly the First Amendment. . . . These institutions that restrain the mass will are precious in the conservative view, not just because they protect the few from being trampled by the many, but also because they protect the majority from its own mistakes. . . .

An outgrowth of these attitudes—and one with particular value—is the humor that the skeptical turn of the conservative mind can bring to bear on confused, disaster-prone but unreservedly grand schemes for the betterment of mankind. . . .   Susannah Lessard, "Civility, Community, Humor: The Conservatism We Need," *The Washington Monthly*

(3) Clarify an important term by marking it off from related terms that cover similar ground. We often introduce a new concept by contrasting it with a related familiar term. In the following excerpt, the student writer defines a controversial new term by contrasting it with a more familiar idea:

Calibrating the Wage Scales

Single women know how difficult it is to make ends meet on the salaries offered to women holding predominantly female jobs. When women suggest that comparable pay for jobs of equal value should supplant the current system of pay equity for the same job, they shake the foundations of the male establishment in this country. . . .

Pay equity, the system under which employment law currently functions, guarantees equal pay for equal work, and it is protected by existing antitrust and civil rights legislation. As long as female and male cashiers or truck drivers or supervisors are paid the same, employers have obeyed the law. . . .

Comparable worth, on the other hand, would require equal pay for work of equal value. In the words of Jane Bryant Quinn, writing in *Newsweek*, it would require "equal pay for jobs that, although different from those held by men, call for a comparable amount of knowledge, skill, effort, and responsibility." Every study indicates that the more an occupation, no matter how valuable or important to society, is dominated by women, the less it tends to pay. . . .

Legally, pay equity is much more clear-cut than comparable worth. What is the relative value of brains and brawn, education and experience, indoor work and outdoor work? How do we compare the value of a secretary's work with that of a garbage collector? . . .

Nevertheless, women need ways to advance economically without taking on "men's work." Like many others, I have tried taking on "different" jobs with unpromising results. For five months during the rainy season, I lifted fifty-pound bundles of newspapers and threw the Sunday edition. . . .

(4) Show how the history of a term helps explain its current uses. Major sections of your paper could show the most important stages in the development of the word. The following outline shows three major stages in the development of the word *democracy*:

We the People

THESIS: Over the centuries, the term *democracy* has moved away from its original Greek meaning of direct rule by the people.

I. Ideally, democracy gives people a direct voice and vote in the common business of the community.
   A. The Greek beginnings
   B. Early town meetings
II. In practice, participation in the political process is often indirect and ineffectual.
   A. Parliamentary democracy
   B. Checks and balances
III. In modern "popular democracies," an authoritarian leadership claims to exercise power in the name of the people.

In practice, an **extended definition** will often require a combination of approaches. Suppose that you have become interested in stereotypes and contradictory associations that cluster around the term *feminism*. In group discussion, you have an opportunity to compare brainstorming notes with material collected by others. Your group may decide to set up a **discovery frame** covering the range of questions that seem particularly productive for this topic. Look at sample materials that students in one group contributed under each heading. (In writing your own paper on this topic, would you use the major headings in their present order, or would you reshuffle them for a somewhat different strategy?)

Feminism

1. *Surface Meaning:* What popular associations cluster around this term? What stereotypes does it bring to mind?

    When people hear the term *feminism*, the stereotypical women's libber image may flash through their minds. They may picture tough-looking, loud, boisterous man-haters, with unshaven legs and no makeup.

2. *Historical Background:* What do you know about the history of the movement? What are some famous names and events associated with it? Who are some outstanding women who symbolize feminist ideals?
    - women's suffrage movement: campaigning for women's right to vote (Susan B. Anthony, Elizabeth Cady Stanton)
    - tie-in with abolitionist movement: Sojourner Truth at the Women's Rights Convention in 1851
    - symbolic figures: Amelia Earhart was the first woman to pilot a plane across the Atlantic. Outstanding athletes: Florence Chadwick (swam the English Channel), Wilma Rudolph (runner)

3. *Media Coverage:* How do the media reflect changing attitudes? What images of women are projected by current movies, TV shows, advertising?

Increasingly, in order to cash in on the large female market, the media cater to the image of the confident woman who is in control of her life. However, the images they project are often *ambiguous* (or dishonest?): The female pilot has the hair and smile of a Clairol model and advertises deodorant.

4. *Personal Experience:* Where have the issues raised by the feminist movement played a role in your own life? How can you relate the term to your own experience?
   ■ I grew up with many girls whose parents were leading them down the road to housewifery, motherhood, or menial jobs by not urging them on to excel the way they did their sons. When the brother went out for varsity sports, the sister became a cheerleader. I remember being the only girl in my trigonometry class.

5. *Related or Contrasting Terms:* What similar terms or near-synonyms come up in discussions of feminism? What opposite terms—or antonyms—can help clarify the term?
   ■ similar or related terms: women's rights, women's liberation, the women's movement; emancipation—setting free from slavery or restraints
   ■ contrasting terms: sexism, chauvinism; patriarchy—a society or way of life where the male "father figure" rules

6. *The Common Denominator:* What is the core meaning of the term?

   A feminist need not be female but could be anyone—male or female—who believes in equal rights for both sexes. Feminism as a movement is designed to help women discover their own powers and their own self-worth. Its aim is to help women achieve equality in all areas of life—private, artistic, social, economic, and political.

Consider the following when trying to strengthen your definition paper:

■ **Learn to clarify possibly confusing terms in passing:**

Medicine and *neurology*—the teasing, endless puzzle of how the brain controls our every thought and activity—has captivated me to this day.   Roger Bannister

■ **Try to sum up the meaning of a key term in a one-sentence definition. A formal definition** first places a term in a larger class and then spells out distinctive features. It presents two kinds of information: First, we sum up what makes the term to be defined part of a larger group, or **class**. Then we spell out distinctive features that set off, or differentiate, the term from other members of the same class.

TERM	CLASS	FEATURES
Oligarchy	is a form of government	in which power lies in the hands of a few.
A martyr	suffers persecution	for refusing to renounce his or her faith.
To double-cross	is to betray someone	whom we have deliberately impressed with our trustworthiness or loyalty.

Note: To make a formal definition informative, you may have to take precautions. If the general class is too shapeless, it will not start focusing your reader's attention. (Classifying an epic as "a type of literature" is less helpful than classifying it as "a long narrative poem.") The specific qualities you list may not be specific enough. (A patriot is "a person who promotes the best interests of the country," but we more specifically apply the term to those who do so *unselfishly*—not for gain or personal glory.) Finally, your definition may not make allowance for important exceptions. (A senator is "an elected representative of a state"—but some senators are not elected but appointed to fill a vacant seat.)

■ **Use a dictionary definition only if it will make your reader think.** Do not start with a dictionary definition only to delay your own investigation. Make sure the definition you quote raises a key issue or sums up an important point. A dictionary definition like the following goes to the heart of the matter (but many are much more colorless or perfunctory):

genocide   "the deliberate and systematic destruction of a racial, political, or cultural group"   *Webster's Ninth New Collegiate Dictionary*

Often the side trip to the dictionary tells readers only what they already know. Trying to define "social justice," you will gain little by quoting a definition of *justice* as the "quality of being just, impartial, or fair."

WRITING PRACTICE 11   In each of the following sentences, a writer clarifies a technical or specialized term. What makes each of these informal *capsule definitions* informative or helpful? What do you learn that you didn't know before? Write five similar capsule definitions, choosing technical or specialized terms from a range of different fields.

1. Brief definition of a psychologist's or sociologist's term:

> People with Type A personalities—those uptight, compulsive, competitive, aggressive, sometimes hostile, insecure overachievers—can greatly reduce their chances for a heart attack by modifying their behavior.

2. Capsule definition of a current issue or problem:

> One of the most stubborn environmental problems continues to be acid rain—the chemical-laden precipitation that has already browned or defoliated vast stretches of forest in the eastern United States and Europe and is spreading throughout the industrialized world.

3. Summary of a scientific theory or prediction:

> The theory of nuclear winter—the deadly worldwide blockage of the sun's rays that would follow an atomic conflict—was first presented to a conference in October 1983.

PEER EDITOR 12 Which of the following student-written sentences are good examples of *formal definitions*? What makes them accurate, informative, or useful? Which of the definitions fall short, and why?

1. Privacy is the privilege of having one's personal belongings, space, and thoughts free from intrusion.
2. Islam is the religion of the Muslims and is widely practiced in the Near East.
3. A referendum is a method of giving the public a voice in political decisions.
4. A sorority is a private association that provides separate dormitory facilities with a distinct Greek letter name for selected female college students.
5. Conformity is the adjustment from a unique individual state of being to a more socially acceptable, clonelike existence.
6. Ecology is the study of the closely webbed interrelationships between organisms and their environment.
7. Initiative is a personal quality that makes people attempt new and difficult things.
8. Pacifism is the belief that disputes between nations can and should be settled without war.
9. Jazz is a form of strongly rhythmic music played by black musicians.
10. Due process is a traditional set of legal procedures that protect us against swift and arbitrary punishment.

WRITING PRACTICE 13 Write formal *one-sentence definitions* for five of the following terms:

censorship	human rights	expediency	primaries
dictatorship	avant-garde	jury trial	pollution
soap opera	Peace Corps	Puritanism	bigotry
evolution			

WRITING PRACTICE 14 Write a *two-paragraph paper* in which you draw the line between two overlapping terms. Devote one paragraph to each term. Choose a pair like the following:

- privacy and secrecy
- dissent and disobedience
- justified force and violence
- authoritarian and totalitarian
- justice and getting even
- love and infatuation
- love and a relationship

WRITING WORKSHOP 15 Working with a group or with your class as a whole, prepare a preliminary collection of material for an extended definition of a term important to an understanding of contemporary American life. Your group may decide to choose a term like *permissiveness, pluralism, multiethnic, neoconservatism, assimilation, the work ethic, prejudice, fundamentalism,* or *women's rights.* Have the members of the group pool their answers to the questions in the following discovery frame. Use the resulting material as background for a possible definition paper.

1. *Surface Meaning:* What common associations cluster around the term? What images does it bring to mind? What popular misconceptions or stereotypes does it bring into play?
2. *History:* What are the historical roots of the term? What is the derivation of the word? When and how was it first used? What stages did it go through?
3. *Media Coverage:* When and where do you see the term in print? Has it recently been in news coverage? Does it appear as a theme in current movies or television entertainment? Does it play a role in a current controversy?

4. *Personal Experience:* What has been your own firsthand experience with permissiveness, or the work ethic, or prejudice? What incidents have you witnessed, and what have you learned from them?

5. *Related Terms:* What related terms cover similar ground? How does the word differ from its synonyms? What opposed terms, or antonyms, help bring the term into focus?

6. *Major Applications:* Does the word have several major different meanings or uses? Are they related?

7. *Common Denominator:* Is there a common strand in the different uses and applications of the term? What is the clue to its central meaning?

WRITING TOPICS 12

1. Write a paper in which you *analyze major causes* (or one single major cause) for one of the following. (Make a list of possible or alleged causes for preliminary class discussion.)
   - unsafe city streets
   - athletic success
   - long-lasting marriages
   - depression among young people
   - charges of sexual harassment
   - sexual discrimination
   - high divorce rates
   - the success of recent blockbuster movies
   - popularity of television personalities

2. Write a paper in which you critically *examine alternatives* in order to lead up to the one you consider most desirable or satisfactory. Choose one of the following topics:
   - relieving traffic congestion
   - combating sexual harassment
   - promoting equal employment opportunities for minorities
   - reducing vandalism at public schools or crime on campus
   - securing better pay for women
   - replacing the traditional family
   - reducing drug abuse among young people
   - countering violent or extremely rude behavior

3. Do you hold any unpopular views? On an issue on which you have a strong opinion, are you aware of powerful objections or strong opposing arguments? Take on the opposition, using a *"Yes, but" approach.*

4. Choose a key term from an area about which you can write as an insider. Write an *extended definition* that would initiate the newcomer or outsider. Choose a term like the following: *high tech, aerobics, human rights, environmentalism, vegetarian, modern dance, punk.*

5. Which of the following is for you more than just a cliché? Write an *extended definition* that shows your readers why the term is important. Aim at the common element that underlies different uses of the term, or at its most important different or related meanings.

consumerism	born-again Christians	sibling rivalry
assimilation	equal opportunity	teacher burnout
pluralism	law and order	privacy
permissiveness	bureaucracy	bigotry
the work ethic	computer literacy	police brutality

11h   *log*   Logical Fallacies

Revise for faulty logic and common logical fallacies.

Guides to straight thinking have traditionally been filled with advice on how *not* to think. These guides to applied logic catalogue the most common **logical fallacies**—common kinds of defective thinking that skew our reasoning. Guidelines for thinking straight warn us of our tendency to

- leap to conclusions
- look for simple solutions to complex problems
- find scapegoats for what went wrong
- mount investigations that lead to foregone results

Much of our reasoning in a systematic argument proceeds from basic assumptions—from what we assume to be true or known—to conclusions they justify. We call the assumptions from which we start the **premises** of our argument. The kind of reasoning that takes us from accepted premises to justified conclusions is deductive reasoning, or **deduction**.

Just as we tend to move too fast from an isolated example to a general conclusion, so we tend to move too fast when applying a general principle to specific instances. Much deductive reasoning can be charted as a three-step argument, called a **syllogism**:

FIRST PREMISE: All executives of the company are nephews of the founder.
SECOND PREMISE: Biff Malone is an executive of the company.
CONCLUSION: He must be a nephew of the founder.

FIRST PREMISE: This fraternity admits no roundheaded Irishmen.
SECOND PREMISE: I am a roundheaded Irishman.
CONCLUSION: I am not eligible for this fraternity.

If the premises are true and the deduction logical, the conclusion is valid. Remember the following advice:

(1) Distinguish between necessary and only probable conclusions. In all of the above examples, the conclusion necessarily follows because the first premise applies to *all* members of a group—it includes or rules out all members of a group. Arguments that use *some* or *many* in the first premise are much less airtight. They are not true syllogisms; at best, they lead to a *probable* conclusion:

FIRST PREMISE: *Most* members of the Achievement Club are business majors.
SECOND PREMISE: Linda is a member of the Achievement Club.
CONCLUSION: Linda is **probably** a business major.

(2) Do not read too much into your premises. Even when a premise uses a term like *all, no,* or *only,* you can easily draw unjustified conclusions. The word *all* includes all members of a group, but it does not *exclude* members of other groups; it often means "all these—and maybe others." When you overlook this nonexclusive nature of the word, you may be headed for a familiar kind of shortcut reasoning:

FIRST PREMISE: All Marxists read the works of Karl Marx.
SECOND PREMISE: My political science professor constantly quotes Marx.
CONCLUSION: She must be a Marxist.

A rough chart of possible readers of Karl Marx will help you avoid this kind of **false syllogism**:

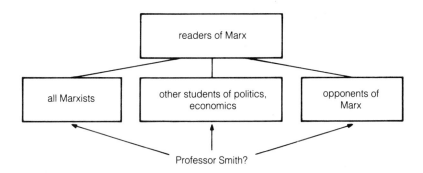

(3) Avoid circular arguments. Some arguments merely circle back to the initial assumptions. **Circular arguments** *seem* to move from premise to conclusion, but in fact they tread water:

CIRCULAR: True ability will always assert itself.
             People of true ability see to it that their talents are recognized.
             Therefore, true ability will not want for recognition.

SEE 11b FOR HIDDEN PREMISES.

Much shortcut thinking illustrates familiar fallacies—kinds of false logic seductive enough to make them hard to resist. Avoid the following among others:

HASTY GENERALIZATION   If you are insulted and abused twice in one week by a person from Lithuania, you are likely to conclude (too hastily) that Lithuanians tend to be arrogant.

FOREGONE CONCLUSIONS   It is human nature to bypass contradictory evidence and to favor instead the evidence that reinforces a foregone conclusion. If you share a widespread prejudice against bureaucrats, you are likely to pounce gleefully on all evidence of bureaucratic bungling. You are likely to ignore or overlook useful bureaucratic activities, such as blocking the sale of a drug with disastrous side effects. If you are prejudiced against woman drivers, you are likely to pounce gleefully on every instance of a female motorist in trouble, ignoring the accidents and near-accidents caused by males.

OVERSIMPLIFICATION We are partial to the quick fix; we welcome the quick and simple answer to a complicated problem. Why is public transportation in such a sorry state? Why so many complaints about stalled commuter trains, late buses, or abandoned routes? One answer may well be the economic interests of car makers and oil companies. But we **oversimplify** if we ignore other factors. For instance, many people stubbornly use their own cars, braving congestion and pollution.

FALSE DILEMMA A true dilemma puts us in a tight spot and leaves us only two ways out—both bad. A true dilemma faces medical researchers conducting animal experiments. Should they heed advocates of animal rights and abandon experiments that torture laboratory animals? Or should they continue experiments that promise to benefit suffering human beings? A **false dilemma** sets up a bad situation with only two ways out—while the author tries to block our view of a third. A false dilemma is often set up by people who want to push us toward an *either-or* choice. A developer might argue that the only alternative to further deterioration of a downtown area is to raze the area and rebuild. A third way out, tried successfully elsewhere, might be restoration and selective renovation. Many an "either-or" choice presented to us turns out to be a false dilemma.

POST HOC FALLACY We tend to look for immediate, easily observable causes. We read about empty beer cans in the backseat of a car that smashed into a tree; these become a satisfying clue to why the accident occurred. *Post hoc ergo propter hoc*—Latin for "It happened *after* this; therefore, it happened *because* of this." Often, the *post hoc* fallacy makes us overlook more distant causes, or combined causes that work together to produce a result. Perhaps the beer cans had been in the car for some time, and the driver had a stroke. Someone gets married after the future spouse is left a trust fund—cause and effect? An office worker develops headaches after the company installs a new computer—cause and effect? Remember that political, economic, or medical conditions are often the result of combined causes, perhaps with roots in the distant past.

FALSE ANALOGY A writer may compare the federal budget to a family budget in order to warn us against excessive debts or to promote the idea of a balanced budget. This analogy will sooner or later *break down:* A family cannot print money. It cannot raise taxes or implement policies that affect supply and demand. To make an analogy convincing, we have to trace the comparison through various related key features. Is the current world banking crisis similar to the situation that produced a crash in the thirties? If we were to answer yes, we would have to show several strong parallels.

RATIONALIZATION   When we rationalize, we find comforting explanations for things that are unwelcome or unflattering. We find an explanation that will put us, or people close to us, in a better light: "I did poorly in algebra because the teacher did not like people from the South." (Therefore my possible lack of ability or effort is no longer the issue.) "Ambitious foreign-aid projects are often wasted when local populations are too backward to work with modern technology." (By blaming the locals, we absolve ourselves of charges of poor planning.)

AD HOMINEM   **Ad hominem** attacks, directed "at the person," shift attention from the issues to the personal lives of their advocates. Slurs aimed at a person's ethnic origin, marital history, sexual preference, or psychiatric record boomerang with a responsible audience. (Sometimes, of course, the person's honesty or personal competence *is* the issue.)

BANDWAGON   When we are told that "everybody thinks so" or "everybody uses it," it is hard to swim against the tide. But the majority may of course be wrong.

SCAPEGOATING   When things go wrong, we tend to look for a convenient scapegoat. When a plane crashes, a train derails, a nuclear plant melts down, or a ship sinks to the bottom of the sea, it is easier to blame the person at the helm than to reevaluate safety margins for equipment or to reexamine established procedures. (It is of course quite possible that a single individual's "human error" played a large role.)

SEE **12b** FOR PERSUASIVE TECHNIQUES OFTEN LISTED AS LOGICAL FALLACIES.

PEER EDITOR 16   How sound is the logic in each of the following arguments? How sound are the premises? (Are there unstated premises?) What kind of logic is at work? How would you argue in *support* of the writer? On what grounds would you *challenge* the writer?

1. The main argument used by those, like myself, who believe in the existence of extraterrestrial civilizations is statistical. There are billions of suns. Some of these suns must have planets. As for these planets, the statistical chances are that some of them are habitable.

2. Public colleges are financed through taxes. They should therefore provide the kind of education that a majority of the taxpayers want them to provide.
3. Alcoholism is a terrible disease; therefore, beer should not be sold on college campuses.
4. The catalog makes it clear that this scholarship is reserved for business majors. As a music major, I need not apply.
5. Philip disappeared from the city a few days after the police started a crackdown on drug pushers. Philip must have been involved in the narcotics trade.
6. Where there is smoke, there is fire. If a public official comes under attack for misappropriating public funds, it is a good sign that some kind of wrongdoing has been committed. Officials accused of dishonesty should be removed before they can do further harm.
7. After the President ordered an air strike in retaliation for terrorist attacks on Americans, no further attacks took place during the following months. This shows that terrorists understand and respect the language of force.
8. A law has to be approved by the majority of the people before it becomes the law; therefore, everyone should obey the laws.
9. Students study because of the expectation of reward or the fear of punishment. Therefore, when there is no tough grading system to offer reward or punishment, students have no incentive to do their best.
10. There are cases on record of someone else confessing a murder after another person had already been found guilty of the crime "beyond a reasonable doubt." This proves that if we return to the death penalty, innocent people are bound to be executed, with no hope of a later correction of the jury's "mistake."

12　Writing to Persuade

OVERVIEW Persuasion attempts to change attitudes or behavior. It often aims at a tangible result: a vote, a contribution, a subscription, or a sale. It often solicits support for a cause: to save a historic building or the wolves in Alaska. Writing a letter to the editor of a local newspaper, you might ask people in your community

- to support (or stop) a new freeway project
- to provide more jobs for the disabled
- to build shelters for the homeless

Writing for the general reader, you might ask them to support (or challenge) stiffer no-smoking laws or stiffer sentences for drunk driving.

Argument and persuasion are often treated together. They are part of the same spectrum and shade over into each other. However, they differ in what the writer expects of (or wants from) the reader. At one end of the spectrum, we may expect nothing of the reader except an open mind, a willingness to look at the evidence and follow an argument to its logical conclusions. Although we may be aiming at a practical result—a vote, a change in policy—we respect our readers' right to make up their own minds.

At the other end of the spectrum, the result—a sale, a vote, a promotion, or a client's freedom—has become the true test of a writer's effectiveness. When this happens, our attention shifts from the merits of the issue to the psychology of the audience. What goes on in the minds of the customers, the voters, or the jurors? What does it take to make them change their minds and their ways? Here are some key requirements for effective persuasion:

■ **Persuasive writers know their audience.** They know that teachers and owners of small businesses tend to have different attitudes toward public spending. They know that police officers tend to feel hamstrung in their work. They reckon with established loyalties and long-standing commitments.

■ **Persuasive writers know how to get the audience involved.** To make our readers care, we often have to do more than argue logically and present the facts. To move people to action, we need to stir their emotions. We try to arouse their compassion or their generous enthusiasm for a cause. Statistics about the slaughter of baby seals may remain dry and abstract. But a graphic account of the clubbing, of skinned carcasses and bloodied pelts, is likely to stir outrage.

■ **Persuasive writers know how to appeal to shared values.** They know how to mobilize the reader's sense of fairness. They know how to appeal to their readers' love of the land, their distaste for red tape, or their sympathy for the underdog.

Persuasive writers know how to motivate their audience. They know that logical argument alone is often not enough. Successful persuasion is often the right blend of convincing logical argument, factual evidence, and effective emotional appeals.

12a | Strategies of Persuasion

Know how to involve and motivate your reader.

Persuasive writers know how to keep after the reader. They know how to make a strong plea, insisting and persisting until we feel like saying: "Enough! I got your message." Remember advice like the following when trying to make a strong plea:

(1) Know your reader. Size up the audience. With a like-minded, receptive audience, we can build a strong sense of solidarity by voicing shared grievances. We can hiss familiar villains and champion the goals shared by the group. A newsletter for owners of small businesses and business executives is likely to find its audience receptive to proposals designed to "keep the taxpayers' money from going down the drain." This audience is likely to cheer at phrases like "derail the gravy train . . . slash the fat from government waste . . . crack down on inefficiency . . . blow the whistle on free-spending bureaucrats." The same newsletter, however, is likely to have a different effect on a *hostile* audience. For instance, for an audience of mail carriers, teachers, or social workers, cut-the-budget rhetoric will seem to promise belt-tightening, layoffs, speedups, and tinkering with pension rights.

(2) Establish your authority. The persuasiveness of an argument often depends on the credibility of the speaker or writer. If you are to persuade skeptical readers, you may have to show that you are writing from inside knowledge, genuine commitment, or long-standing concern. Notice how the author of the following paper established his credentials. We gather early that this writer is writing as an insider, as someone who "was there."

Too Drunk to Drive

We have all read blood-curdling reports on drinking-related accidents. Several people from my high school contributed to the drunken-driving statistics. In one case, a group of my friends left a beach party in a station wagon; the car was found a short time later wrapped around a tree. Of the five people in the car, four were seriously injured; two of them will be permanently impaired.

Nevertheless, I believe that in most of these cases raising the drinking age for young drivers won't help. Ideally, tougher laws should keep minors from drinking alcohol, but in practice they barely intimidate most. No matter what the legal drinking age may be, an underage party-goer can always obtain liquor. A major effect of raising the legal drinking age is increasing the number of false identifications. Some people cunningly doctor the date of birth on their drivers' licenses to show an earlier date. Others borrow someone else's I.D. I've been carrying a copy of my brother's license since I was sixteen and still use it as proof of my "official" age. In my home state, when the drinking age was raised, many students used various subterfuges to report their licenses missing and to obtain a new license with an adjusted age. Raising the drinking age does little more than to promote dishonesty and forgery; it is just another law to break—quite easily.

By the age of eighteen, a young person takes on a number of responsibilities. Eighteen-year-old citizens are allowed to vote for public officials and thus assume responsibility for the future welfare of the country. An eighteen-year-old criminal is tried as an adult, facing stricter penalties and a hard prison life. Part of an adult's responsibility is to face the dangers of drunk driving and act accordingly.

Raising the drinking age is an example of good intentions producing unintended adverse results. We should direct our efforts toward educating teens about drunken driving rather than toward more legislation. When a drunken driver hits your car head-on, the driver's age is not the issue. Drivers, young or old, have to learn to stay sober at the wheel.

(3) Dramatize the issue. The persuasive writer has to get the reader's attention, to arouse concern. Accident statistics may make us shudder, but they do not jolt us as witnessing an actual accident does. When exhortations about violence in our cities fall on deaf ears, a single horrible event, involving someone widely loved or admired, can dramatize the issue.

Much effective persuasive writing starts with a "grabber"—a dramatic account of an incident that arouses indignation or compassion. The following beginning of a student paper dramatizes an issue by starting close to home:

The Firing Line

I remember being awakened at about four o'clock in the morning. My parents told me they were leaving for the hospital—my brother-in-law, Art, had been shot. He had been at a small all-night store late that night buying some milk. A quarrel started in the store. As he stepped outside to avoid the whole scene, a car pulled up with three men inside. One of the men in the car shot at him, putting a bullet through his head. Art is now partially paralyzed in his left leg and arm, and he has restricted speech and vision.

Because there is little or no restriction on the purchase and use of guns, many innocent people are killed and injured every day. Looking through the local newspaper, I was amazed to find two or three articles a day dealing with gun-related deaths and injuries. One headline read, "Disturbed Composer Shoots Friend, Then Kills Himself." An emotionally disturbed composer wounded a family friend who suggested he seek psychiatric help. After he shot his friend, the composer killed himself. A person in need of help was killed and a person trying to help was almost killed because a disturbed man with easy access to a gun pulled the trigger in a rage of frustration and despair.

(4) Appeal to shared values. Persuasive writers know how to motivate their readers. Sometimes, they can appeal directly to the readers' self-interest, touting the benefits of a product for the consumer or of a change of policy for the voter. Often, however, persuasive writers will try to appeal to the readers' standards, to mobilize their loyalties, to appeal to their better (and sometimes their worse) selves.

Look at the following excerpts from an article that starts in a low key (to put the reader in a relaxed, receptive mood) but becomes serious and emphatic when appealing to the basic values of the reader. (Are you the right kind of audience for this article? Why or why not?)

Boycott Cocaine

Among trendy young professionals in our major cities, there is no stigma attached to using cocaine. In particular, the hip lawyers, doctors, movie stars, and so on who use the drug are not deterred, or even bothered much, by the mere fact that it happens to be illegal. But perhaps they will be receptive to a more fashionable approach. After all, many cocaine consumers are the same sort of people who will boycott lettuce or grapes because farm workers are underpaid, or a cosmetic because the company tortures rabbits, or tuna to protest the killing of dolphins. . . .

Most of the coke sold in America originates in two South American countries whose preeminence in the drug trade is due mainly to the ruthlessness of their native practitioners. Several winters ago, rival gangsters broke into the New York home of an expatriate who was making a fortune importing coke from his native land. The thugs stole $15,000 in cash, abducted a ten-year-old son and a seventeen-year-old baby-sitter, and hanged the five-year-old daughter with a length of nylon Christmas wrapping. . . .

Murder is as much a part of cocaine culture as tiny silver spoons and rolled-up hundred-dollar bills. There is seldom a major coke bust that doesn't also turn up an arsenal of automatic weapons. In a recent year in Miami, the cocaine capital of the Northern Hemisphere, a quarter of the city's 614 murders were committed with machine guns. There was so much drug-inspired bloodshed in southern Florida that the Dade County medical examiner was forced to rent a refrigerated truck trailer to store corpses he couldn't squeeze into the morgue. . . .

The victims are not all businessmen, who might only be getting what they deserve. Cocaine hit men tend to be casual in their aim. "Children have been killed in cross fires, and so have innocent adults," says Brent Eaton, a special agent in the Miami division of the Drug Enforcement Administration. "We've had machine-gun fights as people were driving down expressways here in town. We've had people riddled with machine-gun bullets as they were waiting for traffic lights."

At the very least, cocaine has rent the social and economic fabric of two South American countries and fueled the decay of considerable sections of the United States. To buy cocaine is to subsidize a network of death and despair. Snorting cocaine is at least as bad for the planet as wearing a coat made from an endangered species. Join the cause. Boycott cocaine.   David Owen, *Harper's*

(5) Use persuasive language effectively. Persuasive writers know when and how to speak out. Though they can be diplomatic when necessary, they know how to give key ideas proper **emphasis**—how to make them stand out. They know how to sum up an idea bluntly, so that it will sink in.

> Official war propaganda, with its disgusting hypocrisy and self-righteousness, makes thinking people sympathize with the enemy. George Orwell

Persuasive writers know how to use words that arouse and steer the readers' emotions, that channel their responses in the right direction. In the following passage, look at the words likely to sour us on "commercial civilization." Then look at the words that make us feel good about nature and individuals:

> Dams that **throttle** the Colorado River, tourism in Tellurie and sub-
> urban **sprawl blurring** Phoenix into Tucson, bounty hunters and govern-
> ment coyote-**poisoners**, automobiles that **defile** the wilderness while
> they **slacken** the human body and spirit, all the **tacky trash** of commer-
> cial "civilization"—these are the targets of the author's irritable hu-
> mor. . . . Against them he poses the **mysterious magnificence** of desert
> and mountain and the **saving vitality** of "human bodies and human
> wit . . . **united** in purpose, **independent** in action."   Annie Gottlieb,
> "Putting Down Roots," *Quest*

The boldfaced words in this passage are not neutral or value-free; they carry with them built-in reactions. They are meant to trigger responses, favorable or unfavorable, on the part of the reader. Some of the words— *tacky, trash, define*—denounce or condemn. Some of the words are terms of praise: *magnificence, vitality, united.* But many words that are less ob- viously judgmental carry overtones of praise or blame; they help a writer influence our response. In the context of this passage, to *throttle*, to *sprawl*, to *blur*, and to *slacken* are clearly activities we should view with dismay. These words have negative **connotations**—they suggest unfavorable feel- ings or attitudes. Words like *united* and *independent* have positive conno- tations—they suggest desirable qualities; they put what they describe in a favorable light.

Remember: Emotionally charged language can help you steer the reactions of the reader—but it can also set off the *wrong* reactions. Used with the wrong audience, it can alienate rather than persuade. An audience of teachers is likely to be alienated by a writer who in talking about teachers' salaries keeps up a barrage of loaded terms like *union bosses, the education lobby*, and *the public trough*.

WRITING WORKSHOP 17   Working with a group or with your class as a whole, prepare a set of *audience profiles* that would help an advertiser, pro- moter, or fundraiser reach different target audiences. Help chart strategy and set up procedures. What groups should be targeted? What information should be included about the background, preferences, prejudices, inter- ests, loyalties, or values of a typical member of each group? (Can you steer clear of stereotypes and oversimplification?) Possible target audiences for investigation:

- different types of students at your college, considered as potential customers (or as potential voters)
- minority students at your college (blacks, Hispanics, Asians, foreign students)
- public employees (police officers, social workers, office workers)
- women on campus considered as potential customers for a woman's magazine
- low-income, medium-income, and high-income voters in your community
- single, married, and divorced voters voting on school bonds

---

WRITING WORKSHOP 18   For group discussion prepare a *critique* of an exceptionally effective example of persuasion. For instance, choose a full-page advertisement, a newspaper editorial, a striking commercial, a fund-raising letter, or a promotional flyer for a candidate or a cause. (If you can, provide a photocopy, tape, or transcript of the original.) Explain what makes your choice effective persuasion. What assumptions does it reflect about the target audience? What appeals or strategies does it employ? (Does it have any features that are questionable or objectionable?) What can a persuasive writer learn from this example?

WRITING SAMPLES 19   Examine the following examples of *persuasive writing*. What makes them effective or ineffective persuasion? Ask about each:

- What are the writer's aims?
- What are the writer's assumptions about the intended audience?
- What methods or techniques of persuasion does the writer employ?
- To what standards or values does the writer appeal?
- What use does the writer make of persuasive language?
- What are possible limitations of the writer's approach?

1. Consider this question from a standardized group IQ test. "No garden is without its _____." The desired answer is one of these five: "sun-rain-tool-work-weeds." A child who happens to know the expression will

recognize the missing word (weeds) and complete the sentence "correctly." If he doesn't have that piece of information, he'll have to figure out the answer. He might explain to a tester, "It isn't 'tools' because I once planted a garden with my hands." But there is no tester to tell. He might continue, "I don't know how to choose between sun and rain, so I won't use either one." Again there's no tester to hear his reasoning. "So it's either 'work' or 'weeds.'" Another pause. "Well, if a gardener worked hard, maybe he wouldn't have any weeds—but, if he doesn't work at all, he won't have any garden!" Triumphantly, the clever, logical, analytical young mind has selected—the wrong answer!

When a computer grades that test, "work" will simply be marked wrong, and no one will be there to explain the thought process to the computer. Nor will anyone point out the differences between the child who has personal experience with gardens and the child whose closest contact may be the city park, ten blocks away from his fire escape.   Arlene Silberman, "The Tests That Cheat Our Children," *McCall's*

2. We are encroaching on nature, in the United States and around the world, at an unprecedented rate. A large proportion of the chemicals in use in our present-day civilization were "invented" by nature, not by the chemist in the laboratory. An estimated 40 percent of all drug prescriptions in the United States contain as their chief ingredients compounds derived from plants. There is no end to the potential for discovery in nature, because we have only begun the chemical exploration of nature. Tragically, we are burning our library of priceless genetic treasures with our reckless destruction of species.

3. Day   1: I was conceived today. My sex, the color of my eyes, my physical features, and my special talents and gifts are already determined in my genes.

   Day 28: My heart started beating today. I think I will be strong and healthy.

   Day 49: All my vital organs are present. I have tiny fingers, feet, and toes. I can move my body, arms, and legs for the first time. My mother also could tell that I'm going to be a little girl if she wanted to. I have buds for little milk teeth, and you can record my brain waves.

   Day 56: I can grasp objects and even make a fist.

   Day 70: I have fingerprints and footprints, and I can suck my thumbs, fingers, or toes.

   Day 84: I am very sensitive to touch, heat, sound, discomfort, and pain. I have vocal cords, and sometimes I go through the motion of crying. I am also starting to look like my parents; I think I have my father's nose and my mother's eyes.

Day 112:   I have fingernails, eyebrows, and eyelashes. I kick my feet and curl my toes. I think I'm going to be good-looking when I grow up.

Day 114:   Today my life was terminated. (Four months, two days)

WRITING WORKSHOP 20   Working with a group or your class as a whole, help orchestrate a *letter-writing campaign* designed to influence decisions on a current local issue. Help the group identify an issue of urgent common concern. Help identify the audience to be targeted: officials, newspaper editors, local radio or TV stations, civic organizations, and the like. Assist in planning strategy and developing model letters. Arrange for a final evaluation of the effectiveness of the group effort. Some possible issues:

- saving a historic landmark
- saving trees threatened by progress
- permitting campus vendors or street performers to pursue their livelihood
- changing the route of a proposed freeway
- expanding public parks
- fighting or promoting a no-growth ordinance
- securing affordable housing for the elderly or for minorities
- constructing new jails

12b   Limits of Persuasion

Respect the intelligence of your reader.

Experienced persuasive writers use devices that make their side look good while weakening the case for the opposition. However, they also respect the intelligence of the audience. They know that effective persuasion easily shades over into propaganda and the hard sell. Know where to draw the line when tempted to use the following:

SLOGANS Persuasive writers know how to sum up an idea or a program for action in a catchy phrase. **Slogans** like the following for a time (until they wear out) rally people to a common cause: *pluralism, computer literacy,*

249

affirmative action, comparable worth, right to life. An imaginative analogy or striking metaphor—*spaceship earth, lifeboat ethics*—can help crystallize ideas and make them persuasive. But remember that catch phrases easily become too pat (*tax and spend, runaway arms race*); when people use them too often and too thoughtlessly they start to alienate the thinking reader.

SLANTING   Carefully selected evidence can effectively put an issue "in perspective"; it can help us magnify or belittle a problem. The following passage uses carefully selected evidence to make a strategic comparison:

> Japanese children are testing higher than any other children in the world. American children lag far behind, ranking with children in some Third World countries. The reasons for this astounding difference are obvious. Japan devotes 8.6 percent of its gross national product to education, the United States only 6.8 percent. To match the Japanese effort, we would need to spend about $1,000 more per student every year. Teacher pay in Japan is comparable with the wage levels in business, industry, and the professions.

The strategic selection of supporting evidence becomes **slanting** when you systematically (and too obviously) ignore or discount evidence on the other side.

ABUSIVE LANGUAGE   When writers let their emotions get the better of them, emotional language turns into personal insult, or **invective**. Terms like *redneck, gun nut, fem-libber, peacenik, ecofreak,* and *Uncle Tom* alienate fair-minded bystanders and bring out the worst in the opposition.

SUPERLATIVES   Advertisements, editorials, and political speeches are full of **superlatives** or exaggerated claims. Most consumers tune out voices that promise "the best," "the whitest," or a "once-in-a-lifetime opportunity." Most voters have learned to discount inflated political rhetoric: "fatal to our most cherished institutions," "unparalleled in recorded history."

INNUENDO   When we pledge to support welfare payments to the "truly needy," we imply, or insinuate, that others who claim to be needy are not truly so. When we claim that a candidate has been known to associate with kingpins of organized crime, we insinuate that their lack of ethics has rubbed off. Fair-minded readers resist **innuendo**; they expect us not to hint and whisper but to make charges openly and support them as best we can.

FLAG WAVING People cheapen shared ideals when they make a great show of patriotism or religion in order to sell insurance. Do not represent minor annoyances as threats to cherished American values. Let those who died at Lexington, at the Alamo, or at Pearl Harbor rest in peace. Many (says e.e. cummings) "unflinchingly applaud all/songs containing the words country home and/mother." But many also object to the use of such words to place a halo over the passing causes of the day.

WRITING WORKSHOP 21 Letters to the editor, ranging from eloquent to inane, are a favorite means of influencing the course of debate on current issues. Find a striking current example and photocopy it for discussion in class. Explore questions like the following:

- What is the writer's aim?
- Who is the intended audience?
- What methods or techniques of persuasion does the writer employ?
- How does the letter use persuasive language?
- What are special strengths of the letter?
- What are weaknesses of the letter or limitations of the writer's approach?

WRITING WORKSHOP 22 Find an editorial or full-length ad that goes beyond the limits of legitimate persuasion or insults the intelligence of the reader. (Provide a photocopy if you can.) Spell out your standards, and show how they apply to the example you have chosen. Be prepared to defend your judgments in group discussion.

WRITING TOPICS 13

As you write on one or more of the following topics, keep in mind three questions: Who is my intended audience? What am I trying to achieve? What is my overall strategy?

1. Write a paper in which you persuade other students to opt for or against a law or regulation designed to promote the public welfare:
   - a maximum speed limit
   - a higher (or lower) driving age
   - a higher (or lower) drinking age
   - a smoking ban in public places or in the workplace
   - special reserved lanes for buses and car pools
   - mandatory use of helmets for cyclists or bicycle riders
   - compulsory use of seat belts or air bags

2. Addressing yourself to the general public, write a paper "In Defense of . . ." an organization or institution whose critics claim its time has passed: the Boy Scouts, the fraternity system, ROTC, the D.A.R., the Democratic Party, labor unions, college football, the nuclear family, the family farm. Or write to persuade supporters of the institution that the time has come for serious change.

3. Take on a reluctant or hostile audience and persuade them to change their attitudes or their ways. Know your readers: Read, investigate, interview to develop a good sense of what you are up against. For instance, try to do one of the following:
   - persuade confirmed smokers to give up smoking
   - persuade members of the National Rifle Association (or unaffiliated gun enthusiasts) to support some form of gun control
   - persuade firm believers in the separation of church and state to allow recognition of religious holidays by schools or public agencies
   - change the minds of tradition-bound males about the need for changing gender roles
   - persuade fans of horror movies to support efforts to reduce violence in movie and television fare for young Americans

4. Write a promotional letter in which you champion a cause dear to your heart, such as community support for the arts, better employment opportunities for the disabled, Little League baseball, exchange programs for foreign students, or the like. Try to make your letter persuasive for readers wary of huckstering or promotional hype. Try to find fresh and effective ways to enlist support for your cause.

5. Write a guest editorial or guest column for a student newspaper in order to help improve the public image of a group to which you have personal ties or in which you have a special interest. Try to change your readers' minds about a group that you think has received undeserved negative publicity: politicians, rock musicians, welfare recipients, illegal immigrants, producers of television commercials, yuppies, police officers, participants in beauty contests.

4

Grammar for Writers

Instructions Look at the blank in each of the following sentences. Of the three possible choices that follow the sentence, which would be right for *serious written English*? Write the number of the sentence, followed by the letter for the right choice.

1. Federal witnesses have changed their names to protect _____ .
   a. themself   **b.** oneself   **c.** themselves

2. Tourists were warned to beware of sharks and _____ gradually.
   a. should tan   **b.** to tan   **c.** tanning

3. Being a debtor nation is a new concept for _____ Americans.
   a. us   **b.** we   **c.** ourself

4. The huge oil spill _____ lasting harm to wildlife.
   a. done   **b.** did   **c.** doing

5. Spectators at the air show _____ hit by flying debris.
   a. been   **b.** was   **c.** were

6. Eskimos always _____ and are still hunting whales for food.
   a. have   **b.** have hunted   **c.** been hunting

7. The accuracy of her predictions _____ questioned.
   a. was   **b.** were   **c.** be

8. The leaflet warned senior citizens about _____ kind of scam.
   a. this   **b.** these   **c.** them

9. When _____ our bicycles, drivers eyed us suspiciously.
   a. riding   **b.** we riding   **c.** we were riding

10. There was no ill feeling between _____ and his female coworkers.
    a. he   **b.** him   **c.** hisself

11. As we came in, the first thing that _____ is a garish poster.
    a. is seen   **b.** we see   **c.** we saw

12. She admired people _____ told jokes at their own expense.
    a. who   **b.** which   **c.** whom

13. An officer stopped us and _____ us out of the car.
    a. order   **b.** orders   **c.** ordered

14. The press did not treat the candidates _____ .
    a. very respectful   **b.** very respectfully   **c.** real respectful

15. If her father had been rich, she could have _____ to Harvard.
    a. went   **b.** gone   **c.** going

16. He went to the bank for a loan, but _____ turned him down.
    a. they   **b.** it   **c.** them

17. She delivered singing telegrams but did not do _____ .
    a. real good   **b.** very good   **c.** very well

18. There _____ constant feuds between tenants and landlords.
    a. were   **b.** was   **c.** being

19. We lost the competition, although we _____ very hard.
    a. trained   **b.** have trained **c.** had trained

20. Drivers became more aware of how much gas _____ used.
    a. they   **b.** one   **c.** you

---

13   A Writer's Grammar

OVERVIEW Writers study grammar to understand how words work together in a sentence. Grammar enables us to take isolated words and work them into meaningful patterns. Taken separately, words like *check, agent, passport, trip,* and *brochure* are like entries in a crossword puzzle. To make them carry a message, we arrange them in patterns like the following:

The agent checked my passport.
Our trip was a disaster.
The travel bureau sent me a brochure.

When such a statement fits one of the several patterns we use to convey complete messages, we call it a **sentence**. (Questions can also be complete sentences.) In writing, we start a complete sentence with a capital letter and end it with a period (or, more rarely, an exclamation mark or a question mark).

How much grammar do you need to know as a writer? You need to know enough about English grammar to understand how well-written sentences work and why badly written ones break down. Effective writers know something about how good sentences are put together. They recognize sentence-building techniques that help them develop, expand, or combine sentences:

BASIC PATTERN:	Americans love sports.
MODIFIERS:	**Many** Americans love the **traditional spectator** sports.
COMPOUNDING:	Many Americans love **football, baseball, and basketball**.
COORDINATION:	Many younger Americans love the traditional spectator sports, **but** they also practice every kind of exercise.
SUBORDINATION:	The older generation drinks beer at football games **while** the younger generation jogs or works out.

Knowing basic grammatical concepts and terms will enable you to profit from expert advice. It will enable you to talk about editing problems with your instructor and with your peers. The following writer's grammar will start by looking at basic sentence parts and how we put them together in simple statements. It will then look at how we expand these simple statements and link them in larger combined sentences.

13a g^2 Basic Sentence Parts

Study the basic building blocks of the English sentence.

We assign words to major word classes, or **parts of speech**, according to how they work in a sentence. The basic model of the English sentence has only two basic parts. A complete sentence normally has at least a **subject** and a **predicate**. Somebody acts, or something happens, or something exists:

SUBJECT	PREDICATE
The driver	stopped.
Volcanoes	erupt.
God	exists.

Even when we complete or expand such bare-bones sentences in various ways, we can still identify the two basic parts that serve as underpinnings for the rest of the sentence:

EXPANDED: **The** startled **driver** / fortunately **stopped** the car at the last minute.

EXPANDED: Long-dormant **volcanoes** / suddenly **erupt** with disastrous results.

The major word classes are the building blocks we use to make up the two basic parts and to round out the bare-minimum sentences they provide. The four most important word classes are nouns, verbs, adjectives, and adverbs. Look at the way these work in simple sentences:

(1) The subject of a sentence calls something to our attention. It brings something into focus, so that the rest of the sentence can make a statement about it. The most important part of the subject is usually a **noun**: *car, student, bulldog, college, education.* We use nouns to name or label things, places, people, animals, ideas. The consumer looking up entries in the Sears catalogue, the chemist giving names to new plastics, the advertiser naming new products—all rely on the naming function of the noun. The names of products we buy are nouns (*flashlight, exercycle, kayak*); so are the labels that show people's occupations (*violinist, chiropractor, technician*).

Remember that some other words or groups of words may serve as a substitute for a noun and work like a noun in a sentence. (Instead of "*Hang gliders* are exhilarating," you may find "*They* are exhilarating" or "*Floating in hang gliders* is exhilarating.")

The following clues will help you recognize nouns:

■ Many nouns stand for things we can count. We can usually add the -*s* ending to change a noun from one (**singular**) to several (**plural**): one *car,* several *cars;* one *boy,* several *boys;* one *airplane,* several *airplanes;* one *idea,* several *ideas.* Not all nouns use the -*s* ending for the plural:

REGULAR PLURALS: books, students, buildings, laws, regulations
IRREGULAR PLURALS: men, women, mice, children, teeth
UNMARKED PLURALS: sheep, deer, offspring, people, cattle

(Some nouns are used only in the singular: *chaos, courage, rice.*)

■ Nouns often follow a noun marker like *a, this, my,* or *your:* a *dog,* this *car,* my *friend,* your *neighborhood.* We use three kinds of noun markers over and over:

ARTICLES:
> *the, a, an*
> the tide, a tree, an apple, a riot, the bill, a surprise

DEMONSTRATIVE ("POINTING") PRONOUNS:
> *this, these; that, those*
> this street, these tickets; that detour, those requests

POSSESSIVE PRONOUNS:
> *my, your, his, her, its, our, their*
> my hat, your gloves, his directions, their surprise

■ Nouns often have noun-making endings (**suffixes**) like *-acy, -ance, -ence, -dom, -ness,* or *-hood:*

-acy:	literacy, celibacy, delicacy, lunacy
-ance:	importance, attendance, remittance, admittance
-ence:	occurrence, reference, competence, impotence
-dom:	wisdom, kingdom, Christendom, boredom
-ness:	happiness, darkness, illness, sadness
-hood:	neighborhood, childhood, adulthood, nationhood

■ The place of nouns may be taken by noun substitutes, such as the **personal pronouns**: *I, you, he, she, it, we, they.*

He	reads.	*We*	sang.
It	stopped.	*She*	answered.
They	bark.	*You*	win.

SEE 17 FOR AN OVERVIEW OF PRONOUNS.

(2) The predicate makes a statement about the subject. (Sometimes the predicate asks a question about the subject.) The most important word, or group of words, in the predicate is the **verb**: *reads, stopped, has left, will return, was driving, has arrived.* Verbs report actions, events, or conditions. A noun may *name* an action: *theft, arrival, movement, investigation.* A verb refers to present, future, past, or possible performance: *steals, will arrive, has moved, may investigate.*

259

PARTS OF SPEECH

NOUNS:	The **jogger** waved a **hand** in my **direction**. **Drivers** shouted **insults** at **pedestrians**.
PRONOUNS:	**I** introduced **them** to **her**. **My** brother left **this** package for **your** friend.
VERBS:	We **greeted** them as they **entered**. They **will screen** those who **have applied**.
ADJECTIVES:	A **young** doctor needs a **big** cemetery. Proverb Her **younger** sister wants the **best** grades.
ADVERBS:	We **quickly** closed the window **again**. The train stopped **there unexpectedly**.
CONJUNCTIONS:	She **and** her assistant tried **but** failed. Wake me **if** I am asleep **when** he calls.
PREPOSITIONS:	People **without** umbrellas get wet **in** the rain. We waited **on** the hill **until** sundown.

Verbs set things in motion; they often stand for something we can do: *eat* your food; let us *celebrate*; we should *notify* him. The following clues will help you recognize verbs:

■ Verbs are words that can show a *change in time* by a change in the word itself: *steals* (now), *stole* (then); *lies* (now), *lied* (then); *eat* (now), *ate* (then). This change in time is called a change in **tense**. We can change many verbs from present tense to past tense by adding the ending *-d* or *-ed*:

PRESENT:	ask	arrive	request	investigate
PAST:	asked	arrived	requested	investigated

In the present tense, most verbs add *-s* when *he, she,* or *it* could substitute for the subject (**third person singular**). We use this form when speaking about a third party, with "action now":

THIRD PERSON:	My brother **works**.	(He **works**.)
	Jean **travels**.	(She **travels**.)
	The phone **rings**.	(It **rings**.)

VERB TENSES

PRESENT (NOW OR USUALLY):
I **work** at home.

PAST (OVER AND DONE WITH):
We **sold** the house.

PERFECT (COMPLETED RECENTLY OR TRUE UP TO NOW):
I **have received** your invitation.
She **has** always **supported** us.

PAST PERFECT (BEFORE OTHER PAST EVENTS):
His mother **had worked** in a factory.

FUTURE (STILL TO COME):
Your friends **will help** you.

■ Verb forms often consist of several words. The main part of the verb may follow a word like *can, will, have,* or *was: can* work, *was* looking, *will* travel, *have* arrived. Such words are called **auxiliaries**, or helping verbs. More than one auxiliary may come before the same main verb: *will be calling, has been elected, should have known.*

If there are several auxiliaries, an auxiliary like *will (would), shall (should), can (could), may (might)* often comes first. After these there may be a form of *have (has, had).* In the next slot, there may be a form of *be (is, am, are, was, were, be, been).* Here are some examples of complete verbs using one or more auxiliaries:

	(HAVE)	(BE)	MAIN VERB
can			happen
	has		arrived
		is	waiting
could	have		called
may		be	canceled
will	have	been	sold
should	have	been	revised

By changing the form of a verb or by using auxiliaries, we can show the major differences in tense (see chart).

■ Verbs often have verb-making suffixes like *-fy*, *-en*, or *-ize*:

-fy:	notify, magnify, ratify, indemnify, rectify
-en:	darken, weaken, redden, sharpen, lighten
-ize:	organize, synchronize, sympathize, analyze

(3) Additional words may cluster around a noun. In practice, we seldom use the simple noun-and-verb sentence (Birds fly). Usually, we already include **modifiers** that develop, expand, or narrow the meaning of the basic sentence parts:

Most American songbirds fly **south in the winter**.

Some of these modifiers are single words. **Adjectives** modify nouns, answering questions like "Which one?" or "What kind?" (the *red* convertible, a *tall* order, the *right* answer, *high* hopes). Number adjectives answer questions like "How many?" (*three* blind mice) or "Which in order?" (the *first* date).

The following clues will help you recognize adjectives:

■ Adjectives appear in typical adjective positions: "a *reasonable* price," "The price is *reasonable*," "a very *reasonable* price." The most typical position is immediately before a noun (often between a noun marker and the noun):

ADJECTIVE:	the **tall** building	**good** news
	a **long** lecture	my **foolish** friend
	expensive cars	**many** visitors
	the **cheap** fare	the **first** train

■ Most adjectives name qualities that vary in **degree**. Such adjectives fit in after words that show differences in degree, such as *very, rather,* or *quite:* very *cold*, fairly *tall*, extremely *dangerous*. Unlike nouns or verbs, adjectives have special forms for use in comparisons: *small—smaller—smallest; good—better—best; important—more important—most important.*

POSITIVE (OR PLAIN FORM)	COMPARATIVE	SUPERLATIVE
tall	taller	tallest
speedy	speedier	speediest
envious	more envious	most envious
bad	worse	worst

■ Suffixes that help us derive adjectives from other words include *-able, -ic, -ish, -ive,* and *-ous:*

-able:	washable, reasonable, usable, dispensable, disposable
-ic:	basic, tragic, allergic, synthetic, generic
-ish:	foolish, Spanish, lavish, squeamish, sheepish
-ive:	expensive, representative, competitive, compulsive
-ous:	famous, enormous, anonymous, ridiculous, marvelous

(4) Additional words may cluster around a verb. The most important of these are **adverbs**. Adverbs answer questions like "How?" "When?" or "Where?" (They also answer questions like "How often?"):

HOW?	carefully, cautiously, silently, quickly, awkwardly
WHEN?	now, then, tomorrow, yesterday, immediately
WHERE?	there, upstairs, downtown, everywhere
HOW OFTEN?	once, twice, frequently, rarely, seldom

The following clues will help you recognize adverbs:

■ Many adverbs, but not all, show the *-ly* ending: *rapidly, individually, basically, dangerously.* (Note that some exceptional adjectives also have the *-ly* ending: the *friendly* natives, a *leisurely* drive.)

■ Adverbs typically go with a verb: reads *slowly*, spoke *thoughtfully*, asked *twice*. But they have greater freedom of movement than other kinds of words:

The bell rang **suddenly**.
The bell **suddenly** rang.
Suddenly the bell rang.

■ Adverbs, like adjectives, often follow words that show degree: very *cheaply*, more *cheaply*, most *cheaply*.

SEE **19a** FOR PROBLEMS WITH ADVERB FORMS.

Note: Nouns, pronouns, verbs, adjectives, and adverbs are five word classes that we use over and over in putting together short sentences. Two additional parts of speech become important as links between other sentence parts:

■ **Prepositions** are words like *at, of, with, in, on, for, to, with,* or *without*; we use them to tie a prepositional phrase to the rest of the sentence: "Thousands *of* cars were stalled *on* the approaches *to* the bridge." A

phrase is a group of words that work together, but it does not have its own subject and verb.

■ **Conjunctions** are words like *and, but, if, because, though,* and *whereas.* They become important when we start combining several clauses in a larger, more elaborate sentence. "*Before we left*, we called the agency, *but* a machine answered." A **clause** is a group of words that has its own subject and verb.

SEE **13d** FOR PREPOSITIONS; **13e** FOR CONJUNCTIONS.

DISCOURSE EXERCISE 1   Test your ability to recognize five major word classes, or *parts of speech*. In each of the following sentences, one word or group of words has been italicized. What kind of word is it? Write the number of the sentence, followed by the right abbreviation:

N	for noun
V	for verb
Adj	for adjective
Adv	for adverb
Pro	for pronoun

(*Note:* In the **discourse exercises** in this book, sample sentences appear the way they would in someone's actual writing—as part of a longer passage that has meaning and purpose.)

Losing the Space Race

1. The *conquest* of space has long been front-page news.
2. The Russians first sent a *satellite* into orbit.
3. An early Russian space capsule *carried* a dog.
4. Americans *immediately* mobilized their resources.
5. They *gradually* caught up with their competition.
6. *They* poured millions into Project Apollo.
7. American *astronauts* finally landed on the moon.
8. Millions watched the *first* footprints on the lunar surface.
9. *Disastrous* setbacks marred the space race.
10. Three astronauts met a *fiery* death in their capsule.
11. People *had heard* rumors of similar disasters in Russia.
12. A space shuttle crashed *soon* after takeoff.
13. The early space travelers became *celebrities*.
14. Soon an astronaut *was running* for President.
15. Russian astronauts *would tour* the United States.

16. Our *government* slowly deemphasized space travel.
17. Space probes brought back *photographs* of Jupiter.
18. Meanwhile the Russians *were building* space stations.
19. They invited foreign astronauts to travel in *their* spacecraft.
20. They *may be leading* in the space race for good.

| **13b** | *gr* | Sentence Patterns |

Study the basic patterns of the complete English sentence.

Some English sentences need only two basic parts: a subject and a complete verb. But many sentences need one or two additional basic parts to be complete. We call these added essential parts completers, or **complements**.

INCOMPLETE:	The carpenter fixed _____ (What?)
COMPLETE:	The carpenter fixed **the door**.
INCOMPLETE:	Her grandmother had been _____ (What?)
COMPLETE:	Her grandmother had been **a photographer**.

In several typical sentence patterns, the predicate is completed by one or more complements. These become parts of the basic structure. We can sort out English sentences by asking: Are there any completers? Does the sentence have just one—or more? What *kind* of completers are they?

(1) Some sentences need only the subject and a complete verb. In the simplest sentence pattern, the verb alone can make up the predicate; it can tell the whole story. Such a verb "is not going anywhere"; we call it an **intransitive** verb. Sentences built on this pattern need only two basic parts:

SUBJECT	VERB
Planes	fly.
The victims	suffered.
Your letter	has arrived.

(In practice, one or more modifiers may cluster around an intransitive verb. "The victims suffered *terribly*." "Your letter has arrived *on time*." However, these added parts are not needed to make a complete sentence.)

265

THE COMPLETE SENTENCE: BASIC PATTERNS

S–V:	Bees buzz.
S–V–O:	Ranchers dislike coyotes.
S–LV–N:	Her friends were musicians.
S–LV–ADJ:	Silence is golden.
S–V–IO–O:	The delay gave our rivals a chance.
S–V–O–N:	Her lawyer called the driver a menace.
S–V–O–ADJ:	Beer made Milwaukee famous.

(2) In several sentence patterns, a single complement completes the predicate. Sentences that follow these patterns have three basic parts. In the first of these patterns, an action verb carries its action across to a target or result. We call this target or result the **direct object**. The object adds a second noun (or equivalent) to the sentence. The kind of verb that "goes on" to an object is called a **transitive** verb.

SUBJECT	ACTION VERB	OBJECT
The student	reads	a book.
Dudley	made	sandals.
A storm	has delayed	the plane.
Our group	will choose	the winner.

In other sentences, the verb is a **linking verb**, which introduces a description of the subject. A linking verb pins a label on the subject. The label may be a noun. (This noun is often called the **predicate noun** to distinguish it from a noun used as an object.)

SUBJECT	LINKING VERB	NOUN
This ape	is	a gorilla.
The supervisor	was	his fiancée.
His story	may have been	a lie.

Note the difference between these two patterns: In the first pattern, someone does something that aims at something else; *A* affects *B*. In the second pattern, the second noun merely puts a different label on the first; *A* is the same as *B*. In the second pattern, the added noun is not the target or product of an action; it merely puts a new label on the first. The two nouns refer to the same thing or person. "Susan loved a biker" involves two people; "Susan was a biker" only one.

In addition to the many forms of the verb *be* (*is, are, was, were, has been, will be, may have been*, and so forth), linking verbs like the following fit this pattern:

SUBJECT	LINKING VERB	NOUN
Jeffrey	**became**	an ornithologist.
Her resignation	**seemed**	a mistake.
Their disappearance	**has remained**	an enigma.

In a third pattern with three basic parts, an adjective instead of a noun follows a linking verb. (When an adjective is used to complete the predicate, it is called a **predicate adjective**.)

SUBJECT	LINKING VERB	ADJECTIVE
Our bus	was	late.
The price	seemed	reasonable.
The food	tasted	bland.

Note: Linking verbs are considered a special kind of intransitive verb.

(3) In several common sentence patterns, the verb is followed by two completers. Sentences that follow these patterns have four basic parts. For instance, they may have a slot for not just one noun (or equivalent) after the verb; they may have slots for two.

INCOMPLETE:	Maria sent the agency _____ (What?)
COMPLETE:	Maria sent the agency **a letter**.
INCOMPLETE:	The accused called the trial _____ (What?)
COMPLETE:	The accused called the trial **a farce**.

In the first of the four-part patterns, an action verb like *give, lend, send, sell, ask*, or *write* carries the pattern first to the destination (**indirect object**) and then goes on to what was given or sent (**direct object**). The officer gave what to whom? The officer gave *the tourist* (indirect object) *directions* (direct object). In sentences like the following, the first noun (or equivalent) after the verb tells us *where* something is headed:

SUBJECT	VERB	INDIRECT OBJECT	DIRECT OBJECT
The company	sent	**the victims**	an apology.
Stacey	writes	**her teachers**	notes.
A friend	will lend	**them**	the money.

Many other verbs also work in this pattern:

The manager	**promised**	**me**	a promotion.
Igor	**tossed**	**the panhandler**	a coin.
The witness	**had told**	**the jury**	the truth.
Brazil	**owes**	**the bank**	. billions.

Another pattern also adds a second noun (or equivalent) after the verb but uses the added noun in a different way. A verb like *call, name, consider, elect,* or *appoint* carries the pattern first to a direct object and then pins a label on the direct object. (The second completer is traditionally called the **object complement**.) The last two parts of such a sentence point to the same person or thing. In "The editorial called *the official a crook*," the official and the crook are the same person.

SUBJECT	VERB	OBJECT	NOUN
She	called	her ex-husband	**a sponge.**
Marcia	had considered	her manager	**a friend.**
The voters	elected	a Texan	**President.**

A slightly different pattern also pins a label on the object but uses an adjective instead of a noun. (Instead of calling a friend *an idealist*, we call her *idealistic*.)

SUBJECT	VERB	OBJECT	ADJECTIVE
Jean	called	her work	**monotonous.**
Textiles	had made	the town	**famous.**
The tenants	painted	the walls	**green.**

Remember that in your own writing the basic sentence patterns will usually appear in sentences that have been expanded in various ways. ("*In spite of our protests*, the *new* tenants painted the *bathroom* walls green.") When you study the basic patterns, you focus on the *essential* building blocks needed to make an English sentence complete.

DISCOURSE EXERCISE 2 The following sentences illustrate *seven basic sentence patterns*. In some of the sentences, added adjectives and adverbs have been used to expand the basic pattern. Do you recognize the basic pattern in each sentence? Write the number of the sentence, followed by the right abbreviations: S–V, S–V–O, S–LV–N, S–LV–Adj, S–V–IO–O, S–V–O–N, or S–V–O–Adj.

Sayings for All Occasions

1. Ben Franklin collected proverbs.
2. Times have changed.
3. His sayings are still good advice.
4. The used key is always bright.
5. You cannot teach an old dog new tricks.
6. A cheerful look makes a dish a feast.
7. Debt makes another person your master.
8. Laziness makes all things difficult.
9. Little strokes fell great oaks.
10. A small leak will sink a great ship.

REVIEW EXERCISE 3   In each of the following sets, two sentences illustrate the same basic sentence pattern. The remaining sentence is different. Write the number of the set, followed by the letter of the *different* sentence.

EXAMPLE:

    4. (a) Our country offered the refugees asylum. (S–V–IO–O)

    (b) Exams gave Timothy a headache. (S–V–IO–O)

    (c) Her teacher had called the idea brilliant. (S–V–O–Adj)

ANSWER:

    4. c

1. **(a)** Her grandparents had been Lithuanian immigrants.
   (b) The newcomers became American citizens.
   (c) The judge asked the candidates simple questions.
2. **(a)** The city will host the convention.
   (b) Our computer has made a mistake.
   (c) The signature was illegible.
3. **(a)** Lenders were charging customers exorbitant interest.
   (b) The angry customer called the charges a scandal.
   (c) The governor had labeled deregulation a disaster.
4. **(a)** The school board banned our humor magazine.
   (b) Malnutrition had become a national menace.
   (c) Bromo-Seltzer will cure that headache.
5. **(a)** The authorities had denied her husband a passport.
   (b) The parents gave the happy pair their blessing.
   (c) Her decision will keep the voters happy.
6. **(a)** Leonard foolishly lent strangers money.
   (b) The voters had elected an actor governor.
   (c) The couple named their first child Miranda.

Study the adaptations that help us convert simple statement patterns to different uses.

Obviously, not every English sentence is a simple statement that tells us who does what. Many sentences ask questions, tell us what to do, or focus on what *was done*. **Transformations** are changes or adaptations that help us convert the simple statement patterns of basic grammar to other uses. Several simple transformations rearrange (and sometimes delete or expand) familiar sentence parts.

(1) A simple change in word order can help us turn statements into questions. To change a statement to a question, we can move all or part of the verb in front of the subject: "You *are* his friend" becomes "*Are* you his friend?"

	SUBJECT	VERB	COMPLETER
Have	our guests	arrived?	
Is	the package		ready?
Will	your friend	pay	the bill?

Sometimes we need to add a form of *do* (*does, did*) and place it in front of the subject:

	SUBJECT	VERB	COMPLETER
Do	your friends	agree?	
Does	the guide	speak	English?
Did	the officer	write	a ticket?

(2) A common transformation helps us turn statements into requests. It changes the verb to the form used in requests or commands (**imperative**). It omits the subject. "*You* should pay your dues" becomes "Pay your dues!" (Who is supposed to pay is understood.)

VERB	COMPLETER
Shut	the door.
Be	my friend.
Keep	quiet.

(3) A third transformation changes active to passive sentences. It produces the **passive**, which makes the original object the subject of a new

270

sentence. The passive reverses the order of the original **active** sentence, which goes from the "doer" through the action to the target. The new sentence puts the spotlight on the target:

ACTIVE: Edison invented **the lightbulb**.
PASSIVE: **The lightbulb** was invented by Edison.

In the passive sentence, the original subject appears after *by* toward the end of the sentence. (It may also be left out altogether: "*The police caught the thief*" may become "The thief was caught.")

The verb appears in its passive form, which uses a form of *be* and the form that usually follows *have*: have *caught*, had *brought*, has *admired*. (This form is called the **past participle**—see **13g** and **15a**.)

SUBJECT	PASSIVE VERB	
Children	**are taught**	(by teachers).
The champion	**was defeated**	(by the challenger).
Roses	**should be pruned**	(by the gardener).
The suspect	**has been questioned**	(by the police).
Workers	**are being hired**	(by management).

FOR WEAK OR AWKWARD PASSIVE, SEE **22c** AND **25c**.

REVIEW EXERCISE 4   In each of the following sets, two sentences are very similar in their basic structure. Even though they may have been expanded somewhat, they follow the same basic sentence pattern, or they have been adapted or transformed the same way. The remaining sentence is different. Write the number of the set, followed by the letter for the *different* sentence.

1. **(a)** The city will host the convention.
    (b) Our computer has made a mistake.
    (c) Has the manager interviewed the applicant?
2. **(a)** Paper is made from wood pulp.
    (b) The documents had been hidden in a suitcase.
    (c) The tenants will pay by the month.
3. **(a)** Reports from the field arrived daily.
    (b) Take your complaints to the manager.
    (c) Report the incident in detail.
4. **(a)** Corruption was common in high places.
    (b) The apartment was searched by the police.
    (c) His sister looked different without her wig.

271

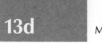

5. **(a)** Charitable people give generously to charities.
    (b) Please contribute freely to our special fund.
    (c) My father contributed reluctantly to the heart fund.

13d   *gr* | Modifiers

Recognize the modifiers that flesh out the basic patterns.

In a typical sentence, **modifiers** develop or narrow the meaning of the basic sentence parts. A modifier may be a single word. Or it may be a group of closely related words—a **phrase**.

BARE BONES:	A parcel arrived.
MODIFIED:	A **big** parcel arrived **yesterday**.
	A parcel **with books** arrived **from Chicago**.
BARE BONES:	The burglar opened the door.
MODIFIED:	The burglar **cautiously** opened the **heavy** door.
	The burglar opened the door **to the garden** *by mistake*.

We divide modifiers into two main groups: The modifiers in the first group modify nouns. Those in the second group modify verbs and, sometimes, other parts of a sentence.

(1) Different kinds of modifiers may cluster around a noun. They tell us more about the noun; they tell us which one or what kind. All of the modifiers italicized in the following examples modify the noun *dog*:

A **shaggy** dog barred my way.
A **big, yellow** dog was chewing the rug.
A **police** dog tracked me down.
A dog **with droopy eyes** dozed in the sun.
Let **sleeping** dogs lie.

Of these modifiers, the first three (*shaggy, big, yellow*) are adjectives. Other words or groups of words may modify a noun and serve the same function as an adjective. *Police* in *police dog* is a noun used as an adjective (sometimes called a **modifying noun**). Nouns are also used as adjectives in combinations like *sales* tax, *vacation* home, or *space* travel. *With droopy eyes* is a prepositional phrase—see (3). *Sleeping* is a **verbal**—a word that is derived from a verb but that can no longer be used as a complete verb by itself (see **13g**).

272

A CHECKLIST OF PREPOSITIONS

The following words may all be used as prepositions. Many point out relationships in *time* or in *space*:

about	behind	from	since
above	below	in	through
across	beneath	inside	to
after	beside	into	toward
against	between	like	under
along	beyond	near	until
among	by	of	up
around	despite	off	upon
as	during	on	with
at	except	outside	within
before	for	over	without

The following *combinations* are also used as prepositions:

aside from	in spite of	on behalf of
as to	instead of	out of
as well as	in view of	regardless of
because of	on account of	

ADJECTIVE:	**yellow** line, **handsome** stranger, **final** offer
MODIFYING NOUN:	**police** dog, **track** coach, **home** computer
PREP. PHRASE:	house **at the corner**, room **with a view**
VERBAL:	**leaking** roof, **scrambled** eggs, **burnt** toast

(2) Different kinds of modifiers may cluster around a verb. They fill in details, answering questions like how, when, where, or how often. All of the modifiers boldfaced in the following examples modify the verb *rang:*

The bell rang **twice**.
Suddenly the bell rang.
The bell rang **loudly**.
The bell rang **at intervals**.

Twice, suddenly, and *loudly* are adverbs. *At intervals* is a prepositional phrase used to modify a verb.

273

(3) Prepositional phrases may serve the same function as either adjectives or adverbs. Combinations introduced by *with, at, on,* and similar words may modify either nouns or other parts of a sentence:

> The woman **from Chicago** disappeared.   (modifies noun)
> The woman disappeared **from Chicago**.   (modifies verb)

With, at, on, and *from* are **prepositions.** They tie a noun (or equivalent) to the rest of the sentence. Other common prepositions are *about, by, during, in, of, through, to, under, until,* and *without.* A preposition with the noun it introduces is a prepositional phrase. Often several prepositional phrases appear in the same sentence:

> We read **about the accident** *in the newspaper*.
> His fear **of earthquakes** kept him **from traveling** *to California*.
> The portrait **of her predecessor** hung **behind her desk**.

Such prepositional phrases may in turn include *other* modifiers:

> **In** *traditional* **textbooks**, our leaders appeared **as** *great* **men on** *white* **horses**.

CAUTION: A prepositional phrase alone cannot make up a complete sentence:

FRAGMENT: The travelers crossed the river. **On a raft**.
COMPLETE: The travelers crossed the river **on a raft**.

PRACTICE EXERCISE 5   Build up the following simple sentences by adding adjectives, adverbs, and prepositional phrases. Use at least one of each kind of modifier in your expanded sentence.

EXAMPLE: The cowboy rode the horse.
ANSWER: The **handsome screen** cowboy **slowly** rode the **magnificent** horse **into the sunset.**

1. The comic strip showed characters.
2. The detective questioned the suspect.
3. Reporters trailed the candidate.
4. The tourist asked the guide questions.
5. The conquerors destroyed civilizations.
6. The woman approached the gate.
7. Athletes are tested.
8. The victims had been attacked.

9. Movies feature aliens.
10. The judge admonished the lawyer.

PRACTICE EXERCISE 6   What *prepositions* are needed to fill the blanks in the following sentences? Write down the number of the sentence, followed by the missing prepositions. (Choose those that to you seem to fit best.)

1. The President traveled _____ China _____ a large contingent _____ reporters.
2. _____ the rally, speakers _____ many nations pleaded _____ an end _____ the arms race.
3. Small newspapers _____ many American cities are losing the battle _____ powerful newspaper chains.
4. The restaurant barred customers _____ jackets or _____ bare feet.
5. The road _____ the other side _____ the mountains led _____ tunnels and _____ spectacular bridges.

13e   Compounding

Study the way compounding enables us to expand simple sentences.

Compounding enables us to pack a sentence with closely related information. Compound structures are several sentence parts of the same kind, usually tied together by *and* or *or*. A sentence may have two or more subjects; it may have one subject but two or more complete verbs. Look at the doubling up of different sentence parts in the following examples:

NOUNS: **The walrus and the carpenter** were walking close at hand.
VERBS: The hooves **slipped and struggled** on the mountain path.
ADJECTIVES: Korea started to build **cheap and reliable** cars.

A set of three or more sentence parts of the same kind is called a **series**. (Note the commas that separate items in a series.)

NOUNS: The journalist serves as **monitor, critic, and rival** of the politician.
VERBS: In the movie, a robot **is struck** by lightning, **runs** amok, and **achieves** true human consciousness.

275

DISCOURSE EXERCISE 7   Find the *compound structure* in each of the following model sentences. Then write a similar sentence of your own. Use or adapt the sentence frame that follows the model.

EXAMPLE: Europeans thought of Americans as wealthy, advanced, efficient, and invincible.

IMITATION: Americans thought of Germans as orderly, ruthless, goal-oriented, and emotionless.

The American Image

1. Europeans have fought insane wars, started disastrous revolutions, and followed fanatical leaders.
    (Americans) (Southerners) (other) have _____
2. To many Europeans, America meant affluence, efficiency, and techno-logical progress.
    To many _____ , _____ meant _____
3. In Western movies, Americans appeared decent, plucky, and generous.
    (In TV shows) (In war movies) (In science fiction movies), _____
4. Refugees discovered people of different races, origins, religions, and values.
    _____ discovered _____
5. Europeans still imitate American fashions, sports, and gadgets.
    _____ imitate _____

| **13f** |  | The Combined Sentence |

Recognize the units that make up the larger combined sentence.

Two or more statements may join in a larger combined sentence. When a short sentence becomes part of the larger whole, we call it a **clause**. A clause has its own subject and verb (unless it is a request, with the subject omitted or understood).

We have many ways of joining one clause to another. Traditionally, we sort these out under two major headings. The examples in the following pair each combine two **independent** clauses:

INDEPENDENT: The company had sent the bill, **but** the mail was slow.
                  The climber slipped; **however**, the rope held.

Independent clauses remain self-sufficient enough to stand by themselves; they could still be punctuated as complete separate sentences. Like railroad cars that are part of a freight train, they can easily be separated again:

SEPARATE: The climber slipped. **However**, the rope held.

In the examples in the following pair, the second clause is a **dependent** clause:

DEPENDENT: Sue will notify us **if** her plans change.
We need a mechanic **who** knows this kind of car.

In these examples, the second clause cannot stand by itself. Like a two-wheel trailer, it depends on something else. It is subordinated to the main clause. A dependent clause alone does not make up a complete sentence.

FRAGMENT: Oil prices will rise. **If consumption goes up**.

Remember: A complete English sentence contains at least one independent clause. Study the different links we use in joining two or more clauses in a larger combined sentence:

(1) Clauses remain independent when they are joined by a coordinator. The simplest way to coordinate independent clauses is to use a coordinator. **Coordinating conjunctions** (or **coordinators** for short) are easy to remember: *and, but, for, so, yet, or,* and *nor.* Coordinators make two equally important parts of a message "work together." The typical punctuation is a comma between the two clauses, before the *and* or *but* that ties them together:

Legislators make laws, **and** judges interpret them.
Many are called, **but** few respond to telephone solicitations.
The tombs contained food, **for** the dead needed nourishment on their journey.
Conditions changed, **so** the dinosaurs became extinct.
We are drowning in information, **yet** we are thirsting for knowledge.
Communities must support artists, **or** the arts will wither.
The new law did not lower taxes, **nor** did it simplify them.

(2) Clauses are still considered independent when they are joined by a conjunctive adverb. A second way to coordinate two or more independent clauses is common in serious explanation and argument. We often use more formal links called **conjunctive adverbs** (or adverbial conjunctions). These include *however, therefore, moreover, nevertheless, consequently, besides, accordingly,* and *indeed,* as well as combinations like *in fact, on the other hand,* and *as a result.*

> The assembly passed the law; **however**, the governor vetoed it.
> The price of gas went up; **therefore**, we bought a smaller car.
> We warned them of the dangers; **nevertheless**, they continued.

Like other adverbs, these words may change their position in the sentence. They often interrupt or follow the second clause. The typical punctuation is the semicolon, which stays at the juncture between the two clauses even if the adverb shifts its position. Note the commas that set off the adverb from the rest of the second clause in relatively formal prose:

> The assembly passed the law; the governor, **however,** vetoed it.
> We warned them of the dangers; they continued, **nevertheless**.

Note that coordinators are locked in place. Unlike the word *however,* the word *but* cannot shift to a later position in the second clause:

ADVERBIAL: Irene was born in Greece; she spoke little Greek, **however**.

COORDINATOR: Irene was born in Greece, **but** she spoke little Greek.

SEE **34b** AND **34c** FOR PUNCTUATION OF INDEPENDENT CLAUSES.

DISCOURSE EXERCISE 8 In the following *sentence-combining* exercise join each pair of short statements in a larger combined sentence. Of the connecting words given as choices, use the one that seems to fit best. (Be prepared to explain or defend your choices.)

EXAMPLE: American steel mills used to dominate the market.
               Steel from Korea now floods the country.

ANSWER: American steel mills used to dominate the market, but steel from Korea now floods the country.

It's a Different Campus

(Choose one: *and, but, so, for, yet, or.* Use a comma.)

1. Older students returning to college are in for a surprise.
   The campus scene has changed.

KINDS OF CONNECTIVES

COORDINATORS:	and, but, for, or, nor, yet, so
CONJUNCTIVE ADVERBS:	however, therefore, moreover, accordingly, furthermore, nevertheless, besides, indeed, consequently, instead, otherwise, hence, thus; in fact, on the other hand
SUBORDINATORS:	when, whenever, while, before, after, since, until, as, if, because, unless, provided, though, although, whereas; so that, no matter how, no matter what, as if, as though
RELATIVE PRONOUNS:	who, whom, whose; which, that
SPECIAL CONNECTIVES:	that, why, whether, how, where, who, what, whoever, whatever

2. Many students tune out political issues.
   Attendance at political rallies is often low.
3. Some of the students may be partying in the pub.
   Others are competing hard for grades.
4. Critics protest against the tyranny of tests.
   Students are taking more tests every year.
5. Today's students have to learn to relax.
   Campuses will turn into deadly serious places.

(Choose one: *therefore, however, moreover, nevertheless, besides, indeed, in fact.* Use a semicolon.)

6. Fraternities still get into trouble for noisy parties.
   Many students today are older and more mature.
7. Student loans have been cut back.
   More students work part-time at scroungy jobs.
8. More students live off campus.
   Many have long commutes every day.
9. For many students with children, day care is a pipedream.
   Some come to campus with their tots in tow.
10. Each campus has a different mix of students.
    The average age of students has gone up nationwide.

(3) A clause becomes a dependent clause when it is joined to the main clause by a subordinator. Subordinating conjunctions, or subordinators for short, are words like *if, when, while, as, unless, where, because, though, although,* and *whereas.* The kind of dependent clause that starts with a subordinator is called an **adverbial clause.** It gives the same kind of information as many adverbs.

Either no punctuation at all or a comma separates the two clauses, depending on how essential the added clause is to the meaning of the sentence. In each of the following examples, the added clause states an essential *if* or *when:*

NO COMMA: Customers get a discount **if** they buy now. (only then)
             You will be arrested **unless** you pay the fine.
             Vince became vague **when he was asked about marriage**.
             No flights will depart **until the fog lifts**.

In each of the following examples, the first half of the combined sentence is true *regardless* of what is added:

COMMA: We have a phone, **although** we are not in the phone book.
          Sharks are fish, **whereas** whales are mammals.
          The plant will close, **no matter how** much we protest. (It will close regardless.)

A complete inventory of subordinating conjunctions would make a long list. Just to specify time, we have *when, while, before, after, until, as, since,* and *whenever,* as well as *as soon as.* Try a simple test to tell subordinators apart from other links between clauses. When you use a subordinator you can reverse the order of the two clauses, with the dependent clause first. A comma then shows where the main clause starts:

COMMA: **If you act humble**, you may avoid a ticket.
          Where women are honored, the gods are pleased.
          Arab proverb

CAUTION: A dependent clause *alone* cannot be a complete sentence. Look out for fragments like the following:

FRAGMENT: The manager will notify you. **If a position opens**.
COMPLETE: The manager will notify you **if a position opens**.

FRAGMENT: Oil had become scarce. **Whereas coal was in plentiful supply**.

COMPLETE: Oil had become scarce, **whereas coal was in plentiful supply**.

DISCOURSE EXERCISE 9   In the following *sentence-combining* exercise, join each pair of short sentences in a larger combined sentence. Of the connecting words given as choices, use the one that seems to fit best. (Be prepared to explain or defend your choices.)

EXAMPLES: The rich get richer.
                The poor get poorer.
ANSWER: The rich get richer while the poor get poorer.

The Imbalance of Trade

(Choose one: *when, where, before, after, until, while, as, if, unless, because*. Use no comma.)

1. Unions complain.
   Imported goods take over the market.
2. Domestic industries go out of business.
   They are protected by special tariffs.
3. Hi-tech companies move manufacturing plants to Korea or Taiwan.
   Labor costs are low.
4. Companies prefer to relocate.
   Local taxes are low there.
5. Americans of the future will work for foreign employers.
   Current predictions come true.

(Choose one: *though, although, whereas, no matter how, no matter what*. Use a comma. Put the dependent clause first when it seems appropriate.)

6. The Japanese outperform us in world markets.
   We try hard.
7. They used to be accused of producing cheap imitations.
   They now are known for high-quality goods.
8. Often the merchandise is made in Japan.
   The package carries an American label.
9. The Japanese are leaders in electronics and automotive engineering.
   Americans still dominate a few other areas.
10. American-built airplanes dominate the sky.
    Some airlines are flying European-built midsize planes.

---

(4) A clause becomes a dependent clause when it is joined to the main clause by a relative pronoun. The second way to subordinate an added clause is to use a **relative pronoun**: *who* (*whom, whose*), *which*, or *that*. The clause that follows a relative pronoun is called a **relative clause**. Relative clauses modify a word in the main clause (*the pause* that refreshes; *people* who care). As a result, they may either follow or interrupt the main clause:

> The tickets went to people **who signed up early**.
> The company shut down the reactor, **which had been built in 1972**.
> A friend **who recognized me** called out my name.
> A Chicago dating service **that helps clients with their image** costs $1,250 a year.

Punctuation depends: Use *no comma* when you need the added clause to narrow choices—to specify which one or what kind, to single out one among several:

RESTRICTIVE: The candidate **who plagiarized his speeches is** no longer running.
We righted the boat **that had capsized during the storm**.

When the added clause does not single out but merely adds details, we use a *comma*, or commas:

NONRESTRICTIVE: President Johnson, **who had been majority leader**, knew the workings of the Senate.

The relative pronouns *whom* and *that* are often left out. The brackets in the following examples enclose the missing links:

> The witnesses [whom] **he had threatened** refused to testify.
> Inmates wrote books about the crimes [that] **they had committed**.

CAUTION: A relative clause alone cannot be a complete sentence. Look for fragments starting with *which* and *who*:

FRAGMENT: He owned pit bulls. **Which frightened his neighbors**.
COMPLETE: He owned pit bulls, **which frightened his neighbors**.

SEE **34d** AND **34e** FOR PUNCTUATION OF DEPENDENT CLAUSES.

DISCOURSE EXERCISE 10   In the following *sentence-combining* exercise, join each pair of short statements in a larger combined sentence. Choose one: *who, whom, whose, which,* or *that.* Use a comma, or commas, for the first three examples. Use no comma for the remaining two.

The Natural History of the Sandwich

1. The Reuben sandwich was invented by Reuben Kay.
    He was a wholesale grocer in Omaha.
2. The Earl of Sandwich wanted to snack without using fork and knife.
    His creation was named after him.
3. During a lifetime, the average American eats 2,900 pounds of beef.
    This is equal to six head of cattle.
4. The barbecue sandwich is made up of shredded pork in sauce on a bun.
    People eat it in North Carolina.
5. The hero sandwich was originally eaten by Italian construction workers.
    They had a strong appetite.

(5) A special type of dependent clause is not joined to the main clause but replaces one of its nouns. Such a clause-within-a-clause is called a **noun clause**. Noun clauses often start with question words like *who, what, why, where,* and *how*:

NOUN:	The reporters asked her **the reason**.
NOUN CLAUSE:	The reporters asked her **why she had resigned**.
NOUN:	She was excited by **the news**.
NOUN CLAUSE:	She was excited by **what she had heard**.
NOUN:	**The thief** returned my documents.
NOUN CLAUSE:	**Whoever stole my wallet** returned my documents.
NOUN:	**Their fate** remains a mystery.
NOUN CLAUSE:	**What happened to the crew** remains a mystery.

That, frequently used as a relative pronoun, also serves to introduce a noun clause, often after words like *say, tell, explain,* or *deny*:

NOUN CLAUSE:	The contractor denied **that the parts were defective**.
	The ad campaign told teenagers **that spray painting the subways with graffiti was not cool**.

Noun clauses blend into the larger combined sentence without punctuation. Do not use a comma in sentences like the following:

NO COMMA: The article explained **how people without talent become celebrities**.

Finer Points   Words like *who, what,* and *that* all have uses other than joining two clauses in a larger combined sentence. So do words like *for, before, after,* and *since*:

COORDINATOR: We had no choice, **for** the lease had expired.
PREPOSITION: He needed a license **for** his pretzel stand.

SUBORDINATOR: We left **before** the movie reached its gory ending.
PREPOSITION: We left **before** the end of the movie.

Note: Traditionally, we call a sentence that coordinates two or more independent clauses a **compound** sentence. A sentence that subordinates one or more dependent clauses is a **complex** sentence. A combined sentence using both coordination and subordination is **compound-complex**.

COMPOUND: He hummed, and she sang.
COMPLEX: He hummed when she sang.
COMPOUND-COMPLEX: When they heard the news, he hummed, and she sang.

DISCOURSE EXERCISE 11   How have the two clauses in each of the following sentences been combined? After the number of the sentence, write CO for *coordination*, SUB for *subordination* with a subordinator or relative pronoun, or NC for *noun clause*.

Our Polluted Habitat

1. Government reports show that pollution levels are high.
2. When factories discharge mercury into rivers, fish become toxic.
3. Farm children become sick if adjoining fields are frequently sprayed.
4. Contractors forget where they have dumped toxic wastes.
5. The sites are filled in, and developers build houses.
6. The buyers later wonder why their families suffer from mysterious illnesses.
7. Government agencies reluctantly order cleanups, which cost millions.
8. The injured parties find that law suits drag on forever.

9. Politicians debate how effective our current laws are.
10. Whether the voters will support stronger laws is a matter of dispute.

13g   *gr* | Appositives and Verbals

Recognize special sentence resources like appositives and verbals.

We can greatly extend our sentence resources by putting familiar sentence parts to special uses. Many of the words we use do double duty. They serve more than one kind of purpose.

(1) Recognize nouns used as appositives. A noun alone often replaces an adjective that modifies another noun: a *group* effort, our *track* coach. But a noun may also come *after* another noun to modify that noun and bring added information into the sentence. We call such an added noun an **appositive**: my son, *the doctor*; my friend, *the dean.*

The appositive may bring its own noun marker (*a, the, our*) along with it. It may in turn be modified by other material:

APPOSITIVE: Her best friend, **a sophomore,** finished second.
               The book attacked Margaret Mead, **a famous anthropologist.**
               Aunt Minnie, **a vigorous woman of fifty-five,** had come in to help.   Dorothy Canfield Fisher

Look at the way we can lift an appositive from an additional statement and insert it into a sentence pocket in the original sentence:

SEPARATE: The Siberian tiger _____ may soon survive only in zoos. It is an endangered species.
COMBINED: The Siberian tiger, **an endangered species,** may soon survive only in zoos.

CAUTION: An appositive alone cannot be a complete sentence:

FRAGMENT: She was driving the same car. **An old station wagon.**
COMPLETE: She was driving the same car, **an old station wagon.**
COMPLETE: She was driving the same car. **It was an old station wagon.**

SEE **20d** ON FAULTY APPOSITIVES.

285

(2) Know the difference between verbs and verbals. **Verbals** are parts of verbs or special forms of verbs. However, a verbal cannot by itself be the complete verb of a sentence. For instance, "he *writing*" and "the letter *written*" are not complete sentences. We would have to add an auxiliary to turn each verbal into a complete verb: "He *was writing*": "The letter *had been written*."

The following are major kinds and uses of verbals:

■ Two kinds of verbals can take the place of adjectives and serve as modifiers. The first kind is a form like *burning, falling, hiding, inflating* (**present participles**). The second kind is a form like *burnt, fallen, hidden, inflated* (**past participles**):

VERB:	The hall was **burning**.
VERBAL:	The spectators fled the **burning** hall.
VERB:	The leaves **had fallen**.
VERBAL:	**Fallen** leaves make me sad.
VERB:	The prices **had been inflated**.
VERBAL:	The store charged **inflated** prices.

Again, such verbals may carry along other material, making up a **verbal phrase**:

Hiding in the cellar, he heard the officers **searching the house**.
Nobody had found the papers **hidden in the attic**.

Study the range of possible positions for such added verbal phrases:

Swiss researchers **studying joggers** have found lacerations from bird attacks.
I lay on the couch in the kitchen, **reading** The Last Days of Pompeii and **wishing I were there**.   Alice Munro

■ The *-ing* form is not always used as a modifier. When it takes the place of a noun, we call it a **verbal noun** (or **gerund**). In the following examples, verbal nouns serve as subjects or objects, taking the place of nouns:

SUBJECT	VERB	COMPLETER
Speeding	causes	accidents.
Teachers	discourage	**cheating**.
Parting	is	such sweet sorrow.

286

Verbal nouns may have their own objects; together with the object, the verbal then forms a verbal phrase:

The manager   disliked   **paying the help**.

■ Another verbal that can replace a noun is the *to* form, or **infinitive**: *to run, to organize, to have succeeded, to be loved.* In the following examples, infinitives serve as subjects or as completers, taking the place of nouns:

SUBJECT	VERB	COMPLETER
The guests	refused	**to pay**.
To err	is	human.
Herman	hated	**to be ignored**.

Infinitives, like other verbals, keep important features of verbs. For instance, they may have their own objects:

Joan	refused	to pay **her dues**.
To know **me**	is	to love **me**.

Note: Infinitives have many other uses besides taking the place of nouns. For instance, we use them in combinations like the following:

OBLIGATION: We ought **to go**.
                     Aliens had **to register**.

FUTURE: It is going **to rain**.
                     I was about **to call you**.

We also use infinitives to modify various parts of a sentence:

We were looking for a place **to stay**.
The thing **to do** is to stay calm.
It seemed a good time **to strike out on her own**.
They would drive five hundred miles **to hear the Grateful Dead**.

CAUTION: Infinitives and other verbals alone cannot be complete sentences. Revise fragments like the following:

FRAGMENT: We stopped at a gas station. **To make a phone call**.
COMPLETE: We stopped at a gas station **to make a phone call**.

FRAGMENT: He arrived late for the interview. **Wearing a bandanna**.
COMPLETE: He arrived late for the interview, **wearing a bandanna**.

SEE **19b** FOR DANGLING OR MISPLACED VERBALS.

DISCOURSE EXERCISE 12 Combine each of the following statements in a single sentence. Work the material from the second statement into the first as an *appositive*, using a comma (or commas) to set the appositive from the rest of the sentence.

EXAMPLE: Bible scholars study Hebrew.
It is the language of the Old Testament.

ANSWER: Bible scholars study Hebrew, *the language of the Old Testament.*

The Gift of Tongues

1. Many famous writers share a hobby.
   It is the study of foreign languages.
2. Chaucer translated poems from the French.
   He was the best-known English poet of the Middle Ages.
3. John Milton had written poems in Italian.
   He was the author of *Paradise Lost.*
4. The author of "The Ancient Mariner" had studied German poetry.
   It is a poem known to every student.
5. Margaret Mead studied the native language of New Guinea.
   She was the famous American anthropologist.

PRACTICE EXERCISE 13 For each blank in the following sentences, write an *appositive* (a second noun and any additional material) that would provide a brief capsule description.

EXAMPLE: King Kong, _____ , has been the subject of several Hollywood movies.

ANSWER: *the big ape with a heart*

1. Penicillin, _____ , was discovered accidentally.
2. Sitting Bull, _____ , defeated General Custer at the battle of Little Bighorn.
3. Iran, _____ , suddenly became the center of media attention.
4. Cities began to convert downtown streets into malls, _____ .
5. Columbus, _____ , landed at San Salvador, _____ .
6. Sigmund Freud, _____ , changed the modern view of the mind.
7. Amelia Earhart, _____ , disappeared over the Pacific during a flight around the world.
8. Tarzan, _____ , travels through the forest with Cheetah, _____ .

9. The new coin was to commemorate Susan Anthony, _____ .
10. Marilyn Monroe, _____ , experienced both success and failure in Hollywood, _____ .

DISCOURSE EXERCISE 14   Combine each of the following statements in a single sentence, working the material from the second statement into the first as a *verbal or verbal phrase*. Make sure the verbal points clearly to what it modifies.

EXAMPLE: Oliver asked for more.
                  He was still feeling hungry.
ANSWER: *Still feeling hungry*, Oliver asked for more.

A Sentimental Favorite

1. Many people have laughed and cried over the novels of Charles Dickens.
   They are living in all parts of the world.
2. His books have sold millions of copies.
   They have been translated into many languages.
3. His stories usually have an earnest moral message.
   They were written in Victorian England.
4. Dickens reforms the old miser Scrooge.
   He turns him into a warm-hearted, generous employer.
5. In *David Copperfield*, the hero does well.
   He leads an upright moral life.
6. Steerforth perishes in a shipwreck.
   He had strayed from the right path.
7. Dickens had a flair for melodrama.
   He often put extreme unselfishness next to grotesque evil.
8. The heroine of *Hard Times* is Rachel.
   She bears misfortune with saintly patience.
9. *A Tale of Two Cities* shows us bloodthirsty revolutionaries.
   They are driven by the spirit of revenge.
10. Dickens found a huge audience around the world.
   He was called sentimental by his critics.

DISCOURSE EXERCISE 15 (Review)   In the following set of sentences, the information from a paragraph has been laid out in bite-sized statements. Reassemble the paragraph, using the resources of *modification, coordination, and subordination*. Try to fill in the logical links that show the writer's train of thought.

Foiling Spoilage

An Italian scientist had turned priest.
He was named Lazzaro Spallanzani.
Back in 1765 he heated up meat extracts and other foods.
They were in sealed glass flasks.
He found out something.
They would last several weeks without going bad.
Other scientists repeated his experiments.
Neither they nor Spallanzani understood.
How did the sealing and heating process preserve food?
We now know the reason.
Bacteria inhabit all raw and unsterilized food.
They feed and multiply.
They break the food down.
They turn it rancid and inedible.
Bacteria can be killed by heat.
An airtight seal will prevent something.
Airborne microorganisms cannot reenter and recontaminate the food.

---

14   Fragment and Comma Splice

OVERVIEW   What are the most basic tests of literate English? Whatever else you attend to in final editing, check for sentence fragments—incomplete sentences split off from the larger statement of which they should be a part. Check for the opposite problem: fused sentences—two complete sentences blurred without a visible dividing line. Check for comma splices—two complete sentences spliced together loosely without a logical link, connected only by a comma.

FRAGMENT   Complete English sentences have at least a subject and a complete verb: Birds/*fly*. Dogs/*bark*. Evangelists/*preach*. Verb forms like *flying* and *flown*, or *writing* and *written*, do not by themselves make complete verbs. They need a helping verb like *have* (*has, had*) or *be* (*am, is, was, were*): "The birds *were flying* south."

Sentence fragments happen when a possible subject, a possible verb, or *part* of the complete verb is missing:

NO SUBJECT: The wing hit the ground. **Spun the plane around**. (What spun?)
COMPLETE: The wing hit the ground **and spun the plane around**.

NO COMPLETE VERB:	We spent hours on the road. **Fighting the traffic**.
COMPLETE:	We spent hours on the road, **fighting the traffic**.
NO SUBJECT OR VERB:	We found the host. **In the jacuzzi**.
COMPLETE:	We found the host **in the jacuzzi**.

Some fragments do have a subject and complete verb—but they start with a word meant as a *link* to another part of the sentence:

FRAGMENT:	We will get a raise. **If the governor signs the budget**.
COMPLETE:	We will get a raise **if the governor signs the budget**.
FRAGMENT:	The left brain is analytical. **Whereas the right brain is creative**.
COMPLETE:	The left brain is analytical, **whereas the right brain is creative**.

FUSED SENTENCE A **fused sentence** runs together two complete statements *without* any grammatical link or any punctuation—not even a comma. Supply a semicolon or a period:

FUSED:	The county was dry no beer was to be had.
REVISED:	The county was dry; no beer was to be had.
	The county was dry. No beer was to be had.

COMMA SPLICE A **comma splice** uses only a comma to splice together two related statements. (There is no coordinator like *and* or *but*, no subordinator like *if* or *whereas*.) Use a semicolon instead of the comma:

COMMA SPLICE:	The cabin was empty, they had gone back to Maine.
SEMICOLON:	The cabin was empty; they had gone back to Maine.

14a	*frag*	Sentence Fragments

Use periods to mark off complete sentences.

Except for requests and commands, a sentence needs a subject and a complete verb: *My friends* (S) *vote* (V) for losers. *The team* (S) *was studying* (V) insects. When a period marks off a group of words without a subject and complete verb, the result is a **sentence fragment**. Most sentence fragments transfer to the written page the afterthoughts and asides of stop-and-go conversation:

FRAGMENT:	My friends vote for losers. **Most of the time**.
	The team was studying insects. **Roaches, as a matter of fact**.

291

As a first step toward dealing with fragments, learn to identify two major kinds:

■ Most sentence fragments are **phrases**—groups of words that work together but that do not stand up as separate statements. They lack a subject, or they lack all or part of the verb:

ADJECTIVES:	The grizzly is a magnificent creature. **Magnificent but deadly**.
PREP. PHRASE:	Sarah was studying Hebrew. **In Israel**.
APPOSITIVE:	They invited Sandra O'Connor. **The Supreme Court Justice**.
VERBAL:	Each day he spent hours on the road. **Fighting the traffic**. Kevin had quit the band. **To start a dry-cleaning business**.

■ Many other fragments are **clauses**—dependent clauses that do have their own subject and verb. However, they start with a word meant as a link with an earlier part of the sentence. The unused link causes a fragment. The link may be a subordinating conjunction (subordinator, for short): *if, because, unless, when, before, after, while,* and especially also *whereas* or *although*. Or the unused link may be a relative pronoun: *who, which,* or *that*.

Subordinators and relative pronouns cause fragments like the following:

SUBORDINATORS:	We will refund the money. **If you return the part**. Lawrence is in Kansas. **Whereas Kansas City is in Missouri**.
RELATIVE PRONOUNS:	The birds were storks. **Which are common in Egypt**. Our neighbor was an ex-convict. **Who was still on parole**.

Some fragments are a combination of the two kinds: a phrase and a dependent clause. ("My roommate was a foreign student. *An Iranian whose father had served the Shah*.") To revise a sentence fragment, do one of the following:

(1) Reconnect the fragment to the main sentence without a break. Most prepositional phrases and infinitives (*to* forms) should blend into the sentence without punctuation to show the seam:

REVISED: Sarah was studying Hebrew **in Israel**.

Kevin had quit the band **to start a dry-cleaning business**.

(2) Reconnect the fragment, using a comma. Use the comma when an appositive or a verbal adds **nonrestrictive** material—nonessential information (or "extras") not used to eliminate possibilities or limit the main point. (See **35b**.)

REVISED: They invited Sandra O'Connor, **the Supreme Court Justice**.

Each day he spent hours on the road, **fighting the traffic**.

(3) Use a colon to introduce a list or an explanation. The colon then says "as follows"; note that it comes after a complete statement:

FRAGMENT: Jerry devoted his weekends to his two great loves. **Football and beer**.

REVISED: Jerry devoted his weekends to his two great loves**: football and beer**.

(4) Use a comma when an explanation or example follows a transitional expression. Use a comma before (but not after) *especially* and *such as*:

COMMA: The school attracted many foreign students, **especially** Arabs.

Our laws protect religious minorities, **such as** Mormons or Quakers.

Add a second comma after *for example, for instance,* and *namely.* (The second comma, however, is often left out in informal or journalistic writing.)

TWO COMMAS: We learned to like strange food, **for example,** raw fish.

(5) Join a dependent clause to the main clause. Use no punctuation if the added clause is **restrictive**—if it spells out an essential condition or limits our choices:

NO COMMA: We will refund the money **if you return the part**. (only then)

He befriended people **who had money**. (only those)

Use a comma if the added clause is **nonrestrictive**—if the first statement is true regardless or if what it maps out will not be narrowed down. (See **34d** and **34e**.)

COMMA: Lawrence is in Kansas**, whereas Kansas City is in Missouri**. (both true)
The birds were storks**, which are common in Egypt**. (true of all storks)

(6) Turn the fragment into a complete separate sentence. If all else fails, convert the fragment to a complete sentence with its own subject and verb:

FRAGMENT: I appealed to the officer's sense of humor. **Being a futile effort**.
REVISED: I appealed to the officer's sense of humor. **The effort was futile**.

Note: Experienced writers occasionally use **permissible fragments** for a thinking-out-loud effect:

DESCRIPTION: On the left, a bank of elevators. **Straight ahead, a long burnished corridor, spooky as a lit tunnel. And empty, all empty.**   Cynthia Ozick
NARRATION: There he is: the brother. **Image of him. Haunting face.** James Joyce

---

14b   *fs*   Fused Sentences

Separate two sentences that have been run together.

The opposite of the fragment is the complete sentence that has become the Siamese twin of another sentence—linked without punctuation or a connecting word like *and, but, if,* or *because.* Use a period to separate the two parts of such a **fused sentence**—or a semicolon to show that the two parts are closely related:

FUSED: Matthew no longer lives there **he moved to Katmandu**.
PERIOD: Matthew no longer lives there**. He moved to Katmandu**.

FUSED: She took the exam over **this was her last chance**.
SEMICOLON: She took the exam over**; this was her last chance**.

DISCOURSE EXERCISE 16   Some headlines are *complete sentences*—with a subject and complete verb. Others are incomplete, lacking a possible subject, or all or part of a verb. The following were selected by the managing editor of the *New York Times* as the ten most important headlines of the twentieth century. Mark each *C* (complete) or *I* (incomplete).

Extra! Extra!

1. Man's First Flight in a Heavier-than-Air Machine
2. The Great Powers Go to War in Europe (1914)
3. The Bolshevik Revolution in Russia
4. Lindbergh Flies the Atlantic Alone
5. Hitler Becomes Chancellor of Germany
6. Roosevelt Is Inaugurated as President
7. Scientists Split the Atom, Releasing Incredible Power
8. The Nightmare Again—War in Europe
9. Surprise Japanese Bombing of Pearl Harbor
10. Men Land on the Moon

PEER EDITOR 17   Find the *sentence fragments* in the following passages. If the second part of a pair is a fragment, write *frag* after the number of the sentence. If the second part is a complete sentence, write *C* for complete.

1. Many communities no longer want rapid growth. Free of all controls.
2. The story begins like a typical short story. A story about a small town having a drawing once a year.
3. The "good woman" in Victorian literature is the angelic wife and mother. Her opposite is the "fallen woman."
4. She left the convent after two years. To take over her father's business.
5. Many minority students went out for sports. Because it gave them their only real chance.
6. People used to grow up in larger families. For example, parents, grand-parents, Uncle Salvatore, and three or four children.
7. The place was called the loft. It was a big room at the top of the building.
8. The veterinarian told us the animal had died of a heart attack. While he was preparing to operate.
9. A regulation target resembles an upside-down saucer. Measuring five inches in diameter.
10. She simply could not satisfy anybody's standards. Not those of her su-periors and not those of her co-workers.

PEER EDITOR 18   Revise *sentence fragments* and *fused sentences* in the following examples. Write the italicized part of each example, adding or changing punctuation as necessary. Use a period followed by a capital letter to separate two complete sentences.

1. We were studying pre-Columbian *architecture. Such as Aztec pyramids and Mayan temples.*
2. Outside Mexico City, construction workers found priceless *murals. In buried buildings.*
3. Jobs were plentiful *in the area rents were reasonable.*
4. The lone survivor had hiked *down into the valley. To get help.*
5. One woman was a *jockey the other woman interviewed was a commercial pilot.*
6. Tom Peters co-authored *In Search of Excellence. The best-selling business book in history.*
7. The men of the tribe had *clearly defined roles. Hunting and fishing.*
8. The new management promoted a highly touted *sales technique. With meager results.*
9. Science fiction takes us to the brink *of the impossible. For example, robots with human emotions.*
10. Americans neglect the languages *of the Third World. Especially Arabic and Chinese.*

14c   *cs*   Comma Splices

Use the semicolon to correct comma splices.

We often pair two closely related statements. They form part of the same picture; they are part of the same story. Use a semicolon (as in the pair you just read) to show the close tie between the paired sentences. Note that there is no connecting word or logical link like *and, but, or, if, unless, although,* or *whereas.* Correct **comma splices**, which use a comma instead of the semicolon and result in a pair of complete statements (independent clauses) too loosely spliced together:

COMMA SPLICE: Paula loved London, it was a wonderful city.
REVISED: Paula loved London; it was a wonderful city.

COMMA SPLICE: Some doctors inform their patients, others keep them in the dark.
REVISED: Some doctors inform their patients; others keep them in the dark.

(1) Use the semicolon also with conjunctive adverbs. A word like *therefore* or *however* may link the two paired sentences. These and similar words are **conjunctive adverbs**: *therefore, however, nevertheless, consequently, moreover, accordingly, besides, indeed,* and *in fact.* Again, a comma used instead of the semicolon would result in a comma splice. (Often a comma is used as *additional* punctuation to set the conjunctive adverb off from the second statement—see **34c.**)

COMMA SPLICE:	The weather turned ugly, **therefore** the launch was post-poned.
REVISED:	The weather turned ugly**; therefore,** the launch was post-poned.

(2) Use commas in a set of three parallel clauses. In a set of three or more, commas instead of semicolons are all right. ("I came, I saw, I conquered.")

COMMAS:	Students in India demonstrate against the use of English, African nationalists protest against the use of French, young Israelis have no use for the languages once spoken by their parents.

Note: Some writers use the comma with two **parallel** clauses—statements where the logical connection or the similarity in structure is especially strong. However, many teachers and editors frown on this practice; avoid it in your own writing.

PEER EDITOR 19 In each of the following pairs, use a semicolon to join two independent clauses. (A comma would cause a *comma* splice.) Write the last word of the first clause and the first word of the second, joined by a semicolon.

EXAMPLE:	His hair was very neat every strand was in place.
ANSWER:	neat; every

1. I enjoy running it becomes an almost unconscious act.
2. Everyone did calisthenics executives joined the workers and supervisors.
3. The class was inventing imaginary new products one of them was a stringless yo-yo.
4. Cost overruns were horrendous therefore, the project was abandoned.
5. People were shouting commands everyone with a flashlight was directing traffic.

6. The suspect had stepped out of the lobby he was walking down the street.
7. Zoos used to be dismal places however, modern zoos provide more natural habitats.
8. The sloth is genuinely lethargic its metabolim runs at half the normal rate for animals of its size.
9. Factories in Japan maintain a minimal inventory supplies are used right away.
10. A pawnshop is on the ground floor above it is a fleabag hotel.

---

15 Verb Forms

OVERVIEW Verbs are high on the list of items that frequently need revision. Verb forms differ noticeably in the **standard** English of school and office and the **nonstandard** English that many Americans hear at home, in their neighborhood, or on the job. And verbs are a familiar stumbling block for students speaking English as a second language.

Study and use the verb forms that are right for serious written English. Do not let nonstandard forms carry over into your writing. Look for the following especially:

THIRD PERSON SINGULAR Do not use the plain form of a verb (*look, investigate*) as an all-purpose form. Do not leave off the -*s* ending for one third party (**third person singular**), with action now (**present tense**):

STANDARD: What **does** the motorist do when she **starts** the car? She **puts** the key in the ignition, **turns** it, **puts** the car in gear, **backs** it out of the garage, **looks** both ways, and **avoids** pedestrians.

Don't is nonstandard when used instead of *doesn't* for third person singular, present tense. Use *doesn't* after *he, she,* or *it*, or any single subject:

NONSTANDARD: She **don't** live here. He **don't** like it. It **don't** matter. The insurance **don't** cover it.
STANDARD: She **doesn't** live here. He **doesn't** like it. It **doesn't** matter. The insurance **doesn't** cover it.

STANDARD ENGLISH: AN OVERVIEW

Nonstandard	Standard
VERB FORMS:	
he (she) **don't**, I says	he (she) **doesn't**, I **say**
we **was**, you **was**, they **was**	we **were**, you **were**, they **were**
knowed, growed, brang	**knew, grew, brought**
I **seen** him, had **went**, has **wrote**	I **saw** him, had **gone**, has **written**
PRONOUN FORMS:	
hisself, theirself	**himself, themselves**
this here book, **that there** car	**this** book, **that** car
them boys, **them** barrels	**those** boys, **those** barrels
CONNECTIVES:	
without you pay the rent	**unless** you pay the rent
on account of he was sick	**because** he was sick
being as they missed the plane	**because** they missed the plane
DOUBLE NEGATIVES:	
we **don't** have **no** time	we have **no time**
it **never** hurt **no** one	it **never** hurt **anyone**
wasn't nobody there	**nobody** was there

-ED FOR PAST TENSE   Many English verbs (**regular verbs**) show a change from present to **past** by adding the *-ed* (or *-d*) ending: We *travel* now/We *traveled* in the past. They *investigate* now/they *investigated* in the past. Do not leave off the *-ed* that shows past:

STANDARD: The founders of our country **battled** the British, **secured** our independence, **created** new institutions, **passed** new laws, and **separated** church and state.

IRREGULAR VERBS **Irregular** verbs signal the past by a change in the word itself: *know* it now/*knew* it then. They typically change again when they appear after *have* (*has, had*): I *had* always *known*. This third form also appears after forms of *be* (*am, is, was, were, has been*) when the subject is the target or product of the action: The truth *will be known* (**passive voice**). Know the standard forms for sets of three like the following:

STANDARD:
It **grows** now/it **grew** in the past/it **had grown**
We **go**/we **went** then/we **had gone** before
It **takes** time/it **took** longer then/nothing **was taken**

> SEE THE GLOSSARY OF USAGE FOR DOUBLE NEGATIVE, *A/AN*, AND OTHER
> NONSTANDARD FORMS.

15a Regular Verbs

Use the standard forms of regular verbs.

Verbs are words that can show a change in time by a change in the word itself: We *meditate* (now); we *meditated* (then). Prices *rise* (in the present); prices *rose* (in the past). We call the forms that show different relationships of events in time the **tenses** of a verb. Most English verbs, the **regular** verbs, make up these different forms in predictable ways. They use or adapt two basic forms to make up the whole range of forms that show action in the present, the future, the past, or the more distant past: *ask, will ask, asked, had asked*. (For an irregular verb, a foreign student would have to learn *three* different basic forms: *speak, spoke, had spoken*.) See the chart for the tenses of regular verbs. Remember:

(1) Use the -*ed* (or -*d*) ending for the past. Regular verbs draw on two basic forms: *ask/asked, repeat/repeated*. We use the plain form for the **present** tense—something happening now, or done regularly, or about to happen: we *travel* often, I *consent*, they *exercise* regularly, they *depart* tomorrow. We add -*ed* or -*d* for the **past** tense: we *traveled* often, I *consented*, they *exercised*, they *departed* yesterday.

PAST:
Many pioneer families **perished** in the desert.
The witness **invoked** the Fifth Amendment.

TENSES OF ACTIVE AND PASSIVE VERBS

Tenses of Active Verbs

	NORMAL	PROGRESSIVE
Present	I ask, he (she) asks	I am asking
Past	I asked	I was asking
Future	I shall (will) ask	I shall be asking
Perfect	I have asked	I have been asking
Past Perfect	I had asked	I had been asking
Future Perfect	I shall (will) have asked	I shall have been asking

Tenses of Passive Verbs

	NORMAL	PROGRESSIVE
Present	I am asked	I am being asked
Past	I was asked	I was being asked
Future	I shall (will) be asked	____
Perfect	I have been asked	____
Past Perfect	I had been asked	____
Future Perfect	I shall (will) have been asked	____

(2) In the present tense, use -*s* for the third person singular. Use the special -*s* ending when talking about one single person or thing, with action now: he *travels*, she *consents*, it *departs*. The **first person** is speaking (*I* or *we*): the **second person** is spoken to (*you*). The **third person** is a third party (or object or idea) that we are talking about: *he, she,* or *it* for the singular; *they* for the plural. Use the -*s* ending for the third person singular:

THIRD PERSON (PRESENT):
Brian **works** as a shoplifter.   (**He** works.)
Marcia **collects** beer mugs.   (**She** collects.)
Inflation **continues**.   (**It** continues.)

Note: Forms that point to *one* person or thing (*I, she, it*) are **singular**; forms that point to several, or more than one (*we, they*), are **plural**. For nouns the -*s* ending is a signal for plural: two *friends*, my *uncles*, several *requests*. But for verbs, the -*s* ending is a signal for singular:

SINGULAR: My friend **works**.
                               Her request **surprises** me.

(3) Use the -*ed* (or -*d*) ending for the perfect tenses (and all passive forms). Regular verbs make the -*ed* form do double duty as a verbal (past participle) that follows forms of *have* (*has, had*). Together with *have*, this verbal makes up the perfect tenses: *has called, had called, will have called*. The **present perfect** has happened recently, and what has happened usually still matters now: They *have notified* the police. He *has supported* us loyally. The **past perfect** had already happened prior to *other* events in the past: They *had asked* me ahead of time. Often additional auxiliaries come before *have*. The **future perfect** will have happened before some time in the future: The dust *will have settled*.

PERFECT: The police department **has consulted** a psychic.
PAST PERFECT: They **had** already **encased** the reactor in cement.
FUTURE PERFECT: The country **will have depleted** its oil reserves.

The verbal ending in -*ed* or -*d* is also used in all forms of the **passive voice**—forms showing that the subject of the sentence is acted upon rather than acting:

PASSIVE: Many elephants **are slaughtered** by poachers.
                               A protest was **filed** by the Animal Rights Committee.
                               The passages **had been lifted** verbatim.

(4) Use -*ing* for the progressive construction. The verbal ending in -*ing* (present participle) serves in forms showing an action or event in progress, taking place:

PROGRESSIVE: The agency **is processing** your application.
                               The architect **was redesigning** the entranceway.

SEE **22a** FOR SEQUENCE OF TENSES AND SHIFTS IN TENSE.

PRACTICE EXERCISE 20 Put each of the following regular verbs through its paces. For each, write a set of sentences following this pattern:

EXAMPLE: We *exercise* now. He (or she) *exercises* now. We *exercised* then.
We *have exercised* recently. We *had exercised* before then.
We *will have exercised* before then. We *are exercising* regularly.

Use the following five verbs: *work, meditate, relax, improvise, compromise*.

15b Irregular Verbs

Use the standard forms of irregular verbs.

Irregular verbs often have three basic forms, with the past different from perfect: I *write* now. She *wrote* last week. He *has written* regularly. The second and third forms are more unpredictable than those of regular verbs: *begin—began—begun, blow—blew—blown, go—went—gone.* (See chart, "Standard Forms of Verbs.") Remember:

(1) Use the right past tense of irregular verbs. Revise nonstandard forms like *knowed, blowed, ccatched, brung,* and *drug.*

STANDARD: Ancient Greek scientists **knew** that the earth was round.
We cruised all day but **caught** few fish.
Telegrams seldom **brought** encouraging news.

(2) Use the right forms after forms of *have* and *be*. The third of the three listed forms is used after *have (has, had)*. It is the form for the perfect tenses:

STANDARD: Our pious neighbors **had gone** to church.
The python **has** already **eaten** the rabbit.
You **should have taken** the blue pills instead.
Overeager reporter **had** already **written** his obituary.
The balloon **had torn** loose from its moorings.

303

STANDARD FORMS OF VERBS

PRESENT	PAST	PERFECT
begin	began	have begun
bend	bent	have bent
blow	blew	have blown
break	broke	have broken
bring	brought	have brought
burst	burst	have burst
buy	bought	have bought
catch	caught	have caught
choose	chose	have chosen
come	came	have come
dig	dug	have dug
do	did	have done
drag	dragged	have dragged
draw	drew	have drawn
drink	drank	have drunk
drive	drove	have driven
drown	drowned	have drowned
eat	ate	have eaten
fall	fell	have fallen
fly	flew	have flown

The same form (past participle) is used in all passive verbs after a form of *be* (*am, are, is, was, were, has been,* and so on):

STANDARD:
The fish **is frozen** and shipped by plane.
The bicycle **was stolen** during the night.
The bolt **had been worn** out.

(3) Sometimes we have a choice of two acceptable forms. Both are right: *lighted* or *lit, dived* or *dove, waked* or *woke, thrived* or *throve*.

BOTH RIGHT:
She **dreamed** (or **dreamt**) of a vacation in the sun.
Your prediction **has proved** (or **has proven**) wrong.
The ship **sank** (or **sunk**) within minutes.
They gracefully **dived** (or **dove**) into the pool.
The sleepers **waked** (or **woke**) refreshed.

PRESENT	PAST	PERFECT
freeze	froze	have frozen
get	got	have gotten (got)
go	went	have gone
· grow	grew	have grown
know	knew	have known
prove	proved	have proved (proven)
ride	rode	have ridden
run	ran	have run
say	said	have said
see	saw	have seen
sing	sang	have sung
speak	spoke	have spoken
steal	stole	have stolen
swim	swam	have swum
swing	swung	have swung
take	took	have taken
tear	tore	have torn
throw	threw	have thrown
wear	wore	have worn
write	wrote	have written

Finer Points   Sometimes we have two different forms with *different meanings:* "The picture was *hung*," but "The prisoner *was hanged*." "The sun *shone*," but "I *shined* my shoes."

PRACTICE EXERCISE 21   Test your knowledge of *regular* and *irregular* verbs. What form of the word in parentheses would be right for the blank space in each of the following sentences? Put the right form after the number of the sentence. (Use a single word each time.)

1. (steal)   Radioactive material had been _____ from the plant.
2. (throw)   We spotted the swimmer and _____ her a lifeline.

3. (tear)	Someone had _____ open the envelope.
4. (go)	The witnesses should have _____ to the police.
5. (choose)	Last year, the party _____ a new leader.
6. (know)	Without the ad, she would not have _____ about the job.
7. (drive)	The car has been _____ too fast and too carelessly.
8. (see)	Several years ago, we _____ a road company production of *Hair*.
9. (break)	Her cabin had been _____ into several times.
10. (grow)	Everything had _____ well in the moist climate.
11. (develop)	In its early years, the company _____ educational software.
12. (write)	He might have _____ a lukewarm letter of recommendation.
13. (know)	When we came home, she already _____ what had happened.
14. (choose)	Our candidate has not yet _____ a running mate.
15. (take)	Someone has _____ the papers from the file.
16. (investigate)	Last year, a grand jury _____ their dealings.
17. (speak)	You should have _____ to the manager.
18. (drown)	Several vacationers have _____ in the lake.
19. (ride)	You never should have _____ in a stranger's car.
20. (wear)	Coats like these are _____ by construction workers in Alaska.

15c   *ub*   Lie, Sit, and Rise

Use the standard forms of *lie, sit,* and *rise*.

Some verbs have doubles just different enough to be confusing:

(1) Know the difference between *lie* and *lay*. We *lie* in the sun (and we let sleeping dogs *lie*), but we *lay* mines, bricks, tiles, and similar objects of a verb. We *lie*, and *lie down*, without an object (we just *lie* there). For *lie*, the past tense is *lay*, and the third basic form is *lain:*

LIE, LAY, LAIN: Let's **lie** in the shade. We whistled, but he just **lay** there. The statue **had lain** on the ocean floor. You **should lie** down. Coins **were lying** on the ground.

We lay *something*, with *laid* as the past tense (*laid* an egg) and as the form used after *have* (*had laid* the rumors to rest).

LAY, LAID, LAID: Bricklayers **lay** bricks. Our forefathers **laid** the foundation. She **had laid** a wreath at the tomb. He was always **laying** odds.

(2) Know the difference between *sit* and *set*. To *sit* (*sit—sat—sat*) is to be seated. *Sit down* follows the same scheme:

They **sit** in the pew in which their parents **sat** and their grandparents **had sat** before them. (S–V)

Set (*set—set—set*), one of the few verbs with only one basic form, means *place* or *put*. You yourself *sit*, or *sit down*; you *set*, or *set down*, something else:

When you have **set** the timer, **set** the device down gingerly behind the screen we **set** up. (S–V–O)

(3) Know the difference between *rise* and *raise*. The verb *rise* (*rise—rose—risen*) means "get up" or "go up." The verb *raise* (*raise—raised—raised*) refers to lifting something or *making* it go up:

Since you **rose** this morning, the tax rate **has risen** ten cents.
Though they are always **raising** prices, they have not **raised** the salaries of the employees.

PRACTICE EXERCISE 22   Choose the right forms of *sit* or *set*, *lie* or *lay*, *rise* or *raise*.

1. The folders *sat/set* on the desk while we were *sitting/setting* up a new filing system.
2. Her uncle *set/sat* a record for flagpole *sitting/setting*.
3. This time of year, the tourists *lie/lay* in the sun, while the natives *sit/set* in the shade.
4. Broken columns were *lying/laying* on the ground; some fragments had been *laid/lain* end to end.
5. Thick dust *lie/lay* on the artifacts that for centuries had *lain/laid* in the tomb undisturbed.
6. Many perplexing questions were *raised/risen* about the *raising/rising* crime rate.

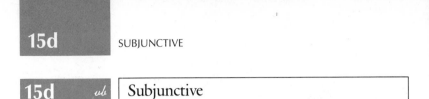

15d   *ub*   Subjunctive

Use the subjunctive in special situations.

Many languages have one set of verb forms for straight facts and another set for maybes, wishes, and hypotheses. The factual form is the **indicative** (I know it *was*); the hypothetical form is the **subjunctive** (I wish it *were*). In English, only a few uses of the subjunctive mode (or **mood**) survive:

(1) Choose the hypothetical *were* or the factual *was* after *if, as if, as though*. Use *were* if a possibility is contrary to fact or highly improbable—a remote chance:

SUBJUNCTIVE: For a moment, the statue looked as if it **were** alive.   (It wasn't really.)
                If I **were** you, I would ask for a refund.   (I'm not really you.)
                The new manager acted as if asking questions **were** a crime.

Use the hypothetical *were* also to show a mere wish:

SUBJUNCTIVE: I wish she **were** more assertive.
                Napoleon wished it **were** spring in Paris rather than winter in Moscow.

Use the factual *is* or *was* when pondering a genuine possibility:

FACTUAL: If the courier **was** ill, he should have declined the assignment.   (Maybe he really was.)
            It looks as if the statue **was** thrown overboard in a storm.   (It probably was.)

(2) Use a subjunctive after verbs asking that something be done. After words like *ask, order, insist, demand, recommend, require,* and *suggest,* use a plain or unmarked form (*be, have, go*) instead of the -*s* ending (*is, has, goes*).

SUBJUNCTIVE: Her supervisor insists that she **spend** more time in the office.
                I move that this question **be** referred to a committee.

Note: A few additional uses of the subjunctive survive in expressions like "*Come* what may" or "*Be* that as it may."

> FOR CONSISTENT VERBS FOR CONDITIONS, SEE **22a**.

PEER EDITOR 23   Choose among *was, were,* or *be,* using the *subjunctive* where appropriate.

1. If *Alice in Wonderland* _____ being written today, Alice would use words like *awesome* and *totally cool.*
2. If neither parent _____ a Catholic, she must be a convert.
3. The measure proposed that utility companies _____ barred from producing nuclear waste within the state.
4. Brian's aunt always acted as if she _____ his mother.
5. Journalists and ministers urged that the sentence _____ commuted.

---

16   Agreement

OVERVIEW   Among the ties that hold a sentence together, one of the most important is agreement between subject and verb. Most nouns and pronouns have different forms for one of a kind (**singular**) and more than one (**plural**): *key/keys, prize/prizes, woman/women, child/children.* Verbs often offer us a similar choice: one *goes*/several *go*; one *is* gone/ several *are* gone; one *has* arrived/several *have* arrived. When we match the right forms, the subject and its verb **agree** in number.

SINGULAR: The clock **ticks**. The listener **was** bored. She **writes** often.
PLURAL: The clocks **tick**. The listeners **were** bored. They **write** often.

Often, other sentence parts besides subject and verb reflect our choice of singular or plural. Look at all the signals that tell the reader "one" or "several" in the following pair:

SINGULAR: **This student has** saved **her** strongest **point** for the **end** of **her paper.**
PLURAL: **These students have** saved **their** strongest **points** for the **ends** of their **papers.**

Note: For nouns, the *-s* ending is a plural signal: *boys, cars, tickets, houses, promotions.* But for verbs, the *-s* is a signal for singular. We use it when we talk about one single thing or person (**third person singular**), with action now (**present tense**):

SINGULAR:	He talk**s**.	She write**s**.	It bark**s**.
PLURAL:	They talk.	They write.	They bark.

SEE 17e FOR AGREEMENT OF A PRONOUN WITH ITS ANTECEDENT.

16a   *agr*   Irregular Plurals

Know irregular plurals borrowed from other languages.

Most English nouns use the familiar *-s* plural (car*s*, building*s*, tree*s*, book*s*, petition*s*). But some words borrowed from Greek and Latin have kept irregular plural forms:

SINGULAR	PLURAL	SINGULAR	PLURAL
crisis	crises	criterion	criteria
thesis	theses	phenomenon	phenomena
analysis	analyses	medium	media
hypothesis	hypotheses	stimulus	stimuli
curriculum	curricula	nucleus	nuclei

Study the difference between singular and plural in the following examples:

SINGULAR:	The artist's favorite **medium was** acrylic paint.
PLURAL:	The **media were** turning the trial into a circus.
SINGULAR:	**This phenomenon has** been discovered only recently.
PLURAL:	**These phenomena have** been extensively studied.

Finer Points

- Acceptable Anglicized plurals are *indexes* for *indices* and *formulas* for *formulae*. Sometimes the earlier plural survives in a specialized or technical use: the *antennae* of insects.
- Use *data* as a plural to be safe: Data *are* items of information.

■ A few foreign words have separate forms for **gender**, like *fiancé* (the man) and *fiancée* (the woman). One male graduate is an *alumnus*; several are *alumni*. One female graduate is an *alumna*; several are *alumnae*.

EXERCISE 24   In a college dictionary, find the acceptable plural (or plurals) for *appendix, beau, cactus, cherub, oasis, stigma, vertebra,* and *species.*

16b   *agr*   Singular or Plural

Know which subjects are singular and which plural.

Sometimes form seems to point one way and meaning another. Remember:

(1) Some pronouns seem plural in meaning but are singular in form. Treat as singular *each, either, neither, everybody,* and *everyone.* Though they point to more than one, look at them *one at a time:*

SINGULAR: Each of the students **is** going to receive a diploma.
Either of the candidates **seems** weak.
Everybody (every single one) **approves** of your decision.

(2) Some nouns look plural but are treated as singulars.   Words ending in *-ics—aeronautics, mathematics, physics, aerobics—*are often singular names for a field or activity: Modern physics *allows* for uncertainty. Some words ending in *-ics* can go either way:

SINGULAR: Politics **bores** me. Statistics **attracts** math majors.
PLURAL: Her politics **have** changed. These statistics **are** suspect.

Collective nouns like *audience, committee, family, police, group, jury,* or *team* are singular when we think of the whole group. They are plural when we think of the *members* of the group:

SINGULAR: The nuclear family **is** the exception, not the rule.
PLURAL: The family **were** gathered around the table.

311

(3) Expressions showing the whole amount may be singular even when plural in form. They are singular when they point to the sum or total:

SINGULAR: Thirteen dollars **seems** excessive for a small cutlet and two carrots.
One third of the world is rich, and two thirds **is** poor.

Number of is singular when it stands for a total: *The number of* joggers *has* declined. It is plural when it stands for "several": *A number of* joggers *were* still on the trail.

16c   *agr*   Compound Subjects

Check agreement when there is more than one subject.

When the word *and* joins several subjects, the resulting **compound subject** is normally plural. But the word *or* may merely give us a choice between two singular subjects:

PLURAL: Rafting **and** canoeing **clear** the smog from the lungs and the fumes from the brain.
SINGULAR: Either the surgeon **or** the anesthesiologist **is** to blame.

(1) Two nouns joined by *and* may describe a single thing or person. Corned beef and cabbage *is* good to eat; the President and chief executive *is* one person.

SINGULAR: **Pork and beans *is*** one of my favorite dishes.
My closest friend and associate *was* a cocker spaniel.

(2) *As well as, together with,* and *in addition to* do not add one subject to another. They merely show that what is said about the subject applies also to other things or persons. (They introduce a prepositional phrase.)

SINGULAR: The mayor's **office**, together with other agencies, **is** sponsoring the event.
The **memo**, as well as the other documents, **has** been shredded.

Finer Points   In some sentences, an *or*, an *either . . . or*, or a *neither . . . nor* gives the reader a choice between a singular subject and a plural one. Make the verb of such a sentence agree with the subject closer to it.

> Either laziness or excessive social obligations **have** kept him from his work.

DISCOURSE EXERCISE 25   In each of the following sentences, solve an *agreement problem* by changing the verb or first auxiliary. Write the changed word after the number of the sentence.

Surviving the Interview

1. Often each of several candidates for a job are reasonably well-qualified.
2. Much feinting, chutzpah, and false humility is required in a successful job interview.
3. Competence or a good track record alone are not enough to assure a good rating.
4. An impressively presented résumé, together with glowing letters of recommendation, put the interviewers in a receptive mood.
5. Statistics about past performance often impresses the listener.
6. A number of topics, like politics and sex, is to be avoided at all costs.

16d *agr* Blind Agreement

Make subject and verb agree even when they are separated by other material.

Avoid **blind agreement**: Do not make the verb agree with a word close to it that is *not* its subject.

(1) Check agreement when a plural noun comes between a singular subject and its verb.   Disregard any wedge between subject and verb:

SINGULAR: **An ad** [in these small local papers] **produces** results.
Understanding [the opponent's motives] **is** important.

Beware of blind agreement whenever the subject of a sentence is one thing singled out among several, one quality shared by several members of a group, or one action affecting different things or persons:

SINGULAR:	Only **one** of my friends **was** ready in time.
	(not "**were** ready")
SINGULAR:	The **usefulness** of these remedies **has** been questioned.
	(not "**have** been questioned")
` SINGULAR:	**Arresting** the local crack dealers **puts** an impossible strain on the courts.
	(not "**put** a strain")

(2) Check agreement when the subject follows the verb. Do not make the verb agree with a stray noun that stands in front of it·

PLURAL:	Inside the yellowed envelope **were** several large **bills**.
	(What was inside? **Bills** were inside.)

(3) Check for agreement in sentences starting with *there is, there are,* and the like. After *there*, the verb agrees with the **postponed subject**—with whatever is "there":

SINGULAR:	There **was** polite **applause** from the better seats.
PLURAL:	There **were** scattered **boos** from the balcony.

In formal usage, the plural verb is required even when followed by a compound subject of which each part is singular:

PLURAL:	There **were** a bed and a chair for each patient.
PLURAL:	On the crown of the hill, there **are** a miniature plaza, miniature cathedral, and miniature governor's palace. Arnold J. Toynbee, "The Mayan Mystery," *Atlantic*

(4) Make a linking verb agree with its subject, not the completer. In the following sentence, *problem* is the subject; *parts* is the completer (or complement): "Our chief *problem* is (not *are*) defective parts." If you can, however, avoid an apparent clash of singular and plural:

RIGHT:	**Another example** of unneeded technological progress **is planes** flying faster than the speed of sound.
BETTER:	**Another example** of unneeded technological progress **is the supersonic plane**, flying faster than the speed of sound.

DISCOURSE EXERCISE 26 Rewrite each of the following sentences, changing both subject and verb from singular to plural. Make *no* other changes.

Banning the Dinosaurs

1. The biology teacher in the local high school teaches evolution.
2. The scientific theory about the origin of life has become controversial.
3. A biology textbook is likely to have been revised several times.
4. In California, a chapter about evolution was first yanked and then put back in.
5. Meanwhile, the typical American youngster learns all about dinosaurs and fossils from TV.

PEER EDITOR 27 Correct *blind agreement* in the following student sentences by changing the verb or first auxiliary. Write the changed word after the number of the sentence.

1. The description of his appearance and manners hint at turbulent hidden emotions.
2. As we enter the post-modern period, the style of the office towers subtly change.
3. For every miracle drug, there is unexpected side effects and tremendous variations in individual response.
4. The weak chemical bonds among oxygen atoms in ozone allows the molecules to break apart.
5. Many crime shows make the viewers feel tough by association and boosts their egos.
6. Computer monitoring of coffee breaks and phone calls are turning offices into electronic sweatshops.

16e *agr* | Agreement After *Who, Which,* and *That*

Check for agreement problems caused by relationships among several clauses.

Who, which, and *that* may point back to either a singular or a plural. These words often serve as subjects in relative clauses that modify a noun (or pronoun). The verb following the *who, which,* or *that* agrees with the word that is being modified:

SINGULAR: I hate a **person** who **stares** at me.

PLURAL: I hate **people** who **stare** at me.

Watch for agreement in combinations like "one of those who *know*" and "one of those who *believe*." Look at the contrast in the following pair:

PLURAL: Jean is one of **those students who go** to classes after work.
               (Many students go to classes after work.)

SINGULAR: Jean is **the only one** of those students **who goes** to classes
               after work.
               (Only one student goes to classes after work.)

16f   *agr*   Logical Agreement

If necessary, carry agreement beyond subject and verb.

Where the meaning requires it, extend agreement beyond the subject and verb of a sentence.

ILLOGICAL: Average newspaper **readers** go through their whole **life**
               knowing a little about everything but nothing well.
REVISED: Average newspaper **readers** go through their whole **lives**
               knowing a little about everything but nothing well.

ILLOGICAL: Many advertisers now beam their messages at women
               who are a **wife, mother, and executive** at the same time.
REVISED: Many advertisers now beam their messages at women
               who are **wives, mothers, and executives** at the same
               time.

SEE THE GLOSSARY OF USAGE FOR *THESE KIND*.

PEER EDITOR 28 Correct faulty agreement in the following student sentences by changing a single word—a verb (or first auxiliary) or another word that should show logical agreement.

1. I am not one of those who believes in letting vigilantes restore law and order.
2. She is one of several officers who was attacked by the suspect.
3. The deep thinkers in the student union solve the world's problems by the use of their powerful mind.
4. These are students with poor academic preparation who nevertheless wants to become educated.
5. Employers were fined for hiring workers who were classified as illegal immigrant.

DISCOURSE EXERCISE 29 (Review) Choose the right forms, paying special attention to common sources of *faulty agreement*. Write the correct form after the number of the sentence.

Made (Poorly) in USA

1. Complaints about poor quality *has/have* hurt American efforts to capture overseas markets.
2. The steps that American companies have taken to improve quality control *is/are* producing only limited results.
3. Ford Motor Company as well as other leading manufacturers *has/have* recalled large numbers of cars and trucks.
4. Having to admit that the front seats tend to shake loose *does/do* little for the image of a new car.
5. True, few customers wind up with one of those cars that *spends/spend* more time in the shop than on the road.
6. But a buyer may discover that there *is/are* an electronically controlled door that doesn't open and a windshield wiper motor that has shorted out.
7. According to some foreign customers, computer chips made in America *tends/tend* to be chipped.
8. Gauges in a new jumbo aircraft *was/were* crosswired so that a fire in one engine showed on the gauge for another.
9. Fire suppression nozzles in the cargo hold *was/were* spraying fire retardant in the wrong direction.
10. The ability to turn out high-quality products *is/are* essential if American industry wants to compete around the world.

17 Pronoun Reference

OVERVIEW When you revise for clarity, pronouns like *it*, *they*, *which*, or *this* will be high on your list. Confusion results when the reader has to ask: "Who are *they*?" "What does the *this* point back to?" Pronouns provide a welcome shortcut because they can take the place of a lengthy original. *American policy in Central America* can simply become *it* when we mention it the second time. But the *it* has to point clearly to its **antecedent**—to what "went before."

Check for the following especially:

AMBIGUOUS *HE, SHE,* OR *THEY* When several people have been mentioned, a *he* or *she* may not point clearly to one of them. The sentence remains **ambiguous**; it can be read two different ways:

AMBIGUOUS:	When **Marianne** explained the procedure to **her new assistant, she** looked bored. (Who looked bored—Marianne or the assistant?)
CLEAR:	When Marianne explained the procedure, **her new assistant** looked bored.
	Marianne looked bored when she explained the procedure to her new assistant.

VAGUE *THIS* OR *WHICH* A *this* or *which* often points back in a general way to one of several ideas earlier in a sentence or paragraph. The *this* or *which* may not be anchored firmly enough to what came before.

VAGUE:	The senator attacked the funding for the exhibit, **which** we considered ridiculous. (What was ridiculous—the exhibit or the attack?)
CLEAR:	When the senator attacked the funding for the exhibit, we considered **his move** ridiculous.

ORPHANED *IT* OR *THEY* An *it* or *they* may appear with nothing specific to refer to:

WEAK:	When Sean went to college, he wanted to be a musician, but **they** discouraged **it**. (Who are they? What is it?)
REVISED:	When Sean went to college, he wanted to be a musician, but **his teachers** discouraged **him**.

AGREEMENT OF PRONOUNS Does the pronoun point back to a singular or plural? Informal spoken English often shifts to the plural *they* or *their* where written English requires a singular:

SPOKEN: **Every girl** on the team did **their** best.
WRITTEN: **Every girl** (every single one) on the team did **her** best.

17a *ref* Ambiguous Reference

Make a pronoun point clearly to one of several possible antecedents.

Pronouns easily become confusing when we mention several people in the same sentence (or paragraph). Look at the pronoun *she* in the following sentence: "*Linda* disliked *Ann* because *she* was very competitive." Which of the two was competitive? The sentence is **ambiguous**; it confuses the reader because of an unintended double meaning. Reshuffle the material in such a sentence:

CLEAR: Because **Linda** was very competitive, **she** disliked Ann.
             Because **Ann** was very competitive, Linda disliked **her**.

If a *they* follows two plural nouns, you might point it at the right one by making the other singular. (Similarly, you might change one of two singular nouns to a plural.)

AMBIGUOUS: **Students** like **science teachers** because **they** are realistic and practical.
CLEAR: A **student** usually likes **science teachers** because **they** are realistic and practical.
             (**They** can no longer be mistakenly referred to **students**.)

CAUTION: The farther removed a pronoun is from its antecedent, the greater the danger of ambiguous reference. Do not make a reader go back through several sentences in a paragraph to check what *he, this,* or *they* stands for.

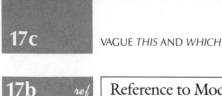

17b   *ref* | Reference to Modifiers

Revise awkward reference to modifiers.

Make pronouns refer to basic sentence parts rather than to modifiers. The *it* in sentences like the following seems misdirected: "James worked in an *asbestos plant*, and *it* got into his lungs" (the plant?). Similar double takes result when a pronoun refers to a **possessive** noun—the form that shows where something belongs: "I reached for *the horse's saddle*, but *it* shied away" (the saddle?).

CLEAR: James worked in an asbestos plant, and **the asbestos** got into his lungs.
                        As I reached for **its** saddle, **the horse** shied away.

Note: Reference to a possessive accounts for awkward sentences like the following: "In *John Steinbeck's* novel *The Grapes of Wrath*, he describes the plight of the marginal farmer." Better: "In *his novel . . . John Steinbeck* describes . . ."

17c   *ref* | Vague *This* and *Which*

Revise vague idea reference.

Vague idea reference results when a *this* or *which* refers to the overall idea expressed in an earlier statement:

AMBIGUOUS: The police knew the employees were stealing, but management was not aware of **this**. (of the stealing, or of the police knowing?)
CLEAR: The police knew the employees were stealing, but management did not realize **word had got out**.

We can often make a vague *this* more specific: "this *assumption*," "this *practice*." A vague *which* is more difficult to improve. You may have to rewrite the sentence without it:

AMBIGUOUS: Newspapers give prominence to youths who get into trouble, **which** gives a bad name to all young people. (What gives a bad name—the slanted coverage or the trouble-making youths?)

320

CLEAR:	Newspapers give prominence to youths who get into trouble. **This slanted coverage** gives a bad name to all young people.

17d   *ref*   Vague *They* and *It*

Spell out implied antecedents of *they* and *it*.

Talking informally, we often make a pronoun point to something not actually mentioned but merely understood: "*They* lost my transcript" (the registrar did). In writing, bring back the lost antecedent:

IMPLIED:	In Nebraska, **they** grow mostly wheat.
CLEAR:	In Nebraska, **the farmers** grow mostly wheat.

Avoid the orphaned *it* or *they* when you refer to an implied idea in sentences like the following:

AMBIGUOUS:	My mother was a musician; therefore, I have also chosen **it** as my profession. (The **it** stands not for "musician" but for "music.")
REVISED:	My mother was a **musician**; therefore, I have also chosen **music** as my profession.
AMBIGUOUS:	The prisoner's hands were manacled to a chain around his waist, but **they** were removed at the courtroom door. (What was removed? The prisoner's hands?)
REVISED:	The prisoner's hands were manacled to a chain around his waist, but the **manacles** were removed at the courtroom door.

ON SHIFTS IN PRONOUN REFERENCE, SEE 22b.

PEER EDITOR 30   Rewrite the following student sentences to revise ambiguous or unsatisfactory pronoun reference.

1. A five-year-old boy was shot by a police officer mistaking his toy gun for a real weapon.
2. The book's title sounded interesting, but when I read it I found it boring.
3. My father is extremely intelligent, though he does not always express it in a verbal form.

4.   Prisons are run by undertrained and underpaid individuals, not to mention that they are hopelessly overcrowded.
5.   Many voters know little about Central America, which makes it difficult for the President to gain popular support for his policies.

17e *ref, agr* | Agreement of Pronouns

Make pronouns agree in number with their antecedents.

To make a pronoun point to what it stands for, make pronoun and antecedent agree in number:

WRONG: **Abortions** should not be outlawed because **it** is often required for medical reasons.

RIGHT: **Abortions** should not be outlawed because **they** are often required for medical reasons.

Watch for the following:

(1) Make a singular pronoun point to one representative person. Treat as singular *a person, an individual, the typical student,* or *an average American*—one person that represents many:

WRONG: A person can never be too careful about **their** use of language.

RIGHT: A person can never be too careful about **his or her** use of language.

WRONG: **The typical male** today is expected to assume a larger share of parenting, but **they are** often poorly prepared for this task.

RIGHT: **The typical male** today is expected to assume a larger share of parenting, but **he is** often poorly prepared for this task.

(2) Use a singular pronoun to refer to expressions like *everybody* and *someone.* These **indefinite pronouns** do not point to one particular person or group of people: *everybody (everyone), somebody (someone), nobody (no one), anybody (anyone), one.* Words like *everybody* or *anyone* are very inclusive; they point to many different people. However, in your writing, use them as if you were looking at these people *one* at a time:

RIGHT: **Everybody** on the team did **her** best.
Nobody should meddle in affairs that are none of **his or her** business.
It was part of the knight's code that **one** must value **his** (or **one's**) honor more than life.

None started as the equivalent of "no one," but today either singular or plural forms after it are acceptable to most readers:

BOTH RIGHT: **None** of the women had to interrupt **her** schooling (or "**their** schooling").

(3) Deal with the pronoun dilemma. Informal English uses the plural pronoun in sentences like "Everybody received *their* copy of the test." Handbooks used to prescribe the singular *he* (*his, him*): "Everybody received *his* copy of the test." This **generic** *he*, meant to refer to both men and women, is now widely shunned. For a mixed group, use *he or she* (*his or her*).

NONSEXIST: Today's executive has a computer by **his or her** desk.

If several uses of *he or she* (and perhaps *himself and herself*) would slow down a sentence, convert the whole sentence to the plural:

INFORMAL: **Everyone** I knew was increasing **their** insurance to protect **themselves** against lawsuits.

FORMAL: **All my friends** were increasing **their** insurance to protect **themselves** against lawsuits.

FOR MORE ON GENDER-BIASED PRONOUNS, SEE **30a** AND **30b.**

PEER EDITOR 31 In each of the following student sentences, replace one pronoun in order to solve a problem of *pronoun reference*. Write the changed pronouns after the number of each sentence.

1. Each member had their own private excuse for joining the fraternity.
2. Universities often prove mixed blessings to the towns surrounding it.
3. The bear feeds primarily on roots; to attack livestock, they would have to be desperate.
4. The actress had played roles as a sassy, randy young girl; it had led to her being stereotyped as a hussy.
5. Most medical students are still white males, although admission policies are now less biased in his favor.

6. Nonsmokers are refusing to patronize a restaurant because of the smoke he might inhale.
7. A woman who spends years preparing for a career in the theater might find themselves acting in mattress commercials.
8. Each person runs differently, depending on their body size.
9. The Founding Fathers intended that someone's religion should be their own responsibility.
10. England consistently had a much lower homicide rate because they enforced strict gun control laws.

---

18 Pronoun Case

OVERVIEW Informal pronoun forms are among the telltale features of casual conversational speech. You may hear people say "between you and *I*" or "invited *she* and her cousin." You need to write "between you and *me*" and "invited *her* and her cousin." Study the way we use pronoun forms in edited written English.

How many people are involved in the following scenario? "*He* proposed to *her*, but *she* rejected *him*." Although the sentence uses four different pronouns, it is talking about only two people. *He* and *she* are **subject forms** (also called subjective forms). They point to the subject and often tell us *who* is doing something in the sentence. (*He* called. *She* answered.) *Him* and *her* are **object forms** (also called objective forms); they point to the object of a verb or a preposition and often tell us what an action is aimed at. (The manager interviewed *him*. The customer glared at *her*.)

Only half a dozen pronouns have separate object forms: *I—me; we—us; he—him; she—her; they—them; who—whom*. These differences in form are called differences in **case**.

SUBJECT	OBJECT	OBJECT OF PREPOSITION
I congratulated	**him**.	
He recommended	**me**	to **them**.
They prejudiced	**her**	against **me**.

A third possible form shows that the object of an action is the same as the performer. *Himself, themselves, myself, ourselves,* and similar forms are **reflexive forms**:

He blamed **himself**.
They asked **themselves** what had gone wrong.
We introduced **ourselves** to the interviewer.

They are also used as **intensives**, for emphasis:

The dean told me so **herself**.
We should weigh the testimony of the accused men **themselves**.

CAUTION: *Hisself, theirself, theirselves,* and *themself* are nonstandard. Unless you are quoting a speaker using down-home language, use *himself* and *themselves* instead.

18a   *ca*   Subject and Object Forms

Choose the right pronoun forms for subject and object.

Written use of these forms differs from what we commonly hear in informal and nonstandard speech. Though we might hear "*Me and him* go jogging together," we expect "*He and I* go jogging" in writing. *He* and *I* are both subjects of *go* and should appear in the subject form.

(1) Choose the right form when a pronoun is one of several subjects or objects. To find the right pronoun for a compound subject or compound object, try the parts one at a time:

SUBJECT: The supervisor and **I** [not: **Me** and the supervisor] worked hand in hand.
(Who worked? **I** worked.)

OBJECT: She asked my brother and **me** [not: my brother and **I**] to lower the volume.
(Whom did she ask? She asked **me**.)

(2) Be careful with pronoun-noun combinations. Choose between *we girls—us girls* or *we Americans—us Americans*. Use the subject form when the combination serves as the subject of the sentence:

SUBJECT: **We Americans** pride ourselves on our good intentions.
(Who does? **We** do.)

OBJECT: The border guard questioned **us Americans** at length.
(Questioned whom? Questioned **us**.)

325

AN OVERVIEW OF PRONOUNS

	SUBJECT FORM	OBJECT FORM
Personal pronouns	I	me
	you	you
	he	him
	she	her
	it	it
	we	us
	you	you
	they	them

	FIRST SET	SECOND SET
Possessive pronouns	my	mine
	your	yours
	his	his
	her	hers
	its	its
	our	ours
	your	yours
	their	theirs

	SINGULAR	PLURAL
Reflexive pronouns	myself	ourselves
(also "intensive" pronouns)	yourself	yourselves
	himself	themselves
	herself	
	itself	

(3) Use object forms after prepositions: *with* her; *because of* him; *for* me. Use the object form for a pronoun that is the second or third object in a prepositional phrase:

OBJECT: This kind of thing can happen to you and **me** [not "to you and **I**"].

	SINGULAR	PLURAL
Demonstrative pronouns *("pointing" pronouns)*	this that	these those
Indefinite pronouns	everybody (everyone), everything somebody (someone), something nobody (no one), nothing anybody (anyone), anything one, each, either, neither	
Relative pronouns	who (whom, whose) which that	
Interrogative pronouns *("question" pronouns)*	who (whom, whose) which what	

OBJECT: I knew there was something between you and **her** [not "between you and **she**"].

OBJECT: She had bought tickets for Jim, Laura, and **me** [not "for Jim, Laura, and **I**"].

(4) Use the right pronoun after *as* and *than*. Often the part of the sentence they start has been shortened. Fill in enough of what is missing to see whether the pronoun would be used as subject or object:

SUBJECT:	He felt as unloved as **I** (did).
	His sister earned more than **he** (did).
OBJECT:	I owe you as much as (I owe) **them**.
	They liked the other candidate better than (they liked) **me**.

(5) Use subject forms after linking verbs. These introduce not an object of an action but a description of the subject:

FORMAL:	The only ones absent were **she** and a girl with measles. (**She** and the other girl were absent.)
FORMAL:	It was **he** who had initiated the proposal.

> SEE THE GLOSSARY OF USAGE FOR *IT'S ME / IT IS I.*

(6) Avoid the *self-* pronouns (reflexive pronouns) as informal substitutes for the plain unemphatic subject or object form. Use forms like *myself* or *himself* to point *back*: "*I* questioned *myself.*" "*The owner herself* showed me the door." Use forms like *I, me, him,* or *her* (personal pronouns) to point:

SPOKEN:	My friend and **myself** made a low-cholesterol pact.
WRITTEN:	My friend and **I** made a low-cholesterol pact.
SPOKEN:	The jury listened spellbound to his lawyer and **himself**.
WRITTEN:	The jury listened spellbound to his lawyer and **him**.

Finer Points

- Use the object form when a pronoun combines with the *to* form to make up an infinitive phrase: "We asked *her to leave.*" "They had chosen *him to replace the bouncer.*"
- Use the subject form when a modifier points back to a subject: "Only two passengers—*she* and her husband—survived." "Only two passengers survived: *she* and her husband." (Who survived? *She* did.)

PEER EDITOR 32   In each of the following sentences, change *one pronoun* to the form that is right for written English. Write the changed form after the number of the sentence.

1. Jane's lawyer brought bad news for she and her mother.
2. I recognized the man's face; it was him who had thrown the pie.
3. This information should remain strictly between you and I.
4. Visitors from space might snigger at the technology that us Earthlings possess.
5. He constantly enriched the conversation of my friends and I with sardonic remarks.
6. The report cited she and her fellow officer for bravery.
7. Teachers do not necessarily always know more than us students.
8. My brother and myself were always bickering, but now we tolerate each other.
9. I asked his fellow bigots and himself to lower the volume.
10. The losing candidate seemed as well qualified as her.

18b   *ca* | *Who* and *Whom*

Know when to replace *who* with *whom.*

Who is replacing *whom* in speech (*Who* do you love?), and *whom* is often used in the wrong places by writers who have only a dim memory of the rules (*Whom* should I say is calling?). In your writing, use *who* as the subject form, *whom* as the object of a verb and also of a preposition:

SPOKEN: **Who** are you working with?
WRITTEN: With **whom** will the new people be working?
                 Whom to vote for is becoming an existential dilemma.

To choose the right forms, you need to look at how they fit into the sentence:

(1) Choose *who* or *whom* at the beginning of a question.   *Who* asks a question about the subject. *Whom* asks a question about an object. Apply the *he-or-him* or *she-or-her* test:

SUBJECT:	**Who** didn't put the ice cream back in the freezer? (**He** didn't.)
OBJECT:	**Whom** did the jurors believe? (They believed **her**.)
OBJECT:	To **whom** did she leave her fortune? (To **him**.)

In more complicated questions, it may not be obvious whether a *who* asks about a subject or about an object. However, the *he-or-him* or *she-or-her* test will always work:

SUBJECT:	**Who** do you think will win? (I think **she** will win.)
OBJECT:	**Whom** did you expect to come? (I expected **her** to come.)

(2) Choose *who* or *whom* at the beginning of a dependent clause. To apply the *he-or-him* or *she-or-her* test to a dependent clause, separate it from the rest of the sentence. In the following examples, *who* (or *whoever*) is the subject of a verb:

SUBJECT:	We asked/**who** discovered the body. (**He** did.)
	Rita was the auditor/**who** had discovered the forgeries. (**She** had.)
	He offered a gold doubloon to/**whoever** first saw the whale. (**He** did.)

In the following examples, *whom* is the object of a verb or of a preposition:

OBJECT:	**Whom** we should test and when/are difficult questions. (We should test **him** or **her** or **them**.)
	She adored her brother, **whom** most people detest. (People detest **him**.)
	We all need coworkers/on **whom** we can rely. (We can rely on **them**.)

Finer Points In applying the *he-or-him* or *she-or-her* test, leave out the interspersed *do you think* or *should I say* in sentences like the following:

SUBJECT:	**Who** (do you think) will be axed first? (**He** will.)
	Who (should I say) is calling? (**She** is.)
OBJECT:	With **whom** (did you say) you had talked? (You had talked with **her**.)

PEER EDITOR 33   Choose *who* or *whom* and write it after the number of the sentence.

1. People *who/whom* we knew only slightly called and offered to board the cat.
2. Some people never discover *who/whom* their real friends are.
3. The visitors had little respect for the people with *who/whom* they worked.
4. People *who/whom* are asked to play themselves are often less convincing than actors.
5. For *who/whom* the message was intended never became clear.

> SEE THE GLOSSARY OF USAGE FOR *WHO, WHICH,* AND *THAT.*

19   Adverbs and Misplaced Modifiers

OVERVIEW   In written English, we pay more attention than in informal speech to how modifiers fit into a sentence. Modifiers, which help us build up bare-bones sentences, range from single words to long prepositional or verbal phrases:

ADJECTIVES:	The **angry** customer called the **escape** clause a **cheap** trick.
ADVERB:	The primadonna will **probably** stalk off the set **again soon**.
PREP. PHRASE:	A woman **in grimy overalls** was standing **on the ladder**.
VERBAL PHRASE:	The pot **waiting at the end of the rainbow** is not always gold.

Check your sentences to see if the right form of a modifier is in the right place. You might hear people say "The motor seems to be running *good*," but you would write "*Glasnost* seemed to be working *well*." You might say "*Bursting at the seams*, we loved Mexico City," letting the listener guess that the city (and not you) was bursting at the seams. But you would write: "*Bursting at the seams, Mexico City* amazed and fascinated us."

19a	*adv*	Adjectives and Adverbs

When you have a choice, use the distinctive adverb form.

Often the only difference between an adjective and an adverb is the *-ly* ending: *sad/sadly, probable/probably, careful/carefully.* We use the **adjective** to modify nouns, telling the reader which one or what kind: the *sad* song, *probable* cause, a *careful* driver, an *easy* answer, *high* praise, an *immediate* reply. We use the **adverb** to modify verbs, telling the reader how, when, or where something is done: talk *sadly, probably* left, drove *carefully,* won *easily,* had praised her *highly,* should reply *immediately.* We also use the adverb to modify adjectives and other adverbs in turn, often showing degree: *extremely* sad, *surprisingly* easy, *incredibly* high; talked *extremely* fast, worked *surprisingly well,* did *surprisingly* poorly. (Note that adverbs like *fast, well, soon, today,* and *outside* do not have the *-ly* ending.)

Adverbs modify verbs in each of the following sentences:

HOW?	The engine ran **smoothly**.
	She answered **reluctantly**.
	We lifted the lid **cautiously**.
WHEN?	The bus will leave **soon**.
	Your brother called **yesterday**.
WHERE?	We ate **outside**.
	The guests went **upstairs**.

(1) Use the adverb form to modify a verb. Often, we convert adjective to adverb by activating the *-ly* ending: *bright—brightly, cheerful—cheerfully, considerable—considerably, happy—happily.* Choose the distinctive adverb form to tell the reader *how*—how something was done or how something happened:

ADVERB:	The inspectors examined every part **carefully**.
	We have changed the original design **considerably**.
	No one took the new policy **seriously**.

Note: Some words ending in *-ly* are not adverbs but adjectives: a *friendly* talk, a *lonely* life, a *leisurely* drive. And for words like *fast, much,* and *early,* the adjective and the adverb are the same:

ADJECTIVE:	The **early** bird gets the worm.
ADVERB:	The worm should not get up **early**.

(2) Avoid the informal adverbs of casual talk. Use *well* and *badly* as adverbs instead of *good* and *bad*. Change "I don't hear *good*" to "I don't hear *well*"; "I write pretty *bad*" to "I write *badly*."

WRONG:	This morning, the motor was running **good**.
RIGHT:	This morning, the motor was running **well**.

Replace informal adverbs like *slow, quick,* and *loud*: drive *slowly*, react *quickly*, speak *loudly*.

(3) Use adverbs to modify other modifiers. Use the adverb form to modify either an adjective or another adverb:

ADVERB + ADJECTIVE: It was a **surprisingly beautiful** bird.
ADVERB + ADVERB: You sang **admirably well**.

Edit out informal expressions like *real popular, awful expensive,* and *pretty good*. Use *very* in such combinations or a distinctive adverb form like *really, fairly,* or *extremely*: Punk rock was *extremely popular*. The crowd was *fairly well-behaved*.

Finer Points   Adjectives instead of adverbs follow linking verbs. After a **linking verb**, an adjective points back to the subject; it pins a label on the subject:

ADJECTIVE: These bottles are **empty**. (**empty** bottles)
The speaker seemed **nervous**. (a **nervous** speaker)
The rains have been **heavy**. (**heavy** rains)

The most common linking verb is *be* (*am, is, are, was, were, has been,* and so on). Other common linking verbs are *become, remain,* and similar words (become *poor*, remain *calm*, grow *rich*, turn *pale*). Additional linking verbs stand for perceptions of the five senses (look *fine*, sound *scary*, taste *flat*, smell *sweet*, feel *moist*). Study the difference between words used as linking verbs or as ordinary verbs (action verbs) in pairs like the following:

ADJECTIVE:	The suspect turned **pale**.
ADVERB:	The suspect turned **abruptly**.

333

ADJECTIVE: Watching the train pull out, we felt **sad**.
ADVERB: We **barely** felt the train move.

Remember:

- *Feel* is a linking verb in "We *felt bad* when we heard the news."
- *Well* used as an adjective means healthy: "He is not *well*."

PEER EDITOR 34   In each of the following sentences, change one word to the distinctive *adverb form*. Write the changed word after the number of the sentence.

1. When the witness testified, she spoke nervously and very defensive.
2. He was tired and unable to think logical.
3. I read the questions as careful as panic allowed.
4. Toward the end of the story, the events unfold very sudden, as they sometimes do in real life.
5. My father regarded life more philosophical than most plumbers do.
6. Macbeth interpreted the prophecies of the weird sisters very literal.
7. During the time Judy spent in France, her horizon widened considerable.
8. Computers solve math problems faster and more efficient than the fastest human mathematician.
9. An experienced cryptographer can decipher a simple code very easy.
10. Sebastian went in for arm wrestling because he didn't do good in other sports.

19b ᴅᴍ, ᴍᴍ | Misplaced Modifiers

Make modifiers point clearly to what they modify.

Moving a modifier will often change the meaning of a sentence:

ADVERB: Riots **almost** broke out at every game.   (but they never quite did)
Riots broke out at **almost** every game.   (they did frequently)

PREP. PHRASE:	The man **with the parrot** started a conversation.
	The man started a conversation **with the parrot**.
VERBAL:	Manuel watered the plants **wilting in the heat**.
	Wilting in the heat, Manuel watered the plants.

Look for wandering modifiers that have drifted from the right place in the sentence. (Sometimes what the modifier should point to has disappeared from the sentence, leaving the modifier unattached.)

(1) Shift a misplaced modifier to the right position. If necessary, rewrite the whole sentence:

MISPLACED:	The manager looked at the room we had painted **with ill-concealed disgust**. (painted with disgust?)
REVISED:	**With ill-concealed disgust**, the manager looked at the room we had painted.
MISPLACED:	**Made of defective material**, the builder had to redo the sagging ceiling.
REVISED:	**Since it was made of defective material**, the builder had to redo the sagging ceiling.

(2) Link a dangling modifier to what was left out of the sentence. Look for danglers like the following. Give them something to attach themselves to. Dangling modifiers usually start with verbals like *to fall, falling, fallen,* or *having fallen.*

DANGLING:	**To become a computer specialist**, an early start is essential. (Who wants to become a computer specialist?)
REVISED:	To become a computer specialist, a **student** needs an early start.
DANGLING:	**Having watched *Dallas* and *Dynasty***, real people will seem dull.
REVISED:	Having watched *Dallas* and *Dynasty*, **viewers** will find real people dull.

(3) Keep a squinting modifier from pointing two ways at once:

SQUINTING:	I feel **subconsciously** Hamlet wanted to die.
	(Are we talking about **your** subconscious feelings—or Hamlet's?)
REVISED:	I feel that Hamlet **subconsciously** wanted to die.

335

Finer Points   Some verbal phrases are not meant to modify any one part of the main sentence. These are called **absolute constructions**. The most common ones clarify the attitude or intention of the speaker:

RIGHT: **Generally speaking**, traffic is getting worse.
                 They had numerous children—seven, **to be exact**.

Some of these absolute constructions carry their own subjects along with them:

RIGHT: **The air being warm**, we left our coats in the car.
                 Escape being impossible, we prepared for the worst.

DISCOURSE EXERCISE 35   In each of the following pairs, work the added material into the original statement as a *verbal phrase*. Where should the added modifier go in the large combined sentence? Use the punctuation indicated to set off the modifier. (There may be more than one right position for the modifier.)

A Pun-Loving Columnist

1. People either love or hate puns.
    often called the lowest form of humor
    (Use a comma or commas.)
2. Herb Caen's column has long been a treasure trove for lovers of word play.
    written for the *San Francisco Chronicle*
    (Use a comma or commas.)
3. According to Caen, a college president had an edifice complex.
    going on a building spree
    (Use no comma.)
4. Restaurant-goers suffer from a reach impediment.
    failing to reach for the check
    (Use no comma unless you put the modifier first.)
5. They show signs of shellout falter.
    hesitating to pick up the tab for their friends
    (Use a comma if you put the modifier first.)

PEER EDITOR 36 Rewrite each of the following student sentences to eliminate unsatisfactory *position of modifiers*.

1. Having run for an hour, the carrot juice tasted great.
2. The car was towed away by John, having exploded on Interstate 59.
3. Unsure of my future, the navy was waiting for me.
4. After ringing for fifteen minutes, the bellhop answered the phone.
5. He was hit by a rotten egg walking back to the dorm.
6. After graduating from high school, my stepfather asked me to vacate the premises.
7. When traveling during the night without sufficient lighting, other motorists will have difficulty seeing the vehicle.
8. These magazines appeal to immature readers with torrid love affairs.
9. I watched a television show with my aunt on a weekend that ended with the murderer throwing himself from the top of a skyscraper.
10. I just wrote to my family for the first time since I came here on the back of a postcard.

---

20   Confusing Sentences

OVERVIEW Some of your sentences, especially in a rough first draft, may give confusing signals to the reader. Like the improvised (and sometimes half-finished) sentences of casual conversation, they may start one way and finish another. They may skip a beat, or they may backtrack over ideas already covered.

Final editing is your last chance to catch sentences that are awkwardly put together, with badly matching parts. Often such a sentence seems to set up one pattern but then switches to another:

MIXED: The typical background of women who get abortions are two-thirds white and more than half childless. (The background . . . are . . . **white**?)

CONSISTENT: Of the women who get abortions, **two thirds are white**, and more than half are childless.

When a sentence is poorly put together, try to straighten out basic relationships by asking questions like "Who does what? What is compared to what? What causes what?"

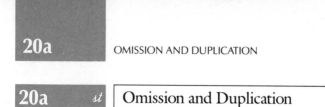

20a   *st*   Omission and Duplication

Check for omitted or duplicated elements.

Revise omission or duplication that results from hasty writing, inaccurate copying, or careless typing.

(1) Supply sentence parts that you have left out. Fill in the missing *a, the, has, be, we,* or *they*:

INCOMPLETE: Our astronauts walked on the moon but have faltered since.   (**Who** faltered?)

COMPLETE: Our astronauts walked on the moon, but **we** have faltered since.

(2) Delete duplicated words. Check especially for doubling up of words like *of* and *that*:

DUPLICATED: They had built a replica of the Eiffel Tower **of** which they were very proud **of**.

REVISED: They had built a replica of the Eiffel Tower **of** which they were very proud.

DUPLICATED: Economists claim **that** because of political pressures in an election year **that** the deficit will grow.

REVISED: Economists claim **that** because of political pressures in an election year the deficit will grow.

DISCOURSE EXERCISE 37   Train yourself to catch *omission and duplication* in careful proofreading. Retype the following hastily written passage with all necessary corrections.

All the Trivia Fit to Print

Some readers look in newspaper for trivia, of which they never tire of. They love read that because of an ancient law that a citizen of Lower Liguria not allowed to wash clothes on a Saturday. They ponder the information that stamp machines in hotel lobbies take two quarters but only one 25-cent and two 5-cent stamp. They love ads for toy sumo wrestlers fight in ring that can made out package in which they came in.

My favorite example of trivia article described muskrat dinners served at restaurant in Delaware. Ingenious traps drown the muskrats and call them "marsh rabbits" when this local delicacy appears on menu.

20b *mx* Mixed Construction

Do not mix two ways of expressing the same idea.

We sometimes start a sentence one way and finish it another. To revise such a sentence, retrace your steps. Disentangle the two ways of saying what you had in mind:

MIXED:	My mother **married** at the age of nineteen, as **were** most of her friends.
REVISED:	My mother **married** at the age of nineteen, as **did** most of her friends. (She **married**, and so **did** they.)
	My mother **was** married at the age of nineteen, as **were** most of her friends. (She **was** married, and so **were** they.)
MIXED:	**In case of** serious flaws in design **should have been reported** to the regulatory agency.
REVISED:	*Serious flaws* in design **should have been reported** to the regulatory agency.
	In case of serious flaws in design, **the regulatory agency** should have been notified.
MIXED:	The course was canceled because of not enough students registered.
CONSISTENT:	The course was canceled **because not enough students registered**.
	The course was canceled **because of insufficient enrollment**.

Avoid the "Because . . . does not mean" sentence, where the adverbial clause starting with *because* appears as if it were the subject of a verb. Use a noun clause starting with *that*:

MIXED:	**Because** we listened to his proposal **does not mean** we approve.
REVISED:	**That** we listened to his proposal **does not mean** that we approve.

339

20c ᵈᵗ | Faulty Predication

Make sure what the predicate says applies logically to the subject.

The subject of a sentence calls our attention to something. The predicate then makes a statement about the subject: "The choice (subject) *was difficult* (predicate)." Make sure the statement made by the predicate can apply logically to the subject:

ILLOGICAL: **The choice** of the new site **was selected** by the mayor.
(What was selected? The site, not the choice.)
LOGICAL: **The new site was selected** by the mayor.

ILLOGICAL: **The participation** at her séances **is always overcrowded**.
(What is overcrowded? The séance, not the participation.)
LOGICAL: Her séances **are always overcrowded**.

Check for special cases of mismatched subjects and predicates:

(1) Revise equations when they link two labels that do not stand for the same thing. In "*Dinosaurs* were *giant reptiles*," the dinosaurs are reptiles, and the reptiles are dinosaurs. But in "*Her job* was *a mail carrier*," the mail carrier is not really a job but a person: "She *worked* as a mail carrier." (Or "Her job was *that* of a mail carrier.")

ILLOGICAL: **A student** with a part-time job **is a common cause of** poor grades.
(A student is not a cause.)
LOGICAL: A student's **part-time job** is a common cause of poor grades.

(2) Revise faulty equation caused by *is-when* or *was-when* sentences. Avoid sentences like "Conservation is *when* we try to save energy." Conservation is not a time when something happens but a practice or a goal.

ILLOGICAL: Parole **is when** a prisoner is set free on condition of good behavior.
LOGICAL: Parole **is the practice of** setting prisoners free on condition of good behavior.

340

(3) Revise faulty equation caused by prepositional phrases. Such phrases typically tell us not what something is but how, when, or where it is done. Use an infinitive (or a similar noun equivalent) instead:

WRONG: Their only hope is **by appealing** to the governor.
RIGHT: Their only hope is **to appeal** to the governor.

20d *at* Faulty Appositives

Make sure appositives apply logically to the nouns they follow.

An **appositive** is a noun that tells us more about another noun: "Ferraro, *the vice-presidential candidate*, had served in Congress." Here, Ferraro and the candidate are the same person. Revise sentences when the second label does not logically fit:

ILLOGICAL: They had only one **vacancy, the assistant manager**.
               (The manager is not vacant; the position is.)
LOGICAL: They had only one **vacancy, the position of** assistant
               manager.

PEER EDITOR 38   Revise each of the following confusing sentences. Look for examples of hasty writing, mixed construction, mismatched subjects and predicates, and faulty labels.

1. Usually it takes a minimum of brain power to watch *Dallas* than it does to read a book.
2. She tried to promote peace among each individual.
3. Young people smoke because it makes them feel sophisticated or perhaps a rebellion against adults.
4. While attending college and working at the same time makes it hard to shine as a scholar.
5. Typical playground equipment fails to keep in mind the needs of the tot.
6. A woman is more likely to understand another woman's anger better than a man.
7. The players up for the team were about even in ability and was a hard decision to make.
8. A person who fails in various things might give him an inferior feeling.

9. Radical opinions are too biased and will not accept realistic compromise.
10. Assimilation is when we try to make every Spock a clone of Captain Kirk.
11. In an era of dwindling resources, we will all have to give up conveniences to which we are used to.
12. Because little of the pledged money actually came in does not mean we have to abandon the project.
13. Scientists know how to distill drinking water from salt water, but the cost of such a project is too unprofitable.
14. By cutting the number of jurors in half greatly reduces the time used in selecting a jury.
15. The legislators were flooded with angry letters, mostly members of the NRA.

---

21 Incomplete Constructions

OVERVIEW In writing, we spell out logical relationships that are often left implied in informal speech. When talking casually, we may take shortcuts like the following: "Americans are more loved and hated than any country on the globe." What we mean is that Americans are more loved and hated than *people* from any *other* country (since literally *any* country would include the United States itself). When we say, "We always have and always will honor our commitments," we mean that we always *have honored* them (in the past) and *will honor* them (in the future).

Look for comparisons that do not spell out fully or clearly what is being compared. Look for combined statements that have telescoped elements that may carry the same idea but need to be different in form. Study ways to complete such incomplete constructions as you edit your writing.

21a   *inc*   Incomplete Comparison

Complete incomplete comparisons.

Many English words—most adjectives and adverbs—have three different forms that we use in comparisons: as *fast* as lightning, *faster* than sound, the *fastest* gun in the West. We use the plain (or **positive**) forms to compare things similar or alike in **degree**: *good* as gold, *sweet* as honey, as *popular* as a tax cut. We use the **comparative** forms to compare *two* things (or two sets) that are different: *better* than cash, *sweeter* than wine, *more popular* than the Beatles. We use the **superlative** form for ranking more than two: *best* performer, the *sweetest* dessert, the *most popular* American president.

	POSITIVE	COMPARATIVE	SUPERLATIVE
Regular	tall	taller	tallest
	happy	happier	happiest
	cautious	more cautious	most cautious
Irregular	good	better	best
	bad	worse	worst
	much	more	most
	little	less	least

Complete or clarify unsatisfactory comparisons:

(1) Spell out what is being compared. Revise incomplete comparisons using *more* and *the most*: "That girl has *more* luck" (than who or than what?). "I had *the most* wonderful experience" (of the day? of a lifetime?).

INCOMPLETE:	The company seemed to employ **more tax lawyers**. (than what?)
COMPLETE:	The company seemed to employ **more tax lawyers than engineers**.
INCOMPLETE:	The author turned the life of Mozart into **the most exciting play**.
COMPLETE:	The author turned the life of Mozart into **the most exciting play of the season**.

(2) Compare things that are really comparable. Revise sentences like the following: "The *fur* was as soft as a *kitten*." The fur was as soft as a *kitten's* (fur), or as soft as *that* of a kitten.

ILLOGICAL:	**Her personality** was unlike **most other people** I have known.
LOGICAL:	**Her personality** was unlike **that of** most other people I have known.

343

(3) Clarify three-cornered comparisons. When you mention three comparable items, which two are being compared?

CONFUSING: **We** distrusted the **oil companies** more than the **local governments**.

CLEAR: **We** distrusted the oil companies more than **we did** the local governments.

We distrusted the oil companies more than the local governments **did**.

(4) Correct overlapping comparisons. Comparisons like the following are blurred: "The forward was faster than *any player on her team.*" The forward is part of the team and cannot be faster than *any player* on the team, including herself.

RIGHT: The forward was faster than **any other player** on the team.

Note: Avoid nonstandard forms that add *-er/-est* or *more/most* for good measure to a word that is already a comparative or superlative form: *worser* instead of *worse*, *more better* instead of *better*, *most cheapest* instead of *cheapest*.

Finer Points Many readers object to the superlative as illogical when it is used to rank only two. They expect you to write "the *better* of the two," not "the *best* of the two."

ILLOGICAL: Of the two superpowers, America is the **richest** but Russia the **strongest**.

LOGICAL: Of the two superpowers, America is the **richer** but Russia the **stronger**.

SEE THE GLOSSARY OF USAGE FOR SUPERLATIVE IN REFERENCE TO TWO AS WELL AS FOR *SO* AND *SUCH.*

DISCOURSE EXERCISE 39 Rewrite the following passage to complete or clarify unsatisfactory comparisons.

The New Yellow Journalism

Readers of today's newspapers find as much blood and gore as the yellow journalism of old. Journalists looking for lurid scandals track politicians as eagerly as evangelists. Nevertheless, tabloids serve up a fare more sensational than any national publications. In the world of tabloids, the death of a husband who swallowed seven fish hooks as part of his fish dinner is more important than John Kennedy. A headline like "Fisherman Hooked on Wife's Soup" attracts more readers than the Polish economy. There seem to be more stories about aging widows piling an unbelievable twenty tons of garbage three feet high in a neglected rat-infested home. The balance sheet of a firm marketing a bad-breath detector rates more attention than the Bank of America.

21b   *inc* | Incomplete Coordination

Check coordinate elements for excessive shortcuts.

When items of the same kind are coordinated by *and, or,* or *but,* leave out only those forms that would cause unnecessary duplication.

(1) Check for completeness when shortening one of several similar verbs. Leave out only words that would be exactly identical: "It can [*be done*] and will *be done.*"

INCOMPLETE: The bear **was given** an injection and the instruments **made** ready.

COMPLETE: The bear **was given** an injection, and the instruments **were made** ready.

(2) Revise shortcuts of the "as-good-if-not-better" type: "Korean cars turned out to be *as good if not better than* ours." The complete forms would be *as good as* and *not better than*:

REVISED: Korean cars turned out to be **as good as, if not better than**, ours.

BETTER: Korean cars turned out to be **as good as ours, if not better.**

(3) Check several linked prepositional phrases. Keep prepositions that are not identical but merely express a similar relationship.

WRONG: I have great **respect and faith in** our leadership.

RIGHT: I have great **respect for** and **faith in** our leadership.
I have great **admiration and respect for** our leadership.

345

Notice the use of different prepositions in the following examples:

RIGHT: He was jealous **of** but fascinated **by** his rival.
RIGHT: Her behavior during the trial adds **to** rather than detracts **from** my admiration for her.

PEER EDITOR 40 Make each of the following *incomplete sentences* more complete by rewriting the italicized part. Write the rewritten part after the number of the sentence. Look for incomplete comparisons and other incomplete constructions.

1. People today live longer and eat up more resources *than the previous century.*
2. *Juries have always and will always be swayed* by the grandstanding of a lawyer.
3. An older person's need for love is *as big as a child.*
4. Taxpayers are already *familiar and hostile to the usual explanations.*
5. The population of China is already *bigger than any country.*
6. *The club had in the past and was still barring* "undesirables" from membership.
7. The Sears Building in Chicago is *as tall or taller than any building in New York City.*
8. People in show business *seem to have more bad luck.*
9. The statistics for rape are much less complete *than robbed banks or stolen bicycles.*
10. Few of my friends were *preoccupied or even interested in the love lives of celebrities.*
11. In much of Europe, American films are *more popular than any other country.*
12. Children understand other children *better than adults.*
13. The impact of American books, magazines, and comics in Great Britain is *much greater than British publications in the United States.*
14. The liberal arts are excellent preparation *for such practical professions as engineers and lawyers.*
15. Critics of our schools must realize that *they can and are doing great harm by indiscriminate attacks.*

---

22 Shifts and Parallelism

OVERVIEW Our sentences set up patterns that steer our readers in the right direction. We locate events in time; we identify the people we are talking to or about; we start sets or lists that make our readers expect more of the same. When we suddenly change the pattern, our readers get their signals crossed. They expect **consistency**—they want us to maintain a perspective or carry through a pattern long enough so that they can get their bearings.

Who refuses to lie in the following sentence? "*I* would never take a job where *you* have to lie to the customer." ("I," the writer—or "you," the reader?) When was the person in the following sentence in Hitler's army? "The president of Austria *admitted* that he *was* an intelligence officer in Hitler's army." (He *was* not while president of Austria but *had been* forty years earlier.)

Sentences should stay within a consistent time frame or maintain a consistent perspective. When they do not, they are like a road full of unexpected twists and turns—or like an intersection with too many confusing traffic signs. They slow down and confuse the reader. Learn to edit your writing for confusing shifts in time, reference, or grammatical perspective.

22a Shifts in Tense

Revise confusing shifts in time.

Verbs have a built-in reference to time: We *agree* (now). We *agreed* (then). When describing a situation or telling a story, be aware of the **tense** forms you are using to show time.

PRESENT:	Nuclear energy **poses** a serious problem for political leaders. (action now)
PAST:	The U.S. **exploded** the first atom bomb in Nevada. (action happening and concluded in the past)
PRESENT PERFECT:	The President **has called** for a halt to the nuclear arms race. (action in the recent past or with special relevance for the present)
PAST PERFECT:	By then, the two countries **had agreed** on a moratorium on tests. (action in the more distant past, before other past events)

(1) Avoid shifting from past to present. Do not switch to the present when something becomes so real that it seems to be happening in front of you:

SHIFT:	We **were waiting** for the elevator when suddenly all lights **go** out.
REVISED:	We **were waiting** for the elevator when suddenly all lights **went** out.
SHIFT:	The pedestrians **scattered** as the car **careens** around the corner.
REVISED:	The pedestrians **scattered** as the car **careened** around the corner.

(2) Show differences in time to avoid confusion. For instance, signal the difference between what *happened* in the past and what *had happened* before then in the more distant past (**past perfect**).

SHIFT:	Linda **was** only a messenger, but she **was** now the supervisor of the whole floor.
CONSISTENT:	Linda **had been** only a messenger, but she **was** now the supervisor of the whole floor.
	(Working as a messenger came before promotion.)
SHIFT:	My uncle always **talked** about how farming **has changed**.
CONSISTENT:	My uncle always **talked** about how farming **had changed**.
	(about how it **had changed** up to the time when he talked)

(3) Be consistent when dealing with possibilities. Note the difference between factual reference to a possibility and the **conditional**, which makes the possibility seem less probable, more remote:

SHIFT:	If they **come** here, the government **would** refuse them asylum.
FACTUAL:	If they **come** here, the government **will** refuse them asylum. (*Both* arrival and refusal are real possibilities.)
CONDITIONAL:	If they **came** here, the government **would** refuse them asylum. (Both arrival and refusal are more remote possibilities.)
FACTUAL:	If terrorists **threaten** to use a nuclear weapon, what **will** we do?
CONDITIONAL:	If terrorists **threatened** to use an atomic weapon, what **would** we do?

(4) Adjust tense forms in indirect quotation. In **direct quotation**, a speaker may talk about events in the past, but they were then the present time: She *said*: "I *feel* elated. I *am* proud to be here." In **indirect quota-**

tion, we are no longer using the speaker's exact words. When *we* talk about her feelings, they are in the past: She *said* that she *felt* elated and *was* proud to be there.

DIRECT:	Roosevelt said, "We **have** nothing to fear but fear itself."
INDIRECT:	Roosevelt said that the nation **had** nothing to fear but fear itself.
DIRECT:	Nixon said: "I **am** not a crook."
INDIRECT:	Nixon said that he **was** not a crook.

Failure to adjust the tenses in indirect quotations can lead to sentences like the following:

| SHIFT: | Chamberlain **said** that there **will** be peace in our time. |
| CONSISTENT: | Chamberlain **said** that there **would** be peace in our time. |

Finer Points   A statement made in the past may say something that is *still true* in the present:

| STILL TRUE: | Galileo **said** that the earth **moves** and that the sun **is** the center of our solar system. |
| | Thatcher **has been quoted** as saying that she **can** do business with Gorbachev. |

22b   *⅟*   Shifts in Reference

Revise confusing shifts in reference.

When talking about yourself, as in accounts of personal experience or in eyewitness reports, you are going to use the pronoun *I* (*me, my, myself*)—**first person singular**. Sometimes you will be speaking for a group and use the **editorial *we***: "At the *Daily*, *we* feel that spring breaks should come more than once a year"—**first person plural**. When talking directly to your reader, as in giving instructions, directions, or advice, you will use *you*: "A good way to lose *your* friends is to give them constant well-meant advice"—**second person singular and plural**. In talking about a third party or parties, you will be using *he* or *she* and *them*—**third person singular and plural**.

In checking your writing, edit out the shifts and confusions that result when your system of referring to people is not clearly worked out:

(1) Edit out the informal generalized *you*. In your writing, use *you* only to mean "you, the reader." Avoid the indefinite anonymous *you* that is in a twilight zone between "you, the reader" and "people in general":

SPOKEN:	Sailing to the colonies, **you** had to worry about pirates. (Your reader wasn't there.)
WRITTEN:	Sailing to the colonies, **travelers** had to worry about pirates.
SPOKEN:	These articles expect **you** to worry about **your** hemline and new shades of lipstick for spring. (Your reader may be male.)
WRITTEN:	These articles expect **women** to worry about **their** hemlines and new shades of lipstick for spring.

By doing without the indefinite generalized *you*, you will avoid one of the most common shifts in reference: shifting to *you* after the person involved has already been identified:

SHIFT:	**I** would not want to be a celebrity, with people always knowing what **you** are doing.
CONSISTENT:	**I** would not want to be a celebrity, with people always knowing what **I** am doing.
SHIFT:	When questioned by police, **a person** should be willing to identify **yourself**.
CONSISTENT:	When questioned by police, **people** should be willing to identify **themselves**.

(2) Avoid shifts to the request form. Giving directions or instructions, we naturally use the form for requests or commands (**imperative**): *Dice* the carrots. *Remove* the hubcaps. But avoid shifting to the request form when giving more general advice:

SHIFT:	Managers **should stop** tallying every move of the employee and every trip to the restroom. **Build** employee morale and **stimulate** group loyalty, as the Japanese do.
CONSISTENT:	Managers **should stop** tallying every move of the employee and every trip to the restroom. **They should build** employee morale and **stimulate** group loyalty, as the Japanese do.

(3) Avoid shifts in references to groups. Make up your mind whether you are talking about all members or one typical member:

350

SHIFT: Some **nonsmokers** might not patronize a restaurant because of the smoke **he** might inhale. (You were talking about more than one.)

CONSISTENT: Some **nonsmokers** might not patronize a restaurant because of the smoke **they** might inhale.

Finer Points   The impersonal generalized *one* goes with *one's* and *oneself*. But when one *one* leads to another, a sentence begins to sound stilted and old-fashioned:

CORRECT: **One** should not expose **oneself** and **one's** friends to idle gossip.

BETTER: **People** should not expose **themselves** and **their** friends to idle gossip.

22c ⅘ Shifts to the Passive

Do not shift to the passive when the same person is still active in the sentence.

Active sentences put the spotlight on who does what: *Poachers are decimating* the herds (**active voice**). Passive sentences put the spotlight on the target or the victim: *The elephants are being slaughtered* (**passive voice**). Avoid an unmotivated shift in perspective when the same person is still active and important. Do not shift from the active "*She remodeled* her own house" to the passive "*The roof was put on* by her."

SHIFT: He **retyped** his résumé, and it **was mailed** the same day. (by whom?)

REVISED: He **retyped** his résumé and **mailed** it the same day.

Avoid awkward shifts to the passive in instructions or advice:

SHIFT: After **you complete** the form, **it should be returned** to the agency.

REVISED: After **you complete** the form, **you should return** it to the agency.

PEER EDITOR 41   Rewrite the following sentences to revise shifts in *time, pronoun reference, or grammatical perspective*. More than one such shift may occur in a sentence.

351

1. A sure-fire prescription for disaster is for a cocaine addict to come off a binge and try to drown your depression in alcohol.
2. As I was getting ready to leave the elevator, I notice two men who are watching me out of the corner of their eyes.
3. Office workers discovered that computers monitored the time you took to staple memos or open envelopes.
4. The police were warning us that if the crowd did not calm down, arrests will be made.
5. Only when one faces the decision of whether to have an abortion can you really feel what a tough issue it is.
6. Parents must take an active interest in what their children are doing. Coach a ball team or be a counselor to a scout troup.
7. My favorite television program was already in progress, but right in the middle of a dramatic scene, the station goes off the air.
8. As the world grew dark, he dreams of a place he will never see.
9. Teenagers armed with rags and towels swarmed around the still dripping car, and quickly the outside is wiped dry and the chrome polished.
10. I became bored with my monotonous job, although it offered quarterly raises as your skills increased.

22d Faulty Parallelism

Use parallel structure for repeated sentence parts.

Sentence parts joined by *and, or,* and *but* should be **parallel**, fitting into the same grammatical category. If you put an *and* after *body*, readers expect another noun: "body and *mind*," "body and *soul*." The words in a set like "red, white, and blue" are parallel (three adjectives); the words in a set like "handsome, personable, and in a red convertible" are not (two adjectives and a prepositional phrase). Look at the way parallel sentences like the following line up identical sentence parts:

INFINITIVES: Two things that a successful advertisement must accomplish are **to be noticed** and **to be remembered**.

PARTICIPLES: I can still see my aunt **striding** into the corral, **cornering** a cow against a fencepost, **balancing** herself on a one-legged milking stool, and **butting** her head into the cow's belly.

CLAUSES: The young people **who brood** in their rooms, **who forget** to come down to the dining hall, and **who burst out** in fits of irrationality are not worrying about who will win the big game.

Faulty parallelism results when a part of your sentence snaps out of the expected pattern:

(1) Revise mismatched sentence parts joined by *and, or,* or *but.* For instance, "*ignorant* and a *miser*" is off balance because it joins an adjective and a noun. You could change *ignorant* to a noun ("He was an *ignoramus* and a miser") or *miser* to an adjective ("He was ignorant and *miserly*").

FAULTY: They loved **the wilderness** and **to backpack** to solitary lakes.

PARALLEL: They loved **to explore** the wilderness and **to backpack** to solitary lakes.

FAULTY: She told me of **her plans** and **that she was leaving**.

PARALLEL: She **informed** me of her plans and **told** me that she was leaving.

Look especially for an *and who* or *and which* that changes a pattern in midstream:

FAULTY: We met a painter **living** in Paris and **who had known** Picasso.

PARALLEL: We met a painter **who lived** in Paris and **who had known** Picasso.

(2) Avoid mixing a noun and an adjective as modifiers. Much bureaucratic prose seems lumpy and awkward because of badly matched pairs like "*hygienic and health* needs" or "*race and ethnic* quotas."

LUMPY: The schools must serve **personal and society** needs as they evolve.

PARALLEL: The schools must serve **personal and social** needs as they evolve.

(3) Check for parallelism when using paired connectives. Such pairs (**correlative conjunctions**) are *either . . . or, neither . . . nor, not only . . . but also,* and *whether . . . or*:

FAULTY: I used to find him either **in the spa** or **chatting with his friends**.

PARALLEL: I used to find him either **soaking in the spa** or **chatting with his friends**.

FAULTY: Reporters wondered whether **to believe** her or **should** they try to verify her story.

PARALLEL: Reporters wondered whether they should **believe** her or **try** to verify her story.

These paired words can seem to set up the wrong pattern when one of them is not placed strategically next to one of the parallel parts:

MISPLACED:	Judge Hardball **not only** threatened the lawyer with expulsion **but also** jail. (We expect to hear that the judge not only **threatened** but also **did** something else.)
REVISED:	Judge Hardball threatened the lawyer with **not only** expulsion **but also** jail.

(4) Avoid faulty parallelism in a series of three or more elements. The **series** that concludes the following sentence has three parallel parts:

PARALLEL:	Computer programs now check student papers for **spelling errors, awkward sentences,** and **sexist phrases**.

But sometimes we read what looks like a series, only to have the last element snap out of the expected pattern:

FAULTY:	He loved to **talk, drink wine,** and **good food**.
PARALLEL:	He loved **conversation**, good **wine**, and good **food**. He loved to **talk, drink** good wine, and **eat** good food.

If the elements in a series are not really parallel in meaning, your revision might break up the series altogether:

FAULTY:	The new manager was **ambitious, hard-driving,** and **an MBA from Harvard**.
REVISED:	The new manager, **an MBA from Harvard**, was ambitious and hard-driving.

Finer Points   Writers will sometimes repeat structural links to highlight or strengthen parallelism in a sentence: "Do not ask *for whom* the bell tolls or *for whom* the paddy wagon came." Repeating a preposition like *for* or *to* or a subordinator like *when* or *whether* may help you realign mismatched parts:

FAULTY:	The story focuses on whether **the old man will capture** the large fish or **will the fish elude** him.
PARALLEL:	The story focuses on **whether** the old man will capture the large fish or **whether** the fish will elude him.

DISCOURSE EXERCISE 42   Rewrite the following passage to revise all examples of faulty parallelism.

Updating the Vampire

Fans of vampire movies should neither be committed vegetarians nor made easily sick by the sight of blood. In the classic vampire story, the vampire lives in a gloomy castle, tricks unwary tourists, and sucking their blood during the night. Today's vampires are more up-to-date and definitely catering to a modern audience. Coming to our modern world, they neither totally abandon their blood-sucking ways nor their costumes. They can read minds but perhaps unable to use a touch-tone phone. At a rock concert, they can blend in without a special costume or needing special makeup. The modern vampire zaps roaches in a microwave, lifts jets into orbit around a different planet, and similar high-tech exploits. Audiences are not always sure whether to thrill with horror or should they laugh at a biting satire of the modern world.

PEER EDITOR 43   Rewrite the following sentences to make them parallel.

1. Stacey's friends surfed, partied, and a recreation major.
2. Corporations, like governments, quibble over whether an ecological disaster was caused by inadequate safeguards or was it a case of individual negligence.
3. A combination of school and legal problems had driven him to the brink.
4. Robots with artificial vision will not only lift and weld but also putting in car windows and installing taillights.
5. The success of a television program depends on how well the program has been advertised, the actors taking part, and is it comedy or serious drama.
6. As a legal secretary, I had to prepare wills, depositions, and basically run the office.
7. Stricter gun control laws would be difficult to enforce, resented by many citizens, and only a doubtful method of preventing crime.
8. The television news always includes stories about a sniper with a rifle or someone murdered a relative.
9. The boy described how he was beaten by his masters, taken advantage of by the older servants, and the meager meals of bread and porridge he received.
10. The affluent American has a large income, a nice house, and lives in the nice part of town.

5

Writing Better Sentences

Instructions Which of the sentences in each of the following pairs is clearer, more direct, or more effective? Write the number of the pair, followed by the letter of the better sentence.

1. **a.** As a doctor, one should demonstrate respect for a dying patient's wishes.
   b. A doctor should respect a dying patient's wishes.

2. **a.** If people seriously look for work, they will usually find a job if they are willing to move.
   b. People looking seriously for work will usually find a job if they are willing to move.

3. **a.** A crowd of over a hundred thousand people turned out for an antigovernment demonstration.
   b. There was an antigovernment demonstration participated in by a crowd of over a hundred thousand people.

4. **a.** It was felt that an element of deliberate deception was present in the speaker's words.
   b. My friends and I felt that the speaker was deliberately deceiving the audience.

5. **a.** The editorial attacked the government's continued policy of suppressing information about the accident.
   b. The editorial accused the government of a continuation of its policy of a blackout of information about the accident.

357

6. **a.** People eating fish from contaminated waters may become the victims of severe mercury poisoning.
   b. If fish from contaminated waters are eaten, severe mercury poisoning may be contracted.

7. **a.** There will be an investigation by the institution of the unauthorized distribution of confidential information about students.
   b. The college will investigate the unauthorized release of confidential information about students.

8. **a.** All parts of the questionnaire should be completed by the applicant.
   b. The applicant should complete all parts of the questionnaire.

9. **a.** The crowd booed the officers who arrested the sun worshippers who had disregarded the swimsuit ordinance.
   b. The crowd booed the officers arresting the sun worshippers who had disregarded the swimsuit ordinance.

10. **a.** Employees will be exempted from taking the training course if they pass a test.
    b. Employees may take a test and pass it, and they will then be exempted from taking the training course.

---

23 Effective Sentences

OVERVIEW When you work on sentence style, you focus on what helps your sentences carry their message. You work on what makes sentences effective. Many simple sentences are built on the "Who does what?" model. They move clearly and directly from a person or cause that is active to the action and to any target or result:

> Our pets eat better than our poor.
> Death devours all lovely things.   Edna St. Vincent Millay

Other simple sentences go clearly and directly from a concept to a label or explanation that helps us understand it:

> A riot is the language of the unheard.   Martin Luther King, Jr.
> Our political constitution is the hope of the world.   Ralph Waldo Emerson

Your job as a writer is to keep your sentences equally clear and direct when they carry more complicated information—when they carry a rich array of detail, when they include necessary *ifs* and *buts*. A fully developed sentence does not merely string together pieces of information the way computers print out strings of data. It does not merely record what we know; it shows how we think. We are not likely to write: "The Beatles were playing in obscure clubs. Record company executives discouraged them. They went on to become the idols of a generation." Instead we are likely to write:

COORDINATION: The Beatles were playing in obscure clubs, **and** record company executives discouraged them, **but** they went on to become the idols of a generation.

Similarly, we are not likely to write: "The space shuttle had several successful flights. The last flight of the *Challenger* turned into a disaster. It had been touted as a special event." We are more likely to write:

SUBORDINATION: Although the space shuttle had had several successful flights, the last flight of the *Challenger*, **which** had been touted as a special event, turned into a disaster.

Well-written sentences carry their load easily. They have the right **emphasis**: They help us take in the main points and keep lesser points in perspective. They have a satisfying **rhythm**: They line up related ideas and balance off opposing points. They make us say: "That is a good sentence."

SEE **13** FOR A REVIEW OF BASIC SENTENCE ELEMENTS.

23a *st, emp* | Effective Predication

Rewrite weak sentences on the "Who does what?" model.

The subject and the predicate are the two basic structural supports of a sentence. The subject brings something to our attention. The predicate then makes a statement about it. The core of the predicate is a verb. Often the verb sets things in motion or brings action into the sentence:

The car / **swerved**.
The judge / **stayed** the order.
The building / **collapsed**.

Try the following to strengthen weak sentences:

(1) Make the subject and verb answer the question: "Who does what?" Try to make the subject name the key agent or doer—put the spotlight on whoever took action or whatever was the cause. Then let the verb and the rest of the predicate make the point:

UNFOCUSED:	**It was not the usual procedure** of the nuns to pamper their students.
FOCUSED:	**The nuns** did not usually pamper their students.
UNFOCUSED:	**An example** of the trend toward vigilantism **is** the father who shot the suspect accused of kidnapping his son.
FOCUSED:	**An outraged father illustrated the trend** toward vigilantism by shooting the suspect accused of kidnapping his son.

(2) Shift the action from a noun to a verb. In rewriting sentences on the "Who does what?" model, you may have to shift the action from static nouns to active verbs. When a noun ending in *-ion, -ment, -ism,* or *-ing* serves as the subject of a sentence, it may blur our view of who does what. When such nouns label actions, events, or activities, try specifying the agent or doer while shifting the action to a verb. Verbs make things happen; they help us dramatize key points:

STATIC:	Violent **arguments took place** in front of the children.
ACTIVE:	**Our parents** often **argued** violently in front of us.
STATIC:	**Confusion marked** the opening speech.
ACTIVE:	**The opening speaker confused and lost** the audience.
STATIC:	**A criticism** often found in modern poetry **is** that we have cut ourselves off from our natural roots.
ACTIVE:	**Modern poets** often **charge** that we have cut ourselves off from our roots in nature.

(3) Convert a weak use of *to be* to a more active verb. Many electronic editing programs flag uses of *to be* (*is, was, has been, will be,* and so on) to make you check whether you should use a stronger, more active verb. "Excessive tanning *is* a cause of cancer" then becomes "Excessive tanning *causes* cancer."

TO BE:	The parents' income **was** the criterion of eligibility.
NOT *TO BE*:	The parents' income **determined** eligibility.

| STATIC: | **One crucial factor** in the current revolution in our social structure **is** the relationship between the white police officer and the black community. |
| ACTIVE: | **The white policeman** standing on a Harlem street corner **finds himself at the very center** of the revolution now occurring in the world.   James Baldwin |

(4) Do without tag statements that shift the main point to a dependent clause. To make the subject and predicate of a main clause carry your main point, eliminate tag statements like "The simple fact is that . . ." and "The question now confronting us is whether . . .":

| WEAK: | **The question** now confronting us **is** whether we should yield to intimidation, and thus encourage other groups to resort to the same tactics. |
| DRAMATIC: | **Should we yield** to intimidation and thus encourage other groups to resort to the same tactics? |

PEER EDITOR 1   Rewrite the following sentences for more *effective predication*. If possible, make the subject and the predicate tell the reader who does what.

1. The result of restrictive new laws will be to force women back to illegal abortion mills.
2. The question is whether this country should stand idly by while the democratic opposition is crushed.
3. Vigorous discussion of current political events often took place among the patrons.
4. It is very probable that intimidation of witnesses will result from such threatening remarks by the defendant.
5. A recent development is the encouragement of new technology for extracting oil by the Canadian government.
6. There has been vigorous support among the voters for rent control measures of different kinds.
7. As the result of unruly demonstrations, repeated interruptions of the committee's deliberations took place.
8. The conclusion is inevitable that considerable impairment of our country's military strength has come about as the result of these cuts.
9. A plan for safe driving is of no use if the cooperation of the individual driver is not present.
10. The contribution of the alumni to the growth of the college will be in proportion to their information about its educational needs.

23b   *coord*   Effective Coordination

Use coordination when two ideas are equally important.

When we coordinate two things, we make them work together. In sentences like the following, both clauses are about equally important. A simple *and* or *but* coordinates the two ideas:

EQUAL:
We tried to locate the files, **but** we were unsuccessful.

Matthew was a subeditor on a large London newspaper, **and** Susan worked in an advertising firm.   Doris Lessing

Our press is essentially provincial in this country, **and** except for a few syndicated columnists the reputation of our newspaper reporters is mainly local.

If you doubt the appropriateness of a coordinator like *and* or *but*, test the sentence by inserting "equally important":

EFFECTIVE:
Under one of the plans, reservists spend only six months on active duty, **but** [equally important] they remain in the ready reserve for seven and a half years.

EFFECTIVE:
Radioactivity is a threat to workers at nuclear plants, **and** [equally important] radioactive wastes are a threat to the environment.

Weak or **excessive coordination** results when we merely string ideas together loosely as they come to mind. To correct excessive coordination, remember that *and* merely says "more of same." In the revisions of the following sentences, modifiers and compounding helped the writer tighten the relationship between ideas:

LOOSE:
Salmon return to the same spot upstream where they were hatched, **and** they have to go against the stream to get there, **and** that takes much strength and determination.

TIGHTER:
Salmon return to the same spot upstream where they were hatched, **struggling against the current to get there, showing tremendous strength and determination**.

LOOSE:
Fingerlings hatch a few days after the female salmon has laid the eggs, **and** they learn to swim on their own, **and** they head for the ocean.

TIGHTER: A few days after the female salmon has laid the eggs, the fingerlings **hatch, learn** to swim on their own, **and head** for the ocean.

Finer Points A special use of "add-on" coordination is the reporter's *and*, which merely registers events without editorializing about cause and effect:

> There was a shock, **and** he felt himself go up in the air. He pushed on the sword as he went up and over, **and** it flew out of his hand. He hit the ground **and** the bull was on him.   Ernest Hemingway

---

PEER EDITOR 2   Rewrite the following passages to correct *excessive coordination*. Tighten relationships by replacing coordinators with subordinators (such as *if, when, because, although*) or relative pronouns (*who, which, that*).

1. Gun owners were fighting back against the new restrictions, and the city council passed a new ordinance, and it omitted the requirement for a 14-day records search.
2. My father came from a wealthy family, and my mother came from a very poor home, and it was strange that she held the purse strings in the family.
3. Many high school teachers follow a textbook word for word, and they go over each page until everyone understands it. In college, many teachers just tell the student to read the textbook, and then they start giving lectures on the material covered in the text, but they don't follow it word for word.

23c *sub, emp* | Effective Subordination

Use subordination to tighten relationships in a sentence.

Often subordination helps us integrate sentences that are loosely strung together. Subordinators (*when, while, since, because, if, though*) and relative pronouns (*who, which,* and *that*) add a **dependent** clause to the main clause. Sometimes the dependent clause is only technically or grammatically subordinate; it actually carries the main point of the sentence:

"The society admitted students *who had maintained a 4.0 average.*" Often, however, the main clause makes an idea stand out. Subordinators or relative pronouns then can make the material they subordinate seem less important. They fit well when the main clause states a major point, with the dependent clauses establishing relations in place, time, or logic:

PLACE: The edge of the cape was wet with blood **where** it had swept along the bull's back as he went by.   Ernest Hemingway, "The Undefeated"

TIME: El Salvador had always been a frontier, even **before** the Spaniards arrived.   Joan Didion, *Salvador*

REASON: We need to demand more, not less, of women . . . **because** historically women have always had to be better than men to do half as well.   Adrienne Rich, *On Lies, Secrets, and Silence*

When sentences are too loosely strung together, use effective subordination to show the relationships between ideas:

(1) Use subordination to help the main idea stand out in a larger combined sentence. Use the main clause for the idea that deserves special emphasis:

SIMPLE: The term *democracy* originated in ancient Greece. Different people have used it to describe quite different political systems. Often the person who uses the word thinks it has only one meaning.

COMBINED: **Democracy**, a term that originated in ancient Greece, **has been used to describe quite different political systems**, though the person who uses it usually thinks it has only one meaning.

(2) Use subordination to clarify relationships in a sentence. Merely placed next to each other, the following two statements may seem disjointed: "Mertens was kidnapped and held hostage for eleven months. He had been a bureau chief for the CIA." They make more obvious sense when one is subordinated to the other:

EFFECTIVE: Mertens, **who had been a bureau chief for the CIA**, was kidnapped and held hostage for eleven months.

(3) Avoid upside-down subordination. "*I was four* when men landed on the moon" focuses our attention on your age. "When I was four, *men landed on the moon*" focuses our attention on the moon. **Upside-down**

364

subordination results when the wrong item seems to stand out—when it catches the reader unaware, with an unintended ironic effect:

IRONIC: The wage was considered average by local standards, **though it was not enough to live on**.

STRAIGHT: **Although it was considered average by local standards**, the wage was not enough to live on.

UPSIDE-DOWN: He had a completely accident-free record up to the last day of his employment, **when** he stepped on a power line and almost lost his life.

IMPROVED: On the last day of his employment, **after** ten years without a single accident, he stepped on a power line and almost lost his life.

DISCOURSE EXERCISE 3   Combine the separate sentences in each of the following sets, making use of *effective subordination*. In each new combined sentence, use at least one dependent clause, starting with a subordinator (*if, when, because, where, although, whereas,* or the like) or with a relative pronoun (*who, which,* or *that*).

Our Cousins the Apes

1. Human beings are constantly encroaching on animal habitats. Many species are already extinct.
2. The great apes are endangered. We are fascinated with them. They include gorillas and orangutans.
3. Monkeys are of low intelligence. They are imitative. They can be trained to perform simple tasks.
4. Primates are our close cousins biologically. They are ideally suited for experiments. These cannot be performed on human beings.
5. Animal rights advocates appeal to our sympathy for these animals. They suffer atrociously. They are used for medical experiments.

23d   *st*   Effective Modifiers

Use modifiers to help a sentence carry added freight.

A skillful writer often uses modifying words and phrases where an inexperienced writer might use separate clauses. Observe the tightening of relationships when separate statements are combined in a compact sentence:

SEPARATE:	Dolphins can send distress signals to other members of their group. They communicate by beeps and clicks.
COMBINED:	Dolphins, **communicating by beeps and clicks**, can send distress signals to other members of their group.
SEPARATE:	I lay on the couch in the kitchen. I was reading *The Last Days of Pompeii*. How I wished I could have been there.
COMBINED:	I lay on the couch in the kitchen, **reading** *The Last Days of Pompeii* and **wishing** I were there. Alice Munro
SEPARATE:	We caught two bass. We hauled them in briskly, as though they were mackerel. After we pulled them over the side of the boat, we stunned them with a blow on the back of the head.
COMBINED:	We caught two bass, **hauling them in briskly** as though they were mackerel, **pulling them over the side of the boat** in a businesslike manner without any landing net, and **stunning them with a blow on the back of the head**. E. B. White

Remember:

(1) Use the full range of modifying phrases. In addition to single words, we use the following modifiers to make a sentence carry added freight:

PREP. PHRASE:	They crossed the swollen river **in a small rubber raft**.
ADJECTIVE PHRASE:	The climbers, **weak from days without food**, gave up the attempt.
APPOSITIVE:	The rhinoceros, **an animal built like a tank**, faces extinction.
VERBALS:	**Goaded beyond endurance**, Igor turned on his pursuers, **shaking his fists**.
ABSOLUTE CONSTRUCTIONS:	**Her face drawn, her lips tight,** the mayor announced her decision.

(2) Use the full range of possible positions for added modifiers. The following sentences, from a bullfighting story by Ernest Hemingway, illustrate the effective use of one or more modifiers *at different positions* in the sentence:

■ Breaking up subject and verb:

The horse, **lifted and gored**, crashed over with the bull driving into him.

Manuel, **facing the bull, having turned with him each charge**, offered the cape with his two hands.

■ At the end of the sentence:

Manuel walked towards him, **watching his feet**.

The bull was hooking wildly, **jumping like a trout, all four feet off the ground**.

■ At the beginning of the sentence:

Now, **facing the bull**, he was conscious of many things at the same time.

Heads up, swinging with the music, the right arms swinging free, they stepped out.

■ More than one position:

The bull, **in full gallop**, pivoted and charged the cape, **his head down, his tail rising**.

SENTENCE PRACTICE 4 Use *modifiers* to build up the following simple sentences with additional details. Use different kinds of modifiers in various positions. Example:

SIMPLE: A girl plays "Silent Night."
MODIFIED: A small, skinny girl plays "Silent Night" with two fingers on an untuned piano in a garage.

1. A woman runs.
2. A dog crossed the road.
3. The rider mounted the horse.
4. Energy is in short supply.
5. Her cousin bought a new car.

SENTENCE PRACTICE 5 Study the following examples of *effective sentences*. They make exceptionally full use of the sentence resources that we can draw on to help load a sentence with information. For each of the model sentences, write a sentence of your own on a subject of your own choice. As much as you can, follow the sentence structure of the original. Try to come close—you need not follow the model sentence in every detail.

MODEL 1:   Your photographs will be more artistic if you use the film that has chromatic balance.
IMITATION: Your checks will be more welcome if you draw them on an account that has money in it.
MODEL 2:   Everyone is a moon and has a dark side which he never shows to anybody.   Mark Twain

367

MODEL 3:	Lonnie wore the composed, politely appreciative expression that was her disguise in the presence of grown-ups. Alice Munro
MODEL 4:	Using their dreams alone, creative people have produced fiction, inventions, scientific discoveries, and solutions to complex problems. Jean Houston
MODEL 5:	The fullback held the ball lightly in front of him, his knees pumping high, his hips twisting as he ran toward the end zone.

---

24   Sentence Variety

OVERVIEW Effective writers know how to keep their readers from being lulled to sleep. They know how to use the infinite variety of our sentence resources to bring a plodding passage to life.

SENTENCE LENGTH Linguists tell us that no two sentences we write need ever be the same. Some sentences are short. They stick to the essentials. They make a single point. (The last three sentences are very short.) Other sentences are more elaborate, providing a full explanation, marshaling a range of supporting details, noting reservations, and spelling out implications until the reader is ready to say "Enough!" (This sentence is much more elaborate.)

| POINTED: | Punctuality is the thief of time.   Oscar Wilde |
| ELABORATE: | Few themes have gripped the imagination of Americans so intensely as the discovery of talent in unexpected places—the slum child who shows scientific genius, the frail youngster who develops athletic ability, the poor child who becomes a captain of industry.   John Gardner |

EMPHASIS A good sentence puts the emphasis on what matters. The writer may frontload the sentence, pulling a key idea to the beginning for special attention. Or a writer may give a sentence added punch by withholding a key point to the last:

| POINT FIRST: | **To conquer fear** is the beginning of wisdom.   Bertrand Russell |
| POINT LAST: | You should write, first of all, **to please yourself**.   Doris Lessing |

368

Keep your sentences from becoming plodding and monotonous. Study the way effective writers use sentences of different length and structure for variety and emphasis.

| 24a | *var* | Sentence Length |

Vary sentence length to bring a plodding passage to life.

Short sentences can briefly make a point; long sentences can fill in detailed explanation and support. A short sentence is often right for summing up a key idea or for giving pointed advice. It is often memorable and quotable:

SHORT: Economy is the art of making the most of life.   G. B. Shaw
          Cooking is the art of making the most of food.   Student imitation

A long sentence is often right for detailed description, explanation, or argument, with all specifics in place and all *ifs* and *buts* fully spelled out:

LONG: There will never be a really free and enlightened State until the State comes to recognize the individual as a higher and independent power, from which all its own power and authority are derived, and treats him accordingly.   Henry David Thoreau, "Civil Disobedience"

Remember the following points:

(1) Avoid choppy short sentences in explanation and argument. In description and narrative, we sometimes use a series of short sentences to create a bare-fact, one-at-a-time effect:

I arrive at my office. I work, taking frequent breaks. I visit the water cooler. I gossip with friends on the phone.

But in explanation and argument, a series of short sentences, unless intended for special emphasis, is likely to seem disjointed:

CHOPPY: We listened to AM radio most of the day. The format never seemed to change. There was one advertising jingle after the other. The fast-talking DJ would give a number to call. You name the song and you win a prize. You could call an agency for tickets to this concert or that.

369

The DJ would play oldies but goodies and then the current number-one song, the big hit.

REVISED: We spent most of the day listening to AM radio, whose format never seemed to change. Punctuating the advertising jingles, the DJ would give a number to call so listeners could name the song to win a prize or order tickets to this concert or that. The DJ would play oldies but goodies and then the current number-one song, the big hit.

(2) Learn how to make a short summary sentence and a long elaborating sentence work together. We often use a short, pointed sentence as the opening sentence or topic sentence of a paragraph. Then we follow up in longer sentences that fill in details. Look at how short and long work together in the following examples:

Newspapers give a distorted view of life. They overemphasize the unusual, such as a mother's giving birth to quintuplets, the development of a Christmas tree that grows its own decorative cones, the minting of two pennies that were only half engraved, gang fights, teenage-drinking, or riots.

Most of Wyoming has a "lean-to" look. Instead of big, roomy barns and Victorian houses, there are dugouts, low sheds, log cabins, sheep camps, and fence lines that look like driftwood blown haphazardly into place.   Gretel Ehrlich

(3) Occasionally make your reader stop short at a brief, memorable statement of an important point. A short sentence can be especially effective if it sets off a key observation at the end of a passage:

With the great growth in leisure-time activities, millions of Americans are turning to water sports: fishing, swimming, water skiing, and skin diving. **Clean water exhilarates and relaxes.**   Vance Packard

Games are supposed to bring out the highest standards of sportsmanship in people. **They often bring out the worst**.   Glenn Dickey

---

SENTENCE PRACTICE 6   Study the following examples of *short, pointed statements* as model sentences. For five of these, write a sentence of your own that follows the structure of the original as closely as possible. (You need not follow the model in all details.)

1. Love is as necessary to human beings as food and shelter.
   Aldous Huxley

SAMPLE IMITATION: Attention is as essential to children as are clothes and shoes.

2. Curiosity, like all other desires, produces pain as well as pleasure. Samuel Johnson

3. Perversity is the muse of modern literature. Susan Sontag

4. The man with a new idea is a crank until the new idea succeeds. Mark Twain

5. Real old age begins when one looks backward rather than forward. May Sarton

6. Better be a nettle in the side of your friend than an echo. Ralph Waldo Emerson

7. I've been too busy living lately to know what is happening. May Sarton

8. Those who cut their own wood are twice warmed.

9. Work expands so as to fill the time available for its completion. C. Northcote Parkinson

10. A nail that sticks out will be hammered down. Japanese saying

---

SENTENCE PRACTICE 7 Study the following examples of *long, elaborate sentences* carrying along many details. Choose five of these as model sentences. For each, write a similar sentence of your own, carrying nearly as much freight as the original. (You need not follow the structure of the original except in its large outlines.)

1. (a news event) On an early January day in 1968, a volcanic eruption pushed some steaming rocks above the surface waters of the South Pacific, adding a new island to the remote Tonga Archipelago.

2. (a snapshot of a person) A dirty, long-haired young man in a faded army fatigue jacket, weary from walking, reached through the barbed-wire fence to pet a mud-covered Jersey milk cow grazing in a field alongside the country road.

3. (a capsule view of a place) The name Bell Labs usually conjures up images of white-coated physicists sequestered in cubicles, equipped with super computers, and subjecting ions to megawatt laser blasts in an effort to "improve communications."

4. (a sentence that traces a process) We begin as children; we mature; we leave the parental nest; we give birth to children who, in turn, grow up, leave, and begin the process all over again. Alvin Toffler

5. (a capsule summary of a plot) Sir Thomas More, a man of high position, enjoying the respect of his peers and the friendship of his king, is brought to ruin by his inability to betray his conscience.

6. (a sentence that explains an important requirement) An interview need not be an ambush to be good, but it should set up a situation in which

371

the subject can be surprised by what he says—that is, a situation in which he has to do some audible thinking.   Richard Todd

7. (a capsule portrait of an author) Whereas most science-fiction writers spend their time predicting, say, the discovery of planets ruled by angry, invisible dogs, Clarke has largely confined himself to predicting things that actually come to pass.   David Owen

8. (a moment of self-realization) I felt I'd just waked from some long, pillowy dream and taken a look at where I was: still friendless, sallow, peculiar, living alone with my mother, surrounded by monstrous potted plants taller and older than I was.   Anne Tyler

9. (a media watcher's generalization) In most housewife commercials, the housewife is portrayed as little more than a simpering, brainless jelly, almost pathologically obsessed with the world of kitchen floors or laundry, or of the celebrated "bathroom bowl."   Michael J. Arlen

---

SENTENCE PRACTICE 8   In the following examples, study how *a short summarizing sentence and a long elaborating sentence* can work together. Then write three similar pairs of your own.

1. *Training is everything*. The peach was once a bitter almond; cauliflower is nothing but cabbage with a college education.   Mark Twain
    SAMPLE IMITATION: *Confidence helps*. The self-assured young woman smiled inwardly when the interviewer announced that the job was hers.

2. *Good families are hospitable*. Knowing that hosts need guests as much as guests need hosts, they are generous with honorary memberships for friends, whom they urge to come early and often and to stay late. Jane Howard

3. Although the automotive industry moved to Detroit early in this century, Indianapolis is still a motor city, swarming with car washes and auto-parts stores, and the sign on the road into town from the airport, WELCOME TO INDIANAPOLIS: CROSSROADS OF AMERICA, seems to imply that you're entering a place best reached by car. *Here, nobody walks*.   Paul Fussell

---

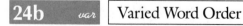

24b   *var* | Varied Word Order

Vary normal word order to keep your sentences from being too much alike.

Sentences may become monotonous when they march down the page in a simple subject-verb pattern. Break up the monotony by experimenting with variations in word order. To perk up a sentence, you might pull another sentence part out in front of the subject (as this sentence does). Or you might first fill in various details or conditions and then complete the main part of your statement at the end.

(1) Pull a modifier to the front of the sentence. Dear to writers of *Time*style, the introductory modifier (or modifiers) can give a sprightly or energetic quality to a passage:

VARIED: The Trans World Terminal stems from the work of contemporary architects like Corbusier of France and Nervi of Italy, masters of the curve in concrete. **Like a true eagle**, this building is all curves and muscle, no right angles. **Built of reinforced concrete**, the whole structure swoops and turns and rises.   Ken Macrorie

VARIED: **Wandering among the shoppers, standing on O'Connell Bridge, walking the quays**, I turned the past and the present over and over in my mind. , Elizabeth Cullinan

(2) Shift a completer to the beginning of the sentence. A writer may move an object or other completer from its usual position after the verb and pull it out in front. This turning around of the usual sentence pattern we call **inversion**. (In the preceding sentence, inversion calls attention to *this turning around*.) The introductory complement is common in exclamations like "*What a liar* you are!" or "*How true* that is!" In other sentences, it often links two sentences by taking up something mentioned earlier:

VARIED: **Gone** are the days when gas stations had eager attendants and clean restrooms.

LINKED: Ma's Café catered to locals and tourists. **The tourists** she charged extra.
           The committee asked him to betray his friends. **That** he refused to do.

(3) Save the predicate of the main clause till the end. Work modifiers or other supporting material into the sentence earlier before you go on to the main verb. Try improving a loosely structured sentence by shifting the main point toward the end, especially if a **belated modifier** sounds like a lame afterthought:

373

LAME: Richard Wagner became one of the most successful composers of all time **in spite of the jeers of his contemporaries.** (This version may make your readers remember the jeers rather than the composer's success.)

IMPROVED: Richard Wagner, **though jeered at by his contemporaries**, became one of the most successful composers of all time.

We can sort our sentences into roughly two kinds according to how late the main point or punch line appears in the sentence. The **cumulative** sentence (also called **loose** sentence) gives us the main point early and then gradually elaborates, leading to further details, proceeding to further comments and ramifications. The resulting sentence is an expandable sentence; it reads as if it had been built in stages:

CUMULATIVE: She liked a simple life and simple people,
 and would have been happier, I think, if she had
 stayed in the backlands of Alabama
 riding wild on the horses she so often talked about,
 not so lifelong lonely for the black men and
 women who had taught her the only religion
 she ever knew.   Lillian Hellman

A **periodic** sentence, though also using considerable detail, does not fully state the central point until the end. An essential part of the main statement is held in suspense; the sentence ends when the main statement ends. Everything else is worked into the sentence along the way. A periodic sentence is often appropriate for a tightly organized summary or definition:

PERIODIC: **Comedy**, though often showing us cranks or eccentrics, nevertheless **aims its ridicule**, as many critics have said, **at common failings of human nature**.

(4) Revive the reader's attention with an occasional pointed question. What else can you do to bring variety into a group of plodding sentences? At strategic points, you may decide to turn to the reader with a key question:

Where do the terms of businessese come from? Most, of course, are hand-me-downs from former generations of business people, but many are the fruit of crossfertilization with other jargons.   William H. Whyte

24c *var* | Varied Structure

Use the full range of our sentence resources.

Inexperienced (or timid) writers often use only part of our common sentence potential. Variety results naturally from variations that are part of our normal sentence resources. For instance, the *to* form, or **infinitive**, may replace the subject or a noun later in the sentence: *To err* is human. *To know me* is *to love me*. Like other verbals, such infinitives often carry along other material. To experiment with such infinitive phrases (as this sentence does) is a step toward sentence variety:

> **To live day by day** is **not to live at all**.
> **To do good is noble: to teach others to do good** is nobler, and no trouble.   Mark Twain
> **To envision a human being without technology** is **to envision a dead naked ape**, not a happy noble savage.   Ben Bova

Another verbal we can substitute for a noun is the *-ing* form, then called a **gerund**, or verbal noun: *Seeing* is *believing*. *Speeding* causes accidents. Again the verbal may carry other material with it to form a verbal phrase: *Speeding on curving roads at night* causes accidents. Using such verbal phrases at different points in a sentence can help a writer counteract monotony:

> **Stealing** has always been a means of **redistributing the wealth**.   John Conyers
> **Helping the country look more like Harvard** won't necessarily make it more humane.   Ralph Keyes

A major departure from the normal patterns is the substitution of a **noun clause** as the subject. What would normally be a noun is then a clause with its own subject and verb:

NOUN:	**The migrations** of birds remain a mystery.
NOUN CLAUSE:	**How migrating birds navigate** remains a mystery.
NOUN:	**The truth** was at first known only to a few.
NOUN CLAUSE:	**What is now proved** was once only imagined. William Blake

SENTENCE PRACTICE 9   Each of the following sentences starts with a variation from the usual subject-verb or noun-verb-noun order. Choose five of these as model sentences. For each, write a similar sentence of your own.

1. Stronger than the mighty sea is almighty God.
   SAMPLE IMITATION: Bleaker than a misspent youth is life without experience.
2. On a huge hill, cragged and steep, truth stands.   John Donne
3. To err is human; to forgive, divine.   Alexander Pope
4. To describe with precision even the simplest object is extremely difficult.   Aldous Huxley
5. In this country, at least in theory, no one denies the right of any person to differ with the government, or the right to express that difference in speech, in the press, by petition, or in an assembly.   Charles E. Wyzanski
6. Having chosen what she wants to become, a woman must be prepared to commit herself over a long period of time to reach her goal. Margaret Mead
7. What makes democratic politics different from most other professions is that, occasionally, the politician has a duty to risk his job by performing it conscientiously.   George F. Will
8. Building a beautiful cabinet is a labor of days; destroying it with an ax takes only a minute.
9. To create a little flower is a labor of the ages.   William Blake
10. What I call my self-respect is more important to me than anything else.   Dorothy Lessing

---

24d   *emp*   Emphatic Position

Use variations in sentence structure for emphasis.

Changes in sentence structure do not only promote variety. They change **emphasis**—they call different parts of a sentence to our attention. "*His horses* he loved more than his family" highlights the person's love of horses. "He loved his horses more than his family" allows us to give equal attention (and sympathy) to both. Note the following especially.

The beginning of a sentence can pull a key idea out for special attention:

Enormous amounts of time, money, and talent go into commercials. **Technically**, they are often brilliant and innovative, the product not only of new skills and devices but of imaginative minds.   Marya Mannes

More often, however, the most emphatic position in the sentence *is the end*. If we allow a sentence to build up to the main point, the payload comes last. The key idea stays imprinted on the reader's mind:

> Earth dwellers now have the choice of making their world into **a neighborhood or a crematorium**.   Norman Cousins

> What my sons have is a world that is small enough to be readily understood, where those responsible **wear a human face**.   Carolyn Lewis

The choice of the emphatic final position channels the reader's attention in the following pair:

> Although he died bankrupt, Rembrandt had been a **successful painter who commanded high fees**. (emphasis on success)

> Although Mozart had played at the royal courts of Europe, he was **buried in a pauper's grave**. (emphasis on failure)

DISCOURSE EXERCISE 10   Study the way the following model sentences save the key point till the end. For each, write a similar sentence of your own, following the structure of the original as closely as you can. (You need not follow it in all details.)

Slang Comes and Goes

1. One of the troubles of colorful language, slang or other, is that its color rubs off.
2. Slang terms for money, like *lettuce* and *grand*, first had their highest frequency in those districts where police officers would prefer to go in pairs.
3. College professors had to learn that the expression "dig that crazy course," coming from their students, was not a criticism but high praise.
4. What sounds cute and clever to the young often sounds merely banal to older ears.
5. Among my friends, *louse* had the plural *lice* when it referred to insects but *louses* when it referred to people.

---

25   Awkward Sentences

OVERVIEW   Ideally, we write sentences in which every word counts and in which every word is in the right place. In sentences like the following, each word carries its share of the load. We take in the basic pattern of the sentence without awkward backtrackings or doubletakes:

The great enemy of clear language is insincerity.   George Orwell

O'Keeffe tramped across the New Mexico landscape, and her camera found beauty in the bleached skulls of long-dead animals.

In practice, however, sentences are seldom this clear and direct on a first attempt. Some writers linger over each sentence, trying to get it right the first time. But most push ahead, planning to polish rough sentences while writing a second or third draft. Whatever your own practice, learn to diagnose and improve sentences that turned out stiff, awkward, or roundabout. Many awkward sentences are simply too wordy:

WORDY:	At the present point in time, the company is not in a position to give employment to additional workers.
IMPROVED:	Right now, the company cannot afford to hire additional workers.

Other awkward sentences get entangled in *that-if* or *and-which* constructions that make the reader lose the thread:

AWKWARD:	I think **that if** an actor with moderate acting ability can earn over fifty million in one year something is wrong with our system of incentives and rewards.
IMPROVED:	In my opinion, **if** an actor with moderate acting ability can earn over fifty million in one year, something is wrong with our system of incentives and rewards.

Still other awkward sentences are weak because of a tagged-on modifier or lame afterthought:

LAME:	A threatening epidemic can be prevented if the proper authorities take firm action from the start, **usually**.
IMPROVED:	**Usually** a threatening epidemic can be prevented if the proper authorities take firm action from the start.

An awkward sentence, like a fogged-over windshield, keeps us from getting a clear view of where we are headed. Revise awkward and confused sentences to give your readers a clearer view of who does what, what is truly important, and how parts fit into a larger whole.

25a *w, awk* | Deadwood

Prune your sentences of deadwood.

Effective writers avoid padding; they know how to write sentences in which every word counts. Revise sentences where too many words are unnecessary props or mere filling. Remember to cross out **redundant** words, which merely duplicate a meaning: Write *October* instead of *the month of October, consensus* instead of *consensus of opinion, combine* instead of *combine together*.

Try trimming down sentences that carry too much deadwood. Look for the following especially:

(1) Take out wordy, roundabout tags. Edit out **circumlocutions**— talky constructions that "take the long way around." Instead of "it is unfortunate that," write *unfortunately*; instead of "it is possible that we will," write "we may."

INFLATED	BRIEF
because of the fact that	because
during the time that	while
a large number of	many
at an early date	soon
in the event that	if
at the present point in time	now

(2) Remove unneeded props. Instead of "*those of* adolescent *age*," write *adolescents*. Trim superfluous *there are*'s and *who were*'s, especially if several pad the same sentence.

AWKWARD:	I wrote little, **because of the fact that** my childhood had been **an** uneventful **one**.
BETTER:	I wrote little, **because** my childhood had been uneventful.
AWKWARD:	**There are** many farmers in the area **who are** planning to attend the protest meeting **which is** scheduled for Memorial Day.
REVISED:	Many farmers in the area plan to attend the protest meeting scheduled for Memorial Day.

Sentences like the following become less flabby when an unneeded *is* or *are* has been trimmed:

FLABBY:	Navratilova **is a tough competitor** and bounced back after her defeat at Wimbledon.
TRIM:	**A tough competitor**, Navratilova bounced back after her defeat at Wimbledon.

(3) Make effective use of pronouns. Pronouns, provided they are clear and well placed, help us avoid awkward repetition of names and labels:

AWKWARD: A child of preschool age often shows a desire to read, but the **child's** parents often ignore this **desire**.

BETTER: A child of preschool age often shows a desire to read, **which** the parents ignore.

25b *rep* | Awkward Repetition

Avoid unintentional repetition of sounds, syllables, words, or phrases.

Carelessly repeated sounds or sentence elements can grate on the reader's ears. Revise for awkward repetition like the following:

AWKWARD: Commercials seldom make for entertain**ing** and relax**ing** listen**ing**.

BETTER: Commercials seldom entertain and relax the listener.

AWKWARD: Close examin**ation** of the results of the investig**ation** led to a reorganiz**ation** of the organiz**ation**.

BETTER: Close study of the results of the inquiry led to a reorganization of the company.

AWKWARD: We listened to an account **of** the customs **of** the inhabitants **of** the village.

BETTER: We listened to an account of the villagers' customs.

Revise for unintentional repetition especially when the similarity in sound covers up a *shift in meaning or relationship*.

My father lost his savings during the depression because he had **banked on** [better: "relied on"] the well-established reputation of our hometown **bank**.

DISCOURSE EXERCISE 11 Rewrite the following sentences to eliminate *deadwood and awkward repetition*.

The Bionic Athlete

1. As an athlete, it is essential to attain the best physical shape as far as body conditioning is concerned.

2. It is an unfortunate fact, however, that many of today's athletes in this modern day and age excel because of the fact that chemicals build up their muscles and speed up their performance.
3. Doctors warn of the risks of pumping the body full of drugs of different kinds.
4. This year has been a discouraging one for those who are committed to keeping steroids from skewing athletic competitions in the sports arena.
5. Increasingly, runners and swimmers more and more find themselves stripped of their medals and well-paying lucrative advertising contracts in the event that banned chemicals are found in their bodies.

25c *pass, awk* | Awkward Passive

Avoid the passive when it makes sentences awkward or roundabout.

An active sentence goes from the "doer" through the action to the target or result. A passive sentence turns this perspective around and puts the target first. The original object becomes the subject of the new sentence:

ACTIVE:	NASA aborted the mission.
PASSIVE:	*The mission* was aborted by NASA.

The passive highlights the target or result. As a result, it works well when the target or product seems more important than the performer:

PASSIVE:	The **dusky**, a subspecies of the seaside sparrow, **has never been found** anywhere except on Merritt Island and along the St. John's River.
PASSIVE:	Among the Ibo, **the art of conversation is regarded** very highly, and proverbs are the palm oil with which **words are eaten.** Chinua Achebe, *Things Fall Apart*

The passive is also appropriate when the doer or performer of an action is beside the point or hard to identify. In many legitimate uses of the passive, we focus on the result, not the cause:

LEGITIMATE:	**Marcia's parents were killed** in a car accident when she was very young.
	In World War II, **millions of people were driven** from their homes.

381

Avoid *unneeded* passives that make sentences roundabout and impersonal:

(1) Avoid the awkward passive. Many verbs work best in an active sentence; they work best when a sentence tells us who does what. When the source of an action is known and important, the passive makes us look at what happens from an awkward angle.

AWKWARD: Monumental traffic jams **are endured by** many motorists on the way to work.

ACTIVE: Many motorists **endure** monumental traffic jams on the way to work.

AWKWARD: After each simplification of the tax laws, longer and more impenetrable instructions **must be puzzled out** by the taxpayer.

ACTIVE: After each simplification of the tax laws, the taxpayer **must puzzle out** longer and more impenetrable instructions.

(2) Avoid the pretentious passive. Do not use the passive under the mistaken impression that it will make your sentences more formal or impressive. Learn to convert weak passives back to the active:

WEAK PASSIVE: Today the **effort** of the average person seems **to be** largely **placed** in trying to ignore commercials and advertisements.

ACTIVE: The average **consumer** seems **to make** a constant effort to ignore commercials and advertisements.

WEAK PASSIVE: My experiences at writing **were** greatly **increased** due to two long essays due each week.

ACTIVE: I **wrote** more than ever, **having to turn in** two long essays each week.

Finer Points   In a passive sentence, the doer or performer is often left out. Do not use this **short passive** to leave responsibility vague or ill defined.

EVASIVE: **Pollution** should be fought unrelentingly. (By whom?)
ACTIVE: Every **citizen** should unrelentingly fight pollution.

Revision of evasive sentences like the following helps a writer avoid mere hearsay and well-meaning platitudes:

EVASIVE: A plan for popular election of Supreme Court justices **is now being advanced**. (By whom?)

EVASIVE: The racial problem is clearly one that **could** and **should have been solved** long ago. (By whom?)

ON SHIFTS TO THE PASSIVE, SEE 22c.

PEER EDITOR 12   Rewrite the following sentences to convert *awkward or unnecessary passives* back to active statements. Who does what? Who should do what?

EXAMPLE: When writing about actions being performed, the awkward passive should be avoided.

REVISED: When writing about what people do, writers should avoid the awkward passive.

1. When an application for a badly needed loan is turned down by a bank because of the customer's gender, a feeling of impotent rage may be experienced.
2. All instructions should be read carefully and all blank spaces filled in before this form is signed by the applicant.
3. If any experimenting endangering human lives is to be done by the government, the voters should be consulted first.
4. When information about summer school is received, the necessary deadlines may have already passed.
5. Various ways of living are being tested today and experimented with by youth whose dominant characteristic is the desire for flexibility.

25d   *awk* | Impersonal Constructions

Revise impersonal constructions to make sentences more direct.

The introductory *there is/there are* and the impersonal *one* (meaning anybody, a person) can make a sentence roundabout and impersonal. Sometimes an introductory *It is* or *There are* sets up the main point of a sentence for needed emphasis:

It is **the result** that matters—not good intentions.
There are **a thousand** hacking at the branches of evil to one who is
striking at the root.   Henry David Thoreau

More often, the *it is* or *there is* merely postpones the main point and
causes an awkward reshuffling later in the sentence:

AWKWARD:	In 1986, **there was** a protest march to the state capitol participated in by 15,000 people.
REVISED:	In 1986, 15,000 protesters marched to the state capitol.

Equally expendable is the impersonal **one** when it serves as a mere
prop in a sentence:

ROUNDABOUT:	**When teaching, one** should be patient.
DIRECT:	**Teachers** should be patient.
ROUNDABOUT:	**If one is a citizen of a democracy, she** should exercise her voting rights.
DIRECT:	**A citizen of a democracy** should vote.

25e   *auk*   Sentence Overloads

Lighten the load in overburdened sentences.

In a well-written sentence, several dependent clauses or added modifiers may specify time, place, or conditions, bringing in material that dove-
tails neatly into the sentence:

If all the world hated you and believed you wicked, **while** your conscience approved you and absolved you from guilt, you would not be
without friends.   Charlotte Brontë

In an overburdened sentence, different parts of a sentence may begin
to crowd and jostle each other. Look for the following:

(1) Revise interlocking dependent clauses. In an overloaded sentence, several dependent clauses may create a logjam of confusing provisos
and specifications. For instance, interlocking *that-if, if-because, which-
when* constructions are often awkward:

AWKWARD:	I think **that if** there were less emphasis on conformity in high school, college students would be better prepared for independent thinking.

IMPROVED: In my opinion, college students would be better prepared for independent thinking **if** there were less emphasis on conformity in high school.

(2) Revise "house-that-Jack-built" sentences. In "house-that-Jack-built" sentences, several dependent clauses of the same kind follow each other, causing the sentence to trail off into a confusing succession of explanations:

AWKWARD: Nitric oxides have an overfertilizing effect on deciduous trees, **which** are trees **that** lose their leaves during the winter, **that** has the effect of encouraging them to keep their leaves far into the winter, **which** makes them sensitive to frost.

REVISED: Nitric oxides have an overfertilizing effect on deciduous trees—trees **that** lose their leaves during the winter. The excess fertilizer encourages them to keep their leaves too far into the winter and thus makes them vulnerable to frost.

(3) Revise an awkward string of introductory clauses. Sometimes too many similar dependent clauses delay the main point:

AWKWARD: **When** children are constantly watched **when** they are born and **while** they are babies, the reason is that parents want to see whether their children are developing as the books say they should.

IMPROVED: Some parents constantly watch their young children to see whether they are developing as the books say they should.

(4) Revise seesaw sentences. Seesaw sentences start with what seems like an important reason or condition but later end with a reason or condition that seems to ignore or overrule the first:

AWKWARD: **Because** many students change their majors, they take more than four years to graduate, **because** most majors are loaded with requirements.

REVISED: Most majors are loaded with requirements. As a result, students who change their majors often take more than four years to graduate.

(5) Keep lengthy modifiers from breaking up the pattern of a sentence. Lengthy appositives, verbal phrases, or dependent clauses sometimes separate elements that belong together:

AWKWARD: The pilot told his friends that he had flown Clinton Morris, **a resident of New York City sought by the government for income tax evasion**, out of the United States.

REVISED: The pilot told his friends about a passenger he had flown out of the United States: Clinton Morris, **a resident of New York City sought by the government for income tax evasion**.

PEER EDITOR 13 Rewrite the following *awkward, overburdened, or confusing* sentences.

1. We watched the officer who questioned the suspects who had been apprehended.
2. There was an antinuclear demonstration participated in by over 20,000 people.
3. There will be an investigation by the mayor's office of the unauthorized distribution of this information.
4. From small incidents, like receiving too much change and pocketing it, to larger issues, like cheating on a test, a lifelong pattern may be established.
5. When people are constantly under supervision when at work and asked immediately where they are going when they leave their station, a feeling of harassment is experienced.
6. Saturday mornings used to be my best time for studying, because I knew nothing was due the next morning (which was Sunday), until I started working.
7. Motorists are quickly informed of the whereabouts of restaurants, motels, and, of course, speed traps set by the police, by other CB operators.
8. The dreary weather, mainly rain, that never seemed to stop, and my problems with my parents, which were serious, upset me.
9. A child's first impressions of people and places shape the course of her future life, frequently.
10. Financial independence between partners was rarely practiced in a traditional marriage.

---

26 Repetition and Balance

OVERVIEW Good sentences have a satisfying rhythm. They fall into a pattern. They use repetition and parallel structure to channel our attention, to underline connections, or to lead up to a high point. They balance off similar or opposed ideas, fitting related ideas into a neat frame ("It is better to be active today than radioactive tomorrow"). Sentences like the following use **parallel structure** to line up parallel ideas, fitting much related detail into a satisfying whole:

> Commercials try to sell us **cars that** attract women, **scents that** attract men, **seasonings that** enhance the flavor of food, and **mouthwash that** will kill the odor later.   Student paper

> **When financial reverses** prompt a young person to quit school and go to work, **when marriage** does not happen at the hoped-for time, **when a child** is born unusually early or late, **when people** simply can't seem to find themselves and their occupational achievement is delayed—these are what we might call untimely events.   Gail Sheehy

Sentences like the following play off opposites:

> Athletes are supposed to break **records, not rules**.

> The sweet-and-lovely look **is out**; the tough-kid pose with unkempt hair and sloppy clothes **is in**.

Remember that sentence style is not a matter of isolated sentences. In the following example, the repetition of an identical pattern accounts for the rhythm and emphasis of the whole passage:

> **We need** more patterns of desire. **We need** models of women—and men—who expect everything, and set out to get it. **We need** people in novels as well as in life to show us how to have the courage to walk out.   Gail Godwin

26a *rep, emp* | Emphatic Repetition

Use intentional repetition for emphasis.

Intentional, deliberate repetition can help emphasize important points—reinforce them, drive them home. Repetition at strategic points shows that an idea matters, that we mean to insist. Look at the way a key term echoes in passages like the following:

EMPHATIC: In the meantime, the oiler **rowed**, and then the correspondent **rowed**, and then the oiler **rowed**.   Stephen Crane

I cannot remember when I was not surrounded by **sports**, when talk of **sports** was not in the air, when I did not care passionately about **sports**.   Joseph Epstein

Less dramatic and more common than the actual repetition of words or phrases is the insistent repetition on the same idea in different words:

> If we are constantly presented with what we are not or cannot have, the **dislocation deepens, contentment vanishes,** and **frustration reigns.** Marya Mannes

26b //, 9p | Parallel Structure

Use parallel structure to help channel the reader's attention.

When we make parts of a sentence parallel, we put related ideas in similar grammatical form. We thus channel the reader's attention, laying out related material in a satisfying pattern, setting up the rhythm that makes a well-balanced sentence a pleasure to read:

> Studies serve **for delight, for ornament,** and **for ability.**   Sir Francis Bacon
> Cars serve **for transportation, for recreation,** and **for ostentation.** Student imitation

Chart the **parallel structure** that makes each of the following sentences a well-balanced whole:

> It is about time we realize that many women make
> **better teachers than mothers,**
> **better actresses than wives,**
> **better diplomats than cooks.**   Marya Mannes
> **The attempt to suppress the use of drugs**
> is as futile as
> **the wish to teach cooking to an ape.**   Lewis H. Lapham
> The only advice one person can give another about reading is
> **to take no advice,**
> **to follow your own instincts,**
> **to use your own reason,**
> **to come to your own conclusions.**   Virginia Woolf

Remember:

(1) Parallel structure helps us line up related ideas. It helps the reader see that several things are part of the same picture or the same story:

PARALLEL: To succeed as a writer, you must have **the perseverance of Sisyphus, the patience of a saint,** and **the hide of an armadillo,** as well as **ambition, energy,** and **thorough mastery of your craft.**   Student paper

(2) Parallel structure helps us line up different ideas for comparison or contrast. When two opposing ideas are neatly polarized, we call the resulting balance of opposites an **antithesis:** "To err is human; to forgive, divine." Sentences like the following owe their pointed, quotable quality to their antithetical style:

Propaganda is a monologue which seeks **not a response but an echo.** W. H. Auden
The idols of every campus generation have always been **against everything** and **for nothing.**   Peter F. Drucker

(3) Parallel structure is often cumulative. It frequently builds up to the most important or climactic item in a series:

The choice made, she could surrender her will to **the strange, the exhilarating, the gigantic** event.   Graham Greene
India **is a poetic nation, yet it demands** new electrical plants. It **is a mystical nation, yet it wants** new roads. It **is traditionally a peaceful nation, yet it could,** if misled, **inflame** Asia.   James A. Michener

ON FAULTY PARALLELISM, SEE **22d.**

SENTENCE PRACTICE 14 Study the use of *parallelism* in the following passages. For each, write a passage of your own on a subject of your own choice, following the structure of the original as closely as you can.

1.   Studies serve for delight, for ornament, and for ability.   Sir Francis Bacon

2.   The press as an institution has evolved through alternating chapters of disgrace and honor, of prostitution and martyrdom, of somnolence and vigilance, gradually assuming the role of public protector.   Jack Anderson

3.   To assign unanswered letters their proper weight, to free us from expectations of others, to give us back to ourselves—there lies the great, the singular power of self-respect.   Joan Didion

4.   Women feel just as men feel; they need exercise for their faculties and a field for their efforts as much as their brothers do; they suffer from too

389

rigid a restraint, too absolute a stagnation, precisely as men would suffer.   Charlotte Brontë

5. It is about time we realize that many women make better teachers than mothers, better actresses than wives, better diplomats than cooks. Marya Mannes

---

SENTENCE PRACTICE 15   Study the way the following well-balanced sentences play off *opposites*. For each, write a similar balanced or antithetical sentence of your own, following the structure of the original as closely as you can.

1. Cunning is the art of concealing our own defects and discovering other people's weaknesses.
    SAMPLE IMITATION: Politics is the art of making one's own record look good and making the other person's look bad.
2. We must begin the journey to tomorrow from the point where we are today.   Garrett Hardin
3. We vow to teach our young the virtues of resistance as well as those of allegiance; we vow to teach them a love of conscience stronger than their love of the state.   Peter Marin
4. We have exchanged being known in small communities for being anonymous in huge populations.   Ellen Goodman
5. Democracy substitutes selection by the incompetent many for appointment by the corrupt few.   George Bernard Shaw

---

REVIEW EXERCISE 16   Study the following passages. Point out any features that make for *effective sentence style*. Look for features like varied sentence length, emphasis, parallel structure.

1. We are informed that marriage should be a place where we can grow, find ourselves, be ourselves. Interestingly, we cannot be entirely ourselves even with our best friends. Some decorum, some courtesy, some selflessness are demanded. As for finding myself, I think I already know where I am. I'm grown up; I have responsibilities; I am in the middle of a lifelong marriage; I am hanging in there, sometimes enduring, sometimes enjoying.   Suzanne Britt Jordan, "My Turn," *Newsweek*
2. There was a photo on the front page of *The New York Times*, a midair shot of an Indy racer all blown to shrapnel, the driver battered unconscious, his limp arms helplessly flung upward by the centrifugal forces contained in the whirling asteroid of junk that only a millisecond before had been a $180,000 automobile. The TV cameras were late to the

scene. They give no clue to what happened. From a great distance you see an orange fireball as the March hits the inner retaining wall. Only pieces emerge from the glow, nothing bigger than your easy chair, some of them still spewing flame, all of them bounding, caroming, cartwheeling through the air, spraying turf as they recoil again and again from the infield grass, still paying dividends of racing speed, a gust of fragments moving forward to litter the entire north end of the Speedway.   Patrick Bedard, "The Anatomy of a Crack-Up," *Esquire*

6

The Right Word

Instructions Look at the three possible choices for the blank space in each sentence. Which word or phrase would be the best choice for serious written English? Write the number of the sentence, followed by the letter for the best choice.

1. The refinery complied _____ the court order.
   a. to   b. with   c. for

2. The company attorney did not _____ for the hearing.
   a. show up   b. show   c. appear

3. The questionnaire asked about students' _____ origins.
   a. ethical   b. ethnic   c. external

4. In a biblical movie, a steam engine would be an _____
   a. anachronism   b. anarchy   c. anathema

5. Students learned the _____ of marketing.
   a. basic essentials   b. basic fundamentals
   c. essentials

6. People starting their own businesses encounter many _____ .
   a. problems   b. hassles
   c. obstructive occurrences

7. Students seldom talked back to the _____ .
   a. profs   b. instructional personnel
   c. instructors

8. Minorities are well represented in our _____ student body.
   a. homogeneous   b. heterogeneous   c. disingenuous

9. In the backlash against nuclear power, Chernobyl played a central
_____ .
   a. factor   b. contribution   c. role

10. _____ costs soared, Congress lost interest in the space race.
   a. In view of the fact that   b. Due to the fact that   c. Because

11. Young Turks are expected to dissent _____ majority opinion.
   a. from   b. with   c. against

12. Students at the academy were allowed to _____ .
   a. sink or swim   b. make it or flunk out
   c. succeed or fail on their own

13. An exclusive trade agreement between two countries is _____
   a. unilateral   b. bilateral   c. multilateral

14. The whole community _____ to help pay the hospital bills.
   a. contributed   b. attributed   c. chipped in

15. Flowers that grow back every year are _____
   a. annual   b. biannual   c. perennial

16. Motorists lost in the desert quickly become _____ .
   a. dehydrated   b. defoliated   c. deracinated

17. Our deficit spending will be judged harshly by _____
   a. propriety   b. posterity   c. prosperity

18. A salesclerk's _____ was not keeping up with inflation.
   a. remuneration   b. income situation   c. income

19. Spanish-speaking voters were _____ in the district.
   a. predominate   b. predominant   c. predisposed

20. Computers have changed the work habits of the _____ in every
office.
   a. gals   b. ladies   c. workers

---

27   Using Your Dictionary

OVERVIEW   Some users turn to the dictionary only to check a spelling (*develop* or *develope*?) or an unusual word (*phlegmatic, serendipity*). Others appeal to the dictionary in order to settle an argument (to prove themselves right and someone else wrong). But many writers think of the dictionary not as a final authority but as a guide; they turn to it regularly for information, advice, and inspiration.

To use words effectively, you have to be a word watcher—alert to their meanings and overtones, to their manifold uses and unintended side effects. Regular use of your dictionary will benefit you as a writer in several basic ways:

- **Your dictionary will help you with baffling new words.** If you have trouble with *modem, digital,* or *analog,* you can turn to your dictionary for quick and accurate information.
- **Your dictionary will help you with unusual meanings.** When you read that Luther spoke at the Diet of Worms, you will realize that *diet* here has nothing to do with food (or with worms). Your dictionary will tell you that *diet* can mean a legislative or parliamentary assembly (in this case, meeting in the city of Worms). Dictionaries help us choose the word that fits the **context**—that goes with what comes before and after.
- **Your dictionary will help you extend your range.** The vocabulary of a good writer is like a memory bank that stores not only the single word *glad* but also many **synonyms**, or words with similar meaning (*delighted, gratified, pleased, lighthearted, happy*), as well as **antonyms**, or words with nearly opposite meaning (*sad, blue, dejected, downcast, heavyhearted, depressed*).
- **Your dictionary will make you aware of shades of meaning.** To be *autonomous* is to be independent—but completely independent and self-ruled, not directed by any other authority. *Coercion* is force—but it is crude, resented force that compels people against their will.
- **Your dictionary will alert you to emotional overtones.** Many words tell us something about the attitudes, feelings, or values of the speaker or writer. Words like *manipulative* or *Big Brother* carry a strong charge of disapproval. Such words carry strong **connotations**—positive or negative associations.

27a   College Dictionaries

Familiarize yourself fully with the information your dictionary provides.

Like mass-volume cars, college dictionaries are becoming more alike. They compete in including new words: *sitcom, skyjacker, unisex, upscale, hot tub, pro-life, interface, preppie.* They vie with each other in covering the language of science and technology, from *entropy* and *laser* to *microfiche* and *quark.* They provide **usage notes**, debating the pros and cons of *disinterested, hopefully, prioritize,* and *impact* used as a verb. Increasingly, they put names of famous people and places in separate biographical and geographical appendixes at the end. Nevertheless, the most widely recommended dictionaries differ in how they present information and in how they envision their intended audience.

■ *Webster's Ninth New Collegiate Dictionary* is published by Merriam-Webster, Inc., whose collection of several million citation slips has been called the "national archives of the language." The *Collegiate* is based on *Webster's Third New International Dictionary*, the most authoritative unabridged dictionary of American English. Historical information about a word comes first, followed by meanings in the order they developed. The current *Ninth New Collegiate* includes the year of the first recorded appearance of a word. The editors do not use the label *informal* (too arbitrary or subjective); they rarely use the label *slang.* Sample entry:

> **fem·i·nism** \'fem-ə-,niz-əm\ *n* (1895) **1** : the theory of the political, economic, and social equality of the sexes **2** : organized activity on behalf of women's rights and interests — **fem·i·nist** \-nəst\ *n or adj* — **fem·i·nis·tic** \,fem-ə-'nis-tik\ *adj*

■ *Webster's New World Dictionary* stands out because of its clear and helpful definitions. Historical information comes first; lists of idioms provide an excellent guide to the manifold uses of a word. The editors have a good ear for informal English and slang; they pay special attention to Americanisms—expressions first found in the U.S.A. Sample entry:

> **Goth·am** (gäth′əm, gō′thəm; *for 1, Brit.* gät′-) **1.** a village near Nottingham, England, whose inhabitants, the "wise men of Gotham," were, according to legend, very foolish **2.** *nickname for* NEW YORK CITY —**Goth′am·ite′** (-īt′) *n.*

■ *The Random House College Dictionary,* Revised Edition (based, like *Webster's Ninth New Collegiate,* on a larger unabridged dictionary), caters to a conservative clientele. The most frequently used meanings come first; historical information is last. Both informal English and slang are marked; usage notes recognize many traditional restrictions. Sample entry:

> **cal·i·ber** (kal′ə bər), *n.* **1.** the diameter of something of circular section, esp. that of the inside of a tube. **2.** *Ordn.* the diameter of the bore of a gun taken as a unit of measurement. **3.** degree of competence, merit, or importance: *a mathematician of high caliber; the high moral caliber of the era.* Also, *esp. Brit.,* **cal′i·bre.** [var. of *calibre* < MF < early It *calibro,* ? alter. of Ar *qālib* mold, last < Gk *kalópous* shoemaker's last = *kālo(n)* wood + *poús* foot] —**cal′i·bered;** *esp. Brit.,* **cal′i·bred,** *adj.*

vocabulary entry ——————
pronunciation
syllabication dots

beau·ty (byōō′tē), *n., pl.* **-ties** for 2–6. **1.** a quality that is present in a thing or person giving intense aesthetic pleasure or deep satisfaction to the senses or the mind. **2.** an attractive, well-formed girl or woman. **3.** a beautiful thing, as a work of art, building, etc. **4.** Often, **beauties**. that which is beautiful in nature or in some natural or artificial environment. **5.** a particular advantage: *One of the beauties of this medicine is the absence of aftereffects.* **6.** a person or thing that excels or is remarkable of its kind: *His black eye was a beauty.* [ME *be(a)ute* < OF *beaute*; r. ME *bealte* < OF, var. of *beltet* < VL **bellitāt-* (s. of **bellitās*) = L *bell(us)*

synonym lists ——————

fine + *-itāt-* -ITY] **—Syn. 1.** loveliness, pulchritude.

part of speech and ——————
inflected forms

be·gin (bi gin′), *v.,* **be·gan, be·gun, be·gin·ning.** —*v.i.* **1.** to proceed to perform the first or earliest part of some action; commence or start. **2.** to come into existence; originate: *The custom began during the Civil War.* —*v.t.* **3.** to proceed to perform the first or earliest part of (some action): *Begin the job tomorrow.* **4.** to originate; be the originator of: *Civic leaders began the reform movement.* [ME *beginn(en)*,

etymology ——————

OE *beginnan* = *be-* BE- + *-ginnan* to begin, perh. orig. to open, akin to YAWN] **—be·gin′ner,** *n.*

synonym study ——————

—Syn. 3. BEGIN, COMMENCE, INITIATE, START (when followed by noun or gerund) refer to setting into motion or progress something that continues for some time. BEGIN is the common term: *to begin knitting a sweater.* COMMENCE is a more formal word, often suggesting a more prolonged or elaborate beginning: *to commence proceedings in court.* INITIATE implies an active and often ingenious first act in a new field: *to initiate a new procedure.* START means to make a first move or to set out on a course of action: *to start paving a street.* **4.** inaugurate, initiate. **—Ant. 1.** end.

antonym ——————

be·la·bor (bi lā′bər), *v.t.* **1.** to discuss, work at, or worry about for an unreasonable amount of time: *He kept belaboring the point long after we had agreed.* **2.** to scorn or ridicule persistently. **3.** *Literary.* to beat vigorously. Also, *Brit.,*

variant spelling ——————

be·la′bour.

hyphenated entry ——————

belles-let·tres (*Fr.* bel le′tRᵃ), *n.pl.* literature regarded as a fine art, esp. as having a purely aesthetic function. [< F: lit., fine letters] **—bel·let·rist** (bel le′trist), *n.* **—bel·let·ris·tic** (bel′li tris′tik), *adj.* **—Syn.** See **literature.**

word element ——————

bene-, an element occurring in loan words from Latin where it meant "well": *benediction.* [comb. form of *bene* (adv.) well]

consecutive
definition numbers

be·neath (bi nēth′, -nēᵺ′), *adv.* **1.** below; in or to a lower place, position, state, or the like. **2.** underneath: *heaven above and the earth beneath.* —*prep.* **3.** below; under: *beneath the same roof.* **4.** further down than; underneath; lower in place than: *The first drawer beneath the top one.* **5.** inferior in position, rank, power, etc.: *A captain is beneath a major.* **6.** unworthy of; below the level or dignity of: *beneath contempt.*

usage note ——————

bent¹ (bent), *adj.* **1.** curved or crooked: *a bent bow; a bent stick.* **2.** determined, set, or resolved (usually fol. by *on*): *to be bent on buying a new car.* —*n.* **3.** a direction taken by

example contexts ——————

bet·ter¹ (bet′ər), *adj., compar. of* **good** *with* **best** *as superl.* **1.** of superior quality or excellence: *a better coat.* **2.** morally superior; more virtuous: *He's no better than a thief!* **3.** of superior value, use, fitness, desirability, acceptableness, etc.: *a better time for action.* **4.** larger; greater: *the better part of a lifetime.* **5.** improved in health; healthier: *Is your mother better?* —*adv., compar. of* **well** *with* **best** *as superl.* **6.** in a more excellent way or manner: *to behave better.* **7.** to a greater degree; more completely or thoroughly: *I probably know him better than anyone else.* **8.** more: *I walked better than a mile to town.* **9. better off, a.** in better circumstances. **b.** more fortunate; happier. **10. go (someone) one better,** to exceed another's effort; be superior to. **11. had better,** would be wiser or more reasonable to; ought to: *We had better stay indoors today.* **12. think better of,** to reconsider and decide more favorably or wisely: *She was tempted to make a sarcastic retort, but thought better of it.* —*v.t.* **13.** to make better; improve; increase the good qualities of. **14.** to improve upon; surpass; exceed: *We have bettered last year's production record.* **15. better oneself,** to improve one's social standing, financial position, or education. —*n.* **16.** that which has greater excellence: *the better of two choices.* **17.** Usually, **betters.** those superior to one in wisdom, social position, etc. **18. for the better,** in a way that is an improvement: *His health changed for the better.* **19. get the better of, a.** to get an advantage over. **b.** to prevail against. [ME *bettre,* OE *betera*; c. OHG *bezziro* (G *besser*), Goth *batiza* = *bat-* (akin to BOOT²) + *-iza* comp. suffix] **—Syn. 13.** amend; advance, promote. See **improve.**

idiomatic phrases ——————

- *The American Heritage Dictionary*, Second College Edition, is intended as a sensible (moderately conservative) guide, less forbidding than traditional dictionaries. Definitions branch out from a central meaning that may not be historically the earliest sense of the word. Sample entry:

> **im·promp·tu** (ĭm-prŏmp′tōō, -tyōō) *adj.* Performed or conceived without rehearsal or preparation: *an impromptu speech.* —*adv.* Spontaneously. —*n.* **1.** Something made or done impromptu, as a speech. **2.** *Mus.* A short lyrical composition esp. for the piano. [Fr. < Lat. *in promptu,* at hand : *in,* in + *promptus,* ready. —see PROMPT.]

DISCOURSE EXERCISE 1   Which of the italicized words in the following sentences would you have to look up in your dictionary? What does your dictionary tell you about the meaning or uses of each new or difficult word?

The Sleeping Giant

1. China is a *homogeneous* nation with a traditional respect for its *mandarins* and the wisdom of its *sages*.
2. Mao's revolution destroyed the ancient *caste* system and the power of *feudal* warlords.
3. He maintained revolutionary *fervor* by mass rallies, propaganda *tirades*, and media *fanfare*.
4. After his death, the new leaders stretched the *procrustean* bed of Maoism to fit new needs.
5. Reformers accused the *staunchly* loyal upper ranks of the army of having become a *stagnant gerontocracy*.
6. China's students have repeatedly been in the *vanguard* of *cataclysmic* change.

DICTIONARY WORK 2   Familiarize yourself with your dictionary by investigating the following:

1. Read the definitions of *high tech, cliché, graffiti, gobbledygook, kitsch.* What do they say? Are they clear and informative?
2. Chart some of the major meanings of a word like *hard, hand, foot, head,* or *mind.* Study the order in which the meanings are arranged.
3. How clear and helpful are the definitions of technical terms like *laser, DNA, dialysis, ozone, microwave*?
4. Are there synonym studies for words like *alien, dogmatic, emotion, expedient*? How helpful are they? Find one set of synonyms that you find particularly helpful or instructive.

5. Are there usage labels or usage notes for any of the following: *go-go*, (being) *hip, persnickety, hopefully, bloke, boffo, starkers, funky, hit it off?*
6. What and where are you told about Sappho, Albert Einstein, Theodore Roosevelt, Stalingrad, Peoria, Susan B. Anthony?

27b *d* | Dictionary Definitions

Use your dictionary as a guide to the full range of meaning of a word.

Dictionaries furnish several kinds of useful information before they explain the meaning of a word: spelling and division into syllables (in•aus•pi•cious), pronunciation, and grammatical label. However, the heart of a lexicographer's (or dictionary maker's) job is the writing of definitions that tell us what a word means and how it is used. To make the most of a dictionary definition, remember advice like the following:

(1) Take in exact technical information. For scientific and historical terms, for instance, dictionaries try to provide exact and helpful information in a very short space. Learn to take in essential points and key details. A good dictionary will try to convey information like the following:

TECHNICAL: A *laser* is a device that amplifies light rays (including rays with the frequencies of ultraviolet and infrared) and concentrates them in extremely narrow, intense, powerful beams that are used, for instance, in surgery, communications, and various industrial processes.

HISTORICAL: *Populism* was a (late nineteenth-century) political movement that championed the interests of the common people (and especially farmers) against the rich and powerful, in particular the large monopolies (like the railroads); today, a populist champions the rights and aspirations of ordinary people against self-appointed political and cultural elites.

RELIGIOUS: *Penance* is an act or ritual of self-punishment designed to show true repentance for sins; often, it is an arduous task taken on to show true regret and renewed devotion.

399

(2) Take in shades of meaning. Look beyond the general area or general idea covered by a word to its special implications. For instance, *terse* means more than "brief"; *mannerism* adds a special twist to "manner":

terse:	intentionally brief and pointed; deliberately avoiding the superfluous, devoid of idle chatter
mannerism:	a habitual, noticeable manner, especially a recurrent quirky or eccentric feature of behavior

(3) Choose the right meaning from the full range of meanings of a word. Most English words have multiple meanings and many uses. The simple word *heel* may stand for part of the foot, part of a shoe, the crusty end of a loaf of bread, and (informally) a contemptible person. Dictionaries try to arrange the several meanings of a word in a natural flow that shows how related meanings branch out from an original or central one.

Often you will have to work your way down a numbered list of meanings, like the meanings listed for the word *cell* in the following entry:

cell \'sel\ *n* [ME, fr. OE, religious house and OF *celle* hermit's cell, fr. L *cella* small room; akin to L *celare* to conceal — more at HELL] (bef. 12c) **1 :** a small religious house dependent on a monastery or convent **2 a :** a one-room dwelling occupied by a solitary person (as a hermit) **b :** a single room (as in a convent or prison) usu. for one person **3 :** a small compartment, cavity, or bounded space: as **a :** one of the compartments of a honeycomb **b :** a membranous area bounded by veins in the wing of an insect **4 :** a small usu. microscopic mass of protoplasm bounded externally by a semipermeable membrane, usu. including one or more nuclei and various nonliving products, capable alone or interacting with other cells of performing all the fundamental functions of life, and forming the least structural unit of living matter capable of functioning independently **5 a (1) :** a receptacle (as a cup or jar) containing electrodes and an electrolyte either for generating electricity by chemical action or for use in electrolysis **(2) :** FUEL CELL **b :** a single unit in a device for converting radiant energy into electrical energy or for varying the intensity of an electrical current in accordance with radiation **6 :** a unit in a statistical array comprising a group of individuals and formed by the intersection of a column and a row **7 :** the basic and usu. smallest unit of an organization or movement; *esp* : the primary unit of a Communist organization **8 :** a portion of the atmosphere that behaves as a unit

From *Webster's Ninth New Collegiate Dictionary*

From its root meaning—"a small enclosed place"—the word *cell* has branched out into various historical and technical uses. Starting with its first use in English sometime before the twelfth century, we can sketch a rough history of this useful term as follows:

(1)   a small cabin-like house for a religious person

(2a)   a hermit's cell

(2b)   a monk's or nun's cell in a monastery or nunnery

(3a)   a cell in a beehive

(3b)   a cell in an insect's wing structure

(4)   a biological cell

(5)   an electric cell

(6)   a statistical cell

(7)   a (Communist) party cell

(8)   a meteorologist's term

(4) Let your dictionary guide you to the right meaning for the context. The **context** of a word may be another word (*square* meal), a whole sentence or paragraph ("*Square* your theories with your practice"), a whole publication (a treatment of *square* roots in an algebra text), or a situation (a tourist asking for directions to a *square*). Depending on the context, a *program* may be the list of offerings for a concert, a scheduled radio or television broadcast, or the coded instructions for the operation of a computer. Dictionaries show how context determines meaning by showing a word in a phrase or sentence and by specifying an area like economics or geometry:

> **pro·duce** (prə dōōs′, -dyōōs′; *for n.*, präd′ōōs, -yōōs; prō′dōōs, -dyōōs) *vt.* **-duced′, -duc′ing** [L. *producere* < *pro-*, forward + *ducere*, to lead, draw: see PRO-² & DUCT] **1.** to bring to view; offer for inspection [to *produce* identification] **2.** to bring forth; bear; yield [a well that *produces* oil] **3.** *a*) to make or manufacture [to *produce* steel] *b*) to bring into being; create [to *produce* a work of art] **4.** to cause; give rise to [war *produces* devastation] **5.** to get (a play, motion picture, etc.) ready for presentation to the public **6.** *Econ.* to create (anything having exchange value) **7.** *Geom.* to extend (a line or plane) —*vi.* to bear, yield, create, manufacture, etc. something —*n.* something that is produced; yield; esp., fresh fruits and vegetables —**pro·duc′i·bil′i·ty** *n.* —**pro·duc′i·ble** *adj.*

From *Webster's New World Dictionary*

DICTIONARY WORK 3   How does your dictionary help you with the different meanings of each of the following words? Show how the *context* guides you to the right meaning of each phrase.

1. straight to the point, straight party line, straight alcohol, thinking straight
2. a head of government, a head of steam, heads or tails, head off complaints
3. committed to the cause, committed to an institution, committed no crime
4. a sense of duty, an off-duty police officer, duty-free shop, the duties of a nurse
5. an undertakers' convention, the conventions of punctuation, revolt against convention, the Geneva Convention

---

  d   Synonyms and Antonyms

Let the dictionary help you distinguish between closely related terms.

The quickest way to show the meaning of a word is to give a double, or **synonym** (*systematic* for *methodical*). We often get further help from its opposite, or **antonym** (*legitimate* for *illicit*).

Synonyms usually mean *nearly* the same; they are not simply interchangeable. *Burn, char, scorch, sear,* and *singe* all refer to the results of exposure to extreme heat, but whether a piece of meat is charred or merely seared makes a difference to the person who has it for dinner. *Arrogant, insolent,* and *haughty* all go a step further than *proud.* "Synonymies" like the following help the writer who wants to make accurate distinctions:

> *SYN.*—**alien** is applied to a resident who bears political allegiance to another country; **foreigner,** to a visitor or resident from another country, esp. one with a different language, cultural pattern, etc.; **stranger,** to a person from another region who is unacquainted with local people, customs, etc.; **immigrant,** to a person who comes to another country to settle; **émigré,** to one who has left his country to take political refuge elsewhere See also EXTRINSIC—

From *Webster's New World Dictionary*

DISCOURSE EXERCISE 4   Study the *synonyms* or related terms italicized in each of the following sentences. What meaning do the words in each set have in common? How do they differ, or what sets them apart?

The Theory of Revolution

1. Revolutions may start with a localized protest against *inequities* and develop into a full-blown attack on *injustice*.
2. In Russia, a sailors' *mutiny* led to widespread *revolt* and finally full-scale *revolution*.
3. Often *idealistic* leaders develop a *visionary* or *utopian* blueprint for a new society.
4. The more *zealous* or *doctrinaire* elements may steer the revolution in a more *fanatical* direction.
5. Or a more *pragmatic* leadership may adopt *expedient* or even *opportunistic* policies.
6. A revolution may in turn produce a *paternalistic, authoritarian,* or *totalitarian* government.
7. *Education* then becomes *indoctrination*.
8. Citizens are expected to be *obedient* and *docile* if not *obsequious*.
9. In propaganda movies, people do not *shuffle* or *slink* but *stride* purposefully toward a better future.
10. Again, as before the revolution, the government labels *dissent* as *treason* or *sedition*.

27d   *d*   Denotation and Connotation

Use the dictionary as a guide to the associations of words.

Words carry attitudes and emotions as well as information. They do not just report; they praise and condemn, warn and reassure. *Demagogue, politician, mercenary, speculator, crony,* or *bureaucrat* do not simply point to people. They point the finger; they reveal the likes and dislikes of the speaker. We call the added freight of attitudes, feelings, or value judgments the **connotations** of a word. Many words denote—that is, point out or refer to—roughly the same objects or qualities. But they connote—that is, suggest or imply—different attitudes, ranging from approval or admiration to disapproval or disgust. A *demagogue* was once literally a "leader of the people," but now the word vents our resentment at being led by the nose.

Connotative words most commonly mirror our likes and dislikes. When we like the bright colors of a shirt, we call it *colorful*; when we dislike it, we call it *loud*. But connotations often activate feelings more complicated than simple approval or disapproval. For example, the term *parenting* implies an enlightened or earnest view of the task; *biological father* sounds cold and uncaring; *stepmother* carries the burden of a centuries-old negative stereotype.

Here are some sets of words that show differences in connotation:

FAVORABLE	UNFAVORABLE	NEUTRAL
public servant	bureaucrat	government employee
financier	speculator	investor
law officer	cop	police officer
legislative consultant	lobbyist	representative of group interests
stage personality	ham	actor
labor leader	union boss	union official
captain of industry	tycoon	business success
investigator	spy	detective
captive	jailbird	prisoner

Often synonymies alert us to the attitudes and feelings different words activate. To make a scheme sound impressive, we call it a *project*; to belittle a project, we call it a *scheme*:

> *SYN.*—**plan** refers to any detailed method, formulated beforehand, for doing or making something [vacation *plans*]; **design** stresses the final outcome of a plan and implies the use of skill or craft, sometimes in an unfavorable sense, in executing or arranging this [it was his *design* to separate us]; **project** implies the use of enterprise or imagination in formulating an ambitious or extensive plan [a housing *project*]; **scheme,** a less definite term than the preceding, often connotes either an impractical, visionary plan or an underhanded intrigue [a *scheme* to embezzle the funds]

From *Webster's New World Dictionary*

CAUTION: Remember that words carrying an emotional charge may set off the *wrong* reaction on the part of the reader. Some words are too negative (or too favorable) for what you are trying to say:

JARRING:	She sings music that pleases listeners of all races and **emits** a feeling of love and warmth. (The word *emit* is too cold; we expect something to "emit" radiation or shrill sounds of warning.)
REVISED:	She sings music that pleases listeners of all races and **creates** a feeling of love and warmth.

SEE 31a FOR MORE ON ACCURATE WORDS.

DISCOURSE EXERCISE 5 How do the words italicized in each sentence differ in *connotation*? What attitudes, feelings, or judgments does each word bring into play?

The Media as Mirror

1. The media have the power to *shape, slant,* or *manipulate* our perceptions of reality.
2. Action taken by an official may be labeled *rash, timely,* or *precipitate.*
3. People who are dissatisfied may be said to *protest, complain, squawk,* or *whine.*
4. A new law may be described as *tough, severe,* or *punitive.*
5. A governor may take the advice of *associates, insiders,* or *cronies.*
6. Resistance to change may be labeled *caution, delay,* or *obstruction.*
7. A program to help the poor may be called *compassionate, sentimental,* or (a favorite) *misguided.*
8. A response to insults by a foreign government official may be called *temperate, timid, gutless,* or *abject.*
9. An unconventional suggestion for solving a problem may be called *bold, novel,* or *far-fetched.*
10. Nevertheless, today's journalists like to think of themselves as *aggressive* rather than *biased* or *partisan.*

27e   *d*   Grammatical Labels

Use the dictionary as a guide to the functions a word serves in a sentence.

Many English words serve different possible functions in a sentence. Here is the kind of grammatical information that dictionaries provide about such words:

- The word *human* is usually labeled both as an **adjective** (adj.) and as a **noun** (n.), with some indication that the latter use ("a human" rather than "a human being") is not generally accepted.

- The word *annoy* is labeled a **transitive verb** (v.t.); it is incomplete without an object. In other words, we usually annoy somebody or something; we don't just annoy. *Set* also is usually transitive ("*set* the bowl on the table"), but it is labeled **intransitive** (v.i.) when applied to one of the celestial bodies. The sun doesn't set anybody or anything; it just sets.

- A noun like *air* may be followed by the abbreviation *attrib.* for "attributive"—used instead of an adjective to modify another noun. *Air* is used attributively in combinations like *air traffic* and *air terminal*. The word *computer* is used attributively in *computer printout*.

Here are some other common grammatical labels:

adv.	adverb		*prep.*	preposition
conj.	conjunction		*prp.*	present participle (of verb)
pl.	plural		*sg.*	singular
pp.	past participle (of verb)			

DICTIONARY WORK 6   Answer the following questions about *grammatical functions* of words after consulting your dictionary.

1. Is *incompetent* used as a noun?
2. Which of the following words are used as verbs: *admonition, loan, lord, magistrate, minister, sacrilege, spirit, war*?
3. Are the following words used as adjectives: *animate, predominate, very*?
4. What idiomatic prepositions go with the following words when they are used as verbs: *glory, care, marvel*?
5. Are the following used as intransitive verbs: *entertain, censure, promote*?

27f   *id* | Idiom

Use the dictionary as a guide to idiomatic phrases.

A word often combines with other words in a set expression. Such expressions are called **idioms**. To write idiomatic English, you have to develop an ear for individual ways of saying things. For instance, we *do* a certain type of work, *hold* a job or position, *follow* a trade, *pursue* an occupation, and *engage in* a line of business.

Study the following list of idiomatic phrases using the word *mind*. Can you think of half a dozen similar phrases using the word *eye* or the word *hand*?

—bear (or **keep**) **in mind** to remember **—be in one's right mind** to be mentally well; be sane **—be of one mind** to have the same opinion or desire **—be of two minds** to be undecided or irresolute **—☆blow one's mind** [Slang] to undergo the hallucinations, etc. caused by, or as by, psychedelic drugs **—call to mind 1.** to remember **2.** to be a reminder of **—change one's mind 1.** to change one's opinion **2.** to change one's intention, purpose, or wish **—give (someone) a piece of one's mind** to criticize or rebuke (someone) sharply **—have a (good** or **great) mind to** to feel (strongly) inclined to **—have half a mind to** to be somewhat inclined to **—have in mind 1.** to remember **2.** to think of **3.** to intend; purpose **—know one's own mind** to know one's own real thoughts, desires, etc. **—make up one's mind** to form a definite opinion or decision **—meeting of (the) minds** an agreement **—never mind** don't be concerned; it doesn't matter **—on one's mind 1.** occupying one's thoughts **2.** worrying one **—out of one's mind 1.** mentally ill; insane **2.** frantic (*with* worry, grief, etc.) **—put in mind** to remind **—set one's mind on** to be determined on or determinedly desirous of **—take one's mind off** to stop one from thinking about; turn one's attention from **—to one's mind** in one's opinion

From *Webster's New World Dictionary*

To avoid unidiomatic English, do the following:

(1) Revise garbled or upside-down idioms. Look out for expressions that mix or reverse familiar expressions:

WRONG IDIOM:	Older people are worried about the ardent **devotion** that young people **pay** to new religious cults. (We **show** devotion; we **pay** attention.)
RIGHT:	Older people are worried about the ardent **devotion** that young people **show** to new religious cults.
WRONG IDIOM:	He served in the Peace Corps, but the ideal **did not live up** to the reality. (The **reality** fails to live up to or measure up to ideal standards.)
RIGHT:	He served in the Peace Corps, but reality **fell short of** his ideals.

(2) Use idiomatic prepositions. A special problem for inexperienced writers is the idiomatic use of prepositions: confide *in*, prevent *from*,

407

IDIOMATIC PREPOSITIONS—AN OVERVIEW

abide **by** (a decision)
abstain **from** (voting)
accuse **of** (a crime)
acquiesce **in** (an injustice)
adhere **to** (a promise)
admit **of** (conflicting
    interpretations)
agree **with** (a person, **to** (a
    proposal), **on** (a course of
    action)
alarmed **at** (the news)
apologize **for** (a mistake)
aspire **to** (distinction)
assent **to** (a proposal)
attend **to** (one's business)
avail oneself **of** (an
    opportunity)

capable **of** (an action)
charge **with** (an offense)
collide **with** (a car)
compatible **with** (recog-
    nized standards)
comply **with** (a request)

concur **with** (someone), **in**
    (an opinion)
confide **in** or **to** (someone)
conform **to** (specifications)

deficient **in** (strength)
delight **in** (mischief)
deprive **of** (a privilege)
derived **from** (a source)
die **of** or **from** (a disease)
disappointed **in** (someone's
    performance)
dissent **from** (a majority
    opinion)
dissuade **from** (doing
    something foolish)
divest **of** (responsibility)

find fault **with** (a course)

identical **with** (something
    looked for)
ignorant **of** (a fact)

succeed *in*. (See chart.) In particular, avoid the informal prepositions in *borrow off* and *wait on*:

INFORMAL: He constantly **borrowed** money **off** his friends.
FORMAL: He constantly **borrowed** money **from** his friends.

INFORMAL: The audience was **waiting on** the next performer.
FORMAL: The audience was **waiting for** the next performer.

PEER EDITOR 7   Where did each writer use an unidiomatic preposition? Write a more idiomatic preposition after the number of each unsatisfactory sentence.

inconsistent **with** (sound procedure)

independent **of** (outside help)

indifferent **to** (praise or blame)

infer **from** (evidence)

inferior **to** (a rival product)

insist **on** (accuracy)

interfere **with** (a performance), **in** (someone else's affairs)

jealous **of** (others)

long **for** (recognition)

object **to** (a proposal)

oblivious **of** (warnings)

part **with** (possessions)

partial **to** (flattery)

participate **in** (activities)

persevere **in** (a task)

pertain **to** (a subject)

preferable **to** (an alternative)

prevail **on** (someone to do something)

prevent someone **from** (an action)

refrain **from** (wrongdoing)

rejoice **at** (good news)

required **of** (all members)

resolve **on** (a course of action)

rich **in** (resources)

short **of** (cash)

secede **from** (the Union)

succeed **in** (an attempt)

superior **to** (an alternative)

threaten **with** (legal action)

wait **for** (developments), **on** (a guest)

---

1. To seek a good grade at someone else's expense would be a violation to our standards of conduct.

2. During the past fifty years, deaths caused by highway accidents have been more numerous than those incurred from two world wars and the war in Korea.

3. Plans for cost reduction have been put to action by different agencies of the federal government.

4. Several families volunteered to take care for the children of flood victims.

5. Only the prompt help of the neighbors prevented the fire of becoming a major disaster.

6. During the first years of marriage, we had to deprive ourselves from many things that other people take for granted.

7. The arrival of the ship to its destination caused general rejoicing.
8. Though I support Mr. Finchley's candidacy, I take exception with some of his statements.
9. We will not hesitate to expose businesses that deprive their employees from these benefits.
10. As an instrument of the popular will, the Senate suffers from defects inherent to its constitution.

---

28   Word History

OVERVIEW   Often we understand a word better when we know its history—when we can see how it developed its current meanings and associations. If we know the common root in words like im*pel*, com*pel*, com*pul*sive, and re*pul*sive, we can still sense the force of the Latin word for *push*—pushing us on, or ahead, or away. If we know that the root *eco-* goes back to the Greek word for household, we get a vivid sense of the interdependence (as of the elements in a household) emphasized in words like *ecology, ecosystem,* and *ecosphere.*

College dictionaries often give a quick rundown of a word's **etymology**, or history, using abbreviations like OE and ME (for Old and Middle English), ON (for Old Norse or early Scandinavian), or IE (for Indo-European, the hypothetical common parent language of most European languages). Here is a capsule history of a word that came into English from Latin by way of Italian and French:

> **pop·u·lace** \'päp-yə-ləs\ *n* [MF, fr. It *popolaccio* rabble, pejorative of *popolo* the people, fr. L *populus*] (1572) **1** : the common people : MASSES **2** : POPULATION

From *Webster's Ninth New Collegiate Dictionary*

In addition to tracing words to other languages, the etymologist is concerned with **semantic** change—gradual changes in meaning. The most complete record of such changes is the unabridged *New English Dictionary on Historical Principles*, reissued in 1933 as the *Oxford English Dictionary* (OED). This monumental reference work gives the earliest date

410

a word occurs and then provides quotations tracing its development down through the centuries.

The basic vocabulary of English goes back to the language the Anglo-Saxon tribes brought to England after A.D. 450 from what is now Denmark and Germany. Many everyday words come from these **Anglo-Saxon** or **Old English** roots: *father, mother, hand, house, bread, water, sun, moon.* But roughly three fourths of the words in your dictionary came into English from other sources.

Throughout its history, English has borrowed heavily from Latin, which Christian missionaries first brought to England as the language of the Roman Catholic church. For centuries, to be educated meant to know Latin and often also Greek, the language of ancient Greek literature, science, and philosophy. When the French-speaking Normans conquered England after A.D. 1066, French became for a time the language of law, administration, and literature. Over the next two centuries, thousands of words from the French of the Norman overlords were absorbed into **Middle English**.

Since the beginning of Modern English (about 1500), English has borrowed words from languages like Italian, Spanish, and Portuguese. This process of borrowing and assimilation continues today, as we are getting used to seeing words from Arabic, Russian, and Japanese.

28a *d* | Latin and Greek

Know some of the most common Latin and Greek roots.

English has borrowed heavily from Latin and Greek. Latin had been the language of the Roman Empire. It became the official language of the Roman Catholic church, which established itself in England in the seventh century and remained the supreme spiritual authority until the sixteenth century. English early took over Latin words related to the Bible and to the teachings and rituals of the church:

altar   candle   mass   pope   relic   shrine

Greek was the language of the literature, philosophy, and science of ancient Hellenic culture, flourishing both in Greece and in other parts of

411

the Mediterranean world. Either in the original Greek or in Latin translation, this body of knowledge helped shape Western civilization during the Middle Ages and Renaissance. Modern English uses thousands of words that came originally from Greek or Latin. Modern scientific and technological terms draw heavily on Latin and Greek roots.

LATIN: history, index, individual, intellect, legal, mechanical, rational

GREEK: anonymous, atmosphere, catastrophe, chaos, crisis, skeleton

(1) Know the most common Latin and Greek roots. Writers trying to fortify their vocabularies profit from the way dictionaries highlight Latin and Greek roots, especially if these are still active in the formation of new words. Knowing the Latin root *mal-* for "bad" helps us understand *malpractice, malfunction, malnutrition, malformation,* and *malfeasance.* Knowing that the Greek root *bio-* means "life" helps us with *biopsy, biochemistry, biomass, biofeedback,* and *bionics.* Here is a brief list of common Latin and Greek roots:

ROOT	MEANING	EXAMPLES
arch-	*rule*	monarchy, anarchy, matriarch
auto-	*self*	autocratic, autonomy, automation
capit-	*head*	capital, per capita, decapitate
chron-	*time*	chronological, synchronize, anachronism
doc-	*teach*	docile, doctrine, indoctrinate
graph-	*write*	autograph, graphic, seismograph
hydr-	*water*	dehydrate, hydraulic, hydrogen
phon-	*sound*	euphony, phonograph, symphony
port-	*carry*	portable, exports, deportation
terr-	*land*	inter, terrestrial, subterranean
urb-	*city*	suburb, urban, urbane
verb-	*word*	verbal, verbiage, verbose
vit-	*life*	vitality, vitamin, revitalize
vol-	*will*	volition, involuntary, volunteer

(2) Know common prefixes and suffixes. **Prefixes** and **suffixes** are exchangeable attachments at the beginning or end of a word: *pre*war, *post*war, *anti*war; organ*ize*, organ*ic*, organ*ism*. Knowing that the Latin prefix *sub-* means "under" helps explain *subconscious, submarine, subterranean,* and *subzero*. The Latin suffix *-cide* means "killing"—helping us understand not only *homicide* and *suicide* but also *fratricide* (killing of a brother) and *parricide* (killing of a parent). Here is a brief list of common Latin and Greek prefixes:

PREFIXES	MEANING	EXAMPLES
bene-	*good*	benefactor, benefit, benevolent
bi-	*two*	bicycle, bilateral, bisect
contra-	*against*	contraband, contradict, contravene
dis-	*away, apart*	disperse, disorganize, discourage
ex-	*out*	exclude, exhale, expel
extra-	*outside*	extraordinary, extravagant, extrovert
mono-	*one*	monarch, monopoly, monolithic
multi-	*many*	multilateral, multinational, multiethnic
omni-	*all*	omnipotent, omnipresent, omniscient
per-	*through*	percolate, perforate, permeate
poly-	*many*	polygamy, polysyllabic, polytheistic
post-	*after*	postpone, postwar, postscript
pre-	*before*	preamble, precedent, prefix
re-	*back*	recall, recede, revoke, retract
tele-	*distant*	telegraph, telepathy, telephone
trans-	*across, beyond*	transatlantic, transmit, transcend

DICTIONARY WORK 8 What does your dictionary tell you about the *history* of the following words? Select ten, and report briefly on the history of each. What language did it come from? How did it acquire its current meaning?

algebra	hogan	paradise	pundit
crusade	immigrant	pogrom	Sabbath
disaster	laissez faire	police	slalom
ecology	millennium	primadonna	virtuoso
gospel	nirvana	propaganda	xenophobia

DICTIONARY WORK 9 What is the meaning of the common element in each of the following sets? How does the *shared root or suffix* help explain each word in the set?

1. anesthetic—anemic—amoral
2. antibiotic—biography—biology

3. audiovisual—audition—inaudible
4. cosmic—cosmopolitan—microcosm
5. disunity—discord—dissent
6. eugenics—eulogy—euphonious
7. heterogeneous—heterosexual—heterodox
8. magnify—magnificent—magnitude
9. monarchy—oligarchy—anarchy
10. synchronize—symphony—sympathy

DICTIONARY WORK 10 Explain the basic meaning of each *Latin and Greek prefix* used in the following words: *ambivalent, antedate, antipathy, circumvent, concord, hypersensitive, international, introvert, multimillionaire, neofascist, pseudoscientific, retroactive, semitropical, ultramodern, unilateral.*

28b *d* | Borrowings from Other Sources

Recognize major sources of our English vocabulary.

Here are some kinds of historical information that you will find in a good dictionary:

(1) Thousands of words came into English from French. England was conquered by the French-speaking Normans in the years following 1066. At the beginning of the **Middle English** period (about 1150), the Norman conquerors owned most of the land and held the most important offices in state and church. The language of law, administration, and literature was French. When English gradually reestablished itself, thousands of French words were retained. Many of these words mirror the political and military role of the Normans: *castle, court, glory, mansion, noble, prison, privilege, servant, treason, war.* But hundreds of other words absorbed into Middle English were everyday words.

FRENCH: avoid, branch, chair, desire, envy, praise, table, uncle

(2) Foreign languages have influenced the vocabularies of special fields of interest. Since the beginning of **Modern English** (about 1500), many words have come into English from French, Italian, Spanish, and other sources. French supplied words for fashions, the arts, and military organization. Italian furnished words to help us talk about opera and music. Spanish supplied words related to the discovery of new continents, often words first brought into Spanish from New World sources.

FRENCH:	apartment, ballet, battalion, cadet, caress, corps, façade, infantry, negligee, patrol
ITALIAN:	concert, falsetto, solo, sonata, soprano, violin
SPANISH:	alligator, banana, cannibal, cocoa, mosquito, potato, tobacco, tomato

(3) Foreign words are continuing to come into English from other languages. We use *apartheid*, from the kind of Dutch spoken in South Africa, to describe the system of racial segregation there. We have seen French restaurants reduce portions and raise prices as they switch to *nouvelle cuisine*. Reporters use the Arab word *jihad* for a holy war against the enemies of Islam. We are getting used to encountering words from Russian or Japanese:

RUSSIAN:	troika, apparatchik, sputnik, gulag, nomenklatura, glasnost
JAPANESE:	samurai, shogun, kamikaze, hibachi, karate, haiku

When such words are not yet fully naturalized, your dictionary may put a special symbol in front of them or label them French, Chinese, or whatever is appropriate.

FOREIGN WORDS:	uhuru (Swahili), mensch (Yiddish)

DICTIONARY WORK 11 What does each of the following expressions mean? What language did it come from? Which of them does your dictionary still consider foreign rather than English?

ad hoc	El Dorado	paparazzo
aficionado	fait accompli	quod erat demonstrandum
blitz	habeas corpus	reich
Bushido	karma	samurai
de jure	kung fu	shiksa

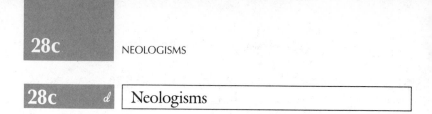

28c   *d*   Neologisms

Make discriminating use of recent coinages.

Our language is always creating new words for new needs. Lexicographers, who at one time frowned on new words, now compete in their coverage of **neologisms**, or newly coined expressions. Technology, space exploration, genetics, medicine, and computers create a constant demand for new words, as do the drug culture and changes in lifestyle (a fashionable new word). Many new words fill an obvious need and are rapidly accepted: *astronaut, fallout, data base, flextime, space shuttle, aerobics, fax, high tech.* Other new words at first sound clever or imaginative but soon become simply convenient shorthand for what they stand for: *palimony, no-show, baby boomer, floppy disk, joystick, boat people, laugh track.*

Remember, however, that some coinages sound cute, awkward, or far-fetched and alienate conservative readers. Avoid coinages that smack of media hype, advertising prose, or bureaucratic jargon:

MEDIA HYPE:	megabuck, docudrama, infomercial, sexploitation
ADVERTISING WORDS:	jumboize, paperamics, outdoorsman, moisturize, usership
BUREAUCRATIC:	escapee, definitize, prioritize, socioeconomic

FOR MORE ON JARGON, SEE 32c.

DICTIONARY WORK 12   What's *new* in dictionaries? How up to date, or how far behind, is your dictionary in its coverage of the following words? Report on its treatment of *ten* of the words. For several of those that are missing, write a short but informative definition that would help an editor bring the dictionary up to date.

acid rain	CAT scan	no-show
aerobics	Chicano	payload
aerospace	cosmonaut	replay
airbag	fast breeder	residuals
bleep	hospice	schlock
body stocking	hydrofoil	sexism
brain dead	interface	skydiving
buzzword	kibbutz	skyjacker

survivalist	transplant	upscale
tokenism	unisex	voiceover

29   Appropriate Words

OVERVIEW Not all words are right for all occasions. Dictionaries use **usage labels** to show that a word might be out of place or out of date in your writing. Traditionally, dictionaries have identified three varieties of *spoken* English likely to seem out of place in serious explanation or argument:

NONSTANDARD **Nonstandard** English is for many Americans the work-aday speech of street, neighborhood, or construction site; it differs from the **standard** English of the media, of school and office. Nonstandard expressions like "*don't* pay it *no* mind" and "brought it on *hisself*" stand out in writing because we usually associate them with the folk speech of people with limited formal education and with little occasion to write. *Anywheres, nohow,* and *irregardless* are likely to be labeled nonstandard in your dictionary.

INFORMAL **Informal** language is the variety of standard English we use in casual conversation; it is the chatty kind of language we use when at ease or with our friends. Some dictionaries label it **colloquial**—"conversational, right for informal talk." *Mom-and-pop store, booze, panhandler,* and *skedaddle* are likely to be labeled informal in your dictionary.

SLANG **Slang** is extremely informal language, usually too freewheeling and disrespectful (not to mention crude) for use in serious discussion. *Klutz, knock it off, blah,* and *humongous* are likely to be labeled slang in your dictionary.

In addition, dictionary makers use usage labels to show that a word is used only in part of the English-speaking world or that it is no longer in common use. Before the mass media helped homogenize a national language, different regions developed local varieties or **dialects** that often drifted far apart. The people who first sang "Auld Lang Syne" were speaking Scots rather than standard British English. In this country, dialects are less distinct, although periodically a wag will publish a "Texas Dictionary" to explain words like *hunker down*. **Obsolete** words or meanings (*coy* in

417

the sense of quiet) have gone out of use altogether; **archaic** words (*thou* and *thine*) survive only in special uses.

In the following dictionary entry, several of the meanings of *brass* carry special labels. These alert us to the specialized use of the word in *brass band*, the British use of the word for a commemorative plaque, or the slangy use of the word in *top brass*:

brass (bras, bräs), *n.* **1.** any of various metal alloys consisting mainly of copper and zinc. **2.** an article made of such an alloy. **3.** *Mach.* a partial lining of soft metal for a bearing. **4.** *Music.* **a.** an instrument of the trumpet or horn family. **b.** such instruments collectively. **5.** *Brit.* **a.** a memorial tablet or plaque incised with an effigy, coat of arms, or the like. **b.** *Slang.* money. **6.** *Furniture.* any piece of ornamental or functional hardware. **7.** *U.S. Slang.* **a.** high-ranking military officers. **b.** any very important officials. **8.** *Informal.* excessive assurance; impudence; effrontery. —*adj.* **9.** of or pertaining to brass. [ME *bras*, OE *bræs*; c. OFris *bres* copper, MLG *bras* metal] —**brass'ish,** *adj.*

— subject label
— geographic label
— usage
— usage

From *The Random House College Dictionary*

In addition to such labels, dictionaries provide **usage notes** to discuss objections to expressions often considered informal, newfangled, or illogical. Here, for instance, is a discussion of the word *media*—historically a plural form (of the Latin word *medium*), as in "Radio and television *are* mass *media* of communication." This usage note discusses the use of *media* as a singular, as in "The *media sensationalizes* the news":

usage The singular *media* and its plural *medias* seem to have originated in the field of advertising over 50 years ago; they are apparently still so used without stigma in that specialized field. In most other applications *media* is used as a plural of *medium.* The great popularity of the word in references to the agencies of mass communication is leading to the formation of a mass noun, construed as a singular ⟨there's no basis for it. You know, the news *media* gets on to something —Edwin Meese 3d⟩ but this use is not as well established as the mass-noun use of *data* and is likely to incur criticism esp. in writing.

From *Webster's Ninth New Collegiate Dictionary*

Recognize words that suggest nonstandard speech.

To function well in today's society, we need a confident command of the kind of standard English that, except for minor variations, is the same throughout the English-speaking world. **Standard** English is the language of education, business, journalism, and government. It is the language of teachers, lawyers, office workers, and others whose work keeps them in daily contact with books, records, forms, memos, notes, and other uses of the written word.

Nonstandard English is for many people the natural speech of home, neighborhood, or job. Historically, nonstandard speech has often been associated with a way of life that required little formal schooling or with jobs that required little reading of instructions and writing of reports.

Standard English is essential to success in school and office. In any dealings with public officials, insurance agents, social workers, or business people of all kinds, the person who does not have an adequate command of standard English is already at a disadvantage.

Many of the features of nonstandard speech stand out and are clearly out of place in writing. Here are some examples of nonstandard usage:

NONSTANDARD:	ain't	being that	nohow	off of
STANDARD:	isn't, hasn't	because	not at all	off, from
NONSTANDARD:	irregardless	hisself	theirself	nowheres
STANDARD:	regardless	himself	themselves	nowhere

SEE THE GLOSSARY OF USAGE FOR *A/AN*, DOUBLE NEGATIVE, DOUBLE COMPARATIVE

PEER EDITOR 13 Rewrite each sentence, editing out all *nonstandard* expressions.

1. Being that their parents died young, my cousins early learned to take care of theirself.
2. He was determined to have hisself promoted irregardless of the cost.
3. If she ain't eligible, we'll have to take her name off of the list.
4. We couldn't find the records anywheres.
5. He bought hisself a new car at hundreds of dollars off of the listed price.

29b *inf* Informal Words

Recognize words that are too informal for serious writing.

The right kind of English for most of your college writing will be **edited written English**—more formal than casual everyday talk, serious enough for the discussion of issues and ideas. People who are comfortable in sports clothes over the weekend put on business clothes when going to the office on Monday morning. Like our clothes, the language we use "makes a statement"—it shows how serious we are about the job at hand.

Much of the best modern prose is **moderately formal**—serious without being solemn, formal with an occasional lighter touch:

VERY FORMAL:	There is a heavy legal presumption against prior restraint of adult journalists, and student journalists need similar protection.
MODERATELY FORMAL:	The Freedom of Information Act is now under attack, on the grounds that it is interfering with the administration's defense of the Republic. James Reston
INFORMAL:	Democracy is a gabby business. There is no way to shut people up. James Reston

In most of your writing, the right tone will be near the midpoint between extremely formal and extremely informal language. Avoid a breezy, chatty style—without lapsing into hyperformal language that would make your writing stiff and pretentious. Excessively informal English becomes a problem when a writer fails to shift gears as needed to move away from casual speech. The following guidelines should help you avoid excessive informality:

(1) Sift out the catchall words that punctuate everyday talk. Avoid the routine use of words like *nice, neat, cute, terrific, great, wonderful, awful, terrible.*

(2) Limit words with a distinctly folky or casual touch to informal personal writing. Words like the following suggest casual talk:

INFORMAL	FORMAL	INFORMAL	FORMAL
boss	superior	kid	child
brainy	intelligent	skimpy	meager
bug	germ	sloppy	untidy
faze	disconcert	snoop	pry
flunk	fail	snooze	nap
folks	relatives	splurge	spend lavishly
hunch	premonition	stump	baffle

Other familiar words are generally acceptable in one sense but informal in another. Informal are *alibi* in the sense of "excuse," *aggravate* in the sense of "annoy," *funny* in the sense of "strange," and *mad* in the sense of "angry."

420

As needed, replace informal combined verbs like the following:

INFORMAL	FORMAL	INFORMAL	FORMAL
chip in	contribute	come up with	find
get across	communicate	cut out	stop
check up on	investigate	get on with	make progress

(3) Edit out informal tags and abbreviations. Avoid informal tags like *kind of, sort of, a lot, lots*. Revise clipped forms that have a "too-much-in-a-hurry" effect: *bike, prof, doc, fan mag, exec, econ*. But note that other shortened forms, like *phone, ad,* and *exam,* are now commonly used in serious writing.

(4) Improve on tired informal expressions. Avoid the familiar overused figurative expressions of informal speech. (See **32b** for more on trite language, or **clichés**.)

TRITE: have a ball   polish the apple   jump the gun
         butter up   shoot the breeze   play ball
         hit the road   jump on the bandwagon   small potatoes

Remember: The word that is right for one audience may be wrong for another. A campus group using words like *buddies, blast,* and *laid-back* in an informal party invitation is not likely to use those words in a letter apologizing to the dean after the party got out of hand. Part of the search for the right word is avoiding words that might have unintentional side effects, misleading or alienating the reader.

Finer Points   Where traditional rules banned all personal reference, much first-rate modern prose uses the personal *I* ("*I* think," "in *my* opinion") or the personal *we*. Informal expressions can set a casual, affectionate, or leisurely tone:

> There was a broad streak of mischief in Mencken. He was forever **cooking up** imaginary organizations, having **fake** handbills printed, inventing exercises in pure nonsense.   Phillip M. Wagner, "Mencken Remembered," *The American Scholar*

But remember that more often informal English will suggest that you are not taking your subject (or your reader) seriously enough.

DICTIONARY WORK 14 How good is your ear for *formal and informal* language? Rank the expressions in each of the following sets from the most formal to the most informal. Be prepared to compare your rankings with those of your classmates and to defend your decisions. (Check selected items in your dictionary.)

1. sales talk—presentation—spiel
2. hook up the equipment—hooked on drugs—got her off the hook
3. no sweat—sweat out a decision—sweat shirt
4. tear into someone—tear up a bill—that tears it
5. arrested—busted—taken into custody
6. go all out—go for it—have a go at it
7. live it up—live it down—live up to expectations
8. crack down on crime—his voice cracked—crack a book
9. go broke—go bankrupt—go belly-up
10. lush—alcoholic—problem drinker

DISCOURSE EXERCISE 15 The following sentences are written in a very breezy *informal* style. Rewrite the sentences, replacing each italicized word or expression with one more appropriate in serious writing.

The Rise of the Yuppie

1. The student hero of the seventies had been John Belushi, *pigging out* and *yukking it up* with his *frat brothers*.
2. By the early eighties, *grinds* were *in*, and slobs were no longer considered *cool*.
3. Yuppies were becoming role models for everyone who did not *hate their guts*.
4. MBAs were becoming a *hot item, mediawise*.
5. Business schools *packed in* students whose goal was to *cash in*.
6. They looked for the financial *savvy* that would help them pay for their BMWs.
7. Law students aimed at careers in the *well-heeled* law factories that service corporations.
8. Others dreamed of becoming Justice Department *hotshots*.
9. Their style of dress showed that the *eager-beaver* ethos had *socked in*.
10. Companies *shelled out* amazing sums as starting salaries rose *sky high*.

REVIEW EXERCISE 16 Which of the following passages are written in formal English? Which in informal English? Is any one of these passages formal with an informal touch? Identify specific words and expressions that make for a serious formal style. Point out words and expressions that make for a breezy or jazzy informal style.

1.　　　The National Institute of Health is, in the words of Author-Physician Lewis Thomas, "one of the nation's great treasures." In the past few decades, the letters NIH have become almost as familiar to Americans as FBI or IRS. The federal research center has been a leading force in the U.S. and around the world for the study of cancer and heart disease, the development of vaccines and treatments for infectious illness (most recently AIDS), and the investigation of mental illness. Its scientists are at the forefront of probes into such fundamental mysteries as gene regulation, the workings of the immune system, and the structure of complex organic molecules. Says Historian Stephen Strickland, author of two books on the NIH: "There is no other biomedical institution that has its scope." The NIH has underwritten the training of one-third of the nation's biomedical researchers; it has sponsored the work of two-thirds of those U.S. scientists who have won Nobel Prizes for Physiology or Medicine since 1945. It is clearly a major factor in America's primacy in medical research.　　　Claudia Wallis, *Time*

2.　　　Advertising is relatively a Johnny-come-lately. It did not exist in the mass-market form that we know much before World War I, and did not exist in any form at all before the late nineteenth century. But before advertising, there were newspapers and magazines. They were very much as we know them today, except of course that the pages were filled with news instead of paid hustle. Since they had almost no other source of revenue, the publications of that time lived or died by the reader's penny spent, and charged an honest price; if a publication cost five cents to produce, you can bet a publisher charged at least five cents for it and hoped like hell that what the paper had to say was interesting enough to get enough people to pony up their nickels. It is no coincidence that the great muckraking magazines of American legend flourished under these game conditions; who pays the piper calls the tune, and the only paymaster was their readers, who apparently liked what the muckrakers were playing.　　　Warren Hinckle, "The Adman Who Hated Advertising," *Atlantic*

3.　　*From a review of Shirley Abbott's* Womenfolks:
　　　The South that Abbott's maternal ancestors knew is far removed from the antebellum world of great plantations and a slave economy. It's a South without recorded historical tradition, a South of red-dirt farms and poor white folk of Scotch-Irish descent, the hillbillies who never owned a slave and very likely never saw one. Driven from Ulster in the 18th century by their English landlords, they arrived in Charleston only to find themselves among the English gentry again. Immediately they decamped for the back country, setting up lean-tos in the woods. These people were not, Abbott insists, merely benighted, but fiercely inde-

423

pendent, even anarchistic: specialists in survival, they preferred to do without schools and churches than to submit to institutions and taxation. For them, the Civil War, to which they were obliged to surrender their men and their goods, was no glorious cause; it was the cause of endless desolation.   Peter S. Prescott, *Newsweek*

29c   *sl* | Slang

Use slang only in the most informal kinds of writing or for special effects.

No one can fix the exact point at which informal language shades over into slang. Generally, slang is more drastic in its disregard for what makes language formal and dignified. Dictionaries may disagree, but for most readers, words like *zilch, crock, the fuzz, far out, yo-yo, ballsy,* and *mooning* will have the true slung-about quality of slang.

SLANG: The **crazies** will have poured in, already **blotto** on beer.   Peter Fussell

Slang often has a zing missing in more pedestrian diction; it often, as it were, hits the spot: *blowhard, drunk tank, downer, pep pill, squeal rule, fat farm, junkie, clip joint, whirlybird.* New slang is often colorful or pointed (*spaced out, ripoff*), but much of it wears out from repetition. At any rate, much slang is too crude or disrespectful for most writing: *pig out, chew the fat, blow one's top, lay an egg.*

TOO SLANGY: What **folks** have **dumped on marriage** in the way of expectations, selfish interests, and **kinky kicks** needs prompt removal if the institution is to survive.

TOO SLANGY: People didn't live as long, so a spouse could safely assume that the partner would **kick the bucket** in five or ten years and the one **still breathing could have another go at it.**

Note: Usage labels vary from dictionary to dictionary. Most dictionaries have dropped labels like *substandard* and *illiterate* as derogatory or insulting. Some dictionaries no longer label words *informal,* so that you may have to decide for yourself that *umptieth, no-no,* and *party pooper* would sound very unbuttoned in serious writing. Even when a dictionary uses the term *slang,* it may apply the term very sparingly.

DICTIONARY WORK 17 Dictionaries published ten years ago may not yet include words like the following or do justice to their current uses: *wimp, nerd, klutz, guru, jock, hacker, punk*. Check these in your dictionary. Write a paragraph about one of these, explaining and illustrating its meaning and uses.

29d *d* | Regional Labels

Notice geographic labels for words in use mainly in one region.

During the centuries before travel, books, and finally radio and television exercised their standardizing influence, languages developed regional varieties. Sometimes, as with German and Dutch, they drifted far enough apart to become separate languages. Here are regional variations that you are likely to encounter:

(1) Vocabulary differs somewhat from one English-speaking country to another. American travelers in England notice the British uses of *tram, lorry, lift, torch, wireless, fortnight*.

BRITISH: lorry, lift (elevator), torch (flashlight), wireless, fortnight, bonnet (hood of a car), chemist (druggist)

Here is a passage with many British terms:

> A scale or two adhered to the **fishmonger's** marble slab; the **pastry-cook's** glass shelves showed a range of interesting crumbs; the **fruiterer** filled a long-standing void with fans of cardboard bananas and a "Dig for Victory" placard; the **greengrocer's** crates had been emptied of all but earth by those who had somehow failed to dig hard enough. Elizabeth Bowen

Dictionaries increasingly discuss special terms or special uses of words in Canadian, Australian, or South African English:

CANADIAN: province, governor general, Grey Cup, permanent force, Calgary Stampede
SOUTH AFRICAN: apartheid, veldt, trek

425

(2) Regional varieties within a country are called dialects. A poet to whom a church is a "kirk" and a landowner a "laird" is using one of the **dialects** of Scotland and Northern England rather than standard British English. American speech shows some regional differences. However, the intermingling of settlers from many areas and the rapid growth of mass media have kept American dialects from drifting very far apart.

DIALECTAL: dogie, poke (bag), reckon (suppose), tote (carry), you all

---

29e   *d* | Obsolete and Archaic

Know how dictionaries label words no longer in common use.

Some words, or meanings of words, have gone out of use altogether. They are called **obsolete**. Examples of obsolete meanings are *coy* (quiet), *curious* (careful), and *nice* (foolish). Some words or meanings are no longer in common use but still occur in special contexts. Such words and meanings are called **archaic**. The King James version of the Bible preserves many archaisms that were in common use in seventeenth-century England: *thou* and *thee, brethren, kine* (cattle).

In the following dictionary entry, five of the numbered meanings of *brave* are labeled obsolete:

> **brave** (brāv) *adj.* **brav·er, brav·est 1.** Having or showing courage; intrepid; courageous. **2.** Making a fine display; elegant; showy. **3.** *Obs.* Excellent. — *v.* **braved, brav·ing** *v.t.* **1.** To meet or face with courage and fortitude: to *brave* danger. **2.** To defy; challenge: to *brave* the heavens. **3.** *Obs.* To make splendid. — *v.i.* **4.** *Obs.* To boast. — *n.* **1.** A man of courage. **2.** A North American Indian warrior. **3.** *Obs.* A bully; bravo. **4.** *Obs.* A boast or defiance.
>
> From *Standard College Dictionary*

Here are some archaisms familiar to readers of poetry and historical fiction:

anon	(at once)		*fere*	(companion)
brand	(sword)		*forsooth*	(truly)
childe	(aristocratic youth)		*methinks*	(it seems)
erst	(formerly)		*rood*	(cross)
fain	(glad or gladly)		*sprite*	(ghost)

DICTIONARY WORK 18 Which of the following words carry usage labels in your dictionary? Which are labeled informal or slang? Which have regional or dialect uses? Which are archaic or obsolete?

bonkers	cove	habitant	prexy
boodle	Franglais	hangup	Sooner
boot	gig	one-liner	sweetie
bower	goober	one shot	tube
complected	goodman	petrol	wonted

30 Sexist Language

OVERVIEW In many situations, avoiding the wrong word is as important as choosing the right one. Fair-minded readers are turned off by language that in crude or subtle ways mirrors prejudice. They will have no patience with outright racial or ethnic slurs: *limey, frog, greaser,* and others too ugly to mention. But they will also object to expressions that slight people because of race, sex, age, national origin, sexual orientation, or disability. Many government agencies and many publications require authors to observe guidelines on how to avoid offensive or prejudiced language.

In particular, readers are increasingly sensitive to language that belittles women. Doing without sexist language is not just a matter of avoiding obviously insulting or condescending terms, such as *chick, doll, gal,* or *old maid.* Many readers increasingly object to terms once considered neutral and used freely by both men and women writers. For instance, *man* as a **generic** term for the human species (*early man, the history of mankind*) was said to include both men and women. It made people picture primarily the male of the species nevertheless. Current textbooks therefore use terms like *humanity, humankind, human beings,* or just plain *people* instead.

Learn how to change language habits that make traditional sex roles seem carved in stone or coded in our genes. Avoid ways of talking that make us think of doctors, pilots, bosses, managers, professors, owners, movers, and shakers as male and of the people who work for them (nurses, flight attendants, secretaries) as female. Avoid gauche invitations implying that the spouses of important people are likely to be female rather than male. Be formal and respectful, or informal and chummy, evenhandedly—regardless of the other person's sex.

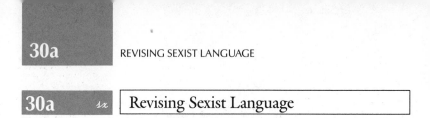

30a	*sx*	Revising Sexist Language

Revise gender-biased language.

The following guidelines should help you steer clear of sexist language:

(1) Replace biased labels for occupations. Unisex labels for occupations or careers include *doctor, lawyer, carpenter, artist, teacher, mayor,* and *senator.* Replace labels that seem to reserve some occupations for men while shunting women off into others. Look especially for occupational labels ending in *-man* or *-ess*:

STEREOTYPED	UNBIASED
fireman	firefighter
policeman	police officer
mailman	mail carrier
weatherman	meteorologist
salesman	sales representative
Congressman	Representative
stewardess	flight attendant

Some balanced pairs, like *actor/actress,* are still acceptable to many people, but avoid the condescending *poetess* (use *poet*). Some terms, although recommended in official guidelines, still sound artificial to many writers, causing them to try alternatives:

STEREOTYPED	UNBIASED	ALTERNATIVES
chairman	chairperson	chair, head
spokesman	spokesperson	voice, representative, speaker
businessmen	businessperson	business people, executives, the business community

(2) Revise expressions that imply there is something odd about men or women in a given situation or line of work. Avoid the condescending *lady doctor* or *lady lawyer.* Do not make a big point about a *female* pilot or a *male* secretary. You can often fill the reader in simply by using the right pronoun: "The new secretary handled *his* workload well."

(3) Mention sex, marital status, or family evenhandedly. Provide such information equally for people of either sex, or omit it when it is irrelevant. Use courtesy titles impartially, and use first names, first-names-only, or nicknames only when you do so evenhandedly for either sex. (*Ms.,* like *Mr.,* allows people to keep their marital status their own business, although women who prefer the traditional *Mrs.* or *Miss* may so indicate by using them in signing their correspondence.)

NO:	Mr. John Greuber, local builder, and Mrs. Vitell, mother of three, were elected to the board.
YES:	John Greuber and Ann Vitell, both long active in community affairs, were elected to the board.
NO:	Dreiser and Edith Wharton are little read by today's students.
YES:	Dreiser and Wharton are little read by today's students.
NO:	Mr. Pfitzer and Jane will show you around the plant.
YES:	Mr. Pfitzer and Ms. Garner will show you around the plant.

30b *sx* | The Pronoun Dilemma

Avoid using pronouns with sexist implications.

English does not have a personal pronoun that refers impartially to persons of either sex. There is no single pronoun (like the made-up *s/he*) that would help us avoid choices like the following: "A police officer needs strict guidelines for the use of (*his? her? his or her?*) gun." Remember:

(1) Replace gender-biased pronouns. Beware of stereotyping occupations by using *he* or *she* selectively when talking about typical representatives. Avoid loaded pairs like "the doctor—*he*, the nurse—*she*" or "the manager—*he*, the secretary—*she*." Use the **double pronoun** he or she (or *his or her*) to refer to a typical doctor, nurse, teacher, secretary, or executive. You can often sidestep the pronoun problem by talking about typical doctors, teachers, or secretaries *in the plural*:

STEREOTYPED:	A successful manager keeps a certain distance from **his** employees.

DOUBLE PRONOUN:	A successful manager keeps a certain distance from **his or her** employees.
PLURAL:	Successful **managers** keep a certain distance from **their** employees.

The plural usually works best when several *he-or-she, his-or-her,* and *himself-or-herself* combinations in a row would make a sentence awkward.

(2) Replace the generic *he*. Use the double pronoun *he or she* also to replace the **generic** *he* in reference to the generalized expressions like *everyone, somebody, anybody, anyone, nobody,* or *one* (**indefinite pronouns**). Everyday speech uses the plural *they* or *their* after these: "*No one* should be required to inform on *their* own family." Grammarians used to require the singular *he* or *him* (or *himself*): "*Everyone* has the right to make *his* own mistakes." In your own writing, use the unbiased *he or she*, or change the generalized pronouns to a plural:

UNBIASED:	**Everyone** has the right to make **his or her** own mistakes.
PLURAL:	We **all** have the right to make **our** own mistakes.

Finer Points   Some writers alternate *he* and *she* in pointing back to pronouns like *somebody* and *everyone* or in talking about a typical student, a typical writer, a representative citizen. Sometimes you can sidestep the pronoun issue altogether:

> A police officer needs strict guidelines for the use of **a** gun.

PEER EDITOR 19   Rewrite the following sentences to eliminate *sexist language*. Discuss the merits of different revisions with your classmates.

1. Thoreau, the Concord sage, and Emily Dickinson, the Amherst poetess, take us on fascinating explorations of inner space.
2. Risking his life for unconcerned or unappreciative citizens is part of a policeman's or a fireman's job.
3. Evolutionists are rewriting the history of mankind to show that early man branched off the evolutionary tree before the chimpanzee.
4. A doctor can walk away from his patients after a brief consultation; the nurse spends most of her day dealing with their pain and fear.
5. Everybody takes American history at least three or four times in his career as a student.

6. Justice Marshall and Sandra O'Connor, the first lady judge appointed to the Court, voted with the majority.

7. On Secretaries' Day, the boss is expected to show his appreciation for the ladies in the office.

8. A business traveler may take out his anger on the stewardess if he misses his connecting flight.

9. The ambition of every Congressman is to become the chairman of an important House committee.

10. While the convention-goer attends his meetings, his spouse can do her shopping or use the legendary recreational facilities.

---

31   Effective Language

OVERVIEW Effective writers know how to choose the right word—the word that brings an idea clearly into focus, the word that brings a vivid image to the reader's mind. People with an impoverished vocabulary can give us only a blurred view of the world. Effective writers use language that does justice to important distinctions and shades of meaning; they use language that makes us see, hear, and feel.

Using effective language is more than a matter of correcting words that are only half right or just plain wrong:

INACCURATE:	Thorough reforms would be hard to *induce* upon our society, (bring about in? implement in?)
INACCURATE:	Good students have learned to listen to teachers and retain the knowledge they have *expelled*. (shared? communicated?)

PRECISE WORDS Often the word that is just right *tells us more* than a blurry all-purpose word. **Precise** words add the right shades of meaning: *Toil* adds something to the idea of ordinary work; we *squander* with more abandon than when we just waste. An *arduous* task is difficult—but so difficult as to require strenuous or dedicated effort. A *serene* feeling is a peaceful feeling—but so peaceful as to calm the spirit and leave us especially happy or contented.

CONCRETE WORDS Effective writers bring their writing to life by using **concrete** words—words that take us close to what we can see, hear, smell, and feel. *Gnarled* makes us visualize the texture of twisted wood. Words

431

like *toss, pitch, lob, hurtle, drill,* and *zing* all help us see motions more specific than the averaged-out *throw.*

FIGURATIVE WORDS **Figurative** language helps writers translate ideas and emotions into vivid images that capture our attention and stir our emotions. It uses imaginative comparisons to help us see, feel, and imagine:

> The historic function of the American school, and especially of the high school, has been to serve as a social and economic **ladder**— though today's school personnel, referring to a more passive clientele, sometimes thinks of it as an **escalator**.   Edgar Z. Friedenberg

31a   *d*   Accurate Words

Aim at accurate words and exact shades of meaning.

In serious writing, we use much of the common stock of language, but we also use words that tell our readers more than a more familiar, all-purpose word might. A diversified vocabulary enables us to do the fine-tuning that makes words bring in exactly the right meanings and associations:

WORD	GENERAL MEANING	SPECIAL ASSOCIATIONS
incongruous	out of place	sticking out in a weird or ridiculous fashion
lucid	clear	making something *exceptionally* clear that might otherwise have been muddy or obscure
precarious	risky	already tottering on the brink
spurious	false	claiming to be authentic but actually completely fake

Speaking or writing in a hurry, we often settle for words that merely come close—words that express the intended meaning almost but not quite. In revising a quick first draft, look for the following:

(1) Use the exact word, not a roundabout description. Often when someone uses a **circumlocution** ("taking the long way around"), we want to say: "English has a word for it!"

ROUNDABOUT:	The skipper and **the people working for him on the boat** were lost.
EXACT:	The skipper and **the crew** were lost.

(2) Use the exact word, not one that is only half right. Your revision of a first draft is your opportunity to replace a near-miss, approximate word with the word that is exactly right:

BLURRED:	Many parents today do not have time to **adhere** to the needs of their children. (We **adhere to**—or stick to—an agreement. We **attend to**, or **satisfy**, someone's needs.)
ACCURATE:	Many parents today do not have time to **attend to** the needs of their children.

(3) Watch out for the right word used the wrong way. Some words carry the right idea but are used the wrong way in a sentence:

WRONG:	**The news** about widespread corruption was first **exposed** in the local press.
RIGHT:	Widespread **corruption** was first **exposed** in the local press.
ALSO RIGHT:	**The news** about widespread corruption first **broke** in the local press. (Evildoers are **exposed**; the news about their doings **breaks** or is **reported**; the truth about them is **revealed**.)
GARBLED:	Most American teenagers do what they want without **consenting** their parents.
REVISED:	Most American teenagers do what they want without **consulting** their parents (or without **obtaining** their consent).
GARBLED:	Many young people have **lost their appeal** for fraternities.
REVISED:	Fraternities have **lost their appeal** for many young people.

(4) Watch out for words with the wrong connotation. Disapproving words used to express approving attitudes (or vice-versa) have a jarring effect on the reader:

INEXACT:	Life in the suburbs **subjects** a family to the beauties of nature.

REVISED: Life in the suburbs **brings** a family **closer** to the beauties of nature.
(The connotations of **subject** are unfavorable; it implies that we are exposed to something unwillingly.)

(5) Watch out for words easily confused. Some words are just plain wrong. One way to go wrong is to confuse words close in sound or meaning:

CONFUSED: The work was sheer **trudgery** (should be **drudgery**).
Similar choices **affront** every student (should be **confront**).
Self-control is an **envious** asset (should be **enviable**).

PEER EDITOR 20 Write down a *more accurate* word or expression for each word or phrase italicized in the following sentences.

1. My parents have always *placed a high standard* on a good education.
2. Having high-spirited parents has given me a *jest* for life.
3. Diane soon discovered some of the problems *coherent* in managing a large department.
4. Her parents were idealists and tried to raise healthy, *opinionated* children.
5. Berlin became the decadent postwar capital where all kinds of sexual *deprivations* were practiced.
6. *Immortal* books should be removed from the library.
7. In my *analogy* of this essay, I hope to show its strengths and weaknesses.
8. The woman *braved* her life to save her fellow passengers.
9. The authoritarian father gave the orders, with no *lip service* in return.
10. Her press agent *contributed* the low attendance to poor publicity.

31b *d* Specific Words

Use specific, informative words.

When we write about the concrete examples or situations that bring ideas to life, we need specific words that bring the reader close to first-hand experience. Words that remain too general keep people and events colorless and anonymous:

GENERAL:	An unidentified individual relieved the passer-by of his valuables.
SPECIFIC:	The mugger made the dazed tourist hand over his digital watch, airplane tickets, and crammed wallet.
GENERAL:	Rodeo artists lived a strenuous life, eating poorly, always exposed to injury.
SPECIFIC:	Rodeo artists lived off hot dogs at county fairs and ruptured their intestines while twisting the necks of steers.

Do the following to make your writing more vivid and informative:

(1) Call things by their names. Instead of lumping something in a general category, use names that call up shapes, textures, and colors. "Small animal" is colorless; *gopher, chipmunk, squirrel,* and *raccoon* call up contours, movements, habits.

GENERAL	SPECIFIC
tree	birch, elm, pine, fir, eucalyptus, poplar, cypress
weeds	dandelion, crabgrass, tumbleweed, thistle

Instead of a colorless, general word like *building*, use a more expressive word like *barn, mansion, warehouse, bungalow, tenement, shack, workshop,* or *cabin. Tenement* carries more information than *building*, making it possible for the reader to visualize an actual structure.

(2) Use concrete words—words that appeal to our five senses. **Concrete** words bring us close to what we can see, hear, and feel; they seem to conjure up sights, sounds, smells, textures, and motions.

Here are some all-purpose words with the more concrete choices that could take their place. What does each of these concrete words add to the general idea? What does it make you see or hear?

GENERAL	CONCRETE
look	gaze, stare, peer, squint, ogle
walk	stride, march, slink, trot, shuffle, drag
sit	slump, squat, lounge, hunch, crouch
take	seize, grab, pounce on, grip
cry	weep, sob, sigh, bawl
throw	hurl, pitch, toss, dump, flip

The concrete words in the following passage from a *New Yorker* article make us feel what it is like to be pitched about the deck of a lurching boat:

> As the boat **lurches**, pails and shovels go **flying** from one side of the deck to the other; foul-weather gear hanging on a clothesline by the port bulkhead **swings out** until it is nearly horizontal, **slaps back** against the wall, and **swings out** again. A pot **skitters** past me across the engine housing, **smacks** the bulkhead, and **falls open** on the deck. Fried chicken—an enormous amount of fried chicken—**tumbles** out. James Stevenson

---

DISCOURSE EXERCISE 21   Ernest Hemingway was known as a stickler for the right word—the word that accurately carried information or created the right picture in the reader's mind. Look at the general, colorless word at the beginning of each of the following sentences. Then compare it with the more *concrete word* that Hemingway used in one of his short stories. What does the concrete word add to the more general meaning?

Camping in the Michigan Woods

1. (throw) The handler had *pitched* Nick's bundle out of the door of the railroad car.
2. (move) The river *swirled* against the logs of the bridge.
3. (rock) There were big *boulders* at the bottom of the stream.
4. (flow) A mist of sand gravel was raised in *spurts* by the current.
5. (reflection) Looking for the river, Nick caught *glints* of the water in the sun.
6. (turn) There were big grasshoppers with wings *whirring out* from their sheathing.
7. (eat) He saw the grasshopper *nibble* at the wool of his sock.
8. (shiny) The jointed belly of the grasshopper was black, *iridescent*.
9. (stand) By a *grove* of trees was a bare space for his tent.
10. (branch) Nick broke off some *sprigs* of the heathery fern.
11. (piece) With the ax he slit off a large *slab* of pine.
12. (burn) When he tucked the chips under the grill, the fire *flared* up.
13. (fill) Nick *dipped* the coffeepot half full of water.
14. (noise) A mosquito he had caught made a satisfactory *hiss* in the flame.
15. (fog) He saw a *mist* rising in the swamp across the river.

SENTENCE PRACTICE 22   Write five two-part sentences that first state a general idea and then make it concrete by means of a striking example. Use *specific language* to make the abstract concrete.

EXAMPLE 1:	The phrase "mass culture" conveys emotional overtones of passivity; it suggests someone eating peanuts at a baseball game. Northrop Frye
EXAMPLE 2:	We are more interested in success than in failure; we are more interested in the exploits of upwardly mobile young entrepreneurs than in the stories of people who spend their nights sleeping on heating grates.
EXAMPLE 3:	Many young people today are always in a hurry; they are on the go so much that their answering machines answer the phone more often than they do.

31c   *d*   Technical Terms

Use technical terms to enlighten and not to confuse the outsider.

We use **technical terms** where they are clearly useful or functional, making sure they are clear to the newcomer or outsider. A mechanic cannot operate efficiently without terms like *carburetor, alternator,* or *differential.* Science, engineering, medicine, and many other fields rely on precise, impersonal technical language to convey reliable specialized information:

TECHNICAL:	High-yield airbursts will chemically burn the nitrogen in the upper air, converting it into **oxides of nitrogen**; these, in turn, combine with and destroy the protective ozone in the Earth's **stratosphere**. Carl Sagan on nuclear winter
TECHNICAL:	The **primates** are our nearest biological relatives; they have the same **neurochemical** pathways that mediate **affective states** like anxiety and apprehension—emotions once thought to belong only to humans.

Like the best technical writing, these sample passages use vigorous plain English (*airbursts, burn, destroy, pathways*) along with the necessary technical terms.

An audience of fellow experts will take current technical terms in stride. But make sure technical language does not confuse or befuddle the outsider. Explain and illustrate new or difficult terms. In a paper on a mountain-climbing trip, you may need to define terms like the following:

> *bivouac:* a temporary encampment in the open, with only tents as an improvised shelter

> *traverse:* to move sideways across a mountain slope, making a slanting path

Whenever you write about a field on which you are more of an expert than the general reader, watch out for technical terms that might need explanation:

COMPUTERS: mainframe, off-line, interface, dot matrix, byte, modem, low-resolution, binary

In a passage like the following, a writer uses the necessary technical terms while making sure their meaning is clear to the newcomer or outsider:

> The **disk drive** works like a very fast tape recorder, recording information on a magnetic medium, the **floppy disk**. When the user needs that stored information, she tells the computer to load the information into its own **short-term** memory (RAM—for "random access memory"), where the data can be examined and revised.

SENTENCE PRACTICE 23   What specialized fields do the following *technical terms* represent? Which of these terms would you expect a college student to know? For five of these, write a one-sentence definition for the newcomer or outsider.

EXAMPLE: *Type-A* personalities are those uptight, compulsive, competitive, aggressive overachievers likely to suffer early heart attacks unless they modify their behavior.

a priori	hard disk	symbiosis
black box	lien	syncopation
black hole	meltdown	thyroid
camshaft	solstice	venire
de facto	sonata	ventricle

31d   *d* Figurative Language

Use figurative language to bring color and life into your writing.

Figurative language brings color into the black and white of literal speech. Effectively used, it can light up a whole sentence or paragraph.

Figurative language employs imaginative comparisons, or **figures of speech**, to exploit the similarities that will translate ideas into striking images. A brief comparison signaled by *as* or *like* is called a **simile**: "In much modern fiction, happiness is found only briefly and in unexpected places, *like a flower growing in the crack of a sidewalk.*" An implied comparison that presents one thing as if it actually were the other is called a **metaphor**: "For many beginning poets, the traditional rhymed four-line stanza is *a jug into which the syrup of verse is poured.*" An **allusion** is a brief mention that brings to mind a familiar story or set of facts; it makes us transfer the appropriate ideas or attitudes from the original to a parallel situation: "We are all *Custer.*"

Figurative language accounts for much of the color and life of ordinary language: *whistleblower, hiring freeze, insurance crunch, deep pockets, brain drain, population explosion, green revolution, fast breeder.* Effective writers use fresh, well-chosen figurative expressions to catch our attention and to make us see the point:

> In this movie, "understanding" is sprinkled into both sides of the conflict **like meat tenderizer.**   Peter Rainer

> Getting complete sentences out of him was like trying to put together *Homo sapiens* from **a few bones in a cave.**   Anita Strickland

> People who keep a journal turn experience into words before the sun sets twice; **sometimes, like dry cleaners, they give same-day service.**

Remember the following advice:

(1) Figurative expressions should be apt. The implied analogy has to fit:

APT: In many of the author's stories, language is **like signals from vessels in distress, telling us of desperate needs.**
(Distress signals are a particularly urgent kind of language.)

INEPT: **Lacking the ignition** of advertising, our economic engine would run at a slower pace.
(An engine without ignition would not run at a slower pace; it would just be dead.)

(2) Figurative expressions should be consistent. If several figurative expressions appear together, they should mix well; they should blend into a harmonious whole:

> Everyone who is born holds **dual citizenship**, in **the kingdom** of the well and in **the kingdom** of the sick. Although we all prefer to use only

439

the good passport, sooner or later each of us is obliged, at least for a spell, to identify ourselves with the citizens of that other place. Susan Sontag

Avoid the **mixed metaphor**, which at first sails smoothly along and then suddenly jumps the tracks (hard to do on the trackless sea). Mixed metaphors create the impression that you are not listening to what you are saying:

CONSISTENT:	If the new industrial robots have become the **arms and eyes** of our factories, computers have become their **brains**.
MIXED:	America's colleges are the **key** to national survival, and the future of the country lies in their **hands**. (Keys do not have hands.)
MIXED:	Enriched programs give the good student a chance to **dig** deeper into the large **sea** of knowledge. (We dig on solid ground rather than at sea.)

(3) Figurative language should not be strained. Reaching for a striking image, we can easily strain our metaphor. Imaginative comparisons should create a graphic image in the reader's mind, but sometimes the image becomes *too* graphic:

DISTRACTING:	Helplessly, Fred watched from his desk while his stomach tied itself into knots.
REVISED:	As Fred watched the event helplessly from his desk, he experienced a sick, tense feeling in the pit of his stomach.

(4) Figurative language should not be stale. Some figurative expressions, though already familiar, still have some mileage on them; to change the metaphor, they still serve as a convenient shorthand for ideas:

Corporate law practice has always been **the Rolls-Royce** of legal careers. Fred Graham

A graduate student looking **for the fast track** at a university tends to avoid controversy.

But some figurative expressions have been used over and over and over. Avoid **clichés**, including *the bottom line, the cutting edge,* and *the melting pot,* not to mention *smart as a whip* and *blind as a bat.*

SEE **32b** FOR MORE ON CLICHÉS.

DISCOURSE EXERCISE 24 Find and discuss *figurative expressions* in the following passage. What images or associations do they bring to mind? Which of these figurative expressions are familiar? Which are fresh or provocative? (Which are familiar but used or adapted in new ways?)

Loaded Words

A great many words bring along not only their meanings but some extra freight—a load of judgment or bias that plays upon the emotions instead of lighting up the understanding. These words deserve careful handling—and minding. They are loaded. Such words babble up in all corners of society, wherever anybody is ax-grinding, arm-twisting, back-scratching, sweet-talking. Political blather leans sharply to words (*peace, prosperity*) whose moving powers outweigh exact meanings. Merchandising depends on adjectives (*new, improved*) that must be continually recharged with notions that entice people to buy. In casual conversation, emotional stuffing is lent to words by inflection and gesture: The innocent phrase, "Thanks a lot," is frequently a vehicle for heaping servings of irritation. Traffic in opinion-heavy language is universal simply because most people, as C. S. Lewis puts it, are "more anxious to express their approval and disapproval of things than to describe them."

The trouble with loaded words is that they tend to short-circuit thought. While they may describe something, they simultaneously try to seduce the mind into accepting a prefabricated opinion about the something described.   Frank Tippett, "Watching Out for Loaded Words," *Time*

SENTENCE PRACTICE 25 Point out uses of *figurative language* in the following examples. (Which are sustained or extended metaphors? Which are allusions? What images does each figure of speech call up? What emotions or attitudes does it activate?) Choose *three* of these as model sentences. For each, write a very similar sentence, using your own figure of speech.

EXAMPLE: If life is in some sense a status race, my parents never noticed the flag drop.   Aristides

IMITATION: If life is meant to be a treadmill, my friends never got on it.

1.   If life is in some sense a status race, my parents never noticed the flag drop.   Aristides

2. It seems to me that any number of people have been through earth-quakes in their private lives that haven't even made a crack in the walls of their philosophy. Ellen Goodman

3. Each generation must get on the same old merry-go-round, only dis-guised in a new coat of paint. Katherine Anne Porter

4. The last of the cyclical postwar recessions was ending, and a quarter century of burgeoning prosperity was on the launch pad. Laurence Shames

5. The 1950s built for women in the United States a world of too-narrow walls, too-early marriage, too-little productivity. Margaret Mead

6. Intelligence is a very real kind of armor, and like any armor it inhibits its owner's ability to float with the prevailing currents. Peter S. Prescott

7. It is frightening to step off onto the treacherous footbridge leading to the second half of life. Gail Sheehy

8. The advice that most Southern mothers pass on is that men are the enemy: a pack of Yankees. Shirley Abbott

---

PEER EDITOR 26 Rewrite the following sentences. Use *more apt or fresh* figurative language to replace expressions that are mixed, stale, or overdone.

1. The original educator is the family, which plants the seeds that teachers later build upon.

2. Immigrants bring new blood into our country to help us recharge our batteries.

3. Family ties going back several generations have become deeply en-trenched in many rural areas.

4. Many times a creative person is thrown into the limelight because she has created something totally new.

5. Frustration and depression will take over our minds the way bacteria do our bodies if we do not harness them.

6. The grocery store is alive with the stuffed carts that will fill the growling stomachs of the customers.

7. We sat in a circle on the floor, pouring out the paths and roads we had traveled since we graduated.

8. This cat was in our driveway when the kiss of death took him by surprise.

9. It is common for people to be unaware of the more difficult gut issues that are propelling them forward.

10. The jagged teeth of the powerful saw bit into the flesh of the tree like a hungry shark crushing its prey.

---

32   ## Plain English

OVERVIEW   Ideally, we would all write vigorous plain English that carries our message without static. In practice, however, words may get in the way, slowing down, confusing, or misleading the reader. Professional writers devote much of their final editing to the rewording of passages that missed the mark. Watch out for verbal habits that, like other bad habits, are easy to pick up but hard to shake:

WORDINESS   Brevity may not always be the soul of wit, but wordiness is its enemy. Writing is wordy if it uses too many words to say too little. Outright **redundancy** duplicates words that say the same: *important essentials* (essentials are always important); a *terrible tragedy* (it wouldn't be a tragedy if it weren't terrible). Padding like the following makes us wonder when the writer will actually start grappling with the subject:

PADDED: **In this fast-moving day and age of today, the area of education** is more important than ever.

BRIEF: Today, education is more important than ever.

CLICHÉS   Fresh language makes us pay attention; it can make us think. ("Harvard—across the river in Cambridge—and Boston are two ends of one mustache." Elizabeth Hardwick) The temptation, however, is to use ready-made, prefabricated language that we can use without thinking. Expressions like *to be brutally frank, from all walks of life, no sooner said than done,* and *in the nick of time* are **clichés**—they are verbal hand-me-downs that have become tattered and threadbare through overuse.

JARGON   People use an inflated pseudoscientific **jargon** to make themselves and what they do seem important. They write "during the preplanning phase" when they mean "during the planning"; they write "desired educational outcomes" when they mean "educational goals." They love words like *prioritize, interface, impact* ("the decision *impacted* our program"), not to mention *aspects* and *factors*.

EUPHEMISMS   **Euphemisms** are meant to shield us from unpleasant realities like age (*senior citizen*), death (*bereavement, memorial park*), or disability (*vision-impaired*). Euphemisms become a problem when manipulative people use them to make bad things sound good: Firing is called "outplacement"; an arsenal for nuclear warfare is called a "nuclear deterrent."

443

Note: As you prune your writing of wordiness, clichés, or pretentious jargon, remember that pruning and weeding are not the whole of the gardener's art. Trim the wild growth, but do not become suspicious of everything that gives life or color or sparkle to your writing.

32a   *w* | Wordiness

Avoid wordiness.

Redundancy is the use of more words than are necessary. The phrase *basic fundamentals* is redundant because fundamentals are already basic by definition, just as it is in the nature of circles to be round. *Newly renovated* and *free gift* are redundant because they tell us nothing that *renovated* and *gift* wouldn't tell us on their own.

Do the following to trim superfluous words:

(1) Avoid direct duplication. In the following sentences, one or the other way of expressing the same idea should be omitted:

REDUNDANT:
> **As a rule**, summers in Chicago are **usually** unbearably hot.
> Prisoners were awakened **in the morning** at six **a.m.**
> The President knew more about the events than **seemed apparent**.
> This common **mis**conception is completely **wrong**.

(2) Watch for redundant pairs. Prune the adjectives in *future plans* (plans are always for the future) or *true facts* (facts are supposed to be true).

REDUNDANT	ECONOMICAL
consensus of opinion	consensus
past memories	memories
anticipate in advance	anticipate

(3) Avoid familiar wordy tags. Much inflated language is caused by tags like the following:

WORDY	BRIEF
at the present time	now
due to the fact that	because
under the prevailing circumstances	as things are
in this time and age	today
at a period of time when	when
the question whether	whether

(4) Use simple, direct transitional expressions. Often a simple logical link like *for example, however,* or *therefore* can take the place of a lengthy preamble like *Taking these factors into consideration, we must conclude that.*

WORDY: **In considering the situation, we must also take into account the fact that** the current residents often do not share our enthusiasm for redevelopment.

BRIEF: The current residents, **however**, often do not share our enthusiasm for redevelopment.

(5) Avoid vague all-purpose words. All-purpose words like *element, factor, aspect, situation,* or *angle* are often mere padding.

PADDED: Another **aspect** that needs to be considered is the consumer relations **angle**.

REVISED: We should also consider consumer relations.

Words like *kind of* and *sort of* are often mere filler:

PADDED: The inflation **situation** was getting **kind of** out of hand.

REVISED: Inflation was getting out of hand.

PEER EDITOR 27   What makes each of the following sentences wordy? Rewrite each sentence to eliminate wordiness.

EXAMPLE: The reason that married students have high grades academically is that they have definite goals in the future to come.

REVISED: Married students have high grades because they have definite goals.

1. We are planning to move because in terms of employment there are few jobs in this area at the present time.
2. Mormons fleeing persecution founded the beginning of our community.
3. In due time, a new fad will eventually replace this current craze.
4. Many plants are closing due to the fact that a flood of cheap products is inundating the market.
5. In my opinion, I have always felt that a popular entertainer should be a happy, smiling type of person.
6. The central nucleus of the tribe was based around the institution of the family.
7. The weather bureau announced that at times there would be occasional rain.
8. At a period of time when schools face skyrocketing insurance costs, the aspect of insurance pools deserves consideration.
9. The setting of the play took place in a rustic part of rural Virginia.
10. In the modern world of this day and age, computer projections are among the basic fundamentals of business planning.

32b *d* Clichés

Phrase ideas freshly in your own words.

Clichés are ready-made phrases, worn out from overuse. Like phrases stored in the memory of an electronic typewriter, they practically type themselves: "*few* and . . . *far between*," "easier said . . . *than done*," "last but . . . *not least*." Many folksy clichés have outlived a rural past (*put the shoulder to the wheel, put the cart before the horse*). Other trite phrases survive from old-fashioned, flowery oratory (*intestinal fortitude, dire necessity, the bitter end*). Still others sound like part of a sales talk that has been replayed too many times (*let's look at the facts, look at the big picture, look at the bottom line*).

To the cliché expert, ignorance is always abysmal, fortitude intestinal, and necessity dire. Daylight is always broad, silence ominous, and old age ripe. People make a "clean break" and engage in "honest toil" till the "bitter end." They make things "crystal clear"; they wait "with bated breath"; they work "by the sweat of their brow." To *say the least*, for *all intents and purposes*, the *bloom is off* such expressions, and *in the final analysis*, they *do more harm than good*.

Clichés make the reader feel that nothing new is being said; the writer has not bothered to take a fresh look. ("For a while it seemed as if things were falling apart, but when our backs were to the wall and the chips were down, everyone in the group seemed to come through and did a great job.") When you first encounter a cliché, it may seem vivid or imaginative ("this is only *the tip of the iceberg*"), but you have to remember that everyone has used it before you. Resist the pull of the cliché; phrase your ideas freshly, in your own words:

TRITE: He was always **wrapped up** in his own thoughts and feelings.

FRESH: Only the **cocoon** of his own thoughts and feelings existed for him.

TRITE: The dean let us have it, **straight from the shoulder.**

FRESH: The dean spoke to us directly and urgently, **like a scout just returned from the enemy camp**.

Avoid clichés like the following:

believe it or not	burn the midnight oil
better late than never	couldn't care less
beyond the shadow of a doubt	crying shame
bolt out of the blue	dire straits
easier said than done	Mother Nature
the facts of life	off the beaten track
few and far between	pride and joy
fine and dandy	proud owner
the finer things	rear its ugly head
first and foremost	rude awakening
good time was had by all	a shot in the arm
green with envy	sink or swim
in one fell swoop	a snare and a delusion
it goes without saying	sneaking suspicion
it stands to reason	something tells me
last but not least	straight and narrow
the last straw	tender mercies
let's face it	to all intents and purposes
malice aforethought	truth is stranger than fiction

PEER EDITOR 28 Which expressions in the following sentences are *clichés*? Rewrite each sentence to get rid of trite language, substituting language fresh enough to revive the reader's attention.

EXAMPLE: You will never rise to the top of the heap if every setback makes you throw in the sponge.

REVISED: You will never make it to the top if every setback makes you think of defeat as inevitable, like the rain.

1. We try to give foreign competition a run for their money, but in many areas, cheap foreign labor has forced American management to throw in the towel.

2. In a very real sense, politicians dealing with tax legislation often cannot see the forest for the trees.

3. Catching the street-corner pusher has become small potatoes. The major effort now is international, and it is a pathway strewn with political pitfalls.

4. Our new educational division has become an integral part of our marketing effort and will play a vital role in the challenging days ahead.

5. In the final analysis, party platforms never get down to brass tacks.

6. The meetings scheduled with the candidate will give people from every walk of life a chance to stand up and be counted.

7. When we try to give our neighborhoods a shot in the arm, appealing to self-interest is our best bet.

8. The opposing candidate was a Johnny-come-lately picked because he could be counted on to play ball with the real estate interests in the legislature.

9. Constantly testing students who don't know how to learn is putting the cart before the horse.

10. After all is said and done, its rabid fans are not going to turn their backs on boxing in the foreseeable future.

32c   *d*   Jargon

Do not try to impress your reader with pretentious pseudoscientific language.

Familiar problems of diction result when a writer tries to impress the reader. **Jargon** is pretentious, pseudoscientific language using two highbrow words where one lowbrow word would do. Jargon tries to make the trivial sound important: "Mandatory verification of your attendance record is required of all personnel exiting the work area." (Punch your time card when you leave.) Jargon creates a pseudoscientific air by using indirect, impersonal constructions and technical-sounding Latin and Greek terms:

JARGON:	He was **instrumental in the founding of** an Irish national theater.
PLAIN ENGLISH:	He helped found an Irish national theater.
JARGON:	**Procedures were instituted with a view toward the implementation** of the conclusions reached. (Note the impersonal passive.)
PLAIN ENGLISH:	We started to put our ideas into practice.

In much technical, scientific, or scholarly writing, technical and impersonal language is necessary. Jargon is the *un*necessary use of technical-sounding terms in order to borrow the prestige of science and scholarship. Remember advice like the following:

(1) Deflate inflated substitutes for straightforward words. In each of the following pairs avoid the big word if the simple word will do:

BIG WORD	SIMPLE WORD	BIG WORD	SIMPLE WORD
ameliorate	improve	residence	home
magnitude	size	maximize	develop fully
interrelationship	relation	insightful	intelligent
methodology	methods	preadolescence	childhood
prioritize	rank	correlate	match

(2) Lower the abstraction count. Watch for such symptoms as the piling up of too many words ending in *-ion: verification, utilization, implementation, modification, conceptualization.* Avoid using terms like the following to wrap personal opinions in a pseudo-objective aura: *factors, phases, aspects, elements, criteria, facets, phenomena, strata.*

JARGON:	**An element of society that is most prevalent** in advertising is the desire for a carefree existence.
PLAIN ENGLISH:	Advertising mirrors the yearning for a carefree life that is strong in our society.

(3) Avoid impersonal tags. Even in formal research reports, overuse of phrases like the following produces a stilted effect. Avoid them in ordinary prose:

STILTED	PLAIN
reference was made	I mentioned
the hypothesis suggests itself	we can tentatively conclude
careful consideration is imperative	we should study carefully
a realization of desired outcomes	producing the desired results

(4) Avoid using or overusing buzzwords. Buzzwords are currently fashionable terms that people use to make themselves sound like insiders. They are words that most people have already heard once too often: *parameters, bottom line, user-friendly, interface, cost-effective, upscale.*

> SEE 25c FOR THE AWKWARD PASSIVE.

PEER EDITOR 29 Translate the following examples of *jargon* into plain English.

1. I sincerely believe that the government should divulge more on the subject of socialism and its cohorts, because its impetus has reached a frightening momentum.
2. In camp, cooking is done over open fires, with the main dietary intake consisting of black beans and rice.
3. To be frank about it, today an inadequacy can bring about the ruination of a person in later life when it happens in education.
4. Being in social situations in Washington subjected me to some embarrassing instances due to my deficiency in etiquette, which was superfluous at home because of its nonexistence.
5. The English language and its use have become very important factors in correlation with communication to large audiences.
6. In these two books, there are basic differences in character representation that are accountable only in terms of the individual authors involved.
7. Further insight into the article discovered that the writing insinuated a connection between the conviction of the accused and his working-class background.
8. Advertisements similar to those of Certs and Ultra-Brite are creating a fallacy in the real cause of a person's sex appeal.
9. The fact that we are products of our environmental frame of reference ensures that each of us has deeply ingrained within the fiber of our being preconceived ideas that influence our thoughts, actions, and reactions.

10. We say we believe in democracy while denying the partaking of its first fruits, justice and equality, to diverse members of our society. This is true in many aspects of our lives, but especially so in the context of racial prejudice.

32d *d* Euphemisms

Prefer plain English to euphemisms and weasel words.

Euphemisms are "beautiful words"—words more beautiful than what they stand for: *memorial park* for *cemetery, waste management* for *garbage disposal, correctional facility* for *jail.* Some euphemisms are merely polite: *intoxicated* for *drunk, stout* for *fat.* But many stem from a desire to upgrade ordinary realities, leaving us inundated with fuzzy, vaguely complimentary terms: *human performance* (physical education), *sanitary engineer* (plumber), *research consultant* (file clerk), *language facilitator* (translator).

In much public-relations prose and other kinds of doublespeak, euphemisms become **weasel words.** They cover up facts that the reader is entitled to know: *straitened financial circumstances* for "bankruptcy"; *resettlement* for "forcible removal"; *negative economic growth* for "recession." Cutting down a redwood grove becomes "harvesting a natural resource."

An effective writer has to know when to be diplomatic but also when to be blunt and direct:

EUPHEMISMS	BLUNT
immoderate use of intoxicants	heavy drinking
lack of proper health habits	dirt
deteriorating residential section	slum
below the poverty line	poor

32e *d* Flowery Diction

Avoid language that is flowery or overdone.

Flowery language attempts to give a poetic varnish to prose. Resist the temptation to weave a flowery garland of fancy words around simple everyday events:

FLOWERY:	The **respite** from study was devoted to a **sojourn** at the **ancestral mansion**.
PLAIN ENGLISH:	I spent my vacation at the house of my grandparents.
FLOWERY:	The visitor proved a **harbinger** of **glad tidings**.
PLAIN ENGLISH:	The visitor brought good news.

Do not imitate writers who habitually prefer the fancy word to the plain word, the elegant flourish to the blunt phrase. Here is a brief list of words that can make your writing seem affected:

FLOWERY	PLAIN	FLOWERY	PLAIN
astound	amaze	nuptials	wedding
betrothal	engagement	obsequies	funeral
commence	begin	presage	predict
demise	death	pulchritude	beauty
emolument	pay, reward	vernal	springlike
eschew	avoid	vista	view

Avoid overwriting or **purple prose** in descriptive writing. Let the fascination or beauty of a natural scene speak for itself instead of smothering it under layers of flowery words:

OVERWRITTEN:	**Invitingly lured from slumber** by the sound of the rhythmic waves **gently caressing** the black rocks, **lying lonely** in their salty pools below, I **witness the dawn's early morning rays thrust** their way through the layer of thick **frigid clouds curtaining** this **uniquely beautiful** spot by the sea.
BETTER:	At low tide, the black rocks are exposed among the saltwater pools. In the narrow channels between the rocks, incoming waves fill the crevices with foaming spray. Sea snails and small crabs hide among the masses of seaweed. Only yards away, sandpipers trot in and out after receding and returning waves.

PEER EDITOR 30 Cut through the *euphemisms* and *flowery language* in the following examples and rewrite them in plain English.

1. Ready to leave the parental nest, I decided to pursue my education at an institution of higher learning.

2. After a most rewarding bout with a social research paper, something stirred my intellect and I possessed a burning desire to stay in school for another three-week session.

3. Offenders who have paid their debt to society at a correctional institution should be given a chance to become productive participants in community life.

4. All personnel assisting in preparation of food should observe proper hygiene after using the sanitary facilities.

5. After the annual respite from their secretarial toil, office workers resume their labors with renewed vigor.

7

Punctuation: When and Why

Instructions Look at the blank in each of the following sentences. Of the three possible choices that follow the sentence, which would be right for serious written English? Write the number of the sentence, followed by the letter for the right choice.

1. The horned owl has become _____ is an endangered species.
   a. rare it   **b.** rare, it   **c.** rare. It

2. Alice Walker, a prize-winning _____ *The Color Purple*.
   a. novelist, wrote   **b.** novelist; wrote   **c.** novelist wrote

3. The million dollars had been the second _____ the first.
   a. prize not   **b.** prize: not   **c.** prize, not

4. The deadline has _____ we return your application.
   a. passed, therefore,   **b.** passed; therefore,   **c.** passed, therefore

5. We lived on an army _____ of us rarely saw the town.
   a. base; most   **b.** base, most   **c.** base most

6. "We recommend," the interviewer _____ you look elsewhere."
   a. said, "that   **b.** said. "That   **c.** said; "that

7. To speed up the _____ faxed the documents to their office.
   a. process we   **b.** process, we   **c.** process; we

8. According to the biography, "Whitman always dreamed of 'the true _____
   a. America."   **b.** America.'"   **c.** America".

9. Students applying for the _____ to fill in endless forms.
   a. grants, have   **b.** grants; have   **c.** grants have

10. Who said: "Ask not what your country can do for _____
    a. you?   b. you"?   c. you?"

11. The Pentagon orders big-ticket _____ ship, and missiles.
    a. items: planes,   b. items, planes,   c. items planes,

12. The injured passenger _____ help arrived.
    a. died. Before   b. died before   c. died, before

13. She was fascinated by controversial new _____ genetic
    engineering.
    a. fields such as,   b. fields, such as   c. fields, such as,

14. The mentally ill were _____ the new round of budget cuts.
    a. hurt. By   b. hurt; by   c. hurt by

15. An aged van—dented, grimy, painted in psychedelic _____ into
    the parking lot.
    a. colors—pulled   b. colors pulled   c. colors, pulled

16. Marcia moved to _____ with her company.
    a. Dallas, Texas,   b. Dallas Texas   c. Dallas, Texas

17. The prosecutor kept asking why she had shredded the _____
    a. documents?   b. documents?"   c. documents.

18. She asked for _____ no one stepped forth.
    a. volunteers but   b. volunteers but,   c. volunteers, but

19. Corporations were getting paranoid about _____ viruses in
    large systems.
    a. hackers: planting b. hackers. Planting c. hackers planting

20. They were training for the _____ grueling endurance test.
    a. decathlon a   b. decathlon, a   c. decathlon; a

OVERVIEW   Punctuation regulates the flow of material on the page.
The most important kind is end punctuation, which brings what we are
saying to a complete stop. We use it to set off complete sentences—units
that can stand by themselves and that we can take in one at a time. Three
kinds of complete sentences call for different end punctuation:

STATEMENTS: Oil prices have been moving up and down.
               Readers love novels about British spies.
               Space probes have landed on Venus.

QUESTIONS:	Do our cities have a future? What has happened to the Democratic Party? What is the official language of India?
REQUESTS OR COMMANDS:	Please spare us the details. Send in your coupon now! Sell real estate in your spare time!

To be complete, a sentence needs at least a subject and a complete verb (Probes/*have landed*). In requests and commands, the subject has been deleted and is understood: (*You* should) sell. (*You* should) send in your coupon. Make sure your sentences are marked off by the right end punctuation. Do *not* mark off as if they were complete sentences groups of words that are **sentence fragments**, lacking a possible subject or all or part of a complete verb.

FRAGMENT:	They estimated the cost of coffee breaks. **At 53 cents a minute**.
COMPLETE:	They estimated the cost of coffee breaks **at 53 cents a minute**.
FRAGMENT:	Police officers were outgunned by criminals. **Brandishing semiautomatic rifles**.
COMPLETE:	Police officers were outgunned by criminals **brandishing semiautomatic rifles**.

33a *frag* Sentences and Fragments

Use the period at the end of a complete statement.

A complete statement normally needs at least a subject and a complete verb. Look at the complete verbs that help turn each of the following into a separate sentence:

COMPLETE:	Malpractice insurance **pays** for your doctor's mistakes. Marcia **was selling** billboard space. Drunk drivers **will be sent** to traffic school.

Revise two familiar kinds of incomplete statements that cause **sentence fragments**.

(1) Do not use a period to mark off fragments without both a subject and complete verb. *In the backyard* is a fragment because it does

---

PUNCTUATION MARKS: REFERENCE CHART

COMMA

before coordinators (*and, but, or*)	**34b**
with nonrestrictive adverbial clauses	**34d**
after introductory adverbial clauses	**34d**
with nonrestrictive relative clauses	**34e**
with nonrestrictive modifiers	**35b**
after introductory modifiers	**35c**
with conjunctive adverbs (*therefore, however*)	**34a**
with *especially, namely, for example*	**36e**
with *after all, of course*	**35c**
between items in a series	**36a**
in a series of parallel clauses	**34a**
between coordinate adjectives	**36b**
with dates, addresses, and measurements	**36c**
with parenthetic elements	**37c**
between repeated or contrasted elements	**36d**
with direct quotations	**38a, 38b**

SEMICOLON

between closely related sentences	**34a, 14c**
before conjunctive adverbs	**34c, 14c**
before coordinators between clauses containing commas	**34b**
in a series with items containing commas	**36a**
outside a quotation	**38b**

---

not tell us who does what in the backyard. *Orbiting around Jupiter* is a fragment because (a) it does not tell us *what* is in orbit around Jupiter and (b) it lacks the *is* or *was* that would turn *orbiting* into a complete verb.

NO SUBJECT:	The wing hit the ground. **Spun the plane around**. (What spun?)
COMPLETE:	The wing **hit** the ground and **spun** the plane around.
NO VERB:	Chung worked in Washington. **A lobbyist for Taiwan**.
COMPLETE:	Chung, a lobbyist for Taiwan, worked in Washington.
NO COMPLETE VERB:	We spent hours on the road. **Fighting the traffic**.
COMPLETE:	We spent hours on the road fighting the traffic.
NO SUBJECT OR VERB:	We found the host. **In the jacuzzi**.
COMPLETE:	We found the host in the jacuzzi.

PERIOD	
at end of sentence	**13a, 33a**
for ellipsis	**38c**
with abbreviations	**46a**

COLON	
to introduce a list or an explanation	**36e, 14a**
to introduce a formal quotation	**38a**

DASH	
to show a break in thought	**37a**
before summary at end of sentence	**37a**
to set off modifier with commas	**37a**

QUOTATION MARKS	
with direct quotations	**38a**
for quotation within quotation	**38a**
with end marks	**38b**
with technical terms	**38e**
to set off titles	**45d, 38f**

EXCLAMATION MARK	**33b**
QUESTION MARK	**33b, 38a**
PARENTHESES	**37b**
SLASH	**38a**

All the sentence fragments in this group of examples are caused by a **phrase**—a group of related words that does not have its own subject and verb.

(2) Do not use a period to mark off fragments starting with an unused link like *if* and *whereas* (subordinators) or *who* and *which* (relative pronouns). Words like *if* and *whereas* are meant to link a dependent clause (*if you need me*) to the main clause (*I'll be here* if you need me). When you mark off the *if*-clause by a period, it will be a fragment—even though it has a subject and a complete verb:

FRAGMENT: The clinic will be closed. **If the governor's veto is upheld**.
COMPLETE: The clinic will be closed **if the governor's veto is upheld**.

FRAGMENT:	Charles Schulz created *Peanuts*. **Which became a national institution**.
COMPLETE:	Charles Schulz created *Peanuts*, **which became a national institution**.

(3) Use a period to separate two complete sentences that have been run together. If there is no punctuation to separate two complete sentences, the result is a **fused sentence**. Supply the missing period (or a semicolon to show an exceptionally close relationship):

FUSED:	*Star Trek* became an American myth **it will run forever**.
REVISED:	*Star Trek* became an American myth. **It will run forever**.
	Star Trek became an American myth; **it will run forever**.

SEE **14a** AND **14b** ON REVISING FRAGMENTS AND FUSED SENTENCES.

33b	*?!!*	**Questions and Exclamations**

Signal questions and exclamations.

Not all of our sentences are simple statements, marked off by periods.

(1) Use the question mark to mark direct questions. These appear exactly as you would ask them of another person. ("Who shredded the documents?") Do you remember to use question marks at the end of questions that are long or involved?

QUESTION:	Are our needs shaped by advertisers, or do advertisers cater to our needs**?**

CAUTION: Do not keep the question mark when you convert a direct question to an indirect question. In an indirect question, you no longer use the exact words of the original speaker or writer. You change time and pronouns to show that you are looking at what is said from your own perspective:

DIRECT:	She asked the guide: "Why **do you call** the *Mona Lisa* La Gioconda**?"**
INDIRECT:	She asked the guide why **he called** the *Mona Lisa* La Gioconda.

460

WRONG: She asked the guide why he called the *Mona Lisa* La
                Gioconda?

(2) Use the exclamation mark (rarely!) for emphasis. Use it to
mark an order or a shout, to signal indignation or surprise. Note that the
exclamation mark appears rarely in ordinary prose.

EMPHASIS: Win a trip to Tahiti!
                The jury found him not guilty!

> FOR END MARKS INSIDE OR OUTSIDE A QUOTATION, SEE **38b**.

DISCOURSE EXERCISE 1   Check the following for *sentence fragments,
fused sentences, and unmarked direct questions.* Rewrite the italicized part
of each example, using the right punctuation. Use a period to separate the
two parts of a fused sentence. Join any sentence fragments you find here to
the main sentence *without* punctuation.

EXAMPLE: Voting is a privilege and *responsibility. In democratic
                countries.*
ANSWER: responsibility in democratic countries.

The Voter's Dilemma

1. Many voters have become *disillusioned they stay home.*
2. What is the use of choosing between two *candidates who both dance
   around the issues.*
3. Presidential campaigns have become a media *circus. Why should voters
   bother.*
4. Candidates heed the *polls. And not their own judgment.*
5. Old political warhorses go foraging among the *grassroots. Before they
   support a candidate.*
6. A whistlestop used to be a chance to sway local *voters it's now little
   more than a photo opportunity.*
7. Why does a campaign have to be a demolition *derby won by the last
   battered survivor.*
8. Voters who really care still *exist. In other parts of the world.*
9. In 1989, voters in Moscow for the first time had a *choice they went to
   the polls in large numbers.*
10. Eighty-nine percent voted against the party *candidate. Endorsed by the
    government and the media.*

34	Linking Punctuation

OVERVIEW When several short statements become part of a larger whole, we call each subsentence in the new combined sentence a **clause**. Independent clauses are self-contained; they could easily be separated again by a period.

INDEPENDENT:	We hear much about miracle drugs; however, they often have severe side effects. (one combined sentence)
ALSO RIGHT:	We hear much about miracle drugs. However, they often have severe side effects. (two separate sentences)

Dependent clauses have been welded together more permanently, so that (as in this sentence you are reading) they cannot just be simply pulled apart. In the following example, a dependent clause follows the main clause:

DEPENDENT:	Addiction sounds less grim **when we call it substance abuse**.
WRONG:	Addiction sounds less grim. **When we call it substance abuse**.
	(The dependent clause has become a sentence fragment.)

Much of the basic punctuation on a page signals the connection between two or more clauses that work together in a larger combined sentence. You typically have three choices: semicolon, comma, or no punctuation.

■   The **semicolon** signals a fairly strong break; it could easily be replaced by a period. Think of it as a semi-period; remember that it looks like a hybrid between a period and a comma.

SEMICOLON:	I think; therefore, I am.
PERIOD:	I think. Therefore, I am.

■   The **comma** signals a slighter break. Two linked statements are closely related, but each would still be true without the other:

COMMA:	You may consider rock lyrics harmless, but the censors disagree.
	(Both true separately: You may think them harmless. The censors disagree.)

462

LINKING PUNCTUATION—AN OVERVIEW

SEMICOLON ONLY:

_____ ; _____ .

COORDINATORS:

_____ , and _____ .
_____ , but _____ .
_____ , so _____ .

CONJUNCTIVE ADVERBS:

_____ ; therefore, _____ .
_____ ; however, _____ .
_____ ; _____ , however, _____ .
_____ ; _____ , nevertheless.

SUBORDINATORS:

Restrictive   _____ if _____ .
                       _____ when _____ .

Nonrestrictive   _____ , although _____ .
                       _____ , whereas _____ .

Introductory   If _____ , _____ .
                  When _____ , _____ .

RELATIVE PRONOUNS:

Restrictive   _____ who _____ .
                       _____ that _____ .

Nonrestrictive   _____ , who _____ .
                  _____ , which _____ , _____ .

SPECIAL CONNECTIVES (WITH NOUN CLAUSES):

_____ what _____ .
_____ how _____ .
_____ that _____ .

Country music flourishes, whereas serious jazz is hard to find.
(Both true separately: The one flourishes. The other is hard to find.)

■ We typically use *no punctuation* when the second statement significantly changes (and sometimes turns around) the meaning of the first:

NO COMMA: The Housing Authority evicts its tenants **when they deal drugs**.
(Only when they do.)

To make the right choices, you need to recognize the different links we use to combine two or more clauses in a larger combined sentence. (See also **13f.**)

34a   *CS or /;*   Semicolon Only

Use a semicolon between two paired statements.

Often two statements go together as related information; they are part of the same story: "Power corrupts; absolute power corrupts absolutely." When a semicolon replaces the period, the first word of the second statement is *not* capitalized:

SEMICOLON: The thin look is in; yogurt sales soared.
We constantly coin new words: Governments spread *disinformation*; executives are protected by *golden parachutes*.

CAUTION: Do not use a comma alone to join two independent clauses. A **comma splice** runs on from one independent clause to the next with only a comma between them. (See **14c.**)

COMMA SPLICE: I loved London, it is a wonderful city.
REVISED: I loved London; it is a wonderful city.

COMMA SPLICE: Carol is twenty-eight years old, she might go back to school.
REVISED: Carol is twenty-eight years old; she might go back to school.

Finer Points If you wish, use *commas* instead of semicolons to link three or more clauses that are exceptionally close in meaning and parallel in form:

COMMA: Be brief, be blunt, be gone.

           Students in India demonstrate against the use of English, African nationalists protest against the use of French, young Israelis have no use for the languages once spoken by their parents.

Some writers use the comma between only *two* independent clauses when the logical connection or similarity in structure is especially close. Many teachers and editors object to this practice; avoid it in your own writing.

PEER EDITOR 2 In each of the following combined sentences, two independent clauses would cause a comma splice if joined only by a comma. Help edit these sentences by putting a *semicolon* at the point where the two clauses join. Write down the last word of the first clause and the first word of the second clause; put a semicolon between the two words.

EXAMPLE: Carl's appearance had changed he had spiked hair.
ANSWER: changed; he

1. A boutique is on the ground floor above it is a cheap tourist hotel.
2. A flaming car wreck cannot daunt our superhero he emerges from the inferno intact.
3. Automobile plants in Japan maintain a minimal inventory things are used right away.
4. The sloth is genuinely lethargic its metabolism runs at half the normal rate for animals of its size.
5. A modern zoo is less crowded the animals live in more natural habitats.
6. Poverty is a major problem in our world it is found in every city in the United States.
7. I enjoy running it becomes an almost unconscious act.
8. People were shouting commands everyone with a flashlight began directing traffic.
9. We were once urged to buy and spend urgent messages to conserve are now coming at us from all directions.
10. We fished in the stream until midnight it was illegal really to fish after dark.

465

34b *p or ʌ* | Coordinators

Use a comma when a coordinator links two clauses.

Use a comma before a **coordinating conjunction** (coordinator, for short): *and, but, for, so, or, nor,* and *yet*. Put a comma before—but not after—the *and, but,* or *so*:

COMMA:
The lights dimmed, **and** a roar went up from the crowd.
She remembered the face, **but** she forgot the name.
The picnic fizzled, **for** it started to rain.
The star was late, **so** the warmup band played forever.
We had better apologize, **or** we will never be invited again.
Her parents did not approve of divorce, **nor** did her spouse.
Reporters knew the truth, **yet** no one dared to print it.

(1) Do not use a comma with a coordinator when it merely joins two words or two phrases. In a sentence like the following, the *and* merely adds a second verb to the same clause: "The earthquake *rattled* windows *and toppled* shelves."

NO COMMA:
Farmbelt legislators clamored for tariffs on imports **and** for subsidies for their constituents.

(2) If it is needed for clarity, use a semicolon between clauses with internal commas. The semicolon then marks the major break:

SEMICOLON:
Now in the Big Bend the river encounters mountains in a new and extraordinary way; **for** they lie, chain after chain of them, directly across its way.   Paul Horgan

---

Finer Points   Some writers leave out the comma before a coordinator if the two clauses it links are very short. Some writers prefer a semicolon before *yet*:

NO COMMA:
The rain pelted us **and** the wind howled.
SEMICOLON:
The critics praised Oliver's work; **yet** no one bought his collages.

Technically, a coordinator leaves an added clause grammatically independent, and a period could replace the comma: "We called your answering service twice. *But* there was no message. *So* we went ahead without you." But see the Glossary of Usage for a traditional objection to an *and* or *but* at the beginning of a sentence.

34c   *p ar l;* | Conjunctive Adverbs

Use a semicolon when a conjunctive adverb joins two clauses.

Conjunctive adverbs are adverbs used as connectives: *therefore, however, nevertheless, furthermore, consequently, moreover, accordingly, besides,* as well as *hence, thus, indeed,* and *in fact.* The two statements they join are often linked by a **semicolon** rather than by a period. A period, nevertheless, would still be acceptable:

RIGHT: Business was improving**; therefore**, we changed our plans.

ALSO RIGHT: Business was improving**. Therefore**, we changed our plans.

RIGHT: The hall was nearly empty**; nevertheless**, the curtain rose.

ALSO RIGHT: The hall was nearly empty**. Nevertheless** the curtain rose.

(1) Do not use just a comma with a conjunctive adverb. If a comma replaces the semicolon, the sentence turns into a **comma splice**:

COMMA SPLICE: The weather turned ugly, **therefore** the launch was postponed.

RIGHT: The weather turned ugly**; therefore**, the launch was postponed.

(2) If the conjunctive adverb moves, keep the semicolon at the juncture between the two clauses. Put the semicolon where the two clauses join, even if the connective follows later. Like other adverbs, conjunctive adverbs can shift their position in a sentence:

RECOGNIZING CONJUNCTIVE ADVERBS

Commonly used conjunctive adverbs signal the following relationships:

ADDITION:	furthermore, moreover, similarly, besides, likewise, also
LOGICAL RESULT:	therefore, consequently, accordingly, hence, thus, then
OBJECTION:	however, still, nevertheless, nonetheless, on the other hand
OPTION:	otherwise, instead
EMPHASIS:	indeed, in fact
TIME:	meanwhile, subsequently

Demand had dropped off; **nevertheless**, prices remained high.
Demand had dropped off; prices, **nevertheless**, remained high.
Demand had dropped off; prices remained high, **nevertheless**.

(3) In relatively formal writing, use additional commas. We often pause slightly for conjunctive adverbs; commas, therefore, often set them off from the rest of the second statement. Formal writing usually requires the added punctuation; however much popular writing does without it.

FORMAL: We liked the area; rents, **however,** were impossible.
INFORMAL: We liked the area; rents **however** were impossible.

Note the *two* additional commas when the conjunctive adverb interrupts the second clause.

DISCOURSE EXERCISE 3   Write the italicized part of each combined sentence, adding punctuation as necessary. Which sentences require a *semicolon*; which require a *comma*? (Include the added commas that set off conjunctive adverbs from the second clause.) Do not add punctuation if a coordinator merely joins parts of a single clause.

EXAMPLE: Gershwin developed a brain *tumor and the studio* fired him.
ANSWER: tumor, and the studio

Hollywood and Small-Town America

1. Most early movie moguls came from immigrant *backgrounds but their pictures* showed a sanitized WASP America.
2. The cities were crowded with poor *immigrants therefore the movies* showed idealized rural towns.
3. These idyllic towns had white clapboard houses with *broad verandas and tidy streets* with quaint little shops.
4. The boys living in these houses looked like *Mickey Rooney so the studio* dyed Danny Kaye's hair blond.
5. Selfish people might cause *trouble the people of good will however always* won out in the end.
6. The banker might *be a skinflint a kindly Jimmy-Stewart type would best him nevertheless.*
7. This idyllic Anytown of the early movies is *not really dead in fact Michael J. Fox* recently lived there.
8. Goldwyn and Mayer *are dead but Beaver Cleaver lives on forever* in reruns.
9. Small-town values are *alive and well or our politicians* wouldn't cater to them so eagerly.
10. We dream of a more *innocent America for we want* a world without conflict, drugs, and crime.

34d *p or ʌ* | Subordinators

Use a comma or no punctuation with subordinators.

Subordinating conjunctions (subordinators for short) start **adverbial clauses**—clauses that, like adverbs, tell us when, where, why, or how. Subordinators include words like *if, when, unless, because, although,* and *whereas.*

An *if* or a *because* changes a self-sufficient, independent clause into a **dependent clause**, which normally cannot stand by itself. "If I were in charge" does not become a complete sentence until you answer the question "If you were in charge, *then what?*" ("If I were in charge, *elevator music would be banned.*") Beware of dependent clauses added to a main statement as an afterthought:

FRAGMENT: He failed the test. **Because he ran out of time**.
REVISED: He failed the test **because he ran out of time**.

When you use a subordinator, you need to ask yourself: Should I go on *without punctuation?* Or do I need *a comma?*

(1) Use no comma when a restrictive clause comes last. A **restrictive** clause limits the scope of the main clause, narrowing the possibilities, imposing essential conditions. "I will raise wages" sounds like an unqualified promise. "I will raise wages *after we strike oil*" puts a restriction on the offer. Such restrictive clauses are essential to the meaning of the whole sentence. We do not set them off *when they follow the main clause.*

RESTRICTIVE: Hundreds will perish **if the dam breaks**.
                        Gold prices rise **when the dollar falls**.
                        They would not treat the patient **unless we signed a release**.
                        Check for leaks **before you light the pilot**.
                        I will follow **wherever you go**.

(2) Set off a nonrestrictive clause. Use a comma before *though, although,* and *whereas.* These introduce **nonrestrictive** material, which does not impose essential restrictions or conditions. Rather, they set up a contrast; both statements are separately true. Similarly, *whether or not* and *no matter how* show that the main statement is true regardless:

NONRESTRICTIVE: Hundreds applied for the job, **although the salary was low**.
                        Reactors produce nuclear wastes, **whereas coal leaves inert ash**.
                        The figures were wrong, **no matter what the computer said**.

Note that a word like *when* or *where* may merely introduce extra information when the time or place has already been specified—and stays the same:

NONRESTRICTIVE: She never went back to Georgia, **where she was born**.
                        They arrived in **February, when the almond trees were in bloom**.

(3) Set off any adverbial clause that comes first. When a subordinator joins two clauses, you can reverse their order: Vote for me *if you trust me. If you trust me,* vote for me. When the dependent clause comes first (restrictive or not), use a comma to show where the main clause starts:

COMMA: **If the dam breaks,** hundreds will perish.
                  After we noticed the police car, we drove more slowly.

RECOGNIZING SUBORDINATORS

Subordinators (subordinating conjunctions) signal relationships like the following:

TIME AND PLACE:	when, whenever, while, before, after, since, until, as soon as, as long as, where, wherever
REASON OR CONDITION:	because, if, unless, provided
COMPARISON:	as, as though, as if
CONTRAST:	though, although, whereas, no matter how, even though
RESULT:	so that, in order that

Finer Points Note special uses of some connectives: *though* used as a conjunctive adverb (with a semicolon); *however* used as a subordinator (with a comma):

Henry Ford II went to Yale; **he didn't graduate, though.**
(used like *however*)
His underlings could not please him, **however hard they tried.**
(used like *no matter how*)

34e *p or ʌ* Relative Clauses

Use commas or no punctuation with relative clauses.

Relative clauses are clauses that start with a **relative pronoun:** *who (whose, whom), which,* or *that.* Such clauses add information about one of the nouns (or pronouns) in the main part of the sentence. They may, therefore, appear at different points in the sentence, *interrupting* rather than following the main clause:

AT THE END: The odds favor candidates **who raise tons of money.**
They dug in Kenya, **which is rich in fossil remains**.

471

WEDGED IN:
The address **that they gave us** does not exist.
Those **who know how to talk** can buy on credit.
Creole proverb

To punctuate relative clauses, you need to ask: comma or no comma?

(1) Do not set off restrictive relative clauses. They are **restrictive** when we need them to know "Which one?" or "What kind?" ("A mole is a spy *who burrows into the enemy's bureaucracy*.") Such relative clauses narrow the possibilities. They help us identify; they single out one person or group: the runner *who tripped*; drugs *that kill pain*. Restrictive clauses are *essential* to the author's message.

NO COMMA:
People **who live in glass houses** should not throw stones.   (only those)
Call the woman **whose name appears on this card**. (only her)

Note: The pronoun *that* almost always introduces a restrictive clause. Shortened relative clauses with a pronoun like *that* or *whom* left out are always restrictive:

NO COMMA:
The forms **[that] we sent** were lost in the mail.
The lawyer **[whom] she recommended** charged large fees.

(2) Set off nonrestrictive relative clauses. A **nonrestrictive** clause does not limit the scope of the main clause; it does not single out one from a group or one group among many. We know which one or what kind; we merely learn more about something already identified: Beethoven, *who was deaf*; aspirin, *which kills pain*. Nonrestrictive clauses are *nonessential*; the essential point would come through without them.

COMMA:
Sharks differ from **whales, which surface to breathe**. (all do)
We drove down **Pennsylvania Avenue, which leads past the White House**.

Use *two* commas when the nonrestrictive clause interrupts the main clause:

TWO COMMAS:
Computers, **which perform amazing feats,** do break down.

472

CAUTION: Watch out for commas used mistakenly to set off a restrictive relative clause:

WRONG: Ex-convicts, **who carry guns**, should be sent back to jail.
RIGHT: Ex-convicts **who carry guns** should be sent back to jail.
      (not all ex-convicts, only those who carry guns)

Finer Points   Punctuate other clauses that modify nouns as you would relative clauses. Sometimes a clause starting with *when, where,* or *why* modifies a noun:

RESTRICTIVE: The place **where I work** has no heat.   (which place?)
NONRESTRICTIVE: Minnesota, **where I was born**, has cold winters.

DISCOURSE EXERCISE 4   Which of the following combined sentences need a comma? Check dependent clauses starting with a subordinator or a relative pronoun, paying special attention to the difference between *restrictive and nonrestrictive*. Write the italicized part of each sentence, adding a comma if and where needed.

EXAMPLE: Geological maps stay *the same whereas political* maps become obsolete.
ANSWER: the same, whereas political

The Politics of Maps

1. Nations often change *place names that carry* an unwanted legacy from the past.
2. The name *Stalingrad which acquired a symbolic meaning in World War II later* disappeared from the map.
3. *St. Petersburg which was the capital of Czarist Russia is* now Leningrad.
4. English and French names were widely used *in Africa until the new nations* became independent.
5. After the Belgians *left the Congo names like* Leopoldville disappeared.
6. Maps no longer *show Rhodesia which was named* after a British explorer.
7. Older names *usually survive only if they are not linked* with the colonial past.
8. Similar changes took place *in the Far East where Batavia turned* into Jakarta many years ago.

473

9. A Malaysian city had been named *after Jesselton who was a British empire builder*.

10. The *city that bore his name is now* called Kinabalu.

34f   *p*   Noun Clauses

Do not set off noun clauses.

Use no punctuation when the place of a noun is taken by a clause within a clause. Clauses that take the place of a noun are called **noun clauses**:

NOUN:	The mayor announced **her plans**.
NOUN CLAUSE:	The mayor announced **that she would retire**.
NOUN:	The *Post* first revealed **his identity**.
NOUN CLAUSE:	The *Post* first revealed **who had leaked the news**.

Noun clauses start with words like *that, why, how, where, who,* and *which*: tell me *that you love me*; explain *why you came back*; ask her *where she lives*. Other words that might start a noun clause are *whoever, whatever, whichever*:

NOUN CLAUSE:	They voted for **whomever the party picked**.

CAUTION: Watch out for commas used mistakenly to set off noun clauses.

WRONG:	I finally remembered, **that the store had moved**.
RIGHT:	I finally remembered **that the store had moved**.

PEER EDITOR 5 Each of the following examples *combines two clauses* in a larger sentence. How are the two clauses related, and what would be the right punctuation for the combined sentence? Choose the right answer for the blank space left in each sentence. After the number of the sentence, write *C* for comma, *SC* for semicolon, or *No* for no punctuation.

1. We need regulations to ensure safe working conditions _____ however, some regulations infringe on individual rights.

2. She wasn't a big-time photographer _____ but she had enough work to keep up her studio.
3. Students who needed financial aid _____ were grilled like suspects in a bank robbery.
4. Space exploration is astronomically expensive _____ therefore, only the richest nations take part.
5. The new law aimed at drug dealers _____ who carry guns.
6. If a marriage becomes unglued _____ the partners tend to blame each other.
7. Lawmakers must stop computer crime _____ before it reaches epidemic proportions.
8. When meteors hit the surface _____ they form craters like those made by volcanoes.
9. Her parents tolerated her friends _____ though one was a body builder with a shaved head.
10. The plaintiff was never told _____ why the application was denied.
11. Freedom of speech includes freedom for those _____ whose views make us ill.
12. Jobs were scarce and insecure _____ so my parents left town.
13. The sun, which is the final source of most of our energy _____ is a gigantic nuclear furnace.
14. The furniture was all glass and steel _____ and the walls were a bright red.
15. Human beings could not survive on other planets _____ unless they created an artificial earthlike environment.

---

35   Punctuating Modifiers

OVERVIEW   Modifiers help us build up the basic "Birds fly" or "Americans worship cars" sentences. Much of the added information that we feed into a short sentence blends in without a break:

NO COMMAS:	Botanists sort out plants.
STILL NO COMMAS:	Botanists sort out plants **according to an elaborate system of classification**.
NO COMMAS:	Scientists have ridiculed newcomers.
STILL NO COMMAS:	**Established** scientists have **often** ridiculed newcomers **with revolutionary new ideas**.

At what point do commas or other internal punctuation become necessary as we expand a single subject-verb sentence? To use internal commas, you need to recognize modifiers that may be either essential to the meaning of a sentence—or merely added on as nonessential detail.

Restrictive modifiers are "musts"; they are needed to narrow the possibilities or single out one among several. They are essential to the sentence and are not set off. We use them to narrow the field, to limit a term that otherwise would apply too broadly: cars *built in Japan* (only those); students *eligible for aid* (only those).

Nonrestrictive modifiers are "extras"; they merely add information about something already identified. They are set off by a comma, or *two* commas if they interrupt the sentence. They leave the term they follow unrestricted or generally applicable: the sparrow, *a pesky bird* (applies to all of them); soap operas, *watched by millions* (applies to the whole type).

RESTRICTIVE: Cars **built in Japan** are the nemesis of car makers in other parts of the world. (specifies which cars)

NONRESTRICTIVE: The BMW, **built in Germany**, quickly became the status symbol of the yuppie. (We know which car.)

35a *p* | Unnecessary Commas

Do not use commas between basic sentence elements.

Do not use a comma between the subject and its verb, or between the verb and one or more objects. In the following sentence, there should be no comma between the **compound** (or double) **subject** and the verb:

SUPERFLUOUS COMMA: Unfortunately, **information and common sense, do** not always **prevent** the irresponsible use of dangerous substances.

In addition, do *not* set off the many modifiers that blend into a simple sentence without a break. These include many single-word modifiers: adjectives and adverbs. They also include most prepositional phrases. (See the chart on pp. 478–479.)

WRONG: Forms **with unanswered questions,** will be returned.
RIGHT: Forms **with unanswered questions** will be returned.

WRONG: The next Olympic Games were to be held, **in 1992.**
RIGHT: The next Olympic Games were to be held **in 1992.**

35b ꝑ or ʌ | Restrictive and Nonrestrictive

Know when to use commas with modifiers.

Punctuation may be required when a modifier follows a noun (or a pronoun). **Restrictive** modifiers help us narrow the possibilities or single out one among several. They are an essential part of the sentence and are *not* set off:

RESTRICTIVE: Gamblers **willing to place $1,000 bets** were invited to the tournament. (a somewhat exclusive group)

Nonrestrictive modifiers merely give added information about something already identified. They are set off by a comma, or *two* commas if they interrupt the sentence. They leave the term they follow unrestricted or generally applicable:

NONRESTRICTIVE: My friends, **willing to risk a few quarters,** joined me in the casino. (They all joined in.)

Look for the following:

(1) Set off most appositives. An **appositive** is a second noun that modifies the first. Most appositives are nonrestrictive. They do not winnow one possibility from among several; they answer questions like "*What else* about the person?" or "*What else* about the place?" ("Her aunt, *a lawyer,* lived in Boston, *my favorite city.*") A proper name is usually adequate identification, and the appositive that follows it is set off:

COMMA: She joined the Actors' Theater**, a repertory company**.
COMMAS: H. J. Heinz, **the Pittsburgh pickle packer,** keeps moving up in the food-processing industry.

Occasionally, however, a restrictive appositive helps us tell apart two people of the same name:

NO COMMAS: I find it hard to distinguish between Holmes **the author** and Holmes **the Supreme Court Justice**.

(2) Set off nonrestrictive verbals and verbal phrases. A verbal phrase modifying a noun usually starts with a form like *running, explaining, starting* or like *dressed, sold, taken.* Such phrases are restrictive when used to narrow down a general term or single out one among several:

477

UNNECESSARY COMMAS—A SUMMARY

CAUTION: Avoid commas in the following situations. Omit the circled commas.

■ between subject and verb:

> **The needle** on the dial⊘ **swung** erratically.

■ before an ordinary prepositional phrase:

> She had first flown a plane⊘ **in Ohio** in 1972.

■ with restrictive modifiers and clauses:

> The hunt was on for migrants⊘ **entering the country illegally**.
> American diplomats⊘ **who speak Chinese**⊘ are rare indeed.

■ with coordinators joining words or phrases:

> The Vikings reached Greenland⊘ **and the coast of North America**.

■ after coordinators:

> WRONG: He promised to call **but**⊘ he never did.
> RIGHT: He promised to call, **but he never did**.

NO COMMAS: The person **running the place** talked like a drill sergeant.
                   The restaurant excluded guests **dressed in togas**.

Verbal phrases are nonrestrictive when they merely *tell us more* about something we have already identified:

COMMAS: Our singing telegram, **smiling broadly,** stood in the doorway.
                   We saw the bride, **dressed in white**.

(3) Set off nonrestrictive adjective phrases. An **adjective phrase** is made up of several adjectives, or of an adjective and other material:

- before coordinators joining two dependent clauses:

    He told the court **that** the building had been only partially insured◌ **and that** the policy had lapsed.

- before noun clauses:

    We already know◌ **what the future holds** for the poor of the world.

- after *such as:*

    The new plan called for more teaching of basics, **such as**◌ English and algebra.

- between adjective and noun:

    Clint Eastwood movies are known for their crude, **brutal**◌ **violence**.

- after last items in a series:

    Natives, tourists, **and pickpockets**◌ mingled in the city square.

Note: Other elements *added* to a sentence may require commas in situations similar to those above.

RESTRICTIVE:	We collected containers **suitable for recycling**. (We discarded the others.)
NONRESTRICTIVE:	The climbers, **weary but happy,** started down. (applies to all the climbers) We approached the lake, **smooth as a mirror**. (We have already focused on one lake.)

(4) Use dashes to set off a modifier that already contains one or more commas. The **dashes** then signal the major breaks:

DASHES:	Her sister—**a stubborn, hard-driving competitor**—won many prizes.

Set sentence modifiers off by commas.

Modifiers may modify sentence elements other than nouns. They may also modify the sentence as a whole rather than any part of it. Look for the following:

(1) Know when to set off verbals and verbal phrases modifying a verb. They may be either restrictive or nonrestrictive. Notice the **comma** showing the difference:

RESTRICTIVE:	He always rushed into the office **reading from fan letters just received**.
	(contains main point)
NONRESTRICTIVE:	Deadline newspaper writing is rapid because it cheats, **depending heavily on clichés**.
	(elaborates main point)

(2) Set off long introductory modifiers. Use a **comma** to show where the main sentence starts. Use this comma after prepositional phrases of three words or more:

COMMA:	**Like many good reporters,** they deplored the low status of the journalistic rank and file.
	In the etiquette books of colonial times, females were carefully instructed in the art of passivity.

Set off *introductory verbals and verbal phrases* even when they are short:

COMMA:	**Smiling,** the officer tore up the ticket.
	To start the motor, turn the ignition key.

(3) Always set off verbal phrases modifying the sentence as a whole. Such phrases are often called **absolute constructions**:

COMMA:	**To tell you the truth,** I don't even recall his name.
	The business outlook being rosy, he invested his savings in stocks.
	Our new manager has done well, **considering her lack of experience**.

(4) If you wish, use the optional commas with transitional expressions. Expressions like *after all, of course, unfortunately, on the whole, as a rule,* and *certainly* often help us go on from one sentence to another. Depending on the amount of emphasis you would give such a modifier when reading, make it stand out from the rest of the sentence by a comma:

COMMA:
After all, we are in business for profit.
On the other hand, the records may never be found.
You will submit the usual reports, **of course**.

Sentence modifiers that are set off require *two* commas if they do not come first or last in the sentence:

COMMAS:
Institutions do not, **as a rule,** welcome dissent.
A great many things, **to be sure,** could be said for him.

DISCOURSE EXERCISE 6 Rewrite the following sentences, adding all commas needed for *nonrestrictive and introductory* modifiers.

EXAMPLE:
On the main island of Britain the Welsh hearing English constantly are now mostly bilingual.
ANSWER:
On the main island of Britain, the Welsh, hearing English constantly, are now mostly bilingual.

Bilingual Americans

1. Now as in the past millions of Americans immigrants or native-born are bilingual.
2. In many American homes the older people speak Spanish to kids answering back in English.
3. Some rural folks in Louisiana a former French colony still speak Cajun French.
4. To help Chinese-speaking children some schools offer classes taught in Chinese.
5. The English-Only movement supported by some educators but fought by many others opposes bilingual education.

PEER EDITOR 7 Punctuate the following sentences. For each blank, write C for comma, NC for no comma, or D for dash.

1. In spite of repeated promises _____ the shipment never arrived.
2. The agency collected debts _____ from delinquent customers.
3. Whipped by the wind _____ five-foot swells splash over the deck.

4. The book told the story of Amelia Earhart _____ a true pioneer.

5. An engraved receipt was promised to listeners _____ sending in large donations.

6. I looked with amazement at the pots _____ filled with large snapping Dungeness crabs.

7. Working on the pitching and rolling deck _____ we hauled up the heavy nets.

8. The owner, a large woman with mean eyes _____ watched us the whole time.

9. Back at the wharf _____ we sipped hot coffee, trying to get warm.

10. The city, on the other hand _____ has shown no interest in the proposed arena.

11. The mechanics working on a competitor's car _____ are racing against the clock.

12. The wooden benches, bolted to the planks _____ were torn loose by the waves.

13. My uncle—a jovial, fast-talking man _____ sold earthquake insurance.

14. Their performance has been unsatisfactory _____ to say the least.

15. A blizzard of invoices _____ marked "Past Due" is designed to frighten the customer.

---

36   Coordination

OVERVIEW   When we coordinate parts of a sentence, we make similar or related sentence parts work together. We pull together bits of information that might have appeared in separate statements: "The Russians took *first place*. They also took *second place*. And (surprise!) they took *third place*." Coordination enables us to line up the three related sentences in a single sentence: "The Russians finished *first, second, and third*." The commas together with the coordinator *and* help us tie the three related sentence parts together.

When and how do we use commas with several sentence elements of the same kind? Look at the following preview:

SERIES: Russian gymnasts **finished first, second, and third.**

COORDINATE ADJECTIVES: Hearst newspapers were legendary for their **slanted, sensational** reporting.

DATES:	The world went back to war on **September 1, 1939**.
ADDRESSES:	The return address was **48 Broadway, Phoenix, Arizona**.
MEASURES:	Our new center stood **six foot, three inches** in his bare feet.
CONTRAST:	**People, not regulations,** should come first.
ENUMERATION:	New sports became popular: **soccer, jogging, lacrosse**.

36a *p or ⌃* | Series

Use commas between items in a series.

A **series** is a set of three or more parts of the same kind: *red, white,* and *blue; single, married,* or *divorced; life, liberty,* and the *pursuit* of happiness. Link the elements in a set of three by commas, with the last comma followed by an *and* or *or* that ties the whole group together. The three elements in a series might be verbs, adjectives, or nouns among other sentence parts:

VERBS:	On the trail, we **talked, laughed, and sang**.
ADJECTIVES:	The hills were bright with **red, white, and brown** poppies.
NOUNS:	Only 18 percent of this country's 56 million families are conventionally "nuclear," with **breadwinning fathers, homemaking mothers, and resident children**. Jane Howard

Not every series follows the simple one,-two,-and-three pattern:

(1) The basic *A, B, and C* pattern can be stretched to four elements or more:

COMMAS:	The stand sold **nuts, raisins, apples,** and **every other kind** of organic lunch.
	The repertory of the humpback whales includes **groans, chirps, clicks, bugles,** and **roars**.

483

(2) Groups of words that form a series may already contain commas. To prevent misreading, use **semicolons** to show the major breaks:

SEMICOLONS: Three people were left out of her will: **John, her greedy brother; Martin, her no-account nephew;** and **Helen, her one-time friend**.

CAUTION: In informal or journalistic writing, the last comma in a series is often left out. Many teachers, however, require the use of the last comma. Use it to be safe:

LAST COMMA: Computer programs can now check student papers **for spelling errors, awkward sentences,** and **sexist phrases**.

Finer Points The *and* or the *or* that usually ties the series together may be left out. In the following example, the writer makes sure we give equal weight to each item in a set of four that uses commas only:

COMMAS ONLY: The idea was to pool all the needs of all those who had in one way or another been bested by their environment—**the disabled, the sick, the hungry, the ragged**.

PEER EDITOR 8 Rewrite the following sentences, adding *series punctuation* and other needed marks.

1. In the tabloids homelessness the national debt and economic disaster do not exist.
2. The room is fitted with three turntables a huge electric clock and a cantilevered microphone over a console of switches buttons and dials.
3. For their new friends yoga was a way of life a cause and a religion.
4. Advertising sells good services candidates and ideas.
5. The electronic message center can store incoming calls signal waiting messages distribute the same message to many recipients and route outgoing calls on the least expensive lines.
6. After a while the messenger arrives with the cholesterol special a triple order of bacon two fried eggs over easy and bagels split and buttered.
7. The squatters lived in shantytowns without sanitation garbage pickup or running water.
8. Women began to speak and write openly about sexism harassment and abuse.

36b *p or ʌ* Coordinate Adjectives

Use a comma between coordinate adjectives.

Coordinate adjectives work together to modify the same noun: a *tall, handsome* stranger. They are interchangeable adjectives; use a comma between them when you can reverse their order: *slanted, sensational* reporting or *sensational, slanted* reporting.

COMMA: The **snoopy, brash** new magazine pilloried the most **annoying, appalling** people in New York and the nation.

Use the comma only when an *and* could take the place of the comma:

RIGHT: a **hypocritical, cliché-ridden** speech   (hypocritical and cliché-ridden)
a **disappointed, angry** customer   (both disappointed and angry)

Do not use the comma when the order of two adjectives cannot be changed, or when an added *and* would not sound right:

NO COMMA: a **heavy wooden** table   (NOT: a **wooden heavy** table)
warm woolen socks   (NOT: **woolen warm** socks)

CAUTION: Often an adjective combines with a noun to indicate a type of person or object: a *public servant*, a *short story*, a *black market*. An adjective that comes before such a combination modifies the combination as a whole.

NO COMMA: a **long** *short story* (not "long *and* short")
a **dedicated** *public servant* (not "dedicated *and* public")

36c *p or ʌ* Dates and Addresses

Use commas with information in several parts.

Dates, addresses, page references, and the like often come in several parts, kept separate from each other by a comma. The last item is followed by a comma if the sentence continues:

DATE:	The date was **Tuesday, January 30, 1990.** On **March 28, 1979,** several water pumps stopped working at Three Mile Island, a nuclear power plant near Harrisburg, Pennsylvania.
ADDRESS:	Please send my mail to **113 Robin Street, Birdsville, Alabama,** starting the first of the month.
REFERENCE:	The quotation is from **Chapter 5, page 43, line 7,** of the second volume.

Remember the comma that separates city and state:

At the **Lordstown, Ohio,** and **South Gate, California,** plants, laser-equipped robots measure car bodies to make sure they meet exact specifications.

Commas also separate the parts of *measurements* employing more than one unit of measurement. Here the last item is usually *not* separated from the rest of the sentence:

MEASURE:	The boy is now **five feet, seven inches** tall. **Nine pounds, three ounces** is an unusual weight for this fish.

Note: The comma is left out if the day of the month precedes rather than follows the month: "12 November 1989."

36d *p or ʌ* Repetition and Contrast

Use commas to signal repetition or contrast.

Use commas between expressions that repeat the same idea:

REPETITION:	**Produce, produce!** This is the law among artists.
RESTATEMENT:	We were there in the nine days before Christmas, **the Navidad**.

Use the same comma in sentences that line up several examples or implications of the same idea in parallel form:

Undergraduate education must prepare the student **not to walk away from choices, not to leave them to the experts**.   Adele Simmons

Use commas also to separate words or phrases that establish a *contrast*:

CONTRAST: The prices were **stunning,** the food **average.**
We should **welcome, not discourage,** dissent.

Many entering freshmen and their parents seek an education that leads to **job security, not critical and independent thinking.**　　Adele Simmons

---

36e :/ or ∧ | Enumeration

Use a colon or comma to introduce examples and explanations.

We often need punctuation when we continue a sentence to illustrate (give examples) or to enumerate (list several items).

(1) Use the colon to introduce an explanation or a more detailed list for something already mentioned. The **colon** then means "as follows":

EXPLANATION: Marcia had a single wish**: a home computer.**
LIST: Military life abounds with examples of regimentation**: fixed hours, a rigid meal schedule, the dress code.**

Avoid a colon after a verb (unless you are introducing an elaborate chart or list, usually set off as a separate column or the like).

WRONG: His two mistakes were: obeying orders and offending Congress.
RIGHT: His two mistakes were obeying orders and offending Congress.
RIGHT: The park rules forbade:
　　(1) walking on the grass
　　(2) sleeping in the park
　　(3) picking flowers
　　(4) riding bicycles
　　(5) kissing in public
　　(6) otherwise acting like a human being

487

(2) Use a comma when explanation or illustration follows transitional expressions. Use the comma before *such as* or *especially*:

COMMA:	The article described computer languages, **such as** Fortran.
TWO COMMAS:	Recent immigrants, **especially** Vietnamese, now live downtown.

Use a comma before and after *namely, for example, for instance,* and *that is*:

TWO COMMAS:	American colleges neglect major world languages, **for example, Chinese and Russian.**

DISCOURSE EXERCISE 9   Where do the following sentences need commas to show *coordination* of similar or related sentence parts? Which of them need additional punctuation, such as colons or semicolons? Rewrite the sentences, adding all necessary punctuation.

The Buck Starts Here

1. The Bureau of Engraving and Printing in Washington D.C. and the mints in Philadelphia Pennsylvania and Denver Colorado are the nation's money factories.
2. For Americans today money is the ticket to the good life not the source of all evil.
3. For the Bureau money is a product made according to strict specifications durable washable paper gummy sticky ink and colored specks of fiber designed to foil counterfeiters.
4. Part of the Bureau's job is to replace currency that has been torn burned soaked and chewed.
5. Banks weed out bills too limp too faded or too creased to be of further use.
6. Citizens from Columbia South Carolina and Corpus Christi Texas send in evidence of lost currency incinerated mattresses scorched filing cabinets and a cow's stomach with the remains of several hundred dollars.
7. The printing presses print sheet after sheet of shiny new ones fives and tens.
8. The Philadelphia mint produces 35 million sparkling gleaming coins a day.
9. Inspectors weed out mistakes such as one-dollar bills with the five-dollar imprint on the back.
10. Collectors pay good money for botched coins for example off-center pennies.

PEER EDITOR 10   Help choose the right punctuation for *coordinated sentence parts*. What should be the punctuation at the blank space in each of the following sentences? Put *C* (for comma) or *NC* (for no comma) after the number of the sentence.

1. Bumper stickers _____ graffiti, and buttons give inarticulate people a chance to express themselves.
2. The company had moved its offices to Atlanta _____ Georgia.
3. Young journalists dream of exposing corrupt _____ public officials.
4. Seven feet, two inches _____ was unusual even for a basketball player.
5. The final clue appeared in Chapter 8 _____ page 148.
6. They had started their shop as a hobby _____ not as a business.
7. Kidnappings _____ bombings, and armed attacks had become commonplace.
8. Jonathan had come to Jamestown, Virginia _____ from Liverpool, England.
9. He loved Italian opera, such as _____ *Madame Butterfly*.
10. She used the new software to conduct a quick _____ thorough search for articles on tax reform.

---

37   Parenthetic Elements

OVERVIEW   Use dashes, parentheses, or commas to set off parenthetic elements—elements that interrupt the normal flow of thought. They suspend the normal traffic of sentence elements for a while the way an officer might briefly halt motor traffic to let a pedestrian cross.

Where and how do we use dashes, parentheses, and commas to signal such brief interruptions? Look at the following preview:

SHARP BREAK:	He opened the door—**a serious mistake**.
ASIDE:	The trophy **(her first)** stood on the mantelpiece.
DIRECT ADDRESS:	Your friends, **John,** are worried about you.
COMMENT:	The loan was denied, **it seems**.
TAG OPENING:	**No,** she is not here.
TAG QUESTION:	She is your friend, **isn't she**?
UNUSUAL ORDER:	Work, **for her father's generation,** was a religion.

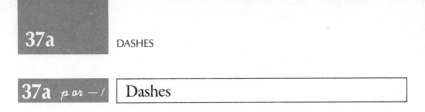

37a par —/   Dashes

Use the dash—sparingly—to signal a sharp break.

A speaker may pause for dramatic effect. Or a speaker may stop in the middle of a sentence to supply some missing detail or additional clarification. In writing, set such material off from the rest of a sentence by **dashes** (made up of two hyphens in typed manuscript).

Overuse of the dash in ordinary prose creates a disjointed, thinking-out-loud effect. Use dashes to do the following:

(1) Make a word or phrase stand out for emphasis. Use the dash (or dashes) to produce a dramatic or climactic effect:

DRAMATIC BREAK: Every time we look at one of the marvels of modern technology, we find a by-product—**unintended, unpredictable, and often lethal**.

It seems possible that more than two billion people—**almost half of the human beings on earth**—would be destroyed in the immediate aftermath of a global thermonuclear war.   Carl Sagan, "The Nuclear Winter," *Parade*

(2) Set off a complete sentence that interrupts another sentence. Use the dash when there is no connective or relative pronoun to provide a transition. (Note that the first word of the interrupting sentence is *not* capitalized.)

INSERTED POINT: The cranes—**these birds were last sighted three years ago**—settled down on the marsh.

(3) Set off modifiers that would normally require commas but that already contain internal commas. Dashes then signal the stronger breaks:

COMMAS IN MODIFIER: The old-style family—**large, closely knit, firmly ruled by the parents**—is becoming rare.

(4) Set off a list that interrupts rather than follows a clause. Dashes take the place of the colon that would normally signal that a list follows:

INSERTED LIST: The group sponsored performers—**dancers, poets, musicians**—from around the world.

(5) After an introductory list, show where the sentence starts over with a summarizing *all, these,* **or** *those*:

LIST FIRST: **Arabs, Japanese, Vietnamese, South Americans**—all these are a familiar part of the campus scene.

Finer Points   For special effect, set off a humorous afterthought or an ironic aside. The dash then signals a meaningful pause:

IRONY: Traditionally, novels are read in the United States by 1.7 percent of the population—**which somewhat reduces their clout.**   Richard Condon, "That's Entertainment!" *Harper's*

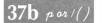

Parentheses

Put parentheses around less important material (or mere asides).

Parentheses signal facts or ideas mentioned in passing:

ASIDE: The University of Mexico was founded in 1553 (almost a century before Harvard).

Parentheses are useful in the following special situations:

(1) Use parentheses for a quick interspersed explanation or clarification:

QUICK HELP: The lowest forms of life, such as the amoebae, normally **(that is, barring accidents)** do not die.   Susanne K. Langer

(2) Use parentheses for optional backup information. Use parentheses around dates, addresses, page references, chemical formulas, and similar information if it might interest some readers but is not an essential part of the text: (*p. 34*) (*first published in 1910*) (*now called Market Street*).

CAUTION: When the inserted aside is a complete sentence (*this is an example*), do not capitalize the first word. When a sentence in parentheses begins *after* end punctuation, end punctuation is required inside the final parenthesis:

OUTSIDE:	The Liverpool fans arrived early **(to start the riot)**.
INSIDE:	Local British soccer teams were banned from the continent. **(The national team was allowed to play**.)

FOR THE USE OF PARENTHESES IN PARENTHETICAL DOCUMENTATION, SEE 51a.

37c Commas for Parenthetic Elements

Use a comma, or commas, to signal slight interruptions.

Use commas with parenthetic elements that blend into a sentence with only a slight break.

(1) Use commas when you address the reader or comment on what you are saying:

DIRECT ADDRESS:	Few remember, **dear reader,** the crash of 1929.
COMMENT:	A good divorce, **you must remember,** will last you a lifetime.
	Romance, **it seems,** is not the same as a relationship.

(2) Use commas to set off introductory tags. These include greetings and exclamations, as well as an introductory *yes* or *no*. Such introductory tags frequently precede a statement in conversation and in informal writing:

TAG OPENING:	**Why,** 'tis a loving and a fair reply. *Hamlet*
	Yes, beggars can't be choosers.

(3) Use commas to set off echo questions. Such **tag questions** are often added to a statement to ask for agreement or confirmation:

TAG QUESTION:	You are my friend, **aren't you?**
	They signed the agreement, **didn't they?**

(4) Use commas for slight breaks caused by unusual word order. In sentences like the following, the italicized parts have changed their usual position in the sentence:

UNUSUAL ORDER: Laws, **to be cheerfully obeyed,** must be both just and practicable.
The Spaniards, **at the height of their power,** were great builders of towns.

(5) Use commas to suggest a thoughtful pause. Commas may take the place of dashes to set off a word for emphasis. They suggest a thoughtful pause rather than a dramatic break:

PAUSE: We should act, **and suffer,** in accordance with our principles.
People cannot, **or will not,** put down the facts.

DISCOURSE EXERCISE 11   What marks—dashes, parentheses, commas—need to be added to the following sentences for satisfactory punctuation of *parenthetic elements*? Rewrite the italicized part of each sentence, adding all necessary punctuation.

EXAMPLE: *Fusion (the philosopher's stone of modern alchemists promises* unlimited cheap and safe energy.
ANSWER: Fusion (the philosopher's stone of modern alchemists) promises

Running Out of Energy

1. Most of the energy we use—whether *from coal oil or water ultimately comes* from the sun.
2. We use up our fossil *fuels (as ecologists have told us for years at an alarming rate*
3. Politicians (and investors) talk less now about alternative *sources (wind power solar energy*
4. Geothermal power in one's backyard, unless there is *a geyser on the property is just not feasible*.
5. *Nuclear power though first heralded* as a boon to humanity, has become a huge headache for utility companies.
6. Nuclear fuel would create an enormous waste problem (as indeed *there is already with our existing uranium plants*
7. Plants like *Three Mile Island you will remember were once thought* perfectly safe.

8. The Chernobyl disaster (at first *played down by the Soviet authorities* cast a *radioactive pall* over the prospects for nuclear power in Europe.
9. *Americans Russians Germans the French these and other nations are* having second thoughts about the atom.
10. New parties like the Greens clamor for nuclear-free zones. *(The Greens are German environmentalists*

PEER EDITOR 12   When editing quoted passages or transcriptions of dialogue, look for the interruptions and asides that are part of spoken English. Copy the following sentences, adding all punctuation needed for *parenthetic elements*.

1. Why this town my friends has weathered far worse storms.
2. Well Your Honor that is only one version of the incident. Other witnesses you realize have told a different story.
3. To change the rules all the time we revised them twice last year does not make sense does it?
4. Well this theory it seems to me was rejected long ago.
5. Pride in the immigrant past loyalty to family and compassion for the unfortunate these it appears will be the themes of our campaign.
6. Why if I were you I would return the whole shipment to the company.

---

38   Quotation

OVERVIEW   One of our basic responsibilities as writers is to distinguish between our own words or ideas and those of others. Whenever we report what someone else has said—and whenever we draw on a printed source—we need to choose between two ways of handling quoted material. We use **direct quotation** when we quote someone verbatim, exactly word for word. We then use quotation marks as a signal that says: "Transcription of someone else's *exact* language coming up." Direct quotation ranges from complete sentences or longer passages to quoted words or phrases:

FULL QUOTATION: Mark Twain said: "One man's comma is another man's colon."

PUNCTUATING QUOTATIONS—AN OVERVIEW

STANDARD:	Keats said, "Truth is beauty."
FORMAL:	The rules were explicit: "No guns allowed."
QUOTED PHRASE:	The cry of "Yanks go home" was heard again.
SPLIT QUOTATION:	"Today," she said, "we start anew."
	"We accept," she said. "We cannot wait."
QUOTE-WITHIN-QUOTE:	He said, "Stop calling me 'Honey.'"
QUOTED QUESTION:	She always asked, "Where were you?"
QUESTIONED QUOTE:	Did she really say, "I don't care"?
OMISSION:	The law says: "All businesses . . . require a license."
ADDITION:	The entry read: "My birthday [April 4] was a disaster."
INDIRECT:	He always asked where I had been.

PARTIAL QUOTATION: One engineer called the company's drug-testing program "a paranoid overreaction."

We use **indirect quotation** when we put someone else's ideas in our own words. Indirect quotation enables us to condense and get at the gist of a statement or a passage (and to show that we understood what the person said). In indirect quotation, we do *not* use quotation marks. We rely on an introductory source statement or credit tag to inform the reader who is likely to ask: "Who said?"

INDIRECT QUOTATION: The National Academy of Sciences reports that the cholesterol we were supposed to give up may not be bad for us after all.
Dreams, according to Freud, revealed repressed conflicts buried in the subconscious.

Study different ways of introducing and marking direct quotations. Look at how we place quotation marks in relation to other punctuation. Know how to show deletions, additions, or other changes in the original text.

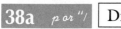

38a *p or "/* | Direct Quotation

Use quotation marks whenever you repeat someone's exact words.

Use quotation marks to enclose material you quote directly, word for word. Use a comma to separate the quotation from the **credit tag**—the statement that identifies the source. Use a colon for a somewhat more formal or emphatic introduction:

COMMA: The Irish essayist Robert Lynd once said, "The last person in the world whose opinion I would take on what to eat would be a doctor."
                 "News stories deal with food as if it were a foreign agent," the article said.
COLON: The rule says: "No tools will be taken from this building."

(1) Check punctuation if the credit tag interrupts a quotation. Use commas before and after if the credit tag splits one complete sentence:

COMMAS: "Both marijuana and alcohol," **Dr. Jones reports,** "slow reaction times on a whole spectrum of tasks."

Use a comma before and a period (or semicolon) after if the credit tag splits two complete sentences. Avoid a **comma splice**:

COMMA SPLICE: "Language habits are changing," the article said, "a lover is now a significant other."
PERIOD: "Language habits are changing," the article said. "Love is now a relationship."
SEMICOLON: "Language habits are changing," the article said; "forming close ties is now called bonding."

No comma is required when the credit tag follows a question or exclamation:

NO COMMA: "To rest is to rust!" the poster said.

(2) Use no comma with partial quotations. Use no comma when you quote only part of a sentence, or when a very short quoted sentence becomes part of a larger statement:

NO COMMA: Goodman said that food should not be considered a potential poison; it "should be eaten and enjoyed."
"The small family lives better" was the official slogan of the campaign to curb population growth.

(3) Use single quotation marks when you shift to a quotation within a quotation:

SINGLE MARKS: He said, "People who say 'Let me be honest with you' seldom are."
As Goodman says, "The urge to take charge of our lives has led us headlong into the arms of the 'experts.'"

(4) Type long quotations as block quotations. Set off quotations of more than four typed lines—*no* quotation marks, indented *ten* spaces. Do not indent the first line of such **block quotations**:

```
The sense of outrage felt by the relatives of
homicide victims was expressed, for instance, by
David H. Berg, a criminal lawyer, in an article in
Newsweek:
```

(10 spaces) ⟶

```
                      A deputy sheriff held my brother's skull for
          a photograph that appeared in the center of
          the front page. . . .  The suffering of my
          family is not unique.  Someone is murdered
          by a gunshot every 48 minutes in America,
          about 10,000 people a year, a figure that
          has quadrupled since my brother's death.
```

Finer Points   Set off lines of poetry as block quotations, but center them on the page (indent fewer than ten spaces if necessary):

SET OFF: Plath had an uncanny gift for setting up ironic contrasts,
             as in the opening lines of her poem "The Water Rat":
                  Droll, vegetarian, the water rat
                  Saws down a reed and swims from his limber grove,
                  While the students stroll or sit,
                  Hands laced, in a moony indolence of love . . .

You may run in one or two lines of poetry with your continuous text. A **slash** (with a space on either side) then shows where a new line begins:

RUN-IN: With her usual gift for upsetting conventional expecta-
                 tions, Plath makes the rat seem amusing and harmless:
                 "Droll, vegetarian, the water rat / Saws down a reed. . . ."

| **38b** *p or "/* | **End Marks in Quotations** |

End quotations correctly.

Remember to use quotation marks to *end* your quotation, and know where to place them in relation to other marks.

(1) Keep commas inside, semicolons outside a quotation:

COMMA: As he said, "Don't worry about me," the boat pulled
                 away.
SEMICOLON: You said, "I don't need sympathy"; therefore, I didn't
                 offer any.

(2) Keep end punctuation inside the quotation except in special situations. Make sure a period comes before a final quotation mark:

PERIOD: The letter said: "You have been selected to receive a
                 valuable gift."

Usually, a question mark or exclamation mark will also come before the final quotation mark. However, keep it *outside* the quotation if you are asking a question or exclaiming about the quotation:

QUOTED QUESTION: He asked, "Where are they now?"
QUESTIONED QUOTE: Who said, "To err is human"**?**

QUOTED SHOUT: She shouted: "The dam broke!"
SHOUTED QUOTE: He actually said: "You don't count"**!**

(3) Do not normally duplicate a terminal mark at the end of a quotation. Use only one question mark when you ask a question about a question:

Did you ever ask, "What can I do to help?"

DISCOURSE EXERCISE 13 Rewrite the italicized part of each sentence to add marks needed for satisfactory punctuation of *quoted material*. Pay special attention to the marks at the end of a quotation.

EXAMPLE: Tabloids love headlines like "Fergie Pregnant *with Sextuplets?*

ANSWER: with Sextuplets?"

Alien Space Mummy Found in Glass Coffin

1. A recent article in *Smithsonian* magazine was titled: "With Tabloids, 'Zip! You're *in Another World!*

2. The world of tabloids is what science fiction writers call a "parallel *universe*

3. In the words of the *Smithsonian* author, "It's like ours, but *with more gusto!*

4. "Cave Explorers Find *Alien Mummy! proclaimed one* screaming headline.

5. The article claimed that a Turkish scientist had found a humanlike creature with green skin and wings "in a glass coffin that dates back to the *Ice Age*

6. "With a creature such *as this the scientist said I'm not* at all certain it really is dead."

7. "300-lb. Mom Swaps Twins *for Cookies said another* recent heading.

8. Perhaps this was the same mom who "dyes twins red and green so she can *tell them apart!*

9. Favorite topics include homicidal spouses ("Ghoulish Husband *Turns Wife into Goulash*

10. Who could pass up another recent classic, "Woman *Eaten by Pigs*

PEER EDITOR 14 What punctuation, if any, is missing at the blank space in each of the following passages? Write it after the number of the passage. Write *No* if no punctuation is necessary. (Make no changes in capitalization.)

1. The psychologist said _____ The accidents will be simulated."

2. The lead actor had what *Time* magazine calls "shirt-ad looks _____

3. Where does it say, "No minors are allowed _____

4. According to Rachel Carson, "Sir James Clark Ross set out from England in command of two ships 'bound for the utmost limits of the navigable globe _____

5. The first wheelchair races in the history of the Olympic Games marked an "emotional milestone _____ for disabled spectators and athletes.
6. "The main problem," the commission said _____ is insufficient training of personnel."
7. "The main problem is not mechanical defects," the report said _____ it is human error."
8. "What do you mean—'deep pockets _____ the governor asked.
9. He just mumbled _____ Excuse me" and staggered on.
10. She asked, "Why have the regulations not been followed _____

38c   *p or "/* | Insertions and Omissions

Use special marks to show changes you have made in the original text.

Signal insertions and omissions:

(1) Identify comments of your own. Put them in **square brackets**:

ADDITION: The note read: "Left Camp B Wednesday, April 3 [actually April 4]. Are trying to reach Camp C before we run out of supplies."

If your keyboard does not have square brackets, compose them by using a slash and two horizontal lines:

```
In the words of the judge, "the members of the tribe
/‾the Paiutes‾/ have clearly been denied their treaty
rights."
```

(2) Show that you have left out unnecessary or irrelevant material. Indicate the omission by three spaced periods (called an **ellipsis**):

OMISSION: The report concluded on an optimistic note: "All three patients . . . are making remarkable progress toward recovery."

If the omission occurs after a complete statement in the original text, use a sentence period and then add the ellipsis. (Use four spaced periods if you leave out a whole sentence.)

"To be a bird is to be alive more intensely than any other living creature, man included. . . . They live in a world that is always present, mostly full of joy." So wrote N. J. Berrill, Professor of Zoology at McGill University.

Finer Points To indicate *extensive omissions* (a line or more of poetry, a paragraph or more of prose), you may use a single typed line of spaced periods.

38d *p or "/* Indirect Quotation

Do not use quotation marks when you put someone else's ideas into your own words.

In an **indirect quotation**, you look at the time frame and the people from your (and not the original author's) perspective. "She said, 'I adore you'" becomes "She said *she adored me*." Look at two ways of introducing indirect quotations:

(1) Use no comma when an indirect quotation comes into a sentence as a noun clause. Indirectly quoted statements are often noun clauses introduced by *that*. Indirectly quoted questions are often noun clauses introduced by words like *whether, why, how,* and *which*. Remember: *No* introductory comma or colon, *no* quotation marks.

DIRECT:	The mayor replied, "I doubt the wisdom of such a move."
INDIRECT:	The mayor replied **that she doubted the wisdom of such a move**.
DIRECT:	The artist asked, "Which of the drawings do you like best?"
INDIRECT:	The artist asked **which of the drawings I liked best.**

(2) Use a comma (or commas) when an indirect quotation is introduced or interrupted by a parenthetical credit tag.

COMMA:	**According to the mayor,** the initiative was a foolish move.
COMMAS:	Which of the drawings, **he wondered**, did I like best?

501

As Gandhi remarked, the first consequence of nonviolent action is to harden the heart of those who are being assaulted by charity. But, **he continued,** all the while they are being driven to a frenzy of rage, they are haunted by the terrible knowledge of how wrong they are. Michael Harrington

Even in an indirect quotation, you may want to keep part of the original wording. Use quotation marks to show you are repeating selected words or phrases exactly as they were used:

QUOTED PHRASE: Like Thackeray's daughters, I read *Jane Eyre* in childhood, carried away **"as by a whirlwind."**   Adrienne Rich

---

DISCOURSE EXERCISE 15   The following quotations are from Richard Rodriguez' *Hunger of Memory*, the story of a young Mexican-American and his assimilation into American society. Convert all sentences to *indirect quotation* (but keep special quoted phrases in quotation marks).

A Bilingual Childhood

1. Richard Rodriguez remembers: "I was a bilingual child, but of a certain kind: 'socially disadvantaged.'"
2. He tells us: "I had been preceded by my older brother and sister to a neighborhood Roman Catholic school."
3. He was surprised: "I was fated to be the 'problem student.'"
4. Rodriguez says about his family: "We were the foreigners on the block."
5. Speaking Spanish at home, he and his family felt: "We are speaking now the way we never speak out in public—we are together."

38e "/ or ital | Words Set Off

Use quotation marks or italics (underlining) for words outside your normal vocabulary.

Set off the following:

(1) Use quotation marks to show that an expression is not your own:

IRONIC: At a New York restaurant, lone diners share companionship over pasta at a special **"friendship table."**

However, avoid apologetic quotation marks for slang or offensive language:

APOLOGETIC:	Many highly skilled positions have been "infiltrated" by women.
BETTER:	Many highly skilled positions have been filled by women.

(2) Use quotation marks or italics for technical words or words discussed as words. Italics are shown by underlining in a typed manuscript.

TECHNICAL:	She described the "Skinner box," a device used by behaviorist psychologists.
WORD AS WORD:	The word *comet* comes from the Greek *aster kometes,* meaning long-haired star.

(3) Use italics to identify foreign words. Italicize words borrowed from foreign languages and not yet fully assimilated:

FOREIGN:	For a Bolivian *campesino,* the pay for a bird for the illegal parrot trade is not bad.
	Young Latin American men are very touchy these days about *machismo,* best translated as "an emphasis on masculinity." Linda Wolfe, "The Machismo Mystique," *New York*

Many legal and scientific terms borrowed from Latin or Greek belong in this category:

LEGAL:	A writ of *certiorari* is used by a superior court to obtain judicial records from an inferior court or a quasi-judicial agency.
BOTANICAL:	The California live oak—*Quercus agrifolia*—began to evolve more than ten million years ago.

38f *"/ or ital* | Titles or Names Set Off

Use quotation marks or italics as required to set off titles or names.

Know the kinds of titles and names that need to be set off:

(1) Distinguish between whole publications and their parts. Put quotation marks around the titles of poems, articles, songs, and other pieces that would normally be *part* of a larger publication ("The Tiger"). Italicize (underline in typing) the title of a *complete* publication—a magazine, newspaper, or book (*The Poems of William Blake*).

PUBLICATION: The index to *The New York Times* devoted three column inches to the heading "Sex" in 1952.
Joan Didion's "Notes of a Native Daughter" was reprinted in *Slouching Towards Bethlehem*.

Do *not* use italics when naming the Bible or its parts (or other sacred writings: Talmud, Koran).

SCRIPTURE: She opened the Bible and read from the Book of Job.

(2) Italicize the titles of works of art or entertainment. Italicize (underline) the titles of plays, major musical works including operas and ballets, movies, television and radio programs, and such works of art as paintings and sculptures:

ENTERTAINMENT: My aunt wanted us to watch *Romeo and Juliet* or *Swan Lake* rather than *I Love Lucy* or *The Price Is Right*.
ART: Every summer, an army of tourists troops past the *Mona Lisa*.

(3) Italicize the names of ships and aircraft. Italicize (underline) the names of ships and other craft, including space vehicles, planes, or trains: the *Queen Mary, Apollo IX*, the *Hindenburg*.

SHIPS: The ill-fated *Titanic* became one of the best-known ships of all time.
TRAINS: The *California Zephyr* and the other great trains will live only in legend.

FOR MORE ON ITALICS, SEE **45d**.

PEER EDITOR 16 Rewrite the following sentences, *setting off words and phrases* as needed.

1. In the chapter titled Pestilence in her History of Medieval Europe, Grumberg blames the black rat for the spread of the plague.
2. Our word assassin, from the Arabic hashshashin, originally meant hashish smoker.

3. The loss of the Titanic, the Hindenburg, or the Challenger seems pale when compared with disaster movies like The Poseidon Adventure or The Towering Inferno.

4. Adrienne Rich reexamined the novel Jane Eyre in an essay titled Jane Eyre: The Temptations of a Motherless Woman, included in her collection On Lies, Secrets, and Silence.

5. Blake included The Lamb in his Poems of Innocence and The Tiger in his Poems of Experience.

6. The Los Angeles Times, in an editorial titled A Face from the Past, called the appointment a setback for glasnost and perestroika.

8

Spelling and Mechanics

Instructions Look at the blank in each of the following sentences. Of the three choices that follow the sentences, which is the right one? Write the number of the sentence, followed by the letter for the right choice.

1. The group was _____ a candlelight vigil.
   a. planing   b. planning   c. plannyng

2. After horrible accidents, we want to know _____ to blame.
   a. whose   b. whos   c. who's

3. The almond trees started to bloom in _____ .
   a. February   b. Febuary   c. Febuerry

4. The police _____ intervened sooner.
   a. should of   b. shouldve   c. should have

5. She spent a lifetime championing _____ rights.
   a. womans   b. women's   c. womens'

6. Researchers were _____ the mutant virus.
   a. studying   b. studing   c. studding

7. The test results were _____ wrong.
   a. definately   b. definitly   c. definitely

8. Socialist waiters are not allowed to _____ gratuities.
   a. accept   b. except   c. acept

9. The city printed bilingual ballots for _____ voters.
   a. chinese american   b. Chinese American
   c. Chinese-American

10. According to the President, the economy was _____ sound.
    a. basicly   **b.** basicaly   **c.** basically

11. Working in a defense plant was against her _____ .
    a. principals   **b.** principal's   **c.** principles

12. Both _____ houses had been burglarized.
    a. family's   **b.** families'   **c.** familys

13. Drunk drivers were beginning to _____ jail sentences.
    a. receive   **b.** recieve   **c.** receave

14. The _____ mayor had been indicted for corruption.
    a. citys   **b.** city's   **c.** cities'

15. A job seeker needs _____ .
    a. self confidence   **b.** self-confidance   **c.** self-confidence

16. The rule _____ apply to students from out of state.
    a. dosen't   **b.** doesn't   **c.** doesnt

17. The play had just had its _____ consecutive performance.
    a. forty-fourth   **b.** fourty-fourth   **c.** forty fourth

18. Vivien Leigh played Scarlett O'Hara in *Gone* _____ .
    a. *with the Wind*   **b.** *with the wind*   **c.** *With the Wind*

19. When the statue was removed, _____ was hardly noticed.
    a. its absents   **b.** its absence   **c.** it's absence

20. He loved the parades and fireworks on the _____ .
    a. Fourth of July   **b.** Forth of July   **c.** fourth of july

39   Spelling Problems

OVERVIEW Poor spelling, like static, comes between you and the audience. It undercuts what you have to say. Anticipate predictable spelling problems by studying the words in high-risk categories. If your word processing software or electronic typewriter has a built-in spelling check, use it to check spellings that are suspect. Allow time for careful, word-by-word proofreading of a final draft. (If possible, wait a few hours or a day after you finish writing.)

Heeding advice like the following will help you develop good spelling habits:

(1) Check for the true unforgivables. A handful of common words again and again trip up poor spellers. No matter how capable you are, misspelling one of these will make you look ignorant. Copy them, read them over, spell them out—until the correct spelling becomes second nature:

accept	definite	occurred	probably
all right	environment	occurrence	receive
a lot	believe	perform	similar
athlete	conscience	preferred	studying

(2) Start a record of your own personal spelling problems. Whenever a piece of writing is returned to you, write down all the words that you misspelled. Work your way through a list of common spelling demons (see **41**). List those that have given you trouble in your writing.

(3) Put in twenty minutes three times a week over a period of time. Unless you work on your spelling regularly, you will make little progress. You cannot unlearn in two or three hours the spelling habits that you developed over many years.

(4) Fix each word firmly in your mind. At each sitting, take up a group of ten or twenty spelling words. If you are a visualizer, place your spelling words before you in clear, legible handwriting. Try putting them on a set of small note cards that you can carry around with you. Run your eyes over each word until you can see both the individual letters and the whole word at the same time. If you learn mainly by ear, read each word aloud. Then spell each letter individually: *Receive*—R-E-C-E-I-V-E. If you learn best when you can bring your nerves and muscles into play, try writing each word in large letters. Trace it over several times.

(5) Make use of memory devices. For instance, to help you tell apart *its* and *it's*, remember: "Use *it's* only when *it's* short for *it is*." Remember the following, or make up your own:

acquainted:	MAC got ACquainted.
all right:	ALL RIGHT means ALL is RIGHT.
beginning:	There's an INNING in begINNING.
believe:	Don't beLIEve LIEs.
business:	The drive-IN stayed IN busINess.
criticism:	There's a CRITIC in CRITICism.
environment:	There's IRON in the envIRONment.
government:	People who GOVERN are a GOVERNment.
library:	The LiBRarians BRought BRicks for the LIBRARY.
performance:	He gave a PERfect PERformance.
recognition:	There's a COG in reCOGnition.
surprise:	The SURfer had a SURprise.
villain:	There's a VILLA in VILLAin.

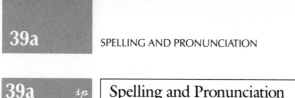

39a sp Spelling and Pronunciation

Watch for differences between speech and writing.

Some words become spelling problems because the gap between spelling and pronunciation is unusually wide.

(1) Watch for sounds not clearly heard in informal speech. Include the boldfaced letters in the following words:

accidentally	can**d**idate	library
basic**all**y	govern**ment**	proba**bl**y
Feb**r**uary	inciden**tally**	quan**ti**ty

(2) Watch for silent consonants. Know how to spell the following:

SILENT LETTERS:	condem**n**	de**b**t	mortgage
	forei**gn**	dou**b**t	soverei**gn**

(3) Watch for vowels in unstressed positions. The vowels *a*, *e*, and *i* blur in endings like *-ate* and *-ite*, *-able* and *-ible*, *-ant* and *-ent*. As a memory aid, link the word with a close cousin: *definite* (fin*i*sh, defin*i*tion); *separate* (sep*a*ration); *ultimate* (ultim*a*tum); *indispensable* (dispens*a*ry).

- *a:* accept**able**, accept**ance**, advis**able**, attend**ance**, attend**ant**, brilli**ant**, perform**ance**
- *e:* consist**ent**, excell**ence**, excell**ent**, exist**ence**, experi**ence**, independ**ent**, persist**ent**, tend**ency**
- *i:* irresist**ible**, plaus**ible**, poss**ible**, suscept**ible**

(4) Never write *of* for *have* in combinations like *could have been* and *might have been.*

WRONG:	could of been	should of known	might of failed
RIGHT:	could **have** been	should **have** known	might **have** failed

---

SPELLING PRACTICE 1   Have someone dictate the following sentences to you. Then check your sentences for predictable *spelling problems*. (Or trade your sentences with classmates for peer checking.)

510

1. They will *probably* never *receive* full *recognition.*
2. The *independent candidate condemned business* for polluting the *en-vironment.*
3. The *brilliant athlete* put in an *excellent performance.*
4. We were *surprised* by the huge *debts* owed by *foreign governments.*
5. We were *beginning* to *believe* that none of it had *occurred.*
6. *Basically* she *doubted* the *existence* of *plausible evidence.*
7. We *should have* asked someone *acquainted* with the *library.*
8. We *definitely accept* the idea that *criticism* is *indispensable.*
9. *It's possible* that they *preferred studying.*
10. They had *shipped* a *similar quantity* in *February.*

39b   *sp* | Variant Forms

Watch for different forms of the same word.

Some words are confusing because they appear in different forms.

(1) Watch out for different spellings of the same root. The root
-*cede* is spelled with a single *e* in *secede* (from the union), *recede* (like a
swelling), *precede* (causing a *precedent*), *concede* (making a concession), and
intercede (stepping in). However, *exceed* and *proceed* have a double *e*, as do
the *proceeds* of a sale. (Then, the double *e* disappears again in *procedure.*)
Watch out for similar pairs:

till/until:	**till** dark	but	**until** dark
four/forty:	**four** and **fourteen**	but	**forty** thieves
nine/ninth:	**nine** and **ninety**	but	the **Ninth** Symphony

**(2) Know how to spell pairs representing different parts of
speech.** The spelling of a noun may be different from that of the corresponding verb or adjective. For instance, when we *absorb* something well
(verb), the result is complete *absorption* (noun). Study similar pairs:

advise/advice: We **advise** somebody (verb), but we give **advice** (noun).
conscience/conscientious: If we are not **conscientious** (adjective) in
   dealing with money, we may suffer from a bad **conscience** (noun).
dissent/dissension: When we **dissent** frequently (verb), the result is **dis-
   sension** (noun).

511

genius/ingenious: A clever person is not really a **genius** (noun) but may be merely **ingenious** (adjective).

pronounce/pronunciation: When we **pronounce** a word wrong (verb), someone may correct our **pronunciation** (noun).

Other similar pairs: *courteous/courtesy, curious/curiosity, generous/generosity.*

(3) Watch out when spelling changes because of a change in grammatical form. For instance, we "ch*oose*" and "l*ead*" in the present, but we "ch*ose*" and "l*ed*" in the past. Some plurals trip up the unwary: one *man* but several *men*, one *woman* but several *women*. Similarly, we write one *freshman* but several *freshmen*, one *Irishman* but several *Irishmen*.

■ Most words like *piano* simply add *-s* for the plural (*pianos, radios, studios, rodeos, sopranos*). Some words ending in *-o* add *-es* instead:

SINGULAR:	hero	potato	tomato	veto
PLURAL:	hero**es**	potato**es**	tomato**es**	veto**es**

■ Most words like *roof* simply add *-s* for the plural (*roofs, chiefs, chefs, reefs, beliefs*). Some words change the final *-f* to *-ves*:

SINGULAR:	life	wife	calf	wolf	knife	loaf
PLURAL:	li**ves**	wi**ves**	cal**ves**	wol**ves**	kni**ves**	loa**ves**

Be sure to add the *-ed* (or *-d*) for *past tense* or *past participle* in words like the following:

used to: He use**d** to sell used cars.
supposed to: She was suppose**d** to be opposed.
prejudiced: They were prejudice**d** (bias**ed**) against me.

Finer Points For some nouns, two different spellings are acceptable for the plural:

■ zero/zeros or zeroes, buffalo/buffalos or buffaloes, cargo/cargos or cargoes, hobo/hobos or hoboes, motto/mottos or mottoes, tornado/tornados or tornadoes

■ scarf/scarfs or scarves, hoof/hoofs or hooves, elf/elfs or elves, wharf/wharfs or wharves

Check your dictionary for other plurals that might be confusing or unusual.

SPELLING PRACTICE 2   What form of the missing word would fit the context? Write the missing form after the number of the sentence.

1. use — China _____ to experience large-scale famines.
2. woman — We recognized the voices of several of the _____ .
3. freshman — A _____ was expected to live in the dorms.
4. prejudice — The townspeople were _____ against the new immigrants.
5. pronounce — The French teacher kept correcting my _____ .
6. advise — Her counselors had given Donna bad _____ .
7. hero — The new movies presented vigilantes as _____ .
8. veto — Repeated _____ of the big powers were commonplace in the Security Council.
9. proceed — The college had elaborate _____ for handling student complaints.
10. woman — The convention chose a _____ for its vice-presidential candidate.

39c   *sp* | Confusing Pairs

Watch for words that sound similar or alike.

Distinguish between sound-alikes or near sound-alikes:

accept/except	**accept** responsibility (take it on); make an **except**ion (take it out)
Capitol/capital	the **Capitol** (buildings) is in the **capital** (the whole city)
cite/site/sight	**cited** for careless driving (give a **citation**), the **site** of the new school (where it is **situated**), the miracle of **sight**
conscious/conscience	we are **conscious** (aware); we have a **conscience** (moral sense)
council/counsel	**councilors** are part of the city **council** (they meet as a group); camp **counselors counsel** young people (they give advice)

513

desert/dessert	**deserts** appear on maps, **desserts** on menus (and when a friend **deserts** us, we hope he will get his just **deserts**)
effect/affect	it has **effects** (results); it **affects** (alters) my grade
lose/loose	win or **lose**; fast and **loose**
personal/personnel	a **personal** (private) matter; a **personnel** (staff) matter
presents/presence	bring **presents** (gifts); **presence** or absence
principal/principle	the **principal's** office, the **principal** (main) reason; against my **principles** (convictions)
quite/quiet	**quite** (entirely) true; peace and **quiet**
than/then	bigger **than** life (comparison); now and **then** (time)
there/their	here and **there**; they and **their** friends
to/too	back **to** Georgia (direction); **too** much **too** soon (degree); you **too** (also)
whether/weather	**whether** or not (choice); foul **weather** (climate)

SPELLING PRACTICE 3   Which choice fits the context? Write it after the number of the sentence.

1. The governor *accepted/excepted* the resignation of two top aides.
2. The decision *affected/effected* thousands of commuters.
3. Macbeth was tormented by a guilty *conscious/conscience*.
4. Marcel was *to/too* tall to play Napoleon.
5. Brokers know dozens of ways to *lose/loose* money.
6. Basques invoked the *principal/principle* of self-determination.
7. Several people had parked *their/there* motorcycles in the driveway.
8. No one knew *whether/weather* we could meet the deadline.
9. Anything was better *then/than* going back down the mountain.
10. Three members of the city *council/counsel* had resigned.
11. Most farms were *then/than* family-owned.
12. He always lectured us about sound business *principles/principals*.
13. The new rules applied to all *personal/personnel*.
14. He loved the town, but staying *their/there* had become impossible.
15. She cherished the *quiet/quite* moments between visits.

---

40 Spelling Rules

OVERVIEW English spelling is highly irregular. It is more like a fossil record of our language history than a simple consistent code. The same *ee* sound is spelled three different ways in *believe, conceive,* and *bereave*; the same *f* sound is spelled one way in *foam* and another in *phone*. As a result, it sometimes seems that we have to memorize spellings one word at a time.

Nevertheless, we often find words that follow a common pattern. In all of the following words, the final letter is doubled as we shift from the present to the past:

stop/stopped, drop/dropped, plan/planned, trot/trotted

In all of the following words, the final *y* changes to *ies* as we shift from singular to plural:

city/cities, family/families, community/communities

Spelling rules help you memorize words that follow a common pattern. Let a few simple rules help you with some familiar spelling problems.

40a *sp* | *I* Before *E*

Put *i* before *e* except after *c.*

The combinations *ie* and *ei* often stand for the same sound. (*Relieved* rhymes with *received.*) If you sort out the words in question, you get the following:

ie: achieve, believe, chief, grief, niece, piece (of pie), relieve
cei: ceiling, conceited, conceive, perceive, receive, receipt

In the second group of words, the *ei* follows the letter *c.* It is *i* before *e* except after *c.* Exceptions:

ei: either, leisure, neither, seize, weird
cie: financier, species

SPELLING PRACTICE 4 Insert *ei* or *ie*: ach __ vement, bel __ ver, dec __ tful, f __ ld, inconc __ vable, misch __ f, perc __ ve, rec __ ving, rel __ f, s __ ze, w __ rd, y __ ld.

40b	*sp*	Doubled Consonant

Know when to double a final consonant.

Often, a single final consonant is doubled before an ending (or **suffix**) that begins with a vowel: *-ed, -er, -est, -ing.* The word *plan* has a single final *n*; we double the *n* in *planned, planning,* and *planner.* The word *big* has a single final *g*; we double the *g* in *bigger* and *biggest.* Two conditions apply:

(1) Double the final consonant only after a short or single vowel. There is no doubling after a long or double vowel: *ai, oo, oa, ea, ee,* or *ou* (boat/boating, read/reading). Some long vowels are shown by a silent final *e* (bite/biting, hope/hoping, bare/baring):

DOUBLING	NO DOUBLING
stop—stopping	stoop—stooping
wrap—wrapped	rape—raped
red—redder	raid—raider

(2) Double the final consonant only at the end of a stressed syllable. There is no doubling when the stress shifts *away* from the final syllable.

DOUBLING	NO DOUBLING
ad**mit**, admitted, admittance	**ed**it, edited, editing
for**get**, forgetting, forgettable	**ben**efit, benefited
be**gin**, beginning, beginner	**hard**en, hardened
re**gret**, regretted, regrettable	pro**hib**it, prohibited, prohibitive
over**lap**, overlapping	de**vel**op, developing
pre**fer**, preferred, preferring	**pref**erence, **pref**erable
re**fer**, referred, referring	**ref**erence

516

Avoid several high-frequency spelling errors by fixing the following firmly in your memory:

NO DOUBLING: (write) wri**ti**ng, wri**te**r (but wri**tt**en)
DOUBLING: (occur) occu**rr**ed, occu**rr**ence; (refer) refe**rr**ed

---

Finer Points   Words that used to be exceptions (doubling at the end of the *un*stressed syllable) now usually follow the rule. However, both forms are right:

BOTH RIGHT: worshiped (worshipped) | traveled (travelled)
        programed (programmed) | quarreled (quarrelled)

SPELLING PRACTICE 5   Which choice fits the context? Write it after the number of the sentence.

1. bared/barred   Commoners were _____ from the club.
2. bating/batting   He knew the _____ average of every player.
3. hoping/hopping   The prisoners were _____ for a reprieve.
4. planed/planned   The raid had been meticulously _____ .
5. robed/robbed   The choristers were _____ in white.
6. pined/pinned   The rejected lover _____ away.
7. biding/bidding   The agents were _____ their time.
8. caned/canned   The expedition lived on _____ meat.
9. doted/dotted   The grandparents _____ on the child.
10. cuter/cutter   They set out for the island in a _____ .

40c   *sp* | ϒ as a Vowel

Change *y* to *ie* before *s*.

As a single final vowel, *y* changes to *ie* before *s* (one city—several cit*ies*; the sixt*ies*, the eight*ies*). It changes to *i* before all other endings except *-ing* (*dried* but *drying*, *burial* but *burying*).

ie: family—famil**ies**, fly—fl**ies**, study—stud**ies**, try—tr**ies**, quantity—quantit**ies**

i: beauty—beautiful, bury—burial, busy—business, copy—copied, dry—drier, lively—livelihood, noisy—noisily
y: burying, copying, studying, trying, worrying

When it follows another vowel, *y* is usually preserved: *delays, joys, played, valleys.* Exceptions: *day—daily, gay—gaily, lay—laid, pay—paid, say—said.*

40d   *sp* | Final *E*

Drop the final silent e before an added vowel.

Drop a silent *e* at the end of a word before an ending that starts with a vowel. Keep it before an ending that begins with a consonant:

	DROPPED e	KEPT e
bore	boring	boredom
hate	hating	hateful
like	liking, likable	likely
love	loving, lovable	lovely

Remember the following exceptions:

DROPPED e: (argue) argument, (due) duly, (true) truly, (whole) wholly, (judge) judgment, (acknowledge) acknowledgment
KEPT e: (mile) mileage, (dye) dyeing (tinting or coloring as against *die—dying*)

Note: A final *e* may signal the difference in the final sound of *rag* and *rage,* or *plastic* and *notice.* Keep such a final *e* not only before a consonant but also before *a* or *o*:

ge: advantage—advanta**ge**ous, change—chan**ge**able, courage—coura**ge**ous, outrage—outra**ge**ous
ce: notice—noti**ce**able, peace—pea**ce**able

SPELLING PRACTICE 6   Combine the following words with the suggested endings: accompany ___ ed, advantage ___ ous, argue ___ ing, benefit ___ ed, carry ___ s, come ___ ing, confide ___ ing, differ ___ ing, excite _____ able, friendly ___ ness, lively ___ hood, occur ___ ing, prefer ___ ed, remit __ ance, sad __ er, satisfy __ ed, shine __ ing, sole __ ly, study __ ing, tragedy __ s, try __ s, use __ ing, valley __ s, whole __ ly, write __ ing.

SPELLING PRACTICE 7 For each blank space, what would be the right form of the word in parentheses? Put the right form after the number of the sentence.

1. (family)   Several _____ were reunited.
2. (plan)   The holdup had been _____ by experts.
3. (study)   My friends were _____ in the library.
4. (regret)   I have always _____ this oversight.
5. (city)   We visited three _____ in one week.
6. (pay)   They had already _____ the bill.
7. (love)   They never stopped hating and _____ each other.
8. (quantity)   Great _____ of food had been consumed.
9. (beauty)   She always described her aunts as famous _____ .
10. (occur)   The thought had _____ to us.
11. (begin)   My patience was _____ to wear thin.
12. (copy)   He had _____ whole paragraphs.
13. (refer)   Your doctor should have _____ you to a specialist.
14. (stop)   You should have _____ at the light.
15. (lay)   We had _____ the tile ourselves.
16. (admit)   Marcia had _____ her mistake.
17. (refer)   She was _____ to a famous incident.
18. (bore)   The speaker was _____ the audience.
19. (forget)   She kept _____ my name.
20. (apply)   Sue had _____ to several colleges.

---

41   Words Often Misspelled

Watch for words frequently misspelled.

The following are among the words most frequently misspelled in student writing. Take up one group of twenty or twenty-five at a time. Find the ones that would cause you trouble.

absence	accidentally	accompanied
abundance	acclaim	accomplish
accessible	accommodate	accumulate

accurately
accuses
accustom
achievement
acknowledgment
acquaintance
acquire
acquitted
across
actuality
address
adequate
admit
adolescence
advantageous
advertisement
afraid
against
aggravate
aggressive
alleviate
allotted
allowed
all right
already
altar
altogether
always
amateur
among
amount
analysis
analyze
annual
anticipate
anxiety
apologize
apology
apparatus
apparent
appearance
applies
applying

appreciate
approach
appropriate
approximately
area
argue
arguing
argument
arising
arrangement
article
artistically
ascend
assent
athlete
athletic
attendance
audience
authority

balance
basically
basis
beauty
becoming
before
beginning
belief
believe
beneficial
benefited
boundaries
breath
brilliant
Britain
buses
business

calendar
candidate
career
careless
carrying

category
ceiling
cemetery
challenge
changeable
character
characteristic
chief
choose
chose
clothes
coarse
column
comfortable
comfortably
coming
commission
committed
committee
companies
competition
competitive
completely
comprehension
conceivable
conceive
concentrate
condemn
confident
confidential
conscience
conscientious
conscious
considerably
consistent
continually
continuous
control
controlled
convenience
convenient
coolly
courageous

course
courteous
criticism
criticize
cruelty
curiosity
curriculum

dealt
deceit
deceive
decision
definite
definitely
definition
dependent
describe
description
desirability
desirable
despair
desperate
destruction
devastate
develop
development
device
difference
different
difficult
dilemma
dining
disappear
disappearance
disappoint
disastrous
discipline
disease
disgusted
dissatisfaction
dissatisfied
doesn't
dominant

due
during

ecstasy
efficiency
efficient
eighth
eliminate
embarrass
embarrassment
eminent
emphasize
endeavor
enforce
enough
entertain
environment
equipped
especially
etc.
exaggerate
excellent
exceptionally
exercise
exhaust
exhilarate
existence
experience
explanation
extraordinary
extremely

familiar
families
fascinate
finally
financial
financier
foreign
forward
friend
fulfill

fundamentally
further

gaiety
generally
genius
government
governor
grammar
guaranteed
guidance

happily
happiness
height
heroes
heroine
hindrance
hopeful
huge
humorous
hundred
hurriedly
hypocrisy
hypocrite

ignorant
imaginary
imagination
immediately
immensely
incidentally
indefinite
independent
indispensable
inevitable
influence
ingenious
insight
intellectual
intelligence
interest
interpret

interrupt
involve
irrelevant
irresistible
itself

jealous

knowledge

laboratory
laid
leisure
likelihood
literature
livelihood
loneliness
losing

magnificence
maintain
maintenance
manageable
manufacturer
marriage
mathematics
meant
medieval
merely
mileage
miniature
minute
mischievous
muscle
mysterious

naive
necessarily
necessary
ninety
noticeable

obstacle
occasion

occasionally
occurred
occurrence
omit
operate
opinion
opponent
opportunity
optimism
original

paid
parallel
paralysis
paralyze
particularly
passed
past
peace
peculiar
perceive
perform
performance
permanent
persistent
persuade
pertain
phenomenon
philosophy
phrase
physical
piece
pleasant
possess
possession
possible
practical
precede
prejudice
prepare
prevalent
privilege
probably
procedure

proceed
professor
prominent
propaganda
prophecy
psychology
pursue

quantity

really
recommend
regard
relief
relieve
religion
repetition
representative
resource
response
rhythm
ridiculous
roommate

safety
satisfactorily
schedule
seize
sense
separate
sergeant
shining
significance
similar
sincerely
sophomore
speech
sponsor
strength
stretch
strictly
studying
subtle
succeed

successful	tragedy	various
summarize	transferred	vengeance
surprise	tries	villain
temperament	undoubtedly	weird
tendency	unnecessary	writing
therefore	useful	
thorough	using	
together		

SPELLING PRACTICE 8   Test your knowledge of words often misspelled. Have someone dictate these sentences to you. Make a list of the words that give you trouble.

1. *Amateurs benefited* more than other *athletes.*
2. The *committee* heard every *conceivable opinion.*
3. *Manufacturers developed* a new *device.*
4. We kept all *business decisions confidential.*
5. Her *appearance* was *definitely a surprise.*
6. She *accused* her *opponent* of *hypocrisy.*
7. The *absence* of *controls* proved *disastrous.*
8. We met a *prominent professor* of *psychology.*
9. Their *marriage succeeded exceptionally* well.
10. These *privileges* are *undoubtedly unnecessary.*
11. The *sponsor* was *dissatisfied* with the *performance.*
12. Their *approach* was *strictly practical.*
13. *Companies* can seldom just *eliminate* the *competition.*
14. A *repetition* of the *tragedy* is *inevitable.*
15. This *subtle difference* is *irrelevant.*

42   The Apostrophe

OVERVIEW The apostrophe, which can't be heard, is the typist's nemesis. (There's no way to hear the two apostrophes in that sentence.) This special mark causes trouble two ways: People who spell by ear leave it out where it clearly belongs ("a *mothers* love" should be "a *mother's* love"). Then people with a shaky grasp of the rules put it in where it's clearly wrong ("the *player's* were leaving the field"). The most common case of the runaway apostrophe is the misused *it's*: "divorce and *it's* aftermath." (Remember: Use *it's* only when it's short for *it is*.)

The apostrophe has two basic uses:

CONTRACTIONS   The apostrophe shows that something has been *left out*. "She cannot be part of the class of 1985 because she is only twenty years old" becomes "She *can't* be part of the class of '85 because *she's* only twenty years old." Such shortened forms are called **contractions**.

POSSESSIVES   The apostrophe shows where something *belongs*: the *star's* dressing room, a *photographer's* dream. These forms are called **possessives** because they show possession or similar close relationships.

Know the basic rules and stay clear of familiar pitfalls when you use apostrophes in contractions and possessives.

42a   *ap* | Contractions

Use the apostrophe in informal shortened forms.

Use the apostrophe to show that part of a word has been left out: *o'clock, ma'am, class of '85*. Avoid common misspellings.

(1) Use the apostrophe in common contractions or shortened forms.   Remember that *they're* is short for *they are*; *let's* is short for *let us*.

(we *are* ready)	**we're** ready
(she *is* a friend)	**she's** a friend
(he *will* be back)	**he'll** be back
(they *are* late)	**they're** late
(you *are* right)	**you're** right
(let *us* ask)	**let's** ask

(2) Use the apostrophe in combined forms that include a shortened form of *not*.   Remember that *can't* is short for *cannot*; *won't* is short for *will not*.

(we *cannot* leave)	we **can't** leave
(she *will not* say)	she **won't** say
(he *could not* stay)	he **couldn't** stay
(they *have not* paid)	they **haven't** paid
(you *are not* safe)	you **aren't** safe
(it *is not* true)	it **isn't** true

CAUTION: Make sure not to misspell *don't* and *doesn't*. These are shortened forms of *do not* and *does not*.

do not: We **don't** usually hire in the summer.
does not: The new converter **doesn't** work.

(3) Know familiar confusing pairs. Use *it's* (= it is) only when it's really an abbreviation. Otherwise use *its*—the possessive pronoun that shows where something belongs: a nation and *its* leaders (tells us *whose* leaders); the bird beat *its* wings (tells us *whose* wings).

it's (it *is*, it *has*):	**it's** true, **it's** raining, **it's** a shame; **it's** been cold
its (of it):	took **its** course, lost **its** value, heavy for **its** size
who's (who *is* or *has*):	**Who's** to blame? **Who's** seen him? the one **who's** guilty
whose (of whom):	**Whose** turn is it? friends **whose** help counts
they're (they are):	**they're** late, **they're** glad, if **they're** here
their (of them):	**their** belongings, **their** friends, they and **their** parents

Note: Contractions are common in informal speech and writing. Avoid them in formal reports, research papers, and letters of application. Use them sparingly in ordinary prose.

42b *ap* | Possessives

Use the apostrophe for the possessive of nouns.

The **possessive** form of nouns shows who owns something (*Macy's*) or to whom something belongs (*the driver's seat*). We usually produce the possessive by adding an apostrophe plus *s* to the plain form:

WHOSE?		
	my **sister's** car	Mr. **Smith's** garage
	her **aunt's** house	the **student's** name
	the **family's** debts	one **person's** opinion
	our **mayor's** office	the **mind's** eye

Besides ownership, the possessive signals other relationships that tell us whose: the *senator's* enemies, the *defendant's* innocence, a *crook's* exposure, the *committee's* activities. Usually the possessive comes before another noun, but sometimes it's been cut loose from it:

WHOSE?	For once the fault was not the **governor's.** (not the **governor's fault**)
	It's either the owner's car or her **son's.** (her **son's car**)

(1) Distinguish between singular and plural possessives. If a plural noun already ends in *-s*, we add only the apostrophe—not a second *s*: a *lovers'* quarrel, the *slaves'* revolt.

SINGULAR:	the **twin's** bicycle, a **parent's** duties, one **family's** home
PLURAL:	the **twins'** birthdays, both **parents'** duties, both **families'** homes

However, use the regular possessive when a plural noun does not end with the plural *-s*. Examples of such unusual plurals are *children, women, men,* and *people*:

PLURAL:	**children's** toys	**women's** rights
	men's wear	**people's** prejudices

Note the two different kinds of plural in the following sample sentence:

PLURAL:	**Judges'** gowns now come in **men's** and **women's** sizes.

CAUTION: Do not start using the apostrophe with nouns that are *not* possessives.

WRONG:	The **player's** went on strike.
RIGHT:	The **players** went on strike. (Who?)
RIGHT:	The **player's** jersey had ripped. (Whose?)

(2) Use the apostrophe in familiar expressions dealing with time or value. Distinguish between singular and plural:

SINGULAR	PLURAL
a **week's** pay	two **weeks'** pay
an **hour's** drive	three **hours'** drive
a **dollar's** worth	two **dollars'** worth
a **month's** salary	three **months'** salary

Expressions like the following are possessive forms and need the apostrophe:

a **moment's** notice   **today's** paper   a **day's** work

(3) Know when to use the apostrophe with pronouns. Use the apostrophe with the possessive forms of **indefinite pronouns**: *everyone (everybody), someone (somebody), anyone (anybody), no one (nobody),* and *one*:

to **everybody's** surprise	**anyone's** guess
at **someone's** suggestion	**nobody's** fault
(also: at someone **else's** house)	**one's** best friends

CAUTION: Do *not* use the apostrophe with **possessive pronouns**: *its, hers, ours, yours, theirs.* Remember *its* as a major exception to the use of apostrophes with possessives (the movie and *its* sequel, the college and *its* faculty). Use *it's* only to mean *it is*: "*It's* too late."

NO APOSTROPHE: both **its** ears | it was **hers** | this is **yours**

(4) Know how to use the apostrophe with combinations or groups of words. Treat compound words or combinations that stand for a single entity the way you would single words. Put the apostrophe plus *-s* or the apostrophe alone at the end of the last word in the group:

SINGULAR: the **commander-in-chief's** orders
                 a **father-in-law's** hopes
PLURAL: her **brothers-in-law's** store
                 my **in-laws'** support

Follow the same rule when using the possessive of words that jointly name a group or a team: *Simon & Schuster's* spring list, *Laurel and Hardy's* comedies. But use two separate possessives for members of a team when differences or separate identities are important:

SHARED: **Laurel and Hardy's** comedies left audiences helpless with laughter.
SEPARATE: **Laurel's and Hardy's** origins had been very different.

Note: When you refer to couples, either joint or separate possessives are all right, depending on whether you think of them as a unit or as individuals:

BOTH RIGHT: **Simon and Adele's** marriage   or   **Simon's and Adele's** marriage

Finer Points Follow your preference when the singular form of a noun already has a final -s. After the apostrophe that signals the possessive, you may or may not add another s, depending on whether you would expect an extra syllable in pronunciation. With words like the following, the additional syllable seems clearly required: the *boss's* office, the *waitress's* tip. We usually do *not* add the extra syllable to the word *Jesus* or to Greek names: for *Jesus'* sake, in *Sophocles'* plays. With many other proper names, either form would be right:

BOTH RIGHT:	**Dolores'** trip	**Dolores's** trip
	Jones' raise	**Jones's** raise
	Dickens' novel	**Dickens's** novel

SPELLING PRACTICE 9 Change each of the following to the *possessive* form. Examples: pay for a month—a *month's* pay; the wedding of my brother—my *brother's* wedding.

1. the budget of the President
2. wages for two weeks
3. the friends of her family
4. the homes of many families
5. the future of America
6. the locker room for girls
7. the worth of a dollar
8. the employment record of a person
9. the fringe benefits of the employees
10. the vote for women

SPELLING PRACTICE 10 Choose the right spelling in each of the following pairs. Make sure both *contractions and possessives* are spelled correctly.

1. The *judge's/judges* ruling made necessary some quick changes in both *lawyer's/lawyers'* strategies.
2. Since the *mayor's/mayors* resignation, many *voter's/voters* have been worrying about *whose/who's* going to succeed her.
3. *Mens/Men's* and *womens/women's* cycling found enthusiastic *spectators'/spectators* when introduced as new Olympic sports.

4. In *today's/todays* competitive world of sports, a *gymnast's/gymnasts* training takes up many hours every day.
5. My *friend's/friends'* face fell, as if she were looking at an empty mailbox on *Valentines/Valentine's* Day.
6. *It's/Its* not easy for *parent's/parents* to let a child find *it's/its* own answers.
7. *Lets/Let's* borrow *someones/someone's* car and go for an *hour's/hours'* drive.
8. *Charles/Charles's* father murmured that the *relatives/relative's* had consumed twenty *dollars/dollars'* worth of food.

42c *ap* | Plurals of Letters and Symbols

Know how to use the apostrophe for plurals of letters, numbers, abbreviations, and words discussed as words.

Traditionally, the apostrophe has been used before the plural *-s* added to the name of a letter, to a number, to an abbreviation, or to a word named as a word: the early 1900's, average I.Q.'s.

LETTERS: Teachers were giving more **C's** and **D's**, fewer **A's**.
NUMBERS: The phone number started with **3's** and ended with **7's**.
ABBREVIATIONS: People with **Ph.D.'s** were driving cabs.

Remember that letters of the alphabet and words discussed as vocabulary items should be italicized (or underlined in typing). Do not italicize the plural *-s*:

ALPHABET: She spelled her name with two **e's** and two **s's**.
WORDS: She punctuated her monologue with many ***Honey's*** and ***Darling's***.

However, in recent years, writers more and more tend to leave out the apostrophe for the plural except with letters of the alphabet and abbreviations using a period.

BOTH RIGHT: the **1830's** or the **1830s**
                  several **6's** in a row or several **6s** in a row
                  too many **if's** and **but's** or too many **ifs** and **buts**

529

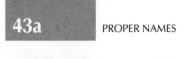

43 Capitals

OVERVIEW Capital letters, like the apostrophe, are historical accidents, and their use varies widely from one language to another. (You may have seen ancient Roman inscriptions that are all capitals.) In English, we capitalize the first word of a sentence and the pronoun *I*. In addition we use capital letters for names and for words in titles.

We capitalize not only names as such (*Maria, John Hancock, Godzilla*) but also ordinary words that become parts of names (*Professor Chan, the Birchwood School for the Blind*). We capitalize not only the names of people but also the names of places, times, vessels, and institutions (the *Badlands,* the *Middle Ages,* the *Queen Mary,* the *CIA*). We capitalize not only the names of countries but also the labels that show national origin (*American, Mexican, Arabic, Japanese*).

We use capitals (along with italics or quotation marks) to highlight the titles of publications and creative works, from *Paradise Lost* to *Star Wars.* Study the basic rules and the finer points for using capitals for names and titles, including the titles you give to your own writing.

43a *cap* Proper Names

Capitalize proper names.

Capitalize names—of people, places, languages, periods, ships and other craft, days of the week, months, organizations, institutions, and religions: *Daniel Boone, Kalamazoo,* the *Everglades, Zimbabwe, Arabic,* the *Middle Ages,* the *Challenger, Saturday, July,* the *Salvation Army, Harvard, Islam.* Do not capitalize the names of the seasons: *spring, summer.*

(1) Capitalize words derived from proper names. Capitalize words that use the name of a country, place, or religion. In particular, capitalize the names of languages and nationalities:

CAPITALS: Imports from **Japan** replaced **German** cameras, **Swiss** cuckoo clocks, **British** motorcycles, and **American** cars. **Marxist** intellectuals criticized the role of **Christian** missionaries and **Buddhist** monks.
Few **Americans** study **Arabic, Chinese,** or **Japanese.**

In some words, the proper name involved has been lost sight of, and a lowercase letter is used:

LOWER CASE: **pasteurized** milk, **guinea** pig, **india** rubber

(2) Capitalize words that become part of a name. When it combines with a proper name, capitalize the general label for a title, family relationship, institution, or geographic feature: *Sergeant Bilko, Grandma Moses, Nuclear Energy Commission, Silicon Valley.* Some titles point to one person only and are capitalized like a proper name: the *Pope*, the *Queen* (of England).

(3) Capitalize a general word put to special use as a proper name. A general label may double as a proper name for one person, institution, organization, or place. Historically, republicans (lowercase) hated kings and preferred a republic; in the United States, Republicans (capitalized) are members of one major party.

GENERAL WORD	PROPER NAME
democratic (many institutions)	**D**emocratic (name of the party)
orthodox (many attitudes)	**O**rthodox (name of the church)
history (general subject)	**H**istory 31 (specific course)
west (general direction)	**M**iddle **W**est (the specific area)
my mother (common relationship)	**M**other (name you call the person)

Note: Practice varies for the *President* or *president* (of the United States), the *Federal* or *federal* government, the (U.S.) *Constitution* or *constitution*, the *Bible* or the *bible*. (Always use lowercase when the word is used figuratively for a trusted guidebook: the *bible* of amateur radio operators.) Believers capitalize pronouns used in reference to the deity: "She believed that *God* would not abandon *His* people."

Finer Points We usually do not capitalize generic job descriptions: "The meeting will be chaired by Grace Mehanos, our *director of marketing.*" We do capitalize formal titles that are used to give a person status or make the person seem important:

FORMAL: Wilbur Kaspin, **V**ice **P**resident for **O**verseas **T**rade, will preside over the meeting.

  The speaker was Thurgood Marshall, **S**upreme **C**ourt **J**ustice.

A CHECKLIST OF CAPITALIZED NAMES

PEOPLE:	Eleanor Roosevelt, Langston Hughes, Albert Einstein, Edna St. Vincent Millay
TITLES:	Dr. Brothers, Senator Kennedy, Queen Elizabeth, Pope John Paul, the President
CONTINENTS:	Asia, America, Europe, Australia, the Antarctic
COUNTRIES:	United States of America, Canada, Great Britain, Mexico, Denmark, Japan, Zimbabwe
LANGUAGES:	English, Spanish, Chinese, Russian, French
REGIONS:	the South, the East, the Middle East, the Midwest
STATES:	Kansas, North Dakota, Louisiana, Rhode Island
CITIES:	Oklahoma City, Dallas, Baltimore, Los Angeles, Washington, D.C.
SIGHTS:	Lake Erie, Mount Hood, Death Valley, the Grand Canyon
ADDRESSES:	Park Lane, Fleet Avenue, Oak Street
MONTHS:	January, March, July, October
WEEKDAYS:	Monday, Wednesday, Saturday, Sunday
HOLIDAYS:	Labor Day, Thanksgiving, Easter, the Fourth of July
INSTITUTIONS:	the Supreme Court, the Department of Agriculture, the U.S. Senate, the FBI
BUSINESSES:	Ford Motor Company, General Electric, Sears
SCHOOLS:	Oakdale High School, Las Vistas Junior College, University of Maine
GROUPS:	the Democratic Party, the American Legion
FAITHS:	Christian, Muslim, Jewish, Buddhist
DENOMINATIONS:	Methodist, Mormon, Unitarian, Roman Catholic

43b   *cap*   Titles of Publications

Capitalize major words in titles.

A capital letter marks the first and last word and all major words in the title of a book, other publication, or work of art. Words not counting as major are articles (*a, an,* and *the*) and also prepositions (*at, in, on, from, with*) or conjunctions (*and, but, if, when*). Even these are usually capitalized when they have five or more letters (*Through, Because*).

Observe these conventions in writing headlines (*Man Revives During Autopsy*) and the titles of your papers:

Raising the Mirth Rate
Travels with a Camel Through Arid Country
How I Quit Drugs and Learned to Love the Police

The same conventions apply to titles of publications cited in a sentence:

TITLES: *New York Times Magazine's* "About Men" column is the weekly counterpart of the older "Hers" column; *Esquire* has published numerous articles on subjects like "Men, Babies, and the Male Clock" or "The Pain of the Divorced Father."

Lange, who titled her book *An American Exodus*, was becoming famous for photographs like "Ditched, Stalled, and Stranded" and "Ex-Slave."

PEER EDITOR 11   Which of the words in the following sentences should be *capitalized*? After the number of each sentence, write down and capitalize all such words.

1. Players from brazil and argentina have played for france and italy in the world cup.
2. The authenticity of some of rembrandt's most popular paintings—*the man with the golden helmet* and *polish rider*—has been challenged.
3. Pistol shots crackled in dearborn, the detroit suburb that was home to the ford motor company's sprawling river rouge plant.
4. In october, a huge and very ugly statue of sir winston churchill was unveiled in parliament square, london.
5. As he was helped aboard, egyptian mohammed aly clutched a small blue-bound koran that had been given to him by the arab mayor of hebron.

6. The sprawling city of canton, 110 miles by rail from hong kong, has for centuries been china's principal gathering place for asian and european traders.

7. Delegates met in manhattan to celebrate the centennial of the union of american hebrew congregations, founded in cincinnati by rabbi isaac wise.

8. At columbia and barnard, at atlanta's morehouse college and the university of virginia, economics was the subject to take.

9. Seven novels by mickey spillane are among the thirty best-selling novels of all time, along with *gone with the wind, peyton place, lady chatterley's lover,* and *in his steps*, by charles monroe sheldon, 1897.

10. Like other newspapers, the *new york journal-american* had learned the art of catering to irish catholics.

---

44   The Hyphen

OVERVIEW The easy-to-miss **hyphen** provides an example of slow-moving, long-term change. A pair of words may start as two words (*baby boom*), pick up a hyphen (*baby-sitter*), and finally become one word (*crybaby*).

Watch out for high-frequency uses of the hyphen. Here are some situations where a missing hyphen would be conspicuous:

in-law words	daughter-in-law, father-in-law, in-laws
self-words	self-conscious, self-confidence, self-correcting
double numbers	twenty-four, sixty-seven
ethnic labels	Irish-American, Asian-American, Polish-American
new blends	trade-off, cancer-causing, cost-effective, gender-neutral

Study some basic guidelines for using the hyphen in these and other situations. When in doubt, use the most recent edition of a good dictionary as your guide.

44a   *hy*   Compound Words

Know which compound words require a hyphen.

Some **compound words** differ from ordinary combinations in both speech and writing: "a wild LIFE" but "our WILDlife"; "a strong MAN"

COMMON TYPES OF HYPHENATED WORDS

in-laws, off-season, drive-in, sit-in, off-duty, take-off, trade-off

ten-speed, six-pack, one-sided, three-cornered, second-rate, one-way, two-dimensional

Polish-American, Asian-American, Anglo-Saxon, Graeco-Roman

law-abiding, Spanish-speaking, cancer-causing, award-winning, money-losing

dark-haired, Washington-based, air-conditioned, computer-aided, career-oriented, middle-aged, foreign-born, college-bound, single-handed

fuel-efficient, cost-effective, oil-rich, water-repellent, image-conscious, toll-free

self-conscious, ex-husband, all-purpose, great-grandfather, co-star, pro-Arab, non-Catholic

south-southeast, north-northwest

two-by-four, cash-and-carry, fly-by-night, father-in-law

but "a STRONGman"; "a dark ROOM" but "a DARKroom." Such unmistakable compounds are *headache, highway,* and *stepmother.* In many similar pairs, however, the parts are kept separate: *high school, labor union.* Still other compound words conventionally require the hyphen: *cave-in, great-grandfather, mother-in-law.*

(1) Know how to spell common compound words: Recognize typical words in each of the three categories.

ONE WORD: bridesmaid, stepfather, checklist, highlight, headquarters, blackout, bittersweet

TWO WORDS (OR MORE): commander in chief, goose flesh, vice versa, off year, high command

HYPHEN:	able-bodied, bull's-eye, drive-in, court-martial, merry-go-round, six-pack, in-laws, vice-president, Spanish-American, one-sided, off-season, in-group, President-elect

(2) Hyphenate compound numbers from *twenty-one* to *ninety-nine*. Also hyphenate fractions used as modifiers:

NUMBERS:	There were **twenty-six** passengers. The plan was **one-third** empty. The tank was **three-quarters** full.

Practice varies for other uses of fractions:

FRACTIONS:	**Two thirds** (or **two-thirds**) remained poor.

CAUTION: Be sure to spell correctly combinations that are often misspelled:

ONE WORD:	today, tomorrow, nevertheless, nowadays
TWO WORDS:	all right, a lot (of time), be able, no one, even though

---

44b   *hy*   Prefixes

Know which prefixes require a hyphen.

Many hyphenated compounds combine a word and its prefix. A **prefix** can be attached at the beginning of many different words. Watch for the following:

(1) Use a hyphen with *all-*, *ex-* (in the sense of "former"), *quasi-*, *self-*, and sometimes *co-*. Hyphenate words like *all-knowing, ex-husband, quasi-judicial, self-contained, co-worker*.

all-:	all-powerful, all-American, all-male, all-star
ex-:	ex-champion, ex-convict, ex-wife, ex-governor
self-:	self-confident, self-conscious, self-image, self-destruct

(2) Use a hyphen with all prefixes before words beginning with a capital letter. Hyphenate *anti-American, pro-British, un-American, non-Catholic, Pan-Arabic*.

(3) Use a hyphen to prevent the meeting of two identical vowels or three identical consonants. Hyphenate *anti-intellectual, semi-independent, fall-like*.

Finer Points   Sometimes a hyphen distinguishes an unfamiliar use of a prefix from a familiar one: *recover—re-cover* (make a new cover), *recreation—re-creation* (creating again or anew).

44c   *hy*   Group Modifiers

Use the hyphen with group modifiers.

Hyphenate words that work together like a single modifier before a noun (a *thirty-page* report):

HYPHENS:	a **middle-of-the-road** policy	**off-the-cuff** remarks
	a **low-income** neighborhood	**wall-to-wall** carpeting
	an **in-depth** interview	a **down-to-the-wire** race
	after-school activities	a **step-by-step** account

HYPHENS: San Francisco has always been a happy hunting ground for painters producing **seagull-and-cable-car** kitsch. *Time*

Use no hyphens when the same combinations serve some other function in a sentence: tend toward the **middle of the road**; explain a process **step by step**.

HYPHEN:	We often stayed for **after-school** activities.
NO HYPHEN:	We often stayed for activities **after school**.
HYPHENS:	Gradually, the drug user's **twice-a-week** habit changes to a **four-times-a-week** need.
NO HYPHENS:	Gradually, we reduced the frequency of treatment from **four times a week** to **twice a week**.

No hyphen is used when a modifier before a noun is in turn modified by an adverb ending in *-ly*: a *fast-rising* executive but a *rapidly growing* city; a *well-balanced* account but a *carefully documented* study.

PEER EDITOR 12   After the number of each sentence, write all combinations that should be *hyphenated or written as one word*.

  1. New style managers developed cost effective procedures for labor intensive industries.

2. Italian Americans protested against the poor self image and low self esteem created by negative stereotypes.
3. The room was about one fourth full, with forty five people scattered in two hundred seats.
4. This is the story of a flabby middle aged two pack a day smoker who transformed himself into a 160 pound marathon runner.
5. Though at times her son in law seemed self conscious, he never the less had a well balanced personality.
6. The self righteous law and order candidate promised to crack down on ex convicts.
7. The ex ambassador complained about anti Soviet demonstrations by pro Israeli citizens.
8. The Connecticut based subsidiary produces computer aided high performance robots for state of the art factories.
9. Now a days few self respecting candidates conduct old fashioned campaigns taking them to out of the way places.
10. Jane Andrew and her co author have written a well documented account of the un democratic procedures followed by quasi judicial agencies.

---

45   Manuscript Mechanics

OVERVIEW The outward appearance of your manuscript sends a message—preferably, that you care about your readers' convenience and respect their standards. A paper scribbled on a page torn from a notebook, a smudged and heavily erased typescript on see-through paper, a pale printout—all of these create reader's block, a reluctance to read and a tendency to block out your message.

Remember that the outward appearance of your manuscript is the first thing to strike your reader. A good first impression is likely to put the reader in a receptive mood.

45a   *ms* | Penmanship and Typing

Prepare a legible and attractive manuscript.

Finished copy that is easy to read and pleasing to the eye shows your consideration for the reader. Write legibly, pruning your handwriting of excessive loops and curlicues. (Do *not* print or leave every other line blank unless instructed to do so.) Type on unlined paper of standard size and weight, double-spacing all material. When in doubt about the quality of the printout delivered by a word processor, show a sample to your instructor.

(1) Observe conventional spacing. Leave one space after most punctuation marks (comma, semicolon) but *two* spaces after end punctuation.

TWO SPACES: `They invested in a restaurant.  It failed.`

After a colon, leave one space if the colon appears before the end of the sentence. Leave two spaces if it appears at the end.

ONE SPACE: `We saw new construction: offices and hotels.`
TWO SPACES: `The news was out:  The test had been post-poned.`

Use two hyphens—with no space on either side—to make a **dash**:

DASH: `Use two hyphens--with no space on either side.`

Note: Leave no space after a period that occurs *within* an abbreviation—but leave one space each if several initials are part of a person's name:

ABBREVIATIONS: `The U.S. Supreme Court   T. S. Eliot`

(2) Leave adequate margins. Leave about an inch and a half on the left and at the top, an inch on the right and at the bottom. *Indent* the first line of a paragraph—about an inch in longhand, or five spaces in typed copy.

(3) Make necessary final corrections. Always make time for final proofreading. If necessary, make handwritten last-minute corrections. Draw a line through a word to delete it or to write the corrected word in the space above. (Use a snaking line to revise the order of two transposed letters.)

```
                                    deep
Film critics have found ~~profound~~ maening in in Laurel
and Hardy.
```

To separate two words, draw a vertical line; to close up a space, use two curved lines. Insert a **caret** (∧) to show where a missing word is to go:

Film|critics have in⌣vestigated *the* symbolism of King
Kong.

To start a new paragraph, insert the symbol ¶; to take out a paragraph break, insert "no ¶" in the margin.

45b   *ms*   Titles of Papers

Use standard form for the titles of your papers.

Capitalize words in the titles of your papers as you would in titles of publications (see **43b**). Capitalize the first and last word. Capitalize all other words except articles (*the, a, and*) and prepositions (*in, at, with*) or conjunctions (*and, when, if*). Capitalize even prepositions or conjunctions when they have five or more letters (*around, because*).

TITLES: My Teacher the Computer
          Was Granddad a Monkey?
          Drugs on the Job
          All About Graft

CAUTION: Do not italicize (underline) your own title. Do not put it in quotation marks unless you want to identify it as a quotation. Use a question mark or exclamation mark as appropriate, but do not use a period even if your title is a complete sentence.

QUOTATION: "A Kinder, Gentler America"
QUESTION: Marriage: Bond or Bondage?
SENTENCE: Chivalry Is Dead

45c   *div*   Dividing Words

Observe conventional syllabication.

Use a hyphen to divide words at the end of a line. Dictionaries generally use centered dots to indicate where a word may conventionally be divided:

ad•dress   af•fec•ta•tion   en•vi•ron•ment   mal•ice

540

(1) Recognize recurrent patterns. For instance, divide words before the *-ing* ending, but keep the added consonant with the ending when you have doubled a final consonant:

play·ing	sell·ing	edit·ing
plan·ning	hum·ming	submit·ting

Divide between two consonants when they go with two separate syllables in slow pronunciation:

op·tics *but* neu·tral | fac·tor *but* su·preme

(2) Do not divide names and combinations that in the reader's mind form a single unit. Avoid dividing names (*Kiplinger, Washington*). Do not divide contractions (*doesn't, wouldn't*) and abbreviations (*NATO, UNESCO, UCLA*). Do not split sums (*$1,175,000*) or expressions using abbreviations like *a.m.* and *B.C.*

(3) Do not set off single letters. Do not divide words like *about, alone,* and *enough* or like *many* and *via.* Similarly, do not set off the ending *-ed* in words like *complained* or *renewed.* (Do not divide one-syllable words: *strength, through.*)

(4) Divide hyphenated words at the original hyphen. Do not break up the *American* in "Un-American" or the *sister* in "sister-in-law."

(5) Do not divide the last word on a page.

45d *ital* | Italics

Use italics to set off special words and phrases.

Italics (or slanted type) are signaled in handwritten and most typed manuscript by underlining.

(1) Italicize for emphasis. Use italics (underlining) to call attention to important words or to words that will prevent misunderstanding. (Use italics and other attention-getters *sparingly*.)

EMPHASIS: The group was a professional ***association***, not a union.

541

(2) Italicize words discussed as words or words still considered foreign.

WORD AS WORD: Dictionaries lag behind, only slowly beginning to include **hot tub**, **prime time**, **gulag**, **preppie**, and **putdown**.

FOREIGN: He developed a taste for **tostadas** and the music of the **mariachis**.

(3) Italicize titles of whole publications. Italicize or underline titles of books (*Veil: The Secret Wars of the CIA*), magazines (*Popular Mechanics*), newspapers (*Chicago Tribune*), and other complete publications. Put in quotation marks the titles of articles, poems, short stories, songs, and other items that are normally *part* of a larger publication: "The Love Song of J. Alfred Prufrock"; "The Lottery"; "I Got You, Babe."

WHOLE: Her latest book, **A Distant Mirror**, was reviewed in **Time**, **Newsweek**, and **Saturday Review**.

PART: The earliest essays had titles like "California Dreaming" and "Marrying Absurd."

Note: The name of the Bible and the names of its parts (Genesis, Book of Job) are usually *not* italicized.

(4) Italicize the names of works of art, music, and entertainment. Use italics (underlining) for the names of paintings, ballets, operas, major orchestral works, plays, movies, radio and television shows. (See also **38f.**)

ART: He dreamed of seeing Michelangelo's **David** in Florence or listening to **Lohengrin** in Bayreuth.

ENTERTAINMENT: From **The War of the Worlds** to **Star Wars**, some of the greatest successes of popular entertainment have been works of science fiction.

(5) Italicize the names of trains, aircraft, ships, and other vessels. (See also **38f.**)

VESSELS: Legendary ships from the **Mayflower** and the **Titanic** to the **Hindenburg** and **Apollo IX** have been symbols of human hopes and fears.

OVERVIEW Abbreviations and numerals save time and space. We are grateful for abbreviations like NASA for a mouthful like National Aeronautics and Space Administration. It takes us much less time to write $1,543.89 than it would to spell out the amount on a check. The flow of information would slow down considerably if media people could not use shortcuts like DNA, AIDS, SAT scores, or PC (for personal computer).

Nevertheless, in ordinary writing we avoid shortcuts making it appear that we are too much in a hurry. Abbreviations like *Mr.* and *a.m.* are all right anywhere, but we expect to see *NY, lb.,* and *in.* only in addresses, invoices, charts, and other very businesslike kinds of communication. We expect numerals for exact sums, but we prefer to have the figures spelled out in "2 out of 3 voted for the 3rd party candidate." Study and observe basic guidelines for using abbreviations and numerals in your own writing.

46a *ab* Abbreviations

Spell out inappropriate abbreviations.

Some abbreviations (*Mr., CIA, a.m.*) are generally acceptable in ordinary prose. Others (*lb., Ave., NY*) are appropriate only in invoices, reports, addresses, and other special contexts.

(1) Use the acceptable abbreviations for titles and degrees. Before and after names, use the titles *Mr., Mrs., Ms., Dr.,* and *St.* (Saint), and the abbreviations *Jr.* (Junior) and *Sr.* (Senior). Use standard abbreviations for degrees: *M.D., Ph.D.* Use *Prof.* only before the full name.

TITLES: **Mr.** John J. Smith, **Jr.**
Dr. Alice Joyce *or* Alice Joyce, **M.D.** (*but not* Dr. Alice Joyce, M.D.)
Prof. Shelby F. Jones *but* Professor Jones

(2) Use familiar initials for organizations. Use initials (*KGB*) or **acronyms** (UNICEF) for agencies, organizations, firms, technical processes, chemical compounds, and the like when the full name is awkward or unfamiliar:

INITIALS:　　　　IBM, AFL-CIO, FBI, CIA, UNESCO, PTA, FM radio, CBS, NATO

(The current tendency is to use such abbreviations without periods. *I.R.S.* has become *IRS; I.R.A.* has become *IRA*.)

If you are not sure that your readers know an abbreviation, explain it when you first use it:

The Nuclear Regulatory Commission (NRC) denied any knowledge of the accident.

Note: Use the **ampersand** (&) and abbreviations like *Inc.* and *Bros.* only when organizations use them in their official titles: *Smith & Company, Inc.*

(3) Use familiar abbreviations related to time and number. Before or after numerals, use *A.D.* and *B.C., a.m.* and *p.m.* (also *A.M.* and *P.M.*), *no.* (also *No.*):

YEARS:　　　　Augustus reigned from 27 **B.C.** to **A.D.** 14.
HOURS:　　　　Planes leave at 11 **a.m.** and 2:30 **p.m.**
NUMBER:　　　This issue was Volume 7, **no.** 2.

(4) Spell out addresses and geographic names. Use abbreviations like *NY* or *CA* only when writing an address for a letter or the like. (Exceptions: *USSR; Washington, D.C.;* and *U.S.* in combinations like *U.S. Navy.*)

WRONG:　　　When in the **U.S.**, she lived on Grant **Ave.** in San Francisco, **Calif.**
RIGHT:　　　　When in the United States, she lived on Grant Avenue in San Francisco, California.

(5) Spell out most measurements. In ordinary prose, *lb.* (pound), *oz.* (ounce), *ft.* (foot), and *in.* (inch) are usually spelled out. Some units of measurement are more unwieldy and are abbreviated, provided they are used with figures: *45 mph, 1500 rpm.* Spell out % (percent) and ¢ (cent), but use $ for exact figures: $287.55.

MEASUREMENTS:　He used to weigh 305 **pounds**, which made him a bit sluggish in competition.

Finer Points   Some Latin abbreviations used to serve as links or tags in ordinary prose: *e.g.* (for example), *etc.* (and so on), *i.e.* (that is). The modern tendency is to prefer the corresponding English expressions.

PEER EDITOR 13   Rewrite the following sentences, using only *abbreviations appropriate in ordinary prose.*

1. Cab drivers in NYC are as likely to be from the USSR as from Boston Mass. or Athens GA.
2. Doctor Brenner was then a lit. prof. teaching Gen. Ed. classes at Baylor U.
3. The Internal Rev. Service office is out on N. Front St. and is open only in the a.m.
4. She spent eighty % of her time lobbying for the U.S. Navy in Washington, D.C.
5. A local cheese co. made a cheese that was two ft. long and weighed twenty lb.

46b   *num* | Numbers

Use figures in accordance with standard practice.

Figures are generally appropriate in references to the day of the month (*May 13*), the year (*1917*), street numbers (*1014 Union Avenue*), and page numbers (*Chapter 7, page 18*). For other uses of numbers, the following conventions are widely observed:

(1) Spell out round numbers.   Numbers from one to ten, and round numbers requiring no more than two words, are usually spelled out: *three dollars a seat, five hundred years later, ten thousand copies, about seventy-five reservations.*

WORDS: My aunt came from Ireland a **hundred** years ago, when she was **seven** years old.

FIGURES: The church was **350** years old and had withstood a major earthquake **125** years ago.

Note: In ordinary prose, the words *million* and *billion* are usually preferable to figures using large numbers of zeros: *4.8 million* (instead of *4,800,000*). However, even very large numbers are likely to appear as figures in charts and statistical reports.

(2) Use numerals for exact figures. Use numerals for exact counts, exact sums, technical measurements, decimals, numbers with fractions and percentages:

FIGURES:	500,867 inhabitants	$3.86	65 mph	4.3 miles
	3½ hours	92% (or 92 percent)		

Use numerals also for references to time using *a.m.* or *p.m.*

TIME: 2:30 p.m. (*but* three o'clock, half past twelve)

(3) Avoid numerals at the beginning of a sentence. Write "Fifteen out of 28 replied" or "When questioned, 15 out of 28 replied." Except in special situations like this one, avoid changes from figures to words (and vice versa) in a series of numbers.

(4) Hyphenate compound numbers. When spelled out, compound numbers from 21 to 99 are hyphenated: *twenty-five, one hundred and forty-six.*

DISCOURSE EXERCISE 14   Rewrite the following passage, using *abbreviations and numerals* in accordance with standard practice:

Spelling Out No.s and Abbrev.

Mister Geo. Brown had resided at Eighteen N. Washington St. since Feb. nineteen-hundred and forty-four. Though he weighed only one hundred and twenty-six lb. and measured little more than 5 ft., he was an ardent devotee of the rugged life. He did his exercises every A.M. and refused to send for the Dr. when he had a cold. 3 yrs. after he moved here from Chicago, Ill., the Boy Scouts of America made him an honorary member, & he soon became known in scout circles for the many $ he contributed to the Boy Scout movement. One Sat. afternoon B. forgot to spell out the amount on a check for one hundred and twentyfive dollars intended for a bldg. drive and payable to the B.S. of A. The treasurer, Bernard Simpson of Arlington, Va., wrote in 2 additional figures, spelled out the charged amount, and left the U.S. after withdrawing B.'s life savings of twelve-thousand five-hundred and fifty dollars from the local bank. "Ah," said Geo. when he found 2$ and 36 cts. left in his account, "if I had only spelled out the No.'s and abbrev.!"

9

The Research Paper

47   Starting Your Search

OVERVIEW   In a research paper written for a composition class, you investigate a limited subject by bringing together information and comment from several sources. In your finished paper, you present something that was worth finding out—and worth sharing with others. A successful research paper sheds light on a question about which many readers might have only superficial or contradictory ideas. It provides solid, reliable information on a subject about which many readers have only vague general impressions.

The research paper will take you two steps beyond ordinary writing projects: First, you will be *synthesizing* material from a wider range of sources. You will draw on the best available information or the best current thinking on your subject. Second, you will *document* your sources, identifying them fully, enabling your reader to trace them and check the use you have made of them.

As you start your project, formulate preliminary plans under three familiar headings:

TRIGGERING   *Why* are you interested in your topic? What previous experience or exposure will help you with your project? What do you hope to learn? What do you hope to prove? Who would make a good audience?

GATHERING   *What* sources are likely to prove helpful? Who has written about this topic, and from what perspective? Who are the experts in this field? Will there be opportunities for firsthand investigation—field trips, interviews?

549

SHAPING *How* are you going to proceed? What is your tentative plan for laying out your subject? What might be a workable strategy for covering major parts of your topic?

47a | Guidelines for Research

Think of your research paper as a writing task.

As you go through the ritual of the research paper, keep in mind your goals as a writer and the needs of your reader. It's easy to get bogged down in details; keep your eyes on the *purposes* they serve. Remember the following guidelines when choosing a promising topic and charting your course:

(1) Work on a subject that is worth the time and energy you invest. A topic may be right for you because it satisfies a latent curiosity: You might want to investigate space stations, solar energy, or nineteenth-century railroads. Or a topic may be right for you because it relates to a personal commitment, like Amnesty International or computers for the blind.

(2) Close in on a limited part of a general subject. The threat to animal life on our planet is a vast general subject—a story that would take many installments to tell. To arrive at a workable topic, you may want to focus on changing attitudes toward predators like the wolf or the coyote or on the vanishing habitats for the big birds: the condor, the whooping crane, or the bald eagle.

(3) Make full use of your library. Discover the full range of library resources and of more informal sources available to you. A good researcher needs the perseverance (and the optimism) of a prospector, always hunting down promising leads and managing not to be discouraged by those that don't work out.

(4) Synthesize material from a range of sources. Avoid subjects that would make you lean heavily on one main source, such as an encyclopedia entry or a survey article in a magazine. Your task is to sift the best current information and the most authoritative opinion and to funnel it into conclusions of your own. Be prepared to bring together scattered data and to weigh conflicting points of view.

(5) Stay close to the evidence you present. A research paper tests your ability to be **objective**, to follow the evidence where it leads. Your stance toward the audience should be: "This is the evidence. This is where I found it. You are welcome to check these sources and to verify these facts."

(6) Document your sources. Identify and describe the sources of all material you have used or adapted in your paper. Whenever you quote, make sure your reader knows who said what and where. Give credit for information, opinion, or ideas that you use as evidence. The running text of your paper will identify your sources briefly, usually including an exact page reference in parentheses. A final alphabetical listing of "Works Cited" will give full publishing data, enabling the reader, for instance, to find the right article in a magazine, the right volume in a series, or the right edition of a book. This final list may include both print and nonprint sources and is therefore often more than strictly a **bibliography** (literally, a listing of *books*).

Writing a research paper in a composition class is like taking a crash course in how to become an authority on a subject. Remember that false starts, leads that lead nowhere, and information overload are part of every researcher's day. They will seem a price worth paying as you discover the rich resources available in our information society in the age of the knowledge explosion, and as you develop techniques for making the best use of what you learn.

WRITING WORKSHOP 1   What is your previous experience with research? What is the closest you have come to making yourself an expert on a subject? Prepare a brief account of your experience. What was your interest in the topic? What resources and opportunities were available to you? What were some of the obstacles, and what were some of the rewards? Share your experience and what you learned from it with members of a group.

47b Avoiding Plagiarism

Protect yourself against charges of plagiarism.

Careful documentation helps a writer avoid **plagiarism**. Writers who plagiarize lift material from their sources without acknowledgment. They reap where others have sown. They appropriate the fruits of someone else's research without giving credit where due. The penalties for plagiarism range from failing grades to ruined reputations and wrecked careers.

People engaged in research value intellectual property as highly as material property. To avoid charges of plagiarism, hold yourself *accountable* for whatever use you make of your sources. Whenever you draw on a source, anticipate questions like the following: Who said this? Who found this out? Who assembled this information? Who drew these conclusions?

Granted, many facts and ideas are common knowledge. Major historical dates and events, key ideas of scientific or philosophical movements—these are, as it were, open to the public; they are easily found in reference books. However, identify your source whenever you use information recently discovered or collected, whenever you adopt someone's personal point of view.

You need *not* identify a specific source when you have merely repeated something that is widely known or believed:

NO SOURCE: George Washington was elected to the Virginia assembly in 1758.
(This is common knowledge, the kind of fact recorded in public documents and found in many history books.)

You *do* need to identify the source when someone else invested time and energy in discovering something not generally known, in reexamining familiar assumptions or supposed facts, or in pulling together scattered data.

SOURCE SHOWN: Samuel Eliot Morison describes Washington as "an eager and bold experimenter" in new agricultural methods (62).
(This is a judgment the historian made on the basis of firsthand investigation. The text mentions his name; the number in parentheses directs us to the right page. We will find the exact title and the facts of publication by looking in the list of "Works Cited" under "Morison.")

Remember that people engaged in research disapprove strongly of those who take over other reseachers' data and ideas without acknowledgment. Observe a few simple don'ts:

(1) Never copy whole phrases or sentences without quotation marks. It is true that you will often condense or summarize. You will often **paraphrase**—pulling out and restating important ideas in your own words. Even so, use quotation marks—both in your notes and in your actual paper—whenever you transcribe word for word characteristic phrases, parts of sentences, or whole sentences. Much unintentional plagiarism results when students include in their notes—*without* quotation marks—material that is an only slightly shortened or superficially adapted version of the original text.

ORIGINAL:	The Green parties of Western Europe point to the Industrial Revolution and nuclear power as unmitigated evils, as sins against nature.
BADLY ADAPTED:	The environmentalists of Western Europe blame modern technology and nuclear power as unmitigated evils, as sins against nature.
SAFE:	The environmentalists of Western Europe think of modern technology and nuclear power ''as unmitigated evils, as sins against nature.''

(2) Never cannibalize unidentified sources. Do not include in your writing badly digested lumps of material of uncertain origin.

(3) Never take notes without including a source tag. As a practical precaution, make sure that a brief **source tag**—showing author, publication, and page number—always accompanies borrowed material in your notes and in successive drafts.

(4) Don't simply appropriate other people's thinking. Never simply take over someone else's plan, procedure, or strategy without acknowledgment.

47c | Choosing a Subject

Choose a limited subject that allows you to bring together evidence from several different sources.

Your ideal subject for research is something that has intrigued or puzzled you in the past but that you have not had time to investigate in depth. By definition, research is an expedition into imperfectly known territory. At times, you will recognize landmarks described by earlier travelers, but you will often be revising older maps or filling in blank spaces.

The following are some general areas for research. Carve out a topic from a general area like the following:

1. *Saving the animals:* the history of a major endangered species; the story of the disappearance of the buffalo or other nearly vanished animal; current conservationist efforts to protect endangered species of birds or other animals; the struggle to protect fur-bearing animals; in defense of the wolf or the coyote.

2. *The limits of technology:* Is manned space travel necessary? Are animal experiments necessary for medical research? Do heart transplants have a future? Was the green revolution a success?

3. *Running out of energy:* the future of solar energy; the story of coal; wind power through the ages; fission and fusion; damming the last wild rivers.

4. *The graying of America:* changing attitudes toward age and aging; the passing of the youth culture; traditional stereotypes about old age; the changing self-image of senior citizens.

5. *The price of progress:* the story of the supersonic passenger plane; natural versus synthetic foods; more about additives; the automobile and the environment; acid rain; toxic waste.

6. *Fighting words in American history:* the abolitionist movement; the American suffragette; the tradition of populism; the story of segregation; the roots of unionism; robber barons or captains of industry.

7. *Future shock:* talking computers; the future of space stations; life on other planets; robots.

8. *The story of censorship:* controversial authors and the schools (Kurt Vonnegut, J. D. Salinger, Joyce Carol Oates); creationism and evolution; the definition of obscenity; unwelcome books (*1984, Grapes of Wrath, Brave New World*).

9. *Bilingual Americans:* the pros and cons of bilingual education; Hispanic versus Anglo culture; the politics of a bilingual community; the new immigrants; English as the official language.

10. *Ethnic identity and the writer:* the search for roots (Alexander Haley, Maxine Hong Kingston); the search for black identity (Richard Wright, Ralph Ellison, Lorraine Hansberry, Alice Walker, Gwendolyn Brooks, Toni Morrison, Maya Angelou); the immigrant's America (Willa Cather, Upton Sinclair, William Saroyan); discovering Latin American literature (Jorge Luis Borges, Pablo Neruda, Octavio Paz, Gabriel García Márquez).

11. *The American Indian:* the story of a forgotten tribe; the Cherokee nation; the pueblos of the Southwest; the last wars; assimilating the native Americans.

12. *Nostalgia time:* the vanishing passenger train; a short history of the stage coach; the passing of the American streetcar; ocean liners and their day of glory.

Note: By and large, you will want to stay away from highly technical subjects, which may require more knowledge of mathematics, physics, biochemistry, or the law than you can muster or than you can explain to the nonspecialist reader.

WRITING WORKSHOP 2   Your instructor may ask you to prepare a *planning report* for a paper on a research topic that you have tentatively selected. Include the why, what, and how. What previous interest or exposure can you build on? What do you hope to accomplish? What are possible sources or promising leads? What might be your overall plan or strategy? Are you aiming at a special audience or the general reader? Present your report for discussion by the class or a small group. Take notes on the queries, comments, or suggestions offered by the group. Consider them in refining or giving final shape to your plans.

Study the following example. How is the project shaping up? Does it have a purpose? What is the general strategy behind the outline?

"Unnecessary Force": Police Brutality

My main reason for choosing police brutality as a subject for research is a personal experience I had at age fifteen. While Christmas shopping with a friend, I witnessed a brutal chase by undercover police officers who were in pursuit of a teenage boy accused of shoplifting. The boy had fled from the store to the parking lot, where two huge men caught up with him. Watching them grab the suspect and throw him to the ground as blood dripped with every punch, I felt my stomach in my throat. That scene has always remained embedded in my mind, and I have often wondered how necessary it was for the police to manhandle the boy the way they did.

Merely by entering the words *police brutality* into the computerized periodical index in the library, I have found numerous articles on the subject. In the last few years, publications like *Time, Newsweek,* and *The New York Times* show titles like "New York's 'Bad Apples,'" "13 Police Suspensions," "Police Suspend 2 After Complaint," or "Police Attacks Not Uncommon." Since the topic is of urgent concern in minority neighborhoods, it is not surprising to find many relevant articles in publications aimed at minority audiences: "The Blacks and the Blues: A Special Report on Police Brutality" (*Essence*) or "Excessive Force: A National Look at Police Brutality" (*Nuestro*). I am beginning to look for relevant material in back issues of the local newspaper, and I have already informally interviewed somebody who was an actual victim of police brutality. I plan to schedule interviews with police officers to hear the other side.

I feel that trying to do justice to both sides is a necessity to make this paper work. I plan to establish first the timeliness and urgency of the topic by looking at a range of news reports and current articles. I will then look in detail at the concerns and problems of the person who is charged with a crime and feels he or she was mistreated during or after an arrest. An important facet is how such incidents are perceived by the community, especially in minority neighborhoods. I then will explore the motives or needs of the police officers involved, looking for explanations or justifications. Many young people feel the way I do about police brutality, and I am hoping to uncover some information in defense of the police and to make people see another side to this issue.

47d   Keeping a Research Log

Record the progress of your project in a research log.

Professional writers researching an article or a book often accumulate shoe boxes full of clippings, folders bulging with tattered notes, or disks crammed with stored information. Writing a research paper is your chance to develop your own style of scouting possible sources, storing promising material, and coding it for future use. Consider starting a **research log** or search diary. Use it to write notes to yourself about early leads and tentative plans. Enter lists of promising sources with brief reminders of why they sound useful. Record tentative conclusions and trial outlines as your project gets underway.

You will soon be taking more formal notes (on note cards or as computer entries), quoting and summarizing material for future use. Use your research log as an informal record of your findings, plans, and thoughts. Here are some sample entries from a research log for a paper about changing attitudes toward aging:

PROMISING LEADS—sources the writer has seen mentioned; individuals and organizations that should be investigated; key terms that keep coming up:

Gray Panthers (over 65 years old)
geriatrics - treating the diseases of old age
periodicals: Gerontologist, 50 plus
National Institute on Aging
AARP - American Assoc. of Retired Persons
National Retired Teachers Assoc.
National Council of Senior Citizens

Check: Elis Kübler-Ross, Margaret Mead, Maggie Kuhn, Simone de Beauvoir - book on aging?

CHECKING OF SOURCES—lists of possible sources the writer has copied from reference guides such as *Sociological Abstracts* or *Social Sciences Index*; brief notes on especially promising materials:

Sociological Abstracts (1982)
✓ Aged's status change M 3697
✓ Aged, popular culture centers M 2680
~~Aged, prestige decline M 3699~~
✓ Aging news, no longer negative image M 5180
~~Sociological perspective M 6758~~

✓ Attitudes toward age S 15182
✓ Alex Comfort M 5573

Social Sciences Citation Index (1983)
micro - Mehlinger, L. J., "Intergenerational
    Programs - The Changing Faces of Aging,"
    Gerontologist 23: 227

Check: S. Seixax, "Fighting to Stay on the Job,"
   Money 13 (Feb. 84): 113-14 (ousted 61-yr. old
   executive Ron Anderson)

RECORD OF OBSERVATIONS—the writer's notes on firsthand investigation, including interviews, conversations, viewing of news programs, and the like:

CHANNEL 7 NEWS
WHAT: Senior Swingers' softball - annual event for men and
    women 60 - 80 yrs. old
WHO: "Geritol Giants" and "Amazing A's"
WHERE: St. Mary's in San Francisco
WHY: "to have fun ... and win"
HIGHLIGHTS: 1) changed rules to suit themselves (no
    strikeouts, no walks, 7 pitches, all may bat);
    2) cheerleaders; 3) newscaster's thought: "I
    thought what you were supposed to do
    when you got to be this age was to lie in a
    hammock"

TRIAL OUTLINES AND TENTATIVE CONCLUSIONS—the writer's preliminary attempts to sort out and add up the results of her investigation:

my thoughts:
*1) people who years ago called for changing attitudes
toward aging have helped to bring about much of
what they called for: greater dignity, more self-
assertion, and more independence on the part of
older people*
*2) the baby boom generation is getting older – changing
from glorification of youth to more sympathy with
the feelings of older people*

AGENDA FOR RESEARCH—the writer's notes on issues to be explored, facts
to be checked, data to be updated:

*AARP had 9 million members – how many today?
"fountain-of-youth" drugs – status of current research?
new breed of older people in current TV drama?
check current educational programs offered the elderly
more recent study on retirement preferences?*

Help your plans and ideas take shape by putting them down on paper.
By registering your current research activity as you go along, you can
avoid the backtracking and the hunting for some item only dimly remembered that frustrate researchers relying too much on memory. Remember
that your research log is your personal memory aid and planning aid. Work
out your own system for making the best use of it.

CAUTION: Make sure that any phrases or sentences you copy from
a source are identified as *quotations* and accompanied by a source tag for
possible future use.

WRITING WORKSHOP 3   Although your research log is for your own use,
prepare to share these and other materials with classmates. Be prepared to
compare notes on promising sources, lucky finds, and tentative directions.

---

48   Going to the Sources

OVERVIEW The experienced investigator knows where to look. To conduct a successful search, you have to know how to tap the resources of your college library. Although your search strategy will vary from subject to subject, you will normally explore three major kinds of materials:

- *reference works* (encyclopedias, specialized dictionaries, guides) that provide an overview or summary of your subject
- *magazine or newspaper articles* that deal with limited areas of your subject or with current developments
- *books* (or sections of books) that deal with your subject in some depth

Remember that your library is not the *only* source of information. Your phone book has a special section listing government agencies where you might write for advice or enlightenment. Your college as well as local businesses and organizations will employ experts who might consent to be interviewed. On subjects touching on local history, relatives or neighbors might serve as resource persons for your project.

In a successful search, one find leads to another. For instance, when writing about the competitive edge enjoyed by Japanese industry, you may turn first to classic treatments of the subject—books often mentioned or quoted, such as William Ouchi's *Theory Z* or Ezra Vogel's *Japan as Number One*. Checking one familiar area of competition, you may look in a periodical index under "Automobiles—Export/Import" and find articles with titles like "We're a Colony Again, This Time of Japan." (This article turns out to be an interview with Lee Iacocca, published in *U.S. News & World Report.*) Looking up the broader topic "Balance of Trade," you may find articles like "Japan Is Fanning Protectionist Fires on the Hill" (published in *Business Week*). One of these articles provides a helpful bibliography, listing articles with titles like "Meeting the Japanese Economic Challenge" (*Business Horizons*), "Why the Japanese Seem to Be Eight Feet Tall" (*Fortune*), and "Learning from the Japanese" (*Management Review*). In the meantime, you have found some insiders to interview—a worker in an American plant under Japanese management, a student who spent a year in Japan.

As you sift the input for your paper, think of the library as a resource center and service center. Learn how to retrieve material recorded in miniaturized form on **microfilm** or **microfiche**. Learn how to draw on **data**

banks and other computerized sources of information. Use facilities for photocopying articles or pages from a book. When stymied, ask a librarian about reference works, indexes, library services, or research strategies.

Evaluating Sources

Draw on reliable information from authoritative sources.

At the beginning, you may welcome almost anything in print on your subject, but soon you will turn selective. Your aim is to draw useful information and expert opinion from reliable sources. This means that you will have to distrust some of the more perishable kinds of publication: campaign biographies, chamber-of-commerce brochures, nonbooks improvised to exploit a current trend. More generally, you will have to ask yourself: "Who is talking? How does this author know? What side is the writer on, or what is the hidden agenda?" When evaluating possible sources, keep in mind test questions like the following:

(1) Is the writer an authority on the subject? Experts are not infallible, but it's good to know that an author has written and lectured widely on the subject and is frequently quoted or consulted. It's comforting to find that an author writing about agribusiness has been in the fields to talk with workers and supervisors, has studied government and corporate reports, and has read recent studies of relevant trends.

(2) Is the work a thorough study of the subject? Does it show a grasp of the historical background; does it seriously explore causes and effects? Does it take the opinions of others seriously, carefully weighing the pro and con on debated issues? Is it short on opinion and long on evidence?

(3) Does the author draw on primary sources? Reliable authorities do not simply accept secondhand accounts; they settle important questions by turning to **primary sources**—legal documents, diaries, letters, eyewitness reports, transcripts of speeches and interviews, reports on experiments, statistical surveys. They take us close to unedited firsthand facts.

561

(4) Is the author biased? The bailout of a large automobile manufacturer through government loans will be viewed one way in the autobiography of the company's chief executive. The story will be told differently by an aggressive critic of corporate politics. Whenever possible, try to look at both sides; try to find accounts by less directly interested parties to balance one-sided views.

(5) Is the work up to date? Has it profited from recent research or newly discovered facts? If it was first published ten or twenty years ago, is there a revised, more recent edition? Keep in mind that a writer may have been left behind by new findings and new thinking in a burgeoning field.

WRITING WORKSHOP 4   Team up with classmates to prepare a report on the resources of your library. You might farm out areas like the following to different members of the team:

1. What is the nature of the *central catalog*—card catalog or computerized system? How does it work? What system of classification does it use—Dewey decimal or Library of Congress? Spot check library holdings on a few selected topics, such as fly casting, World War I, body language, the history of English, or bilingual education.
2. How does the library guide you to its periodical holdings? Is there a central *periodical index*? What is the policy for access to current magazines? When are bound volumes available? (And how long does it take for magazines to get back from the bindery?) Spot check the library's subscription list for periodicals in selected areas, such as architecture, computer science, pharmacology, art, or poetry. Try out microfilm or microfiche services.
3. Are there *special collections* or special branches of the library? Are there special collections for rare books, ethnic studies materials, authors' memorabilia, or the like? How accessible are these materials to students? What are the materials like? Is there a special department for government publications?
4. What kind of *media services* does your library provide? Where and how do users obtain records, videotapes, art prints, films, and maps? Spot check the library's holdings in such selected areas as Shakespeare plays, Bach cantatas, and classic films.
5. What access does the library provide to *databases* such as those available from the DIALOG Information Retrieval Service? What are the procedures and the cost? If you can, obtain an example of a computer-generated bibliography on a subject like women in sports, the artificial heart, or English as the official language.

6. What are the special *strengths* or weaknesses of your college library? Interview librarians or instructors who are especially concerned about library resources in their fields.

48b   Using Reference Works

Learn to use the reference tools available to every investigator.

Reference books were the memory banks of the print age. (Many are now being converted to the technology of the chip age.) Commonly available reference works range from weighty multivolume sets to handy manuals and guides. Often a well-established guide becomes the bible of music lovers, car mechanics, or electronics engineers. You will find specialized reference works in a guide like Eugene P. Sheehy's *Guide to Reference Books*, published by the American Library Association. Here is a sampling of reference works that are often consulted:

ENCYCLOPEDIAS   An encyclopedia is sometimes a good place to start—but not to finish—an investigation.

- The *Encyclopaedia Britannica* (an American publication) is the most authoritative of the general encyclopedias. It is brought up to date each year by the *Britannica Book of the Year*. A complete revision, called *The New Encyclopaedia Britannica*, was published in 1974 and has been updated since. It has two major sections: a ten-volume quick-reference index (the *Micropaedia*) and a nineteen-volume guide to more detailed information on many subjects (the *Macropaedia*).
- The *Encyclopedia Americana* is sometimes recommended for science and biography. General subjects are broken up into short articles, arranged alphabetically. The annual supplement is the *Americana Annual*.
- The one-volume *Columbia Encyclopedia* serves well for a quick check of people and places.

BIOGRAPHY   In addition to biographical entries in encyclopedias, libraries usually have ample materials for a paper reassessing the role or reputation of a famous person.

- *Who's Who in America*, a biographical dictionary of outstanding living men and women, provides capsule biographies of impor-

563

tant contemporaries. (The original *Who' Who* is a British publication. Specialized offshoots of the same publication include *Who's Who of American Women*.)

- The *Dictionary of American Biography (DAB)* gives a more detailed account of the lives of significant persons. (The British counterpart is the *Dictionary of National Biography*.)

- The *Biography Index* is a guide to biographical material in books and magazines. It may lead you, for example, to material on the married life of George Washington or the evangelism of Billy Graham.

- *Contemporary Authors* (a frequently updated multivolume work) gives information on authors of current books and includes biographical facts, excerpts from reviews, and comments by the authors.

LITERATURE A library project may deal with an author's schooling or early reading, recurrent themes in the books of a well-known novelist, or the contemporary reputation of a nineteenth-century poet.

- The fifteen-volume *Cambridge History of English Literature* and the *Cambridge Bibliography of English Literature* take stock of English authors and literary movements.

- The Spiller-Thorp-Johnson-Canby *Literary History of the United States*, with its supplementary bibliographies, lists as its contributors an impressive roster of American literary scholars.

- *Harper's Dictionary of Classical Literature and Antiquities* is a comprehensive scholarly guide to Greek and Roman history and civilization. (Books like Michael Grant's *Myths of the Greeks and Romans* and Edith Hamilton's *Mythology*, available as paperbacks, introduce the reader to famous names and stories.)

Note: You will increasingly be able to find special bibliographies and dictionaries for the literature of minorities and of regions.

OTHER FIELDS OF INTEREST Every major field of interest has its own specialized reference guides: specialized encyclopedias, dictionaries of names or technical terms, or yearbooks reporting on current developments. For instance, a student majoring in business administration will come to know books like the *Dictionary of Economics, The Encyclopedia of Management, The Encyclopedia of Banking and Finance,* and the *Handbook of Modern Marketing.* Here is a sampling of specialized reference works frequently consulted:

- *American Universities and Colleges* and *American Junior Colleges* provide basic facts about educational institutions.
- The *McGraw-Hill Encyclopedia of Science and Technology* is kept up to date by the *McGraw-Hill Yearbook of Science and Technology.*
- The *Encyclopedia of Computer Science and Technology* is a multivolume guide to a rapidly growing field. (Harry Thomas' *Electronic Vest Pocket Reference Book* is a classic pocket guide to electronics.)
- The *Dictionary of American History* by J. T. Adams is a six-volume guide.
- Langer's *Encyclopedia of World History* is a long-established reference guide in one volume.
- The *International Encyclopedia of the Social Sciences* is a multivolume reference work.
- *Grove's Dictionary of Music and Musicians,* a multivolume reference guide for music lovers, covers biography, history, and technical terms.
- The *McGraw-Hill Encyclopedia of World Art* has fifteen volumes.
- The Funk and Wagnalls *Standard Dictionary of Folklore, Mythology, and Legend* is one of several well-known guides to basic themes in folk culture and folk tradition.
- *Vital Speeches of the Day* can help you find recent speeches by government officials or business executives on topics like Third World debt, threats to free trade, or the impact of new technologies on employment.

BIBLIOGRAPHIES For many subjects of general interest, you will be able to find a printed **bibliography**—an inventory of important books and other sources of information. Writing about Emily Dickinson, John Steinbeck, or William Faulkner, you should be able to find a book-length bibliography of publications by and about the author. Shorter bibliographical listings often appear at the end of an entry in an encyclopedia or a chapter in a textbook.

Especially helpful are **annotated bibliographies** that provide a capsule description of each source. The following might be a sample entry:

Edsels, Luckies, & Frigidaires by Robert Atwan, Donald McQuade, and John W. Wright (New York: Dell, 1972) is a large-format paperback which resembles nothing so much as a 100-year scrapbook of

American advertising. Over 250 full-page ads are organized under three main headings, "Advertising and Social Roles," "Advertising and Material Civilization," and "Advertising and the Strategies of Persuasion." Chronological arrangement of the ads reflects changes in the "good life" over the last century.

BOOK REVIEWS The *Book Review Digest* excerpts book reviews written shortly after publication of a book. Book review sections are a regular feature of many professional publications. The following is an example of a short book review from the *Library Journal:*

> **De Santis, Marie. Neptune's Apprentice: adventures of a commercial fisherwoman.** Presidio Pr. Jun. 1984. c.256p. illus. by Patricia Walker. ISBN 0-89141-200-X. $15.95.
>
> SOC SCI. PER NAR
>
> There are innumerable books about the lure of the sea but very few are by women. De Santis was a doctoral student in the late 1960s when she heard the siren call and, after brief apprenticeships on California commercial fishing boats, she determined to be her own captain. To describe the way the sea "shaped the spirit of its people" she tells of the people in the fleet for the eight years she fished: toil, fear, acceptance by the fishing fraternity, greed, fish and game bumbling—and always the search for the elusive fish. She left just before much of the fishing collapsed, but the sea remained with her. This is a fine testament to an individual's maturing and to the environment. Recommended, not just for libraries near the sea.—*Roland Person: Southern Illinois Univ. Lib., Carbondale*

LIBRARY WORK 5   Study *one* of the following often-mentioned *reference tools*. Prepare a brief report on its scope, usefulness, and format. Try to provide useful advice to prospective users; include some interesting sidelights.

1. *Books in Print*
2. *National Union Catalog (NUC)*
3. *Library of Congress Subject Headings*

4. *Sociological Abstracts*
5. *Contemporary Authors*
6. *Readers' Guide to Periodical Literature*
7. *Who's Who of American Women*
8. *Wall Street Journal Index*
9. *Historical Abstracts*
10. *Sheehy's Guide to Reference Books*
11. *Dictionary of Scientific Biography*
12. *Bartlett's Familiar Quotations*
13. *Comprehensive Dictionary of Psychological and Psychoanalytic Terms*
14. *McGraw-Hill Dictionary of Art*
15. *Concise Encyclopedia of Living Faiths*

48c | Finding Articles in Periodicals

Know how to find articles in current and past issues of magazines and newspapers.

Much information or comment is published in **periodicals**—publications that appear at regular intervals, ranging from the daily newspaper to monthly and quarterly magazines. Writing about the vanishing whooping crane, you might find useful articles in periodicals such as *National Geographic, National Wildlife, Audubon, Outdoor Life,* and *Smithsonian.* Writing about robots in automobile factories, you might find useful articles in periodicals such as *Car and Driver, Technology Review, Business Week, Omni,* and *Science Digest.*

Most libraries have a compact catalog for all periodicals to which the library subscribes. This catalog, separate from the general catalog of the library, will show the location of recent issues and back issues, as well as availability on microfilm or microfiche.

COMPUTERIZED INDEXES Many libraries now have a central computerized index that will call up for you a battery of current magazine articles on a given subject. Trying to find material on changing patterns of modern marriage, you might punch in the key word MARRIAGE. The following might be a partial printout of what would appear on the screen:

```
                                    InfoTrac Database
                                    1/1/90 at 12:28
MARRIAGE
  —ADDRESSES, ESSAYS, LECTURES
          Changing relationships between men and
      women; scope of the problem.  (transcript)
      Vital Speeches—Oct 1 '84 p757(8)
MARRIAGE
  —ANALYSIS
          What is this state called marriage? by
      Elaine Brown Whitley il Essence Magazine—Feb
      '85 p54(5)
      #32D2299
MARRIAGE
  —CASE STUDIES
          First marriage after 40, by Lynn Normont
      il Ebony—Jan '83 p28(7)
      #15A2292
MARRIAGE
  —ECONOMIC ASPECTS
          The money side of marriage. il Changing
      Times—June '85 p32(6)
      #27K5219
          Equal pay for different work saved our
      marriage.  (physician pays wife for domestic
      duties) by Daniel L. Brick, Medical
      Economics—Feb 4 '85 p95(3)
MARRIAGE
  —FORECASTS
          Changes in marriage and the family:
      looking back from the twenty—first century.
      il Futurist—April '85 p84(3)
      #23B2988
```

PRINTED PERIODICAL INDEXES To find magazine articles on your subject, you will often search the printed periodical indexes in your library. Published in monthly or semimonthly installments, these are later combined in huge volumes, each listing articles for a period of one or more years.

- The *Readers' Guide to Periodical Literature* indexes magazines written for the general reader. These range from newsmagazines like *Time, Newsweek,* and *U.S. News & World Report* to periodicals with more specialized audiences—*Working Woman, Science Digest, Technology Review,* or *The American Scholar.*

In the *Readers' Guide,* articles are listed twice—once under the author's name and once under a subject heading. At times, you will look up a much-quoted, much-interviewed authority—Isaac Asimov on robots, Betty Harragan on corporate gamesmanship for women. More often, you will scout for material under subject headings like "Engineering," split into categories like "Management," "Social Aspects," and "Study and Teaching" and followed by "Engineering and the Humanities," "Engineering Research," and "Engineering Students." Some subject headings in the *Readers' Guide* are the names of people—scientists, artists, politicians, celebrities—written up in an article.

Compare two entries for the same article as listed in the *Readers' Guide.* The first of these is the *author entry,* the second the *subject entry:*

AUTHOR ENTRY: **HARRIS, Michael**
        Junk in outer space. il Progressive 42:16-19 N
        '78
SUBJECT ENTRY: **SPACE pollution**
        Junk in outer space. M. Harris. il Progressive
        42:16-19 N '78

The author entry begins with the full name of the author; the subject entry begins with the general subject: space pollution. The title of the article is "Junk in Outer Space." (The abbreviation *il* shows that the article is illustrated.) The name of the magazine comes next: *Progressive.* Note especially the following information:

- The *volume number* for the magazine is 42. *Page numbers* for the article follow after the colon: 16 through 19. (Sometimes the symbol + appears after the last page number; it shows that the article is continued or concluded later in the magazine.)

569

- The *date of publication* was November 1978. (For magazines published more than once a month, the exact date is given. For example "N 10 '78" means "November 10, 1978.")

Survival hint for the student writer: Whether you use the *Readers' Guide* or a more specialized index, don't miss the introductory page: Study the list of abbreviations and the list of the periodicals indexed. Look at sample entries to study the listing of individual articles and the system of cross-references.

Other guides to periodicals intended for a general audience:

- *Essay and General Literature Index* may help you when you are not satisfied with what you find in the *Readers' Guide*.
- *Poole's Index to Periodical Literature*, covering the years from 1802–1907, is a guide to British and American magazines of the past. You might consult it, for instance, when looking for contemporary reactions to Wagner's operas or Ibsen's plays.
- *Popular Periodicals Index*, published since 1973, will prove helpful to students of popular culture.

The following are guides to periodical literature in specialized subject areas:

- *Applied Science and Technology Index* (see the *Industrial Arts Index* for years before 1958)
- *Art Index*
- *Biological and Agricultural Index* (called *Agricultural Index* before 1964)
- *Business Periodicals Index*
- *Education Index*
- *Engineering Index*
- *General Science Index*
- *Humanities Index* (now a separate publication, combined with the *Social Sciences Index* during the years 1965–1973)
- *Social Sciences Index* (formerly *International Index*; lists articles in sociological and psychological journals)

CURRENT EVENTS A number of special reference guides are useful for papers on a political subject or on current events:

- *Facts on File* is a weekly digest of world news, with an annual index. It gives a summary of news reports and comments, with excerpts from important documents and speeches.
- The *New York Times Index* (published since 1913) is a guide to news stories published in the *New York Times*. Look up an event

or a controversy in this index to find the approximate dates for coverage in other newspapers and magazines.

- The annual index to the *Monthly Catalog of the United States Government Publications* lists reports and documents published by all branches of the federal government.

ABSTRACTS You can often identify useful articles by looking at **abstracts**—short summaries of articles in a field, usually collected and published several times a year. The following is an example from Volume 30 of *Sociological Abstracts:*

82M2679
Fly, Jerry W., Reinhart, George R. & Hamby, Russell (Georgia Coll, Milledgeville 31061), Leisure Activity and Adjustment in Retirement, *Sociological Spectrum,* 1981, 1, 2, Apr-June, 135–144.
¶ A sample of retired persons (N = 134) in a southern metropolitan area responded to a questionnaire designed to investigate the interrelationship between level of leisure activity & adjustment in retirement. Adjustment was measured by two indices, life satisfaction & alienation. Results show that persons who have more leisure activities are more satisfied with their lives & are less alienated than those who have few leisure activities. 2 Tables. HA

COMPUTERIZED RESEARCH Computerized information services and research tools are greatly simplifying and speeding up a writer's search for sources.

- A system like INFOTRAC provides an instant listing of relevant current newspaper and magazine articles from hundreds of publications. By typing in key words or retrieval codes, you can call up on the screen (and print out if you wish) a wide range of sources on subjects like marriage, divorce, acid rain, recessions, or men's fashions. You can call up book reviews, articles by or about a person, or sources of printed information about a company or business.

- The WILSEARCH system provides access to periodical indexes including the *Reader's Guide to Periodical Literature, Biography Index, General Science Index, Social Sciences Index, Art Index,* and *Book Review Digest.* You can instruct the computer to search for background information published on your topic over many years.

- The DIALOG information service provides access to many different **databases**—collections of information stored in large computers. The service allows you to tap into sources of information covering areas like government statistics, science, medicine, law, business, finance, or current news events. A printed index (or a librarian) can help you find the right **descriptors**—subject labels or key words that will help the computer search for material on your topic. If your home computer has a **modem**, or telephone hookup, you may be able to have a complete reprint of an article produced on your own printer.

If you use the DIALOG service in your search for articles on your research topic, it will provide a printout describing possible sources in the following format. For inclusion in your records, note the item number (EJ 281390) and the file number (IR 511297):

```
EJ281390  IR511297
  Censorship Today and Probably Tomorrow.
  Donelson, Ken
  Canadian Library Journal, v40 n2 p83-89 Apr 1983
  Language: English
  Document Type: JOURNAL ARTICLE (080); POSITION
  PAPER (120)
  Journal Announcement: CIJSEP83
  Examines preconceptions of censorship, citing
problems posed to librarians and teachers.
Highlights include censored books; individual
censors (including the Gablers); organized groups
(including Save Our Schools (SOS), Phyllis
Schlafly's Eagle Forum, and the Moral Majority);
teacher and librarian censors (moral, literary,
sociological); and those who aid and abet censors.
(EJS)
```

When using a system like DIALOG, remember the following advice:

■ **Check costs ahead of time.** Your college may be subscribing to a database (such as DIALOG) and make the service available to students at no cost or low cost. Otherwise, costs to you personally may range from reasonable to substantial.

■ **Let a librarian or system specialist help you in your search.** You will need help regarding which databases to tap into. You are likely to need help with translating your research topic into the key word or words that will help the computer track down relevant sources.

■ **Remember possible limitations.** Databases started to file and index material in the early seventies. For earlier materials, you may have to go to conventional library sources.

LIBRARY WORK 6 Interpret and discuss the following sample entries from the *Readers' Guide*. What information do they provide?

Ocean pollution *See* Marine pollution; Oil pollution
Ocean travel
> *See also*
> Cruising
> Voyages
> Voyages around the world

Oceanic
> *See also*
> Nuclear-free zones—Oceanic

Oceanic earthquakes *See* Earthquakes
Oceanographic submersibles
> Deep seeing. W. Sullivan. il *Oceans* 19:18-23 Ja/F '86
> Explorers of dark frontiers [Deep Rover] S. Brownlee. il *Discover* 7:60-7 F '86
> Finding the Titanic [images from the Argo] M. Spalding and B. Dawson. il *Byte* 11:96-100+ Mr '86

Oceanography
> *See also*
> Artificial satellites—Oceanographic use
> International Oceanographic Foundation
> Ocean-atmosphere interaction
> Ocean bottom
> Ocean Drilling Program
> Oceanographic submersibles
> Sea water
> Space flight—Oceanographic use
> United States. National Oceanic and Atmospheric Administration

Oceans (Periodical)
> Changing of the watch. C. du P. Roosevelt. *Oceans* 19:2 Ja/F '86
> Defining Oceans. M. W. Robbins. *Oceans* 19:3 Ja/F '86

O'Connell, Brian F.
> Soviet Christians one year after Gorbachev. il *Christ Today* 30:44-6 Mr 21 '86

O'Connell, Maurice R. (Maurice Rickard)
> Myths in Irish history. *America* 154:200-3 Mr 15 '86

O'Connell, Tom
> Less corn, more hell. il *Progressive* 50:15 Ja '86

O'Connell-Cahill, Catherine
> There's got to be a mourning after [with readers' comments] *U S Cathol* 51:14-19 Mr '86

O'Connell-Cahill, Michael
> Whiskey river please run dry: alcoholism in the Christian family. il *U S Cathol* 51:18-26 F '86

O'Connor, Colleen
> Who's afraid of the F.E.C.? *Wash Mon* 18:22+ Mr '86

LIBRARY WORK 7 In the *Readers' Guide, Social Sciences Index,* or *Humanities Index,* find an article on *one* of the subjects listed below. Write a brief report. Include the facts of publication, the purpose of the article, intended audience, main point or points, overall plan or strategy. Comment on level of difficulty, handling of technical terms or difficult material, and the like. Include one or two key quotations.

- talking computers
- the artificial heart
- sign language for apes
- schizophrenia
- reevaluations of the CIA or FBI
- competency tests for teachers
- women executives
- dissent in the Soviet Union
- drug testing for athletes
- basketball recruiting
- the homeless
- mainstreaming the disabled

 48d Finding Books in the Library Catalog

Learn to use the general catalog of your library.

For the typical research paper in a composition class, you will be expected to find several book-length treatments of your general subject, or to find relevant sections or chapters in several books. An important part of your research itinerary is to go book hunting in the general catalog of your college library.

Many libraries today are in a state of transition from the card catalogs of the print age to the online catalogs of the computer age. The traditional catalog has been a card catalog with rows of drawers holding printed index cards in alphabetical order. Today, users increasingly view computerized catalog information on screens. However, the kind and arrangement of the information will be similar under the different systems. An important difference (and a godsend to the harried researcher) is that the computer catalog is likely to be set up for searches by key word. For instance, if you use the key words SPORTS MEDICINE, the computer will provide a listing of all the books in your library that have the words SPORTS and MEDICINE anywhere in their titles.

Old-style catalog cards use the Library of Congress format, like this:

Q175
K95
1970
	Kuhn, Thomas S
	    The structure of scientific revolutions, by Thomas S. Kuhn. (2d ed., enl. Chicago, University of Chicago Press, 1970)
	
	    xii, 210 p. 24 cm. (International encyclopedia of unified science. Foundations of the unity of science, v. 2, no. 2)
	
	      Includes bibliographical references.
	
	      1. Science—Philosophy. 2. Science—History. ɪ. Title.
	(Series: International encyclopedia of unified science, v. 2, no. 2)
	Q175.K95 1970 501 79-107472
	SBN 226-45803-2 MARC
	Library of Congress 70 [4]

New-style computer entries may look like this:

Call#:	JX 1944.H68 1978b
Author:	Howard, Michael Eliot, 1922—
Title:	War and the liberal conscience / by Michael Howard. New Brunswick, N.J.: Rutgers University Press, 1978. 143 p. ; 23 cm.
Series:	The Trevelyan lectures ; 1977.
Notes:	Includes bibliographical references and index.
Subjects:	Peace—History World politics—To 1900 World politics—20th century War—History Liberalism Europe—Politics and government.
Also listed under:	Trevelyan lectures ; 1977.

In the typical library catalog, the same book is listed several times: by *author* (under the author's last name), by *title* (under the first word of the title, not counting *The, A,* or *An*), and by *subject*. At times, you will be tracking down a promising author or book, following up leads you already have. But often you will ferret out possibly useful books under the right subject headings.

AUTHOR ENTRIES Author entries give you complete publishing information about each separate book by an author, with titles arranged in alphabetical order. Entries for books *about* the author may follow at the end. Know how to read the information on the typical Library of Congress card:

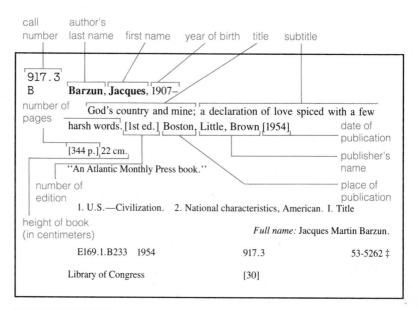

SAMPLE AUTHOR CARD

Look for clues to the nature of the book:

■ *The number or description of the edition.* If the catalog lists both the original edition and another marked "2nd ed." or "Rev. ed.," generally choose the one that is more up to date.

■ *The name and location of the publisher.* For instance, a book published by a university press is likely to be a scholarly or specialized study. The

576

date of publication is especially important for books on scientific, technological, or medical subjects, where information dates rapidly.

■ *The number of pages* (with the number of introductory pages given as a lowercase Roman numeral). It shows whether the book is a short pamphlet or a full-scale treatment of the subject. If the book contains *illustrations* or a *bibliography*, the card will carry a notation to that effect.

■ *The subject headings* (which show under what headings the book will be listed in the catalog). The listing for the Barzun book shows that the book will be of interest to students of the American image or the American national character. An entry for a sociological study of a Midwestern town may carry the following notation concerning various headings under which the study is listed:

1. U.S.—Social conditions.   2. Cities and Towns—U.S.
3. Cost and standard of living—U.S.   4. U.S.—Religion.
5. Social surveys.   6. Community life.

TITLE ENTRIES Title entries carry the same information as author entries—except that the title is repeated at the top for alphabetical listing. The following might be a locally generated title card:

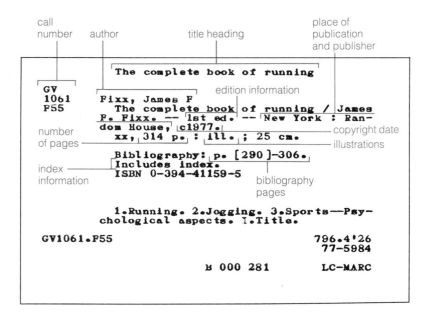

SAMPLE TITLE CARD

SUBJECT ENTRIES   Subject entries will often be your best hope for finding usable books. Under what headings is material for your topic likely to surface? For instance, books on the American Civil War might appear under *U.S.—History—Civil War*, under *U.S.—History—Military*, under *Slavery in the United States*, or under *Abolitionists*. Try to think of other key terms that might appear in the catalog: *Confederacy* or *Emancipation*. Pay special attention to **cross-references** that often appear at the beginning of a set of related subject entries:

```
FISHES, see also
    Aquariums
    Tropical fishes
      (also names of fishes, e.g., Salmon)
```

Librarians recommend that you consult the *Library of Congress Subject Headings* as a guide to finding material by subject in the library catalog. Here is an example of a typed subject card from the card catalog of a special division of a college library:

```
978       MORMONS AND MORMONISM—HISTORY
S

          Stegner, Wallace Earle, 1909-

          The gathering of Zion; the story of the
          Mormons, by Wallace Stegner. 1st ed. New York,
          McGraw-Hill, 1964

          331 p. illus. maps 23 cm (American Trails
          series)

          Bibliography: pp. 315-319
```

SAMPLE SUBJECT CARD

Note: In large libraries, subject entries may appear in a separate alphabetical listing divided from the rest of the catalog.

CALL NUMBERS Once you decide that you should consult a book, copy its call number. The **call number** directs you, or the librarian, to the shelf where the book is located. Your library may use either the Library of Congress system or the Dewey decimal system.

■ The **Library of Congress system** divides books into categories identified by letters of the alphabet. It then uses additional letters and numerals to subdivide each main category. For instance, the call number of a book on religion starts with a capital *B*. The call number of a book on education starts with a capital *L*.

■ The **Dewey decimal system** uses numerals to identify the main categories. For instance, 400–499 covers books on language; 800–899 covers books on literature. The 800 range is then further subdivided into American literature (810–819), English literature (820–829), and so on. Additional numerals and letters close in on individual authors and individual works by the same author.

LIBRARY WORK 8 Through the central catalog of the library, find *one* of the following books. Study its preface or introduction, table of contents, and a key chapter or sample entries. Then prepare a brief *book review* that tells your reader about the purpose of the book, its intended audience, the scope of the book, and its overall plan. Include one or two characteristic or revealing quotations.

■ Bruno Bettelheim, *The Uses of Enchantment*

■ Leo Rosten, *The Joys of Yiddish*

■ G. M. Trevelyan, *History of England*

■ Barbara W. Tuchman, *A Distant Mirror*

■ Kenneth Rexroth, *Classics Revisited*

■ Norma Lorre Goodrich, *Ancient Myths*

■ Margaret Mead, *Male and Female*

- Alden T. Vaughan, *New England Frontier: Puritans and Indians*
- Robert Coles, *Children of Crisis*
- Thomas Pyles, *The Origin and Development of the English Language*
- Mari Sandoz, *Cheyenne Autumn*
- Margaret M. Bryant, *Current American Usage*
- Desmond Morris, *The Naked Ape*
- Konrad Lorenz, *On Aggression*
- Joseph Campbell, *The Hero with a Thousand Faces*
- Simone de Beauvoir, *The Second Sex*
- Alice Walker, *In Search of Our Mothers' Gardens*
- Adrienne Rich, *On Lies, Secrets, and Silence*
- Maxine Hong Kingston, *China Men*
- Richard Rodriguez, *Hunger of Memory*

48e   Your Working List of Sources

Keep a complete record of promising sources.

From the beginning, record complete data for a working list of promising sources. Prepare a separate **source card** or source entry for each book, pamphlet, article, or nonprint source. (Research guides are moving away from terms like *working bibliography* or *bibliography card* because they might imply that research should be limited to *printed* sources—to the exclusion of interviews, for instance, or documentaries.)

Some of the information in your preliminary list of sources is mainly for your own use in locating the book or article: the complete call number or a location in the library. But most of the information will be essential when you identify your sources in your finished paper.

SOURCE CARDS FOR BOOKS   When preparing your source cards for books, use the format that you will need to observe when later typing your final list of works used (or cited) in your finished paper: Start with the last name of the author. Underline (italicize) title and any subtitle. Indent the second line five spaces. A typical entry might look like this:

```
HV
947                Mitford, Jessica.  Kind and Usual
M58                    Punishment:  The Prison Business.
1073                   New York:  Random, 1973
```

SOURCE CARD—BOOK

For accurate identification of a book, you will need to record the author's name, the title of the book, and complete publishing data. Start with the *full name of the author*—last name first to facilitate alphabetizing. Second, give the *full title* of the book, including any subtitle (separate it from the main title by a colon). Underline or italicize title and subtitle of a book, pamphlet, or other work that appeared as a separate publication. (Underlining in a handwritten or typed manuscript converts to italics in print.)

The publishing data, or *facts of publication*, for a book may include the following:

- *editor's or translator's name* if the book has been put together or translated by someone other than the author(s): "Shakespeare, William. *The Complete Works*, ed. G. B. Harrison" or "Chekhov, Anton. *The Cherry Orchard*, trans. Tyrone Guthrie and Leonid Kipnis."
- *number or description of the edition* if the book has been revised or brought up to date: "3rd ed." or "Rev. ed."
- *number of volumes* if a work consists of several and all relate to your investigation: "2 vols."

- *place of publication* (usually the location of the main office of the publishing house, or of the first office listed if several are given).
- *name of the publisher*, leaving out such tags as "Inc." or "and Company": "Random"; "McGraw-Hill."
- *date of publication* (if no date is listed on the title page, use the latest copyright date listed on the reverse side of the title page).
- *number of the volume used* (if only one volume of a larger work seems relevant to your investigation): "Vol. 3."

SOURCE CARDS FOR ARTICLES For accurate identification of an article, you will need to record both the *title of the article* (in quotation marks) and the *title of the periodical* (underlined or italicized). The quotation marks show that an article, story, or poem was *part* of a larger publication. An annotated card, including brief reminders about the article, may look like this:

Periodical Room   Schorer, Mark. "D. H. Lawrence: Then, During, Now," <u>Atlantic</u> March 1974 : 84-88.

The author, one of Lawrence's biographers, traces Lawrence's reputation as a writer from its low point at the time of his death to its present "position of primacy among great twentieth-century prose writers in English" (84).

Normally, your entry for a journal or newspaper article will not include the publisher's name or the place of publication, though the latter is sometimes needed to identify a small-town newspaper: *Daily Herald* [Ely, NV]. Record the *date* of the issue and complete *page numbers: Surfer's Companion* Sept. 1987: 13–18. *The Honolulu Enquirer* 10 Jan. 1988,

24–26. In case you decide later to make or request a photocopy, you might want at this point to include complete page numbers when an article is interrupted and then concluded later in the magazine (12–17, 45–46). However, a plus sign will signal the continuation in your final listing of sources (12–17 +).

To point your readers to the right pages in back issues of a journal or newspaper, you may need additional data like the following:

■ In many professional or technical journals, page numbers are consecutive through the issues of the same *volume*—usually all the issues published in one year. Record the number of the volume (in Arabic numerals), the year (in parentheses), and the page numbers of the article: *Modern Ornithology* 7 (1987): 234–38. When page numbers of different issues are *not* consecutive for the same volume, you may have to include the number of the issue: *Birdwatcher's Quarterly* 17.3 (1988): 17–20 (for volume 17, no. 3).

■ The full-service modern newspaper often publishes more than one daily edition, with several sections whose pages are not numbered consecutively throughout the issue. Include the specifics needed to guide your reader: *Bogtown Gazette* 25 Oct. 1988, late ed.: C18. (Include *p.* or *pp.* for page or pages only if omitting them might cause confusion.)

Remember: Your record keeping at this point serves a double purpose. You register the results of your search for your own use, tagging your finds and setting up a file. But at the same time, you are storing information that you will need to retrieve later when you document your sources in your finished paper.

LIBRARY WORK 9 Prepare *annotated source cards or entries* for three possible sources for a research report on changing public attitudes on a current issue. Choose *one* of the following:

■ nuclear safety
■ prison reform
■ age and aging
■ safe sex
■ damage awards
■ capital punishment

- mercy killings
- space flights

For your sources, choose one book indexed in the central catalog, one article indexed in the *Readers' Guide*, and one current magazine article. Provide full information; include call numbers when appropriate.

OVERVIEW In putting a research paper together, you face two major tasks. First, you collect material that bears on the question you are trying to answer or on the issue you are trying to explore. Second, you sort out and arrange these materials in a coherent presentation, supporting the conclusion or conclusions that you have reached. As you check out possible sources, you will always be looking ahead. You will be asking yourself: What promising material does a source contain? How will the material fit in? What conclusions will it support?

Good writers are often good note takers; they have an eye for material that will serve them well later. When deciding whether to note or not to note, ask yourself whether you can answer yes to the following questions:

- Am I personally *learning* something here about my topic?
- Does this help answer a *question* that has come up in my earlier reading?
- Does this *raise* a question to which I should try to find the answer?
- Does this relate to an *issue* that has come up repeatedly during my investigation?
- Does this furnish *evidence* or support for a working hypothesis or tentative conclusion?
- Does this represent an objection or *contrary evidence* that I will have to address?
- Does this help clarify a *key term* or buzzword related to my topic?

Take notes that will allow you to quote what the experts say, what eye witnesses say, what insiders say. Take notes now that will later allow you to offer detailed statistics or reconstruct key events. Make sure that at a later stage your notes will tell you clearly *who* said *what* and *where*, as well as *why* it seemed to matter.

49a — Taking Notes—Note Cards or Computer Entries

Take accurate notes to serve as raw material for your first draft.

Whether you write your notes by hand, type them, or feed them directly into your word processor, accurate and usable notes provide the essential supply line for your paper. For handwritten or typed notes, 3″ × 5″ or 4″ × 6″ note cards enable you to shuffle your information as the pattern of your paper takes shape. The following procedures will save you time and grief:

■ Include a *heading*—first only a specific identifier, but later also the tentative subdivision of your paper—with each card or entry. If you feed notes into your word processor, use a clear **retrieval code** (like WS for women in sports), followed by a specific identifier (like "track coach interview" or "women's Olympic marathon"). Refine your retrieval code later as subdivisions of your paper take shape (for instance WS—hst for "Women in Sports—history").

■ Include the *author and title* of your source (in shortened form) at the end, along with exact page numbers. (It's frustrating to have to hunt through a book for a lost page reference.) *Make sure a source appears on each card.*

■ Use each card or entry for *closely related information* or for quotations centered clearly on one limited point. (This way you will not have to disentangle material later for use at different points in your grand design.) Include the kind of specific detail that you will need to support generalizations: selected quotations, key examples, statistical figures, definitions of difficult terms.

■ Make sure the material you select is *representative* of the source—not taken out of context. The person you quote should be able to say: "Yes, I'll stand behind that. That's more or less what I meant."

■ Use *quotation marks* to identify all quoted phrases, parts of sentences, or whole sentences. Anticipate the reactions of the reader who will say: "This does not sound like you. Was this first said by somebody else?"

585

When you put borrowed material in your own words, beware of appropriating characteristic phrases or following the pattern of a sentence written by someone else.

In taking notes, do not simply copy big chunks of material. Adapt the material to suit your purposes as you go along. Learn to use several major techniques:

(1) Summarize background information; condense lengthy arguments. Here is a note card that condenses several pages of introductory information in John G. Neihardt's book *Black Elk Speaks:*

```
    Last Battles

        In the fall of 1930, a field agent helped
    Neihardt meet Black Elk, a holy man of the
    Oglala Sioux who was a second cousin to Chief
    Crazy Horse.  Black Elk was nearly blind and
    knew no English.  Neihardt, speaking to him
    through an interpreter, gained his confidence
    partly by respecting the holy man's long si-
    lences.  In the spring of 1931, Black Elk took
    many days to tell his life story, including the
    story of his share in the defeat of General
    Custer, which Black Elk witnessed as a young
    warrior.

    Neihardt, Black Elk vii-xi
```

SAMPLE NOTE CARD

(2) Make strategic use of brief, well-chosen direct quotations. When we quote **verbatim**, we quote directly word for word. Quote characteristic or striking phrases. Quote sentences that sum up well a step in an argument. Look for sentences that show well the point of view or intentions of the quoted author. Apt, brief direct quotations give your writing an authentic touch; they show that you are staying close to the firsthand sources:

```
Indian Education

     Indian children were put in crowded boarding
schools and fed at the cost of 11 cents a day
(with their diet supplemented by food that could
be grown on school farms).  From the fifth grade
up, children put in half a day's labor on the
school farm.  They were taught "vanishing trades
of little or no economic importance."

Johnson, "Breaking Faith"  240
```

(3) Use extended direct quotation for key passages. Quote at some length to let the original author sum up a major argument. Let authors speak in their own words on difficult or controversial points. Quote verbatim an author's striking summing up of a key issue or a current trend:

```
Vegetarianism

     "Welcome to Vegetarian Chic, the latest
consuming consequence of healthier attitudes
among Americans.  While few people have totally
forsworn meat, they're loading their plates high
with veggies and fruits--11 percent more of the
former and 7 percent more of the latter than
five years ago.  According to a 1985 Gallup
poll, some 6.2 million Americans now call them-
selves vegetarians (although many eat the odd
morsel of fish or chicken or even beef)."

Givens, "Going for the Greens"  79
```

(4) Paraphrase less important material. In a **paraphrase**, we put information and ideas into our own words. This way we can emphasize what is most directly useful. We can cut down on what is less important. At the same time, we show that we have *made sense* of what we have read.

Remember: In a true paraphrase we have made the material truly our own. Compare the following passage with the detailed paraphrase that follows it. Study how completely the rewrite has changed the *wording* of the original while doing justice to the *ideas* of the original author:

ORIGINAL:

Running is one of the primal human acts, and the particular human form it takes, using a bipedal stride in a fully upright stance, has played an essential part in shaping our destiny. It was once believed that our hominid ancestors were rather pitiable creatures compared with the other animals of the jungles and savannas; lacking the fangs, claws, and specialized physical abilities of the predators, the hominids supposedly prevailed only because of their large brains and their ability to use tools. But there is now compelling evidence that our direct ancestors of some four million years ago had relatively small brains, only about a third the size of ours. What these hominids *did* have was a fully upright stance.   John Leonard, *Born to Run*

PARAPHRASE:

According to John Leonard in "Born to Run," running is a part of what makes us human, and the way we run—fully upright, striding on two feet—has helped determine what we are today. It was thought earlier that physically our near-human ancestors were pitifully weak creatures, who lacked the formidable teeth, claws, and physical strength of wild animals hunting for food in the jungles and open spaces and who prospered only because of their large brains and their invention of tools. But, according to Leonard, strong evidence proves that our forebears from four million years ago had comparatively small brains—about one third of our own brain size. What these near-humans had was the ability to stand fully erect.

The following sample note card paraphrases an author's statement and support of one key point:

Rehabilitation

     Trades or vocational skills taught in
today's prisons are often outdated or unrealistic. In one case, a New York medium-security
prison provided detainees with a course in
operating diesel trucks. The course was very
popular and was supported by local charitable
organizations. Ironically, after their release
the prisoners found that the law prohibited them
from obtaining a Class One driver's license for
more than five years in most cases. In the
interim, many returned to the professions that
had put them behind bars in the first place. As
a result, over half returned to prison.

Menninger, "Doing True Justice" 6

LIBRARY WORK 10   Select a magazine article or a chapter in a book on one of the topics listed below. Assume that you are extracting information or opinions for use in a larger research project. Prepare five note cards illustrating various techniques of *note taking:* Include examples of summary, paraphrase, mixed indirect and direct quotation, and extended direct quotation. Choose one:

- deregulation
- the history of advertising
- secret wartime codes and how to break them
- the history of photography
- the Long March
- Hollywood's early stars
- the Cherokee nation
- the suffragette (suffragist) movement
- space stations
- the war on drugs

49b | Using Quoted Material

Use quoted material to advantage in your own text.

As you start your first draft, you will have to work material from your notes smoothly into your own text. Study effective ways of integrating material from your notes in your paper. Avoid the temptations to plagiarize that might arise.

See the accompanying chart for a brief overview of how to punctuate quotations (and how to omit part of a quotation or add comments of your own). Review Section **38** of this handbook for a full discussion of basic rules and finer points. In your final draft, quotations of *more than four typed lines* should be set off as **block quotations**—double-spaced, indented *ten* spaces, with *no* quotation marks.

(1) Long quotation—to be used sparingly:

In her biography of President Johnson, Doris Kearns summed up the factors that weakened the role of the traditional political party:

> The organization of unions, the development of the Civil Service, and the rise of the welfare state deprived the party of its capacity to provide jobs, foods, and services to loyal constituents, thus severing its connection with the daily lives and needs of the people. . . . Technology provided access to new forms of amusement and recreation, such as movies and television, which were more diverting than party—sponsored dances and made it unlikely that people would attend political meetings and speeches for their entertainment value. During the 1960's, more and more people declined to affiliate themselves with a party and identified themselves as independents. (162)

PUNCTUATING QUOTATIONS: AN OVERVIEW

DIRECT QUOTATION: quotation marks, introduced by comma or (more formally) by colon:

```
According to the report, "Engineering,
medicine, and law are no longer male bastions."
The author emphasized her conclusion:
"Engineering, medicine, and law are no longer
male bastions."
```

QUOTED WORDS OR PHRASES: *no* introductory comma or colon:

```
Like Horace Mann, Americans have long
considered education the "great equalizer" in
society.
```

QUOTE-WITHIN-QUOTE: single quotation marks when someone you quote is in turn quoting someone else:

```
The article concluded: "She is a hard worker
and, in the words of a fellow judge, 'very much
in charge of herself.'"
```

EXCERPTED QUOTATION: Use an **ellipsis**—three spaced periods—to show that you have omitted material in order to shorten a quotation. (Use four periods, with *no* extra space before the first period, if the omission occurs after a complete sentence.)

```
The reviewer called the book a "searing
indictment of the extent to which
Americans . . . failed to respond to the plight
of European Jews."
```

ADDITIONS: Use **square brackets** to show interpolations:

```
According to the report, "Powerful tribal
antagonisms are a basic political fact of life
in countries like Nigeria and Rhodesia [now
Zimbabwe]."
```

COMMENT: In this example, the introductory sentence sums up the point of the quotation. (Readers easily become discouraged if they do not see the relevance and the point of numerous lengthy quotations.) Then the author's account of an important political change is quoted at some length. The excerpt is set off as a **block quotation**—*indented ten spaces, no quotation marks*. The introductory sentence gives credit to the original author; the full title of her book will appear after her name in the final listing of "Works Cited." The number in parentheses at the end of the quotation directs the reader to the exact page of the book.

Note: Use no additional paragraph indentation with block quotations unless the quotation runs to more than one paragraph. An additional *three* spaces then shows the beginning of each actual paragraph in the original source.

(2) Plagiarized version—illegitimate, unacknowledged paraphrase:

```
The political party no longer plays its traditional
role. The growth of the unions and the welfare state
deprived the party of its capacity to provide jobs,
food, and services to people.  New forms of amusement
and recreation, such as movies and television, were
more diverting than party-sponsored dances and made
it unlikely that people would attend political
meetings for their entertainment value.  More and
more people declined to affiliate themselves with a
party and became independents instead.
```

COMMENT: Much **plagiarism** takes this form. The passage takes over someone else's words and ideas in a slightly shortened, less accurate form—*and without acknowledgment*. Even if the source were identified, this method of adapting the material would be unsatisfactory. Far too much of the original author's way of putting things has been kept—without the use of direct quotation. Much of the wording has been copied: "deprived the party of its capacity," "more diverting than party-sponsored dances."

(3) Legitimate paraphrase—attributed to the original author:

As Doris Kearns reminds us, major changes in our
society weakened the traditional political party.
The old—style party had provided jobs, favors, and
even free food to the party faithful, but the unions,
the Civil Service, or the welfare state took over
many of these functions. People no longer depended
on social events sponsored by the party or on rousing
political speeches for entertainment; they had movies
and television instead. During the 1960's, fewer and
fewer people declared a party affiliation; many
listed themselves as independents (162).

COMMENT: This paraphrase (followed by the page reference) keeps the essential meaning of the original. But the information is given to us in the adapter's own words, sometimes with added touches that help make the point clear or vivid: "the party faithful," "rousing political speeches." The last sentence is parallel in structure to the original, but the other sentences are put together very differently.

(4) Part paraphrase, part direct quotation—worked closely into the text:

In her biography of President Johnson, Doris Kearns
traces the changes that weakened the role of our
political parties. The growing labor unions, the
expanding Civil Service, and the welfare state began
to provide the jobs, the favors, and the free food
that the old—style party had provided for the party
faithful. These changes cut off the party's close
"connection with the daily lives and needs of the
people." Movies and television made the old—style

593

party—sponsored dances and rousing political speeches
obsolete as entertainment. During the 1960's, voters
more and more "declined to affiliate themselves with
a party and identified themselves as independents"
(162).

COMMENT: Here the adapter explains the main points but at the
same time keeps some of the authentic flavor of the original. Direct quotation is limited to characteristic phrases and key points. By using this
technique, you can show that you have paid faithful attention to the original material and yet have made it truly your own.

(5) Legitimate summary—for preview or overview:

Doris Kearns shows how the unions, the Civil Service,
the welfare state, and the mass media all helped
weaken party affiliation. They provided the jobs,
the favors, and the entertainment for which voters
once turned to the traditional party organizations
(162).

COMMENT: This summary, getting at the gist of the passage, could
serve as an overview or recapitulation—reinforcement of major points.

WRITING WORKSHOP 11   Alice Walker, who later wrote the Pulitzer
Prize-winning novel *The Color Purple*, wrote her first published essay in the
winter of 1966–1967 on the topic "The Civil Rights Movement: What Good
Was It?" (*The American Scholar*, Autumn 1967). Suppose that in a paper on
Martin Luther King, Jr., you are making use of the following excerpt from
Walker's essay. Prepare several different versions of a passage that would use
material from this excerpt:

- a passage introducing an excerpted *block quotation* using part of the
  material
- a passage using an extended *paraphrase* of much of the material
- a passage combining paraphrase and *direct quotation*
- a passage using only a brief *summary*

In each version, identify author and source. Introduce the material in
such a way that the reader can see the point or the significance of the
material. Make photocopies of your material for discussion in class or in a
small group.

594

The life of Dr. King, seeming bigger and more miraculous than the man himself, because of all he had done and suffered, offered a pattern of strength and sincerity I felt I could trust. He had suffered much because of his simple belief in nonviolence, love, and brotherhood. Perhaps the majority of men could not be reached through these beliefs, but because Dr. King kept trying to reach them in spite of danger to himself and his family, I saw in him the hero for whom I had waited so long.

What Dr. King promised was not a ranch-style house and an acre of manicured lawn for every black man, but jail and finally freedom. He did not promise two cars for every family, but the courage one day for all families everywhere to walk without shame and unafraid on their own feet. He did not say that one day it will be us chasing prospective buyers out of our prosperous well-kept neighborhoods, or in other ways exhibiting our snobbery and ignorance as all other ethnic groups before us have done; what he said was that we had a right to live anywhere in this country we chose, and a right to a meaningful well-paying job to provide us with the upkeep of our homes. He did not say we had to become carbon copies of the white American middle class; but he did say we had the right to become whatever we wanted to become.

49c Introducing Quoted Material

Lead into quoted material in such a way that its source and its point are clear.

To use material from your sources to advantage, introduce it effectively. In order to set the stage, let the reader know one or more of the following: Who said this and where? What is the writer's authority, or what are the author's credentials? In other words, why should we listen to this person? What is the point of the quotation? Why are you using it here?

SOURCE:	Rachel Carson said in *Silent Spring* that "only within the moment of time represented by the present century" has one species—ours—acquired the power to alter the nature of the world.
CREDENTIALS:	Garrett Hardin, author of "The Tragedy of the Commons" and many other articles and books on "human ecology," has attacked "suicidal policies for sharing our resources through uncontrolled immigration and foreign aid."

595

POINT: Garrett Hardin has used the lifeboat analogy to dramatize
          our limited capacity for helping the world's poor: "Our
          survival demands that we govern our actions by the ethics
          of a lifeboat, harsh though they may be."

Remember the following guidelines:

(1) Link material clearly to its source. As necessary, put in tags like
"According to the governor" or "as Steinem further observed." When you
quote several authors, make sure a *he* or *she* or *the writer* points clearly to
the person you had in mind. The following example of paraphrased material uses several reminders that the same source is still being cited:

> Increases in out-of-state tuition are keeping
> students from Third World countries away from
> American colleges. Stephen Horn, president of
> California State University at Long Beach, told a
> meeting of educators that, of the 27,000 African
> students who attend college away from their home
> countries, 24,000 study in the Soviet Union.
> According to Horn, many of those students are the
> future leaders of their countries. The United States
> does not subsidize foreign students as heavily as the
> Soviets do and therefore attracts far fewer foreign
> students. In the opinion of the speaker, further
> increases in nonresident tuition would discourage all
> but rich foreigners from attending school in the
> United States (64).

**(2) Know how to quote key words and phrases as part of your
own sentences.** When a quotation becomes part of a sentence of your
own, fit it into the grammatical pattern of your own sentence—without
changing the wording of the part quoted directly:

WRONG: Pope Pius described a just war in this way: "If it has been
          forced upon one by an evident and extremely grave in-
          justice that in no way can be avoided." (Fragmentary,
          unrelated *if*-clause)

596

RIGHT: Pope Pius stated that a war is just "if it has been forced upon one by an evident and extremely grave injustice that in no way can be avoided."

49d | Combining Different Sources

Combine material from different sources in a coherent paragraph.

Writing a research paper tests your ability to synthesize, to make things add up. In a well-written research paper, you will often integrate material from several different sources.

A paragraph in your finished paper will often combine material from several different note cards. The paragraph will often begin with the general conclusion that the evidence on several related cards suggests. The rest of the paragraph will then present details selected from the cards. Study the three sample cards on the following page. Then study the way material from these note cards has been integrated in the following finished paragraph:

> For years, nature lovers have been keeping an anxious count of such endangered species as the bald eagle and the whooping crane. When the bald eagle became the national symbol soon after Independence, there were nesting pairs everywhere in what is now the continental United States. Two hundred years later, Frank Graham, Jr., writing in Audubon magazine, reported a current estimate of 5,000 bald eagles left in the lower forty-eight states. According to his figures, only 627 nests remained active, and they produced approximately 500 young (99). In 1981, Steven C. Wilson and Karen C. Hayden, writing in the National Geographic, reported a count of 76 for wild whooping cranes left in the United States, up from a dismal count of 21 thirty years earlier (37–38). Another estimate puts the current population at 95 (Freedman 89).

597

Endangered Species--Counts

    The bald eagle became the national symbol in 1782, and there were nesting pairs in all the lower 48 states. The current bald eagle population has been estimated at 5,000 in the lower 48 states. As of 1975, only 627 nests remained active, and they produced approximately 500 young.

Graham, "Will the Bald Eagle Survive?" 99

Card 1

Endangered Species--Counts

    "In 1948, the wild whooping crane population was up by just two from a decade earlier--to 31. The count sank to 21 in the winter of 1951-52, then rose gradually to an encouraging 74 in 1978-79. Last spring there were six yearlings to join the flight north. . . . The wild whooping crane count now stands at 76, an improvement deriving in large measure from protective practices at Arkansas."

Wilson and Hayden, "Where Oil and Wildlife Mix" 37-38

Card 2

Endangered Species--Counts

    "Whooping cranes, the largest cranes inhabiting North America, are on the U.S. endangered species list. The big birds' population dwindled to 14 in the late 1930s but is now estimated at 95."

Freedman, "Whooping Cranes" 89

Card 3

Remember: Taking notes to work up a rich backlog of usable material and funneling your notes into a rough first draft are not mutually exclusive stages of your project. They overlap. While already working on your draft, you may decide to hunt further for missing material. What counts is that you feed in an ample supply of usable material that your finished paper will synthesize.

WRITING PRACTICE 12   Assume that the following passages are part of your reading notes about the effect of television on young viewers. What general conclusion(s) do these passages support? Write a passage in which you use the material from these notes to support a conclusion. Identify your sources; use both direct quotation and paraphrase. (Remember that in your actual paper you would use exact *page numbers* for all material you use.)

1. Two passages from *The Plug-In Drug: Television, Children and Family* by Marie Winn, author of many children's books:

    "By its domination of the time families spend together, it destroys the special quality that distinguishes one family from another, a quality that depends to a great extent on what a family *does*, what special rituals, games, recurrent jokes, familiar songs, and shared activities it accumulates."

    "The decreased opportunities for simple conversation between parents and children in the television-centered home may help explain an observation made by an emergency room nurse at a Boston hospital. She reports that parents just seem to sit there these days when they come in with a sick or seriously injured child, although talking to the child would distract and comfort him. 'They don't seem to know *how* to talk to their own children at any length,' the nurse observes."

2. A passage from a magazine article by Bruno Bettelheim, famous psychoanalyst and author of *The Uses of Enchantment*, a book about fairy tales:

    "Children who have been taught, or conditioned, to listen passively most of the day to the warm verbal communications coming from the TV screen, to the deep emotional appeal of the so-called TV personality, are often unable to respond to real persons because they arouse so much less feeling than the skilled actor. Worse, they lose the ability to learn from reality because life experiences are much more complicated than the ones they see on the screen."

3. A selection from an interview with Jerzy Kosinski—Polish-born author of *Being There*—published in the periodical *Media and Methods:*

"Recently I heard of a college class in media communication which had been assigned to watch two hours of television and record the content of those two hours. They were asked to describe each element—including commercials—in as much detail as possible, classifying every incident and every character in terms of its relative importance to the story. All these students had been raised in front of TV sets and were accustomed to being bombarded by TV images; many of them hoped to be employed in the communications industry after graduation. Yet not a single one could complete the assignment. They claimed that the rapidity and fragmentation of the TV experience made it impossible to isolate a narrative thought-line, or to contemplate and analyze what they had seen, in terms of relative significance."

WRITING PRACTICE 13 Combine closely related material from different note cards in a finished *sample paragraph*. Prepare three note cards that all bear on the same limited point. Turn to sources that you have used for one of the previous exercises, or to sources related to your own current research paper project. Use the material on your cards in a sample paragraph that introduces the material clearly and helpfully to your reader. Hand in the note cards with your finished paragraph. (Include page references in parentheses.)

---

50   First Draft and Revision

OVERVIEW In a successful research project, the gathering and sorting of material go hand in hand. Even while you are collecting material, you will be ordering and shaping it so that you can channel it into a first draft.

PLANNING With some research projects, you may truly be mapping uncharted territory. But often the nature of the subject or its history will suggest a tentative working plan. Writing about bilingual education, you are likely to operate tentatively with a rough pro-and-con sorting. On the con side, you may accumulate material from articles titled "Against a Confusion of Tongues," "In Defense of the Mother Tongue," "Avoiding Canada's Problem," or "Bilingual Classes? In U.S. But Few Other Nations." On the pro side, you may gather material from articles titled "Progress in Bilingual Education" or "Bilingualism: The Accent Is on Youth." Soon you may set up a third category for sources weighing advantages and disadvantages, from articles titled "Bilingualism: An Answer from Research" or the like.

As you proceed, you will be pushing from such tentative groupings toward a definite outline for your paper. One major function of your first draft will be to let you see how your outline works—and to let you adjust it or reorganize it if necessary.

DRAFTING Once you have settled on a working outline, you use it as a guide in organizing and shuffling your notes. When your notes are in the right order, you can start writing your first draft. As you push ahead, keep in mind the needs you have to meet:

- Make the reader see your *plan* and guide the reader's attention in the right direction. You need to raise the issue or dramatize the topic; you need an early preview or early hints of your general strategy; you need to mark major turning points.
- Show that your conclusions are not just *one person's opinion*. Throughout, you need to satisfy the reader who asks, "Who said this? What is the source of this information? What do the experts say? Is there another side?" All the way through, you will be feeding into your draft information, testimony, and commentary from your sources.
- *Integrate* the material from your notes in your text. This means that you have to select, adapt, and splice together material from your sources in such a way that there will be a smooth, natural flow.

REVISING When you write a paper drawing on sources, you have your hands full choosing the right material, adapting it for use, and feeding it into your draft at the right points. When you revise your first draft, you can look at what you have done from the point of view of the reader. Do not limit yourself to final editing for better sentences, clear punctuation, or the right word. Adjust your plan as necessary. If necessary, shift important background information to an earlier part of your paper. Revise your strategy if you decide to leave the more controversial parts of a proposal till later in your discussion.

50a	Developing an Outline

Go from tentative groupings to a definite outline for your
materials.

How do you work out a tentative outline that will guide you in the
writing of your first draft? Early in your collecting of material, begin to
set up tentative major categories. From the beginning, look for details and
ideas that seem *related*—they bear on the same major point, or they point
toward the same tentative conclusion.

Remember the following advice:

(1) Group together notes that contain related material. Assign
tentative common headings to groups of notes that deal with the same
limited question or the same part of a larger issue. For a paper on prison
reform, you might decide early that your major groupings should include
"Old-style penitentiaries," "Rehabilitation," "Experiments—U.S.," and
"Experiments—Abroad." As you continue your reading, additional headings and subheadings may become necessary.

(2) Work toward a unifying thesis. Ask yourself, "What is this
paper as a whole going to tell the reader?" Try to sum up in one sentence
the overall conclusion that your research has led you to. Present this sentence as your thesis early in your paper—preferably at the end of an
effective but short introduction:

The Isolated Americans

THESIS: The failure of Americans to learn foreign languages is producing a growing isolation of our country from the rest of the
world.

(3) Work out a clear overall plan for your paper. Suppose you are
writing about the threatened survival of the American bald eagle. You
may decide early to group your note cards under major headings like the
following:

Population counts
Dangers from pesticides
Dangers from sheep ranchers
Conservation measures

602

These headings suggest a plausible general strategy: You may want to start with a review of past history, go on to a discussion of current problems, and then conclude by discussing promising solutions. Here is a preliminary outline for a paper about the bald eagle as an endangered species:

Saving the Bald Eagle

THESIS: The bald eagle will become extinct unless we come to understand and respect the special needs of this endangered species.

I. The history of the bald eagle
II. Dangers to the bald eagle
    A. Pesticides used by farmers
    B. Poisoned bait, traps, and bullets used by ranchers
    C. Technological dangers
III. Steps toward improvement
    A. New eagle refuge
    B. Stricter control of poisons
    C. Better power line structures

(4) Use your outline as a working outline. As your overall plan takes shape, it serves as your agenda in the final stages of the paper. The more definite your plan becomes, the more clearly you will see which of your notes deal with unrelated materials and should be set aside. By the same token, you will see more clearly in which areas your notes should be supplemented by further reading.

WRITING WORKSHOP 14   Prepare a *trial outline* for discussion in a small group or in class. Present it as an informal working outline, subject to refining and revision. Study the following example as a possible model: What kind of paper is it sketching out? What are likely to be the strong points of the paper? What are likely to be weak points or problems?

PURPOSE:
I feel very strongly about population control and putting into practice zero population growth if necessary. I want to show that having large families can have disastrous effects on the world's population and on the quality of life.
PLAN:
why population control is a vital health issue—introduction
pollution as a result of overpopulation
    environmental pollution
    noise pollution

population in history of world
  population stable 10,000 years ago
  how Agricultural Revolution created rapid growth
  how Industrial Revolution created rapid growth
problems facing family planning
effects of overcrowding in rats—used to show comparison with
  humans
    behavioral disturbances in males
    maternal problems in females
    high infant mortality rate
built-in population control in animals
culturally acceptable population control in humans prior to
  Agricultural Revolution
population problems in America
conclusion—Having large families is not a right. Basic rights are
  threatened unless a population control is enforced.

50b   Writing the First Draft

Funnel the material from your notes into a rough first draft.

The best advice during the first-draft stage is: Push on; polish and fine-tune later. You need to see the whole take shape; you need to see that your legwork is paying off. Keep the following guidelines in mind to help you produce a stronger first draft:

(1) Start with a strong overview. Do not just sketch out a "let's-see-what-we-find" program. Focus the readers' attention and arouse their interest by a more definite preview. Pinpoint the issue; sum up key findings; summarize the pro and con.

TOO OPEN: Surrogate motherhood is an area filled with suc-
                cesses and problems. Some people believe in the surro-
                gate program and others condemn the practice. Here we
                will explore some of the seemingly good and bad aspects
                of the program.

FOCUSED: Conflicting voices on the use of animal experiments
                in medical research leave us unsure of which side to take.

Our hearts tell us to listen to often-inflated news reports of cruelty and abuse. Our brains tell us that if it weren't for research involving other living creatures, many of the lifesaving techniques that are common today would not exist.

(2) Avoid the "dumped" quotation. Do not just spring a quotation on the reader. Prepare the ground for it, summing up who says what and why.

DUMPED: Susan Jacoby is a "First Amendment junkie."

REVISED: Susan Jacoby, who has written widely on women's issues, disagrees with the feminists on the issue of pornography. She is first and foremost a journalist who believes in free speech and the protection of the First Amendment. She is unequivocally a "First Amendment junkie."

(3) Bundle related quotations effectively. Add a lead sentence that shows what a set of quotations is supposed to prove. Look at the lead sentence of the following paragraph:

Infertility, now affecting one in five couples, has many causes. J. H. Guenero, writing in *Science News*, identifies familiar medical problems: failure to ovulate, inflammatory disorders, blockage of the fallopian tubes. Hilary Rose, a professor of Social Policy at Bradford University, points to modern birth control methods as a more recent culprit. The prolonged use of the pill, damage due to badly fitted coils, and poorly performed abortions all help explain the rising incidence of infertility.

(4) Look out for weak links. Avoid lame transitions using *also* or *another*. Help the reader who wonders, "Why is this in here at this point?"

WEAK: Another expert on the dinosaur puzzle is Janice Rotha, who writes in the *American Scientist*. . . .

BETTER: An expert who disagrees strongly with the sudden-extinction theory is Janice Rotha. She writes in the *American Scientist*. . . .

Study the texture of writing that integrates substantial material from sources, and use it as a model. In much of your draft, you will have to do the splicing together that produces a smooth blend of quotation, paraphrase, and interpretation:

ONE SOURCE:

> Phyllis Schlafly has long been one of the most
> prominent critics of the women's movement. For the
> founder of the conservative Eagle Forum, twenty years
> of NOW have added up to an "anti-family" crusade that
> has contributed to the deterioration of family life
> in America. "The first goal the feminist movement
> set for itself was divorce on demand—easy, no-fault
> divorce," Schlafly has said. "The result has been
> incredible social, financial, and emotional
> devastation for women." She charges that the
> ideology of the women's movement aims at a "gender-
> neutral" society in which we "are forbidden to make
> reasonable distinctions" (22-23).

Much of the time your task will be to confront your sources with each other—to correlate information, to compare similar testimony, to line up the pro and con. Study the way the following paragraph integrates material from several different sources:

SEVERAL SOURCES:

> Every month, it seems, produces a new spate of
> articles about the new career woman, telling us, for
> instance, that American companies "have discovered
> that selecting only male candidates means ignoring
> about half of the best talent available, and many are
> now actively recruiting women as managers" (Castro
> 64). For many young women, unfortunately, this media

publicity creates a misleading picture of the actual job market. Even though 55 percent of all women are working today (Kitch 229), over half of them are either clerical or service workers (Smith 46–47), not highly paid executives as glossy magazine ads would lead us to believe. In her book <u>90 Highest-Paying Careers for the 80's</u>, Anita Gates has a last chapter entitled "Careers That Didn't Make the List." This list of lower-paying careers includes all of the traditional female occupations (203–6). As Shirley Radl tells young women, "You haven't come a long way, and you're not a baby" (1).

WRITING WORKSHOP 15   Prepare a first draft of your paper. Your instructor may ask you to submit it for suggestions for revision or for peer review.

50c   Revising the First Draft

Allow time for revision of your first draft.

The first draft of your research paper gives you the opportunity to check what you have and to see if it will work. After a day or two, you will be ready to look at your draft with the reader's eye. Will the reader see early what your agenda is? Have you spelled out what you really want to show? Can your reader follow in your footsteps as you marshal the facts or develop your argument? Consult the following checklist as a guide to revision:

(1) Spell out fully what you have learned.   You may have to make explicit what you merely implied; what is obvious to you may not be obvious to your reader. Can you identify a sentence or a passage that sums

607

up what you are trying to prove? Does a strong **thesis** appear in a strategic position—at the beginning or at the end?

(2) Strengthen support for key points. For example, in reading your first draft on the subject of the "Graying of America," you may decide that your statistics on forced retirement are too skimpy and dated. Revision is your chance to bring in updated information or to use a recognized authority to bolster your point.

(3) Reorganize if necessary. Check the flow of your paper and re-channel it as needed. Suppose you are writing your paper on the conflict between ideal and reality faced by many career women today. The central idea of your paper is that Madison Avenue has created a myth of the successful career woman that many women, faced by conflicting demands, find hard to live up to in the real world. In your first draft, you have followed this outline:

I.   The media image of the New Woman
II.   Unresolved conflicts
   A.   The homemaker stereotype
   B.   "Femininity" versus being a professional
   C.   Career and motherhood
III.   The realities of the workplace
   A.   Predominantly female occupations
   B.   Disparity in pay
IV.   The price of progress
   A.   Health problems and stress
   B.   Difficult personal relationships

As you read your first draft, you may decide on some major reshuffling. On second thought, your Part II delves too early into material colored by personal grievances, so you decide to start with a "let's-look-at-the-cold-facts" approach. In your second draft, you reverse the order of Parts II and III. You also plug in some material from the history of women's work to add perspective. The outline you follow in your revised draft looks as follows:

I.   The media image of the New Woman
II.   The working woman then

III. The working woman now
   A. Predominantly female occupations
   B. Disparity in pay
IV. Unresolved conflicts
   A. The homemaker stereotype
   B. "Femininity" versus being a professional
   C. Career and motherhood
V. The price of progress
   A. Health problems and stress
   B. Difficult personal relationships

(4) Integrate quoted material better. A poorly revised research paper often resembles the overloaded barge, ready to sink under the load of lengthy quotations. Should you do more to get your reader ready for a quotation, explaining the what and the why? Should there be a better mix of sentence-length quotations and brief quoted phrases, worked more organically into your text?

(5) Strengthen coherence. Give your readers a reason to keep on reading as they move from point to point. Revise weak links like the following:

WEAK LINK:	**Another** point to consider is . . . We might **also** look at . . . **Some observers** feel that . . .
REVISED:	A **similar, more recent** argument is that . . . People **outside the profession** usually look at the problem from a different perspective . . . A **younger generation of psychiatrists** seems to be departing from . . .

(6) Check for clear attribution. Are the beginning *and* the end of each direct quotation clearly marked? Can the reader tell throughout where your information came from, whose judgment you have trusted, or to whose opinions you have become converted? Remember that full documentation, like the listing of ingredients on a package of supermarket bread, means full disclosure of what went into the final product.

(7) Revise your paper to reflect second thoughts. A first draft may end more optimistically or more pessimistically than it began. It may at first follow your initial plan but then veer off in a different direction. You may at first have stressed common misconceptions about mental illness—only to conclude later that many people are more enlightened on the subject than you thought. Check especially your opening pages to make sure that they are consistent with the rest of the paper.

WRITING PRACTICE 16   Write a final outline that reflects your revision of your first draft. Observe the format of a formal outline.

---

51   Identifying Your Sources

OVERVIEW   Effective **documentation** enables your reader to search out an article or book you have used and turn to the right page. You are not keeping secrets from your readers; they are welcome to check where you found and how you selected your material.

The style of documentation shown in this section was recently developed by the Modern Language Association (MLA). It is similar to the style of documentation recommended by the American Psychological Association (APA) for research in the social sciences. Learning a style of documentation is similar to studying the instruction booklet when applying for a driver's license: At first the many regulations are bewildering, but gradually major principles come into focus. In the end, many minor details are found to serve a purpose.

Three principles underlie the provisos of the new style:

- Identify your sources briefly in your text.
- Give page references in your text, including the author's name and sometimes a shortened title as needed.
- Give a complete description of each source in a final alphabetical listing of "Works Cited."

610

Often your typed text will name the author and the work you are quoting: "Doris Lessing writes in *The Golden Notebook*, . . ." For such standard citations, include only the page reference in your text, putting it in parentheses (93). Your final list of "Works Cited" will give full information about the source:

```
Lessing, Doris.   The Golden Notebook.   New York:
     Simon, 1962.
```

If your text does not identify the author and the work, give the last name with the page reference: "One well-known chronicler of the space program kept referring to the astronauts as 'fighter jocks' (Wolfe 413)." Again, the list of "Works Cited" will give full information:

```
Wolfe, Tom.   The Right Stuff.   New York: Farrar, 1979.
```

You need to include a shortened form of the title with the page reference if you have drawn on more than one work by the same author: (Wolfe, *Right Stuff* 413).

Follow this current MLA style unless told otherwise by your instructor. In preparing research papers in other academic fields, you may be required to follow a different style. Widely followed guides to style for documentation include *The Chicago Manual of Style* and Kate L. Turabian's *Manual for Writers of Term Papers, Theses, and Dissertations*, both published by the University of Chicago Press.

51a   *doc* | Parenthetical Documentation (MLA)

Include page references and, if needed, short identification in parentheses in your text.

Identify your source not only when you *quote directly* but also when you *paraphrase* or *summarize*. In addition, show the source of all facts, figures, or ideas that are the result of someone else's effort or inspiration. You need *not* identify a specific source when you have merely repeated something that is widely known or believed.

Study the following possibilities:

1. SIMPLE PAGE REFERENCE You will often identify the author or the publication or both in your running text. You are naming the author as an important authority, or you are naming a key source that your reader should remember ("As Maxine Hong Kingston says in *China Men*, . . ."). You will then use your parenthetical reference to point the reader to the right page. Put page number (or page numbers) in parentheses after a closing quotation mark but before a final period:

> For Gwendolyn Brooks, the "biggest news" about the
> events in Little Rock was that the people there "are
> like people everywhere" (332).

2. REFERENCE TO THE WHOLE WORK *No* parenthetical page numbers are required if your text refers to a work as a whole.

> In <u>The Woman Warrior</u>, Maxine Hong Kingston dramatizes
> the inferior role of women both in traditional
> Chinese culture and in the Land of the Free.

3. IDENTIFICATION BY AUTHOR Include author's last name with the page reference if author and work do not appear in your text (and if you cite only *one* source by this author):

> The familiar arguments in favor of bilingual
> education have recently been challenged by an
> outstanding Hispanic author (Rodriguez 32, 37–39).

4. IDENTIFICATION BY TITLE Include a shortened form of the title if you are going to use *more than one* source by the same author. Underline (italicize) the title of a book or whole publication; enclose the title of an article or part of a publication in quotation marks.

Frank Graham, Jr., writing in <u>Audubon</u>
magazine, reported a current estimate of
5,000 bald eagles left in the lower forty-
eight states. According to his figures,
only 627 nests remained active, and they
produced approximately 500 young (99). In
1981, Steven C. Wilson and Karen C.
Hayden, writing in the <u>National
Geographic</u>, reported a count of 76 for
wild whooping cranes left in the United
States, up from a dismal count of 21
thirty years earlier (37–38). Another
estimate puts the current population at 95
(Freedman 89). Angered by the notorious
"massacre of Jackson's Canyon"
(Christopherson 39), the author of several
authoritative articles on our endangered
bird populations said, "The notion that
eagles are simply feathered vermin dies
hard, especially in the Far West"
(Lamotte, "Bald Eagles" 168). As D. H.
Lawrence said about another "lord of
life,"

> The voice of my education said to me
> He must be killed.   (218)

page references only

authors identified

one of several articles identified

centered block quotation— poetry

PARENTHETICAL DOCUMENTATION—A SAMPLE PAGE

> Alex Comfort has frequently told us that the blunting
> of abilities in the aged results at least in part from
> "put-downs, boredom, and exasperation" ("Old Age"
> 45); the changes we see in old people, according to
> him, "are not biological effects of aging" (<u>Good Age</u>
> 11).

Note: If you shorten a title, keep the *first word* (other than *The, A,* or *An*) the same in the shortened and in the complete title, so that your readers can find the source in alphabetical order in your list of "Works Cited." For instance, shorten "Facts and Fancies About Old Age" to "Facts" and not to "Old Age."

5. IDENTIFICATION BY AUTHOR AND TITLE Include author's name and a short title if you use more than one source of an author you have not identified in the text. Put a comma between author and title, *no* comma between title and page number.

> The traditional stories that the Arabs brought with
> them into medieval Spain were always fairly short
> (Grunebaum, <u>Medieval Islam</u> 294, 305-10).

6. REFERENCE WITHIN A SENTENCE Put page reference and identification *where needed* for clarity part way through a sentence:

> As Mahoney (14) had predicted, recent surveys show
> that many who are forced to retire would prefer to
> continue working (Bensel 132).

7. MORE THAN ONE AUTHOR Include names of several authors with page reference if you have not specified authors in your text. If there are more than three, give name of first author and then put et al. (unitalicized), Latin for "and others."

> Tests and more tests have often been a substitute for
> adequate funding for our schools (Hirsenrath and
> Briggers 198). When not clamoring for more tests for
> students, legislators clamor for tests designed to

```
check "if the teachers know anything themselves"
(Rathjens et al. 112).
```

8. REFERENCE WITH BLOCK QUOTATION   Although a parenthetical reference usually comes before a comma or a period, put it *after* final punctuation that concludes a block quotation. (Leave two spaces before the parenthesis.)

```
        alone.  Few of them show signs of mental
        deterioration or senility, and only a small
        proportion become mentally ill.  (114)
```

9. REFERENCE TO ONE OF SEVERAL VOLUMES   Use an Arabic numeral followed by a *colon* for one volume of a work if in your "Works Cited" you list several volumes:

```
According to Trevelyan, the isolationist movement in
America and the pacifist movement in Britain between
them "handed the world over to its fate" (3: 301).
```

10. REFERENCE TO A PREFACE   Use lowercase Roman numerals if you find them used in a book for the preface or other introductory material:

```
In his preface to The Great Mother, Erich Neumann
refers to the "onesidedly patriarchal development of
the male intellectual consciousness" (xliii).
```

11. REFERENCE TO A LITERARY CLASSIC   Use Arabic numerals separated by periods for such divisions of literary works as act, scene, and line (*Hamlet* 3.2.73–76) or "books" and lines of epic poems (*Odyssey* 2.315–16). However, some authors prefer the more traditional use of capital and lowercase Roman numerals (*Hamlet* III.ii.73–76).

```
In Shakespeare's Tempest, Gonzalo, who would prefer
to "die a dry death," fits this archetype  (1.1.66).
```

12. REFERENCE TO THE BIBLE   Use Arabic numerals for chapter and verse (Luke 2.1), although some authors prefer to use a traditional style (Luke ii.1).

ABBREVIATIONS AND TECHNICAL TERMS FOUND IN SCHOLARLY WRITING

©	copyright (© 1981 by John W. Gardner)
c. or ca.	Latin *circa*, "approximately"; used for approximate dates and figures (c. 1952)
cf.	Latin *confer*, "compare"; often used for **cross-references** instead of "see"; "consult for further relevant material" (Cf. Ecclesiastes xii.12)
et al.	Latin *et alii*, "and others"; used in references to books by several authors (G. S. Harrison et al.)
f., ff.	"and the following page," "and the following pages" (See p. 16 ff.)
Ibid.	an abbreviation of Latin *ibidem*, "in the same place." (When used by itself, without a page reference, it means "in the last publication cited, on the same page." When used with a page reference, it means "in the last publication cited, on the page indicated.")
loc. cit.	Latin *loco citato*, "in the place cited"; used without page reference (Baugh, loc. cit.)
MS, MSS	Manuscript, manuscripts
n.d.	"no date," date of publication unknown
op. cit.	short for *opere citato*, "in the work already cited"
passim	Latin for "throughout"; "in various places in the work under discussion" (See pp. 54–56 et passim.)
rev.	"review" or "revised"
rpt.	"reprint"; a reprinting of a book or article
q.v.	Latin *quod vide*, "which you should consult"

13. QUOTATION AT SECOND HAND Show that you are quoting not from the original source but at second hand. Your list of "Works Cited" will list only the second-hand source. (But quote from and cite the original source if you can.)

> William Archer reported in a letter to his brother
> Charles that the actor playing Pastor Manders never
> really entered "into the skin of the character" (qtd.
> in Ibsen 135).

14. REFERENCE TO NONPRINT MATERIALS When you refer to an interview, a radio or television program, or a movie, make sure your text highlights the name of the interviewer, person being interviewed, director or producer, or scriptwriter whose name appears in alphabetical order in your list of "Works Cited"—and whose name will direct your reader to a full description of the nonprint source. Sometimes you may name a production or movie in parentheses to direct your reader to the right entry:

> In an interview in 1988, Silveira discussed the roots
> of his work in Aztec and Inca art.

> The Caldwell production of La Traviata broke new
> ground without alienating traditional opera fans.

> A news special by a local station fanned the long-
> smoldering controversy into bright flames (Poisoned
> Earth).

Note: For unusual situations and a range of different sources, see the sample parenthetical references included in the Directory in **51c**.

51b   *doc* | Works Cited—General Guidelines (MLA) |

Code information accurately for your list of works cited.

At the end of your research paper, you will furnish an alphabetical listing of your sources. This listing, titled "Works Cited," serves as a directory guiding the interested reader to the sources you have drawn on during your search. It will often be more than a **bibliography** (a "book list" or list of printed materials) and include nonprint sources. Before you study a range of sample entries, learn the broad outlines of the style you will be required to follow.

Start your page with the centered heading "Works Cited." Then type your first entry, with the first line *not* indented, but with the *second line* and additional lines indented five spaces. Remember:

(1) Put the last name of the author first. This order applies only to the first author listed when a book has several authors. (The bibliography is an *alphabetical* listing.)

```
Brooks, Gwendolyn.  The World of Gwendolyn Brooks.
    New York: Harper, 1971.
Himstreet, William C., and Wayne Murlin Baty.
    Business Communications: Principles and Methods.
    7th ed.  Boston: Kent, 1984.
```

If *no name of author or editor* is known to you, list the publication alphabetically by the first letter of the title, not counting *The, A,* or *An.*

(2) Show major breaks by periods. Separate the name of the author or editor from what follows by a period. Set off the facts of publication for a book from what precedes and what follows by periods. (Leave *two* spaces after periods separating blocks of information.)

```
Silverberg, Robert, ed.  Science Fiction Hall of
    Fame.  London: Sphere Books, 1972.
```

(3) Underline (italicize) the title of a complete publication; enclose the title of a part in quotation marks. Underlining (when your typewriter has no italics) tells the printer to use italicized print. Italicize titles of books, collections, newspapers, or magazines: *A Brief Guide to Lean Cuisine.* Put in quotation marks titles of articles, reports, stories, or poems that were part of a larger publication: "How to Deep-Freeze Bait." *Angler's Monthly*. Remember: quotation marks for the *part*, italics for the *whole*.

(4) Include complete page numbers for an article. Entries for books do *not* include page numbers, but give the inclusive page numbers for articles in periodicals or for parts of a collection. (If part of an article spills over onto later pages not consecutively numbered with the beginning of the selection, use a plus sign to show that there is more on later pages.)

```
Lane, Chuck.  "Open the Door: Why We Should Welcome
     the Immigrant."  The New Republic 1 Apr. 1985:
     20-24.
Miller, JoAnn.  "The Sandwich Generation."  Working
     Mother Jan. 1987: 47-48.
Kaplan, Janice.  "Politics of Sports."  Vogue July
     1984: 219+.
```

Note: When a periodical uses continuous page numbering through several issues of an annual volume, include the *volume number* as an Arabic numeral. Use a colon before the inclusive page numbers: *PMLA* 96 (1981): 351–62. When page numbering is not continuous from one issue to another, you may need the number of the specific *issue* as well as the volume number. The following would guide the reader to volume 2, issue 2: *Kentucky Review* 2.2 (1981): 3–22.

(5) If you list several publications by the same author, do not repeat the author's name. In the second and later entries, use a line made of three hyphens instead:

```
Comfort, Alex.  A Good Age.  New York: Simon, 1976.
——. "Old Age: Facts and Fancies."  Saturday Evening
     Post Mar. 1977: 45.
——. Practice of Geriatric Psychiatry.  New York:
     Elsevier, 1980.
```

51c *doc* Works Cited—MLA Directory

Study model entries for books, articles, and nonprint sources.

The following directory of model entries has separate sections for books, articles, and nonprint sources. Each section starts with the most basic or most common situations and then gradually goes on to more unusual or more complicated ones. (There is also a final section on still finer points.) The final authority on the MLA style of documentation is the *MLA Handbook for Writers of Research Papers*, Third Edition.

In the following directory, each sample entry for your final list of "Works Cited" comes with a sample reference for parenthetical documentation in the text of your paper. Remember that most of the time you will identify author and source in your actual running text ("Isaac Asimov says in *The Age of Robots* . . ."), so that often your parenthetical references will give *page numbers* only. The sample references in this directory show what you have to do if your text has *not* already identified author or source.

Find what you are looking for in the following overview:

C. NONPRINT SOURCES

36. Personal Interview
37. Broadcast or Published Interview
38. Personal Letter
39. Talk or Lecture
40. Printed Speech
41. Television or Radio Program
42. Movie
43. Videotapes and Other Visuals
44. Computer Software

45. Audio Recording
46. Live Performance
47. Musical Composition
48. Work of Art
49. Cartoon
50. Map or Chart

D. FINER POINTS

51. Informal Local Publication
52. Microfilm or Microfiche

A. Books (and other whole publications)

1. STANDARD ENTRY FOR A BOOK Put last name of author first. Underline (italicize) the title. Include place of publication, name of publisher, and date of publication. Leave *two* spaces after periods.

```
Schell, Jonathan.  The Fate of the Earth.  New York:
     Knopf, 1982.
```

SAMPLE REFERENCE: (Schell 89)

Note: In the current style, identification of publishers is often heavily abbreviated: *NAL* for New American Library, *Harcourt* for Harcourt Brace Jovanovich, Inc. Other examples:

(Oxford University Press)	New York: Oxford UP, 1990
(Prentice-Hall, Inc.)	Englewood Cliffs: Prentice, 1989
(Academy for Educational Development)	Washington: Acad. for Educ. Dev., 1983

Place of publication is often omitted for books published before 1900:

```
London, 1878.
```

2. BOOK WITH SUBTITLE Use a colon to separate title and subtitle (unless the original has other punctuation). Underline (italicize) both the title and subtitle of the book.

```
Rodriguez, Richard.  Hunger of Memory: The Education
     of Richard Rodriguez.  Boston: Godine, 1982.
```

SAMPLE REFERENCE: (Rodriguez 82-83)

621

3. BOOK BY TWO OR THREE AUTHORS For the first author, put last name first. Then give full names of coauthors in normal order. With three authors, note the commas between authors' names.

> Gilbert, Sandra M. and Susan Guber. The Madwoman in
> 　　the Attic: The Woman Writer and the Nineteenth-
> 　　Century Literary Imagination. New Haven: Yale
> 　　UP, 1979.
> Wresch, William, Donald Pattow, and James Gifford.
> 　　Writing for the Twenty-First Century: Computers
> 　　and Research Writing. New York: McGraw, 1988.

SAMPLE REFERENCES:　(Gilbert and Guber 114)
　　　　　　　　　　(Wresch, Pattow, and Gifford 67)

4. BOOK BY MORE THAN THREE AUTHORS Give the first author's name, followed by a comma and the abbreviation *et al.* (Latin for "and others"). Do *not* put a period after *et*, and do not underline or italicize. (However, if you wish, you may give the full names of all coauthors instead.)

> Stewart, Marie M., et al. Business English and
> 　　Communication. 5th ed. New York: McGraw, 1978.

SAMPLE REFERENCE:　(Stewart et al. 34)

5. LATER EDITION OF A BOOK If you have used a book revised or brought up to date by the author, identify the new or revised edition the way it is labeled on its title page. After the title of the book, put *2nd ed.* for second edition, *rev. ed.* for revised edition, or *1989 ed.* for 1989 edition. Leave two spaces before and after this added information.

> Zettl, Herbert. Television Production Handbook. 4th
> 　　ed. Belmont: Wadsworth, 1984.

SAMPLE REFERENCE:　(Zettl 39)

6. REPRINTING OR REISSUE OF A BOOK If a work has been republished unchanged (perhaps as a paperback reprint), include the date of the original edition. Put it before full publishing data for the reprinting you have

used. If new material (like an introduction) has been added, include a note to that effect before the data for the reprinting.

> Wharton, Edith. <u>The House of Mirth</u>. 1905. Introd.
>   Cynthia Griffin Wolf. New York: Penguin, 1986.
> Ellison, Ralph. <u>Invisible Man</u>. 1952. New York:
>   Vintage–Random, 1972.

SAMPLE REFERENCE: (Ellison 7)

7. BOOK WIH EDITOR'S NAME FIRST If the title page lists an editor who has assembled or arranged the materials in the book, use *ed.* after the editor's name or *eds.* if there are several editors. (Use *comp.* if the title page says "Compiled by.")

> Griffin, Alice, ed. <u>Rebels and Lovers: Shakespeare's
>   Young Heroes and Heroines</u>. New York: New York
>   UP, 1976.
> Foster, Carol D., Nancy R. Jacobs, and Mark A. Siegel,
>   eds. <u>Capital Punishment: Cruel and Unusual?</u>
>   4th ed. Plano: Instructional Aides, 1984.

SAMPLE REFERENCES: (Griffin 17)
                     (Foster, Jacobs, and Siegel 86)

8. BOOK WITH EDITOR'S NAME LATER If an editor has edited the work of a single author, put the original author's name first if you focus on the *author's* work. Add *ed.* (for "edited by") and the editor's or several editors' names after the title. (Do not use *eds.*) However, put the editor's name first and the author's name later (after *By*) if the editor's work is particularly significant or important to your project.

> Mencken, H. L. <u>The Vintage Mencken</u>. Ed. Alistair
>   Cooke. New York: Vintage, 1956.
> Cooke, Alistair, ed. <u>The Vintage Mencken</u>. By H. L.
>   Mencken. New York: Vintage, 1956.

SAMPLE REFERENCES: Identify by person mentioned first.
                     (Mencken 98) (Cooke 4)

9. BOOK WITH TRANSLATOR'S NAME Put *Trans.* followed by the translator's name (or translators' names) after the title. But put the translator's name first if the translator's work is particularly significant to your project.

> Lorenz, Konrad. <u>On Aggression</u>. Trans. Marjorie Kerr
>   Wilson. New York: Harcourt, 1966.
> Kerr, Marjorie, trans. <u>On Aggression</u>. By Konrad
>   Lorenz. New York: Harcourt, 1966.

SAMPLE REFERENCES: Identify by person mentioned first.
(Lorenz 34) (Kerr 13)

10. SPECIAL IMPRINT A line of paperback books, for instance, is often published and promoted separately by a publishing house. Put the name of the line of books first, joined by a hyphen to the publisher's name: *Laurel Leaf-Dell, Mentor-NAL.*

> Hsu, Kai-yu, ed. and trans. <u>Twentieth-Century
>   Chinese Poetry</u>. Garden City: Anchor-Doubleday,
>   1964.

SAMPLE REFERENCE: (Hsu 45)

11. UNSPECIFIED OR INSTITUTIONAL AUTHORSHIP Reports prepared by an organization or agency and major reference books may list a group as the author or not specify authorship:

> Carnegie Council on Policy Studies in Higher
>   Education. <u>Giving Youth a Better Chance:
>   Options for Education, Work, and Service</u>. San
>   Francisco: Jossey, 1980.
> <u>Literary Market Place: The Directory of American Book
>   Publishing</u>. 1984 ed. New York: Bowker, 1983.

SAMPLE REFERENCES: (Carnegie Council 29)
(<u>Literary Market</u> 178)

Note: Abbreviate agency or anonymous title but start with first word that would appear in alphabetical listing—*not* "Council on Policy" or "*Market Place.*"

624

12. WORK WITH SEVERAL VOLUMES If you have used *one* volume of a multivolume work (for instance, a historical work published as three books), add the abbreviation *Vol.* followed by an Arabic numeral for the number of the volume: Vol. 3. (You may add the total number of volumes and inclusive dates at the end.) If the separate volumes have their own titles, include the volume title as well as the title of the whole multivolume work.

> Woolf, Virginia. <u>The Diary of Virginia Woolf</u>. Ed.
> Anne Olivier Bell. New York: Harcourt, 1977.
> Vol. 1.
>
> Churchill, Winston S. <u>The Age of Revolution</u>. New
> York: Dodd, 1957. Vol. 3 of <u>A History of the</u>
> <u>English-Speaking Peoples</u>. 4 vols. 1956-58.

SAMPLE REFERENCES: (Woolf 67) (Churchill 115-16)

If you have used *more than one* volume, list the whole multivolume work, giving the total number of volumes: 3 vols.

> Trevelyan, G. M. <u>History of England</u>. 3rd ed.
> 3 vols. Garden City: Anchor-Doubleday, 1952.

SAMPLE REFERENCES: Include volume number as well as page number(s).
(3: 156) (Trevelyan 3: 156)

Note: To refer to one *whole volume*, use (Trevelyan, vol. 3).

13. PART OF COLLECTION OR ANTHOLOGY Identify fully both the article or other short piece (poem, short story) and the collection of which it is a part. Put the part title in quotation marks; underline (italicize) the title of the whole: Asher, Carol. "Selling to Ms. Consumer." *American Media and Mass Culture.* Then go on to publishing data for the collection. Conclude with inclusive page numbers for the part: 43-52.

> Rogers, Carl R. "Two Divergent Trends." <u>Existential</u>
> <u>Psychology</u>. Ed. Rollo May. New York: Random,
> 1969. 87-92.
>
> Oates, Joyce Carol. "Where Are You Going, Where Have
> You Been?" <u>The American Tradition in</u>

<u>Literature</u>. Ed. Sculley Bradley et al. 4th ed.
New York: Norton, 1974. Vol. 2. 1916–30.

SAMPLE REFERENCES: (Rogers 87) (Oates 1928)

If the anthologized part was originally published as a book, underline (italicize) the part title like a book title. If the author of a piece is unknown (as with a folktale), start with the part title.

Hansberry, Lorraine. <u>A Raisin in the Sun</u>. <u>Black</u>
<u>Theater: A Twentieth-Century Collection of the</u>
<u>Work of Its Best Playwrights</u>. Ed. Lindsay
Patterson. New York: Dodd, 1971. 221–76.

SAMPLE REFERENCE: (Hansberry 223–24)

"How Humans Were Fashioned by the Coyote."
<u>Beginnings</u>. Ed. Hans P. Guth and Gabriele L.
Rico. Lexington: Heath, 1981. 47–50.

SAMPLE REFERENCE: ("How Humans" 48)

14. ENCYCLOPEDIA ENTRY Put titles of entries in quotation marks. Page numbers and facts of publication may be unnecessary for entries appearing in alphabetical order in well-known encyclopedias or other reference books. Date or number of the edition used, however, should be included because of the frequent revisions of major encyclopedias. (Include author's name for signed entries. If only initials are given, you may find the full name in an index or guide.)

Politis, M. J. "Greek Music." <u>Encyclopedia</u>
<u>Americana</u>. 1956 ed.
"Aging." <u>Encyclopaedia Britannica: Macropaedia</u>.
1983.
"Graham, Martha." <u>Who's Who of American Women</u>. 14th
ed. 1985–86.

SAMPLE REFERENCES: No page numbers are needed for alphabetical entries.
(Politis) ("Aging") ("Graham")

15. LESS WELL-KNOWN REFERENCE BOOKS Include full publishing data
for less well-known reference books.

> Brakeley, Theresa C. "Mourning Songs." <u>Funk and</u>
>
>   <u>Wagnalls Standard Dictionary of Folklore,</u>
>
>   <u>Mythology, and Legend</u>. Ed. Maria Leach and
>
>   Jerome Fried. 2 vols. New York: Crowell, 1950.

SAMPLE REFERENCE: No page numbers are needed for alphabetical entries.
(Brakeley)

16. INTRODUCTION, FOREWORD, OR AFTERWORD If you cite introductory material or an afterword by someone *other than the author* of the
book, start with the contributor's name, followed by the generic description (*un*italicized, *not* in quotation marks): Introduction. Preface. Foreword. Afterword. Sometimes the introductory material has separate page
numbers, given as lowercase Roman numerals: v–ix or ii–xvi.

> Bellow, Saul. Foreword. <u>The Closing of the American</u>
>
>   <u>Mind</u>. By Allan Bloom. New York: Simon, 1987.
>
>   11–18.
>
> DeMott, Robert. Introduction. <u>Working Days: The</u>
>
>   <u>Journals of</u> The Grapes of Wrath <u>1938–1941</u>. By
>
>   John Steinbeck. Ed. Robert DeMott. New York:
>
>   Viking, 1989. xxi–lvii.

If you cite a preface or introduction written separately by the *original
author* (as for a collection of poems, stories, or essays), start with the
author's name as writer of the introductory material. Then repeat the
author's *last name only* after *By* after the title of the whole book.

> Rich, Adrienne. Foreword. <u>On Lies, Secrets, and</u>
>
>   <u>Silence: Selected Prose, 1966–1978</u>. By Rich.
>
>   New York: Norton, 1979. 9–18.

SAMPLE REFERENCES: (Bellow 13) (DeMott xxxii)
(Rich 16–17)

627

17. GOVERNMENT PUBLICATION References to entries in the *Congressional Record* require only the date and page numbers. For other government publications, start by identifying the government and the appropriate branch or subdivision. Use appropriate abbreviations like *S. Res.* for Senate Resolution, *H. Rept.* for House Report, *S. Doc.* for Senate Document, and *GPO* for Government Printing Office.

> Cong. Rec. 7 Feb. 1973: 3831–51.
>
> California. Dept. of Viticulture. Grape Harvesting.
>   Sacramento: State Printing Office, 1990.
>
> United States. Cong. Senate. Subcommittee on
>   Constitutional Amendments of the Committee on
>   the Judiciary. Hearings on the "Equal Rights"
>   Amendment. 91st Cong., 2nd sess. S. Res. 61.
>   Washington: GPO, 1970.

SAMPLE REFERENCE: (California. Dept. of Viticulture 18–20)

Note: Identify sources with long elaborate names briefly but adequately *in your text*.

18. PAMPHLET OR BROCHURE Treat a pamphlet or brochure the way you would a book, but note that often author (and sometimes place or date) will not be specified.

> Worried Sick About Cholesterol? Boston: Inst. for
>   Better Living, 1989.

SAMPLE REFERENCE: (Worried Sick 12)

19. DISSERTATION If a doctoral dissertation has been locally reproduced but *not* formally published, put the title in quotation marks. If it has been formally published, underline (italicize) the title. If the dissertation is available through University Microfilms International, include the abbreviation *UMI* and the order number.

> Latesta, Philip. "Rod McKuen and the Sense of Déjà
>   Vu." Diss. Columbia U, 1986.
>
> Latesta, Philip. Rod McKuen and the Sense of Déjà Vu.

```
Diss. Columbia U.  Ann Arbor: UMI, 1986.
8509765.
```

SAMPLE REFERENCE: (Latesta 19—21)

20. PART OF A SERIES If the front matter of a book shows it was published as part of a series, include the name of the series (unitalicized, no quotation marks) before the publishing data.

```
Rose, Mike.  Writer's Block: The Cognitive Dimension.
    Studies in Writing and Rhetoric.  Carbondale:
    Southern Illinois UP, 1984.
```

SAMPLE REFERENCE: (Rose 78)

21. BIBLE OR LITERARY CLASSIC Specify the edition you have used, especially if different versions of the text are important, as with different Bible translations or different editions of a Shakespeare play. Put the editor's name first if you want to highlight the editor's contribution.

```
The Holy Bible.  Revised Standard Version.  2nd ed.
    Nashville: Nelson, 1971.
Hubler, Edward, ed.  The Tragedy of Hamlet.  By
    William Shakespeare.  New York: NAL, 1963.
```

SAMPLE REFERENCES: For chapter and verse: (Job 2.8)
                      For act and scene: (Hamlet 3.2) or
                      (Hamlet III.ii)

Note: Even when using specific page numbers for an edition you have used, you can help your reader find the passage in a different edition by adding the number of the chapter or of act and scene after a semicolon: (34; ch. 2).

22. QUOTATION AT SECOND HAND List only the work where the quotation appeared:

```
Ibsen, Henrik.  Ghosts.  Ed. Kai Jurgensen and Robert
    Schenkkan.  New York: Avon, 1965.
```

SAMPLE REFERENCE: (qtd. in Ibsen 48)

23. TITLE WITHIN A TITLE Sometimes, an italicized (underlined) book title includes the name of another book. Shift back to roman (*not* underlined) for the title-within-a-title: *A Guide to James Joyce's* Ulysses.

B. Articles in periodicals

24. STANDARD ENTRY FOR MAGAZINE ARTICLE Start with the last name of the author. Put the title of the *article* in quotation marks; underline (italicize) the name of the *magazine*. Go on to the date (or month), separated from the *complete page numbers* by a colon. Abbreviate most months: Nov. 1990: 23–31. 27 Apr. 1989: 77–80.

```
Hammer, Joshua.  "Cashing In on Vietnam."  Newsweek
     16 Jan. 1989: 38–39.
Weinberg, Steven.  "The Decay of the Proton."
     Scientific American June 1981: 64–75.
```

SAMPLE REFERENCES: (Hammer 78) (Weinberg 69)

Note: If an article is interrupted and continued later in the publication, use a plus sign to show that there is more later after the initial pages: 28 Feb. 1990: 38–41 +.

25. NEWSPAPER ARTICLE If necessary, specify the edition of the newspaper—early or late, east or west: *Wall Street Journal* 14 July 1989, eastern ed.: A3. Sections of a newspaper are often identified by letters (B34) or by numbers (late ed., sec. 3: 7 +). Use the major headline of the article as its title:

```
Hechinger, Fred.  "How Free Should High School Papers
     Be?"  New York Times 5 July 1989, western ed.:
     B7.
```

SAMPLE REFERENCE: No page number necessary for one-page article. (Hechinger)

Note: Leave off the article *The* in the names of newspapers like *The Wall Street Journal* or *The New York Times* when you include them in your list of "Works Cited."

26. ARTICLE BY SEVERAL AUTHORS Give the full names of coauthors. If there are more than three, put *et al.* (Latin for "and others") after the name of the first author instead.

Gale, Noel H., and Zofia Stos-Gale. "Lead and Silver
   in the Ancient Aegean." <u>Scientific American</u>
   June 1981: 176-77.

Martz, Larry et al. "A Tide of Drug Killings."
   <u>Newsweek</u> 16 Jan. 1989: 44-45.

SAMPLE REFERENCES: (Gale and Stos-Gale 176)
                   (Martz et al. 45)

27. UNSIGNED OR ANONYMOUS ARTICLE If the author of an article remains unnamed, begin your entry with the title. (Note, however, that
newsmagazines increasingly give the names of authors of major articles.)

"Environmentalists See Threats to Rivers." <u>New York</u>
   <u>Times</u> 15 July 1981, late ed., sec. 1: 8.

"The Boundaries of Privacy." <u>Time</u> 30 Apr. 1984:
   64-65.

SAMPLE REFERENCES: ("Environmentalists") ("Boundaries" 64)

28. ARTICLE WITH SUBTITLE Have a colon separate title and subtitle.
Enclose both title and subtitle in the same set of quotation marks.

Schmidt, Sarah. "From Ghetto to University: The
   Jewish Experience in the Public School."
   <u>American Educator</u> Spring 1978: 23-25.

SAMPLE REFERENCE: (Schmidt 25)

29. ARTICLE WITH VOLUME NUMBER For most periodicals, the month
or the date is sufficient to steer the reader to the right issue. For scholarly
or professional journals, you will typically include the *volume number* instead, followed by the year in parentheses. (Usually page numbers are
consecutive for the whole volume covering the issues for a year—the second
issue will start with page 90 or page 137, for instance.)

Santley, Robert S. "The Political Economy of the
   Aztec Empire." <u>Journal of Anthropological</u>
   <u>Research</u> 41 (1985): 327-37.

SAMPLE REFERENCE: (Santley 327)

631

30. ARTICLE WITH NUMBER OF VOLUME AND ISSUE If page numbers are not continuous for the whole volume (each new issue starts with page 1), you may have to include the *number of the issue*. Add it after the volume number, separating the two numbers by a period (no space): 13.4.

> Winks, Robin W. "The Sinister Oriental Thriller:
>
> Fiction and the Asian Scene." Journal of
>
> Popular Culture 19.2 (1985): 49–61.

If there is *no volume number* but only the number of the issue, treat it as if it were the volume number:

> Bowering, George. "Baseball and the Canadian
>
> Imagination." Canadian Literature 108 (1986):
>
> 115–24.

SAMPLE REFERENCES: (Winks 51–53) (Bowering 117)

Note: If the issue is part of a *numbered or labeled series*, you may have to identify the series—for instance: 3rd ser. 43 (1986): 594–614. Use *ns* or *os* for "new series" or "old series": "ns 8.4 (1986): 1–43."

31. SIGNED OR UNSIGNED EDITORIAL After the title, add the right label: Editorial (*un*italicized, *not* in quotation marks). If the editorial is unsigned, begin with the title.

> Whitcroft, Jeremiah. "Talking to Strangers."
>
> Editorial. Plainsville Courier 13 Sept. 1989: 7.
>
> "A Frown on the Interface." Editorial. Software
>
> News 3 Sept. 1988: 3–4.

SAMPLE REFERENCES: (Whitcroft) ("Frown" 4)

32. LETTER TO THE EDITOR After the name of the author, add the right label: Letter (*un*italicized, *not* in quotation marks).

> Vinaver, Martha. Letter. Los Angeles Times 14 July
>
> 1989, part II: 6.

SAMPLE REFERENCE: (Vinaver)

33. TITLED OR UNTITLED REVIEW Use the abbreviation *rev.* before the title of the work being reviewed. For unsigned reviews, start with the title of the review (if any) or the description of the review.

```
Bromwich, David.  "Say It Again, Sam."  Rev. of The
    Oxford Book of Aphorisms, ed. John Gross.  The
    New Republic 6 Feb. 1984: 36—38.

Harlan, Arvin C.  Rev. of A Short Guide to German
    Humor, by Frederick Hagen.  Oakland Tribune 12
    Dec. 1988: 89—90.

Rev. of The Penguin Books of Women Poets, ed. Carol
    Cosman, Joan Keefe, and Kathleen Weaver.  Arts
    and Books Forum May 1990: 17—19.
```

SAMPLE REFERENCES: (Bromwich 38)   (Rev. of Women Poets 17)

34. COMPUTER SERVICE For material obtained from a computer service, add the name of the system and access number or file and item number for the article you have used.

```
Schomer, Howard.  "South Africa: Beyond Fair
    Employment."  Harvard Business Review May—June
    1983: 145+.  Dialog file 122, item 119425
    833160.
```

SAMPLE REFERENCE: (Schomer 145)

35. INFORMATION SERVICE Information services like ERIC provide both bibliographic listings and actual printouts of the documents themselves. If the material had been previously published elsewhere, provide standard publishing information, followed by identification of the service and an item number. If the material had not been previously published, cite it as a complete publication published by the service:

```
Kurth, Ruth J. and Linda J. Stromberg.  Using Word
    Processing in Composition Instruction.  ERIC,
    1984.  ED 251 850.
```

SAMPLE REFERENCE: (Kurth 3)

C. Nonprint sources

36. PERSONAL INTERVIEW Start with the name of the person you interviewed. Use the right label—*un*italicized, *not* in quotation marks. Give the date.

> Silveira, Gene. Personal Interview. 23 Oct. 1990.
>
> Duong, Tran. Telephone Interview. 16 Jan. 1989.

SAMPLE REFERENCE: (Duong) No parenthetical reference is necessary if your text names the person you interviewed.

37. BROADCAST OR PUBLISHED INTERVIEW Identify the person interviewed and label the material as an interview. Add the title of the radio or TV program, the name and place of the station, and the date. You may include the name of the interviewer if known.

> Asimov, Isaac. Interview. Science Watch. With
>   Dorothy Brett. KFOM, San Bruno. 19 Mar. 1986.

If an interview appeared in print, identify it as an interview and then give standard publishing information about the printed source. Include page numbers.

> Asimov, Isaac. Interview. Scientists Talk About
>   Science. By Anne Harrison and Webster Freid.
>   Los Angeles: Acme, 1987. 94—101.

SAMPLE REFERENCE: (Asimov) For printed source: (Asimov 98)

38. PERSONAL LETTER For a letter you have received, name the letter writer and label the material as a letter. Give the date. For a published letter, use the name of the *recipient* as the title and then give full publishing data, with inclusive page numbers.

> Chavez, Roderigo. Letter to the author. 15 Jan.
>   1990.
>
> Hemingway, Ernest. "To Lillian Ross." 28 July 1948.
>   Ernest Hemingway: Selected Letters, 1917—1961.
>   Ed. Carlos Baker. New York: Scribner's, 1981.
>   646—49.

SAMPLE REFERENCE: (Chavez)
                     For printed source: (Hemingway 647)

39. TALK OR LECTURE Name the speaker and provide an appropriate label: Lecture. Keynote Speech. Address (*un*italicized, *no* quotation marks). If the talk had a title, use the title (in quotation marks) instead. Then go on to the occasion (often including the sponsoring organization), the place, and the date.

> Freitag, Marilyn. Keynote Speech. Opening General
>> Sess. New World Forum. Atlanta, Apr. 7, 1988.
>
> Jacobi, Jean. "Television News: News from Nowhere."
>> Valley Lecture Series. Santa Clara, 29 Oct.
>> 1990.

SAMPLE REFERENCE: (Freitag)   No parenthetical reference is necessary if
                     your text names the speaker.

40. PRINTED SPEECH If you had access to a printed version of a speech, add full publishing data to the usual information about a talk.

> Partlet, Basil. "Yuppies and the Art of Cooking."
>> Western Chefs' Forum. Phoenix, 19 Aug. 1989.
>> Rpt. West Coast Review Spring 1990: 76–82.

SAMPLE REFERENCE: (Partlet 77)

41. TELEVISION OR RADIO PROGRAM Underline (italicize) the title of a program. The title may be preceded by the name of a specific episode (in quotation marks) and followed by the name of the series (unitalicized, no quotation marks): "The Young Stravinsky." *The Great Composers.* Musical Masterpieces. Identify network (if any), station, and city (with the last two separated by a comma: KPFA, Berkeley). Include information about directors, writers, or performers when it seems especially significant. Pull a name out in front to highlight a person's contribution.

> The Poisoned Earth. Narr. Sylvia Garth. Writ. and
>> prod. Pat Fisher. WXRV, Seattle. 23 Oct. 1988.

635

Rostow, Jacob, dir. "The Last Bridge." <u>A Forgotten
War</u>. With Eric Seibert, Joan Ash, and Fred
Minton. KMBC, Sacramento. 12 Dec. 1987.

SAMPLE REFERENCE: (<u>Poisoned Earth</u>) No parenthetical reference is
necessary if your text names the program.

42. MOVIE Underline (italicize) the title. Identify the director and the production company, and give the date. Include further information as you wish about performers, scriptwriters, and other contributors. Pull a name out in front to highlight a person's contribution.

<u>It's a Wonderful Life</u>. Dir. Frank Capra. With James
Stewart, Donna Reed, Lionel Barrymore, and
Thomas Mitchell. RKO, 1946.
Zeffirelli, Franco, dir. <u>Romeo and Juliet</u>. By
William Shakespeare. With Olivia Hussey,
Leonard Whiting, and Michael York. Paramount,
1968. 138 min.

SAMPLE REFERENCE: (Zeffirelli)

43. VIDEOTAPES AND OTHER VISUALS Label the medium: Videocassette. Filmstrip. Slide program (*un*italicized, *not* put in quotation marks).

<u>Creation vs. Evolution: Battle of the Classrooms</u>.
Videocassette. Dir. Ryall Wilson. PBS Video,
1982. 58 min.
<u>Drugs and the Schools</u>. Slide program. Dev.
Educational Research Associates. New Age, 1990.
38 slides.

SAMPLE REFERENCE: (<u>Creation</u>)

44. COMPUTER SOFTWARE Basic information includes writer of the program (if known), title of the program or material, distributor or publisher,

and date. Because of frequent updatings of computer software, you may have to specify the version: Vers. 1.4. In addition, you may need to tell your readers what equipment and how much memory are required (in kilobytes: 128K).

> Crighton, Irene. <u>Think/Write</u>. Vers. 1.2. Computer
> Software. Celex, 1989. Apple IIe, 128K, disk.

SAMPLE REFERENCE: (Crighton)

45. AUDIO RECORDING Specify label of the recording company, followed by order number and date. (Use *n.d.* for "no date" if date is unknown.) Identify references to jacket notes or the like.

> Holiday, Billie. <u>The Essential Billie Holiday:</u>
> <u>Carnegie Hall Concert</u>. Audiocassette. Verve,
> UCV2600, 1969.

> Shakespeare, William. <u>Twelfth Night</u>. 2 Audio-
> cassettes. Dir. George Rylands. With Dorothy
> Tutin, Derek Godfrey, Tony Church, and others.
> The Marlowe Dramatic Society. Listen for
> Pleasure, 7081, 1981.

> Rifkin, Joshua. Jacket Notes. <u>Renaissance Vocal</u>
> <u>Music</u>. Nonesuch, H-71097, n.d.

SAMPLE REFERENCE: (Rifkin)

46. LIVE PERFORMANCE Normally begin with the title (underlined or italicized). Then specify author or composer and participants. At the end, put the theater or hall, the place, and the date. To highlight one person's contribution, pull the name out in front, followed by *dir., chor.* (for choreographer), *cond.* (for conductor), *actor*, or the like.

> <u>Cats</u>. By Andrew Lloyd Webber. Dir. Kevin Hall.
> Orpheum Theater, San Francisco. 12 June 1988.
> Based on T. S. Eliot's <u>Old Possum's Book of</u>
> <u>Practical Cats</u>.

Huffman, Alan, dir. <u>Mother Courage</u>. By Bertolt
   Brecht. University Theater, San Jose. 19 Nov.
   1986.

SAMPLE REFERENCE: (Huffman)

47. MUSICAL COMPOSITION Underline (italicize) the special titles of specific works (*Don Giovanni, Firebird Suite*). Do *not* underline or put in quotation marks the titles of works identified by generic label (symphony, sonata, quartet) and number or key: Symphony No. 7 in A, op. 92.

Wagner, Richard. <u>The Flying Dutchman</u>.
Brahms, Johannes. Concerto for Violin and Orchestra
   in D-major, op. 77.

However, italicize (underline) the title of a *printed musical score* the way you would a book title:

Beethoven, Ludwig van. <u>Symphony No. 7 in A, Op. 92</u>.
   Orpheus Orchestral Scores 7. Hamburg: Orpheus,
   1988.

SAMPLE REFERENCE: (Beethoven)

48. WORK OF ART Underline (italicize) the title of the work. Show the location.

Klee, Paul. <u>Red Balloon</u>. Solomon R. Guggenheim
   Museum, New York.

SAMPLE REFERENCE: (Klee)

49. CARTOON If the cartoon or the strip has a title, enclose it in quotation marks. Use the right label (unitalicized, not in quotation marks): Cartoon.

```
Trudeau, Garry.  "Doonesbury."  Cartoon.  Los Angeles
     Times 14 July 1989, part V: 8.
Wilkinson, Signe.  Cartoon.  Ms. Nov. 1988: 84.
```

SAMPLE REFERENCE: `(Wilkinson 84)`

50. MAP OR CHART Include the right label: Map. Chart (unitalicized, not in quotation marks).

```
The Historic West.  Map.  Phoenix: Pathways, 1989.
```

SAMPLE REFERENCE: `(Historic West)`

D. Finer points

51. INFORMAL LOCAL PUBLICATION Show when a source you cite is an informally duplicated, photocopied, or mimeographed publication. Put the titles of items not formally published in quotation marks. Note that often part of the publishing data will be missing, so that you may have to use *n.p.* (no known publisher) or *n.d.* (no known date). Put missing data that you supply from the outside (or inside) in square brackets.

```
Lopez, Fernando, ed.  "Tales of the Elders."  Mimeo.
     Albuquerque: n.p. [1989].
```

SAMPLE REFERENCE: `(Lopez 17)`

52. MICROFILM OR MICROFICHE You need not show that you obtained material on microfilm or microfiche—list the source the way you would have listed the original publication.

WRITING WORKSHOP 17   The following are possible sources for a paper exploring advice young women receive on how to be successful in a business career. Prepare an alphabetical list of *"Works Cited,"* following the MLA style of documentation. Prepare photocopies for a meeting in which your class or small group will check and discuss format.

1. A book titled Women Like Us by Liz Roman Gallese, published by William Morrow in New York in 1985.
2. A book by Betty Legan Harragan called Games Your Mother Never Taught You: Corporate Gamesmanship for Women, published by Warner Books in New York in 1977.
3. Several articles by Betty Legan Harragan: How to Take Risks and Make More Money in Harper's Bazaar for August 78, starting on page 82 and continued later in the magazine; and Getting Ahead in Working Woman for December 1982, starting on page 44 and continued later.
4. A book called The Right Moves: Succeeding in a Man's World Without a Harvard MBA, written by Charlene Mitchell and Thomas Burdick, published by Macmillan in New York in 1985.
5. A book edited by Ralph E. Smith and titled The Subtle Revolution: Women at Work, published by the Urban Institute in Washington, D.C., in 1979.
6. The fourth edition of Betty Friedan's The Feminine Mystique, published by W. W. Norton in New York in 1983.
7. An article by Kay Mills in the Los Angeles Times for September 18, 1984, and titled Despite Gains, Job Future Still Uncertain for Women, to be found in Section I on page 1.
8. A book called Letitia Baldridge's Complete Guide to Executive Manners published by Rawson Associates in Toronto in 1985.
9. An article by Barbara Ehrenreich titled Strategies of Corporate Women, printed in The New Republic for January 27, 1986, to be found on pages 28 through 31.
10. An article by Mary Bralove, titled Corporate Politics: Equal Opportunities and printed in a periodical called Masters in Business Administration, to be found in volume 12 for Aug.–Sept. 1978, starting on page 26 and continued on page 30.
11. A personal interview about Harragan's Games Your Mother Never Taught You, conducted with a business school instructor named Kaye Schonholtz on March 17, 1987.
12. An unsigned article in the Oakland Tribune for February 14, 1990, titled Superwoman: Coping with Stress, appearing in a late edition in Section B on pages 7 and 8.
13. A book by Marilyn Loden called Feminine Leadership: Or How to Succeed in Business Without Being One of the Boys, published by Times Books in New York in 1985.

14. A photocopied brochure published by the Fresno Boosters Club, titled Preventing Executive Burnout and written by Jordan K. Pagodian and three coauthors, published in Fresno, California, in December 1986.

51d   *doc* | Using Footnotes/Endnotes

Know how to use endnotes for additional information.

In much traditional scholarly writing, footnotes (now usually **endnotes**) have been used to identify sources and add information. Such notes are usually numbered consecutively. A raised footnote number appears outside whatever punctuation goes with the sentence or paragraph, as in this example.[2] At the bottom of the page (or now usually on a separate page at the end of a paper or article), the note itself appears. It starts with the raised number, is indented like a paragraph, and ends with a period or other end punctuation.

A traditional footnote identifying a source might look like this:

> [2] Robin Northcroft, <u>A Short Guide to Fine British Cooking</u> (New York: Culinary Arts, 1989), p. 85.

Even when you use a system of documentation that does not identify sources in footnotes, you may want to use notes for the kind of backup that can help satisfy an interested reader. For instance, your text may have mentioned the recent outpouring of books with titles like *Aging: Continuity and Change* or *Aging and Society*. For the interested reader, you may decide to provide a more extended listing in a note:

> [3] Books on aging from the publication list of a single publisher include <u>The Social Forces in Later Life</u>, <u>Social Problems of the Aging</u>, <u>Biology of Aging</u>, <u>Human Services for Older Adults</u>, <u>Families in Later Life</u>, <u>The Later Years</u>, <u>Working with the Elderly</u>, <u>Late Adulthood</u>, and <u>Aging: Politics and Policies</u>, among others.

Put such notes on a separate page headed "Notes" at the end of your paper before your "Works Cited." Other common uses of such notes include the following:

- showing your familiarity with earlier research in the field
- dealing with objections likely to be raised by insiders
- clearing up possible confusions over technical terms
- providing additional context (or more of the exact wording) of a key quotation
- pointing to an interesting parallel or precedent

52   The Making of a Sample Paper

OVERVIEW To be a successful researcher, you need to be both an idea person and a detail person. As an idea person, you chart the course of your investigation. You seize on connections between ideas. You quarry the right materials and build them into the grand design of your paper.

As a detail person, you do the groundwork. You follow up leads. You accurately transcribe and identify quotations. You carefully record publishing data, and you place the commas and colons correctly in listing your sources. In a successful project, you attend to detail without losing sight of the larger purposes of your investigation.

The following materials give you a chance to look over the shoulder of a student researcher at work and then to take a detailed look at her finished paper. As you study her work, try to keep in view her handling of both the ideas and the details. Remember that a research paper is a writing task. The thinking and planning that go into it are as important as the spacing and punctuation of information about your sources.

52a   Sample Paper: From Plan to Revision

Trace the making of a sample paper through major stages.

As you study the sample paper that follows in this section, try to reconstruct the process that produced the finished result.

PLANNING REPORT The following **planning report** shows that from the start the author wrote with a purpose. She had an agenda; her topic had a personal significance for her as a writer.

> I want to investigate the area of women in sports. It's a good topic for me because I love sports both as a spectator and as a participant. My thesis has not yet crystallized in my mind, but I want to focus on the *changes* that have occurred in the last 10–15 years with respect to opportunities for women in athletics. I may wish to go back farther for more historical perspective. I know women did not compete in the first Olympics, but they have been in Olympic competition for as long as I can personally remember. In my own experience, however, women who wanted to participate in the drama of competitive sports had to either become cheerleaders or join a small organization of girls rumored to wear combat boots, the GAA or Girls' Athletic Association. I realized last year how much things have changed when I watched a women's sectional volleyball game at the local high school. The local team won a victory that sent them to the state finals. The exciting part was that the entire boys' football team had turned out to cheer the girls on. When the final buzzer sounded, the fans exploded, absolutely jubilant, and total bedlam ensued. One thing was obvious: These women athletes were neither cheerleaders nor truckdriving types—they were a new breed, and they made me feel proud. This incident might make a good introduction.

SEARCH RECORD The following **search record** shows how the author of the women-in-sports paper capitalized on promising leads, useful pointers, and lucky finds. What resources did she draw on? Where did she turn? How did she proceed?

> My plan was to start by scanning periodicals that seemed obvious sources for material on women athletes: *Sports Illustrated, Ms.* magazine, *Womensports, Women's Sports and Fitness.* I was also going to look for material on outstanding professional athletes such as Billie Jean King, Chris Evert, or Babe Zacharias. My older sister earlier in the year had received a brochure that was part of a fund-raising drive for scholarships to women athletes; I decided to try to track down a copy of the brochure. A promising source was the coach of the local volleyball team at the high school—very committed to women's volleyball and consistently coaching championship teams.

During the early informal reading, I found that many magazine articles about female athletes deal with current "sports celebrities" or with current fads, like female body builders. I felt that I needed to find material that focused more directly on the issues faced by women in sports, on their changing self-image, and on future directions. Through the card catalog, I found two key sources providing essential historical background: Janice Kaplan's *Women and Sports* and, in a collection called *Sports in Literature*, an article by Marie Hart ("Sport: Women Sit in the Back of the Bus"), reprinted from *Psychology Today*. The electronic periodical index at the college library had hardly any listings under WOMEN IN SPORTS but had much material under the umbrella heading WOMAN ATHLETES, with numerous subheadings such as "Achievements and Awards," "Competition," and "History."

Some of the most useful material I found was focused on two major topics. The first was Title IX, designed to promote greater equality of opportunity for women in collegiate athletics. Much has been written on the original legislation, its guidelines and applications, and later changes. The second topic was the 1984 Olympics, which for many observers was a turning point in the recognition awarded female athletes.

Lucky find: I found that an author who had written a book on sports sociology was a local resident, and I was able to arrange an interview. While I worked on the paper, I watched the newspaper for relevant news reports, such as a story on a woman who won a dogsled race in Alaska. I learned much by talking to people about my paper.

TRIAL OUTLINE As they digest their material, most writers at first use a rough working outline. They then gradually refine it until they arrive at a trial outline to guide the writing of the first draft. To keep the effort on track, they push toward a tentative thesis, stated early in the first draft. (Often, they find that their tentative thesis needs sharpening as the rest of the paper takes shape.) Here is the **trial outline** that guided the writing of the first draft for "Women in Sports":

Women in Sports

THESIS: The revolution in women's athletics is producing two kinds of fallout: It is leading us to reevaluate the nature of athletics, and it is refashioning the way women see themselves.

I. The historical perspective
   A. 1890–1950: Conventional roles, some advances
   B. 1950s and 60s: Changes begin
   C. 1970s: Commercial money and Chapter IX
   D. The 1984 Olympics
II. Reevaluating Athletics
   A. Challenging excessive competition
   B. Challenging excessive violence
III. Refashioning women's self-image
   A. Physical fitness and emotional fitness
   B. Breaking physical barriers
   C. Increased self-esteem
   D. Carryover into other areas of life

REVISION NOTE Sometimes a trial outline works out well. Revision of a first draft can then focus on page-by-page detail: clarifying points, bolstering evidence, strengthening connections. But often some real rethinking and reshuffling seem advisable. Here is a note on how her view of her audience guided the author of "Women in Sports" in a major reshuffling of material:

I early had a sense of three major sections of the paper: There would be a historical section on the traditional obstacles faced by women in sports and on their slow progress in overcoming them. There would be a section on how the increasing visibility of women in the world of sports has begun to change the spirit of sports, with less emphasis on violence and winner-takes-all competition. There would be a section on women's growth in self-esteem and self-confidence as the result of emphasis on physical fitness and increased participation in sports.

Originally I thought that the section on women and how they see themselves should be last since it contained much eloquent material. But the more I thought about it, the more it seemed that the more general section on changes in sports and our general attitude toward sports should come last. Ending with the section on women and their changing attitudes would have made this a paper primarily on women, aimed primarily at women as an audience. Ending the paper with the section on changing attitudes towards sports made this a paper on sports in general, aiming at both men and women as an audience.

52b | Sample Research Paper: The Text |

As you study the sample research paper, pay attention to content and form.

As you study the sample research paper, do justice to three major dimensions:

LARGER ELEMENTS Make sure you see how the author tackles her subject, guides the reader, and maintains the reader's interest. For instance, in the early pages, study the way she introduces her subject and leads up to her thesis. She *dramatizes the issue* by turning to personal experience: She tells (briefly) the story of the volleyball playoff that helped crystallize her own thinking about the progress of women in sports. This account sets up the "then-and-now" contrast that provides the basic historical perspective for the paper. (Notice the rich array of examples of today's women athletes from tennis players and cyclists to fencers and soccer players.)

USING SOURCES How has the author used and identified her sources? How does she introduce quoted material? What is the mix of short direct quotation, paraphrase, and longer block quotations? What is the range of her sources?

DOCUMENTATION Study the author's use of parenthetical references and her final list of "Works Cited." Where did she have to deal with special problems? How did she handle unusual or unconventional sources?

A Note on Format: Your paper does not need a separate title page. The first page starts with the **author block** (author, instructor, course, and date). Note *double-spacing* throughout, including author block, block quotations, and list of "Works Cited."

Running heads give the student writer's last name followed by the number of the page (plain numeral—no punctuation or abbreviation). A double space separates the running head from the top line on the page.

The **title** is *not* italicized (underlined), put in quotation marks, or typed as all capitals. (Use italics or quotation marks only if your title quotes someone else's title: *Star Trek* and the Myth of Innocence.)

A separate **outline**, when required by the instructor, is double-spaced throughout and follows conventional outline format (see **3e**).

646

Barbara Meier Gatten
Professor Lamont
English 2A
April 9, 1990

*outline if required by
instructor*

Women in Sports

THESIS: The revolution in women's athletics has changed both what women expect of themselves and what we expect of athletics.

I. Today's highly visible women athletes
II. Progress toward equality in sports
   A. Challenging traditional restrictions
   B. Making progress: The 50s and 60s
      1. The Sputnik effect
      2. The spirit of political activism
   C. Breakthroughs: The 70s
      1. Commercial sponsorship
      2. Title IX and its aftermath
   D. Turning point: The Los Angeles Olympics
III. Sports and the changing self-image of women
   A. Fitness: body and mind
   B. Testing the limits
   C. Increased self-esteem
   D. Sports and life
IV. Women's athletics and traditional sports
   A. Competition vs. participation
   B. Downplaying violence
V. A new concept of sport

½″

Barbara Meier Gatten
Professor Lamont
English 2A
April 9, 1990

author block

Women in Sports:
Pushing the Limits

The gym was packed. Each time the home team
scored, there was a roar, followed by a deathly quiet
that magnified the slap of a hand on the ball or the
squeak of rubber on wood. When the final buzzer
sounded, signaling victory for the home team and a
trip to the state playoffs, the gym went wild.
Classmates and friends rushed out onto the floor,
lifting the players up in the air. A few years ago,
this scene could have meant only one thing: the men's
basketball playoffs. Tonight, it was the women's
volleyball sectionals.

Twenty years ago, such a scene would have been
unlikely. Then women who enjoyed sports had two
choices: They could join the Girls' Athletic Association (GAA) and play intramurals, or they could participate vicariously as cheerleaders on the side-
lines. Today, in addition to the highly publicized
women tennis players, runners, ice skaters, and

volleyball players, there are women cyclists, swimmers, squash players, rowing crews, mountain climbers, fencers, soccer players--and a rugby team called "The Gentle Women of Aspen." What has happened? The revolution in women's athletics has changed both what women expect of themselves and what we expect of athletics.   *thesis with preview*

  For many years, progress toward equality of the sexes in sports was slow. Women were free to participate in genteel games like tennis or golf as long as they did not perspire too freely or appear too intent on winning. From the beginning, women athletes had to reckon with the traditional ideal of the ladylike woman, who could not appear tough or assertive. Outstanding athletes like the swimmer Esther Williams or the ice skater Sonja Henie were praised for their beauty and grace rather than for their athletic achievement. In 1936, the editor of Sportsman magazine wrote, "As swimmers and divers, girls are as beautiful and adroit as they are ineffective and unpleasing on the track" (qtd. in Hart 66). Janice Kaplan claims in her book Women and Sports that as recently as the 60s practically the only sport at which a woman could hope to make money was ice skating, since "ice shows were always looking for pretty girls who could stand up on skates" (54). Writing in

paragraph integrating several sources

Background and Commentary

Look at how the author introduces quotations and other material from sources in the opening pages of the paper. Look at how she accomplishes one or more of the following purposes:

- identify the source
- establish the authority or the credentials of the source
- signal the point or the relevance of a quotation or other material

Study examples like the following:

> In 1936, the editor of <u>Sportsman</u> magazine wrote, . . .

> Janice Kaplan claims in her book <u>Women and Sports</u> that as recently as the 60s . . .

> Phyllis Bailey, Assistant Director of Athletics at Ohio State University, described a kind of athletic "Sputnik effect": . . .

> In this area, according to George R. LaNoue, former head of the Task Force on Higher Education of the U.S. Equal Employment Opportunity Commission, "the treatment of women athletes . . . ."

> Linda Schreiber writes about how running helped to increase her energy and change her outlook, how she experienced the sharpened physical and mental edge of being in shape: . . .

Gatten 3

1971, Marie Hart, in an article titled "Sport: Women Sit in the Back of the Bus," concluded that "the emphasis in periodicals is still largely on women as attractive objects rather than as skilled and effective athletes" (66). It was not until the 80s that a swimmer who had just won her third Olympic gold medal could say: "Once the Marilyn Monroe look was really in. Now it's the lean, muscular, runner look" (qtd. in O'Reilly, "Out of the Tunnel" 73).   *quoted at second hand*

In the 1950s and 1960s, real opportunities for women in sports were slowly beginning to open up, partly as the result of political pressures. Phyllis Bailey, Assistant Director of Athletics at Ohio State University, described a kind of athletic "Sputnik effect":

> The international scene of the 1950s and 60s had put pressure on the government to take women's college sports more seriously. The Olympics had become a political battlefield, and our men were getting medals, but our women weren't. We had to do something to protect our standing in the world and get American women on a par with others. (qtd. in Kaplan, Women in Sports 59)

block quotation (no quotation marks—double indentation)

651

*part paraphrase, part
quotation in account of a key event*

Gatten 4

At the same time, the climate of political activism of the 60s and growing agitation for individual rights encouraged women to knock on doors previously closed. In 1967, Kathrine Switzer crashed the then male-only Boston Marathon. She filled out the entrant's application as K. Switzer and then "was nearly shouldered off the course by officials when they noticed she was, in fact, female." The attempted ouster and resulting controversy "infuriated Switzer and galvanized her into action to change the system," making her a major force in the movement that led to the inclusion of the first women's marathon in the 1984 Olympics (Ullyot 44, 50-51).

The major breakthroughs for women's sports occurred in the 70s. First, a few major companies gingerly invested in women's pro sports and soon realized that they had discovered a gold mine. Colgate-Palmolive became the controlling dollar behind women's golf, skiing, and tennis. The company decided to put its advertising money into the women's pro circuit instead of afternoon soap operas, and the gamble paid off. Another company to place a lucky bet was Phillip Morris, the tobacco company. The Virginia Slims tennis tour put women's tennis on the map. The effect of the Slims tour with its lucrative prize money was to establish for the first time the role model of the well-paid, well-respected female athlete. By the early 1980s, Martina Navratilova, a top player on the Virginia Slims circuit, could win over two million dollars in tournament action in one year, not counting the income from endorsements (Sherman 194).

While women were gaining in the professional arena, a landmark event changed women's athletics in academia. In 1972, Congress passed the Education Amendments Act. Chapter IX of the Act barred an institution from receiving federal funds if it practiced any form of sex discrimination. The heated controversies about how to implement the law "focused on the relative facilities and funds available to male and female athletes." In this area, according to George R. LaNoue, former head of the Task Force on Higher Education of the U.S. Equal Employment Opportunity Commission, "the treatment of women athletes by universities was often shabby at best" (28).

The net effect of the new law was to promote sudden growth in women's athletics. Headlines like "Big Ten Begins Women's Program" began to sprout in sports publications. According to Kaplan, before Title IX, colleges spent an estimated 2 percent of their athletic budgets on women's sports; by 1984, the figure was close to 20 percent. Before, there

summary of statistics

Background and Commentary

As the paper unfolds, keep an eye on the writer's use of her sources:

- What kind of sources does she turn to? Do they seem easily accessible or from out-of-the-way places?
- Do the sources represent a *range* of authorities?
- What are their *credentials*? Do they seem qualified, and do they merit attention?
- Does the writer seem *biased* in selecting sources—is there a predictable point of view?
- Which of the quoted sources seem most *relevant* or useful? Which least?
- Do any of the *quotations* seem especially eloquent or memorable? Why?
- Are any of the *facts and figures* surprising or startling? Why? Do any of them seem incomplete or bewildering? Why?

Gatten 6

were virtually no athletic scholarships for univer-
sity-bound women; by 1984, there were more than ten
thousand ("Politics" 219). Robert Sullivan, writing
in Sports Illustrated, said:

> There were 32,000 females participating in
> college athletics in 1972, the year the law
> was enacted; by 1983 the total had
> increased to 150,000. . . . From 1974 to
> 1981 the number of colleges granting athletic
> scholarships to women increased from 60 to
> 500, while expenditures on women's programs
> by NCAA schools soared from $4 million to
> $116 million. This greater commitment to
> women's athletics resulted in vastly
> improved performances by females not just
> in basketball, but also in track and field,
> swimming, and most other sports. (9)

excerpted block quotation

In 1984, a Supreme Court ruling took some of the
teeth out of Chapter IX, stipulating that Title IX
should be regarded as "program specific." In other
words, it would ban sex discrimination only in a specific program (such as math or science) that was
receiving federal funds, not in the institution as a
whole. Since little federal aid goes directly into
sports programs, discriminatory athletic departments
no longer endangered federal aid for a college or

Background and Commentary

Study the way material from these cards has been integrated into the
finished paper.

```
Women in 1984 Olympics                              Card 1

"Title IX became effective only in 1975, and
enforcement has been sketchy.  But the threat of
losing federal funds was enough to raise the
number of women in collegiate athletic programs
from 16,000 in 1972 to more than 150,000 today.
. . . The U.S. Olympic women's basketball team,
probably the best female team ever assembled any-
where, is a direct result of the scholarships
created by Title IX.  As Olympic Basketball Player
Miller says:  'Without Title IX, I'd be nowhere.'"

O'Reilly, "Out of the Tunnel"  73
```

```
        Women in 1984 Olympics

Card 2   "The dazzling accomplishments of U.S. women at
        this year's Games were the direct result of
        changes in personal attitude and public policy
        brought about by two inseparable revolutions:  the
        women's movement and the growth of women's
        sports."
```

```
            Women in 1984 Olympics

            Numbers:  2,500 female athletes from 140 nations
            in 76 events
Card 3
            "Although a far cry from the number of events open
            to male Olympians, it was a quantum leap from the
            first modern Olympics, which denied participation
            to women--and a bigger jump from ancient times
            when even female spectators were hurled from the
            nearest cliff."



            Mosher, "Women in Motion"  82
```

---

quoted key phrases   Gatten 7

university as a whole.   Nevertheless, according to
Sullivan, "having been forced to beef up women's programs by Title IX," most schools now claimed to be
"morally committed" to parity for women's athletics
(9).   Pete Hamill, widely read columnist for The New
York Post and The New York Daily News, said that
Title IX "gave women solid coaching and structured
competition" and that "there now is no going back"
(19).[1]   *endnote will mention dissenting view*

For many women, the twenty-third Olympic Games
in Los Angeles marked a turning point in the quest
for recognition for female athletes.   During the 1984
Olympics, 2,500 female athletes from 140 nations com-
peted in 76 events.   In the words of Cheryl Mosher,

> Although a far cry from the number of
> events open to male Olympians, it was a

*block
quotation
for key
event*

> quantum leap from the first modern Olym-
> pics, which denied participation to women—
> and a bigger jump from ancient times when
> even female spectators were hurled from the
> nearest cliff.   (82)

Like other observers, Jane O'Reilly, writing in
Time magazine, saw the "dazzling accomplishments" of
U.S. women at the 1984 Games as the result of the
advances triggered by Title IX.   She said that the
U.S. Olympic women's basketball team, which she

Gatten 8

called "probably the best female team ever assembled
anywhere," was a "direct result" of the scholarships
and the support created by the law ("Out of the Tun-
nel" 73).   *turning point: major transition*

What have the recent advances in women's sports
done for the self-image of women? When the doors to
free participation in sports swing open, so do other
doors, many of them psychological. The grass roots
movement towards greater fitness among women affects
both body and mind. In <u>Marathon Mom</u>, Linda Schreiber
writes about how running helped to increase her
energy and change her outlook, how she experienced
the sharpened physical and mental edge of being in
shape: *author and book identified*

> The more I ran, the easier hauling grocer-
> ies and carrying babies became. I found I
> had more pep, needed less sleep. Running
> also seemed to allow me to see things in a
> more mellow perspective. . . . I didn't
> feel so narrow and confined, because my day
> had at least included a run. Somehow I
> didn't feel so "small" and events at home
> so petty. (8)

Beyond the joy of simple fitness, there is for
many the added dimension of testing limits, of having
the opportunity to "push back the envelope," in test

first of two publications by same author Gatten 9

pilot jargon. Looking back over the Los Angeles
Olympics, Jane O'Reilly said, "These women tested
their limits, and having a chance to do that is what
sports and feminism are all about" ("Out of the Tunnel" 73). Every athlete has the experience of pushing at the barrier of his or her own limitations, and
many experience the satisfaction felt when the barrier yields to persistent effort. A case in point is
long-distance running for women: Women runners were
always assumed to lack endurance. The 1928 Olympics
were the first games where women were allowed to run
anything longer than a sprint. Eleven women that
year entered an 800-meter race. Officials predicted
disaster and were correct. Five women dropped out,
five collapsed at the finish line, and the strongest
collapsed in the dressing room afterwards. Kaplan
believes that these women failed because they were
expected to fail: "None of them had ever trained for
long distances, and they were psyched out by the
adumbrations of doom and the ambulance waiting at the
finish line" (37). *extended account of case in point*

Ironically, today women are thought to exceed
men in their physical potential for endurance because
of a superior ability to metabolize fat.[2] According
to an article in <u>Science Digest</u>, statistical projections based on available sports records show that
endnote will provide detail

659

Background and Commentary

Although the author of this paper has mobilized an array of printed sources, she also draws on interviews and informal talks. Here is a more extended selection from one of the interviews:

Question: How long have you been involved with horses?
Answer: All my life. My parents owned a small farm with a few horses.

Question: What made you want to compete?
Answer: The thrill of showing off a beautiful horse at its best. I also had friends who were involved in showing.

Question: What kind of financial support is available for top-level competing?
Answer: The cost depends on where you go for shows. At the lower levels, there is no organization to help pay the bills. The USET (United States Equestrian Team) generally helps pay costs for American riders to attend international competitions, but they can't pay the whole bill.

Question: Do judges accept women riders?
Answer: Actually, many of the judges are women themselves and believe that women are better riders. Women can develop the strength needed, and they have the grace needed to ride well. Most men have the strength needed, but it is much more difficult for them to develop grace on horseback.

Question: What explains the large number of women riders now competing at the top level?
Answer: Women riders overall are doing much better than in the past. Equestrian competition is one of the few events where men and women compete on an equal basis. Men used to dominate the sport because they were trained in the military and because of the common misconception that the sport was only for men. Now women are taking the top positions in every area. Maybe this will be one sport where women will prove better than men.

Gatten 10

"women may equal men in certain events, most notably
the marathon, in the next few decades" (Torrey 91).

The experience of overcoming physical and mental
barriers in sports is giving many women increased
confidence and self-esteem. Women athletes are talking about their efforts and achievements with a new-
found pride. In a recent interview, a woman who
trains young riders for competition in equestrian
events said:

> Equestrian competition is one of the
> few events in which men and women compete
> on an equal basis. Men used to dominate
> *material from*
> *interview*　the sport because they were trained in the
> military and because of a common misconcep-
> tion that the sport was only for men. Now
> women are taking top positions in every
> area. Maybe this will be one sport where
> women will prove better than
> men. (Costello)

This increased sense of self-worth is not limited to sports that require money and leisure and may
seem the province of the privileged few. As the
director of International Running Circuit, sponsored
by Avon Cosmetics, marathon runner Kathrine Switzer
has organized races for women from Japan, Brazil,
Malaysia, and Thailand, disregarding warnings that

Gatten 11

women running in the streets would precipitate
chaos. In Sao Paulo, Brazil, 10,000 women ran a
race, 2,000 with no shoes. Switzer said afterwards,
"Some had nothing else in their lives, but they took
part and were changed" (qtd. in O'Reilly, "The Year
of Getting Tough" 292).

Much testimony from women athletes indicates
that self-confidence and determination carry over
from athletics into other areas of life. Sally Voss,
all-American golfer, said that the pressures she
encountered in her work as an anesthesiologist were
easier to deal with because of her experiences in
athletic competition: "Having been exposed to intense
athletic competition, I am better able to assess difficult situations and react in a rational and even
manner." Sally Ride, first American woman in space,
said, "Athletics teaches endurance and the value of
pursuing beyond one's perceived limits to achieve
higher levels of ability" ("A Winning Combination"
1-2).   *brochure with no author given*

The fact that women are participating in sports
in unprecedented numbers is obviously having a strong
impact on women. In turn, what impact, if any, is
this flood of female participants having on sports
themselves? Although the extent of actual change is
difficult to assess, women's athletics is challenging

turning point: major transition

Gatten 12

two features of traditional sports: excessive competition and violence. Many women would agree with
Betty Lehan Harragan, a management consultant, that
"women have to learn about competition and developing
a winning attitude" (qtd. in Kaplan, <u>Women in Sports</u>
112). But they would also agree that excessive
emphasis on competition is one of the main things
wrong with sports, leading to such abuses as "the
ridiculous salaries of the pros (and some college
players!), the rah—rah chauvinism, and the corruption
of recruiting" (Chapin vii—viii).   *quoted from a preface*

     Women's sports have traditionally laid stress on
participation. Because athletic programs for women
tended to be recreational and low—budget, the "everyone—can—play" ethic prevailed. Today, dazzled by the
rewards of increased money and prestige, women's athletics is in danger of losing sight of the ideal of
sport—for—all. Competition systematically narrows
the field of participants to only those who are good
enough to compete. When there are limited recreational facilities or team berths, some get to play
and others become spectators. If the only thing that
counts is being Number One, then only a select few
battle it out while the many watch. Recruiting and
training of top performers become the overriding
priorities.

Background and Commentary

In the revision of her first draft, the author faced a familiar problem for writers of research papers: In her first draft, she had used an excessive number of block quotations, giving the paper too much of a stitched-together effect. In her revision, she made a special effort to excerpt and integrate quoted material more. Read the third and last major part of the paper, and answer the following questions:

- Which paragraphs excerpt and integrate material from *several sources*?
- Where and how does the author use *partial quotations* and sentence-length quotations as part of her running text?
- Where does she use *block quotations*, and why? Is the more extended quotation justified by an important point, by an eloquent personal statement, or by helpful authentic detail?
- What is the proportion of quoted or paraphrased material and *interpretation* or discussion by the author?
- How effective or adequate are the *transitions* that take the reader from paragraph to paragraph?

several related quotations   Gatten 13

From the beginning of the current expansion of women's sports, there have been voices warning against an imitation of the "male model." George R. LaNoue, in an article in <u>Change</u>, said in 1976:

> Among the leaders of women's athletics there is strong opposition to turning women's sports into an imitation of men's. They do not want to engage in widespread off-campus recruiting. They would prefer to remain teachers instead of becoming win-at-any-cost sports promoters. (30)

Sports sociologist Stephen Figler said in <u>Sport and Play in American Life</u> that funding mandated by Title IX was leading to hasty expansion, "fostering the development of the same faulty mechanism that drives men's school athletics" (289). Figler quoted Katherine Ley, a faculty member of the United States Sports Academy, as saying, "as much of a boon as equal opportunity legislation has been," it "derailed the early attempts of women to devise an improved athletic model" (285).   *partial quotation*

Nevertheless, the search for the "improved model" continues, and the rallying cry of "Sport for all!" continues to be heard. Kaplan writes:

> The desire to have sports available to women does not have to translate into programs with the same questionable priorities

Gatten 14

as the men's, where millions are poured
into money-raising games that few can play
but many watch. It's time to raise a generation of participants, not another generation of fans. (<u>Women in Sports</u> 167)

She commends some of the smaller schools that have
opted for cuts in big-budget sports like football in
favor of more even distribution to sports like volleyball, basketball, and tennis. Figler has suggested the broadening of intercollegiate competition
by the creation of parallel, independent teams for
those not skilled enough to make varsity teams. As
he explained in a recent interview:

The element that gives collegiate sports its
excitement is competition between schools--
that's why intramurals don't really fill
the need. A better idea would be a kind of
extramural program in which a team had a
from   budget, a schedule, and a coach, all funded
telephone   by either state money, tuition, student
interview   fees, or some combination. Often P.E.
departments have good former coaches on
their staffs because they didn't like certain aspects of big collegiate sports--
these people would be ideal for a program
of this type.

Gatten 15

Excessive competition and glory–for–the–few is not the only idea being challenged by the women's sport movement. Another area of traditional athletics to come under attack is the notion that violence is an inescapable element of sport. Traditional male sports often seem motivated by "an inherent aggressiveness in man stemming from the Darwinian struggle for existence," with sports serving "as substitutes for actual fighting, mock struggles that satisfied the urge to conquer" (Nash 181). Some of the most popular men's sports—football, ice hockey, boxing—are extremely violent. Don Atyeo says in <u>Blood and Guts: Violence in Sports</u> about football: "Each year it kills on average twenty–eight players and maims thousands more. It leaves everyone who reaches its higher levels with some form of lasting injury." He quotes a former player for the Los Angeles Rams as saying that people who play for any length of time "carry the scars for the rest of their lives." These may not "be showing on the outside, but they'll have knees that are worn out, shoulders that don't work right, fingers that point in a different direction" (219–20). Part of the code of the male athlete has been that one must take the pain to prove his manliness. As Kathryn Lance says in <u>A Woman's Guide to Spectator Sports</u>, the idea of playing with pain, of

Gatten 16

"giving everything, including the integrity of one's body," to the team or club "is so extreme that players will enter a game anesthetized to the point where they can bear the pain of possibly severe injuries" (13).

The growth of women's sports, if not eliminating violence in sport, is at least helping to temper it. Women's sports are not burdened with the tradition of violence linked to the idea of sport as a proving ground for sexual identity. This is not to say that the risk of pain and injury are not part of the challenge of sports for many women athletes. Ann Roiphe, reminiscing about field hockey, her favorite game when a young girl, says:

from printed interview

> I remember a girl named Karen with blood pouring down her face and onto a white middy blouse and a dark accusing hole where her front teeth had been. It is blurred in my mind whose stick was responsible, but I was close enough to feel guilt and fear and the excitement of both those emotions. It never occurred to me that a simple child's game, a ball playing, might not be worth a lifetime of false teeth. (14)

Gatten 17

Increasingly, women are competing in tests of endurance that were once male-only events. In 1985, Libby Riddles became the first woman to win the Iditerod, a 1,000-mile dogsled race from Anchorage to Nome, Alaska. Riddles won by driving her dogs through a howling blizzard that no other contestant would challenge. This race "pits the wits of a cold, sleep-starved musher against the vagaries of weather, trail, and dogs. More than speed and experience, it takes audacity" (O'Hara 40).   *author not identified in text*

While women are increasingly facing up to tests of courage and endurance, at least some men in the world of sports seem ready to turn away from the image of the violent, aggressive man as the male ideal. Former football heroes such as O. J. Simpson and Al Cowlings are telling youngsters to play tennis instead of football because tennis will benefit them longer and because they will not have to spend their lives suffering from football knees (Schmerler 8).

Women's sports are helping society move away from the glorification of violence as media time is increasingly devoted to women's sports like tennis and golf. Both the airing of women's athletics and increased participation in sports by women are creating a wider audience of female spectators, which in turn creates greater demand on the networks for coverage of women's events.

In conclusion, the struggle for the acceptance of women's sports is not a battle between men and women. The real enemies of sport for women are the same as they are for men: the danger of being a mere passive spectator, the philosophy that winning is the only thing, and finally the idea of violence as a normal, inescapable part of sport. What is needed is a new concept of sport that sees the purpose of sport as lifelong enjoyment and pleasure, increased fitness for life, and a feeling of well-being and joy.

Gatten 19

Notes

[1] A sobering dissent, chronicling the negative impact of court decisions and institutional backsliding, is G. Ann Uhlir's article on "Athletics and the University: The Post—Woman's Era" in Academe for July—August 1987 (25—29).

[2] A more complete examination of this point can be found in Kaplan's chapter on "Physiology" in her book Women and Sports. Along with the documentation on fat metabolism, she uses medical research to explode a number of other myths about female physiology. Science Digest (Torrey 91) corroborates the research on fat metabolism and explains the use of sports records in making predictions regarding progress in sports.

endnotes directing reader to additional sources
for details or opposing view

Background and Commentary

This list of "Works Cited" puts in alphabetical order all sources used by the author. It includes not only books and articles but also such informal sources as personal interviews and a locally published promotional brochure.

Study the entries as *model entries* for your own list of "Works Cited." Note the following especially:

- Note variations from the standard entry for books: book listed under an editor's name, book with subtitle, book with more than one author.
- Note inclusive page numbers for articles in magazines and newspapers. (Note the plus sign for articles continued later in the same issue.)
- Note the treatment of an article in a collection, of the locally published brochure, and of the interviews.
- Note the treatment of more than one publication by the same author.

Remember a few basic rules:

- First line of each entry is *not* indented; the remaining lines are.
- Last name of author comes first (only for the first one if there are several coauthors).
- Titles of *whole* publications are underlined (or italicized); titles of parts (articles, poems, short stories) are enclosed in quotation marks.

Gatten 20

Works Cited

Atyeo, Don. <u>Blood and Guts: Violence in Sports</u>. New
York: Paddington, 1979.

"Big Ten Begins Women's Program." <u>Coaching Women's
Athletics</u> Oct. 1981: 20.

Chapin, Henry B., ed. <u>Sports in Literature</u>. New
York: McKay, 1976.

Costello, Arlene. Personal Interview. 6 Jan. 1990.

Figler, Stephen K. <u>Sport and Play in American Life</u>.
Philadelphia: Saunders, 1981.

——. Telephone Interview. 8 Feb. 1990.

Hamill, Pete. "Women Athletes: Faster, Higher, Better." <u>Cosmopolitan</u> Nov. 1985: 19+.

Hart, Marie. "Sport: Women Sit in the Back of the
Bus." <u>Psychology Today</u> Oct. 1971: 64–66.

Kaplan, Janice. "Politics of Sports." <u>Vogue</u> July
1984: 219+.

——. <u>Women and Sports</u>. New York: Viking, 1979.

Lance, Kathryn. <u>A Woman's Guide to Spectator Sports</u>.
New York: A & W, 1980.

LaNoue, George R. "Athletics and Equality: How to
Comply with Title IX Without Tearing Down the
Stadium." <u>Change</u> Nov. 1976: 27–30+.

Mosher, Cheryl. "Women in Motion." <u>Women's Sport
and Fitness</u> May 1985: 82.

Nash, Roderick. "Heroes." <u>American Oblique: Writing
About the American Experience</u>. Ed. Joseph F.

Gatten 21

Trimmer and Robert R. Kettler.   Boston: Houghton,
      1976.   180–88.
O'Hara, Doug.   "Libby Riddles Beat a Blizzard to
      Become Top Musher."   Christian Science Monitor
      28 Mar. 1985: 1+.
O'Reilly, Jane.   "Out of the Tunnel into History."
      Time 20 Aug. 1984: 73.
——.   "The Year of Getting Tough."   Vogue Nov. 1984:
      290–92.
Roiphe, Ann.   Interview.   Ms. June 1982: 14.
Schmerler, Cindy.   "Splitting Ends."   World Tennis
      May 1985: 8.
Schreiber, Linda and JoAnne Stang.   Marathon
      Mom.   Boston: Houghton, 1980.
Sherman, William.   "The World of Tennis's Top Women."
      Tennis News May 1983: 194–97+.
Sullivan, Robert.   "A Law That Needs New Muscle."
      Sports Illustrated 4 Mar. 1985: 9.
Torrey, Lee.   "How Science Creates Winners."   Science
      Digest Aug. 1984: 33–37+.
Uhlir, G. Ann.   "Athletics and the University: The
      Post-Woman's Era."   Academe July–Aug. 1987: 25–
      29.
Ullyot, Joan.   "Forcing the Pace."   Runner's World
      Jan. 1986: 43–51.
"A Winning Combination."   Cardinal Club Brochure.
      Stanford, CA: Stanford U Dept. of Athletics,
      1986.

53   Alternate Styles: APA

OVERVIEW   Styles of documentation vary for different areas of the curriculum. Not only the nature of research but also the expected ways of reporting the results differ from one specialized field to another. Many publications in the social sciences follow the APA style of documentation, outlined in the publication manual of the American Psychological Association. You will encounter this style (with some variations) in periodicals in areas like psychology, linguistics, or education.

For identification of sources in the text of a paper, this style uses the **author-and-date** method. The date of publication appears with the parenthetical page reference: (Garcia, 1985, p. 103), or (1985, p. 103) if the author has been named in your text. Often, the APA style identifies an authority and the publication date of research *without* a page reference; interested readers are expected to familiarize themselves with the relevant research and consider its findings in context: (Garcia, 1985).

53a   *doc* | Parenthetical Identification: APA

Know the major variations of parenthetical identification in the APA style.

Study the following possibilities. Note use of commas, of *p.* or *pp.* for "page" or "pages," of the symbol & for *and*, and of similar distinctive features.

1. AUTHOR AND DATE ONLY:

```
The term anorexia nervosa stands for a condition of
emaciation resulting from self-inflicted starvation
(Huebner, 1982).
```

2. DATE ONLY—author's name in your own text:

```
As defined by Huebner, anorexia nervosa is a
condition of emaciation resulting from self-inflicted
starvation (1982).
```

675

3. PAGE REFERENCE—for direct quotation or specific reference:

> Anorexia nervosa is "not really true loss of appetite" but "a condition of emaciation resulting from self-inflicted starvation" (Huebner, 1982, p. 143).

4. WORK BY SEVERAL AUTHORS—use *et al.* only in second or later reference: (Filmore et al., 1984).

> Much advertising leads young women to believe that weight control equals beauty and success (Filmore, Suarez, & Thomas, 1984, p. 128).

5. SAME AUTHOR—for several publications in same year, use *a, b, c,* and so on, in order of publication:

> Gamarken has conducted several similar experiments (1978, 1981a, 1981b).

6. REFERENCE TO SEVERAL SOURCES—list in alphabetical order, divided by semicolons:

> Statistical estimates concerning the occurrence of the condition have varied widely (Gutierrez & Piso, 1982; Huffman, 1981).

7. UNKNOWN OR UNLISTED AUTHOR—identify source by shortened title:

> The influence of the media is pervasive and more often than not harmful ("Cultural Expectations," 1985).

| List of References: APA

Study model bibliography entries for the APA style.

Use the heading "References" for your final alphabetical listing of works cited or consulted. The APA style provides essentially the same bibliographical information as the MLA style. However, note the author-and-date sequence at the beginning of the entry. Watch for differences in the use of capitals, quotation marks, parentheses, and the like. (The following entries are adapted from *Researching and Writing: An Interdisciplinary Approach*, by Christine A. Hult.)

1. BOOK WITH SINGLE AUTHOR Use initial instead of author's first name. Capitalize only the first word of title or subtitle (but capitalize proper names that are part of a title as you would in ordinary prose).

Bruch, H. (1973). Eating disorders: Obesity,
     anorexia nervosa, and the person within. New
     York: Basic Books.

2. BOOK WITH TWO OR MORE AUTHORS Put last name first for each of several authors. Use the symbol & (ampersand) instead of the word *and*.

Minuchin, S., Rosman, B., & Baker, L. (1978).
     Psychosomatic families: Anorexia nervosa in
     context. Cambridge, MA: Harvard U. Press.

3. MAGAZINE OR NEWSPAPER ARTICLE Do not put titles of articles in quotation marks; do not use italics (or underlining). If there is no volume number, use *p.* or *pp.* for "page" or "pages." If an article is concluded later in the issue, use a semicolon between the two sets of page numbers.

Miller, G. (1969, December). On turning psychology
     over to the unwashed. Psychology Today, pp.
     53–54; 66–74.

4. ARTICLE WITH VOLUME NUMBER Underline (italicize) the volume number for a periodical, with inclusive page numbers following after a comma: *6*, 152–69. If the number of the issue is needed, put it in parentheses between the volume number and the page numbers: *6*(3), 152–69.

> Holmi, K. (1978). Anorexia nervosa: Recent
>   investigations. Annual Review of Medicine, 29,
>   137–48.
>
> Steinhausen, H. & Glenville, K. (1983). Follow-up
>   studies of anorexia nervosa: A review of
>   research findings. Psychological Medicine:
>   Abstracts in English, 13(2), 239–45.

5. UNSIGNED MAGAZINE OR NEWSPAPER ARTICLE Alphabetize by the first word of the title, not counting *The, A,* or *An.*

> The blood business. (1972, September 11). Time, pp.
>   47–48.

6. EDITED BOOK OR NEW EDITION Put abbreviation for "editor" (*Ed.* or *Eds.*) or for number of edition in parentheses.

> Hartman, F. (Ed.). (1973). World in crisis:
>   Readings in international relations (4th ed.).
>   New York: Macmillan.

7. SEVERAL WORKS BY SAME AUTHOR Repeat the author's name with each title; put works in chronological order.

> Bruch, H. (1973). Eating disorders: Obesity,
>   anorexia nervosa, and the person within. New
>   York: Basic Books.
>
> Bruch, H. (1978). The golden cage: The enigma of
>   anorexia nervosa. Cambridge, MA: Harvard U.
>   Press.

8. PART OF A COLLECTION Reverse initial and last name only for author or editor of the part, not of the collection.

> Cherns, A. (1982). Social research and its diffusion. In B. Appleby (Ed.), <u>Papers on social science utilisation</u>. Loughborough U. of Technology: Centre for Utilisation of Social Science Research.

9. ENCYCLOPEDIA ENTRY If the author of an entry is identified, include the name.

> Anorexia nervosa. (1978). <u>Encyclopedia of Human Behavior</u>.

10. NONPRINT MEDIA

> Maas, J. B. (Producer), & Gluck, D. H. (Director). (1979). <u>Deeper into hypnosis</u> [Film]. Englewood Cliffs, NJ: Prentice-Hall.
>
> Clark, K. B. (Speaker). (1976). <u>Problems of freedom and behavior modification</u> (Cassette Recording No. 7612). Washington, DC: American Psychological Association.
>
> Brewer, J. (1979, October). <u>Energy, information, and the control of heart rate</u>. Paper presented at the Society for Psychophysiological Research, Cincinnati, OH.
>
> <u>Problems of Freedom</u>. (1982, May 21). New York: NBC-TV. Hult, C. (1984, March). [Interview with Dr. Lauro Cavazos, President, Texas Tech University].

Society's Effect upon the Rise of Anorexia Victims

A second direct cause of anorexia is the expectation society has regarding beauty. Over the years,
society's ideal of a beautiful body has changed. The
current look is angular and lean. Starved, emaciated
models portray this image in the media, and it is
promoted through diet pills, drinks, foods, weight-
loss centers, and bulge-hiding clothes (Garfinkle,
Garner, Schwartz, & Thompson, 1980). Adolescents,
vulnerable to peer pressure, see these norms and
strive to conform. The male is exposed to ideal
beauty also, through such models as Miss America or
Playboy centerfolds appearing on television and in
magazines. These models tend to exaggerate parts of
the body (DeRosis, 1979). A number of researchers
have linked these sociocultural pressures to the
apparent increase of anorexia victims. Dieting is a
"sociocultural epidemic" and fashion's ideal may
indirectly affect adolescent women who eventually
believe that weight control is equal to self-control
and will surely lead to beauty and success (Garfinkle et al., 1980).   *second reference*
                                             uses et al.

                           Survey

In order to discover whether or not the family
and cultural pressures that lead to anorexia in young

Remember: Part of your job as a newcomer in a field of study or a line of work is to learn to write to an established format and to the specifications that are part of the conventions of your chosen field. Often the people in the field will judge how serious you are about becoming one of theirs by your willingness to master exact details—the little things that count. Note the sample page from a research paper in the social sciences on the facing page.

10

Practical Prose Forms

Writing Summaries

Practice in writing summaries will benefit you in important ways as a student and as a writer:

- It will give you practice in *close, attentive reading*. Too many writers are ineffectual because they have not learned to listen first, to think second, and to formulate their own reactions third.
- It will strengthen your sense of *structure* in writing. It will make you pay close attention to how a writer organizes material, develops a point, and moves from one point to another.
- It will develop your sense of what is *important* in a piece of writing. It will make you distinguish between a key point, the material backing it up, and mere asides.

Often you will be aiming at a summary about *one third* or *one fourth* the length of the original. Remember the following guidelines:

(1) Make sure you grasp the main trend of thought. Identify key sentences: the thesis that sums up the main point of an essay (or section of an essay), the topic sentence that is developed in the rest of a paragraph. Look out for major turning points—a strategic *however* or *on the other hand* that signals an important step in an argument.

(2) Reduce explanations and examples to the essential minimum. Leave out phrases that merely restate or reinforce a point already made. Condense lengthy explanations; keep only the most important details, examples, or statistics.

683

(3) Use the most economical wording possible. Write "negotiate" for "conduct negotiations"; "surprisingly" for "it came as a surprise to many observers that. . . ."

(4) Beware of oversimplification. Preserve an essential *if, but,* or *unless.* Keep distinctions between *is, will,* or *might.* Keep words like *only, almost,* or *on the whole.*

The following three versions of the same passage will help you reconstruct the process by which one writer produced a summary. Notice how in the second version the writer has crossed out everything that merely repeats or expands the main points:

ORIGINAL:

There are numerous cases of societies in which the armies of the night have ridden triumphantly over minorities in order to establish a powerful orthodoxy which dictates official thought. Invariably, the triumphant ride is toward long-range disaster.

Spain dominated Europe and the world in the 16th century, but in Spain orthodoxy came first, and all divergence of opinion was ruthlessly suppressed. The result was that Spain settled back into blankness and did not share in the scientific, technological and commercial ferment that bubbled up in other nations of Western Europe. Spain remained an intellectual backwater for centuries.

In the late 17th century, France in the name of orthodoxy revoked the Edict of Nantes and drove out many thousands of Huguenots, who added their intellectual vigor to lands of refuge such as Great Britain, the Netherlands and Prussia, while France was permanently weakened.

In more recent times, Germany hounded out the Jewish scientists of Europe. They arrived in the United States and contributed immeasurably to scientific advancement here, while Germany lost so heavily that there is no telling how long it will take to regain its former scientific eminence. The Soviet Union, in its fascination with Lysenko, destroyed its geneticists, and set back its biological sciences for decades. China, during the Cultural Revolution, turned against Western science and is still laboring to overcome the devastation that resulted.   Isaac Asimov, ''The 'Threat' of Creationism,'' *The New York Times*

WORKING VERSION:

~~There are~~ numerous ~~cases of~~ societies ~~in which the armies of the night~~ have ridden triumphantly over minorities in order to establish a powerful orthodoxy ~~which dictates official thought~~. Invariably, the ~~triumphant~~ ride is toward long-range disaster.

Spain dominated ~~Europe and the world~~ in the 16th century, but ~~in Spain orthodoxy came first, and~~ all divergence of opinion was ~~ruthlessly~~

suppressed. The result was that Spain ~~settled back into blankness and~~ did not share in the scientific, technological and commercial ferment ~~that bubbled up in other nations~~ of Western Europe. Spain remained an intellectual backwater ~~for centuries~~.

~~In the late~~ 17th century, France ~~in the name of orthodoxy revoked the Edict of Nantes and~~ drove out ~~many thousands of~~ Huguenots, who added their intellectual vigor to lands of refuge such as Great Britain, the Netherlands and Prussia, ~~while France was permanently weakened~~.

~~In more recent times~~, Germany hounded out the Jewish scientists ~~of Europe~~. They arrived in the United States and contributed ~~immeasurably~~ to scientific advancement here, while Germany lost ~~so heavily that there is no telling how long it will take it to regain~~ its former scientific eminence. The Soviet Union, ~~in its fascination with Lysenke~~, destroyed its geneticists, and set back its biological sciences for decades. China, during the Cultural Revolution, turned against Western science and is still laboring to overcome the devastation ~~that resulted~~.

SUMMARY:

Many societies have suppressed minorities to establish a powerful orthodoxy, with disastrous long-range results. Spain, a dominant power in the sixteenth century, suppressed all divergence of opinion; as a result, it did not share in the scientific, technological, and commercial progress of Western Europe. Seventeenth-century France lost the intellectual vigor of the Huguenots who took refuge in Great Britain, the Netherlands, and Prussia. Germany lost its scientific eminence when it drove out Jewish scientists who advanced science in the U.S. The destruction of the geneticists set back Soviet science; the revolution against Western science devastated science in China.

WRITING PRACTICE 1　Study the following passage about artificial intelligence. Then write a summary of about one third the original length. (You may want to compare your summary with those prepared by your classmates.)

Some of the debates about the potential of artificial intelligence are fueled by confusions between intelligence and other elements of human-ness. Philosophers such as Herbert Dreyfus in *What Computers Can't Do* suggest that computers will never be able to pass beyond certain critical limits. For example, they will never "understand" language the way a human being can. A computer program encountering words telling it that "John loved Jane" or that "John felt pain when Jane socked him in the nose" will confront significant limits to what it can comprehend. It may be taught rules of inference based on the meanings of these words or on typical patterns of human interaction so that it could follow or make sense of a story containing these words. It could show that it understood by asking questions about the story, answering questions, or proposing consistent statements that might follow.

On the other hand, according to this view of the limits of artificial intelligence, the computer would never comprehend such notions as being in love or physical pain. It would lack the immediate emotional and physical experience of being a human body and psyche and the years of experiences that we use to flesh out our understandings of communications from others.

The problem with these claims is that intelligence is being confounded with consciousness and human-ness. Artificial-intelligence programs some day will most likely be able to manipulate language and other information in ways that we would judge as intelligent understanding when manifested by other human beings. However, such programs will never be conscious in the way a human being is.

On the other hand, these limitations can be partially overcome. Human beings regularly use the abstraction of language to expand their base of experience. We can converse and make inferences about worlds of which we have no direct experience because we have learned about them through language. Examples are faraway lands and times and uncommon emotions that we don't comprehend in the same way as those who have directly experienced them.   Stephen Wilson, "An Introduction to Artificial Intelligence," *Cadre 84*

---

55   Writing Business Letters

OVERVIEW   Effectively written letters will help you to take care of business. Apart from the letters you might be writing as part of a job, you may be writing to a teacher, college office, government agency, business firm, or future employer. Here are some general guidelines for letters that will get attention and results:

(1) **State your business early in the letter.**   Close to the beginning, bring the issue or the problem into focus. Your readers will need to know: "What is this about? What do you want?" Are you asking for information? Do you want to clear up a mistake? Do you need documents?

(2) Provide essential information. Include essential data such as order or document numbers, dates, or locations. Make sure your readers can locate an item, incident, or situation in their records or files. Where appropriate, give a brief history of the problem or condition to fill your readers in or bring them up to date.

(3) Highlight separate points. When there are several parts to a request or several layers to a grievance, you may find that the first one or two points get attention while the others get lost. Highlight (perhaps number in order) the several related points that need attention.

(4) Spell out what action you expect or request. Make sure your readers understand how they are expected to act on what you are telling them. What do you want them to *do*?

(5) If appropriate, express your personal interest or appreciation. You will often get better service or cooperation if your readers feel that their work is valued or that somebody cares. Try to include a brief positive statement at the beginning or end of your letter.

(6) Remember that appearance counts. A hastily written letter with messy erasures and added scribblings will not inspire confidence. Why should our reader invest time and effort in our problem or need if we ourselves don't seem to care?

55a *form* Using a Modern Format

Use a functional modern format.

Much modern correspondence uses a variation of the **block format**, which does away with paragraph indentation and aligns all elements of the letter flush left. Paragraph breaks are shown by double-spacing between paragraphs. Letters using the block format are easy to produce on the typewriter or word processor, and they have a simple uncluttered look.

In a **modified block format**, the date and often also the closing with the signature block will move out to the center of the page. And some writers continue to prefer traditional indentation—five spaces—for paragraphs.

The following are major elements of the business letter:

LETTERHEAD Most firms or organizations have stationery with a printed letterhead. It usually includes address and zip code, often in addition to a company logo or slogan ("The Sunshine People"). You can then start your typing with the date of the letter and go on to the inside address.

RETURN ADDRESS When you are not using the letterhead of a firm or an organization, type your return address above the date, as follows. Place it on the right side of the page:

```
                              138 South Third Street
                              San Jose, California   95126
                              January 12, 1990


        Ms. Patricia Sobell
        Personnel Manager
        San Rafael Gazette
        2074 Washington Avenue
        San Rafael, CA   94903


        Dear Ms. Sobell:
```

INSIDE ADDRESS If you know the title of the person, include it—on the second line, or after a comma on the same line as the name.

688

```
Ms. Patricia Sobell        Ms. Jane Day, President
Personnel Manager          The Waxo Company
San Rafael Gazette         225 East Elm Street
2074 Washington Avenue     Walls, KS 76674
San Rafael, CA 94903
                           Dear Ms. Day:
Dear Ms. Sobell:
```

Use a courtesy title like *Mr.* or *Ms.* (the latter now widely replacing the traditional *Mrs.* and *Miss*). A woman may show her preference for one of the possible choices in the signature line of her own correspondence:

```
Sincerely,                 Sincerely,
```

Kate Gordon   *Helen Freid*

```
(Mrs.) Kate Gordon         (Ms.) Helen Freid
```

GREETING Whenever you can, address your letter to an individual. Remember that a first name will sound very chummy unless you are on friendly terms with the person. Put a colon after the greeting:

```
Dear Dr. Morton:
Dear Professor Grimaldi:
(No Prof. here—use Prof. only with full name in addresses)
Dear Ms. Freedman:
Dear Mr. Scopaz:
Dear Jonathan:
```

Things get complicated when you address a firm (or institution) or an officeholder not known to you by name. The traditional "Gentlemen:" and "Dear Sir:" are out, since the person reading your letter may be a woman. "Dear Sir or Madam:" avoids sexism but sounds very old-fashioned. Try naming the group or identifying the person by office or status:

```
Dear AT&T:
Dear Ombudsman:
Dear Colleague:
Dear Fellow Student:
Dear Reader:
```

The **simplified style** does without the salutation altogether (thus skirting the gender issue) and puts a **subject line** instead. It often also omits the complimentary close (*sincerely, cordially*).

SIMPLIFIED:
```
The Jackson Manufacturing Company
1334 West Devonshire Road
Bolivar, MO 65613

SUBJECT: Water Rationing During July
```

BODY OF THE LETTER Lay out your message in a series of pointed paragraphs, with a good flow from point to point. Avoid long rambling paragraphs in which information gets lost. Double-space between paragraphs.

COMPLIMENTARY CLOSE AND SIGNATURE The traditional closing is a variation of *sincerely, sincerely yours, cordially,* or *yours truly,* followed by a comma. (This **complimentary close** is omitted in the simplified style.) For people whom you know well (and whom you wish well), a phrase like *Best wishes* or *Regards* might be appropriate.

Leave four lines for your signature and then type your name. Include an official title or function if you are writing in an official capacity. Align the signature block with the *Sincerely*.

```
Sincerely,

Pat Gramat
Pat Gramat
Program Chair
```

NOTES If someone other than the author of the letter has typed it, the typist's initials appear a double space below the signature block, flush left. Other possible concluding notes include *Enclosure* (for instance, a chart, résumé, or offprint is attached) and *cc* to name people who have been copied (that is, sent a copy).

```
jw
Enclosures
cc: Chris Cremona
```

Study the following examples of business letters using the block format or the simplified style. Some of the sample materials in this section have been adapted from Walter Wells, *Communications in Business*, 5th ed. (Boston: Kent, 1988).

690

full block
format

BETTER BUSINESS COMMUNICATIONS
23875 South Campbell Avenue
Tucson, Arizona 85721

April 28, 1990

Dr. LaVerne Prescott, President
Modern Graphics
1987 Ocean View Drive
Los Angeles, CA 90025

Dear Dr. Prescott:

Thank you for your recent inquiry about the format of
current business letters. This letter illustrates
the full block format widely used in business today.
All major elements of the letter begin at the left
margin, including the first word of each paragraph.
The body of the letter is single-spaced, with double
spacing between paragraphs.

This format is easily produced on a typewriter or
word processor. It has a simple and uncluttered
modern appearance. However, some businesses prefer a
modified block format, with the date and the
signature block moved to the center of the page.

Many businesses adopt an official letter format and
then expect everyone in the organization to follow
it. Please feel free to write or call with any
questions about the details of this style.

Sincerely,

Greg Traverse

Greg Traverse
Customer Relations

simplified style

BETTER BUSINESS COMMUNICATIONS
23875 South Campbell Avenue
Tucson, Arizona 85721

May 19, 1990

Dr. LaVerne Prescott, President
Modern Graphics
1987 Ocean View Drive
Los Angeles, CA 90025

SUBJECT: The Simplified Format for Business Letters

As a follow—up to my letter of April 28, I'm writing
this letter to illustrate the simplified format in
action. The simplified format, with its subject line
in place of a salutation, makes it easy for the reader
to identify the subject. But if that subject is
negative, the writer may want to find some phrasing
that avoids a negative impression.

Some teachers now teach the simplified format
exclusively. Others are holding out for one or the
other of the more traditional forms.

Please note that the complimentary close as well as
the initial salutation has been left out in the
simplified style.

Greg Traverse

Greg Traverse
Customer Relations

km

BUSINESS ENVELOPES Here are some examples of well-typed business envelopes. Remember: Accurate names and addresses are essential. Neatness counts.

Lawndale Pharmaceutical Company
170 Medena Road
Akron, Ohio 44321

SPECIAL DELIVERY

Dr. Joan Coulton
10372 White Oak Avenue
Granada Hills, CA 91344

United Bank of Iowa
1640 Medina Road
Des Moines, Iowa 50313

Attention Ms. Pat Corveau

Schrader Lock Company
624 South First Avenue
Sioux Falls, SD 57104

San Marcos Resort,
Country Club & Colony
Chandler, Arizona 85224

Mr. Don Busche, President
Confidential   Northridge Manufacturing Company
402 West Main Street
Northridge, Illinois 60162

MEMO **A memorandum**, or interoffice communication, is different from a business letter. It serves a different purpose—communication *within* an organization.

Connecticut Life Insurance Company

MEMORANDUM

To: Harry M. Brown   Date: March 21, 1990
           cc: Ben Siegel   File No.: 0010
                 Patricia Newman
                 Angela Millel

From: Walter Wells

Subject: A Word About Memorandum Format

    Memos can serve either an expository or a reaction-evoking function. They can be long or short as need demands--but they must be clear, have an appropriate character, and be as impressive in format as any letter.

    Memo format is, of course, more tightly determined by its imprinted heading, as at the top of this memo. Those headings come with minor variations, but this one is typical. Sometimes the From and To lines are positioned more closely together, and the "distribution" indicator is placed after the body of the memo rather than before it. But in its essentials, this model is as good as any.

    As with your letters, you will be measured to a great extent by the memos you write. So be sure to write them neatly, and write them well.

ms   *W. W.*

WRITING PRACTICE 2   Find a project or recent development that merits *publicity or support*. Write a letter about it to the editors of a newspaper or magazine, to a legislator, or to a responsible official. Observe conventional letter form.

55b   Streamlining Your Style

Use a modern plain-English style.

Do not use a special business jargon when writing your business letters. Avoid both extremes: On the one hand, avoid old-fashioned stodgy phrases ("wish to advise that," "beg to acknowledge," "the aforementioned"). On the other hand, avoid a breezy shirtsleeve English ("give it the old college try," "run with the ball," "give them a run for their money").

Current style manuals for business communications recommend a modern plain-English style. Look out for the following:

STIFF OLD-STYLE PHRASES—use simple modern alternatives:

OLD-STYLE	MODERN
as per (your request)	according to (your request)
we beg to acknowledge	thank you for . . .
cognizant of	aware of
we are in receipt of	we have received
pursuant to	according to
subsequent to	after

REDUNDANT WORDS—omit words that merely duplicate a meaning already expressed:

REDUNDANT	PLAIN
the month of October	October
my **personal** opinion	my opinion
consensus **of opinion**	consensus
combine **together**	combine
a **necessary** prerequisite	a prerequisite

695

CIRCUMLOCUTIONS—avoid phrases that take "the long way around":

ROUNDABOUT	BRIEF
during the time that	while
a large number of	many
at an early date	soon
in the event that	if
leaving out of consideration	disregarding
at the present point in time	now
those of adolescent age	adolescents

INFLATED SENTENCE STRUCTURE—shorten "talky" constructions:

INFLATED	ECONOMICAL
it is unfortunate that	unfortunately
it is possible that we will	we may
in order that sufficient time may be allowed	in order to allow enough time

Note: When you work for a company or institution, it will be part of your survival skills to write in the style currently favored by the organization. Such styles may range from advertising hyperbole ("In the secluded hills overlooking spectacular Monteno Bay nestles a romantic hideaway perfect for that long-delayed vacation") to a style that wraps the bad news in resolutely positive phrases ("For your convenience as a valued customer, we will no longer automatically return your canceled checks").

WRITING PRACTICE 3   Rewrite the following letter of complaint in a less breezy and less insulting style.

> SUBJECT: Shipment of broken glassware
>
> We sure like fine glassware, but you bet we didn't expect to be stuck with the broken mess that just arrived.
>
> Just what kind of outfit are you people running? We place a simple order, delivery takes forever, and when

it finally gets here, half the pieces are broken.   To
top it all off, in the same day's mail we get our
bill.   Some joke!

We feel we can do without this kind of rotten service.
There's no time left for us to place an order with a
decent company (although we'd like to), so get on the
ball and send us a replacement order right away.

55c   The Request

State inquiries and requests clearly and positively, and aim
them at the intended reader.

Many of the business letters you write will ask someone else to do
something for you: to provide information, to perform a service, or to
correct a mistake. Make such letters clear, businesslike, and persuasive.

(1) State your request clearly and directly *early* in the letter. The
basic question in your reader's mind is "What do you want?"

**(2) If several points need attention, make sure each stands out
clearly.** Consider numbering them for emphasis. Too often, only the first
major point gets attention; other matters, buried later in a letter, are
forgotten.

**(3) Whenever possible, relate your request directly to the interests
and responsibilities of the person you are writing to.** Avoid a "To-
Whom-It-May-Concern" effect. Avoid using form letters if at all possible.

(4) When you have a complaint, remain courteous. Emphasize the
mutual satisfaction to be derived from a mistake corrected, rather than the
mutual frustration occasioned when an error is first made.

The sample letters on the following pages attempt to put these principles into practice.

request

274 Junipero Hall
Colfax College
Colfax, CA 95030
17 January 1990

Mr. Gerald Bliss, Editor
The Muse, 234 Drake Hall
Redwood College
Madrone Hills, CA 94002

Dear Mr. Bliss:

Largely because of the success of The Muse, your new
campus literary magazine, we at Colfax College feel
the time is right for a similar publication on this
campus. Your help on a few important questions would
get us moving in the right direction.

We would like to know the following:

1. How you went about soliciting manuscripts for
your first edition.
2. How you decided on the space to devote to
fiction, poetry, criticism, reviews, and
advertising.
3. Whether you use university or commercial
printing facilities.
4. What mailing list you used to solicit charter
subscriptions.

Our enthusiasm runs high over the possibility of a
literary review at Colfax. Target date for the first
issue is October 1. We have firm approval from the
administration, and the faculty is solidly behind us.

Sincerely,

Martha Gronowsky

Martha Gronowsky
Student Body Vice-President

request

209 Elm Street
Treeline, WY 82240
February 16, 1990

Dr. Raymond Garcia, Graduate Advisor
Environmental Studies
Midline State University
Midland, WI 53511

Dear Dr. Garcia:

I was surprised to receive your recent request for more transcripts to complete my application to the Graduate School. I will, of course, have them sent if absolutely necessary, but I do feel that your request penalizes me.

Upon coming to State as a transfer undergraduate in 1980, I paid two dollars, for transcripts in duplicate, to each of the three institutions I had previously attended. At that time, you informed me that all my papers were in order, and you admitted me. Now you request the very same transcripts in support of my graduate application.

Would it not be possible for you to refer to the transcripts already in your possession? Or if copies must be sent to the graduate advisor, could you not duplicate my transcripts and send me the bill? In either case, you would save me the time of recontacting each institution, and you would help me avoid possible delays in their responding.

Sincerely yours,

Kenneth Darwin

Kenneth Darwin

WRITING PRACTICE 4   Write a *letter of inquiry or request* in connection with some project in which you are currently interested. Observe conventional letter form.

55d	The Letter of Application

Make your letter of application suggest competence, confidence, and a genuine interest in the position.

Employers look for employees who will prove an asset to their organization and who are at the same time good to work with and good to know. They shy away from applicants who seem to promise problems, trouble, or an inflated ego. Remember the following advice:

(1) If you can, be specific about the position for which you apply. Mention the advertisement or the person that alerted you to the vacancy. (But do not mention leads that smack of the grapevine.)

(2) Find a way in.   If possible, show some knowledge of the company or the institution. Show that the future employer already means something to you. For instance, mention an open house you attended at the company's research facility, a tour of a manufacturing plant, or a newspaper article about the company's plan for a new product or technique.

(3) Present your academic qualifications to advantage.   Mention selected key courses that might relate to the employer's needs; stress what you learned.

(4) Stress previous experience.   Make the most of part-time work. If appropriate, mention volunteer work, fund-raising efforts, campaign organizing, and the like. Stress what you learned from such experiences—

for instance, learning to handle people's special needs by working with disabled students, or learning to budget resources by being in charge of equipment in a youth camp.

(5) Give your letter character. Establish your identity. Many job applications look very much the same. The anonymous, average applicant has little chance to be remembered—and to be preferred. If you have positive convictions about the work of the organization to which you apply, state them.

(6) If you want to list references, first get permission from those whose names you want to use. Quietly drop from your list the names of teachers or former employers who show little enthusiasm when you tell them about your plans.

(7) Consider preparing a separate résumé. If the account of your qualifications is extensive, put it on a separate data sheet. Make sure your letter does not merely duplicate what's on your résumé. Use your letter to pull out and highlight what is most important; use it to show the connections between different parts of your experience.

Study the sample letters on the following pages.

letter of application

892 N. Brendan Ave.
San Jose, CA 95113
November 17, 1990

Ms. Carla Gabriel, Editor
South Valley News
2239 Monterey Highway
Live Oak, CA 95032

Dear Ms. Gabriel:

In answer to your advertisement, I wish to apply for the position as general reporter. I am a journalism major and have worked for a student daily and an urban newspaper. I have come to appreciate the effort and perseverance required in newsgathering and in overcoming the obstacles in its path.

On February 1, I will graduate from San Jose State University. While getting a degree, I have taken a broad range of courses, representing all areas of editing and reporting. Also, I have been a general reporter for the Spartan Daily for two years. Last summer I worked for thirteen weeks on the Santa Clara Journal, as an intern sponsored by the Journalism Department of my college.

My most satisfying assignment was a guest editorial for the Spartan Daily, in which I stressed the role of the journalist in keeping the public informed about community needs, crime, and health hazards and in defending the right to know.

References are available on request. I will be glad to come to your office for an interview. I can be reached at (408) 294-4789.

Sincerely,

Pat Romeros

Pat Romeros

letter of application

95 South Drive
North Hollywood, CA 91607
12 March 1991

Mr. Daniel Levin, Attorney at Law
Peale, Corman, Bishop, Levin & Dilworthy
80 Limita Canyon Boulevard, Suite 7630
Beverly Hills, CA 92025

Dear Mr. Levin:

Edith Winters informs me of an opening in your
secretarial staff, a position for which I should very
much like to become a candidate.

I understand that you need a legal secretary with a
rapid stenographic skill and the ability to handle a
large volume of correspondence. Along with my degree
in legal stenography from Foothill Junior College, I
have four years of secretarial experience in retail
dry goods and in insurance. My shorthand speed is
145 words per minute. On my present job, I handle
between forty and sixty letters every day. I have had
training sufficient to prepare me to handle routine
letters without supervision.

My present job at Southwestern Life & Indemnity has
been quite satisfactory, but, having taken my degree
recently, I seek the further challenges and rewards
of a top-flight legal firm. I hope the enclosed
résumé will help interest the firm in me.

I can be in Los Angeles for an interview any afternoon
convenient for you.

Yours sincerely,

Pat Edmondson

Pat Edmondson

résumé

JEAN LAPORTE

Demmler Hall	Age: 25
Valhalla University	Ht: 6-1 Wt: 170
Kent, OH 26780	Willing to relocate
(613) 428-7600	

Education

B.S. in Industrial Engineering, Valhalla
University, June 1989; top ten percent of class,
with special course work in statistics,
motivational psychology, business law, and
communications.
Dean's Honor Roll 1987–1989
U.S. Paint Company Scholarship 1987
Member of Industrial Relations Club
Secretary of the Student Council
Attended Colfax College, Colfax, Indiana, 1985–1986

Experience

Station Manager, Arco Service Station, Cleveland,
Ohio, 1986–1987.
Staff Supervisor, Cleveland Summer Camp, Kiowa,
Ohio, summer 1986; responsible for housing,
activities scheduling, and occasional discipline of
fourteen counselors and 110 campers.
Camp Counselor, Cleveland Summer Camp, Kiowa, Ohio,
summers of 1983 and 1984.

Personal Interests

Politics, world affairs, camping, chess
Junior chamber of commerce member and volunteer
hospital worker.

---

56   Writing Essay Exams

OVERVIEW   Essay examinations require you to organize your thinking and marshal evidence in a limited time. They force you to abbreviate the process of writing. The premium is on *recall*—assembling quickly what is relevant to the topic. Next and equally essential is *planning*—working out quickly a general strategy. Third in your formula for success is *key detail*—fleshing out your outline in what is usually the first and final draft.

Remember the following guidelines:

(1) Get an overview of the exam.   Know what you are expected to do, especially if the exam comes in several parts. Take in specific instructions: Are you being asked to *summarize* information? *compare* two procedures or historical events? *explain* a point of view and show why you agree or disagree? *define* and illustrate a key term?

(2) Budget your time.   Set aside some time at the beginning to *think*—to collect your thoughts, to organize your thinking. (Take some rough notes.) Allot the right share of time for different tasks. (Be sure to respond to the last part of a three-part or four-part question.) Save some time for last-minute proofreading.

(3) Work from a rough outline.   If you can, have a clear three-point or four-point program in mind as you write. Do not just plunge in—a well-worked-out plan will minimize backtrackings, afterthoughts, and lame repetition.

(4) Make strategic use of detail.   Select a key example to illustrate a concept or to support a point. Include an apt quotation or a striking statistic to show your familiarity with the subject.

705

(5) Write legibly. The people grading essay examinations are only human, and they feel the pressure of time. By and large, they will prefer an answer that is short but well written to one that is scribbled and goes on and on.

Keep in mind that the reader is likely to be reading passage after passage on the same subject. Dispense with long roundabout introductions; avoid a restatement of the exam questions. Make your main points stand out. To set your exam off from the rest, use striking supporting detail or a fresh personal example; quote an instructor's favorite phrase or allude to class discussion.

<hr>

56a | Analyzing a Passage

Read carefully and organize your reactions when asked to analyze a selected passage.

A test in a subject like composition, literature, history, or political science will often ask you to read and react to a passage. Often you will have to do justice to two separate questions: "What does it say? How do I react, and why?" Suppose you are asked to explain a passage that the American poet Walt Whitman wrote about capital punishment. You are then asked whether you agree or disagree with the writer, and to show why. To help you focus your reading and organize your response, remember guidelines like the following:

(1) Sum up the author's central message. Early in your response, give an overview or preview that summarizes the main idea, including important distinctions or reservations:

> In this passage, Whitman does not say outright that he is for or against the death penalty. Instead, he attacks the system that *implements* the punishment—a system riddled by indecision and contradiction. Whitman feels that society should make a definite choice, for or against the death penalty, and then act firmly on that resolve.

(2) Organize your answer around major points. Try to mark off major steps in the argument, major segments in the author's train of thought:

Whitman touches on at least three reasons why the contemporary practice concerning capital punishment is unsatisfactory. First, the application of the law is fitful and *inconsistent*. The law seems undecided whether to inflict capital punishment for murder, and the authorities often find ways to spare or pardon the offender. . . .

Second, the application of the law often seems patently *unfair*. When an execution does take place, as often as not the condemned prisoner belongs to a racial minority. . . .

Third, and above all, the authorities *procrastinate*. Any minor technicality can delay a case indefinitely. . . .

(3) Respond to the author's style. Respond to hints and implications that help you read between the lines. Respond to what makes the writing eloquent, harsh, conciliatory, or different. Quote striking or revealing phrases:

Although Whitman does not state his own position on the justification of capital punishment outright, we can infer that he personally favors it from several remarks he makes in the passage. With a sarcastic tone, he refers to "soft-hearted (and soft-headed) prison philanthropists" who sympathize with convicted criminals. He refers to "penny-a-liner journalists" who write melodramatically about the plight of convicted murderers. He criticizes judges and lawyers who bend the law to give "the condemned every chance of evading punishment."

(4) Take a stand. State your own position clearly and forcefully. Use precedent, parallels, or revealing contrast to clarify and bolster your own point of view:

There are times when our anger makes us clamor for the death of an offender. But in our more thoughtful moments, we are likely to think differently. In Tolkien's *Lord of the Rings*, there is a passage that goes roughly as follows: "There are many who live who deserve to die. There are many who die who deserve to live. Can you give life? If not, do not be so quick to take it."

(5) Back up the stand you take. Fortify your position with reasons or examples:

My main reason for opposing capital punishment is that it is too arbitrary and unpredictable. Too much hinges on the cleverness of lawyers and on the prejudices of juries. One recent study found that good-looking, personable defendants are more likely to be acquitted than those who look threatening, gloomy, or disturbed. To judge from this study, juries may well send a man to his death because he *looks* like a villain; they thus make a mistake that can never be made good.

SAMPLE TEST 6 *Instructions:* In the following passage from *Progress and Privilege*, William Tucker joins in the debate between advocates of progress and advocates of conservation. Where does he take his stand? What is his argument in this excerpt? Is it in any way new or different; does it shed new light on the issue? Where do you stand on the issue raised in this excerpt, and why?

The fact is that, from a human perspective, nature, for all its diversity, is still not very stable. For most of nature, the laws of survival still mean matching the ever-present possibilities for catastrophe against the inborn capabilities of organisms to reproduce fantastic numbers of offspring to continue the genetic line. Let me give an example. In 1963, scientists doing an oceanographic survey in the Indian Ocean came across a 4,000-square-mile area covered with dead fish. The number equaled about one quarter of the world's catch at the time. The fish had not died from human activity but were the victims of the inevitable nutrient cycles that govern most of the ocean environment. . . .

The unpleasant truth is that natural cycles, for all their diversity, are still enormously unstable. Genetic diversity can protect diversified forests from diseases, for example, but fires can still destroy whole forests. It is this uncertainty that evokes the widely used strategy of fantastic procreative abilities among plants and invertebrates.

As mammals, we have tried to overcome these unpredictabilities through a different strategy—by internalizing our environment and building self-correcting controls. That is why we do not need the heat of the sun, as reptiles do, to warm our blood and give us energy at the start of the day. Nor are we as devastated by dryness or changes in the weather. (Some insect populations have been shown to go through population explosions and crashes from temperature changes of only a few degrees.) By building internal controls, we have been able to stabilize the relationship between our internal and external environments.

The business of human progress, then, has been a *continuation* of this evolutionary line of development. Human progress has not been "growthmania" or "growth for growth's sake," as environmentalists often charge. It has been a deliberate effort to extend our control over the external environment so that we are not subject to the instabilities and unpredictabilities of nature's cycles.

Thus, we do not guarantee ourselves any kind of stability in human affairs by foregoing the effort to humanize the environment, and letting nature take its course. That only returns us to nature's unpredictabilities. What we *can* do is be very cautious about disrupting natural systems any more than is necessary, and conserve wildlife whenever possible. This does not have to be strict preservation, but only a matter of taking concern for wild systems where they still exist.

56b   Tests on Your Reading

Learn to write a structured essay examination that makes the best possible use of what you know.

Many tests, whether open-book or written without books or notes, ask you to show how well you know the material you have studied. To do well on such tests (and to reduce test anxiety), study with a sense of purpose. Come to the examination prepared for what lies ahead. Keep in mind guidelines like the following:

(1) Prepare for a writing test. Obviously you want to immerse yourself in the material as much as you can. But much of your preparation will be to chart and to outline, to identify key points—to *prestructure* the material that you might use in a paragraph or short essay. Identify key terms that could provide the focal point for explanation or discussion. Chart the main steps in a procedure or the key parts of an argument: *Photosynthesis*—what are the essential processes that make it work? *Alienation*—what does a character in a short story say and do to show his alienated condition? *Agrarianism*—where, when, and why did it originate?

(2) Memorize key supporting details. Imprint on your memory some pointed definitions, striking examples, and telling statistics. Memorize some key phrases and short pointed quotations. Nothing establishes your credentials as a well-prepared student more reliably than sentences like the following:

> Modern civilization, what D. H. Lawrence calls "my accursed human education," has alienated us from our roots in the natural world.

> According to Barbara Tuchman, dates are fundamental to the historian because they show order in time and thus make possible "an understanding of cause and effect."

(3) Check the exact wording of instructions. Assume the question in a history exam is "What do you consider the most important difference between the fall of Greece and the fall of Rome?" Do not simply put down everything you can remember about the fall of Greece and the fall of Rome. Focus on the key word in the instructions: *difference*. What *is* the difference? How can you line up material that will bring out this difference as clearly and convincingly as possible?

(4) Structure your answer. No matter what the pressure of time, do not simply spill out what you remember. Especially in a paragraph-length response, try to come straight to the point—make your first sentence sum up your answer or your stand on the issue. Proceed to cover major parts of the problem or key reasons in a clear order—for instance, from simple to difficult or from unlikely to probable. (Avoid lame transitions like *also* or *another*.)

Study the following instructions for an essay exam on a literary subject and a student response that a teacher selected as a model:

INSTRUCTIONS: *A common type of character in much contemporary literature is the individual who is trapped by a trick of fate, by the environment, or by his or her own nature. Choose such a character from a short story you have recently read. Define the trap in which the character is caught. Describe any struggle on the part of the character to become free.*

ANSWER: Katherine Mansfield's Miss Brill finds herself trapped by her spinsterhood and the advancement of age. She is old, as the story tells us; she's as old as her out-of-date fox fur. She is alone, with no friends, relatives, or close neighbors. This is her trap. Like a bird that will create its own prison in its own territory, Miss Brill makes hers. She does not socialize, nor does she try to make something useful out of her life but rather preys like a parasite on other people's more interesting, colorful lives. In her own way, Miss Brill struggles to escape her prison. She day-dreams. The world that she lives in is a fantasy world where all people are friendly and related. She "belongs" in this world, whereas in the other world, the real world, she actually belongs to no one.

Quite successfully, Miss Brill loses the real world for a time, but she cannot escape the real world entirely. The real world sticks its head in, in the form of a boy who says "Ah, go on with you now." So she goes home, more aware than ever of her prison's boundaries and helpless (by her own nature) to do anything else. She can only fly on home to the security and solitude of her cold, dark nest.

Note the following points about this answer:

- It responds directly to the *key term* or *key idea* in the assignment. The assignment asks about a character who is *trapped*. This word and its synonyms keep echoing throughout the student's answer: *trapped, prison, boundaries*.
- The first sentence sums up the answer as a whole. It gives the brief, clear definition of the "trap" that the question asks for.
- The point about the character's trying to escape through day-dreaming responds to the *second* part of the question. But note that this point is worked organically into the first paragraph. The student has planned this answer; there are no afterthoughts, no "Oh-I-forgot" effect.

WRITING WORKSHOP 7   Work with a group that shares an interest in one of the topics listed below. Find and study background material in a textbook or encyclopedia. Help set up a timed essay test on the topic chosen by your group. In writing your own short essay on the topic, start with a preview or overview. Trace clearly the major steps, arguments, or dimensions of the topic. Include some striking details or examples. After the test, share in a group critique of the results. Possible topics:

- evidence for the theory of evolution
- Marx's critique of laissez-faire capitalism
- the Ptolemaic and the Copernican views of the solar system
- Luther's criticism of the Roman Catholic church
- diet and heart disease
- the abolitionist movement
- the Mayan civilization
- causes of the Great Depression

11

57 Glossary of Usage

Glossary of Usage

Diagnostic Test

Instructions In each of the following sentences, which of the two italicized choices is right for serious written English? Write the number of the sentence, followed by your choice.

1. We assembled the unit exactly *as/like* the instructions said.
2. The governor reported little progress *in terms of/concerning* new prisons.
3. None of our so-called friends offered us *no/any* help.
4. Mario was *apt/liable* to become an outstanding tennis player.
5. He dislikes *these kind of people/this kind of person*.
6. The vaguely worded letter *implied/inferred* that the bank was about to fail.
7. A psychic had warned the company of *a/an* accident.
8. The stadium was always filled with a large *amount/number* of people.
9. The reason Jim drove on the left side of the street was *that/because* he had grown up in England.
10. Cars *didn't use to/used not to* be permitted inside the park.
11. We had hoped the company would choose Phoenix over Houston, but it chose the *latter/later*.
12. Motorists *couldn't/could* hardly see the road in the dense fog.

13. Her friend was *disinterested/uninterested* in restaurants that featured vegetable burgers and carrot juice.

14. The new manager always made people wait *several/a couple of* minutes in the outer office.

15. It was the kind of secret that is known to *most/almost* everybody involved.

16. The former owner had stubbornly refused to take anything *off of/off* the price.

17. *Being that/Because* fees are constantly going up, many students will have to reconsider their plans.

18. For some people, it is *cheaper/more cheaper* to lease a car than to buy one.

19. We were determined to continue *regardless/irregardless* of our collaborators' decision.

20. This year for the first time, we have had *fewer/less* applicants than the year before.

57   Glossary of Usage

Avoid expressions that many readers find objectionable.

When our readers object to a word or phrase we use, their negative reaction comes like static between our message and its destination. A large part of final editing is *editing out* expressions that at least some of our readers will consider uneducated, excessively informal, or illogical. The best advice for dealing with such potential problems is: Rewrite to avoid them whenever you can do so without sounding stilted or unnatural.

The advice given in this glossary will help you write the kind of *serious edited English*—moderately formal with an occasional informal touch—that is acceptable to a large cross section of educated readers. Many dictionaries now include **usage notes** that deal with problems like those included here. Remember, however, that dictionaries, like readers, range from conservative to more permissive.

Note: Check **39c** for confusing pairs like *advise/advice, affect/effect, lose/loose,* or *than/then.*

a, an Use *a* only before words that begin with a consonant when pro- U1
nounced: *a desk, a chair, a house, a year, a* C, *a university.* Use *an* before
words that begin with a vowel when pronounced (though in writing
the first letter may be a consonant): *an eye, an answer, an honest mistake,
an* A, *an* M, *an uninformed reader.* The *a* before a vowel is nonstandard:

WRONG: a ear, a accident, a automobile, a athlete
RIGHT: **an** ear, **an** accident, **an** automobile, **an** athlete

accept, except See EXCEPT, ACCEPT. U2

aggravate In writing, use to mean "make worse or more grave." Avoid U3
its informal use in the sense of "annoy" or "irritate":

FORMAL: When you **irritate** him, you **aggravate** his condition.

ain't Nonstandard for *am not, isn't, aren't,* or *hasn't* (She *ain't* been seen U4
since).

all right Spell as *two* words. (Although *alright* appears in some diction- U5
aries, most readers will consider it a misspelling.)

allusion, illusion An *allusion* is a brief mention that reminds us of a story U6
or an event (the speaker's *allusion* to Watergate). An *illusion* is a deceptive
appearance or false hope (The Vietnam war destroyed many *illusions*).

a lot Always spell as *two* words. "*A lot* of money" is informal; "*lots* of U7
money" is slang:

FORMAL: She owed us **a large amount** of money.

already, all ready "They *already* (ahead of time) had our equipment *all* U8
(completely) *ready.*"

altogether, all together "It is *altogether* (completely) too late to bring U9
these people *all* (every one of them) *together.*"

among, between See BETWEEN, AMONG. U10

amount, number Use *amount* only when thinking about bulk or a sum U11
(the total *amount* of the debt). Use *number* when thinking about count-
able items (the *number* of whooping cranes).

RIGHT: A large **number** (not **amount**) of people were waiting.
               The **number** (not **amount**) of unsold cars on dealers' lots
               was growing steadily.

and and ***but*** **at the beginning of a sentence** A traditional rule banned U12
and and *but* at the beginning of a sentence. Used at the beginning of a
sentence, they partly cancel out the pause signaled by the period. They
can therefore suggest a sudden or an important afterthought. But many

modern writers start sentences with *and* or *but* merely to avoid weightier, more formal words like *moreover, furthermore, however,* and *nevertheless.* Don't overdo or overuse the initial *and* or *but.*

> He was plagued by financial worries. **But** nothing could cramp his generous heart.   *Time*

U13   **and/or**   *And/or* is sometimes necessary in commercial or official documents. Avoid it in ordinary writing.

U14   **angle, approach, slant**   *Angle, approach,* and *slant* are overused as synonyms for "attitude," "point of view," "position," or "procedure."

U15   **anyone, anybody**   *Anyone* and *anybody* stand for "any person at all." *Any one* singles out: "Take any *one* of those three." *Any body* refers to the physical body.

U16   **anyways, anywheres, anyplace**   In writing, use *anyway* or *anywhere.*

U17   **apt, liable, prone**   In informal English, *apt, liable,* and *prone* all appear in the sense of "likely." In formal usage, *apt* suggests that something is likely because of someone's aptitude ("She is *apt* to become a successful artist"). *Liable* suggests that what is likely is burdensome or undesirable ("He is *liable* to break his leg"). *Prone* suggests that something is almost inevitable because of strong habit or predisposition ("He is *prone* to suspect others").

U18   **as**   *As* is nonstandard as a substitute for *that* or *whether* ("I don't know *as* I can come"). It is also nonstandard as a substitute for *who* ("Those *as* knew her avoided her"). As a substitute for *because* or *while, as* is often criticized as weak or ambiguous:

> **As** (better: "because") we had no money, we gave him a check.

U19   **at**   Omit the redundant *at* in *where at.* Use "*Where* does he live?" instead of "*Where* does he live *at*?"

U20   **attribute, contribute**   *Attribute* means "to trace to a cause" or "to credit to a source." *Contribute* means "to give one's share" or "to have a share" in something.

> RIGHT: She **attributed** her success to perseverance.

U21   **awful, awfully**   In writing, use *awful* only for something truly horrible (The plane went down with *awful* loss of life). Do not use *awful* or *awfully* as an informal substitute for *very* or *extremely* (That was *awful* close).

> INFORMAL: Their parents had been **awfully** mean to them.
> FORMAL: Their parents had been **extremely** mean to them.

U22   **bad, badly**   Use the adjective *bad* after the linking verb *feel,* which shows a condition: "His resignation made everyone feel *bad*." Use the adverb *badly* to show how something is done: "She handled the assignment *badly*."

being as, being that   Nonstandard as substitutes for *because* or *since*   U23 ("being *that* I was ill").

beside, besides   *Beside* means "next to," "to the side of" (the empty lot   U24 *beside* our house). Sometimes *beside* means "outside one's normal calm state" (The other driver was *beside* himself). *Besides*, with the *-s*, means "furthermore" (*Besides*, you are too short).

between, among   Use *between* in references to two of a kind (distinguish   U25 *between* right and wrong). Use *among* in references to more than two (distinguish *among* different shades of color). *Between* is also right when more than two things can be considered in pairs of two:

RIGHT: Bilateral trade agreements exist **between** many countries.

breath, breathe   We take a deep *breath* (noun), but we *breathe* (verb) in   U26 and out.

broke   A very informal word for a familiar condition (being out of   U27 money). Do not use *broke* instead of *broken*: "Someone *had broken* (not *had broke*) the glass."

RIGHT: She **broke** her arm, the same one she **had broken** (not **broke**) before.

burst, bursted, bust, busted   *Bursted* is a nonstandard form of *burst*: "The   U28 tank *burst* (not *bursted*) and killed two of the workers." *Bust* as a verb meaning "*break*" or "*arrested*" is slang.

but what   Use *that* instead of *but what* after words like *doubt*: "We never   U29 doubted *that* (not *but what*) they would return."

but yet, but however   Expressions like *but yet* or *but however* are redun-   U30 dant; they say *but* twice. Use only one of the logical links at a time: "The full amount had been paid, *but* (not *but yet*) the computer kept sending us bills."

calculate, reckon, expect, guess   In written English, *calculate* and *reckon*   U31 imply computing or systematic reasoning. *Expect* implies expectation or anticipation; *guess* implies conjecture. In the sense of "think," "sup-pose," or "consider," these verbs are informal or dialectal.

can and *may*   Formal English uses *can* in the sense of "be able to." It uses   U32 *may* to show permission. The use of *can* to indicate permission, com-mon in speech and writing, is often considered informal:

INFORMAL: **Can** I speak to you for a minute?
FORMAL: Visitors **may** (are permitted to) enter the country only if they **can** (are able to) prove their identity.

U33   **cannot help but**   *Cannot help but* is often criticized as illogical or confused. Use either *cannot help* or *cannot but*:

> RIGHT: I **cannot help** wishing that I had never met you.
> RIGHT: I **cannot but** wish that I had never met you.

U34   **can't hardly, can't scarcely**   These expressions, like double negatives, duplicate the negative idea. Use *can hardly, can scarcely.*

> WRONG: Many countries **can't hardly** pay the interest on their debt.
> RIGHT: Many countries **can hardly** pay the interest on their debt.

U35   **censor, censure**   To *censor* means to meddle with speech or writing to make it conform to the censor's standards (or to ban it outright). *Censorship* is the result. To *censure* is to express disapproval in a very serious official manner (a vote of *censure*).

U36   **center around**   Logical readers expect a discussion to *center on* an issue, not to *center around* it.

U37   **compare with, compare to**   We compare two cities *with* each other to see what they have in common. We compare a city *to* an anthill to show what a city is like.

U38   **complement, compliment**   The first word means "complete" or "supplement." The second word means "say nice things, flatter." *Complementary* findings round out or complete a picture. *Complimentary* remarks flatter. (*Complimentary* tickets are given free of charge to create a good impression.)

U39   **conscience, conscious**   This is one of those spelling errors that jump out from the page at the reader. We are usually *conscious* (*-ious*) and sometimes un*conscious*, and some of our feelings are buried in the sub*conscious*. Our *conscience* (*-ience*) makes us feel guilty when we do something wrong.

> WRONG: His **conscious** (should be **conscience**) told him to return the money.

U40   **couple of**   In formal writing, *couple* refers to two of a kind, a pair. Used in the sense of "several" or "a few," it is informal. Used before a plural noun without a connecting *of*, it is nonstandard:

> INFORMAL: We had to wait **a couple of** minutes.
> NONSTANDARD: We had only **a couple** dollars left.

U41   **credible, credulous, creditable**   Stories may be credible or incredible—easy or hard to believe. The people who read them may be credulous or incredulous—easy or hard to fool. An act that does someone credit is a creditable act.

718

cute, great, lovely, terrific, wonderful Words like *cute, great, lovely, terrific,* and *wonderful* are often used routinely or lightly and can make your writing sound gushy or insincere. — U42

data Though now often used as a singular, the word is originally a Latin plural (meaning "facts"): — U43

SAFE: **These** data **are** part of a growing body of evidence.

different than *Different from* used to be expected in formal English. *Different than,* widely used in speech, is becoming acceptable in writing. — U44

ECONOMICAL: We tried a different method **than** we had used last year.
LESS ECONOMICAL: We tried a different method **from the one** we had used last year.

disinterested, uninterested In formal English, *disinterested* means "not swayed by personal, selfish interest" or "impartial." *Disinterested* used in the sense of "uninterested" or "indifferent" is objectionable to many readers: — U45

RIGHT: We were sure she would be a **disinterested** judge.
He seemed **uninterested** in our problems.

done *Done* is nonstandard when used instead of *did* or *have*. — U46

RIGHT: We **have done** nothing that **has** not **been done** before.
WRONG: The burglars **done** (should be **did**) a thorough job.
WRONG: They **done finished** (should be **finished** or **have finished**) their part.

don't, doesn't Put the apostrophe where the *o* would have been in *do not* and *does not.* Standard English doesn't use *don't* after *he, she,* or *it* (third person singular): She *doesn't* smoke. He *doesn't* work. It *doesn't* matter. — U47

double comparative, double superlative Short adjectives usually form the comparative by adding the suffix *-er (cheaper),* the superlative by adding the suffix *-est (cheapest).* Long adjectives, and adverbs ending in *-ly,* usually employ the intensifiers *more* and *most* instead (*more expensive, most expensive; more carefully, most carefully*). Forms using both the suffix and the intensifier are nonstandard (*more cheaper, most cheapest*). — U48

double negative Double negatives say no twice. The use of additional negative words to reinforce a negation already expressed is nonstandard: "I *didn't* do *nothing*"; "*Nobody* comes to see me *no more.*" — U49

RIGHT: I **didn't** do **anything**.
Nobody comes to see me **anymore**.

Similar to double negatives are expressions like *couldn't hardly* or *couldn't scarcely:*

RIGHT: I **could hardly** keep my eyes open during the talk.

U50 due to as a preposition Use *due to* as an adjective: "His absence was *due to* ill health." "His absence, *due to* ill health, upset our schedule." (In these examples, you could substitute another adjective: "His absence was *traceable* to ill health.") Avoid *due to* as a preposition meaning "because of":

OBJECTIONABLE: Computer chips fail **due to** poor quality control.
SAFE: Computer chips fail **because of** poor quality control.

U51 each other, one another Conservative writers distinguish between *each other* (referring to two persons or things) and *one another* (referring to more than two):

The bride and groom had known **each other** since childhood.
The members of his family supported **one another**.

U52 enthuse, enthused These are very informal shortcuts for "turn enthusiastic" and "enthusiastic."

U53 etc. *Etc.*, the Latin abbreviation for "and so on," often serves as a vague substitute for additional examples or illustrations. Furthermore, *ect.* is a common misspelling. "And etc." and "such as . . . etc." are redundant. To avoid trouble, steer clear of *etc.* altogether.

U54 except, accept Use *except* when you make an *ex*ception—you take something *out*. Use *accept* when you receive something willingly—you take something *in*.

U55 farther, further; all the farther A traditional rule requires *farther* in references to space and distance ("We traveled *farther* than we had expected"). It requires *further* in references to degree and quantity ("We discussed it *further* at our next meeting") and in the sense of "additional" ("without *further* delay"). *Further*, however, is now widely accepted as appropriate in all three senses.

All the farther in the sense of "as far as" ("This is *all the farther* we go") is nonstandard or dialectal.

U56 flaunt, flout We *flaunt* (show off) wealth or possessions ("If you have it, *flaunt* it"). We *flout* (defy or ignore) laws.

U57 flunk Slang for *fail.*

U58 get Several uses of the verb *get* are informal: "We finally *got* to see him" (succeeded); "He never *got* it" (understood); "The police finally *got* him" (arrested); "What *gets* me is that he is always late" (irritates).

For many readers, *get* used instead of *be* (*am, are, was, were*) to form the passive has an informal ring: "Her Mustang *got hit* by a truck."

U59 get, got, gotten In American English, *have gotten* is an acceptable alternative to *have got* in the sense of "have obtained" or "have become." For example: "Her grandparents had *got* (or *gotten*) wealthy after the Civil War."

hadn't ought to   In formal English, *ought*, unlike some other auxiliaries, has no form for the past tense. *Hadn't ought* is informal; *had ought* is nonstandard: U60

INFORMAL: You **hadn't ought** to ask him.
FORMAL: You **ought not to have** asked him.

hopefully   When used instead of "I hope" or "let us hope," *hopefully* is widely considered illogical.   U61

RIGHT: She looked at the bulletin board **hopefully** (with hope).
POOR: **Hopefully**, she will look at the bulletin board.
BETTER: **We hope** she will look at the bulletin board.

if, whether   *If* is sometimes criticized when used to express doubt or uncertainty after such verbs as *ask, don't know, wonder, doubt*. The more formal subordinator is *whether*: "I doubt *whether* his support would do much good."   U62

immigrate, emigrate   People *immigrate* to a new country, where they arrive as *immigrants*. People *emigrate* from the old country, where they leave as *emigrants*.   U63

impact   *Impact* is fashionable jargon when used to mean "affect," "change," or "alter." Try a more exact word like *improve, strengthen*, or *reduce*: "These cuts greatly *worsened* (not *impacted*) the housing situation in the city." There is nothing wrong with traditional uses of the word like "the *impact* of the meteor on the lunar surface" or "several *impacted* teeth."   U64

in, into   Formal writing often requires *into* rather than *in* to indicate direction: "He came *into* (not *in*) the room."   U65

individual   *Individual* is a key word in our political tradition: "the rights of the *individual*." Used outside its political or social context to mean simply "a person," it can sound impersonal and bureaucratic, like a police report: "The *individuals* (better: *people*) in the square were asked to disperse."   U66

infer, imply   Use *imply* to mean "hint or suggest a conclusion." Use *infer* to mean "draw a conclusion on the basis of what has been hinted or suggested." A speaker *implies* something; the audience *infers* what is meant from the speaker's hints.   U67

in terms of   A vague all-purpose connective frequent in jargon: "What have you seen lately *in terms of* new plays?"   U68

721

JARGON:	What did she expect **in terms of** salary?
BETTER:	What salary did she expect?

U69   *irregardless*   Use *regardless*. *Irregardless*, sometimes heard in educated speech, is widely considered illogical and nonstandard.

U70   *it's, its*   Use *it's* (with the apostrophe) only when it's short for *it is*. Use *its* (no apostrophe) to show possession: the band and *its* admirers, the war and *its* aftermath, the orchestra and *its* conductor.

U71   *it's me, it is I*   Grammarians require *it is I* on the grounds that the linking verb *is* equates the pronoun *I* with the subject *it* and thus makes necessary the use of the subject form. *It's me* is now freely used in informal speech. Avoid it and parallel uses of other pronouns (*us, him, her*) in your writing:

INFORMAL:	I thought it was **him**. It could have been **us**.
FORMAL:	It was **she** who paid the bills.

U72   *judicial, judicious*   A judicial decision is reached by a judge or by a court. A judicious decision shows sound judgment.

U73   *kind of, sort of*   Avoid as informal substitutes for *rather* or *somewhat*: "We were all *sort of* (should be *rather*) tired at the end of the lecture."

U74   *later, latter*   *Later* is the opposite of *earlier*. The *latter* is the opposite of the *former*. "Although both Alfred and Francis were supposed to arrive at eight, the *latter* came *later*."

U75   *learn, teach*   In standard English, the teacher *teaches* (rather than *learns*) the learner. The learner is *taught* (rather than *learned*) by the teacher.

STANDARD:	They **taught** (not **learned**) us everything we know.

U76   *leave, let*   In formal usage, *leave* does not mean "allow" or "permit." You do not "leave" somebody do something. Nor does *leave* take the place of *let* in suggestions like "Let us call a meeting."

U77   *lend, loan*   We *lend* money (using the verb), thus giving someone *a loan* (using the noun).

U78   *less, fewer*   To be safe, use *less* in references to extent, amount, degree (*less* friction, *less* money, *less* heat). Do not use it in references to things you can count: *fewer* people, *fewer* homes, *fewer* requirements.

U79   *like as a conjunction*   In informal speech, *like* is widely used as a subordinator replacing *as* or *as if* at the beginning of a clause. Avoid this informal *like* in your writing:

INFORMAL:	Do **like** I tell you.
FORMAL:	Do **as** I tell you.
INFORMAL:	The patient felt **like** he had slept for days.
FORMAL:	The patient felt **as if** (or **as though**) he had slept for days.

In formal usage, *like* is acceptable as a preposition, followed by an object: *like* a bird, *like* a cloud. It is not acceptable as a conjunction that starts a clause, with its own subject and verb: *like* a bird flies, *like* a cloud had passed.

PREPOSITION: Manuel looks exactly **like** his father.

CONJUNCTION: We did everything **like** (should be **as**) the instructions said.

literally   *Literally* literally means "in plain fact." Do not use it figuratively to mean "figuratively."   *U80*

RIGHT: They **literally** leveled the village.

WRONG: They **literally** (should be **completely**) blanketed the city with leaflets. (They did not use an actual blanket.)

media   Though many media people use *media* as a singular, it is originally the plural of *medium*, and many of your readers will expect to see it used as a plural: "The *media are* not just reporting but shaping and sometimes creating political events."   *U81*

moral, morale   We talk about the "moral" of a story but about the "morale" of workers. People with good morale are not necessarily moral, and vice versa.   *U82*

most, almost   *Most* is informal when used in the sense of "almost" or "nearly": "*Most* everybody was there." "Jones considers herself an authority on *most* any subject." Use "*almost* everybody," "*almost* any subject."   *U83*

myself, yourself, himself, herself   The -*self* pronouns are called reflexive pronouns because they usually "point back" to someone already mentioned: *U84*

I blamed **myself** for the accident.
The **woman** introduced **herself**.
He **himself** gave me the key.

Conservative readers object to these pronouns when they do not point back but are used as simple substitutes for *I* or *me, he* or *him*:

FORMAL: My brother and **I** (not **myself**) met him at the station.

FORMAL: We have reserved seats for Jean and **you** (not **yourself**).

nohow, nowheres, nowhere near   *Nohow* and *nowheres* are nonstandard for *in no way* and *nowhere*. *Nowhere near* is informal for *not nearly*: "They were not nearly as clever as they thought."   *U85*

off of   Nonstandard for *off* or *from*:   *U86*

STANDARD: Take it **off** (not **off of**) the table.

STANDARD: She deducted two dollars **from** (not **off of**) the price.

723

U87   ***OK, O.K., okay***   All three spellings are acceptable, but the expression itself is informal:

       FORMAL: The mayor gave us her formal **approval** (not "her formal **OK**").

U88   ***on account of***   Nonstandard as a substitute for *because*:

       NONSTANDARD: When promoted, people may stop trying **on account of** (should be "because") they have reached their goal.

U89   ***parameter***   *Parameter* is a useful technical word for exact margins or outside limits. For ordinary limits, try *limits* or *boundaries*.

U90   ***plan on***   In your writing, plan to substitute *plan to*.

       INFORMAL: My parents had always **planned on** us taking over the farm.
       FORMAL: My parents had always **planned to** have us take over the farm.

U91   ***plus***   *Plus* is acceptable in writing when used about figures, sums, and the like. Avoid using it as an informal substitute for *and* or *also*: "He dresses shabbily, *and* (not *plus*) he smells."

U92   **possessives with verbal nouns**   A traditional rule requires that a verbal noun (gerund) be preceded by a possessive in sentences like the following:

       FORMAL: He mentioned **John's winning** a scholarship.
                     I am looking forward to **your mother's** staying with us.

In informal English, the plain form is common:

       INFORMAL: Imagine **John winning** a scholarship!

A combination of a pronoun and a verbal with the *-ing* ending may express two different relationships. In the sentence "I saw *him returning* from the library," you actually saw *him*. In the sentence "I object to *his using* my toothbrush," you are not objecting to *him* but merely to one of *his* actions. Use the possessive pronoun (*my, our, his, their*) when the object of a verb or of a preposition is not the person but one of his or her actions, traits, or experiences:

       RIGHT: We investigated the chances of **his** being elected.
                     There is no excuse for **their** not writing sooner.

predominate   *Predominate* is a verb: "Shirt sleeves and overalls *predomi-*   **U93**
nated in the crowd." *Predominant* is the adjective: "Antiwar feeling was
predominant." "Democrats were the *predominant* party."

preposition at the end of a sentence   Teachers no longer tell students   **U94**
not to end a sentence with a preposition. The preposition that ends a
sentence is idiomatic, natural English, though more frequent in informal
than in formal use:

INFORMAL:	I don't remember what we talked **about**.
INFORMAL:	She found her in-laws hard to live **with**.
FORMAL:	Let us not betray the ideals **for which** these men died.
FORMAL:	Do not ask **for whom** the bell tolls.

prepositions often criticized   *Inside of* (for *inside*), *outside of* (for *out-*   **U95**
side), and *at about* (for *about*) are redundant.
     Back of for *behind* (*back of* the house), *inside of* for *within* (*inside of*
three hours), *outside of* for *besides* or *except* (no one *outside of* my friends),
and *over with* for *over* (it's *over with*) are colloquial.
     As to, as regards, and *in regard to* often seem heavy-handed and
bureaucratic:

AWKWARD:	I questioned him **as to** the nature of his injury.
PREFERABLE:	I questioned him **about** his injury.

     As to whether, in terms of, and *on the basis of* flourish in all varieties
of jargon.
     Per (a dollar *per* day), *as per* (*as per* your request), and *plus* (quality
plus service) are common in business and newspaper English but inappropriate in a noncommercial context.

prior to, previous to   These sound like old-fashioned business jargon or   **U96**
bureaucratese. Try *before*.

JARGON:	He always had an elaborate strategy session **previous to** (should be **before**) an important exam.

provided, provided that, providing   *Provided, provided that,* and *providing*   **U97**
are interchangeable in a sentence like "He will withdraw his complaint,
provided you apologize." However, only *provided* has escaped criticism
and is therefore the safest form to use.

U98   ***reason is because***   *The reason . . . is because* is often criticized as redundant, since *because* repeats the idea of cause already expressed in the word *reason*.

INFORMAL: **The reason** that the majority rules **is because** it is strongest.

FORMAL: **The reason** that the majority rules **is that** it is strongest.

U99   ***respective, respectful***   When we are respectful, we show respect. The use of *respective* in expressions like "They went to their *respective* rooms" sounds jargony to many readers. Try "They *each* went to their rooms."

U100   ***shall, will***   In current American usage, *will* usually indicates simply that something is going to happen. (I will ask him tomorrow.) The more emphatic *shall* often shows determination, obligation, or command:

We **shall** do our best.
Wages of common laborers **shall** not exceed twenty dollars a day.

   Shall is also common in questions that invite the listener's approval or consent:

Shall I wait for you?
Shall we dance?

   Handbooks no longer require *shall* for simple future in the first person: "I *shall* see him tomorrow."

U101   ***so and such***   Informal English often uses *so* or *such* without going on to the *so . . . what*? "They were *so* frightened" (that what?). "There was *such* an uproar" (that what?). Substitute "They were *extremely* frightened" or add the *so . . . what*?

RIGHT: They were so frightened **that they were unable to speak**. There was such an uproar **that the judge banged the gavel in vain**.

U102   **split infinitives**   Occasionally, a modifier breaks up an infinitive, that is, a verbal formed with *to* (*to come, to promise, to have written*). The resulting split infinitive occurs in the work of distinguished writers, and the traditional rule against it has been widely abandoned. However, a split infinitive can be awkward if the modifier that splits the infinitive is more than one word:

AWKWARD:	He ordered us **to** with all possible speed **return** to our stations.
BETTER:	He ordered us **to return** to our stations with all possible speed.

superlative in reference to two   In informal speech and writing, the   U103
superlative rather than the comparative frequently occurs in comparisons between only two things. This use of the superlative is often considered illogical:

INFORMAL:	Which of the two candidates is the **best** speaker?
FORMAL:	Which of the two candidates is the **better** speaker?

sure   In writing, use *surely* or *certainly* as the adverb: U104

INFORMAL:	The guide **sure** knew all the answers.
FORMAL:	The guide **certainly** knew all the answers.

take and, try and, up and   *Take and* (in "I'd *take and* prune those roses")   U105
and *up and* (in "He *up and* died") are dialectal. *Try and* for *try to* ("I'd
try and change his mind") is colloquial.

these kind   Avoid "*these kind* of cars" and "*those kind* of fish." Agreement   U106
requires "*this kind* of car" (both singular) or "*these kinds* of fish" (both
plural).

this here, that there   Use only the *this* or *that* to avoid these folksy non-   U107
standard expressions.

titles: Dr., Prof., Reverend   In references to holders of academic degrees   U108
or titles, *Dr. Smith* and *Professor Brown* are courteous and correct. *Professor* is sometimes abbreviated in addresses when it precedes the full
name: *Prof. Martha F. Brown.* In references to clergy, *Reverend* is usually
preceded by *the* and followed by the first name, by initials, or by *Mr.*
(*the Reverend William Carper; the Reverend W. F. Carper; the Reverend
Mr. Carper*).

type, type of, -type   Omitting the *of* in expressions like "this *type* of plane"   U109
is colloquial. Avoid *-type* used as a suffix to turn nouns into adjectives:
"an *escape-type* novel," "a *drama-type* program." Use "an *escape* novel," "a
dramatic program."

unique   It is often argued that one thing cannot be *more unique* than   U110
another. Either it is unique (one of a kind) or it isn't. Formal English
therefore often substitutes *more nearly unique.*

U111 **used to, didn't use to, used to could** *Used to* in questions or negative statements with *did* is informal. Avoid it in writing:

INFORMAL: She **didn't use to** smoke.
FORMAL: She **used not to** smoke.

Used to could is nonstandard for *used to be able*.

U112 **wait for, wait on** Informal English uses *wait on* both when we wait *for* others and when we wait *on* (or serve) them. In writing, use *wait for* when someone is keeping you waiting.

INFORMAL: They had been **waiting on** him in the parking lot.
FORMAL: They had been **waiting for** him in the parking lot.

U113 **where, where at, where to** In formal English, *where* takes the place of *where to* ("*Where* was it sent?") and *where at* ("*Where* is he?"). *Where* used instead of *that* ("I read in the paper *where* a boy was killed") is informal.

U114 **who, which, and that** *Who* and *whom* refer to persons ("the man *whom* I asked"). *Which* refers to ideas and things ("my son's car, *which* I bought"). A *who* (*whom*) or *which* introducing a restrictive clause may be replaced by *that*. In such situations, conservative readers prefer the *who* (or *whom*) to *that*. But they prefer the *that* to *which*.

LESS FORMAL: The people **that** I asked liked the car **which** I bought.
MORE FORMAL: The people **whom** I asked liked the car **that** I bought.

U115 **whose** *Of which* and *in which* can easily make a sentence awkward. *Whose* is therefore widely accepted in reference to ideas and things: "the Shank-Painter Swamp, *whose* expressive name . . . gave it importance in our eyes" (Thoreau).

U116 **-wise** People often change a noun into an adverb by tacking on *-wise*; this practice is common in business or advertising jargon:

JARGON: The delay was advantageous **tax-wise**.
BETTER: The delay was advantageous **for tax purposes**.

U117 **without** *Without* is nonstandard when used as a conjunction (subordinator) introducing a clause:

NONSTANDARD: The owner won't let me stay **without** I pay the rent.
STANDARD: The owner won't let me stay **unless** I pay the rent.

728

you **with indefinite reference**   Formal writing limits *you* to the meaning of "you, the reader." Much informal writing uses *you* with indefinite reference to refer to people in general.

INFORMAL:	In ancient Rome, **you** had to be a patrician to be able to vote.
FORMAL:	In ancient Rome, **one** had to be a patrician to be able to vote.
STILL BETTER:	In ancient Rome, **only patricians** were able to vote.

12

Grammatical Terms

58   Grammatical Terms

Know widely used grammatical terms.

Like the technical terminology of other fields, the language of grammarians confuses the newcomer and is a source of pride to the specialist who knows its finer points. It helps us talk about how words work together in sentences and is a useful tool when not allowed to become an end in itself. Modern linguists have often used approaches to language study different from those of the traditional school grammarians, so that you may encounter a range of different terms, old and new. Even our school grammar has moved slowly (very slowly) toward a more English terminology, moving away somewhat from the Latin and Greek terms first used by grammarians whose main business was to analyze Latin and Greek. The entries in this glossary are intended as capsule definitions and quick reminders. The index of this book will lead you to fuller discussion of many of the terms included here.

absolute construction   This is a word or phrase that is not tied to any particular part of a sentence—it goes with the whole sentence: "*The guests having departed*, Arvin started to pick up the debris." Typically, the absolute construction (also called *absolute phrase* or *absolute modifier*) includes a verbal like *breaking, having broken, being broken,* or *broken,* preceded by a noun that functions as if it were its subject: "*Trumpets blaring*, the band marched out onto the field." "*His heart broken*, he returned to Peoria." Sometimes the subject is merely implied: "*Consid-*

731

ering the force of the impact (that is, when *we* consider the force of the impact), the damage was slight."

accusative   Now usually called the **objective** case, or the *objective form*: invited *me*, reprimanded *him*, disappointed *her*, offended *us*, pleased *them*. See also CASE.

active   Verb forms we use when the subject of the sentence is the doer or agent—the active element in the sentence rather than a passive target. See also VOICE.

ACTIVE: The retreating Germans **had blown** up the bridge.
PASSIVE: The bridge **had been blown up** by the retreating Germans.

adjective   Adjectives are words that can point out a quality of a noun (or equivalent). They answer questions like "which one?" or "what kind?": the *cheap* seats, a *fabulous* meal, a *supersonic* plane. They occur characteristically as modifiers of nouns ("the *happy* child") and as predicate adjectives ("The child was *happy*"). Most adjectives can show differences in **degree**; they have distinctive forms for use in comparisons:

POSITIVE	COMPARATIVE	SUPERLATIVE
tall	taller	tallest
happy	happier	happiest
cautious	more cautious	most cautious

Number adjectives do not change form to show degree: *three* musketeers, *second* thoughts. The articles *the, a,* and *an* are sometimes called **limiting adjectives**. Verbals like *changing, broken,* and *scorched* (**participles**) often function as adjectives in a sentence: *changing* winds, *broken* bones, *scorched* earth.

adjective clause   A dependent clause serving an adjective function: "The man *who had startled us* apologized." (The clause modifies the noun *man*.)

adverb   A class of words that answer questions like how, when, where, or how often.

HOW: slowly, cautiously, rashly, clumsily
WHEN: now, then, today, yesterday, soon, never
WHERE: here, there, upstairs, downtown, outside
HOW OFTEN: frequently, seldom, rarely

Adverbs are used to modify verbs, adjectives, other adverbs, or a sentence as a whole:

VERB:	She ran **quickly.**
ADJECTIVE:	He was **strangely** silent.
ADVERB:	She sang **moderately** well.
SENTENCE:	**Surprisingly,** he did not answer.

To make up an adverb, we can usually adapt an adjective by adding the *-ly* ending: (considerable) aged *considerably*; (fierce) blew *fiercely*; (accidental) dropped it *accidentally*. Some notable exceptions: spoke English *well*, drove too *fast*, liked her very *much*.

adverbial clause A dependent clause serving an adverbial function: "We left *after the rain had stopped.*" "We met *where the path ends.*" "*When the bell had ceased to ring*, I opened the door." (The dependent clauses answer questions like when, where, and how.)

agreement Use of matching forms for several related parts of a sentence. Both subject and verb should be singular (A spy *pries*) or plural (Spies *pry*). Both a pronoun and its antecedent (what it points to) should be of the same **number** and **gender**: "Today *a woman* often has to balance the demands of *her* family and of *her* job."

antecedent Pronouns are shortcut words (*he* instead of *the Secretary-General of the United Nations*). What the *he* (or *she* or *it*) points back to and substitutes for is the antecedent—literally, "what has gone before."

appositive A noun placed after another to fill in quick information: Magellan, *the* Portuguese *navigator*; Sandra O'Connor, *the* new *Supreme Court Justice*. (Note that often the appositive carries considerable added freight.) Sometimes, the appositive does come first: "*A teacher of the young all her life*, Margaret Mead wrote and lectured till her last days."

articles *A* and *an* (the **indefinite** articles) and *the* (the **definite** article), used as noun markers: *a* book, *an* honest man, *the* door. They signal that a noun is about to follow. See also DETERMINERS.

auxiliaries Auxiliaries are the helping verbs needed to turn parts of verbs, like *falling* and *fallen*, into complete verbs: *is* falling, *was* falling, *had* fallen. The true workhorse auxiliaries are *be* (*am, is, are, was, were, has been, will be*) and *have* (*has, had, will have, has had*). Another important group is the **modal auxiliaries**: *shall* (*should*) report; *will* (*would*) agree; *can* (*could*) be true; *may* (*might*) end; *must* return; *ought* to know.

case Changing forms of nouns or pronouns to show the role they play in a sentence. The **possessive** of nouns usually goes with another noun to tell us *whose* (the *suspect's* alibi—singular; the *tenants'* grievances— plural). The **subject form** (subjective or nominative case) of pronouns appears as the subject of a verb: *I* (*he, she, we, they*) made the selection.

The **object form** (objective or accusative case) appears as the object of a verb or preposition: They selected *me* (*him, her, us, them*). Vote for *me* (*him, her, us, them*). English once had an elaborate system of case forms, like Latin or German. Those just listed are the few that remain.

clause   A clause has its own subject and predicate; *one or more* such subject-predicate units make up a sentence. The following sentence has two clauses; each follows a basic who-does-what model: "*The parents kept watch*, while *the children slept.*"

Independent clauses are grammatically self-contained and can be punctuated as complete sentences:

INDEPENDENT: I think; therefore, I am.
I think. Therefore, I am.

Dependent clauses are grammatically subordinate to an independent clause (**main clause**):

DEPENDENT: Arvin had a dog, **which barked all night.**
After the rain stopped, we went home.

See also ADJECTIVE CLAUSE, ADVERBIAL CLAUSE, NOUN CLAUSE, RELATIVE CLAUSE.

collective noun   A group noun that is singular in form but may require a plural verb:

SINGULAR: The **jury votes** tomorrow. (thought of as a unit)
PLURAL: The **jury are** out to lunch. (thought of as individuals)

comparative   The form of adjectives and adverbs that is used to indicate higher degree: "Blood is *thicker* than water." "She speaks Spanish *better* than I do."

complement   A sentence part that completes what the verb says about the subject. (It then becomes part of the **complete predicate**.) The complements, or completers, of action verbs are called **objects**. They often specify the target, the result, or the destination:

Edith called **the sheriff (direct** object).
She wrote **my father (indirect** object) **a letter (direct** object).

The complement of a linking verb is a noun or an adjective describing the subject (**subject complement**); it pins a label on the subject:

Her father was **a minister (predicate noun).**
The boy looked **pale (predicate adjective).**

After some verbs, an object is followed by a description of the object (**object complement**):

The editorial called the project **a failure (noun)**.
Arvin labeled the charges **ridiculous (adjective)**.

complete predicate The complete predicate includes not just the verb but any objects or complements as well as modifiers that complete the statement the verb makes about the subject.

SUBJECT	COMPLETE PREDICATE

The threatened takeover / **brought out the worst in the management**.
Most Parisians / **leave their beloved city during August**.

complex sentence See SENTENCE.

compound noun Two or more words that have merged to function as a single noun. Compound nouns may actually be spelled as a single word: *takeover, spacecraft, moonlight*. However, they are often hyphenated: *queen-size, in-laws*. And many are still spelled as two words: *moon shot, labor union, space shuttle*.

compound sentence See SENTENCE.

compounding The doubling up (also tripling or quadrupling) of sentence parts, with two or more sentence parts of the same kind joined by a word like *and, or,* or *but*: "*The eagle and the condor* are both endangered" (compound subject); "The company at first *denied and* then *belittled* the accident" (compound verb); "The hikers were running out of *food, drink, and patience*" (compound object).

conjunction A word that connects two or more clauses (and sometimes other sentence parts). **Coordinating conjunctions**, or coordinators for short, are *and, but, for, so, yet, or,* and *nor*. (They link two independent clauses.) **Subordinating conjunctions**, or subordinators for short, include *if, when, unless, because, though, whereas,* and many more. (They link a dependent clause to the main clause.)

SEPARATE: Survivors hid in caves. Androids took over the planet.
COORDINATOR: Survivors hid in caves, **and** androids took over the planet.
SUBORDINATOR: Survivors hid in caves **while** androids took over the planet.

conjunctive adverb Conjunctive adverbs are also called **adverbial conjunctions** and include words like *however, therefore, nevertheless, moreover, furthermore, consequently, besides, indeed,* and *in fact*. They link two independent clauses, but like adverbs they can shift their position to a different part of the sentence:

The party touted its candidates; **nevertheless**, the voters shunned them.
The party touted its candidates; the voters shunned them, **nevertheless**.

coordinate adjectives   Two or more interchangeable adjectives that describe different qualities of the same noun, with a comma taking the place of *and*: "a *noisy, unruly* crowd."

copula   Now usually called a **linking verb**: "Homer *was* blind." "The survivors *became* slaves."

correlative conjunctions   Paired connectives coordinating sentence parts or clauses: *either . . . or; neither . . . nor, not only . . . but also, whether . . . or.*

declarative   A declarative sentence presents a statement—not a question or a request: "The desert is spreading south from the Sahara."

degree   See ADJECTIVE.

determiners   Noun markers including **articles** (*a, an, the*), **demonstrative pronouns** (*this, these; that, those*), and **possessive pronouns** (*my, your, his, her, its, our, their*).

elliptical constructions   Constructions in which missing elements can be supplied to facilitate grammatical analysis:

The paintings [**that**] he collected filled a large room.
When [**she was**] interviewed, the actress denied rumors of an impending suit.

expletives   The *it* and *there* used as mere introductory words in *it-is, there-is, there-are* sentences.

finite verb   A verb (often more than one word) that can serve as the complete verb in a sentence. *Writing* and *written* are only parts of verbs (they are **verbals**); finite verbs are *wrote, will write, has written, could be written, was writing.*

gender   The quality of nouns and pronouns that determines choice between *he, she,* or *it* (**masculine, feminine,** and **neuter**); between *actor* and *actress, alumnus* and *alumna, fiancé* and *fiancée.* In many situations, you will be expected to avoid gender-specific language—for instance, to use *chair* or *head* instead of *chairman, flight attendant* instead of *stewardess.*

genitive   Now usually called possessive. See CASE.

gerund   A verbal noun: "Favorite hobbies were *surfing* and *snorkeling.*" "*Being fired* was a new experience." See VERBAL.

idiom   An expression that is more than the sum of its parts and that is the customary way of saying something. "Keep it in mind" is idiomatic; "hold it in mind" is not. "Don't twist my arm" is idiomatic; "don't push my arm" is not.

imperative   The request or command form of verbs, usually used without a subject (*you* is understood): *Watch* your head. *Check* your weapons at the door. *Be* prepared. See MOOD.

indefinite article   *A* and *an* (*a* reminder, *an* invitation), contrasted with the definite article *the*, which points or singles out (*the* local jail).

indefinite pronoun   Indefinite pronouns do not point to particular people: *anybody* (*anyone*), *somebody* (*someone*), *everybody* (*everyone*), *nobody* (*no one*), and *one*.

independent clause   See CLAUSE.

indicative   The ordinary factual forms of verbs, used in statements and assertions ("I know it *is* true"), contrasted with the **subjunctive** ("I wish it *were* true"). See MOOD.

infinitive   The basic or generic form of a verb, used without reference to person or number: *ask, run, investigate, organize.* We usually use it in combination with *to* (then used to mark the infinitive): They started *to balk.* We were afraid *to ask.* It was too good *to miss.* Infinitives can show **perfect tense** (I am sorry *to have forgotten*) or **passive** (They were happy *to be included*).

inflection   Inflected forms help us change a word according to how it fits into a sentence. We change nouns from singular to plural (*jewel/jewels*). We change many adjectives and adverbs to show degree (*fast/faster/ fastest*). We use the endings *-s, -ed,* or *-ing* to produce a whole range of different verb forms. Sometimes we do not just add an ending but change the word itself: *mouse/mice; ring/rang.*

intensifier   Words that modify adjectives or adverbs and express degree, also called **intensive adverbs**: *very* hot, *quite* calm, *rather* young.

interjection   A grammatically independent element used to express attitude or emotion: *ah, oh, ouch,* and the like.

interrogative   See PRONOUN, SENTENCE.

intransitive   See VERB.

linking verb   A verb that does not carry an action across to a target or result but instead pins a label on the subject: The campaign *was* a disaster. Sobriety *became* fashionable. The most common linking verb is *be* (*am, is, are, was, were, will be, has been*). Other verbs used as linking verbs are *become, remain, stay, seem, look, sound,* and *taste.* (We *remained* friends. The caller *sounded* desperate.)

modal auxiliary   See AUXILIARIES.

modifier   A word, phrase, or clause that develops or restricts the meaning of another sentence element or the sentence as a whole (see also ADJECTIVE, ADVERB). **Restrictive** modifiers help identify and need no punctuation; **nonrestrictive** modifiers provide additional information for something already identified or known; they are set off, normally by commas:

RESTRICTIVE: The person **who returned my wallet** was a complete stranger.

NONRESTRICTIVE: Mr. Norton, **who found my wallet**, is an old friend.

modifying noun   A noun that modifies another noun and takes the place usually occupied by an adjective: a *steam* engine, a *garbage* truck, a *labor* union.

mood   The classification of verb forms as **indicative** (plain or factual: "I *am* ready"); **imperative** (request or command: "*Be* quiet"); and **subjunctive** (hypothetical or contrary to fact: "I wish he *were* here!").

nominal   A word, phrase, or whole clause that functions as or like a noun in a sentence, serving, for instance, as subject or object. Accordingly, a nominal might be an **infinitive** (*To err* is human), a **gerund** or verbal noun (*Seeing* is *believing*), or a **noun clause** (*What she does with her free time* is none of my concern).

When style manuals warn against excessive **nominalization**, they aim at discouraging the overuse of nouns where active verbs might bring a static sentence to life:

NOMINALS: Their **rejection** of the ruling party's candidates was the voters' **expression** of their **dissatisfaction** with the privileges of the party hierarchy.

VERBS: When they **rejected** the ruling party's candidates, the voters **showed** how much they **resented** the privileges of the party hierarchy.

nominative   Now usually called **subjective case**, or **subject form**. See CASE.

noun   A class of words that name or classify people, animals, things, ideas. They occur typically as subjects of clauses or as objects of verbs and prepositions:

NOUNS: The **pilot** guided the disabled **plane** toward the fog-shrouded **runway**.

Their appearance is often signaled by noun markers like the **articles** (*a, an, the*). Many nouns (**count** nouns) add *-s* to the plain form to form the plural: *dogs, cars, houses, colleges*.

Common nouns start with a lowercase letter (*car, college*); **proper** nouns are capitalized (*Ford, Yale*). **Abstract** nouns name very general concepts or ideas (*democracy, virtue, evil, happiness*).

The **possessive** (possessive case) is a special form of nouns that tell us whose: the *athlete's* grade average (singular); the *athletes'* grade averages (plural).

noun clause   A dependent clause taking the place of a noun: "*That he was late* does not surprise me." "We knew *why he was late.*"

number   Choice of appropriate forms to express **singular** (one of a kind) or **plural** (more than one).

object   A noun (or grammatical equivalent) needed to complete the statement made by a transitive verb. A single object that identifies the target or result is the **direct object**: "The ordinance banned *guns.*" "The medication prevented *clotting.*" After verbs like *send, give, teach,* or *lend,* the sentence often goes on to the destination first (**indirect object**) and then specifies what was sent (**direct object**): "Three guests gave the *newlyweds* (indirect object) *toasters* (direct object)."

object complement   See COMPLEMENT.

object form or **objective case**   See CASE.

participle   A verbal like *throwing* and *thrown* (or *pitching* and *pitched*), used as *part* of a verb (had *thrown*) or as a modifier (stone-*throwing* protesters). See VERBAL.

parts of speech   The eight major word classes listed in traditional grammar: noun, pronoun, verb, adjective, adverb, conjunction, preposition, interjection.

passive   The passive construction (or **passive voice**) reverses the usual **active** who-does-what? model of the English sentence. The passive highlights the recipient, target, or product of the action by pulling it out in front of the verb. The verb changes from *wrote* to *was written,* from *will pay* to *will be paid.* The doer or agent appears after *by* (or may be omitted altogether).

ACTIVE: The working poor, not the idle rich, **pay** most of our taxes.
PASSIVE: Most of our taxes **are paid** by the working poor, not the idle rich.

past   See TENSE.

perfect   See TENSE.

person   Choice of appropriate forms to express the person speaking (**first person:** *I know, we know*); the person spoken to (**second person:** *you know*); or the person spoken about (**third person:** *he knows, she knows, it knows; they know*).

phrase   A group of related words that function together as one grammatical unit—a main verb and its auxiliaries; a preposition or a verbal accompanied by its object or other related material:

VERB PHRASE:	Craig **has been studying**.
PREPOSITIONAL PHRASE:	Irene sat **at the window**.
VERBAL PHRASE:	We should stop **hunting whales**.

Verbal phrases may be further subdivided according to the verbal they use: infinitive (or *to* form), participle (form like *knowing* or *known* used as a modifier), or gerund (*-ing* form used as a verbal noun):

INFINITIVE PHRASE:	He started **to call us names**.
PARTICIPIAL PHRASE:	**Breathing heavily**, we rested in the shade.
GERUND PHRASE:	The rules forbid **running near the pool**.

A phrase, unlike a clause, does not have a subject and a complete verb.

possessive   A special form of nouns that tells us whose: the *doctor's* dilemma (singular); *doctors'* earnings (plural). See CASE.

predicate   The second basic element of the typical written sentence, making a statement about the subject: Birds/*fly*. Crickets/*chirp*. The **simple predicate** is simply the complete (finite) verb: "Her angry ex-lover/*shot* his rival in the parking lot." The **complete predicate** is the verb together with any complements or modifiers that help it complete its statement about the subject: "Her brother/*makes sandals in Oregon*."

predicate noun   The noun that follows a linking verb and completes the predicate: "The orangutan *is* also *an* endangered *species*." See COMPLEMENT.

preposition   A class of words that relate a noun (or equivalent) to the rest of the sentence: "Arvin left *after* dark." "Miriam worked *without* pay." The noun that follows the preposition is called its object; together they make up a **prepositional phrase**: *at night, in the morning, for your own good*.

present   See TENSE.

principal parts   The basic forms of a verb: simple present (*know*), simple past (*knew*), past participle (*known*).

progressive construction   Verb form expressing action in progress: "Fred *was frying* a fish." "Vera *has been looking* for work."

pronoun   A class of words that can take the place of nouns, classified as **personal** (*I, you, he*); **possessive** (*my, your, his*); **reflexive** or **intensive** (*myself, yourself, himself*); **demonstrative** (*this, that*); **relative** (*who, which, that*); **interrogative** (*who, which, what*); and **indefinite** (*one, anyone, everyone*). See also ANTECEDENT, CASE.

relative clause   A dependent clause related to the main clause by a relative pronoun: "The article *that I mentioned* begins on page 5."

relative pronoun   The relative pronouns—*who (whom, whose), which,* and *that*—help us combine two (or more) separate statements in a larger

740

combined sentence. They do not merely link two ready-made clauses but at the same time *replace* one of the sentence elements in the second clause:

SEPARATE: We talked to the lawyer. She had handled the case.
COMBINED: We talked to the lawyer **who** had handled the case.

restrictive   See MODIFIER.

sentence   A grammatically complete and self-contained unit of thought or expression, set off from other such units by end punctuation. The typical written sentence contains at least a subject and a predicate (*Birds/ sing*). The most common exception is the subjectless request or command, in which the subject is said to be understood (*Show* him in).

Sentences may be statements (**declarative**), questions (**interrogative**), or requests or commands (**imperative**):

STATEMENT: My friends voted for Smith.
QUESTION: Did you vote for Smith?
REQUEST OR COMMAND: Vote for Smith!

Actual sentences often combine two or more **clauses**, each with its own subject and predicate. Sentences combining two or more independent clauses are called **compound**. Sentences combining an independent and one or more dependent clauses are called **complex**. A combination of the two types is called **compound-complex**.

COMPOUND: The right wing hit the runway, **and** smoke billowed up.
COMPLEX: The pilot turned back **when** the hydraulic system failed.
COMPOUND-COMPLEX: **As** the night wore on, ambulance crews gathered up the injured, **and** lawyers sought out the survivors.

source sentence   The minimum sentences from which more complicated structures are derived in transformational grammar. They are the bare-bones statement patterns from which actual sentences are generated by successive transformations. See TRANSFORMATION.

subject   The first basic part of the written sentence, about which the predicate makes a statement (*Scientists*/split the atom. *Nuclear power plants*/cost billions). The **simple subject** is a simple noun (or equivalent), along with any noun markers: "*The* first heart *transplant*/attracted worldwide media attention." The **complete subject** is the core noun (or equivalent) with any modifiers that cluster around it.

subject complement   See COMPLEMENT.

subject form or **subjective case**   See CASE.

741

subjunctive   Special verb forms for remote possibilities (or impossibilities) as well as wishes and demands: "If affordable housing *were* profitable, there would be a glut of it." "We insist that the meeting *be* open to the public." See MOOD.

subordinate clause   Another term for dependent clause. See CLAUSE.

superlative   The form of adjectives and adverbs used to express highest degree: "Maria is the *fastest* runner on the team." "She runs *fastest*."

syntax   The study of how words work together in sentences. It focuses on sentence structure, as contrasted with **phonology**, the study of speech sounds, and **morphology**, the study of the elements that make up words.

tense   The system of verb forms expressing mainly different relationships in time:

PRESENT:	I know	PERFECT:	I have known
PAST:	I knew	PAST PERFECT:	I had known
FUTURE:	I will (shall) know	FUTURE PERFECT:	I will (shall) have known

The auxiliary *have* (*has, had*) helps us make up the perfect tenses, which show action recently completed or still relevant (She *has tried* over and over—**present perfect**) or action preceding other action in the past (We *had warned* him repeatedly—**past perfect**).

English verbs have different tenses also for the **progressive** forms (action in progress: *is deteriorating, was thinking, has been working* hard) and for the **passive voice** (*is disliked, was shortened, will be reported, has been denied*).

transformation   One of the successive steps by which more complicated structures are produced from simple ones in a transformational grammar. The reshuffling, addition, or deletion of grammatical elements needed, for instance, to turn present into past tense, active into passive voice, an affirmative into a negative statement, or a statement into a question:

SOURCE:	The plane arrived.
TRANSFORMATION:	**Did** the plane **arrive**?

transitive   See VERB.

verb   A class of words that signal the performance of an action, the occurrence of an event, or the presence of a condition. Verbs appear in typical verb positions: "Let's *leave*." "The boys *left* the scene." Most verbs can show a change in time by a change in the form of the verb: *bring* (present tense)/*brought* (past tense); *laugh* (present tense)/*laughed* (past tense). Verbs typically take an -*s* in the third person singular of the present tense (*asks, leaves, condones*). They use **auxiliaries** in forms consisting of more than one word (*have left, was asked, will be leaving, can talk, may have seen*).

Action verbs are modified by adverbs; **linking verbs** are followed by adjectives:

ACTION VERB:	She **responded** quickly.
LINKING VERB:	His response **seemed** quick.

Regular verbs simply add *-ed* or *-d* for the past, as against irregular forms like *ran* or *swam*. Regular verbs use the same form for the simple past and the past participle. **Irregular verbs** often use a different form: *grew*/have *grown*, tore/was *torn*, took/might have *taken*.

REGULAR:	I **laughed**	I have **laughed**
IRREGULAR:	I **knew**	I have **known**

Transitive verbs normally require an object. **Intransitive verbs** can serve as the complete predicate:

TRANSITIVE:	She **raises** chickens.
INTRANSITIVE:	The sun **rises**.

See also MOOD, TENSE, VOICE.

verbal   A form that is derived from a verb but does not by itself function as a predicate: **infinitive** (*to* form); **present participle** (*-ing* form used as part of a verb, or as a modifier); **gerund** (*-ing* form used as a verbal noun); **past participle** (*-ed* form in regular verbs, irregular in others). Verbals appear as noun equivalents, modifiers, and *parts* of verbs:

INFINITIVE:	The earth began **to shake**.
PRESENT PARTICIPLE:	They are **suing** the company.
	The **melting** snow feeds the river.
	Smiling, Pat started the car.
GERUND:	**Running** burns up calories.
PAST PARTICIPLE:	The tenants had **moved** the furniture.
	We looked at the **burnt** toast.
	He called it a **known** fact.

See also PHRASE.

voice   The verb form that shows whether the subject is acting (**active**) or acted upon (**passive**):

ACTIVE:	Manuel **feeds** the cats.
PASSIVE:	The cats **are fed** by Manuel.

Index

Note: Boldfaced numbers preceding page numbers refer to the numerical handbook key. Page numbers followed by (gl) refer to an entry in the Glossary of Usage. Page numbers followed by (gt) refer to an entry in the Glossary of Grammatical Terms.

Additional Symbols

¶	New Paragraph
no ¶	No Paragraph Break
?/ or ;/	Use Mark Shown
∧	Correct Omission
x	Correct Obvious Error

Guide to Charts and Lists

Guide to Revision

ab	abbreviations
adv	adverb
agr	agreement
ap	apostrophe
awk	awkward
ca	case
cap	capitalization
coh	coherence
coord	coordination
CS or /;	comma splice
d	diction
dev	development
div	dividing words
DM	dangling modifier
emp	emphasis
FP or //	faulty parallelism
frag	sentence fragment
FS	fused sentence
gl	glossary
gr	grammar
hy	hyphen
inc	incomplete
inf	informal
ital	italics
log	logic
MM	misplaced modifier
ms	manuscript
mx	mixed construction
NS	nonstandard
num	numbers
pass	passive
plan	plan
ref	reference
rep	repetition
sf	shift
sl	slang
sp	spelling
st	sentence structure
sx	sexism
trans	transition
var	variety
vb	verb
w	wordiness